VICTORIA

A LIFE

A. N. WILSON

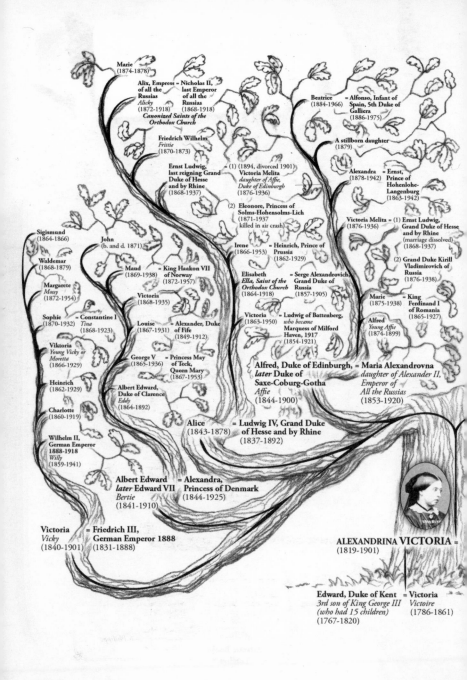

Marie
(1874-1878)

Alix, Empress = Nicholas II,
of all the   last Emperor
Russias   of all the
Alicky   Russias
(1872-1918)   (1868-1918)
Canonized Saints of the
Orthodox Church

Beatrice   = Alfonso, Infant of
(1884-1966)   Spain, 5th Duke of
                 Galliera
                 (1886-1975)

Friedrich Wilhelm
Frittie
(1870-1873)

A stillborn daughter
(1879)

Ernst Ludwig,
last reigning Grand
Duke of Hesse
and by Rhine
(1868-1937)

(1) (1894, divorced 1901)
Victoria Melita
daughter of Affie,
Duke of Edinburgh
(1876-1936)

Alexandra   = Ernst,
(1878-1942)   Prince of
               Hohenlohe-
               Langenburg
               (1863-1942)

(2) Eleonore, Princess of
Solms-Hohensolms-Lich
(1871-1937
killed in air crash!)

Victoria Melita = (1) Ernst Ludwig,
(1876-1936)   Grand Duke of Hesse
                     and by Rhine
                     (marriage dissolved)
                     (1868-1937)

Sigismund
(1864-1866)

John
(b. and d. 1871)

Irene   = Heinrich, Prince of
(1866-1953)   Prussia
              (1862-1929)

(2) Grand Duke Kirill
Vladimirovich of
Russia
(1876-1938)

Waldemar
(1868-1879)

Maud   = King Haakon VII
(1869-1938) of Norway
             (1872-1957)

Elisabeth   = Serge Alexandrovich,
Ella, Saint of the Grand Duke of
Orthodox Church Russia
(1864-1918)   (1857-1905)

Margarete
Mossy
(1872-1954)

Victoria
(1868-1935)

Marie   = King
(1875-1938) Ferdinand I
             of Romania
             (1865-1927)

Sophie   = Constantine I
(1870-1932) *Tino*
             (1868-1923)

Louise   = Alexander, Duke
(1867-1931) of Fife
             (1849-1912)

Victoria   = Ludwig of Battenberg,
(1863-1950)   who became
              Marquess of Milford
              Haven, 1917
              (1854-1921)

Alfred
Young Affie
(1874-1899)

Viktoria
Young Vicky or
Moretta
(1866-1929)

George V   = Princess May
(1865-1936) of Teck,
             Queen Mary
             (1867-1953)

Heinrich
(1862-1929)

Albert Edward,
Duke of Clarence
Eddy
(1864-1892)

Alfred, Duke of Edinburgh, = Maria Alexandrovna
later Duke of   *daughter of Alexander II,*
Saxe-Coburg-Gotha   *Emperor of*
Affie   *All the Russias*
(1844-1900)   (1853-1920)

Charlotte
(1860-1919)

Wilhelm II,
German Emperor
1888-1918
Willy
(1859-1941)

Alice   = Ludwig IV, Grand Duke
(1843-1878)   of Hesse and by Rhine
                (1837-1892)

Albert Edward   = Alexandra,
later Edward VII Princess of Denmark
Bertie   (1844-1925)
(1841-1910)

Victoria   = Friedrich III,
Vicky   German Emperor 1888
(1840-1901)   (1831-1888)

ALEXANDRINA VICTORIA =
(1819-1901)

Edward, Duke of Kent = Victoria
3rd son of King George III *Victoire*
(who had 15 children) (1786-1861)
(1767-1820)

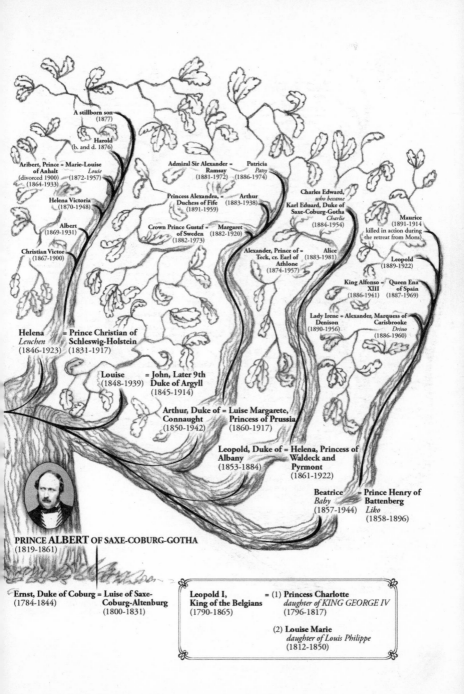

A stillborn son
(1877)

Harold
(b. and d. 1876)

Aribert, Prince = Marie-Louise
of Anhalt   *Louie*
(divorced 1900) (1872-1957)
(1864-1933)

Admiral Sir Alexander = Patricia
Ramsay   *Patty*
(1881-1972)   (1886-1974)

Helena Victoria
(1870-1948)

Princess Alexandra, = Arthur
Duchess of Fife   (1883-1938)
(1891-1959)

Charles Edward,
who became
Karl Eduard, Duke of
Saxe-Coburg-Gotha
Charlie
(1884-1954)

Maurice
(1891-1914
killed in action during
the retreat from Mons)

Albert
(1869-1931)

Crown Prince Gustaf = Margaret
of Sweden   (1882-1920)
(1882-1973)

Leopold
(1889-1922)

Christian Victor
(1867-1900)

Alexander, Prince of = Alice
Teck, cr. Earl of   (1883-1981)
Athlone
(1874-1957)

King Alfonso = Queen Ena
XIII   of Spain
(1886-1941)   (1887-1969)

Lady Irene = Alexander, Marquess of
Denison   Carisbrooke
(1890-1956) *Drino*
             (1886-1960)

Helena   = Prince Christian of
Lenchen   Schleswig-Holstein
(1846-1923)   (1831-1917)

Louise   = John, Later 9th
(1848-1939)   Duke of Argyll
                  (1845-1914)

Arthur, Duke of = Luise Margarete,
Connaught   Princess of Prussia
(1850-1942)   (1860-1917)

Leopold, Duke of = Helena, Princess of
Albany   Waldeck and
(1853-1884)   Pyrmont
                   (1861-1922)

Beatrice   = Prince Henry of
Baby   Battenberg
(1857-1944)   *Liko*
                 (1858-1896)

PRINCE **ALBERT** OF SAXE-COBURG-GOTHA
(1819-1861)

Ernst, Duke of Coburg = Luise of Saxe-
(1784-1844)   Coburg-Altenburg
                        (1800-1831)

Leopold I,   = (1) **Princess Charlotte**
King of the Belgians   *daughter of KING GEORGE IV*
(1790-1865)   (1796-1817)

                       (2) **Louise Marie**
                           daughter of Louis Philippe
                           (1812-1850)

First published in hardback in Great Britain in 2014 by Atlantic Books, an imprint of Grove Atlantic Ltd.

This paperback edition published in Great Britain in 2015 by Atlantic Books.

10 9 8 7 6 5 4 3 2 1

A CIP catalogue record for this book is available from the British Library.

Paperback ISBN: 978 1 84887 958 4
E-book ISBN: 978 1 78239 344 3

Printed in the UK by Clays Ltd, St Ives Plc

Atlantic Books
An imprint of Grove Atlantic Ltd
Ormond House
26–27 Boswell Street
London WC1N 3JZ

www.atlantic-books.co.uk

for
Gillon Aitken

Also by A. N. Wilson

FICTION

The Sweets of Pimlico

Unguarded Hours

Kindly Light

The Healing Art

Who Was Oswald Fish?

Wise Virgin

Scandal: Or Priscilla's Kindness

Gentlemen in England

Love Unknown

Stray

The Vicar of Sorrows

Dream Children

My Name Is Legion

A Jealous Ghost

Winnie and Wolf

The Potter's Hand

THE LAMPITT CHRONICLES

Incline Our Hearts

A Bottle in the Smoke

Daughters of Albion

Hearing Voices

A Watch in the Night

NON-FICTION

A Life of Sir Walter Scott: The Laird of Abbotsford:

A Life of John Milton

Hilaire Belloc: A Biography

How Can We Know?

Landscape in France

Tolstoy

Penfriends from Porlock: Essays And Reviews, 1977–1986

Eminent Victorians

C. S. Lewis: A Biography

Paul: The Mind of the Apostle

God's Funeral: A Biography of Faith And Doubt in Western Civilization

The Victorians

Iris Murdoch As I Knew Her

London: A Short History

After the Victorians: The World Our Parents Knew

Betjeman: A Life

Our Times: The Age of Elizabeth II

Dante in Love

The Elizabethans

Hitler: A Short Biography

The Book of the People: How to Read the Bible

CONTENTS

ACKNOWLEDGEMENTS

I GRATEFULLY ACKNOWLEDGE the permission of Her Majesty Queen Elizabeth II to quote from materials in the Royal Archives and for other items which are in royal copyright. Thanks are also due to David Ryan at the Royal Archives, to all the staff and volunteers in the Round Tower at Windsor, and especially to the Senior Archivist Miss Pam Clark, who not only suggested many useful lines of inquiry, but also read the entire book in typescript and made many corrections and recommendations. Jonathan Marsden, Director of the Royal Collections and Surveyor of the Queen's Works of Art, has been consistently helpful, and I should like to thank Lisa Heighway for the care she devoted to helping with the choice of illustrations, and the openness and generosity with which she revealed the seemingly limitless riches of the royal photographic collection. Thanks are also due to Sir Christopher Geidt for encouragement and kindness.

Dr Simon Thurley of English Heritage took me on an unforgettable tour of Osborne House out of season. Dr Ruth Guilding, formerly of English Heritage (and curator at Osborne), has given me many insights into the life and tastes of Queen Victoria and of the Prince Consort. Michael Hunter, the present curator at Osborne, was helpful and welcoming.

The staff of the Bodleian Library, the British Library, the Lambeth Palace Library and the National Library of Scotland have also been unfailingly obliging. I read much of the secondary material for this book in the Humanities One Reading Room in the British Library, and the bulk of the manuscripts in the Manuscript Room, where the staff are learned and accommodating.

During much of the time that I was doing research, the Special Collections in the Bodleian Library were rehoused, at great inconvenience, I should imagine, to the staff, but the papers of nineteenth-century courtiers and statesmen still mysteriously materialized in seemingly no time at all, even in the unfamiliar setting of the Science Library in Parks Road.

The staff in the London Library were, as always, kind friends.

I am deeply grateful to Dr Horst Gehringer who so generously welcomed me to the State Archives in Coburg, to Dr M. Eckstein who helped me to decipher some of the more illegible examples of the Queen's *Alte Schrifte*, and to Dr Angelika Tasler who gave me useful insights into Duke Ernst II's musical life, and who also introduced me to the library and archive in the Schloss Ehrenberg. I am very grateful to Dr Oliver Walton, who straddles a life in the Royal Collection in England with work for the Prince Albert Society in Coburg and who has given encouragement and good advice throughout.

Alexander and Michaela Reid not only provided me with lavish hospitality at Lanton Tower but were unstinting in their generosity in allowing me full access to Sir James Reid's scrapbooks, diaries and albums. Michaela shared all her great knowledge of the Victorian court with me while I enjoyed their hospitality.

The Marquess of Salisbury has generously allowed me to quote from the archive at Hatfield. While I was there, my researches were helped by the archivist Vicki Perry, by the assistance of Sarah Whale and by the advice of the former archivist Robert Harcourt Williams.

Hugo Vickers gave very particular help.

I owe my knowledge of German largely to the patient teaching of Ute Ormerod. It would not have been possible to write this book without her.

Gillon Aitken and Anna Stein were wonderful agents, as always. My editor at Atlantic, Margaret Stead, is like the unseen deity in the Psalms – 'thou understandest my thoughts long before'. It is impossible to imagine a more inspirational publisher. Tamsin Shelton has been a punctilious and patient copy-editor.

A biography of Queen Victoria is not a task undertaken lightly. The process is a long time in the gestation, as well as in the writing.

This book owes much to conversations which I had long ago, often with friends who, alas, are no longer with us. I was especially fortunate to have Elizabeth Longford as a friend. Her biography, *Victoria R.I.* (1964, revised 1987), is a gigantic achievement which will never be replaced. Often, in the course of writing my own book, I recalled conversations I had with her, either at Osborne House, during a memorable autumn of 1988, or on subsequent occasions in London. I have also been helped, not only by frequent reference to his biography of Disraeli, but also by memories of conversations with Robert Blake. The following have all in different ways helped, either with specific answers to queries or with their knowledge of Queen Victoria, her court or her ways, or with questions which it had not occurred to me to ask, but which set me off on trails of fruitful inquiry: Davina Jones, Anna Keay, Antonia Fraser, Rebecca Fraser, Flora Fraser, my brother Stephen Wilson, the late Gerard Irvine, Lawrence James, Roy Strong, the late Kenneth Rose, Mary Miers, Richard Ingrams, Michael Hall, Rachel Woollen, Allan Maclean of Dochgarroch, Katherine Duncan-Jones, Jane Ridley, Sarah Bradford, A. D. Harvey, John Martin Robinson, Claire Whalley and Susie Attwood.

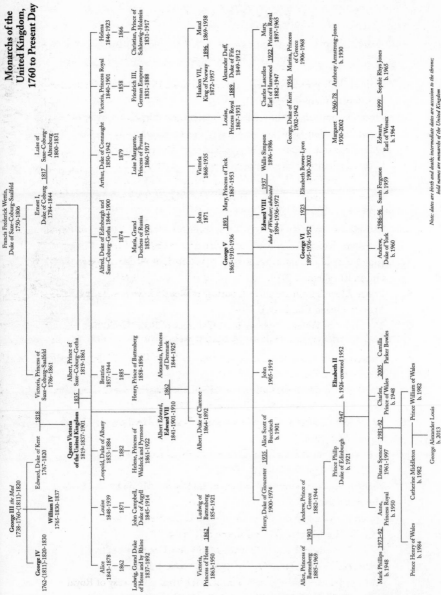

Monarchs of the United Kingdom, 1760 to Present Day

Note: dates are birth and death; intermediate dates are accession to the throne; **bold names are monarchs of the United Kingdom**

ILLUSTRATIONS

1. Thomas Sully portrait of young Queen Victoria, 1838. Wallace Collection. Courtesy of Getty Images.
2. Queen Victoria and Prince Albert when in their thirties. Courtesy of Royal Collection Trust/© Her Majesty Queen Elizabeth II 2014.
3. Queen Victoria reading to her grandchildren. Courtesy of Royal Collection Trust/© Her Majesty Queen Elizabeth II 2014.
3. Victoria, Duchess of Kent, with Prince Alfred and Princess Alice. Courtesy of Royal Collection Trust/© Her Majesty Queen Elizabeth II 2014.
4. Miniature of William Lamb, 2nd Viscount Melbourne. Courtesy of Royal Collection Trust/© Her Majesty Queen Elizabeth II 2014.
5. King Leopold I. Courtesy of Royal Collection Trust/© Her Majesty Queen Elizabeth II 2014.
6. Prince Albert's intimate circle. Courtesy of Royal Collection Trust/© Her Majesty Queen Elizabeth II 2014.
7. The Prince of Wales as a young man. Courtesy of Royal Collection Trust/© Her Majesty Queen Elizabeth II 2014.
8. Princess Alice. Courtesy of Royal Collection Trust/© Her Majesty Queen Elizabeth II 2014.
9. The Royal Family at Osborne in the 1850s. Courtesy of Royal Collection Trust/© Her Majesty Queen Elizabeth II 2014.
10. 'The Allies'. Courtesy of Royal Collection Trust/© Her Majesty Queen Elizabeth II 2014.
11. The mausoleum at Frogmore. Courtesy of Royal Collection Trust/© Her Majesty Queen Elizabeth II 2014.
12. Young royals in mourning. Kindly provided by Sir Alexander and Lady Michaela Reid.
13. Queen Victoria and the Empress Frederick. Courtesy of Royal Collection Trust/© Her Majesty Queen Elizabeth II 2014.
14. Queen Victoria and some of her adult children. Courtesy of Royal Collection Trust/© Her Majesty Queen Elizabeth II 2014.
15. Princess Beatrice and Queen Victoria in the library. Courtesy of Royal Collection Trust/© Her Majesty Queen Elizabeth II 2014.

16. Queen Victoria with Prince Arthur and Princess Margaret of Connaught. Kindly provided by Sir Alexander and Lady Michaela Reid.

17. A family reunion at Coburg. Courtesy of Royal Collection Trust/© Her Majesty Queen Elizabeth II 2014.

18. Lord Palmerston. Courtesy of Royal Collection Trust/© Her Majesty Queen Elizabeth II 2014. Prime Minister Disraeli. Courtesy of Corbis. Third Marquess of Salisbury. Courtesy of the Marquess of Salisbury/ Hatfield House. Prime Minister Gladstone. Photo by William Currey /© National Portrait Gallery, London.

19. Queen Victoria wearing fur stole. Courtesy of Royal Collection Trust /© Her Majesty Queen Elizabeth II 2014.

20. Duke of Cambridge. Courtesy of Royal Collection Trust/© Her Majesty Queen Elizabeth II 2014.

21. Sir Henry Ponsonby. Courtesy of Royal Collection Trust/© Her Majesty Queen Elizabeth II 2014.

22. Sir James Reid. Kindly provided by Sir Alexander and Lady Michaela Reid.

23. Dr Norman Macleod. Courtesy of Royal Collection Trust/© Her Majesty Queen Elizabeth II 2014.

24. Four generations. Courtesy of Royal Collection Trust/© Her Majesty Queen Elizabeth II 2014.

25. Queen Victoria with one of her beloved dogs. Courtesy of Royal Collection Trust/© Her Majesty Queen Elizabeth II 2014.

26. John Brown. Courtesy of Royal Collection Trust/© Her Majesty Queen Elizabeth II 2014.

27. Queen Victoria with Abdul Karim. Courtesy of Royal Collection Trust /© Her Majesty Queen Elizabeth II 2014.

28. 'The Queen of Sheba'. Kindly provided by Sir Alexander and Lady Michaela Reid.

29. The Queen's bedroom at Osborne House. Courtesy of Royal Collection Trust/© Her Majesty Queen Elizabeth II 2014.

30. An elderly Queen Victoria. Courtesy of Royal Collection Trust/© Her Majesty Queen Elizabeth II 2014.

PART ONE

ONE

AUTHORS

O NE GUSTY APRIL day in 1838, Thomas Carlyle was walking in
Green Park, near Buckingham Palace in London, when he
saw the young Queen ride past in her carriage. Forty-two years old,
the Scotsman had been living in the English capital for a little over
three years, and he had lately soared to literary fame. His study of
The French Revolution had been published in the previous year – the
year in which Victoria acceded to the throne – and the popularity of
the two events was not disconnected. Carlyle had made what his first
biographer, J. A. Froude, called a 'vast phantasmagoria'[1] culminating
in the French people getting rid of their monarchy.

The English were not minded, in any very organized sense, to do
the same, but Victoria became queen in hungry times. The monarchy
had not been popular in the first decades of the nineteenth century.
Froude noted that 'the hungry and injured millions will rise up and
bring to justice their guilty rulers, themselves little better than those
whom they throw down'.[2]

Britain in those days was very far from being a democracy. It was
governed by an oligarchy of aristocratic, landowning families. Its
stability as a state depended upon the functioning of the law, the
workings of two Houses of Parliament, the efficiency of the army
and navy, and the balance of trade. Parliament was representative, not
democratic. That is, the members of the Commons were not elected
by the people, but by a small number of men of property. In the reign

previous to Victoria's, that of her uncle William IV, the Reform Bill of 1832 had done a little to extend the franchise and to abolish the more grotesque of the electoral anomalies – the so-called Rotten Boroughs, in which there were only a handful of electors. But the members of the Commons were not elected by more than a tiny handful of those whom they represented. Checking and approving the deliberations of the Commons was the function of the Upper House, the Lords, some hundred or so rich men who owned most of the land, and exercised most of the power, in Britain.

There had, as yet, been no French-style revolution to overthrow these arrangements. And it was to be the care and concern of the British governing classes to make sure that no such revolution occurred. The previous old King, William IV, having had a dissolute life and fathered ten children out of wedlock, died legitimately married and reconciled to God, murmuring the words, 'The Church, the Church.'

The twin institutions of the Church of England and the monarchy clearly played a vital role in the delicate balance of the British Constitution. The Victorians liked to tell one another that the monarch was simply a figurehead, kept in place by the Whig landowners, a figure who signed state papers and gave the nod to the deliberations of the House of Lords. This was not really the case. The monarch still occupied a position of real power in Britain, and if that power were to be exercised recklessly, or if the monarchy were hated by a hungry populace, there was no knowing what anarchy would ensue. The monarch depended upon the peerage; the peerage depended upon economic prosperity, and upon the rising commercial classes who could provide it; the shared powers of Trade, Land, the Law and the Church were all delicately, and not always obviously, interwoven in the destinies of that young woman glimpsed in the park by the historian. It was essential for her future that the other institutions should continue to support her; it was essential for all of them that she should maintain the status quo, that she should not fail.

Victoria's grandfather, King George III, a monarch who was politically active and who had played a pivotal role in the shaping of British political history, was blind for the last ten years of his life, and at sporadic intervals in the last twenty years of his long reign (1760–1820) he had been raving mad. The fear that the royal madness was hereditary was ever-present in the British governing class, and the young Queen's ministers watched every one of her tantrums, each emotional display, every instance of irrational behaviour, with anxiety.

George III's son, who ruled as Regent during the times of blindness and madness, had been extremely unpopular, not least because of the sordid and cruel way in which he had divorced his queen, Caroline of Brunswick. By the time he was succeeded by his brother the Duke of Clarence (William IV) in 1830, it had looked very much as if the supply of possible heirs to the throne had all but dwindled. It was mere luck that William had not, in turn, been succeeded by his extremely unpopular brother Ernest, Duke of Cumberland, a scar-faced brute who was widely believed to have murdered his valet and married a woman who had killed her previous two husbands, and whose extreme Toryism made him hated by the masses.[3] Had the young Victoria not existed, Ernest would have been the King of England, and Britain might well have made a second decision to become a republic.

Carlyle himself was by way of being a republican, certainly one deeply read in the era of the first Republic in the seventeenth century, and a hero-worshipping biographer of Oliver Cromwell. Carlyle was a sardonic and amusing man, whose stock in trade was a refusal to be impressed – by the English, who to his Scottish soul were ever alien; by the Establishment, which he found laughable; by the class hierarchy, very near the bottom of which he had been born. His hero was the German poet Goethe, and Carlyle sought, in the confused state of modern England, with its great social injustices, its teeming poor, its disease-ridden industrial cities, its Philistinism, some means of returning, with that poet, a positive attitude to life, an Everlasting Yea. Carlyle, on that breezy April day, was passed by a carriage: the

Queen taking, as he said in his Scottish way, 'her bit departure for Windsor. I had seen her another day at Hyde Park Corner, coming in from the daily ride. She is decidedly a pretty-looking little creature: health, clearness, graceful timidity, looking out from her young face... One could not help some interest in her, situated as mortal seldom was.'[4]

Carlyle, who went on to write one of the most magisterial royal biographies in the literature of the world – *The Life of Frederick the Great* – was peculiarly well placed to see the strangeness of Victoria's position as she swept past him in the carriage. (They would not meet until years later, when, both widowed and old, they exchanged small talk at the Deanery of Westminster Abbey.)

She was indeed situated as mortal seldom was. This makes her story of abiding fascination. Her father and mother might so easily not have had a child at all. Once born, Victoria's often solitary childhood was the oddest of preparations for what she was to become: not merely the mother of nine and the grandmother of forty-two children, but the matriarch of Royal Europe. She was either the actual ancestor of or was connected by marriage to nearly all the great dynasties of Europe, and in almost each of those crowned or coroneted figure-heads, there was bound up a political story. Her destiny was thus interwoven with that of millions of people – not just in Europe, but in the ever-expanding Empire which Britain was becoming throughout the nineteenth century. One day to be named the Empress of India, the 'pretty-looking little creature' had a face which would adorn postage stamps, banners, statues and busts all over the known world. And this came about, as the Germanophile Thomas Carlyle would have been the first to recognize, because of the combination of two peculiar factors: firstly, that Victoria was born at the very moment of the expansion of British political and commercial power throughout the world; and secondly that she was born from that stock of (nearly all German) families who tended to supply the crowned heads for the monarchies of the post-Napoleonic world.

The moment in the park, when two stars in the Victorian galaxy passed one another, is one of those little conjunctions which happen in capital cities. This was the era when Britain rose, for a few decades, to be supremely the most powerful nation on earth: richer and more influential than any of its European rivals, even than Russia. Thereafter, another power would emerge, formed from the coalescence of the German states, the development of German heavy industry, the building up of German military and naval might. Carlyle and Queen Victoria, like so many figures who shape a new and vibrant civilization, were outsiders, who had seemingly come from nowhere. One of the things which marked them out was an acute consciousness of Germany and its importance in the scheme of things. Mr Casaubon, the inadequate scholar married to the heroine of George Eliot's *Middlemarch*, wrote worthlessly because he had not absorbed developments in German scholarship, and this was a period when it was said that only three of the dons at Oxford could so much as speak German. (It was said that the whole story of religion in the nineteenth century would have been different if the future Cardinal Newman had known German.) Yet the story of Germany, and the story of Britain, and their tragic failure to understand one another, lay at the heart of nineteenth-century history, being destined to explode on the battlefields of the First World War.

There was something else about the young Queen which, had he known it, would have made Carlyle – historian, journalist, biographer – all the more interested in her. Whether or not Benjamin Disraeli, novelist and Prime Minister, really buttered up his Queen by using the phrase 'We authors, Ma'am',[5] it would not have been flattery alone. Disraeli's words are always quoted as a joke, but she really was an author. Disraeli's alleged flannel referred to her published work, *Leaves from the Journal of Our Life in the Highlands*, published in 1868. But this publication and its sequel were but a tiny fragment of her pen's outpouring. Her often solitary childhood made it natural for her to express her feelings in writing. There was often no one but herself to talk to. She kept journals from infancy to old age. She was one of the most prolific letter writers of the nineteenth century, that letter-writing age, and, whether she was conducting state business, or emoting about family crises, or worrying about her health, or noting the passing season, it was her custom to put her feelings and thoughts into writing. In a recent study, Yvonne M. Ward calculated that Victoria wrote as many as 60 million words.[6] Giles St Aubyn, in his biography of the Queen, said that had she been a novelist, her outpouring of written words would have equalled 700 volumes.[7] Her diaries were those of a compulsive recorder, and she sometimes would write as many as 2,500 words of her journal in one day.

When she died she left many volumes of journals, an historical record of political events, conversations, impressions, of the entire cast-list of nineteenth-century public life. There was scarcely a Head of State, or a bishop, or an aristocrat, or a famous writer or composer or painter whom she had not either met (reclusive as she was for much of the time) or of whom she had not formed some impression. She asked her youngest daughter, Princess Beatrice, to transcribe these, and to omit any details which might be upsetting to the family. The princess followed these instructions, and all the evidence suggests that she censored quite a lot, destroying her mother's manuscript journals as she did so. Very few of the original journals in the Queen's own hand survive.

Princess Beatrice was not alone in wishing to obliterate her mother's writings. King Edward VII likewise left instructions to his secretary, Lord Knollys, to go through his papers upon his death. Knollys destroyed freely, especially anxious to cover up the unhappy relations between Edward and his wife, Queen Alexandra. Historians will be even sadder to realize how much of Queen Victoria's correspondence with her wittiest Prime Minister, Disraeli, has also been destroyed. Though nearly twenty morocco-bound volumes of the correspondence survive at Windsor, the hopeful researcher discovers that nearly all of the Queen's letters have been excised from this collection; and of Disraeli's letters, the great majority are anodyne discussions about minor honours being awarded to now-forgotten mayors or Members of Parliament.

The compulsion felt by Victoria's children to expunge her writings from our view leads immediately to the thought that she must have had something to hide. The reader of any modern biography of Queen Victoria is naturally hopeful that some of the indiscretions, so diligently veiled by Princess Beatrice, can be finally unmasked. Here a word of caution must be sounded. Queen Victoria was an instinctively indiscreet person. Much as she would have hated our contemporary habits of prurience, and dismissive as she would have been of a modern writer picking over the details of her private life, she was nevertheless almost compulsive in her need to share that private life with a wider public. To this extent, though she was not an 'author' in the sense that Disraeli might have half-mockingly implied, she was much more like Dickens and Ruskin and Proust than she was like the majority of royal personages who have a quite simple desire for privacy. Victoria was much more complex. On the one hand, she considered any intrusion into the Royal Family by the press to be an abominable impertinence. On the other hand, she was only prevented with the greatest difficulty by courtiers and by her children from publishing her version of her relationship with her Highland servant John Brown.

In our lifetime, the whole convention of discretion about the lives of royal personages has been blown apart by a succession of factors – including the willingness of some members of the Royal Family to tell all, or nearly all, to newspaper and television journalists. Clearly such behaviour would have been unimaginable, indeed horrifying, to Queen Victoria.

In December 1890, for example, she erupted with anger at *The Times* printing a mild story (as it happened, it turned out to be untrue) about a proposed visit to England by the Duke and Duchess of Sparta (the Crown Prince of the Hellenes, Constantine, and his wife, Princess Sophie of Prussia).[8] All the newspaper had said was that the Duke and Duchess of Connaught, rather than accompanying the Queen and the Court to Osborne the previous day, would wait behind in London for the Duke and Duchess of Sparta. An indignant Victoria instructed her Prime Minister to remonstrate with that newspaper's editor for 'the exuberant fancy of his fashionable correspondent, who makes announcements about the Queen and Royal Family at variance with the plain unvarnished Court Circular'. Her private secretary, General Ponsonby, 'told the Queen the newspapers put in the Royal news because they thought it pleased the Royal Family and they knew it pleased the public. Her Majesty replied with some asperity that these notes were most interfering and annoying to the Royal Personages who wish to be left in peace and do not desire their movements to be announced, and that the public were informed of all particulars in the Court Circular & could not be pleased at being misled by erroneous notices'.[9]

So, there could be no doubt that the queen would have deplored anything in the nature of an intrusive journalism, or history, which pried into her private life. And yet – for with interesting personalities there is always an 'and yet', and Queen Victoria was among the most fascinating and self-contradictory of all British monarchs – she also had a desire to write about her life for publication. Her children might cringe, but she was unselfconscious about describing the pleasures of her Highland picnics, her watercolouring expeditions, and her love of the Highlanders themselves. Of course, her published books were not confessional or revelatory in the manner of modern journalism, but her own freedom of expression and lack of caution were closer to the 'modern' approach than were the instincts of her children. When, in the 1920s, the ex-Prime Minister's wife Margot Asquith began to publish indiscreet volumes of autobiography, a step had been taken in the direction of modern 'kiss and tell' conventions. Queen Victoria's daughter Princess Louise (Duchess of Argyll) expressed amazement that her friend Lady Battersea was also going to publish some completely anodyne reminiscences. 'I have been rather taken aback, for your letter says, what you assured me would not be the case, that you would publish your reminiscences. I confess I thought them charming and entertaining, for just your personal belongings and friends, but not the public. This Margo [sic] fever to me is such a pitty [sic]!'[10] In another letter to the same friend, Louise wrote, 'This letter need [sic] the flames after you have read it as I do so dislike any letters being kept these days, you will not wonder?'[11]

It is easy to understand the reluctance of King Edward VII to have all the details of his private life recorded. He had only narrowly avoided being cited in divorce courts as a co-respondent on more than one occasion, and the King, who was nicknamed Edward the Caresser, was a by-word for raffish behaviour. Princess Louise, herself trapped in an unhappy marriage to a homosexual, her name 'linked', as journalists say, to several men not her husband, and desperately lonely in her widowhood, was understandably touchy about vulgar publicity.[12] But it would be a mistake to attribute her views to a fear of scandal. There was a sense, in the pre-1914 world, which extended in most English circles until the Second World War, of two sets of information: things which everyone 'knew' but which were not written down; and matters which were printable. It was not so much that the laws of libel prevented newspapers from printing stories. It was more a matter of what was and was not 'done'. Strong conventions prevented the British public from being told, until a few days before it happened, that their King was on the verge of abdication in 1936. Yvonne M. Ward also makes the powerful point, in her *Censoring Queen Victoria*, that the public image of the Queen, for a good half century and more after her death, was determined by the letters which her editors chose to put into print. Arthur C. Benson and the 1st Viscount Esher, both homosexual men of a certain limited outlook determined by their class and disposition, were the pair entrusted with the task of editing the earliest published letters. It is a magnificent achievement, but they chose to concentrate on Victoria's public life, omitting the thousands of letters she wrote relating to health, to children, to sex and marriage, to feelings and the 'inner woman'. It perhaps comforted them, and others who revered the memory of the Victorian era, to place a posthumous gag on Victoria's emotions. The extreme paradox arose that one of the most passionate, expressive, humorous and unconventional women who ever lived was paraded before the public as a stiff, pompous little person, the 'figurehead' to an all-male imperial enterprise.

This atmosphere of discretion which surrounds the Royal Family has done Queen Victoria a disservice. By destroying so many of her mother's journals, Princess Beatrice makes us suspicious that she was covering up details which would satisfy the eyes of the salacious. Certainly, it is hard to see why Edward VII would have been so anxious to buy letters from a blackmailer, 'some of them most compromising' about his mother's relationship with John Brown, had he not himself believed that they would be scandalous. These matters will be discussed in their due chronological place. They are mentioned here at the outset, however, to alert the reader to the fact that there is a certain amount of the story which has been systematically censored by the Queen's children. At the same time, it is necessary at the outset to realize that just because a letter or a diary has been burned does not mean it was either sinister or even especially interesting. On the contrary, as Princess Louise's reaction to her old friend's memoirs showed, the habits of discretion, the desire to burn perfectly harmless letters in order to cover their traces, might not conceal the garish secrets which the imaginations of a later generation wish to supply. The modern biographer, or the reader of modern biographies, might be so anxious to find the few hidden, or irrecoverably lost, 'secrets' of Queen Victoria's life that they miss the one very obvious reason why her children would have wanted to destroy as much of her archive as possible.

To judge from the surviving letters, one feature of Queen Victoria's written life which must have been especially painful to her family is the free and ungoverned manner in which she criticized her children – both to them directly and behind their backs. Their physical appearance, their dress sense, their capacity to procreate, the frequency with which they did so, the names they gave their children, the manner in which they brought them up were all subjected to a ceaseless and frequently far from complimentary commentary. For her son the Prince of Wales she reserved especially uncompromising vilifications, and it was hardly surprising, when he had the power to do so, that Bertie, having become Edward VII, took matters into his own destructive hands.

The fact that Princess Beatrice destroyed so large a proportion of her mother's journals is not, therefore, a fact which demands only one interpretation: namely, a cover-up of scandals. The Queen expressed herself so forcefully, so freely, so often, that it could be this fact alone, and not any particular 'secret', which Princess Beatrice wished to obliterate from the history books. Luckily for us, an abundance of the Queen's letters still survive, as do the reminiscences, diaries and correspondence of those who knew her. And it is from this primary material in general that the following pages will, wherever possible, derive, as we revisit the story of that 'pretty-looking little creature' glimpsed by Carlyle in Green Park; for we would echo his instinctual judgement, 'one could not help some interest in her'.

TWO

ZOOLOGY

The story starts in Germany. 'Why should we have Germans to
rule over us?' drawled Lady Jersey at a party in 1820.[1] And many
of the British biographers and historians who have written about
Queen Victoria have clearly shared the prejudice, usually wishing to
point out that the German principalities or duchies which serviced
so many European dynasties were smaller than English counties.
The size of the Duchy of Gotha or of Saxe-Coburg might be of
geographical interest, but it should not blind us to the way in which
European royalty actually functioned. It has been rightly pointed out
that until the French Revolution and the ending of the Old Regime,
Europe was ruled by a single family divided into many branches, the
big family of European dynasties. European royalty were all part of
one family, both in the sense that they constituted a sort of political
trade union, and in the genealogical fact that they were often interconnected many times over by ties of blood and marriage.[2]

After the Second World War, it became even easier for British
historians than it was for Victoria's insular aristocratic contemporaries to imagine that the British monarchy was a self-sufficient,
home-grown norm, and to speak of the arrival of 'foreign' spouses
for British monarchs as an exotic whim or a regrettable necessity.
Although the Tudor dynasty was to some extent 'home-grown', the
British monarchy thereafter could have no life detached from the
European mainstream, especially after its own domestic civil wars.

Once these had been eventually resolved, with a victory for the Whiggish aristocracy in 1688, and once it had been decided firmly in 1701, with the Act of Settlement, that the British monarchy must be Protestant in perpetuity, it became essential to find British monarchs among the Protestant members of the European royal 'pool'. Victoria's grandfather, George III, was the first Hanoverian monarch to have been born in England, and her nearest non-German ancestor on her father's side was the daughter of James I – Elizabeth of Bohemia (1596–1662), and she was not English, but half Scots and half Danish. Obviously enough, her mother being German, all Victoria's maternal ancestors were Germans.

Victoria cherished her German ancestry. 'It shocks the people of England that the Queen takes no notice of her paternal relations, treats English ones as alien and seems to consider her German uncles and cousins as her only kith and kin,' complained the diarist Charles Greville in 1840. The following year, when her first son was born, the Queen tried to persuade the College of Arms to quarter the royal arms of England with those of his distinguished European forebears and his arms were gazetted as those of the Duke of Saxony – one of the titles which she bestowed (with what legitimacy some would question) upon the future Edward VII.

It is understandable that members of the House of Lords and their families should have been hypersensitive about the Queen's Germanic predilections. By European standards, the British ruling classes, although they bore coats of arms and titles, were scarcely of ancient lineage. Very few of them, by European standards, could be seen as aristocratic at all. Few of their titles went back beyond the seventeenth century. Only one of the English dukedoms, that of Norfolk, is medieval,[3] and the family which bears the title, the Howards, are descended from mere harbourmasters. Even the 'royal' ancestry of the Stewarts was mingled with that of the Medici, Tuscan peasants who enriched themselves as cloth merchants and bankers; aristocratic purists would see even the French monarchy as the offspring of a 'mésalliance' over which those of more ancient or exalted lineage took precedence. W. M. Thackeray, author of *Vanity Fair*, dismissed Coburg as 'a Pumpernickel state'. It is more amusing, from one perspective, to pretend that England is the centre of the universe, but it was Thackeray, and not the House of Saxe-Coburg, who is made to seem provincial by the use of the epithet.

Victoria and Albert came out of Europe, and they can only be understood in a European context. For Victoria, although she was born in England and became the figurehead of the British Empire, England was also a place of lifelong exile. She grew up as an immigrant in London. Her mother, who had imperfect English, filled her with all the immigrant uncertainties, as well as hopes; and many of her adult characteristics are based upon the classic immigrant insecurity. For example, her cunning ability to hoard wealth is classic immigrant behaviour, replicated in so many first- and second-generation immigrant families. In America, where everyone started, at one stage or another, as an immigrant, this amassing of money is popularly described as the American Dream. Not having the security of belonging, the immigrant tries to make cash a substitute for being at home. Monarchs who came before Victoria were strapped for cash because the Prime Ministers controlled the purse strings. Victoria was much cleverer at extracting money from the system than either of her two uncle-kings or her forebears had been. By lying low during her widowhood, and by negotiating extraordinarily generous allowances for her offspring from her Prime Ministers, she laid the foundation for the prodigious wealth of the present British Royal Family[4] – a mixed blessing for them politically, and in her lifetime a habit which came close to being politically disastrous.

Hitherto, from 1688 to Queen Victoria's time, the wealth of Britain had largely been concentrated in the landed classes, though this was changing thanks to the Industrial Revolution. The English ruling classes acquired armorial bearings, built themselves palaces on the ducal scale, and owned huge acreage and princely rents, all of which bolstered their status as 'aristocrats'. But their 'aristocracy' had the naked purpose of acquiring and retaining power. Since 1689, there had been a very simple relation between the Whig families who exercised power and their monarchs. The English and Scottish oligarchy held the power in Britain. They did not do so, as Oliver Cromwell had unsuccessfully tried to do during the 1650s, without a monarch. But they did so having acquired monarchs from the Continent who would do their bidding – first William of Orange, and subsequently the Hanoverian *Kurfürsten*, so-called electors of the all-but-defunct Holy Roman Empire. Part of the fascination of Victoria's long reign is found in her partial failure to understand this dynamic, particularly in her widowhood. Successive Prime Ministers had to teach her that she was not an absolute monarch in the continental mould. It was this fact which enabled her successors to continue in place, while those of her descendants and relations who conducted themselves as autocrats in Berlin, for example, or in St Petersburg found themselves deposed.

The British ruling class, who had beheaded Charles I and sent James II into exile, might clothe majesty with ceremony, but there was no question about who was in charge. Lenin's fundamental political question – Who? Whom? – was easily answered in Britain in 1819, the year that Victoria was born. Who held control? The landed and titled class. Over whom? The rest of the country. The answer was slightly more complex than this, in so far as the 'gentry', having a firm system of primogeniture, had, since medieval times, intermingled with the mercantile and professional classes. Second sons, such as Dick Whittington, had no land or rent to inherit and had been obliged to go to the cities, usually London, to make their fortune. Following the Industrial Revolution in the closing decades of the eighteenth century, Britain had developed new ways to generate wealth, and in the years of Victoria's reign it would turn out to be necessary greatly to expand 'the governing class' to include the magnates of industry and the princes of commerce. Lady Bracknell's question – 'Were you born into the purple of commerce or did you rise through the ranks of the aristocracy?' – was, when it was first posed in Oscar Wilde's play of 1895, perfectly acute from an economic and political point of view. Power and wealth are the same things, and the British political system evolved to absorb the new super-rich into the 'aristocracy', just as it enfranchised the growing middle classes and eventually extended the franchise to all classes. The monarchy remained part of the system – indeed, an integral part. For the older oligarchy it was a bastion against egalitarianism; for the rising crowds of 'villa conservatives' and working-class Tories, it was a way of maintaining a continuity with the past, and of avoiding the disruptions of political unrest such as were seen in the revolutions abroad of 1848 and 1870. Even for political progressives in England, the monarchy had its uses – its ritualized status could sanction political change even when this change was radically undermining the power of the House of Lords. (The Liberals would never have completed the extension of the franchise without a monarchy to insist that the Lords made the necessary concessions.)

So much hung on a monarchy, and much, therefore, hung upon the fitness of the monarch to occupy the throne; much hung upon her understanding of her role. Yet for Victoria herself, as for her future husband, and cousin, there was a quite other understanding of ancestry. The grand dukes and electors and princes of Middle Europe were literally veins carrying down through the history of the Holy Roman Empire the story of European governance. From infancy to old age, Victoria carried around a consciousness of the huge 'Royal Family' of Europe from which she sprang, and into which her children would, for the most part, marry. Particularly in her letters to her sister-in-law the Grand Duchess of Saxe-Coburg, which covered most of their grown-up lives, she showed an everlasting awareness of the existence, marriages, births, deaths and life stories of this great cloud of royalties. Throughout her reign, while her Cabinet ministers were wrestling with a changing Britain, a Britain that was expanding its overseas Empire, worrying about the future of Ireland, extending the franchise, allowing and then expanding Free Trade, building schools, reforming the army, noting with a mixture of emotions the growth of the petty-bourgeoisie and the expansion and suffering of the working class, Victoria – caught up with these facts of life as political realities – was also keeping up a constant exchange of news about kings, queens, emperors, grand duchesses, their dynastic rise and fall, their intermarriage and their place in the new scheme of things. At times, when you read this copious correspondence, several letters a week on occasion, you are listening to the monologue of a duchess in Proust. But she was no snob, and her awareness of all these royal figures, major and minor, and her interest in their doings, was one way of being aware of European political realities. Victoria, as she grew into the role of the Head of State of the most powerful country in the world, had a relationship with Europe (literally a blood relationship) which was quite different from that of her successive British Governments. While her Prime Ministers and Foreign Secretaries discussed Europe's future, Victoria was personally related to those at the heart of such discussions. It has been well said that 'the dispute with Lord Palmerston, for example, was famously that much worse because Victoria and Albert's truly pan-European family connections provided a communications network rivalling, and very often interfering with that of the Foreign Office'.[5]As her long reign continued, and as she developed her inherited Coburg skills as a marriage-broker, she found herself the matriarch and grandmother of the majority of European governments, and one has to use historical imagination to recall that this was far more than a ritualized symbol.

If Marx was right, that 'the secret of nobility is zoology',[6] this is even truer of royalty. Success in breeding, which Marx saw as the key to aristocratic power and Darwin would erect into the principle of the human dominion over this very planet, lies at the heart of things. Since 1701, the British royal line had depended not merely on the ability to breed, but to breed Protestants. Bismarck, on the opposite end of the political spectrum from Karl Marx, sought to be equally offensive when he said that Sachsen-Coburg was the 'stud farm of Europe', but if the crowned heads of the interconnected and international monarchical system needed replenishment, such stud farms were necessary; 'zoology' had to be effective, and Coburg, by the beginning of the nineteenth century, was some stud farm.

Victoria and Albert's grandmother, dynasty-builder the Duchess Auguste, was beadily aware that she was living in a new Europe. The dynastic and territorial ambitions of Napoleon lay in ruins. And marriage could bring to prominence royal personages who had not necessarily triumphed on the battlefield or inherited extensive domains. Born Auguste of Reuss-Ebersdorf, she was one of the great beauties of her age, painted by Tischbein (Johann Heinrich, the 'Elder'). The canvas, now in the United States, depicts the eighteen-year-old Auguste, two years before her marriage, as the grieving widow Artemisia, whose great monument to her husband Mausolus gave to the ancient world one of its Seven Wonders, and to the languages of Europe the term 'mausoleum'. When it is remembered that Auguste's most celebrated grandchild was to become the inconsolable Widow of Windsor, there seems something prophetic about the painting of the grandmother, still in her youth, gazing mournfully at her husband's urn. The picture was commissioned by her father Heinrich XXIV, Count of Reuss-Ebersdorf, as an advertisement of her charms on the marriage market. The somewhat porcine Franz of Saxe-Coburg-Saalfeld (1750–1806), heir to the dukedom of Saxe-Coburg-Saalfeld, was so taken with her that he paid four times the asking price to the painter. In fact, he was forced into a marriage to another woman, the poor sixteen-year-old Sophie Saxe-Hildburghausen, who died seven months after the wedding, leaving him free to marry Auguste.

Once she had married Franz in 1777, and provided him with seven children, Auguste showed herself to be a matchmaker of formidable energy. In 1795, the German-born Russian Empress Catherine invited Franz and Auguste to the Court of St Petersburg, and they took along their three eldest daughters. It was said that as the three young women arrived for a ball at the Winter Palace, the old Empress and her grandson Constantine were watching them through a window. The eldest daughter, Sophie, tripped on her gown as she emerged from the carriage; the second, Antoinette, anxious not to repeat the tumble, crawled out of the carriage on all fours; the third, Juliane or Jülchen, lifted her skirts and was able to jump out without mishap. 'All right,' Constantine said, 'if it must be so, I'll have the little monkey. It dances prettily.' Had Russia developed in a more liberal direction after the Napoleonic Wars, Constantine might well have been chosen as Emperor. In December 1825, when the mutinous troops called for '*Constantin i Constitutia!*' ('Constantine and the Constitution!'), the more simple-minded believed that 'Constitutia' was the name of his wife. Alas, his marriage to Juliane had long since dissolved when the Decembrists – those who had believed in the possibility of making Russia a constitutional system such as Britain's – were sent to their long Siberian exile.

The marriage was not a success. Constantine 'claimed condescensions from her, such as can scarcely be hinted at'. At fifteen, Jülchen could not cope with the sexual demands of an experienced army officer. By the time she grew up, she sought consolation from other lovers, and, even though he came to Coburg, trying to woo her back as late as 1814, the marriage was really over in 1801.

Auguste had greater success with the marriage of her son Leopold (1790–1865), who, the year after the combined British and Prussian victory at Waterloo, married Princess Charlotte of Great Britain. Charlotte was the daughter of the Prince Regent – the future George IV. She was the prince's only legitimate offspring, and she would one day be Queen of England. Her consort would therefore in effect be king, and king of the country which of all the nations in Europe seemed poised – with its triumph over the Emperor Napoleon, with its pioneering of industrial revolution, with its expanding colonies in India – to be master of the victorious future.

Charlotte, moreover, possessed the advantage not merely of being young, intelligent and beautiful; she was also the daughter of a highly unpopular Prince Regent and niece of his even less attractive brothers. Charlotte was the nation's bright future, the figure in whom the British people could rest their hopes.

Leopold had first visited London in 1815, during the victory celebrations after Waterloo, in the entourage of the Russian imperial party. So flooded was the British capital by visiting dignitaries that all the hotels were full, and Leopold's first lodgings – the only rooms that could be found at short notice – were over a grocer's shop in Marylebone High Street. This did not deter the young man, then twenty-five, from being invited to all the celebratory parties by the Prince Regent.

Leopold had inherited his mother's good looks, and her eye for the main chance. From the 'zoological' point of view, the House of Coburg was a perfectly reasonable option for the British Royal Family: they were the right religion – and the Grand Duchess Catherine, sister of the new Emperor Nicholas I – had primed the pump. The Romanovs believed that the Coburgs would be useful allies to the Russians if married into the British Royal Family.[7] So the wedding took place. Charlotte was ecstatically happy to be separated from her hated father and to have escaped marriage to some of the truly ugly options, such as the Prince of Orange. It would seem to have been a very happy match, and she was soon pregnant.

Princess Charlotte suffered two miscarriages, but in 1817, she appeared to be carrying a baby to full term. This was indeed the case. In the light of her previous misfortunes in pregnancy, she was laid up for several weeks before the *accouchement*. It was to be an important national event; Charlotte was heir presumptive to King George III's throne and, as always happened when a birth was close to the succession, the chief officers of state were required to be present as witnesses. The Archbishop of Canterbury and the Lord Chancellor both made their way to Claremont, Leopold's house near Esher in Surrey. The Secretary of State for War and the Home Secretary also appeared.

At nine in the evening on 5 November, a son was stillborn. The princess appeared to receive with tranquillity the knowledge that her infant was dead. She rallied, and took a little food. As evening turned to night, however, it was evident that all was not well. Charlotte complained of singing in her ears; her heart palpitated and she had violent stomach pains. She felt extremely cold, and however many blankets and hot-water bottles were provided, she shivered convulsively. Since she was haemorrhaging internally, nothing could have been more disastrous than to apply heat to her body. At 2.30 am on 6 November 1817, Princess Charlotte died.

It was an event which caused intense national shock. George III was still alive, but the question of the succession now posed itself insistently. In the immediate future, there was no danger of the line actually fizzling to nothing. Of his fifteen children, twelve survived; but the youngest of these, Princess Sophia, was forty years old, and the only hope of breeding a new heir rested with the sons. The Prince Regent – destined to inherit the throne in 1820 – was out of the running; he was long estranged from his wife, Caroline of Brunswick. The Duke of York, whose German wife was immured in the English countryside, had no hope of a legitimate child. He was fifty-four years old, and deeply involved with a middle-aged mistress. The next in line, William, Duke of Clarence, had suffered no difficulty in producing children. He had ten of them, by the celebrated comedienne Mrs Jordan, but none were legitimate. The Duke of Kent, aged fifty, had been living a quasi-marital existence, very fondly, with his French-Canadian mistress Madame de Saint-Laurent for the last twenty-four years, and even if she were to be made his lawful wife, she was too old to have children. The Duke of Sussex had twice defied the Royal Marriages Act by taking wives without his father's consent. Neither the Duke of Cumberland nor the Duke of Cambridge, at the time of Charlotte's death, had any legitimate successors.

The princess's death therefore triggered a race, among the overweight, late-middle-aged sons of George III, to find a lawful wife who could become the next Queen of England, and the mother of future monarchs. The Duke of Clarence ditched Mrs Jordan and made repeated proposals of marriage to a Ramsgate heiress named Miss Tilney Long. Having been repeatedly refused, he tried a woman in Brighton called Miss Wykeham, and when she turned him down he went down the traditional royal path of seeking a bride among the royal stud farms of Protestant Germany. He selected the plain, evangelical Princess Adelaide of Saxe-Meiningen, aged twenty-six. The Duke of Cambridge, aged a sprightly forty-three, joined the race by marrying Princess Augusta of Hesse-Cassel, a beautiful girl aged twenty who was a great-granddaughter of King George II of England.

Princess Charlotte's desolated widower, Leopold, had lost not only a young wife of whom he was lovingly fond, but also his place on the royal snakes and ladders board. Having been poised to become a king in all but name, he had overnight become a royal nobody. 'And now my poor son stands alone in a foreign country amid the ruins of his shattered happiness,' said his mother. Leopold's instinct, immediately after Princess Charlotte's lugubrious funeral, was to head for home. His wise counsellor, however, the Coburg doctor Baron Stockmar, had other advice. Leopold should hang around and see what turned up. As would often prove to be the case, Stockmar's advice was worth heeding.

In 1876, when she presented new colours to her father's old regiment, the Royal Scots, at Ballater, Queen Victoria said, 'He was proud of his profession, and I was always told to consider myself a soldier's child.'[8]

Edward, Duke of Kent, was brought up in Kew. The Old Palace where King George and Queen Charlotte lived was too small for their numerous progeny, so Edward and William (the future William IV) were put into the hands of a governor and brought up, in some comfort, in a house nearby. When William was sent away to sea, it was decided that Edward should become a soldier, a German soldier, and he was sent for his training at Hanover. He had already, in late adolescence, developed habits of wild extravagance, and no one ever taught him the value of money.

He arrived in Hanover in 1785. The punishing disciplines of German military life – inspired by the successful military genius of

Frederick the Great, King of Prussia, who was still alive – were a rude
shock to the English prince, but he had no choice but to succumb
to them. In 1790, he was given command of the Royal Fusiliers
(7th Foot), who were posted in Gibraltar. The 'Royals', as they were
known, had been looking forward to a light duty on the Rock. It
was a shock to encounter the duke's methods, for, as has been rightly
said, 'Germany had made him a good soldier, but it had made him
a German soldier, completely inhuman and bestially severe with the
troops'.[9] Drills and inspections happened with great frequency. The
smallest infringement of discipline was met with merciless floggings.
The men were on the parade ground for hours at a time. The duke
was detested by his men. By the end of the year, it was agreed in
London and by his commanding officers – Lieutenant General Sir
Robert Boyd and Major General Charles O'Hara – that the best way
of avoiding a mutiny was to send the duke to Canada.

He arrived in Quebec in 1791. Here, he continued to be as cruel to
his men as he had been in Gibraltar. The barrack square echoed to
the screams of men being flogged on 'Edward's orders'. He pursued
in person one deserter, a French soldier called La Rose, exploring
mountainous country and forests before coming upon La Rose in
an inn at Pointe-aux-Trembles. 'You are fortunate, sire, that I am
unarmed,' said La Rose, 'for if I had a pistol, by Heaven, I would
shoot you where you stand.' La Rose was brought back to Quebec,
and Kent insisted upon the maximum sentence under the Mutiny
Act – 999 strokes of the lash. He stood by while this punishment was
administered. La Rose did not utter a whimper, and when it was over,
he went up to Kent and snapped his fingers in his face: 'That's that. It
is the bullet that should punish, my lord. No whip can cow a French
soldier.'[10]

The duke's Jekyll and Hyde personality became apparent when he
met Julie de Saint-Laurent, a beautiful young Frenchwoman with
whom he fell passionately in love, and who remained his devoted
domestic companion for the next quarter of a century. They became
attached while he was still posted in Gibraltar; she seems to have

had at least two aristocratic French lovers before she met the Duke of Kent, but no children. If the intransigent King, his father, had not insisted upon bringing in the Royal Marriages Act of 1772, whereby no member of the Royal Family could marry without their father's permission, there would have been no shortage of heirs after the death of Princess Charlotte!

As things were, the boys had to choose, either to marry in defiance of their father – as the Duke of Sussex did – and thereby remove themselves from the royal succession; or to live with their chosen companions, without matrimony. So it was that William, Duke of Clarence, had his ten children, and many devoted years, with the actress Mrs Jordan. And the Duke of Kent had his beloved 'Julie'. Her real name was Thérèse-Bernardine Montgenet, the daughter of a respectable engineer in the highways department at Besançon. The Duke of Kent always insisted that she had never been an actress – so why she adopted another name in the theatrical mode, and was called 'Madame de Saint-Laurent' remains a mystery to this day.[11] Had Princess Charlotte not died in Claremont in 1817, and had she become the Queen of England upon the death of her father in 1820, there is no reason to suppose that Edward, Duke of Kent, would not have stayed happily with Madame de Saint-Laurent for the rest of his life.

While the portly dukes of Clarence and Cambridge were doing their bit for the advancement of the English monarchy by discarding their mistresses and pursuing brides of childbearing age, their brother the Duke of Kent was not to be outdone. Satirists did their best to make the situation funny, but it was one of those occasions, of which English history provides so many, when events were more grotesque than satire could ever invent.

> Yoicks! The R—l Sport's begun
> I' faith but it is glorious fun

> For hot and hard each R—l pair
> Are at it hunting for an Heir

sniggered 'Peter Pindar'. More (unintentionally) amusing was the author of 'Nature's Policy for Man and Nations', which apostrophized,

> O Kent beloved, in thy return the instrumental
> Arm, destined to consummate the awful purpose,
> Of the long dreadful and eventful times, obey
> Thy God's mysterious will!

> The numerous nuptials of thy illustrious house
> And threatened loss, the intended cause of thy return
> Are Heaven's mysterious language...
> That thou, O Kent, should'st forthwith consummate
>   our good
> In the common bliss of kings, subjects and nations...[12]

The Duke of Kent was in Belgium with Julie de Saint-Laurent when Princess Charlotte died. They had recently moved into an old house which they had enjoyed decorating, papering and whitewashing[13] – as the duke told his brother's old mistress, Mrs Fitzherbert.

On the morning that the news reached Brussels of Princess Charlotte's death, Thomas Creevey, gossip and diarist, happened to be in town. He rushed to the duke's house, where he found him in a state of agitation. 'The country will now look up to me, Mr Creevey, to give them an heir to the crown,' he said.

The bombshell had first exploded over the duke's breakfast table. Julie, opening the weekly bag of letters from England, had fished out the *Morning Chronicle*. When she had read of 'the dreadful catastrophe at Claremont', poor Madame de Saint-Laurent had shrieked and fallen in a faint on the floor. She knew at once that her happy relationship with the duke, which had begun in 1791, would now come to an end. As the duke tactlessly informed Mr Creevey, two possible brides came at once to mind: the Princess of Baden and the Princess of Saxe-Coburg.

The latter was his choice. Armed with letters of introduction from the princess's brother, the bereaved Prince Leopold, the Duke of Kent set out for the Castle of Amorbach.

She was Marie Luise Victoria, known as Victoire, one of the children of the indefatigable matchmaker, the Duchess Auguste. She was the sister of the widowed Prince Leopold. She was born on 17 August 1786, the day that her great-uncle by marriage, Frederick the Great, died. She was only seventeen when they married her off to Prince Emich Charles of Leiningen, a man old enough to be her father, on 21 December 1803. Since the Thirty Years War in the seventeenth century, the poverty-stricken territory of Amorbach in Lower Franconia had scarcely seen more miserable days. Napoleon's armies left it desolate. In 1806, the year that Victoire's father-in-law died and she became the Princess of Leiningen, Napoleon formally brought the Holy Roman Empire to an end. Whatever their political future – whether as a dependency of Austria or Prussia, or as part of a German federation – the people of Lower Franconia were actually starving when Victoire became their duchess. Her husband's income was tiny. Two children were born to her: Charles in 1804 and Feodore – later the devoted companion of Queen Victoria – in 1807. The marriage was not a happy one, and in 1814, Victoire was left a poverty-stricken widow.

Queen Victoria's mother had known the real hazards of the royal snakes and ladders board, and the experience left her with a perpetual sense of insecurity – a sense which the Queen would inherit, and live with until her death. Unlike the prosperous aristocrats and merchants over whom she would rule, Victoria belonged to the class of European monarchy who could be reduced to penury, or killed, at the whims of fate. She always felt the keenest sympathy for those who were in this position – sympathy, and a little horror, for there but for the grace of God might any ruler go. Even those who did not belong to the inner circle of the European stud farm excited Victoria's keen empathy when they were put down from their thrones, whether they were Bonapartes in exile or Indian maharajahs.

Her mother, plump, red-cheeked, brightly dressed in silks and satins as she might have been, was all but an indigent when she met the Duke of Kent in 1818. She had no prospects outside the chance of marriage. She was thirty-two years old.

By now the race for a royal heir to King George IV was on. The Duke of Clarence was still eyeing up Miss Wykeham, a rich heiress. The Duchess of Cumberland, who had lost her first baby at birth in 1817, was pregnant again. The Duke of Cambridge was on the point of marrying Princess Augusta, daughter of the Landgrave of Hesse-Cassel. There was no point in delay. In May, Lord Castlereagh told the House of Commons that the Prince Regent had given his consent for the Duke of Kent to marry the widow of the late Prince of Leiningen. Parliament voted him an increase of his income of £6,000. A prodigiously extravagant man, Edward Kent had been hoping for £25,000, which was what Parliament had voted for his brother the Duke of York. But these were hard times, and, moreover, Prince Leopold, who was hanging on to Claremont and all his emoluments as a field marshal and colonel of a cavalry regiment, refused to give up the colossal annual allowance of £50,000 which he had enjoyed as the consort of Princess Charlotte.

So, by the standards of English royalty, Victoire was marrying a pauper. By the standards of Lower Franconia, she was in clover.

The pair left Amorbach and went to her native Coburg to be married. The ceremony took place in the superb baroque Schloss Ehrenberg which Duke Ernst I, Victoire's brother, had only lately refurbished. They were married according to Lutheran rites in the great Hall of Giants, an assembly room embellished with huge white plaster giants.

Kent took his bride to England, and on 11 July, at Kew, they went through the marriage ceremony again, this time according to the rites of the Church of England. In the same ceremony, his brother

William, Duke of Clarence, was married to Princess Adelaide of Saxe-Meiningen. The service sheet was printed in German and in English, and, such was Victoire's uncertainty of the latter tongue, she was given a phonetic version of her speech of thanks at the wedding breakfast: 'Ei hoeve tu regrétt, biing *aes yiett* so littl cônversent in thie Inglisch lênguetsch, uitsch obleitschës – miy, tu seh, in *averi fiú words*, theat ei em môhst grêtful for yur congratuleschens end gud uishes, *end heili* flatterd, bei yur allucheon, to mei brother.'[14]

They returned to Germany shortly after the ceremony, and returned to Amorbach, where her fifteen-year-old son Prince Charles ruled over the impoverished princedom. With his mania for spending money which he did not possess, and his passion for interior decoration, the Duke of Kent borrowed £10,000 and set about beautifying the Schloss, bringing over English workmen to install stoves, to build new stables and to lay out the gardens. Prince Metternich, who visited the newly-weds, recalled that, 'The Duke regaled me incessantly with his stables, the particular pleasure which his new home affords him.'[15]

No one had pretended that the marriage had been anything other than one of convenience and arrangement. But all the indications are that the pair quickly became very fond of one another.

In November 1818, the duke became aware of an exit and an entrance into the world. On the 17th, he heard that his old mother Queen Charlotte had died. It also became clear that his wife was pregnant. They resolved to spend the winter quietly in Amorbach, but that the *accouchement* should take place in England.

Questions of zoology must arise in any dynastic history such as ours. As it happens, a very dramatic zoological puzzle is posed by Queen Victoria's genetic record. She would have nine children, and through them, she passed haemophilia to her descendants. Of the nine, three children were affected by the condition. Two of her daughters were carriers who passed the gene to some of their sons, who were affected, and to some of their daughters, who in turn became carriers. Prince

Leopold was the only one of Queen Victoria's sons to be a haemophiliac. His son was free of the disease; his daughter became a carrier.

There were no instances of haemophilia in the British Royal Family before Victoria. We would be unable to work out the puzzle of 'Queen Victoria's Gene' were it not for a Moravian monk, Father Gregor Mendel, who was born three years after her. It was his pioneering work on sweet peas which began the modern science of genetics, leading eventually to Francis Crick and James Watson a century later discovering the structure of DNA. As it happens, the genetic history of Queen Victoria's mother is well documented. In 1911, William Bullock and Paul Fildes, working for the Eugenics Society in London, produced a paper on haemophilia, and traced the Duchess of Kent's family back over eight generations. The haemophilia descendants are marked on a chart, in a genealogical table containing over 500 names, kept in the Royal Society of Medicine Library in Wimpole Street, London.[16]

Neither of Victoria's half-siblings carried the gene. The second scroll in the Royal Society of Medicine Library covers Victoria's ancestry over seventeen generations, and there appears to be no mention of haemophilia in her family. Statisticians have calculated that the individual whose mother is a carrier has a 1 in 2 chance of developing as a haemophiliac himself. There is between a 1 in 25,000 and a 1 in 100,000 chance of developing the disease as the result of a mutation in the mother's ovary. If the mutation did occur, it would seem likely that it occurred not in the duchess, but in the Duke of Kent.

In a fascinating book, *Queen Victoria's Gene* published in 1995, D. M. Potts and W. T. W. Potts – professors respectively of population and family planning, and biology – set out the facts. They dwell on the fact that the Duke of Kent and Madame de Saint-Laurent had been without issue; they remind us of the high statistical unlikelihood of a cell mutation in either parent; and they point to the enormous advantage which the duchess would enjoy, if only she could become pregnant. 'If Victoire, keen to produce a child who might well be heir to the British throne, had suspected her husband's fertility, she might well have tried to improve her chances with another man.'[17] Much can hang on those two words, 'might well'.

The theory seems powerful[18] until you acknowledge three things. First, it is all argued from a set of negatives: no children were born to Kent and Madame de Saint-Laurent; no previous members of the British Royal Family appear to have been haemophiliac, etc. Negatives are not evidence. Second, the evidence is that, although they scarcely knew one another when they got married, the duke and duchess were to all appearances extremely fond of one another. Finally, the child, when born, bore an extraordinary resemblance to King George III. Moreover, Potts and Potts try to strengthen their case by stating that there are no subsequent cases, in Queen Victoria's descendants, of George III's porphyria; but this is not true. For example, the late Prince William of Gloucester, a grandson of King George V, when examined at Addenbrooke's Hospital in Cambridge, and again by Professor Ishihara of Tokyo, was found by both medics to be suffering from variegate porphyria, by then in remission – the symptoms of which had been fever and a blistering rash. Since Potts and Potts wrote their book, Professor Timothy Peters has, in fact, cast serious doubt on whether George III had porphyria at all. And this would make half their 'case' collapse. Whether George III did or did not have the condition, the Potts professors' belief that there was no porphyria among the descendants certainly convinced me, when I first read their book, that the odds against the Duke of Kent being Victoria's father were overwhelming. But the fact that they made this mistake made me hesitate. And standing in front of several portraits of George III removed my doubts – for there were the same hooded, protuberant eyes, the same bird-like nose that were so conspicuous in Victoria's mature face. When, in her grown-up life, her ministers feared that she was going mad, like her grandfather, they were surely right to feel that she was recognizably his descendant. (She had other characteristics redolent of him too, including her detailed knowledge of people, high and low, and her kindliness.)

So, although I initially found Potts and Potts very persuasive, with the passing of time my mind has altered. The present book is written with the confidence that Victoria was indeed the daughter of Edward, Duke of Kent, and his wife Victoire.

Despite their ambition that she should be born in England, Queen Victoria's parents left it nail-bitingly late before they returned from Germany. They set out for England on 28 March, when the duchess was nearly eight months pregnant. It was a journey of over 430 miles, at a time when there were no tarmacadamed roads in Europe. Not much had changed in the state of European highways since Laurence Sterne wrote *A Sentimental Journey*, and that whimsical author would no doubt have enjoyed describing the scene as they left Amorbach. The duke drove the duchess himself in a cane phaeton – money was again tight, and he could not find the ready cash to tip a coachman. But he also felt a tender solicitude for her comfort. Then came a carriage containing Victoire's favourite caged birds, cats and dogs. There were English maids, two cooks, Dr Wilson, a retired naval surgeon, and a remarkable obstetrician, Frau Charlotte Siebold. She was a qualified doctor as well as a skilled midwife. (Given the crucial role she played in bringing the future Queen of England into this world – and, a little later, the expertise with which she oversaw the birth of Prince Albert – it is remarkable that Queen Victoria so forcefully disapproved of women training as doctors.) As personal attendants, they brought not only maids and a valet, but also the faithful Baroness Späth, who had been Victoire's lady-in-waiting since her first marriage.

The Duke of Kent's personal equerry, who accompanied them on this journey, was a notably handsome staff officer in the Royal Horse Artillery, John Conroy. He was an Irishman, and his wife, Elizabeth, was the daughter of the duke's aide de camp, Major General George Fisher. Conroy was to play the role of demon-king or pantomime villain in Queen Victoria's childhood mythology, and this story will unfold as we follow her through the years of infancy and youth. At the outset, however, it is worth getting something clear about Conroy, which was almost certainly unknown to any of the players in the melodrama in which he played the villain. During the time of his ascendant role in the Royal Household, it was believed by the gossips that he had become the lover of Victoire, the Duchess of Kent. It was even believed by some that he was the father of Queen Victoria. No evidence for this exists at all, and the more one examines the story, the less probable either supposition appears.

Conroy's demon status remained unimpaired, not least because he was considered beneath mention. In the *Dictionary of National Biography*, for example, published in multi-volume form from 1917 onwards, the editors Sir Leslie Stephen and Sir Sidney Lee omitted Conroy altogether. Lee was a fine biographer of Victoria and of Edward VII and a royal friend. He believed that by concealment of Conroy he would make him less interesting to posterity. The reverse occurred, leading to the inevitable question, what did the guardians of the royal shrine wish to conceal?

For many years, the nature of Conroy's obsession with the Royal Family remained mysterious, even though it was clear from the outset that he saw himself in a role which was quite other than servile to them. His grandson, a science don at Oxford, left the family papers to the college of which he was a fellow – Balliol – and these were unearthed and catalogued by two patient scholars, John Jones, the college archivist, and Katherine Hudson. In 1994, Hudson published a definitive life of Conroy – *A Royal Conflict* – which established beyond question what had been buzzing in Conroy's head even before Queen Victoria's birth. Conroy believed that his wife, Elizabeth, whom he had married in 1808, was the Duke of Kent's daughter. In a purple leather diary, belonging to Conroy's grandson, and preserved at Balliol, there is written, in code – 'Lady Conroy was the only child of General Fisher... Lady Conroy is said to be the daughter of the Duke of Kent who had been sent to Canada to keep him out of mischief.'

Beliefs do not need to be substantiated by evidence in order to be held fervently. It was, in fact, impossible for Elizabeth Fisher to have been the daughter of the Duke of Kent. She was baptized in Quebec on 28 November 1790, when the Duke of Kent was still in Gibraltar, one of the most detested officers in the British Army, meting out terrible punishments to his troops. The relationship between the Fishers and Kent was close. General Fisher was his aide de camp. The general's brother had been the duke's tutor in youth. Some rumours did exist about Elizabeth's legitimacy, with Algernon Seymour, Duke of Somerset and Earl of Hertford, as a far likelier candidate than any. It is not clear how Conroy formed the obsession, nor even whether Elizabeth Fisher, who bore him six children, was aware of it. But the point is that, as his children were born, Conroy was unable to avoid thinking that they were cousins of the royal line; and, as with all thoughts about royal bastardy, whether or not based on fantasy, there was the thought that, had things been only a very little different, and had carnal knowledge been accompanied by a marriage certificate, the supposed royal bastard might be wearing the crown. Had Mrs Fisher been the daughter of Edward, Duke of Kent (which she wasn't), and had the duke married her mother (which he didn't), John Conroy would one day have been Prince Consort to the Queen of England.

The diligence of researchers in the Balliol archive provides us with a vital missing piece of the jigsaw puzzle. Ludicrous as Conroy's misconception was, it explains, even if it does not justify, some of his later behaviour.

When the strange caravan reached Frankfurt, the duke was thinking of his ex-mistress. He wrote an anxious letter to the Baron de Mallet asking after Julie's health, 'for I fear what she has read recently in the papers has had again a very sensible effect on her nerves, which I gather, from her last letter, written, although with her usual affection, evidently under great agitation.'[19]

His heart was sad for Julie, but his duty was now with Victoire, and the next day the entourage rumbled over the cobblestones of Frankfurt am Main, past the house where Goethe was born, and on to the French road. They reached Calais on 18 April, but the gusty weather made it unthinkable that a heavily pregnant woman should cross the Channel. Even after they had waited a week, the sea was still choppy, and the three-hour voyage was uncomfortable. As soon as possible, they made the journey to Kensington, at that time still a village detached from Westminster, set in the rolling fields and lawns of a glorious English spring. At the northern end of London, in the equally leafy village of Hampstead, John Keats was writing his 'Ode to a Nightingale'.

The Kents had been allowed the vacant apartments of the Princess of Wales, Caroline of Brunswick. In one of his vindictive acts against his wife, the Prince Regent had stripped the apartments of their furniture, and they had been neither aired nor heated when the Kents arrived. The larder was unusable because water constantly dripped from its ceiling. Kent, however, had a mania for house-improvement. £2,000 was borrowed from somewhere, and in the next weeks, the rooms were repainted and papered, furniture had been purchased, shelves and a desk adorned his library, and in the duchess's bedroom, the windows were decorated with white curtains and the bed with white cambric. A mahogany crib was in waiting on the new carpet as, on 23 May, at 10.30 in the evening, the Duchess of Kent went into labour. It was her third child, and it was an easy birth after six hours. At 4.15 the following morning, on 24 May 1819, the child was born: 'a pretty little Princess, plump as a partridge', as her mother described her.

In Coburg, when she heard the news, the baby's grandmother Auguste said, 'Another Charlotte! The English like Queens, and the niece of the ever-lamented beloved Charlotte will be very dear to them.'[20]

The christening took place a month later in the Cupola Room at Kensington Palace on 24 June. The gold font, part of the regalia of the kingdom, was brought from the Tower of London, and crimson velvet curtains from the chapel of St James's. There was no question that this was to be a royal baptism. The original name chosen was Georgiana. It was an English name, an eighteenth-century coinage, combining the names of Queen Anne and the Georges. It was originally pronounced 'George-Anna', but later the usual pronunciation was 'George-Ayner'; the most celebrated holder of the name was the Duchess of Devonshire (1757–1806), the radical wife of the fifth duke, and friend of Charles James Fox. There then arose the opportunity to name the infant after the Emperor of Russia, and to have Tsar Alexander as a sponsor. George IV insisted that, if this were to be the case – and the name Alexandrina were to be chosen – the British royal names, compacted into 'Georgiana', could not be secondary to the Russian. If the child were to be Alexandrina, then she must have no other name. So the King appeared to maintain until the day of the christening itself, which was conducted by the Archbishop of Canterbury, Dr Manners-Sutton, assisted by William Howley, Bishop of London. The mother's name, Victoria, was given almost as an after thought. The other two sponsors were the widowed Queen of Württemburg (George III's eldest daughter and the Princess Royal of England) and her maternal grandmother, the Duchess of Saxe-Coburg-Saalfeld. None of the three godparents were present in person, and they were represented by the child's uncle, the Duke of York, and his sisters Princess Augusta and the Duchess of Gloucester.

When Drina, as the infant was called for short, was a month old, her parents went to live in Prince Leopold's residence at Claremont. In August, the princess was vaccinated, the first royal personage to undergo such treatment, against smallpox. By the end of the month, news had reached Claremont, via the princess's old German grandmother, that the family had been blessed by another birth. Madame Siebold, the German *accoucheuse* and doctor who had assisted Drina into the world, had gone back to Germany. In the summer palace of Rosenau, four miles outside Coburg, the present Duchess of Saxe-Coburg-Saalfeld, Luise, had given birth to a son, whose name was Albert.

England was in a bad way. When the old King died, in the following
year, Byron would write in 'The Vision of Judgment',

> A better farmer ne'er brushed dew from lawn,
> A worse king never left a realm undone.

When Victoria was less than three months old, industrial unrest
swept the North of England. At one stage as many as 20,000
Manchester factory workers were on strike. On 16 August, groups of
factory workers, with their wives and children, gathered at St Peter's
Fields, Manchester, to listen to the radical Henry Hunt making a
speech. It was not an angry assembly: it had more the atmosphere
of a carnival, with people holding up banners with legends such as
'Unity and Strength' or 'Liberty and Fraternity'. But, terrified by the
prospects of a riot, the local magistrates summoned the militia, and
as Hunt arrived to speak, forty of the local yeomen cavalry rode into
the crowd with sabres drawn. Thousands of people tried to escape, but
over 400 were wounded, and 11 were killed. It became known as the
Peterloo Massacre.

The working classes and the Establishment were now at war. There
were riots in Macclesfield and in other parts of the North. Meetings
were called all over the country.

A modern reader who knew of the Duke of Kent's 'form' as an
exceptionally fierce army officer might guess that he would have sided
with those who perpetrated the massacre. But one of the fascinating
things about Kent was that he was interested in the new ideas. In 1815,
he had been sent a pamphlet called *New View of Society* by the radical
Lanarkshire factory owner Robert Owen. Owen was a socialist who
believed in sharing the ownership of his factory with the workers.
Kent and his brother the Duke of Sussex attended a lecture by Owen
at 49 Bedford Square in London in which Owen demonstrated the
class system by means of a pyramid. The apex of the pyramid was the
monarch; the sturdy base was the working class. A peer remarked to
Kent at this time that he thought that socialism's levelling tendencies

were dangerous. Kent replied, 'I foresee the results. I know that there will be a much more just equality of our race and an equality which will give much more security and happiness to all than the present system. It is for this reason I so much approve and give it my support.'

Two years later, addressing the St Patrick's Society in 1817, he said, 'My politics are no secret nor am I ashamed to avow them. With some experience of the function which I am now executing I am not at a loss for witnesses to refer to – whether in this or in any other charity meeting I ever introduced a single sentence of a political tendency... True charity is of no particular party but is the cause of all parties.'[21]

At a meeting held in the Freemasons' Hall on 26 June 1819, a month after Queen Victoria's birth, the Duke of Kent took the chair for the purpose of appointing a committee to investigate and report on Mr Owen's plan for providing for the poor and ameliorating the condition of the working classes. The duke commented on 'the anomalous condition of the country arising from the deficiency of productive employment for those who without it must be poor, in consequence of the excess to which manufactures had been extended by the late increase of machinery'.[22]

In the course of the autumn, Kent made plans to visit Owen in Lanarkshire, perhaps after Christmas, and see practical socialism in action. Fate had different ideas.

Kent had been accumulating large debts in the short time he had been back in England, and it was decided to winter beside the seaside in Devon, living modestly and avoiding society. At the end of October, the duke inspected a house at Sidmouth called Woolbrook Cottage and decided that it would suit their purposes. In early December, they set out, breaking the journey at Salisbury where the bishop, Dr Fisher, was none other than the duke's old tutor and the uncle of Mrs John Conroy. They reached Woolbrook Cottage on Christmas Eve.

'My little girl thrives under the influence of a Devonshire climate, and is, I am delighted to say, strong and healthy,' he was able to write to a friend a few days after the festival. He occupied his days in writing to Robert Owen, who had managed to become notorious.

As if it were not sufficiently shocking to propose an improvement in the lives of the working classes, Owen had tactlessly blurted out that socialism could never work until all the 'erroneous religious notions' of Christianity be discarded. 'We must act with prudence and foresight,' the duke warned Owen, while assuring him that he was 'fully satisfied with the principles'.[23]

There was no danger of the Duke of Kent having to part with a fortune in the event of a socialist revolution; in fact, things were quite the other way about, and when strapped for cash, Kent borrowed money from Owen. Life passed quietly in these philosophical reflections in the cottage; and the most dramatic incident occurred when some local boys, taking pot shots at birds, accidentally shot through little Drina's bedroom. The shattered pane fell on the floor, as the child's head was lightly dusted with splintered glass.

One disconcerting episode was when Kent encountered a fortune teller in Sidmouth, who told him, 'This year two members of the Royal Family will die.'

Kent had caught a cold while staying with the Fishers in Salisbury, and in the weeks after Christmas his chill became worse. Young Dr Stockmar, the Coburg medic, came down for a visit and was prevented from returning to Esher by a heavy fall of snow. Kent and Conroy went for a long walk on the cliffs, during which the duke got wet. Stockmar saw no cause for alarm. It was 15 January.

The next day, however, when Sir David Dundas visited Princess Augusta (one of the duke's sisters) in Windsor, he remarked that the Duchess of Kent had written of her worry concerning her husband's health. By 18 January, his condition had worsened, and on the 20th, he had taken to his bed, and was being treated by Dr Wilson and Dr Stockmar. His fever rose and delirium set in. The ineffectual and gruesome medical procedures of the day – blisters, bleeding, cupping and leeches – were gone through, to no avail. The duchess sat at his side for hours at a time. On 22 January, the duke's mind cleared and he realized that he was dying. Stockmar advised him to make his will, and this he hurriedly did, making sure that his child Drina be entrusted to the care of her mother. By evening, a group had gathered around the bed – Dr Maton, Queen Charlotte's personal physician, Dr Wilson, Prince Leopold, who had arrived from Esher, Stockmar, his staff adjutants Generals Moore and Wetherall, and John Conroy.

The duke looked up and said to them all, 'May the Almighty protect my wife and child and forgive all the sins I have committed.' Then, turning to his wife, he said, 'Do not forget me,' and he sank into delirium. On the morning of Sunday, 23 January, his wife having spent five sleepless nights at his side, Edward, Duke of Kent, gave up the struggle.

By slow progress, the desolated duchess, with her brother Prince Leopold, brought the child back to Kensington. Before the month was out, the fortune teller of Sidmouth was proved correct. During the Christmas holiday, the blind old King had a recurrence of his madness, and had spoken for fifty-eight consecutive hours without drawing breath. On 29 January, six days after his son, he breathed his last.

They buried him in the Royal Vault at Windsor. His fatherless granddaughter was even (for a while) deprived of her chance of one day becoming the Queen of England, for the Duchess of Clarence succeeded in having a second child – a daughter – who would be before her in the line of succession. The child was called Princess Elizabeth. She lived just three months. Thereafter, Victoria's position as a would-be heir to the throne looked more secure as year succeeded to year.

'I was friendless and alone,' said the Duchess of Kent, when she looked back on those dreadful times. But she did not remember with total accuracy. Though she had lost her husband, she still had her brother, Prince Leopold. General Wetherall had been appointed by the terms of Kent's will as one of the executors, to protect Victoire and to advise her. There were also her German friends, her lady-in-waiting the Baroness Späth, Feodore's governess Louise Lehzen, and the wise Dr Stockmar. And, from now onwards an unbridgeable presence in the life of both the Duchess of Kent and of little Drina, there was the loyal Irish officer who privately believed that his wife was the late Duke of Kent's daughter: that is to say, there was John Conroy.

THREE

'IT IS ONE STEP'

THE FIRST RECOLLECTION was a yellow carpet. She was crawling upon it, but she must not make a noise. If she screamed or was naughty, then her uncle Sussex would hear it, and punish her. The extraordinary old duke, who resided in the apartment below, became a figure of dread to her. One frightening thing was his wig. The other strange old men who wore wigs were called bishops: these too induced in her feelings of disgusted panic – a feeling which would last through her lifetime, even when the days were long past when the bishops, like the judges, were bewigged.

The era, which had begun in the second half of the seventeenth century, when men covered their natural hair with a wig was about to be supplanted by the modern age. One bishop of the old school who managed to calm her fears was My Lord of Salisbury, who went down on all fours and allowed her to play with his badge, which was that of Chancellor of the Order of the Garter. This was Bishop Fisher, known as the 'Kingfisher' because of his penchant for royalty. Going down on all fours before royalty came naturally to him. (It was his niece who was Lady Conroy, and his great-nieces who were the royal infant's playmates and constant companions.)

It is very vivid, the account, written down by Queen Victoria in 1872, of her childhood. It possesses the vividness of fiction, and also fiction's arbitrariness.

Claremont remains as the brightest epoch of my otherwise rather melancholy childhood – where to be under the roof of that beloved Uncle [Leopold] – to listen to some music in the Hall when there were dinner-parties – and to go and see dear old Louis! – the former faithful and devoted Dresser of Princess Charlotte – beloved and respected by all who knew her – and who doted on the little Princess who was too much an idol in the House…[1]

Claremont was where Victoria first stood upright. Her proud, doting mother noted it down on 21 May 1821 – *'Heute Morgen ist meine geliebstes Kind Victoria allein gegangen.'* ('This morning my much-loved little child Victoria walked on her own.') In her imperfect English many years later, recalling the event, the still-doting mother said, 'It is one step to be independent.'[2] Independent Victoria always was. One senses that, even if she had not been destined for royal greatness, Victoria was one of those rather alarming only children to whose beck and call parents grovel.

The 'melancholy' of her childhood was a fixed part of Queen Victoria's personal mythology. When we speak of unhappy child-hoods, however, we can mean one, or both, of two things. We can speak of the outward circumstances of childhood having been marred by poverty, illness, or the unkindness of those who hold the infant in their charge; and we can mean that childhood is an unhappy memory. Queen Victoria's was of the latter kind of 'unhappy' childhood, but despite her almost unbounded capacity for self-dramatization and self-pity, her childhood, at least her early childhood, could not be described as 'unhappy'. She was well fed and housed; she had devoted nurses and an adoring mother. She was abundantly supplied with toys and entertainments. And by the standards of the age, she was treated with pure indulgence. True, her governess, Fräulein Lehzen, was a strict woman, but she never used corporal chastisement (surely a very unusual thing in those days); and although the prospect of old men in wigs was able to terrify the infant, she was in fact much cosseted, not only by the German women in her immediate circle, but also in the wider family of her late father.

Although as a very small infant she had been known as Drina, she gradually came to be known as Victoria. Perhaps the insistence of so many wiseacres that the name was 'un-English', and that she should change it to Elizabeth accounted for her violent antipathy to Queen Elizabeth I. As Sidney Lee reminds us, she 'always deprecated any association with her'.[3] If Victoria and her mother felt like foreigners, and poor relations, this was because the duchess was a foreigner, and they were – by royal standards – poor relations. It requires no psychiatric genius to see why the relationship between monarchs and their successors is usually tense. The very existence of the heir, so necessary for the functioning of the system, is for the current occupant of the throne an incarnate *memento mori*.

Victoria, however, remembered something worse than this:

> I... led a very unhappy life as a child – had no scope for my very violent feelings of affection – had no brothers and sisters to live with – never had had a father – from my unfortunate circumstances was not on comfortable or at all intimate or confidential footing with my mother... – much as I love her now [June 1858] – and did not know what a happy domestic life was![4]

All the written evidence made at the time of her early childhood contradicts this 'memory'. Indeed, the stark contrast between her 'memory' in adult life and the reality of her mother's love during her actual childhood was only borne in upon Victoria when her mother died. When the Queen was confronted by the extent of her mother's besotted, passionate devotion, grief and remorse turned into a major crisis, amounting to a breakdown. When she had her first lessons, there was a little note (in English) awaiting the princess on her schoolroom table: 'My dear little Girl, I hope you will be very attentive in your repetition and think with what great pleasure it gives to Mamma to witness your progress in learning and good behaviour. God bless you, dearest child. Ever your very affectionate Mother, Victoria.'[5]

On the last day of 1827, when she went to bed, the seven-year-old princess found a tiny pink envelope on her pillow. Inside was a letter, urging, 'Before you shut your dear little eyes, Pray to and thank the Almighty God, for all the good you have experienced in this year.'[6] The next New Year's Eve, there was a letter on even pinker paper, containing another love letter: 'Before you shut your dear little eyes: In some hours this year is closed!... Believe me, my most beloved child, that nobody in this world can love you better than, your true and affectionate Mother. God bless you!!!'[7]

The recipient of these messages could hardly be described as emotionally deprived. This did not mean that her family relationships were uncomplicated. As a child, she lived and breathed the unassuaged hostility between her mother's entourage and the Court. Nor was it true, as she 'remembered', that Victoria 'had no brothers and sisters to live with'. You would never guess, from reading *David Copperfield*, that Charles Dickens had two sisters and a brother, just as you would never guess from reading *À la Recherche du Temps Perdu* that Proust had a brother. Similarly, from reading Queen Victoria's recollections of a solitary childhood, you could be forgiven for overlooking her half-brother and half-sister, Prince Charles and Princess Feodore, Victoire's children by Prince Emich Charles of Leiningen.

Born in 1804 and 1807, these children were old enough to remember all the excitement which burst out in Germany upon the defeat of Napoleon, though the bells of the great baroque church at Amorbach, pealing the victory over the French, were so soon tolling the death of their father. They could remember the celebrations at Coburg when their uncle Leopold married Princess Charlotte, and as a clever thirteen-year-old and a pretty ten-year-old, they had seen their mother marry the Duke of Kent. (In so far as they saw much of the duke, they appeared to have liked him, and he them.)

As Victoria grew up, in Claremont and Kensington, she frequently shared a room, not only with her mother but with her half-sister.

Feodore was Victoria's constant companion for the first nine years of her childhood. The half-sisters were to be part of one another's lives, on and off, until death.

With her English relations, Victoria had a necessarily more distant relationship. The frightening old Duke of Sussex was downstairs at Kensington, with his vast collection of books. The Duke of York, his brother, was fifty-six by the time Victoria was born. Of all her 'wicked uncles', he was perhaps the most popular with the country at large, in part at least because of his vociferous opposition to Roman Catholic Emancipation. He publicly declared that he would go to the scaffold rather than change his mind about the matter; after all, the Hanoverian line of succession would have no legitimacy if the Stewarts had remained, and if Catholics were allowed a part in the legislature, so how could the Hanoverians logically support giving Catholics seats in Parliament or allowing them to go to the University? So much were the British public at one with the dear old duke in this matter that they were prepared to overlook his grosser indiscretions – such as attending the House of Lords to make partisan speeches in support of the Whigs. The public even took a forgiving view of the duke's turning a blind eye, while Commander-in-Chief of the British Army in wartime, to his mistress, Mrs Clarke, openly selling army commissions. (£2,600 for a full-pay majority; £1,500 for a company; £550 for a lieutenancy; and £400 for an ensigncy.[8]) His infant niece was oblivious to these matters.

For the childless duke, his little niece was a ray of light. He bought her a donkey to ride upon. Her visits to him were frequent in his new-built palace Stafford (now Lancaster) House. Lest she find his company too dull, he arranged Punch and Judy shows for her in his garden, and when, in 1826, he was sent for his health down to Brighton, the seven-year-old wrote to him:

MY DEAR UNCLE,
    I offer you many affectionate congratulations on your birthday – very many with my best love – for all your kindness

to me – and it has been a great pleasure to me to be able to write this year to my Uncle, the King, and to you.

We hope to hear that Brighton does you a great deal of good...[9]

Her uncle the King – George IV – was also beguiled by the plump little blue-eyed girl. He entertained her at Carlton House with her cousins, the Cambridges – George and Augusta – who, though not as close as siblings, would remain very close family for their whole lives. And that same year, 1826, in which the little princess wrote a charming birthday letter to the Duke of York in Brighton, Victoria's aunt the Queen of Württemberg (the Princess Royal) made a visit, and George IV invited Victoria, her mother and her half-sister Feodore to Windsor. 'He had been on bad terms with my poor father when he died – and took hardly any notice of the poor widow and the little fatherless girl, who were so poor at the time of his (the Duke of Kent's) death that they could not have travelled back to Kensington Palace without the kind assistance of my dear Uncle, Prince Leopold.'[10]

She recollected going to stay with her aunt the Duchess of Gloucester, and going over to Royal Lodge in Windsor to visit the King. 'The King took me by the hand, saying, "Give me your little paw". He was large and gouty but with a wonderful dignity and charm of manner. He wore the wig which was so much worn in those days.'[11]

This encounter took place in August 1826, when Drina was a little over seven years old. It speaks volumes about the isolation of the Duchess of Kent from the English Court that this was the first formal invitation she had received from the King since the death of her husband six years before. The Duke of Wellington, who was of the party, thought that George IV was involved in an infidelity with Madame de Lieven (wife of the Russian Ambassador); but the duke was inclined to infer romantic liaisons which did not exist; and he had missed something which did not escape the notice of George's existing *maîtresse en titre*, Lady Conyngham, whose nickname was the 'Vice Queen'.[12] The King was much taken with Princess Feodore.

The Duchess of Kent had been flustered by Feodore having been included in the invitation to Windsor, and, as Victoria later recalled, 'The King paid great attention to my Sister, and some people fancied he might marry her!'

It was a gruesome possibility as far as the very pretty eighteen-year-old was concerned – to be chosen to carry the child of this obese, sixty-four-year-old, bewigged, pomaded figure. Lady Conyngham made sure that she brought the flirtation to an end, sending the Duchess of Kent and Feodore home in 'the Large Carriage' while she accompanied the King in the smaller. When Victoria looked back on these matters, half a century later, the visit to Windsor in 1826 would have shimmered with ironies. Had the King decided to re-enter the stakes to provide an heir, he could have married Feodore and had a baby by 1828. Victoria, instead of becoming the Queen of England eleven years after her encounter with George IV, would have been a footnote in history – and probably in German history at that, since, had Feodore married the King, the Duchess of Kent would almost certainly have retired to Coburg to lick her wounds, and Victoria would have been married off to some duke or elector, her English royal childhood becoming nothing but a series of sharply focused memories.

Given the fondness Victoria was to develop for the novels of Sir Walter Scott, and her passion for his native land, it is not unmoving to think of the great novelist meeting her at Kensington Palace when she was nine.

Not the least impressive political achievement of George IV had been the reconciliation he had effected between the British Crown and that hitherto semi-detached British nation, Scotland. Since the 1745 Rising, when the Scottish Highlanders had supported the claims of the Young Pretender (Bonnie Prince Charlie) to the throne, no Hanoverian monarch had gone north of the border. George IV changed all that, and in a celebrated visit to Edinburgh, he allowed himself to be arrayed in Highland dress. (He was so fat that his belly dangled *beneath* the hem of his kilt.) The visit had been stage-managed by that celebrant, or creator, of Scottishness, Sir Walter Scott. Four years after the Edinburgh visit, when Sir Walter was in London, he was invited by the Duchess of Kent to call at Kensington Palace. He was accompanied by Prince Leopold, who presented him to Princess Victoria. 'This little lady is educating with much care,' Sir Walter observed, 'and watched so closely, that no busy mind has a moment to whisper, "You are heir of England." I suspect that if we could dissect the little heart, we should find that some pigeon or other bird of the air had carried the matter. She is fair, like the Royal Family – the duchess herself very pleasing and affable in her manners.'[13]

Scott was not alone in expressing the hope (though in the privacy of his journal) that 'they will change her name'. Two years later, two Members of Parliament, even more dyed-in-the-wool Tories than Sir Walter, urged that the princess 'should as Queen assume the style of Elizabeth II' and repeated the old complaint that the name Victoria did not accord with the feelings of the English people.[14]

Scott's view that Victoria was 'educating with much care' was a sanguine one. When the duchess brought her twelve-year-old daughter Feodore from Germany, she also brought the governess, Louise Lehzen. She was the daughter of a village clergyman from Lagenhagen, near Hanover, thirty-five years older than Victoria, and with experience as a governess to the three daughters of the von Marenholz family.

While the child was a baby, a Mrs Brock was employed as her nursemaid, and Lehzen would read to her. By the time Victoria was five, Lehzen was placed in charge. 'She never for the thirteen years she was governess to Pss. Victoria once left her,' Queen Victoria recalled. 'The Princess was her only object and her only thought. She was very strict and the Pss. had great respect and even awe of her but that with the greatest affection.'[15]

Lehzen did not make much progress with teaching the child to read – she preferred to be read to – nor with teaching her to write. 'I was not fond of learning as a little child – and baffled every attempt to teach me my letters up to five years old – when I consented to learn them by their being written down before me.'[16]

It was when she was eight that a tutor was engaged. This was the Reverend George Davys, a fellow of Christ's College, Cambridge, and Vicar of Willoughby-on-the-Wolds in Leicestershire. Two years after taking up his position at Kensington, Mr Davys was given the London living of All-Hallows-on-the-Wall, in London, a living he retained even after becoming Dean of Chester in 1831; he only forsook All-Hallows when his grateful pupil raised him to the episcopacy and made him Bishop of Peterborough in 1839, where he lived until the age of eighty-four. The first duty of Davys was to make sure that the young Victoria could speak English perfectly; and this he did. She had a beautiful, bell-like voice, and spoke English without accent, though with the German habit of punctuating sentences, and silences, with a sigh and the exclamation 'So!' – pronounced 'Zo!' This was her only Germanism. Her mother had poor English, but had done her best to speak to her in that language.

Mr Davys was not alone responsible for her education. She had a German tutor, a Lutheran clergyman called Henry Barez, a writing-master, Mr Seward, who also taught her arithmetic, at which she excelled, while Mr Davys took charge of her historical and geographical studies.

Her religious views were her own, and always would be. One should never forget, when contemplating Victoria, the church of St Moritz in Coburg, where, in a splendid altarpiece, the worshippers at the Lutheran service can see the kneeling alabaster figures of her and Prince Albert's ancestors – Duke Johann Friedrich II and his wife Elisabeth, the first generation to uphold and guarantee the Reformation in Germany. Victoria's Protestantism was in the blood. Her mother was fervently pious. In one of the little letters she placed on Victoria's pillow each birthday, she wrote:

May 23th [sic]. Oh my beloved Child; Never forget for a moment, that all comes from Him. He has watched over you these twelve years: compare your lot with that of many others: As you advance in years more is naturally expected of you. If you would give me real proves [sic] of your attachment and gratitude: you can but show it by conquering those faults which would certainly make you and those who love you unhappy. You will find Mamma always ready to give you all the pleasure she can, and which belongs to your youth: But I would neither love, or fulfil my duty towards you, if I did not tell you the truth, and warn you against all that could hurt your soul and body.[17]

Mr Davys belonged to the evangelical wing of the Church of England, but of the gentler variety – not too much fire or brimstone or dwelling upon eternal punishment, or insistence upon a Calvinistic predestination. All her life Victoria looked for what she called 'tolerant' clergy, which tended to mean those who agreed, or pretended to agree, with her own set of eclectic prejudices. As a child, she was unaware of what she would later deplore – the High versus Low squabbles of the National Church. But Mr Davys would have found a relatively pious little girl, who said her prayers. She would always do so, and it would remain part of her life.

Some human beings change and develop, and that is their strength. For others, strength consists in their incapacity for change. Victoria never ceased to be the child of Kensington Palace, and never ceased to expect her companions to be as constant, and as affectionate, as had been Lehzen. It was for this reason that her best friends were servants, or those prepared, in her presence, to behave as if they were servants. So long as her husband was constant in his attendance upon her, she was able, for some of the time, to offer him the same 'respect and even awe' which she had shown to her governess. But at other times, she would be as self-willed as she was with Lehzen. There were furious outbursts in her childhood – tantrums far worse than anything Lehzen had ever seen. She had no experience of the Hanoverians. She had not watched Victoria's father growing up, nor witnessed his near-murderous rows with his brothers, nor seen, when Duke of Kent, the soldier trying to knock discipline into his troops on Gibraltar and provoking a mutiny by his furies and by the savagery with which he refused his troops drink, and, on 25 December 1802, rewarding three of them with the Christmas present of being shot by a firing squad, and a handful of other mutineers a merciless lashing. (His brother the Duke of Cumberland, who was, if anything, an even harsher disciplinarian, caused a scandal, when he was colonel of the 15th Dragoons, by thrashing not a private, but one of his fellow officers, with his cane.) If Lehzen had been more aware of Victoria's Hanoverian genes, she would perhaps have been less surprised when the young Victoria hurled a pair of scissors at her. Loving Victoria – which many people were to do – was learning to live with a furious irascibility of temper.

If her childhood was scarred by the hostility between her mother and the Court, it was also, as she grew older, marred by the divisions within Kensington Palace itself. For Lehzen did not have sole charge of her.

The other figure in the story, who was to dominate more and more, was John Conroy. When, in 1827, George IV questioned whether Lehzen were really a fit person to be preparing the child for the task of monarchy, Conroy got the Duchess of Kent to suggest making Lehzen a Hanoverian baroness, and, while they were about it, promoting himself as a knight commander of the Hanoverian Order. Neither of the enemies who had Victoria in their charge were possessed of an English Order, and enemies Lehzen and Conroy certainly were. As Lehzen's influence on her young charge increased, so did Conroy's hold over the Duchess of Kent. And it was through Conroy that the duchess so unwisely came to accept what he called 'the Kensington System'.

This System was to bring up the princess detached from the English Court and from her English uncles, and to be utterly dependent upon the Duchess of Kent and Conroy. But chiefly upon Conroy. The one exception to Conroy's exclusion of the English Royal Family from his circle was Princess Sophia (1777–1848), Victoria's unmarried aunt, who had an apartment in Kensington Palace. The Duchess of Kent and Conroy had dinner with Princess Sophia two or three times a week, Conroy managed her finances, and in 1826, with the princess's money, bought for himself an estate in Montgomeryshire for the sum of £18,000.[18]

While it was obvious that Conroy was feathering his own nest with Princess Sophia's money, the Kensington System was not without its merits. Indeed, both Prince Leopold at Claremont and his old adviser Dr Stockmar agreed that it would be injudicious for the duchess and Victoria to see too much, either of the dissolute and dysfunctional family in Coburg, or the rakish life of George IV, with his overbearing mistress Lady Conyngham and her *mari complaisant*, Henry, who had been made a peer and Lord Chamberlain as a reward for, in effect, lending his wife to the King. Conroy had no money himself and his wife had produced six children – four sons and two daughters. His mania that she was Victoria's half-sister does not justify his deviousness, nor the coolness with which he charmed Princess Sophia out of £18,000 (in today's money, the equivalent of £1.2 million on the retail price index, and over ten times that amount when measured by average earnings[19]). But his fevered brain believed that the Royal Family were in his debt.

It was only after Feodore's marriage, on 18 February 1828, that Victoria's childhood solitude properly began. Feodore was married to Prince Ernst Christian Charles of Hohenlohe-Langenburg, in the very Cupola Room at Kensington Palace where Alexandrina Victoria had been baptized. The Lutheran rite was followed, and the ceremony was conducted by Dr Kuper of the Royal German Chapel. Victoria was a bridesmaid, 'dearest little girl as you were', Feodore recollected in 1843. 'I escaped some years of imprisonment, which you, my poor dear Sister had to endure after I was married.'

As she reflected on those years, Feodore added, 'Thank God they are over!'[20] She wrote at a time when, as she put it, 'God Almighty has changed both our destinies most mercifully, and has made us so happy in our home.' But fairness would make us concede that she also wrote from Germany, far from the Britain which Victoria had been called to govern; and she wrote from a position of absolute irresponsibility.

The Duchess of Kent might have been vacillating in her opinions, and Conroy might have been in part a villain; but they carried a heavy load of duty. The country was in a dangerous state. The condition of the poor had not improved since the Peterloo Massacre of a decade earlier. Owen's pyramid did not look secure. And if it collapsed, what would become of the apex of the model, the monarchy?

From the Continent came reminders that kings could be made and unmade overnight. The conservative Bourbon restoration of the monarchy in France (Louis XVIII, r. 1815–24, Charles X, r. 1824–30) was cast down and replaced by the liberal 'July Monarchy' of Louis-Philippe. In Brussels, the Belgians, who resented their subordination to the Dutch, wanted to be fashioned into an independent kingdom, and they spoke of the Duke of Nemours – Louis-Philippe's son – as the likely candidate. In the event, the prize was given to Prince Leopold, Victoire's brother. He had turned down the throne of Greece in May, but in Belgium he would have the chance to put into practice Stockmar's ideas of modern, constitutional monarchy. He would also, though obliged to leave behind Claremont, and Kensington and his sister and the baby Drina, be sufficiently close to London to maintain an influence.

It left the Duchess Victoire, and Drina, and Lehzen, and Baroness Späth, and Feodore as a predominantly female household in Kensington Palace. True, there were the masters who came to give the child her lessons. But the only figure of dominance was John Conroy. And this dominance was to grow. On 12 January, Adelaide, Duchess of Clarence, and her fellow German, wrote Victoire a candid letter of warning. It was, she wrote, the 'general wish' that the duchess should not allow Conroy 'too much influence over you, but keep him in his place... He has never lived before in court circles or in society, so naturally he offends sometimes against the traditional ways, for he does not know them... In the family it is noticed that you are cutting yourself off more and more from them with your child... This they attribute to Conroy, whether rightly or wrongly I cannot judge.'[21]

FOUR

'WHITE LITTLE SLAVEY'

W HEN IT BECAME clear that George IV was dying, the Marquess of Anglesey, a veteran of the Battle of Waterloo and former Cabinet minister, rushed to Bushy Park with some honest advice for the Duke of Clarence. A king, urged Anglesey, must be seen among his subjects, he must maintain 'a splendid court', and perform 'creditable acts of liberality' but 'without preying upon the pockets of the people'.[1]

William IV, as the Duke of Clarence would become on 26 June 1830, was king during an exceptionally turbulent period of British politics. It did not require a crystal ball to see the perils of a hungry populace, and of an ever-growing middle class who had no political voice. 'I was most sorry,' Anglesey noted after that interview with William at Bushy, 'to find that he was violently anti-Reform, & a bitter enemy to free trade.'[2] The first years of the reign would see the rejection and, finally, the acceptance of the Great Reform Bill. Britain was on the way to becoming a fully parliamentary political system, even though it was a very long way from being a democracy. The monarchy, as Lord Esher, adviser to Edward VII and editor of Queen Victoria's early letters and journals, would later say, was exchanging 'authority' for 'influence'.[3] While the question of Reform was being debated, the monarch was clearly seen to be a bastion of conservatism, standing in the way of progress and the freedoms of his subjects. In the early years of the reign especially, there were ugly mob scenes. William and his brother Prince Ernest of Cumberland, for example, were hooted at and pelted with stones and abuse when they went to the theatre in February 1831.[4] Likewise, when he went to the races at Fernhill in June 1832, some in the crowd threw stones at him. One hit his head.[5]

William IV was rightly perceived by his contemporaries to be a buffoon, albeit sometimes an amiable one. In 1834, Greville confided to his diary, 'There is a very strong impression abroad that the King is cracked and I dare say there is some truth in it. He gets so very cholerick and is so indecent in his wrath.'[6] Yet this was very far from being the whole truth about the Sailor King. He heeded Lord Anglesey's advice, and his reign was notable for displays of genuine royal benevolence, which went some way towards appeasing the public grievance at the slowness of reform. On his birthday in 1830, he feasted 3,000 poor people at Windsor, an event which was much noted in the press. In 1833, accompanied by Princess Victoria, Queen Adelaide and the Duchess of Kent, the King attended four concerts in Westminster Abbey in aid of various musical charities. The festival raised the huge sum of £7,600. There was scarcely a hospital or a missionary society in the land which had not applied successfully either to the King or to Queen Adelaide for help. William gave £1,000 to house indigent Irish Protestant clergymen in London and £3,000 to rebuild the church at Kew, while Adelaide founded the King William Naval Asylum at Penge for the widows of naval officers, and gave money generously for the foundation of new cathedrals in Adelaide in Australia and Valetta in Malta. It has been calculated that Queen Adelaide was one of the most generous royal benefactors in history, giving away some £40,000 per annum out of an income of some £100,000.[7] This more than compensated, in the eyes of a grateful public, for her supposed marital disloyalty to the King. (Her lover was thought to be Earl Howe, in whose seat, Penn House, near Amersham, she spent some of her declining years.) When, in 1835, there was a rumour of her pregnancy – false as it turned out – the wags proposed that the Psalm 'Lord how great are your works,' should be sung.[8]

Queen Adelaide and her fellow German the Duchess of Kent had a somewhat frosty relationship, though Victoria appears to have liked her plain little aunt by marriage. William IV immediately asked the two Victorias, duchess and princess, to attend court functions, one of the first being the Garter ceremony on 20 July, when Princess Victoria appeared, still in deep mourning for her uncle George, with a black train and veil reaching the ground. On 24 February 1831, she attended her first royal Drawing Room in honour of Queen Adelaide's birthday. The King complained that the princess had looked at him 'stonily' during this occasion.

It was Lord Howe, on behalf of the new King, who invited the Duchess of Kent and Princess Victoria to the Coronation in Westminster Abbey, asking the duchess who should carry her coronet. She did not reply to the letter. The King then wrote in person, signing his note 'Wm.R.'. This elicited a response, not from the duchess herself but from Sir John Conroy, who said that if they attended, the duchess's coronet should be borne by Lord Morpeth.[9] But in the event, neither the duchess nor Princess Victoria attended. Victoria wept copiously when told of her mother's decision. 'Nothing would console me,' she would tell her own children in later years, 'not even my dolls.'[10]

When, in August 1831, the duchess took Victoria on holiday to the Isle of Wight, for a hired month at Norris Castle, the ships in Portsmouth Harbour gave them a royal salute. When news of this harmless display of loyal affection reached the ears of the King, William formally requested the duchess to forgo such honours in the future.

In the interests of the monarchy, the Duchess of Kent and the King might have tried to overlook their mutual antagonism and to concentrate on training Victoria, during her teenage years, for the onerous life awaiting her. Although both made stabs at preparing her for becoming queen, however, they were unable to do so together.

And while there was an attempt, largely initiated by Conroy, at following one of Lord Angelsey's triple requirements for the modern sovereign – being seen among the subjects – there was little or no attempt to explain to the princess the political and constitutional role which she was going to have to play in her country's history. Lord Esher, in his introduction to her youthful journals, remarked that, 'There is nothing in her journals or elsewhere to show that before she was eighteen years old she had ever talked seriously and at any length to any man or woman of exceptional gifts. It was only when her uncle King Leopold heard of the illness of William IV, that Stockmar was instructed to speak with due gravity upon important matters to the young girl whose accession to the Throne appeared imminent.'[11] This deficiency, this failure to prepare Victoria for her historic role, was something for which Lord Melbourne, when Prime Minister, would attempt to compensate. He did his best, but he came late. Many of her own troubles as Queen, and certainly many of the troubles of her Prime Ministers, particularly Peel and Gladstone, would have been avoided had her mother thought to offer the young Victoria a basic political education.

Even in a household where both parents are alive and where the atmosphere is harmonious, the rearing of an heir to the throne brings its peculiar tensions and problems. This was certainly to be the case when Victoria had children of her own and when she and her much-adored husband tried to prepare an infant-heir for his future role as a monarch. In Victoria's case things were much more difficult. Her mother was alone, and not merely foreign, but intensely so, with an imperfect grasp of English and absolutely no experience of English life. With the departure of her brother Leopold to the Continent – first to hesitate about the offer of the throne of Greece, and then to accept the throne of Belgium – and with the death of their mother on 16 November 1831, the Duchess of Kent felt increasingly isolated.

Victoria entered puberty with the sharpening sense of the bad blood between the Duchess of Kent and the Court of William IV. As the princess grew through youth to maturity, however, the members of her household were inevitably perceived – both at the time, and by posterity – as working for their own self-interest. For she was 'situated as seldom mortal was'. Those who had influence over this girl had influence over the future Queen of England. The interests and factions could only become more intense as she grew older, and her mother was certainly not in a position to control them.

A recent biographer of Edward VII has suggested that 'no Gothic novelist could have invented a villain blacker than [Sir John] Conroy'.[12] This could be because Conroy exercised undue, or unscrupulous, influence over the Duchess of Kent. Equally, the truth might be more nuanced in history than it is in Gothic novels. The truth might be that, in the imagination of his royal charge, he became a villain in Gothic fiction, but that in reality he was no worse than 'an intriguing vulgarian who saw in his position the means to advancement'.[13] We know from Victoria's later life that her likes and dislikes were capricious. Conroy, too, was someone of strong feelings. When he found himself completely ostracized and dismissed from the life of the Queen, he could meditate upon 'his past services to the ignorant little child that was called to preside over the destinies of this once great country'.[14] Given the depth of his later humiliation and the strength of his feelings, it was perhaps inevitable that Conroy should have nursed the most bitter feelings of hatred towards those who remained at Victoria's side after she became queen. For the Duchess of Kent, he would retain his affectionate regard and loyalty. But of her brothers, he would not retain memories which were especially fond. Leopold, King of the Belgians, was (in Conroy's estimation) 'as great a villain as ever breathed'. Ernst I, Duke of Coburg, was 'a heavy-headed humbugged German. Immoral'. Baron Stockmar appeared in retrospect to be 'a double-faced villain'. His harshest words were reserved for 'that hypocritical and detestable bitch' Louise Lehzen, the governess. Clearly, there was some element of truth in Conroy's claim that, from the beginning, he and Lehzen had been rivals for control over the princess. 'While eating her trusting Mistress's bread in the Palace, that infamous woman wholly stole the child's affections and intrigued with King William through a Miss Wilson.'[15]

Whether you sided with Lehzen or with Conroy – and there were those in high places who saw merits in Conroy – or whether you considered the constant intrigues and feudings to be unseemly, one fact remained undeniable. It was the fact which was the underlying cause of all the factions and politicking. Her half-brother Prince Charles of Leiningen, deeply anxious about the situation he witnessed whenever he visited Kensington Palace, emphasized this one fact when he wrote to his uncle, King Leopold, that 'a young lady' of eighteen was incapable of ruling England by herself. In his view, even if she did live to an age when she had technically reached her majority, she should have a Regent, and in his opinion, Sir John Conroy was indispensable.[16]

Without being blind to Sir John Conroy's faults, it is surely not necessary to paint him as the villain of a Gothic novel. That he was ambitious for power can scarcely be doubted. On the other hand, he had been in the service of the Duke and Duchess of Kent by now for many decades. He had proved himself a good friend to the duchess. He possessed certain elements of common sense which she appeared utterly to lack. And it would be purely sentimental to overlook the fact that Victoria herself was a very difficult person, self-willed and in many ways foolish, 'younger in intellect than in years', as Conroy said.[17]

Conroy used the arrival of a new King as a pretext for strengthening his own power base, and on the Duchess of Kent's behalf he dictated a long letter to the Prime Minister, the Duke of Wellington. 'The weight of my Maternal Station' – a favourite phrase of Conroy's which he often employed in such petitions – made the duchess ask for an increase in her Civil List grant. She also requested Wellington to guarantee her position as Regent, in the event of King William's death. She wanted, with immediate effect, to be placed on the footing of a dowager Princess of Wales. Wellington was scarcely minded to accede to Conroy and the duchess's request. And, besides, there were other things on the Establishment's mind in the opening years of the reign. England was in the grip of the Reform Bill crisis.

The burgeoning middle classes, many of them richer than the small landed gentry, were still unrepresented in Parliament. They simply did not have the vote at all. This was quite apart from the fact that the great majority of the population had no representation in Parliament. The Chartists, who believed in a universal franchise, were regarded as dangerous extremists. In every department of government – at Court, in the Church, in the colonial establishments, in the municipal corporations, in the judiciary – nepotism and bribery were rife. It was calculated that out of the 658 Members of Parliament in the House of Commons, 487 were returned by nomination – that is, there was scarcely even a pretence at an 'election'. Even in constituencies where an election took place, the electors often did not number in triple figures.[18] Before 1832, a borough freeholder, in order to be eligible to exercise a country vote, had to be assessed for the land tax; this requirement was removed by the Reform Act. For years to come, one of the differences between Tories and their opponents was that the Tories wished to restrict the votes of borough freeholders (i.e. the unlanded, those whose property was worth between £10 and £40) to boroughs, not allowing them a vote in county elections. In these improbable circumstances, William IV, and most of his peerage including his bishops, vigorously opposed Reform. If a Reform movement developed a republican colouring, it would not be the first time in British history. The monarchy was therefore deeply connected with the political life of the times. And if the King were seen to be opposed to change of any kind, where would this leave the sovereign after the inevitable change had come? These were questions which William IV was too old, and too stupid, to need to face. But the answers to the questions would dominate the reign of his successor. And his successor was a little girl, living a secluded life in Kensington Palace and being kept in total ignorance of the colossal changes which would be required of the monarchy, and of the political system as a whole.

It is important to bear in mind that democracy, as it is popularly understood today, formed no part of the ideology either of the Whigs, who proposed Reform, nor of the more liberal-minded Tories. If Lord Palmerston (1784–1865) was one of the dominant, if not *the* dominant, political personalities of the early years of Victoria's grown-up life and reign, then we should look to his student days in Edinburgh for the roots of his political thinking.

In that city which saw the origin of Adam Smith's definitions of Free Trade and economic liberalism, Palmerston studied under Smith's successor, Dugald Stewart. Indeed, he not merely studied under Stewart, he lodged in his house. In one of his celebrated lectures on moral and political philosophy, Stewart, quoting Montesquieu, said, 'It was one great fault in most ancient Republics, that the people had a right to influence immediately the public resolutions; – a thing of which they are absolutely incapable. They ought to have no hand in the government but for the choosing of representatives.'[19]

This fundamental idea must always be borne in mind if we are to understand the early-nineteenth-century liberal paternalist mindset – and if we are to understand the unfolding nineteenth-century political debate about the extension of the franchise. In this system of representative paternalism, the monarchy clearly had its vital role to play, and it was not until she allowed herself to be schooled by her husband, her uncle Leopold and Baron Stockmar (and to a smaller extent by Melbourne) that Victoria came to grips with the political realities. As well as recognizing the principle of representative government, however, it was also necessary, as Dugald Stewart had taught Palmerston, to be aware of the mysterious movements of public opinion, to recognize when the public could no longer be imposed upon, and when its own view, however mysteriously arrived at, must be allowed to influence government. (Canning, one of Palmerston's political masters, opined that the State was no longer oligarchical but rested on public opinion which was 'Protestant, patriotic and liberty-loving'.[20] Canning was not a Whig, but a liberal-leaning Tory. This is what Palmerston, that populist of genius, was so good at recognizing. Prince Albert became good at such recognition. Victoria's populist political instincts were, at first, non-existent – in spite of Conroy's attempts to instil them by means of the 'royal progresses' during her teens; then, little by little, thanks to her husband's dislike of Palmerston, they were positively anti-populist; and then, little by little, as she got into her late stride, under the premierships of Disraeli and Salisbury, she triumphantly conformed to Dugald Stewart's guidelines for successful modern political leadership.

Evidently, when compared with alternative political systems abroad, the British system was successful: that is, there were no political revolutions or civil wars during Victoria's reign; no toppling of Metternich, no 1848 revolutions, nothing to resemble the violence and horror of the Paris Communes of 1870. (This is not to say that the system which allowed, or produced, the Irish famine, the workhouses, transportation of criminals, etc., was an ideal; merely that the system of constitutional monarchy and a bicameral parliamentary system seemed to have some, comparatively benign, efficacy.) But Victoria's story is not simply one of an eighteen-year-old ingénue growing into a wise old bird who mastered the British political game. Central to her life story is the extent to which the liberal principles espoused in Britain since 1832 could realisti-cally be exported into the Continent from which she and Albert came and over whose destinies so many of her children and grand-children would reign. It is worth saying these things now, in their chronological place – 1832 – even though at the time, the national drama of Reform either did not interest the young Victoria, or it was withheld from her knowledge. She began her journals, when aged thirteen, in the momentous year of the Reform Bill becoming law; she makes no allusion to it, any more than Jane Austen, in her novels, alluded to the Napoleonic Wars.

Yet the journals do depict a Britain of astonishing contrasts. Having changed horses at Birmingham, which she visited for the second time in 1832, she noted, 'we have just passed through a town where all coal mines are and you see the fire glimmer at a distance in the engines in many places. The men, women, children, country and houses are all black. But I can not by any description give an idea of its strange and extraordinary appearance.'[21]

If this was the New World, her mother and Sir John made sure that she also had plenty of opportunity to acquaint herself with the old. Perhaps no figure more triumphantly embodied the old order than the Archbishop of York, Edward Vernon Harcourt, with whom she stayed when she was sixteen. This great prince of the Church, son of Lord Vernon, but taking the name of Harcourt having inherited the estates of his mother's family at Stanton Harcourt in Oxfordshire, maintained a style which Victoria had never seen before. The father of sixteen children, Harcourt had matriculated at Christ Church College, Oxford, when the Thirteen Colonies still acknowledged allegiance to King George III. He was one of the privy councillors who had charge of King George in his madness. He would live beyond his ninetieth birthday to see Newman a Catholic, and railways trundling through Yorkshire.

Victoria's diary entries for her time at Bishopthorpe have some of the astonishment, some of the eye for social nicety, of a Jane Austen innocent. 'Miss Harcourt is a very nice person. She ought by rights to be called Miss Georgiana Harcourt, the Archbishop's eldest daughter being unmarried, but as she never goes out and does not make the honneurs in the house, Miss Georgiana is always called Miss Harcourt. The Archbishop has 10 sons, 5 of whom were at Bishopthorpe.'[22] The concerts and Oratorio performances at York Minster give us the chance to hear more of Victoria's very distinct musical tastes: she much preferred Rossini and Donizetti to Handel, and found 'The Messiah... with the exception of a few Choruses... very heavy and tiresome'.[23]

Although memory told her that her childhood and youth were miserable, the journals tell a different story. Partly, no doubt, this was because they were written to be read by her mother, and she did not use her diary – as she would do in later years – as a repository of sorrows. Yet, surely, the truth is that until her later teens, Victoria did not find Sir John Conroy intolerable; was not made to suffer unduly by the conflict between the King and her mother; had no reason to question the general consensus that Sir John and her mother were making a good fist of her upbringing.

In Oxford, in the year of Reform, Sir John, accompanied by Princess Victoria and the duchess, entered the Sheldonian Theatre, where he was given an honorary doctorate in Civil Law. At the same time, he was given the Freedom of the City of Oxford. The Regius Professor of Civil Law, Dr Joseph Phillimore, in a Latin speech, commended Sir John's military career, and his loyalty to the memory of the late Duke of Kent. 'Thus having been received into His Household and family, and certain duties being entrusted to his charge, he performed the important trust with singular prudence (which is a great talent) and also with much industry. Can you wonder that he who had gained the esteem of the Husband, should also have pleased His surviving Consort?' The Sheldonian Theatre was packed to capacity and the crowds cheered the Duchess of Kent, and Sir John, and the princess, as they did wherever they went on these royal tours.

Clearly – as on the first occasion that their boat received the salute of the fleet as they crossed the Solent – the extreme popularity of the Duchess of Kent and Conroy rankled with the King. Both the Duke of Wellington and Melbourne were to say in later days that William IV wanted to take Victoria away from her mother and to bring her up at Windsor.[24]

The actual pattern of the princess's days was, for the most part, uneventful and happy. She was not a great reader, but she was developing her talent as a journal writer. She was an above-average watercolourist and there are literally hundreds of highly accomplished watercolour sketches of the many scenes she visited in these years. The boring Conroy girls were her unwished-for companions. Her royal cousins, and in particular the FitzClarences (William IV's ten children), were her mother's *bêtes noires*, and if one of them entered the room, the Duchess of Kent would leave.

Adolescence was the unfolding discovery that she was growing up in a snakepit of mutual hatred and slander. Lehzen had formed an alliance with Miss Martha Wilson, Lady of the Bedchamber to Queen Adelaide. Through this conduit, damaging anti-Conroy and anti-duchess intelligence was passed to the Court.

The final tour of the North – the one during which she stayed with the illustrious Harcourts at Bishopthorpe – exhausted her. At the end of September, they went down to Ramsgate to welcome 'dear Uncle Leopold' who was paying a visit from his new kingdom of Belgium. Victoria was already suffering from a heavy cold, and this worsened into 'an ulcerated sore throat'.

They were staying in the Albion Hotel. Conroy believed that her cold was trivial, but he was anxious 'from a political point of view' that too much might be made of the girl's illness. King Leopold walked Sir John along the sands, berating him. Leopold had watched one English princess – his wife – die; and if Victoria were to do the same, and the hated Duke of Cumberland succeed William IV, the prospects for the English monarchy did not look strong. 'If in consequence of your folly anything happens to the princess, there is of course an end of all your prospects, if the princess lives and succeeds the King, she will abhor you. Though late in the day, still things may be placed on a tolerable footing for you.'[25]

Within a few days, the princess appeared to be fighting for her life. At some point during this illness, Conroy clumsily entered her bedroom and attempted to make her promise to ensure his position, and her mother's as Regent. She refused. It would seem that Sir John was all but violent with her.[26] When the crisis in the illness had passed, his fate was sealed. Henceforward, her hatred of him was out in the open and, together with Lehzen and the King, she was merely waiting for the moment when she reached eighteen in order to be rid of Sir John and his influence.

Conroy tried to force her to make him her official private secretary. She refused. 'And therein,' commented Baron Stockmar, 'lies the whole affair. With every day that she grew older the princess naturally became more aware of her self, more conscious of her own strength, and hence became jealous of what she must have seen as an exercise of undue control over herself'.[27]

In 1836, when Victoria was seventeen, the gruesome warfare over her future took 'zoological' form: the conflicting parties began to select rival marriage partners for her. The King had 'a violent passion' for the princes of Orange – but it was thought the passion was fuelled by the knowledge that there was bad blood between the Dutch Royal Family and the Coburgs. He invited Prince Alexander – grandson of the King of the Netherlands – to London at the very moment when the Duchess of Kent had asked her two young nephews, Ernst and Albert, to come on a visit from Coburg. She had not even told the King that she had invited the nephews, and so angry was William IV when he heard of their visit that he instructed Lord Palmerston, the Foreign Secretary, to forbid it. The duchess was instructed to tell the boys, who had already set out on their journey to England, to turn back while still in Germany.

Palmerston saw that this farce could only make the King seem ridiculous. 'Really and truly I never heard anything like it,' wrote Uncle Leopold to Victoria, 'and I hope it will a little rouse your spirit: now that slavery is abolished in the British Colonies, I do not comprehend why your lot alone should be to be kept, a white little slavey in England.'[28]

At the very moment when the shy young Coburg princes arrived in London, William IV was throwing a lavish ball for the princes of Orange in Windsor. They were lumpen and boring. 'So much for the <u>Oranges</u>, dear Uncle,'[29] Victoria wrote to Leopold.

It was the Duchess of Kent's wish that Victoria should marry her cousin Ernst of Coburg. Had she done so, her life would have continued much as before – in the Houses of Coburg and Hanover. For Ernst, like his father before him, and like Victoria's Hanoverian uncles, was a lecher and a roué. No one would seriously look at the married life of Duke Ernst I of Coburg, or the domestic life of George IV and William IV, and find in it a role model for family virtue. No one would look at these dynasties, as royalty lost its last shreds of political authority, and find in them a moral or spiritual figurehead.

Cousin Ernst brought with him his sixteen-year-old brother Albert, a boy of almost shocking beauty, and of almost equally stunning seriousness and shyness. The first time Victoria set eyes upon him was at the bottom of the staircase in Kensington Palace. It was not love at first sight, but there was an immediate attraction of kinship.

Five years had passed since 'Uncle Ernst's' last visit to England, and neither Albert nor young Ernst had been to the country before. For the first time, Victoria knew what it would have been like to grow up in a family, and to have brothers. 'I sat between my dear Cousins on the sofa and we looked at drawings. They both draw very well, particularly Albert, and are both exceedingly fond of music; they play very nicely on the piano. The more I see them, the more I am delighted with them, and the more I love them. They are so natural, so kind, so very good and well instructed and informed; they are so well bred, so truly merry and quite like children.'[30] They were with her on her seventeenth birthday. 'A very old person I am indeed!' The Coburg cousins stayed a few more weeks and left on 10 June. 'I cried bitterly, very bitterly',[31] but they were not the tears of a lover. They were the tears of a child who had never experienced the spontaneity of family life. She now saw, in all its absurdity, how fantastical it had been to be made to treat 'Jane and Victoire' as her sisters, as they played together in Campden Hill. She had only a year to live through, and the tyranny of Sir John would have no further power over her.

Things came to a head a few weeks later, that summer in 1836, when the King asked the duchess and Princess Victoria to come to Windsor Castle to celebrate the Queen's birthday on 13 August. He wanted them to stay over until the 21st, which was his own birthday. The duchess replied that she would like to celebrate her own birthday at Claremont on the 17th – a tactless response which put the King in a fury.

On 20 August, he was in London to prorogue Parliament, and took the opportunity to go to inspect Kensington Palace. The previous year, the duchess had applied for his permission to occupy a grand suite, which William was keeping for his own use – seventeen rooms in all – and he had refused. Upon his arrival at Kensington Palace, he found that the duchess had defied his orders and was indeed in occupation of the grander royal apartments.

Armed with this infuriating intelligence, the King set off for Windsor, where the Duchess of Kent and Princess Victoria were already awaiting him. He arrived in the drawing room at ten o'clock at night, and took the princess's two hands in his own. He expressed his regret that he did not see his niece more often. Then he made a low bow to the duchess, and said 'that a most unwarrantable liberty had been taken with one of his Palaces; that He had just come from Kensington, where He found apartments had been taken possession of not only without his consent, but contrary to his commands and that he neither understood nor would endure conduct so disrespectful to him'[32].

It was scarcely a good omen for the birthday dinner, held at the Castle the next day. After the dinner, at Queen Adelaide's request, the King's health was drunk, and he replied in a lengthy, furious speech.

I trust in God that my life may be spared for nine months longer, after which period, in the event of my death, no Regency would take place. I should then have the satisfaction of leaving the royal authority to the personal exercise of that Young Lady [pointing to the Princess], the Heiress Presumptive of the Crown, and not in the hands of the person now near me, who is surrounded by evil advisers and who is herself incompetent to act with propriety in the station in which She would be placed. I have no hesitation in saying that I have been insulted – grossly and continually insulted – by that person, but I am determined to endure no longer a course of behaviour so disrespectful to me. Amongst many other things I have particularly to complain of the manner in which that young Lady has been kept away from my Court; she has been repeatedly kept from my drawing-rooms, at which she ought always to have been present, but I am fully resolved that this shall not happen again. I would have her know that I am King and that I am determined to make my authority respected.[33]

He ended his speech with paternal expressions of affection for the princess, who had burst into tears. Without a word, the Duchess of Kent had risen to leave the table. She later called for her carriage.

The incident in the Albion Hotel in Ramsgate when Victoria was sixteen had cooked Sir John Conroy's goose. Victoria's dogged willpower had been demonstrated. If he had been unable to force her, even when she was so weak and ill, to sign away her powers to him, he would never be able to do so again.

The hereditary system reminds rulers and governed alike of their place in the natural scheme of things. Aptly was the Victorian age one in which Nature dominated the human imagination so keenly. In 1831, while Victoria was attending her first Drawing Room, Charles Darwin was on board *The Beagle*, his mind beginning to dwell, not only upon the variety of finches on the Galapagos Islands, but on the processes by which the varieties arrived there. Had he been forced to stay at home and watch the Royal Family instead of the finches, he would have been equally aware of the potency of natural forces. The Duke and Duchess of Kent would never have come together had not the hereditary principle decreed that one Hanoverian baby should succeed, over the rival Hanoverian babies, and come to the English throne. If her very existence began with the Struggle for Life, the start of her reign was, equally, a demonstration of the contention between Nature and the Will. The old King was determined to live long enough to see her reach the age of eighteen. She herself was determined to be of age before she succeeded to the Crown. Her growing hatred of Conroy sustained her as she outgrew adolescence.

On 24 May 1819, she changed English history merely by being born. On 24 May 1837, she came of age, and thereby determined that Sir John Conroy, rather than being any political danger, was merely a grotesque footnote in the history books. Public excitement was intense. At half past three in the afternoon, with Lehzen and Victoria's sister-in-law Marie, Countess of Klebelsberg, she drove out for an hour and a half. 'The parks and streets were thronged and everything looked like a *Gala* day.'[34] In the evening, at half past ten, she attended a ball at St James's Palace, with her mother's entourage – Sir John Conroy, Lady Flora Hastings, Lady Conroy and the Duchess of Northumberland. But all eyes were upon the birthday girl. Though the King had been very ill, he appeared revivified by Victoria's triumphant achievement, of having lived eighteen years.

Her mother had recognized, even before the ball began, that everything was now going to be different. For the first time in her life, the princess travelled in a carriage with her own attendant, but without the duchess, who followed in another carriage. When Victoria arrived at the Palace, the King placed her on his chair of state, while Conroy and friends dined with the also-rans. Conroy could only hope that the King would disgrace himself by making another outburst. This did not happen. Victoria danced with a succession of swells – with Lord Fitzalan, Prince Nicholas Esterhazy, the Marquis of Granby, the Marquis of Douro and the Earl of Sandwich. 'I wished to dance with Count Waldstein, who is such an amiable man, but he replied that he could not dance quadrilles, and as in my station I unfortunately cannot valse and gallop, I could not dance with him.'[35]

There could be no doubt now that the ballroom had been shown the future Queen of England. The next day, hardly coincidentally, Baron Stockmar arrived in England. There was to be no danger of the Coburgs losing their influence. When Princess Charlotte died in 1817, Providence had snatched from Prince Leopold the chance of dominating British affairs; but Providence was offering the Coburgs a second throw of the dice.

The old family doctor, and political *éminence grise*, had hitherto been on reasonably good terms with Conroy, but on this occasion, after a 'heated' conversation, they were no longer friends. Presumably, Stockmar saw the way the wind was blowing. He had come to advise the princess about her future role, and it was clear to him that she was in a difficult position. As the King's health failed, Sir John and the duchess put more and more pressure on Victoria to make the tiresome Conroy her chief adviser when she came to the throne. She found his behaviour and attitude 'impudent and insulting'.[36]

Stockmar, who was anxious for Victoria to be rid of Conroy as easily as possible, did not want to antagonize him to the point where he dug in his heels. The ideal situation would be one in which Conroy could be persuaded, by money or titles, to go quietly when the moment arrived. Meanwhile, Stockmar was anxious for the princess to be clear about two things: the specific matter of her money, and the more generalized matter of her position as a constitutional monarch. He found her to be ill-informed about both.

Upon the princess reaching the age of eighteen, Lord Melbourne, the Prime Minister, had sent a letter via Stockmar to the duchess asking if they would accept a revised offer of money from the King. He was to increase the duchess's allowance to £6,000 and that of the princess to £4,000. Had the princess been acquainted with this letter, and was the duchess's refusal of the King's offer made – as the duchess claimed – with Victoria's consent?

Victoria indignantly told Stockmar, 'Not only have I <u>never seen</u> or heard of this letter, but was never told by my Mother that Lord Melbourne had been here... As I <u>never</u> knew anything of Lord Melbourne's letter, I am, of course, also totally ignorant of the answer.' She made clear to Stockmar her strong objections 'to allowing Sir John any interference in my affairs. Whatever he has done, it has been done by order of my Mother, as I requested in <u>her</u> name, without making me responsible for any of her actions, as Sir

John is <u>Her</u> private secretary and neither <u>my</u> Servant nor Adviser, nor <u>ever was</u>.'³⁷

By Sunday, 4 June, it was clear that the King was dying. Stockmar came to see Victoria in the afternoon, and for half an hour, 'he had a very pleasant and useful conversation with me; he is one of those few people who tell plain honest truth, don't flatter, give wholesome necessary advice, and strive to do good and smooth all dissensions. He is Uncle Leopold's greatest and most confidential attached and disinterested friend, and I hope he is the same to me.'³⁸

Lessons were now suspended. The princess was on the alert, day by day, for the news from Windsor. On 16 June, a little late perhaps, she began to read to Lehzen out of Jean-Louis de Lolme's *The Constitution of England*. They did not get very far with it, and soon turned to the letters of Madame de Sévigné. Stockmar was now calling at Kensington Palace on a daily basis, as the King's life sank towards its close at Windsor.

On 18 June, Waterloo Day, the King said to his medical adviser, 'Doctor, I know I am going, but I should like to see another anniversary of the battle of Waterloo. Try if you cannot tinker me up to last out that day. I know that I shall never live to see another sunset.' His lungs were turgid with blood, his heart valve was ossified, his liver was enlarged and his spleen had swollen to twice its normal size.³⁹ In spite of this incapacity, he managed to receive the Sacrament from the Archbishop of Canterbury, in the company of the Queen, who broke down and wept when the blessing was pronounced. 'Bear up! Bear up!' the King told her. He died at 2.20 on the morning of Tuesday, 20 June.

Two men, who had been in attendance on the dying King, were designated to inform the new Queen of her role. One was the Lord Chamberlain – Lord Conyngham (son of the Vice Queen and her tolerant husband). He was forty years old, the son-in-law of that old Marquess of Anglesey who had been bold enough to offer the incoming King William IV advice on how to conduct himself as a monarch. His daughter, Jane, Lady Churchill, would become one of Queen Victoria's ladies of the bedchamber and a close personal friend.

The other was William Howley, who, at less than five feet tall, must have been one of the shortest Archbishops of Canterbury since Laud. He was the last holder of that office to wear a wig, that habit which had caused Victoria such fear in her infancy. He was also the last Wykehamist Archbishop. Like Laud, he was High Church, and for that reason, he had been vehemently opposed to the measure of Catholic Emancipation in 1829. He was the only bishop in the Lords to speak against the Reform Bill in 1831.

When George IV had died, during the small hours of 26 June 1830, Conyngham's mother, the Vice Queen, had spent the rest of the night hastily packing and had left Windsor at dawn, accompanied by 'wagonloads' of plunder.[40] (She lived on until the age of ninety-two, dying in 1861.) It was perhaps with a memory of this, not entirely dignified, exit that Lady Conyngham's son brought to the new Queen a letter from Queen Adelaide, asking permission to stay at Windsor until after the funeral. One of Victoria's first acts was to write a letter to the Queen Dowager, 'begging her to consult nothing but her own health and convenience, and to remain at Windsor just as long as she pleases'.[41]

What did the two men speak of, as their coach rattled through the night from Windsor towards London? We are not informed, but these two unremarkable men were heralds of a new age.

The princess had been told, on the previous evening, that her uncle was nearly dead. She had burst into tears 'and continued very much affected'. The man who told her was her brother-in-law, Prince Ernst Hohenlohe, the husband of Princess Feodore. He concluded that she had been kept in ignorance of the King's condition, but this cannot have been true, unless (which seems highly improbable) her *Girlhood* journals were all written up after the event – when would she have had the time? The illness of the King was an intermittent theme of Victoria's journal for the previous month. Her outburst of emotion, hours before he actually died, was attributable to the whole situation at last becoming real to her.

That evening, for the last time, she went to bed in the same room as her mother. What happened thereafter passed instantly into history. How could she not have been inwardly preparing for some time how she would meet this moment?

The Duchess of Kent recollected that she woke her daughter with a kiss, to tell her that the archbishop and Lord Conyngham were awaiting her in her sitting room.

Victoria wrote in her journal, 'I got out of bed and went into my sitting-room (only in my dressing-gown) and *alone*, and saw them.'[42]

The two men in wigs, kneeling on the carpet, perhaps for an instant recalled the antics of the Kingfisher, when the Bishop of Salisbury, during her childhood, let her play with his insignia as Chancellor of the Order of the Garter. But if so, the flicker of childhood memory was instantly overwhelmed by the knowledge that she was no longer a child; that she was in control; that these men were on their knees before her because she was the Queen of England. She sent Lord Conyngham back to Windsor at once, to assure the Queen Dowager of her kindly reassurances. The archbishop, scarcely larger than the tiny Queen, informed Victoria that King William 'had directed his mind to religion, and had died in a perfectly happy, quiet state of mind, and was quite prepared for his death'.

Then, she was alone. 'Since it has pleased Providence to place me in this station, I shall do my utmost to fulfil my duty towards my country; I am very young and perhaps in many, though not in all things, inexperienced, but I am sure, that very few have more real good will and more desire to do what is fit and right than I have.'[43]

She had become Queen Victoria.

PART TWO

FIVE

'THE IGNORANT LITTLE CHILD'

HISTORY BELONGS TO the victorious. The morning after the Queen came to the throne, John Conroy, in the words of his son, 'finding his enemies and more especially that most hypocritical and detestable bitch Baroness Letzen [sic] were powerful against him, and that the childish monarch was acted upon by the vengeful cavils of his enemies, resolved to make up his book. He consulted with Baron Stockmar (who was Leopold's agent and who was his friend in part at that time) who proposed certain rewards for his past services to the ignorant little child that was called to preside over the destinies of this once great country.'[1]

Realizing that his luck had run out, Conroy wanted to cash in his chips as soon as possible, before the Establishment closed ranks against him. He proposed, and the Queen apparently gave verbal consent, that he should be rewarded with the Ribbon of the Bath, with a pension of £3,000 a year from the Privy Purse and an English peerage. As far as the duchess was concerned, this was only giving Conroy his just deserts. She would later recall that 'twenty-one of the most valuable and best years of your life have been passed without intermission in my service and that of the Duke of Kent', and remembered how 'His Royal Highness counselled me who was about to become his widow and who was the mother of his child, to avail myself of your assistance, and to be guided by your advice'.[2]

As soon as the Prime Minister heard what was afoot, however, Conroy's ambitions hit the buffers. Stockmar called on the Duchess of Kent on 22 June. He found Sir John already in court dress, in his uniform, ready to kiss the new monarch's hands. He would never be asked to do so. Stockmar had to tell him the bad news. Admission to the Order of the Bath was rejected out of hand. So was the enormous pension. The Prime Minister had no more wish than any other member of the Establishment to see Conroy sitting on the benches of the House of Lords. He cunningly offered an Irish peerage. Only a limited number of Irish peers sat in the Lords, and it would be years before a seat in the Upper House became vacant. Conroy haughtily refused the Irish peerage, and with that, he left the history books. His young friend Lady Flora Hastings – daughter of his late friend the Marquess of Hastings – told him, 'You have nothing to flinch from – if you are not treasured as you deserve. The shame will recoil upon those who do not fulfil their part.'³ Lord Melbourne's view of the Hastings family – 'I don't think there is an ounce of sense between them all' – was a judgement which the Queen endorsed with the two words '*è vero*'.⁴

The Conroys were no doubt intemperate in their language; but they were right. The eighteen-year-old who had just become the British Head of State was an 'ignorant little child'. Since Conroy had been so proud to be in charge of her education, much of the responsibility for this ignorance must rest upon his shoulders.

As is often the case with ignorant people who have a measure of uneducated native wit, the ignorance was patchy. The letters between Victoria and her uncle Leopold for the first half of 1837, for example – and there are many of them – reveal a keen interest in current affairs, both in Britain and in Europe. The King of the Belgians' replies to her reveal an intense desire to control her, and to intervene in British political affairs. The expulsion of Conroy did not leave Victoria alone, still less independent. It left the 'ignorant little child' at the mercy of the major political interest groups: Coburg, represented by King Leopold and Stockmar; the Whigs, represented chiefly by Lord Melbourne, the Prime Minister, but also Palmerston, the Foreign Secretary; and the Tory Party.

The premier who had refused Sir John his reward was William Lamb, 2nd Viscount Melbourne. He was a walking example of an English, as opposed to a continental, aristocrat. A mere three generations earlier, Peniston Lamb, a figure of humble origins in Nottinghamshire, made a success as an attorney. His heir, a nephew named Matthew, married an heiress, bought a country estate – Brocket in Hertfordshire – entered the House of Commons and acquired a baronetcy. His son, Sir Peniston Lamb, married into the Whig aristocracy, and with money he got an Irish barony – becoming the first Lord Melbourne. His wife was Elizabeth Milbanke, who numbered many distinguished men among her lovers. Melbourne's compliance in her affair with the Prince Regent advanced his baronetcy to a viscountcy. The father of the second viscount – Queen Victoria's 'Lord M.' – was generally acknowledged to be another Whig peer, Lord Egremont, an eccentric art collector and patron of Turner, the walls of whose magnificent house in Sussex, Petworth, groaned with great Italian masters.

The second viscount, who now appears in history as Queen Victoria's first Prime Minister, and who will be referred to hereafter as Melbourne, was famous in the early part of his life, not for his good looks – which were striking: short, dark hair, thick brows, a straight nose dividing a quizzical pair of glossy brown eyes, and a sardonic, sensual mouth – nor for his undoubted cleverness, nor for his early venture into politics and his seat in the House of Commons, but for his wife. He had married Lady Caroline Ponsonby, a hoydenish tomboy who was the life and soul of the Whig salons. (The Whigs are 'all cousins', as Melbourne himself used to say.) They all went in for love affairs, though perhaps not as flagrantly as Melbourne's mother. Lady Caroline, however, who was mentally unbalanced, had one of the most notorious love affairs in history – with Lord Byron, who had lately shot to fame as the author of *Childe Harold*. The affair was of short duration, but it obsessed her for the remainder of her days, and its messily protracted ending included Byron's clumsy but characteristic touch – having an affair not only with Melbourne's wife but with his mother too.

> Remember thee! Ay, doubt it not.
> Thy husband too shall think of thee!
> By neither shalt thou be forgot,
> Thou *false* to him, thou *fiend* to me![5]

For Melbourne, who loved his wife, the affair was not something which could blow over. As Lady Caroline descended into alcoholism, obesity and lunacy, he spent a wretched existence at Brocket, with an increasingly fat wife being cared for by nurses from the Bedlam hospital, and their backward, possibly autistic, son. Lady Caroline died in 1828.

Melbourne by then was in his late forties, and he must have assumed that his early political ambitions could never be realized. When Canning became Prime Minister, however, the Ultra Tories such as the Duke of Wellington all resigned, and Canning turned to his Whig friends to fill the vacant ministries. He brought forward Palmerston and Melbourne. When he showed the list of possible Cabinet ministers to old George IV, the King – remembering the convivialities of Carlton House twenty years before, and an enjoyable affair with Melbourne's mother – said, 'William Lamb – put him anywhere you like!'[6]

Melbourne became Home Secretary, a post he continued to occupy when the Whigs came back into office under the premiership of Earl Grey. For one whose reputation was for languor and inactivity, it is superficially[7] surprising that his most famous act, as Home Secretary, was to insist upon the transportation and exile of the Dorset agricultural labourers who formed a trade union and became known – after they were prosecuted for conspiracy and transported with thieves and killers on a prison ship to Australia – as the Tolpuddle Martyrs.

Superficially surprising for those – like the young Queen – who saw chiefly the benign, witty and seemingly indifferent drawing room Melbourne. There were other sides to his fascinating nature, among which was the flagellant. When it became clear that he and Lady Caroline should not risk another child, after the mental deficiencies of their son became clear, they took to adopting a series of orphan girls. Clearly there was collusion between Melbourne and his 'victims', one of whom wrote a letter to him, from the position of a married woman who had named her two children Caroline and William: 'I remember as though it were yesterday the execution, then being thrown into a corner of a large couch there was at Brocket you used then to leave the room and I remember your coming back one day and saying, "Well, cocky, does it smart still?" at which of course I could not help laughing instead of crying... Does the Queen whip the royal princes, I should like to know.'[8]

As the last jokey inquiry shows, we have leapt ahead in time by quoting this letter; but it does reveal one of the many quirky sides to Melbourne's nature. He and the Queen were once discussing floggings at Eton. When Victoria said she considered it 'degrading', Melbourne disagreed. He said his tutor 'had not flogged me enough, it would have been better if he had flogged me more'. Flogging, he told his monarch, always 'had an amazing effect on him'.[9]

The passionate friendship, or *amitié amoureuse*, which sprang up at once between the fifty-eight-year-old Prime Minister and the eighteen-year-old Queen was a liberation for them both. Victoria was set free from the constraints of childhood, and the hated Kensington System; Melbourne was liberated from a scarred emotional life, during which he had retreated from the pains of marriage into a series of platonic encounters with aristocratic women, and spanking and whipping sessions with young girls, sometimes prostitutes. There was something of the pain and bitter-sweet pleasure of the sado-masochist in his last attachment, since he must always have known that the friendship could only end with her growing up, and marrying.

When one considers the weekly audiences of modern Prime Ministers with the sovereign, it is difficult to imagine the subject of flagellation arising – as it did several times between the Queen and her Lord M. But the relationship between Victoria and Melbourne was an extraordinary one, and they discussed a huge range of subjects which she eagerly Boswellized: Shakespeare, the characters of her three predecessors on the throne ('spoke of the singular instance of both George III and Queen Charlotte's being very plain and all their children very handsome'),[10] Whig society gossip, Goethe, religion, French history (Cardinals Richelieu and Mazarin, he informed her, 'were shocking fellows')[11] and mixed race marriages ('He thinks that the children of a woman of colour and a white very handsome, "they breed very fine", he said').[12] Clearly mixed breeding appealed to him, whatever the species, since he commended to the Queen the breed of dogs known as lurchers. 'Talked of a dog Mrs Lamb's bred from an Italian grey-hound and a terrier, which he said made a very fine dog; it had all the swiftness and activity of an Italian greyhound with all the strength and sagacity of a Terrier.'[13]

In many of the journal's pages, during the Melbourne phase, the author seems much younger than her eighteen to twenty years: 'Talked of my having wished to roll in the grass when I was in the garden,' she wrote in Buckingham Palace, 'which made him laugh.'[14] 'I said' – of a Miss Rice – 'that she wanted to be like an innocent, simple, Irish girl, she being such a tall girl. "A great thumping girl," he said, which made me laugh very much.'[15] Perhaps he never seemed more of the old world than when – one New Year's Day in the Brighton Pavilion – he 'Talked of my having taken a bath; his seldom doing so.'[16] To judge from the journal, it was Palmerston, more than Melbourne, who spoke to the Queen of politics and foreign affairs, the Prime Minister being content, for hours on end, to go riding with his young pet, to sit discussing whether they preferred Racine to Corneille, or making disobliging remarks about the duller ladies-in-waiting.

The rapport between the pair established itself instantaneously, so that the political convention, whereby a General Election followed the accession of a new sovereign, was painful to her. The Whigs, with their radical Liberal supporters (whom Melbourne deplored), won it, but not comfortably; and the years that he and Victoria spent together – 1837 to 1841 – could never have lasted: a fact which adds to their poignant quality of holiday romance. Even if, like Queen Elizabeth I, she had never married, the electoral system would one day remove her Lord M. It was some holiday, however, while it lasted.

The defining fact in Victoria's personal mythology would seem to have been her marriage to Prince Albert; but there is no finished truth about a human being, and to see her as the besotted spouse and grief-stricken widow of the German prince is only one truth about the Queen. She lived for eighty-one years, and was married for a mere quarter of that time. In many ways, we can say that we see her most clearly being herself in those platonic male friend-ships which were based on shared humour: with Lord Melbourne, with Disraeli and to a smaller extent with Dean Davidson and Lord Salisbury. The elements of humour and independence are present in her more mysterious relationship with John Brown. One sees her at her vigorous, independent and humorously selfish best in these friendships. The first, and in some ways the sweetest, was that with Lord Melbourne.

It was he who groomed her for her role as Head of State. It was he who prepared her for the ceremonial initiation of the Coronation. Secularist as he may have been (for all his expertise in New Testament Greek and the early Fathers of the Church), Melbourne was a traditionalist, too, who was determined that his protégée should be crowned in the appropriate manner. When Lord Fitzwilliam wrote to him 'a characteristic letter saying it was quite unnecessary to have a Coronation… that did very well in the twelfth century but that in the nineteenth it was quite useless', Lord M. dismissed such talk and proceeded with the arrangements. It was not to be an affair on the lavish scale of George IV's Coronation, which had cost £240,000; but nor need it be the pared-down, almost hole-in-corner arrangement of William IV, who had spent a mere £30,000. Victoria's Coronation cost £79,000 – a fairly modest sum, compared with her extravagant uncle George. (Military expenditure for 1835 was £12.1 million.[17])

Coronation Day, Thursday, 28 June 1838, began for Victoria at 4 am when she was woken by the guns in the park, 'and could not get much sleep afterwards on account of the noise of the people, bands &c, &c'.[18] The crowds were huge. Railways had brought unprecedented numbers into the capital, and for the previous week, as she had seen during carriage drives, there were 'swarms of people'.[19] Feodore and the German relations had come, so there was a sizeable royal procession through the streets from Buckingham Palace. The Queen was overwhelmed by the 'multitudes, the millions of my loyal subjects who were assembled in every spot to witness the Procession... How proud I felt to be the Queen of such a Nation.'

Melbourne, no churchman he, had stage-managed the ceremonies. It was therefore unsurprising that so little attention had been given to the liturgical arrangements. ('Lord M. said he always went to his parish church in London, which made me laugh excessively, as I know he never goes to church in London, never having the time to do so: he laughed very much and could not deny that.'[20]) He had plainly done some research – for instance, discovering that Queen Anne's train had been borne by the daughters of four dukes. The clergy had not rehearsed the ceremony. 'The Bishop of Durham stood on one side near me,' she recalled, 'but he was, as Lord Melbourne told me, remarkably "maladroit" and never could tell me what was to take place.'[21] She herself was no ritualist, but she had managed to learn the names for the various esoteric robes – 'I took off the Dalmatic robe Supertunica &c and put on the Purple Velvet Kirtle & Mantle, & proceeded again to the Throne.' There were certain moments of near-farce, as when she entered St Edward's Chapel, 'as it is called, but which, as Lord Melbourne said, was more unlike a Chapel than anything he had ever seen; for what was called an Altar, was covered with sandwiches, bottles of wine, etc etc. The Archbishop came in and ought to have delivered the Orb to me, but I had already got it, and he (as usual) was so confused and puzzled and knew nothing; – and went away.'[22]

But those who came to witness the ceremonies were no better informed about coronation rituals than the bishops, and so they were less aware of the blunders than were the central participants. The French Ambassador, Count Sebastiani, she noted with amusement, 'had been surprised "*que les Cérémonies Protestantes fussent aussi belles*"'. The dean had fetched out of the wardrobe the very copes worn at the Coronation of James I. The choir was in good voice. And the very sight of so young, and so solitary, a figure on the throne, receiving the homage and oblation of the tottering old peers, was itself impressive.

When the crown was placed on her head, all the peers and peeresses donned their coronets. 'My excellent Lord Melbourne who stood very close to me throughout the ceremony was completely overcome at this moment and very much affected. He gave me such a kind (and I may say fatherly) look.' When the moment came to do homage, 'he knelt down and kissed my hand, he pressed my hand, and I grasped his with all my heart, at which he looked up with his eyes filled with tears and seemed much touched.'

The love – for it was much more than friendship – between Melbourne and Victoria is one of the most touching of all the relationships in her life. She called forth in the cynical worldly Whig reserves of tenderness which he had needed to seal up during the humiliations of his marriage. He, like a gentle tutor platonically in love with his pupil, taught her much, not only about the political process, but about life itself.

Like the relationship between tutor and pupil, however, it could not last forever. And from a political point of view, it had almost no significance. Melbourne was too languid, too oblique, too bored and sceptical to wish to hang on to office, and he was utterly out of sympathy with his times.

The questions facing Britain in the opening years of the Queen's reign were ones in which Melbourne took no interest. While her journals reflect the pair riding together, laughing together, jesting, not always kindly, about their shared acquaintances, it is almost as if the 'condition of England', which meant so much to serious politicians and writers of the day, were little more than 'noises off'. While she notes that 'great riots had broke out at Birmingham again; houses burnt and others plundered, which he [Lord M.] feared was to be expected',[23] the monarch's role in a changing, turbulent nation seemed difficult to define. 'Dawdled about,' she wrote. 'Wrote to Lord Palmerston and Lord Melbourne &c. Dawdled.'[24]

Palmerston, who had been in politics all his grown-up life, was in no doubt about what needed to be done. Much the most dynamic of the Whigs, and one of the biggest players on the political stage for the first half of Victoria's reign, Palmerston believed that he was born to rule, and he was determined to hold on to the power base of the great Whig houses and families – whatever strange political alliances this took. He stood, in foreign policy, for a belligerent, interventionist Liberalism, asserting Britain's influence and power in different parts of the world. At home, he believed in maintaining the notion of Parliament as a representative, not a democratic, body; but if this meant alliances with aspirant radical Liberals, or with disillusioned Tories, that was no difficulty for this, the least doctrinaire of politicians. The 1837 cartoon by John Doyle ('HB') shows the young Queen playing chess with Palmerston. Melbourne, hands behind his back, peeps over her shoulder. The caption is 'The Queen in Danger!' Clearly the impish suggestion of the cartoonist is that the virginal young woman is not safe in the company of these two old rakes – who were, in effect, brothers-in-common-law. (It was generally recognized that Palmerston was the father of three of the five children of Melbourne's sister, Emily Cowper.)

The actual 'danger' was that both Melbourne and Palmerston – but particularly Palmerston – were happy to neuter her sense of party politics, and to emphasize her sympathies with the Whigs. 'Lord M.

and I are quite of the same opinion; these Tories are <u>too</u> vile and monstrous.'[25]

Given the passionate hero-worship which she bestowed on Melbourne, and the Tory Leader Sir Robert Peel's shyness and awkwardness with women, it was not surprising that she should have failed to build up any relationship with the Leader of the Opposition. In July 1839, she 'talked of my having seen Peel coming down the same street I was, and that the moment he saw me he dashed down another street to avoid me, which I thought very rude. "I don't think he meant that," said Lord M. I observed he always formerly looked cross when he met me. "That's his clumsiness," said Lord M.'[26]

Peel was Leader of the Tory Party at a crucial period of its history. Like all parties, it was a coalition, and in the 1820s, it had been a coalition between the Canningites, or liberal Tories, of whom Peel had been one, and the diehards such as the Duke of Wellington. 1829 had seen the first *volte-face* by the diehards when Wellington decided to support Catholic Emancipation. The 1840s, with Peel as the Leader, would see an even more divisive issue than whether Roman Catholics should be allowed to stand for Parliament, or enter the universities or the professions. This was the question of Free Trade, and the issue on which the matter came to a head was the preservation or abolition of the Corn Laws, which imposed a tariff on the import of cheap grain.

This was a matter as basic as the price of a loaf of bread, the matter which, symbolically at least – though not in fact – had undone the French monarchy in 1789. Whether or not Marie Antoinette ever did say 'Let them eat cake', and whatever she meant by it, Victoria in the first three years of her reign was every bit as detached from the realities of her subjects' lives as Marie Antoinette had been from hers.

No doubt some of the agricultural labourers who set fire to hayricks and farm buildings in the Captain Swing riots, and some of the Chartists causing disturbances in Monmouth, Bristol and Birmingham, would have favoured a republic. But the broad stream of political opinion wanted to maintain the Queen in her position, and the main political groups wanted the sovereign either to give them her support, or, if that were emotionally beyond her reach, to recognize their place in the political scale of things.

While Palmerston and Melbourne cocooned the Queen in what was, in effect, a three-year Whig country-house party of plays, balls, rides, gossip and laughter, there were others, in Parliament and in the country, who, 'vile and monstrous' as they might be, had a different perspective on 'the condition of England' question. There were the Liberals, who ranged from economic Liberals, wanting the abolition of the Corn Laws and Free Trade, to those who wanted a much more radical programme of extending the franchise and reforming Parliament much further than it had been reformed in 1832.

There were the diehard Tories, the landed class who wished to protect their incomes from arable land by imposing tariffs on imported corn and driving up the price of bread.

There were Peelite Tories, who knew that this state of things could not long continue and who would eventually look for different political allies.

And there was the monarchy. Everyone agreed that it was a vital, central part of the British political system, but no one could be sure – since it had never been tested to its limits since 1688 – exactly what the nature of royal power and prerogative was, nor how much anyone wished it to be seen as exercising power.

We see from Queen Victoria's journals in the first three years of her reign that she spent almost every day with Melbourne, and that for much of the time he was actually living at Windsor Castle or travelling with her to the Brighton Pavilion. When she was at Buckingham Palace, he often sat up with her until half past eleven, and would then go home and sit up till two or three in the morning to complete his work, in order to give himself time for his royal passion.

But, as in Doyle's cartoon, Palmerston, though not enjoying anything like the degree of intimacy with the Queen enjoyed by Melbourne, was a frequent visitor, dining with her twice a week at least, and keeping her fully abreast of his political thinking abroad.

There is another visitor whose name appears in the journals several times a week, and that is Dr Stockmar. "'Clever man, the Baron,' remarked Melbourne. "He seemed to say 'You English, it's some time before you'll allow a foreigner to be of the same flesh and blood as you are, but when you know him you like him very well', and there's some truth in that." Asked if he had ever told the Baron what he thought of the Germans [a running joke between the Queen and Lord M.]. "Oh! he quite admits it", was his reply; "all Europe admit it." I said the Germans were just as good as other nations; which he wouldn't allow.'[27]

The Duchess of Kent, egged on by Conroy, had quarrelled with Baron Stockmar. ('I never saw so foolish a woman,' Melbourne told the Queen, 'and we laughed at Stockmar's calling her "such a stupid woman".' [28] Conroy had poisoned the duchess's mind against Stockmar, and told her lies. Conroy told the Duke of Sussex, which Victoria vigorously denied, that she had found Stockmar sitting with the Queen 'with all the <u>boxes</u> <u>open</u>!'[29]

With more than a touch of absurdity, given the fact that she had yet to master the English language, the Duchess of Kent purported to find sinister the 'Foreign Influence' at Court. There was, no doubt of it, such influence, and it came from a combination of Stockmar and the duchess's own brother, the King of the Belgians, who wrote to Victoria every week, often several times a week, with minute directions about her conduct of affairs.

Rather than 'dawdling' with Lord Melbourne, the Queen could at least provide one of the traditional functions of a monarchy if she were to marry and establish a dynasty. After the near-disaster of George III's inheritance – his madness, the fifteen children hardly any of whom came even close to producing canonically regular offspring – the zoological function of monarchy was surely closely to be linked with the constitutional. But it was not a limitless field. The violently anti-Catholic passions which came to the surface when Roman Catholics were allowed the vote ten years before had demonstrated that there would be no possibility of the public tolerating a repeal of the Act of Settlement to allow Victoria to marry a Catholic prince.

She was therefore limited to a choice of three: these were the Dutch Royal Family, her cousin George Cambridge and the Coburg cousins. In February 1839, 'I made Lord M. laugh very much by saying it was odd the late King should have fixed upon three such ugly clumsy fellows (for Prince Adalbert is also very plain) for me... Talked of the Cambridges... of George, his being a disagreeable young man.'[30] George himself would ungallantly say in later years that there had been no possibility of his being attracted by his 'plain little cousin', the Queen of England.

This left the Coburgs. Melbourne must have known that a belief in the desirability of this match was one thing which united Stockmar, the Duchess of Kent and King Leopold. Perhaps a little desperately, he tried to tell Victoria that the Coburgs were 'not well thought of, and that Aunt Julia was not well thought of; and I made him laugh by saying that Mary had said to me, that when Mama spoke with astonishment about our suspecting Lady Flora, that it seemed so odd to her that <u>a Coburg</u> should be so surprised at it.'[31]

The inference here was that Coburg, with its notoriously dissolute duke – father of Ernst and Albert – its divorced and banished Duchess Luise (the boys' mother) – and its history of illegitimacies and sexual disease – could scarcely claim to be shocked by love affairs and intrigues in England.

The 'suspicions' surrounding 'Lady Flora', however, to which Victoria callously alluded in her journal were only one of the signs that her immaturity, her lack of judgement and her detachment from public opinion were in danger of causing big trouble unless she could somehow be reined in, and given such benign distraction from 'dawdling' as only marriage could provide.

The Lady Flora in question was Lady Flora Hastings, an old childhood acquaintance of the Queen, a close family friend of the Conroys and now a lady-in-waiting to the Duchess of Kent. As a Conroy friend and a supporter of the Tories, Flora Hastings was fair game, as far as the childish malice of the Queen was concerned. She enjoyed mocking Lady Flora to Lord M. 'I asked him if he thought

Lady Flora plainer than Lady Mary: he replied, "Why, I really do; she is more disagreeable." I am quite of this opinion.'[32]

When limited to catty remarks about Lady Flora's appearance, the Queen's malice could do little harm. But rumours began to circulate that Flora was too close to Sir John Conroy. When the Tory Lady Flora's waistline altered, and a swelling was visible, Lady Tavistock, Whig of the Whigs, put it about that she was pregnant. The Queen, with an intrusiveness which even at this distance in history makes us gasp, insisted that Lady Flora be examined by a royal doctor: Sir James Clark.

Clark, like many of Victoria's medical advisers throughout her life, was an incompetent, but even he could see that the young woman was a virgin. He failed to diagnose a malignant tumour, which was eventually to kill her in July 1839. Not only was it a profound tragedy for the Hastings family, it showed the Queen and her circle in an appalling light. On the very day that the news of Lady Flora's miserable death reached the Court, the Queen continued to stay up late, giggling with Lord M. The Duchess of Kent, whose relationship with her daughter had never been worse, bombarded her with letters of remonstrance that 'we were too merry last night'.[33] The duchess put on mourning for Lady Flora, which – in the Queen's view – 'is too ridiculous'. There followed an absurd, and rather heartless, discussion of whether different members of the Royal Family should send carriages to Lady Flora's funeral, which was held in Scotland. Lord M. thought that sending a carriage was tantamount to attending the obsequies in person, and that the Queen should not send one. But the duchess sent a carriage and so did the Queen Dowager and Lord Howe. While Victoria airily doubted whether the Flora Hastings business was 'really making such a sensation as people said it did',[34] the French Ambassador was reporting home that 'L'affaire de Lady Flora Hastings s'envenima et donne beaucoup de tourments à la Reine.'[35] She received a vicious press, especially in the Tory newspapers, and Conroy made sure that the affair rumbled on and on, with the Morning Post publishing, posthumously, Lady Flora's letters, spitting venom against the Queen and 'violent against Lehzen'.[36] It could not do the Queen, or the monarchy, any good.

The so-called Bedchamber Crisis, which had preceded the Flora Hastings debacle, was in a sense more damaging because it revealed the absolute lack of political nous on the part of the young Victoria. She really was what Conroy so crudely dubbed 'an ignorant little child'.

The political year was dominated by events in Jamaica, with the planters showing great severity to their slaves, with overcrowding in the prisons, and a repeated danger of outright anarchy and rebellion. It was decided to bring in a parliamentary measure to suspend the Jamaica Constitution. The Government had a majority of only five in the Commons when the matter was put to the vote, a significant number of radicals having withdrawn their support from the Whigs. Melbourne felt he had no option but resignation.

Lord M. told the Queen to call for the Duke of Wellington and Sir Robert Peel and ask them to form a Tory administration. When she called for Wellington, he referred her to Peel, who had, after all, been the last Tory Prime Minister (1834–5). Peel told the Queen that he could not serve as her Prime Minister unless she made some concession to the political sensibilities of the Tories, by changing the personnel at Court. Melbourne, when consulted, advised her to make 'some changes' in the ladies. 'You must remember that [Peel] is a man who is not accustomed to talk to Kings; a man of a quite different calibre; it's not like me; I've been brought up with Kings and princes which gives me that ease. I know the whole Family, and know exactly what to say to them; now he has not that ease and probably you were not at your ease.'[37] This was indeed the case, and Victoria had been nervous and shaking when she gave audience to Peel. Nevertheless, when she stubbornly refused to offer a Tory lady a position as a lady of the bedchamber, and when Peel therefore said he that he could not serve under her, she believed she had achieved a sort of triumph.

'You will easily imagine that I firmly resisted this attack upon my power,' she wrote to her uncle Leopold, who replied, 'I approve very highly of the whole mode in which you proceeded.'[38]

Far from demonstrating her power, she had managed in two years, after the glad accession of a young, popular Head of State, to make the monarchy into an institution which was hated. Tories, of all people, no longer felt the monarchy was theirs. Melbourne quietly admitted to her that his Government would have difficulty limping on. This ridiculously trivial matter was in danger of provoking a General Election, since at any moment the Tories could force a vote on some other issue in the Commons and defeat the Melbourne administration.

It was fairly widely agreed that the Queen was neither a wise nor a competent Head of State. Melbourne himself, much as he loved her, must have cringed as she wrote him such letters as, 'The Queen is ashamed to say it, but she has forgotten when she appointed the Judge Advocate; when will the Cabinet be over?'[39] He could see, and feel, her youthful charm. He loved her. The greater political world saw only a capricious little incompetent, and the press, both Tory and radical, saw no reason to be merciful to her.

It was at this stage of things that Stockmar was able to play his trump card. Melbourne and the Queen both agreed to dismiss as an absurdity the notion, put about by Conroy, that Stockmar was exerting a 'Foreign Influence' at Court. But he plainly was doing so; and although the baron's *bons mots* are not quoted as often as Lord M.'s (perhaps because he never made any), he was almost as frequent a visitor at Buckingham Palace and Windsor. She was informed of her accession at six o'clock on the morning of 20 June 1837. At 7.30, while she was having her breakfast, 'good, faithful Stockmar came and talked to me'. After a solitary dinner she saw Stockmar twice, once before and once after the visit of Lord Melbourne.[40] Thereafter, Stockmar was an absolutely repeated and habitual visitor.

If the summer of 1839, with its Bedchamber Crisis and its Lady Flora Hastings affair, had not been so disastrous, Melbourne might have been able to stave off the Coburg match. The Queen, after all, was only twenty. He might have been able to do so anyway, had it not been for the fact that when she met her cousin Albert again in the autumn of that difficult year, she felt an overpowering sexual attraction.

There was no doubt of it being a Coburg-arranged affair. Victoria's only doubt was whether the boy himself had been made 'aware of the wish of his <u>Father</u> and <u>you</u> relative to <u>me</u>', as she put it to the King of the Belgians in July 1839. She made it clear to her uncle that she did not regard herself as engaged to Albert.[41]

The two brothers, Albert and Ernst, arrived in London in October. 'Albert's <u>beauty</u> is <u>most striking</u>, and he so amiable and unaffected – in short, very <u>fascinating</u>', were her initial reactions.[42] Within a fortnight, she was telling her journal, 'Dearest Albert took my face in both his hands and kissed me most tenderly and said, "*ich habe dich so lieb, ich kann nicht sagen wie!*" [I love you so much, I can't say how much.] Dearest Angel, so kind of him, and he said we should be "so *glücklich*" if I can only make <u>him</u> happy.'[43]

There was considerable opposition among the Queen's English family. The Duchess of Gloucester supposed it had all been arranged behind everyone's back by the Duchess of Kent, and the old Duke of Cambridge said that Victoria 'was only brought up for the Cobourg [sic] family and not for the English family' – which was largely true. She skittishly asked Albert himself whether his father had expected things to move forward so quickly and he replied, '*Nein, im Gegentheil, wir haben alle geglaubt dass würde nicht seyn.*' ('No, on the contrary, none of us believed it would happen.') 'He clasped me in his arms and pressed his lips to mine again and again, and leant his head on my shoulders,' and murmured more sweet German nothings in her ear.[44] By 9 November, Albert was showing her his illustrations to a story he had written of 'Herr v. Pumplemus und Herr v. Zigeuner', which she thought 'delightful and <u>so</u> funny'. But they were not funny as Lord M. was funny.

The genuine playfulness and humour in the Queen's nature was not to find companionable outlet for over twenty years, when she began to befriend John Brown; and it would not know a complete flowering until Disraeli became Prime Minister in 1874.

She was so besottedly enraptured by Albert, his beauty and his accomplishments, that she had a far less vivid sense than we do

– who know the future – of how much, in this infatuation, of her own freedom and personality she was surrendering. 'I <u>love</u> him more than I can say,' she gushed to her uncle Leopold, 'and I shall do everything in my power to render the sacrifice he has made (for a <u>sacrifice</u> in my opinion it is) as small as I can'.[45]

Leopold replied, 'Lord Melbourne has shown himself the <u>amiable</u> and <u>excellent</u> man I always took him for. Another man in his position, instead of <u>your</u> happiness, might have merely looked to his own personal views and imaginary interests. Not so our good friend; he saw what was best <u>for you</u>, and I feel it deeply to his praise.'[46]

There could be no doubt that for Melbourne himself it was a personal tragedy. Throughout their three years of conversations, he had ribbed his young monarch about the Germans, and his distaste for the race in general, the Coburg Royal Family in particular. Once the Coburg prince had arrived to claim his cousin as a bride, there would be no more of their old jokey familiarities. He felt as the father of a doted-upon daughter might feel when she meets her first serious lover: but more excluded than this, for they had been half-lovers. Moreover, when the Whigs lost the election in 1841 and Melbourne continued to correspond with the Queen, it was firmly pointed out, to both sides of the correspondence by Stockmar via Albert, that this was constitutionally inadvisable. They slowly began to lose touch. When she met him in 1843, she was shocked to find him an old man. 'Lord Melbourne seemed very nervous, and there is a strained altered look in his face, which it pains me to see. He is grown very thin, and uses his left hand with difficulty. But he talked on all subjects very well and quite like his old self. He said "I am very weak. I am so crippled", but I assured him he looked very well and only begged he would take great care of himself. "Well I will try", he answered.'[47]

He turned down her offers of an earldom, and of the Garter, accepting in preference some lithographs of the Queen, which she gave him: he could not have made it clearer that their relationship had become a purely personal one for him. Driving past Buckingham

Palace became an unbearable experience for him. Through lighted windows he caught glimpses of familiar pictures, or saw someone lighting a candle. The feeling of rejection was so acute because it was real – he had been rejected. Her future was elsewhere.

SIX

'TOO HASTY AND PASSIONATE FOR ME'

Victoria and Albert. The very phrase conveys something institutional: the words gave the name to a royal yacht and, as they do today, to a venerable London museum. Although they were married when it was technically possible to take photographs, no camera was present at their wedding, and the images of their early life together have been immortalized in glossy formality by the German painter Franz Xaver Winterhalter.

In Queen Elizabeth II's private sitting room at Balmoral,[1] however, hang two altogether less formal likenesses of the royal pair – chalk drawings by the Hungarian-born painter Charles Brocky. They formed part of the glorious exhibition 'Victoria and Albert: Art and Love', which was displayed at the Queen's Gallery in 2010. The figures whom Brocky depicted in 1841 are conveyed with a realism which is palpable and instantly recognizable as two likenesses. They are so alive, vibrant, young, sexy, that it almost shocks us to see them. What Brocky captured, before Winterhalter made them into lustrous icons, was, as it were, the raw materials of the legend. We see Victoria as her husband must have seen her on her wedding night when they were alone together. We see Albert as a bright, slightly amused boy, quizzical about the world which he was about to conquer. He is so young that his whiskers are no more than fluff. It is a supercilious face, and his expression suggests that he does not expect us, or his wife, to aspire to his level of intelligence. Victoria looks like someone who has scarcely emerged from childhood; but she is bursting with sexual vitality. Her hair has been dressed but it nevertheless, at the edges of its ringlets, is slightly tousled. The eyes and nose, a little disconcertingly, are those of her grandfather George III. You could not look at this drawing and think she was any other lineage. The eyes, however, are young, joyful, amused. The very moist red mouth is open, just a little.

This pair of extremely strong characters was in for an extraordinary journey together when they married. Both wanted power. Neither wanted to surrender their independence. More than in most marriages, there was a thunderous clash of wills. There was also, however, a deep bond from the very first. Furious as they would be with one another in the first stormy two years, as they were also in the tired last year, they remained everlastingly a team. The strength of their personal attraction, and the Queen's physical stamina, led to the birth of nine children, all of whom survived birth and childhood. This was in itself something of an achievement in the nineteenth century. It was also a political statement. Their private life was not really a private life, however much they might wish it to be so. For each coition was not only an act of love, but a gesture against the swell of European republicanism. Each pregnancy brought forth a potential German empress, the would-be parent of a Russian tsar, the potential for a queen of Spain or a tsar of Bulgaria. In fact, when Brocky drew them, they had already started to have children, and they were twenty-two years old. They look younger. The chalk likenesses show teenagers who have just sprung up from a sofa when their parents came home early. Brocky also immortalizes a couple who are mythological progenitors, like Abraham, the father of many nations. Albert was first photographed in Brighton by William Constable in 1842; the daguerreotype is so dark and indistinct, you can hardly make him out. In 1848, he commissioned William Kilburn to take a daguerreotype which was subsequently coloured. To compare the Brocky drawing of 1841 and the Kilburn photograph of only seven years later is to register a shock. The young man, not yet thirty, in that photograph, taken in the Year of Revolutions, has aged a lifetime. But he had done his bit to stave off the Revolution.

That this was his – and his mentor Stockmar's – ambition is the central fact about Prince Albert's existence. It is sometimes suggested that Albert somehow oversaw the diminution of the power of the monarchy, its demotion from being an institution which had possessed some measure of power but which, by the time he had died, was no more than a figurehead, an emblem, a 'focus of unity'. Almost the opposite was true. He and his Coburg backers – principally Stockmar and King Leopold – had a passionate interest in power, in the day-by-day exercise of political influence. No monarch, or monarch's consort, can ever have worked harder than Prince Albert. It was not pointless work, or work for its own sake: it was work with a purpose: to establish monarchy as a workable modern political institution, strong enough to resist the forces of revolution which, since 1789, had threatened Europe. In the first part of the marriage, the work was devoted to his role in Great Britain. When the children grew to marriageable age, the work branched outwards; the clear idea was that Albert and Stockmar's brand of German liberalism, based on a particular reading of the British Constitution, should become the template by which the whole of Europe could be governed.

The marriage took place on 10 February 1840, at 1 pm: it was a break with tradition, royal marriages having previously been solemnized at night. The ceremony was held in the Chapel Royal, St James's, and despite torrents of rain, violent gusts of wind and extreme cold, there were some crowds to watch the Queen leave Buckingham Palace, with twelve train-bearers wearing white dresses adorned with white roses. One member of the public noted it was 'a quietish affair, creating none of the excitement as at her son's in later years'.[2] The

Queen was given in marriage by her old uncle, the Duke of Sussex, who wore a black skullcap, perhaps against the cold – the fashion for wigs, except among the more old-fashioned bishops and barristers and judges in court, being now all but obsolete. Victoria, less than five feet in height, wore a white satin gown, with a deep flounce of Honiton lace, a diamond necklace and earrings and the magnificent sapphire brooch which Albert, who was ever fascinated by jewellery, had had made for her. Albert, at five feet ten inches[3] towering above his bride, wore the uniform of a field marshal in the British Army.

The guests were nearly all Whigs. Out of 300 people in the congregation, there were only 5 Tories of note – the Lord Great Chamberlains Willoughby and Cholmondeley were there *ex officio*; Ashley – whose name in history is the seventh Earl of Shaftesbury – was asked, as Lord Melbourne's nephew-in-law; Lord Liverpool was an old friend; and she could scarcely avoid inviting the Duke of Wellington, who was a national institution almost as venerable as the monarchy. Although she said, 'It is MY marriage and I will only have those who can sympathize with me', it was generally thought to be tactless to choose such a day to proclaim her political affiliation, but she felt she had been provoked.

In the short period since she had announced her engagement, the Tories in Parliament had made trouble for her. First, the proposal, made by Melbourne's Government, that Albert be granted the same income as Prince Leopold – £50,000 – was done without consulting the Opposition in advance. There was therefore an unseemly debate in which the radical Joseph Hume proposed reducing the grant to £21,000, and Colonel Sibthorp, in his top boots and wide-awake hat, the Ultra of the Ultras, proposed to fix it at £30,000. Sibthorp's motion was carried by a humiliating 262 votes to 158. 'From the Tories, good Lord deliver us,'[4] she had written in her journal on New Year's Day. More embarrassing than the reduced grant was the fact that Melbourne's Government, in proposing Albert's naturalization as a Briton, also tried to accord him precedence for life over the princes of the blood. Cumberland (King of Hanover) violently objected and persuaded Cambridge to do likewise, and this stirred up yet more hatred from the Tories. The Duke of Wellington himself opposed the measure in the Lords on the simple ground that such powers could only be granted by Parliament, and not by the Queen herself – she had wanted to make Albert King Consort, until Melbourne talked her out of it. So things did not start propitiously.[5]

After a wedding breakfast at Buckingham Palace, they went – in 'one of the old travelling coaches', complained Greville, who hoped for something more spectacular – to Windsor.

The wedding night was nervous, but evidently delightful. 'We had our dinner in our sitting room; but I had such a sick headache that I could eat nothing, and was obliged to lie down in the middle blue room for the remainder of the evening on the sofa; but, ill or not, I never, never spent such an evening!! My dearest dearest dear Albert sat on a footstool by my side, and his excessive love and affection gave me feelings of heavenly love and happiness, I never could have hoped to have felt before! He clasped me in his arms, and we kissed each other again and again! His beauty, his sweetness and gentleness, – really, how can I ever be thankful enough to have such a Husband! At ½ p.10 I went and undressed and was very sick, and at 20 m. p. 10 we both went to bed; (of course in one bed), to lie by his side and in his arms, and on his dear bosom, and be called by names of tenderness, I have never yet heard used to me before – was bliss beyond belief! Oh! this was the happiest day of my life!'[6]

The next morning, after walking on the terrace – 'Eos our only companion' (Albert's greyhound) – it was Prince Albert's turn to feel queasy. 'Poor dear Albert felt sick and uncomfortable, and lay down in my room, while I wrote to Uncle Leopold.'[7]

As far as Leopold of Belgium and Baron Stockmar were concerned, it was to be business as usual. What had been so tragically interrupted by the death of Princess Charlotte in 1817 would now be resumed and set to rights in February 1840. A male Coburger would in effect rule

England. 'He is the King to all intents and purposes,' Greville could write in 1845, and both Albert and Leopold would have agreed.

This was not how Queen Victoria herself viewed matters, and there was a paradoxical sense in which, the deeper she fell in love with Albert as a sexual partner, and the more she admired him as a human being, the more she regretted the surrender of her political power to him. In time, a harmony would develop. And from the perspective of widowhood, of course, Albert became a saint whose every view she always echoed. The reality was very different in the early stages of their marriage.

For a start, Albert felt terribly lonely. 'Think of my position. I am leaving my home with all its old associations, all my bosom friends, and going to a country in which everything is strange to me – men, language, customs, modes of life. I have no one to confide in.'[8] This had been his response when told by Melbourne that he was not to be allowed to bring a German secretary or companion with him, but must accept George Anson as his private secretary. Anson, a young man who had been working as Melbourne's secretary and was a scion of the Earls of Lichfield's family, can scarcely have been cheered up, in his first month of working with the prince, to receive the memo, 'Wished to have an opportunity of telling you that I was determined not to appoint you. I felt that it was committing myself by taking one who was confidentially placed about the Prime M. The Q. insisted upon your app. – & resented my opposition.'[9]

A year later, on 19 February 1841, Anson had a conversation with Melbourne in which he said, 'the prince is indolent, & it would be better if he was more so, for in his position we want no activity. I replied the prince may be indolent, but it results from there being no scope for his energy. If you required a cipher in the difficult position of Consort of the Queen you ought not to have selected the prince, having got him, you must make the most of him, & when he saw the power of being useful to the Queen, he will act. He is not ambitious, he wishes for no Power, except such as will enable him to support & assist the Queen'.[10]

Anson had really misread Albert, in this 'indolent' first year. It is true that he wanted to support Victoria, but he also wanted to direct her, and to have political influence. And this he could not do in the early stages of the reign; partly because she continued to rely on Melbourne for political advice and support, until he was voted out of office; and partly because of the influence of the Baroness Lehzen, who resented the power of Stockmar, and did all she could to thwart Albert's path.

This suited the Queen to begin with because, while Melbourne remained in office, and while Lehzen was still at her side, she could resist the pressure from Albert to share political influence with him.

The history of the monarchy in the Victorian age could really be defined as the history of the Queen's Private Secretaries. There were no formal revolutions in nineteenth-century Britain, as there were in nineteenth-century France and Germany; no moments when the Royal Family had to pack its trunks and leave – although Prince Albert did suppose such a moment might be reached in 1848, and withdrew the family to the Isle of Wight. What there was, however, from the earliest years of the Queen's reign to the end, was a series of movements backwards and forwards in which the elected representatives and the Cabinets saw the degree to which they valued the monarchy – even the degree to which they depended upon it; and the monarch worked out how far she could or could not go in the assertion of powers and privileges. There was no specific Act of Parliament, or crisis, after which it could be said that from then onwards the power of the monarchy had diminished or changed. It was more a matter of testing the water, becoming tactful to the atmosphere. And in this matter, the go-between, the private secretary, played a pivotal role. In her widowhood, this man, first General Grey, then General Ponsonby, had a formally acknowledged role. From his arrival in England until his death, the role of secretary, of political adviser to the monarch, was played by Prince Albert, with King Leopold and Stockmar ever anxious to offer their sometimes intrusive advice.

The Queen became pregnant almost at once after she married, and the 1840s were dominated by childbirth. Victoria, the Princess Royal, was born on 21 November 1840; Albert Edward, 9 November 1841 – almost immediately declared Prince of Wales; Princess Alice, 25 April 1843; Prince Alfred in 1844; Princess Helena in 1846; Princess Louise in 1848; Prince Arthur in 1850; with the two youngest following in the next decade – Prince Leopold in 1853 and Princess Beatrice in 1857. Even when we allow for the fact that the Queen was a strong woman, who lost none of her children in infancy, and, fairly obviously, had every possible assistance in the way of nurserymaids, governesses and the like, this was still a mighty distraction. From the first pregnancy, Prince Albert became an effectual political secretary to the Queen. Although his own private secretary, George Anson, was a Whig, Albert, guided by Stockmar, took a view which was absolutely different from his wife's partisan politics. He believed it was essential that the Crown should be above politics. 'The Whigs seek to change before change is required,' he wrote solemnly in a memorandum to himself, preserved in the Royal Archives. 'The love of change is their great failing. The Tories on the other hand resist change long after the feeling and temper of the times has loudly demanded it and at last make a virtue of necessity by an ungracious concession. My endeavour will be to form my opinions quite apart from politics and party, and I believe such attempt may succeed.'[11] This was a clumsy – and inaccurate – picture of the political parties and their situations. It showed that he, like his Queen, had much to learn.

Victoria wanted life to go on as before, only with the addition of Albert as her lover. The happy moments of the journal concern not merely sex ('Albert still complained of weakness in his knees'; 'My dearest Albert put my stockings on for me. I went in and saw him shave, a great delight for me'), but also fun, especially musical fun. 'I danced several Quadrilles and Valses, finishing up with a Gallop with Albert', she wrote from Claremont in March 1841. But too much of the time was taken up with pregnancy and childbirth, which she never enjoyed. She would later confide in her firstborn, Vicky, that 'what made me absolutely miserable was to have the first two years of my married life utterly spoilt by this occupation'– childbearing. 1841 was a low point. 'Lord Melbourne entreats Your Majesty to pick up your spirits,' Melbourne wrote after the first baby, when she was evidently suffering from severe post-natal depression. On the first Christmas after the birth of the Princess Royal, Anson noted, 'The Q. was not at all well again yesterday – being again troubled with lowness... The Baroness [Lehzen] lets no opportunity of creating mischief & difficulty escape her – to keep an influence over the Nursery underlings is one of her great aims.'

The Queen wrote of Vicky's arrival, 'alas! a girl and not a boy as we both had so wished and hoped for.' A wet nurse was employed for the baby, 'a Mrs Ratsey, a fine young woman, wife of a sail maker at Cowes, Isle of Wight'.[12]

Albert and Victoria spent Christmas quarrelling. Clearly, Mrs Ratsey, however fine a young woman, was less than satisfactory as a wet nurse, and on 16 January, when the Queen and the baby were both ill, Albert wrote to his wife, 'Dr Clark has mismanaged the child and poisoned her with calomel and you have starved her. I shall have nothing more to do with it; take the child away and do as you like and if she dies you will have it on your conscience'. On the same day, he wrote to Stockmar that Lehzen was a 'crazy, stupid intriguer, obsessed with the lust of power, who regards herself as a demi-God, and anyone who refuses to recognise her as such is a criminal. I declare to you, as my and Victoria's true friend, that I will sacrifice my own comfort, my life's happiness to Victoria in silence, even if she continues in her error. But the welfare of my children and Victoria's existence as sovereign are too sacred for me not to die fighting rather than yield them as prey to Lehzen.'[13]

Two days later, he told Stockmar, 'Victoria is too hasty and passionate for me to be able often to speak of my difficulties. She will not hear me out but flies into a rage and overwhelms me with reproaches of suspiciousness, want of trust, ambition, envy etc etc. There are, therefore, two ways open to me: (1) to keep silence and go away (in which case I am like a schoolboy who has had a dressing down from his mother and goes off snubbed); (2) I can be still more violent (and then we have scenes like that of the 16th, which I hate, because I am so sorry for Victoria in her misery, besides which it undermines the peace of the home).'14

There was further trouble ahead, since the Whig administration of Lord Melbourne was about to be voted from office, and both the Queen and Lord M. were to begin their painful separation. The semi-tragic situation outlined at the end of the last chapter, in which Lord M. could scarcely pass Buckingham Palace without a pang, did not come into being overnight. It was a slow matter – a lingering sorrow for Melbourne personally, a frustrating dawdle for Stockmar and Albert, who were anxious that Victoria should learn the ways of a constitutional monarch.

The character of the new Prime Minister did not help. Sir Robert Peel is widely, and rightly, seen as a statesman of great integrity and vision, who had the courage to change his mind. In Ireland, the diehard 'Orange Peel' became a man who saw the absurdity of trying to impose Protestantism on the largely Catholic Irish, and who saw the point of allowing the Irish a greatly increased grant towards training the Catholic clergy at Maynooth. The economy was a matter of much more widespread application. As things had panned out since the end of the Napoleonic Wars, the Tories had been the party which opposed the idea of Free Trade, and which defended the imposition of tariffs on foreign corn, thereby keeping the price of bread high in a hungry, unhappy country; but the rents and revenues of the landed classes high too. Peel, with Hamlet-like slowness, changed his mind about this matter and came to see that the Corn Laws had to be repealed. His change of mind was seen as a betrayal of Tory values, especially by the vociferous Lord George Bentinck and his brilliantly devious Commons colleague Benjamin Disraeli. Bentinck and Disraeli led the rebellion against Peel and, when the vote came in 1846, this would cause a split in the Tory Party and make it unelectable for another thirty years.

So, Peel, however you viewed him, was a politician of first importance in the scheme of things. Yet this Harrow-educated son of a cotton- and calico-manufacturer was a dull dog, and the Queen liked to be amused. With his slight Lancashire accent and his red hair, Peel was a shock to her system after the amusing conversations, and the warm affection, she had enjoyed with Lord M. By contrast, Peel was everything of which Stockmar, and hence Prince Albert, most approved. He was, like both of them, moderate, hard-working, principled and clever.

It took a while for the Queen to come round to her husband's love of Sir Robert, but she did so. This was one of the things which softened the blow of losing Lord M. Another factor which made life much easier between Albert and the Queen was that she tearfully consented to the banishment of Lehzen. Albert had not exaggerated Lehzen's love of intrigue, and as soon as she had been dispatched to Germany, never to return, relations improved – between him and his wife; between the Duchess of Kent and the Queen; between the Duchess of Kent and the Queen Dowager, all of whom Lehzen had succeeded in putting at odds with one another.

Moreover, after the miserable incompetence of the Queen's early years – with the Bedchamber Crisis and the Lady Flora Hastings affair; and after the rocky start of the Tories openly scorning Albert in the House of Commons – the Queen was lucky enough to suffer several assassination attempts. Although never slow to let anyone know if she felt slightly bilious or had a mild headache, the Queen was physically courageous in graver circumstances, and the many attempts made during her reign upon her life never saw her reduced to panic, or even to displays of fear. The first of these occurred on 10 June 1840, when Edward Oxford – 'he is seventeen years old, a waiter in a low inn – not mad – but quite quiet and composed'[15] – shot at Albert and Victoria not a hundred yards from Buckingham Palace in Hyde Park.

In May 1842, they were shot at by one John Francis, again as they passed in their carriage. 'The pistol was about a yard from the window,'[16] Albert recollected. He was condemned to death, but, since his pistol had in all probability not been loaded, Victoria and Albert spared his life. In July of that year 'a hunchbacked lad named Bean'[17] also fired at their carriage.

It was a dangerous time. Peel's secretary was assassinated not long afterwards, by a man mistaking him for the Prime Minister himself. Not only did these events raise the royal pair in the public esteem, but the prospect of being shot would appear to have taught them to count their blessings and to be less quarrelsome – though it was always a stormy marriage, and Queen Victoria's children, servants, secretaries and Prime Ministers all knew the force of Prince Albert's judgement that she 'is too hasty and passionate'.

When the Tories won the election, there was no repetition of the Bedchamber Crisis. On the contrary, Prince Albert ensured that there were Tory ladies introduced into his wife's household. Albert, who was himself a skilled home economist, was impressed by Peel's desire to get the economy of the country straight, with income tax of seven pence in the pound being imposed for a limited period of three years as a way of turning the budget deficit into a surplus, which placed him in a position to review the tariffs on imported goods – including corn. He cleverly brought in the Canada Corn Act of 1843, on the one hand appearing to side with the Protectionists – for he was actually bringing into the legislature a protection of a particular imported grain – and on the other defending the Canadian economy against the incursions, fiscal or actual, of the United States.

It is interesting that, as the family grew, neither Victoria nor Albert considered the possibility of moving either to Kew, where George III had led a blameless (if sometimes mad) family existence, or to Kensington Palace, where Victoria had herself grown up, occupying, by the end – to her uncle William IV's disgust – over seventeen rooms. Claremont, though still belonging to King Leopold, was always at their disposal, and they often went there. It was entirely rural and entirely suitable as a house for a young Royal Family. Both Victoria and Albert complained that Buckingham Palace, in spite of the money spent on it by George IV, was unsuited to their needs as royal personages with an expanding number of children. The alterations to the Palace by John Nash, finished as George IV was dying, had cost over £500,000, but it was estimated by a Select Committee that a further £150,000 was needed to make it habitable. Edward Blore was the architect employed to finish Nash's work. Nevertheless, by the time Victoria and Albert started to have children, they found there was no suitable room for the brood. Dr Lyon Playfair, having inspected the kitchens and sanitation, declared them to be worse than many of the places he had visited as Commissioner of Inquiry into the State of Large Towns. Windsor Castle was deemed equally impractical, and the area around the Brighton Pavilion had been so built up as to block the view of the sea from the Queen's windows. It also lacked privacy.[18]

These were the stated reasons, or 'reasons', for the acquisition of a new royal residence. The glaringly obvious psychological reason is that the royal pair, and Albert in particular, needed to start something new. He did not wish to be seen as the young man from Coburg, meekly fitting into the traditions of the English Royal House and living in the houses and palaces of his wife's predecessors.

Sir Robert Peel, who had by now become Prince Albert's friend, made inquiries and lighted upon, of all places, the Isle of Wight, considering two properties to be suitable: Norris Castle, where the child Victoria had spent holidays with her mother and the Conroys, and Osborne where the Conroys actually had a house. In March 1843, it became clear that Lady Isabella Blachford, the owner of Osborne House, would be prepared to sell it, and Prince Albert paid her a flying visit; he decided at once that it was suitable. The Queen could not accompany him. As for much of the 1840s, she was pregnant, this time eight months into her pregnancy with Princess Alice. Peel advised them to make inquiries 'through some very confidential channel as a suspicion of the object of them would probably greatly enhance the price'.[19] Albert took the point, but bombarded the Prime Minister with practical questions: 'Can one see the sea from the House at Osborne or from any part of the Park? Is there any right of way, or a public footpath through the Park? What kind of House is it? How many rooms? Does the wood run down to the sea? Is the Farm on the land side or the sea side of the Park, is it New Barn Farm (as marked on the Ordnance Map?) Is Barton Farm included in the purchase money? & must this Leasehold be purchased with the Freehold?'[20] In spite of all their attempts at secrecy, the prince was obliged to ask Peel, 'Have you seen in the Chronicle our whole scheme about the Isle of Wight detailed?'[21] So they bought Osborne. It must be one of the most idyllic spots in the south of England, with its gentle, natural cove, and its trees framing the views of the Solent. Here the children would grow up. Here Victoria would spend most of her life – certainly, most of the happiest times of her life. And here she would die.

1843 was a happy year and the young parents did not allow the existence of small children to deter them from the pleasures of travel. In the summer, they visited France as guests of the French King and stayed with Louis-Philippe at Château d'Eu. 'The King and Queen are all kindness and affection to us,' the Queen wrote to her Prime Minister, 'and treat us quite as members of their family.' They weren't family exactly, but there was a connection – King Leopold of Belgium having married, *en secondes noces*, Louise, Louis-Philippe's daughter. 'Aunt' Louise had been a kind friend to Victoria during her teenage misery and an ally against Conroy and the Kensington System. The Queen continued, 'this union and harmony which reigns among us does our hearts good. The Château is fine and full of many fine old Family pictures. The country reminds the Queen of Brighton. The people are very friendly, crying, Vive la Reine d'Angleterre! whenever the Queen appears.'[22] She always enjoyed visits to France, and they were a feature of her life until deep old age.

At the end of the year, Prince Albert told Peel that they had decided to have a little English tour, basing themselves at Peel's house, Drayton Park, visiting surrounding nobility, taking in a trip to Birmingham to see the factories, and paying a call on the Queen Dowager at Witley Court in Worcestershire. They made the journey to the Midlands by train. Clearly there were no lavatories on board, since the ever-practical Peel told them that they would be stopping for five minutes at Watford, and again at Wolverton where a room had been made ready, 'in the event of H.M. wishing to occupy it during the short time (five minutes) that the train will stop there'.²³ It is perhaps worth noting in passing that such an earthy mindset was not Prince Albert's. In spite of suffering throughout his life from chronic indigestion, he made efforts to discontinue the habit, in his household, of the men lingering over their dessert, while the ladies withdrew after dinner. Albert was obviously among those who considered that the chief function of this custom was to allow the men to overindulge in alcohol, and perhaps in ribaldry, whereas surely the reason the convention arose was to allow the two sexes to relieve themselves without drawing attention to the prosaic reality of things.

It must have been quite demanding for Peel, on top of his minis-terial duties, to arrange this royal visit at his home in Drayton, but all seems to have passed off happily. Victoria and Albert then went on to Chatsworth, seat of the 6th Duke of Devonshire. Rather tactlessly perhaps, George Anson, thanking Peel for his hospitality on behalf of the royal pair, wrote to the Prime Minister from Chatsworth, 'The weather continues to favour us here & this beautiful place has appeared this morning in a white frost to great advantage. The prince thinks it is the finest place he has yet seen in England.'²⁴

Although the stylish bachelor Duke of Devonshire had been given very short notice for the royal visit, his genius gardener, Joseph Paxton, who had built the superb giant greenhouse nicknamed the 'Great Stove', was stimulated by a challenge. All the garden walks were tidied. The lime trees between the park and the neighbouring village of Edensor were pruned and 'made perfect', in case the royal couple wished to visit the village church. 'The road from the arboretum walk is to be covered with white and yellow gravel... there must be not a drop of water on the arboretum walks.'[25] Paxton then set to work for his greatest extravaganza. He ordered over 13,000 oil lamps, to illuminate the trees, the south front of the house and the Great Stove.

The duke, despite the pretence of being bored by the visit, put on a display which no Prime Minister or royal personage in England (George IV being dead) could dare, or afford, to match. It was a glorious demonstration of the Whig aristocracy at its grandest. A party of uniformed Yeomanry met the train at Chesterfield, and as the Queen and prince were conveyed over the twelve miles of Derbyshire Peaks to this superb Cavendish palace, they were greeted by a twenty-one-gun salute from the hunting tower. It is recorded that 194 gallons of ale and 436 gallons of beer were ordered to keep the crowds happy, 6 oxen and 20 sheep were slaughtered for the guests who included Lord Palmerston, the Duke of Wellington and Lord Melbourne; 45 bedrooms were required and 140 sat to dinner each night. As the royal carriages came into the park, the National Anthem struck up, and Paxton's crystal palace, the Great Stove, was lit up like a pleasure dome in the land of faeries. At 9 pm, from the house, the guests could look at Paxton's great cascade lit with coloured Bengal lights, while 3,000 Russian lanterns flickered from the winter trees and the fountains were lit by lamps. At 10 pm exactly, a rocket was launched, cannons fired from the cascade and the hunting tower, and a magnificent display of fireworks crackled all over the park. The Duke of Wellington said, 'I have travelled Europe through and through and witnessed scenes of surpassing grandeur on many occasions, but never before did I see so magnificent a coup d'oeil as that now extended before me.'[26]

Albert conveyed to the Prime Minister his desire to have Osborne, and Peel at once felt visited by the spectre of the extravagant George IV. Albert insisted that the house could be made habitable by rebuilding the kitchens, and extending the stables and building dormitories for the servants. Blore was put in charge of drawing up the architectural plans. But then, the work was placed in the hands of Thomas Cubitt.

Thomas Cubitt (1788–1856) had started out as a jobbing carpenter. A classic case of 'Self-Help', as defined by that manual of self-made men by Samuel Smiles, Cubitt became a speculative builder at just the moment when the building boom in London took off. His great coup was to build the Calthorpe Estate in Bloomsbury, and on the basis of that he got the contract, in 1825, to start building the Grosvenor Estate near Buckingham Palace. This meant the construction of sewers, paving, street lighting, as well as the handsome and palatial residences of Belgrave Square, Chester Street, Eaton Square and Eaton Place, a colossal undertaking which, by the time Victoria became queen, had made Cubitt a prodigious fortune. He left over £1 million in his will.[27]

He was the natural choice of builder for Osborne House. Professor Henry-Russell Hitchcock, an historian of architecture, criticized Albert for not employing one of the leading architects of the day. 'The stupid result,' he wrote in *Early Victorian Architecture in Britain* (1945), 'confirms the suspicion based on the employment of a builder rather than an architect, that the Royal Family had no real respect for the profession.'[28]

But the architectural historian missed the historical point. Osborne did have an architect: Prince Albert himself; he did not feel the need of Sir Charles Barry or Decimus Burton to tell him what to build. His Italianate villa beside the Solent makes a statement. As a student at Bonn University, he had read the History of the Renaissance, attending weekly two-hour classes with the art historian Eduard Joseph d'Alton, attending the lectures of August William Schlegel. His wide knowledge of European art was in marked contrast to the tastes of Queen Victoria herself, which, until she married, would appear to have been limited to exclamations of rapture when Sir Edwin Landseer captured the likeness of a favourite pony or dog. In the early months of 1839, Albert had visited Italy with Stockmar and an English army officer supplied by King Leopold, Lieutenant Francis Seymour – who had subsequently become part of his household. January and February had been spent in Florence, and in March he had gone on to Rome and Naples. It was the period when the literate world was reading Leopold von Ranke's *History of the Popes* (1834), that gloriously self-confident work of scholarship, in which a liberal Lutheran polymath surveyed with a superior eye the Papacy in the times of Michelangelo, the new St Peter's and the Council of Trent. During his hour-long audience with Pope Gregory XVI, the nineteen-year-old prince had discussed Greek art. When the Pope ventured to say that he thought Greek art owed much to the Etruscan influence, Albert was able to put him right and point to the great influence of Ancient Egypt. Gregory XVI was a scholarly monk, who had encouraged the excavation of the Forum and the Catacombs, and who founded both the Etruscan and the Egyptian Museums in the Vatican.[29] He was too polite, however, not to defer to the German teenager in such matters.

The young man who knew better than the learned founder of Italian museums scarcely needed the assistance of an English architect to construct a seaside villa.

In 1841, Ludwig Grüner came to England. He had started as a scene painter and engraver in Dresden but, after extensive travel in Europe, he had built up an unrivalled expertise, particularly in Raphael, whose work he reproduced in engravings; and in the decoration of Italian churches in fresco and mosaic. Grüner became one of Prince Albert's closest artistic advisers, and helped him build up his considerable collection. He also took a hand himself in the adornment of the Garden Pavilion at Buckingham Palace. (Sadly, the Pavilion was demolished during the 1930s.)

The fire which had devastated the Palace of Westminster in 1834 necessitated the building of new Houses of Parliament. As Barry and Pugin's work was completed, the question of such matters as the decoration of corridors and staircases arose. Peel suggested to the Queen in 1841 that inquiries should be conducted by a select committee under royal chairmanship – Prince Albert being the obvious choice of chair.

Albert's mind turned at once to the work of the German artist Peter Cornelius, who had been responsible for the revival of the art of fresco painting in Rome in 1816, had returned to Germany and made Munich 'the unrivalled queen of modern art'. King Ludwig I of Bavaria commissioned him to embellish the Hofgarten, the Neue Residenz, the Glyptothek, the Pinakothek, as well as various churches with frescoes depicting scenes from German history and mythology. When he visited London in 1841, this Catholic founder of the 'Nazarene' or neo-medieval school of painting was enlisted to instruct English painters in the techniques he had mastered in Italy. 'The effect on British art will be tremendous,' Benjamin Robert Haydon predicted; and the artist who learned the most from Cornelius was undoubtedly William Dyce. Prince Albert was keen from the first to encourage English artists along this path. 'If the same fire was lighted amongst the English,' he wrote to Peel, 'if an encouraging opportunity were afforded them, if some were sent to study at Munich, Florence and Rome, I have not the slightest doubt, that they would produce works equal to the present school of Germans.'[30]

Cornelius was both a leading exemplar of neo-medievalism and a great influence on British neo-medievalists. His work was not confined to frescoes, or even to painting. When Albert Edward, Prince of Wales, was born, Frederick William IV, King of Prussia, commissioned Cornelius to design a silver shield – the Shield of Faith (*Der Glaubenschild*). It took five years to complete. Goldsmith Johann Georg Hossauer worked to Cornelius's designs. In the centre of the shield is the golden head of Christ, surrounded by dark blue enamelling and gilded stars. The circular shield is set with onyx and chrysoprase, with scenes from Christ's life picked out as reliefs in silver. Albert compared the shield to the best efforts of 'the classic Italian masters of the 15th and 16th centuries'.[31] Albert himself designed jewellery, of which a striking example is a brooch of 1841 which he had made as a Christmas present for the Queen. It depicts the Princess Royal, Vicky, as a cherub clutching a string of pearls and wearing a blue enamelled dress dotted with golden stars. Her wings are set with emeralds, diamonds, topazes and rubies. 'The workmanship and design are quite exquisite, & dear Albert was so pleased at my delight over it, its having been entirely his own idea and taste.'[32]

Inspired by the German artistry of Cornelius, then, and encouraged by the prince, artists were invited to submit cartoons of subjects drawn from British history or from Spenser, Shakespeare or Milton to adorn the new Palace of Westminster. The exhibitions of these cartoons in 1844 were tremendously popular and provoked what was called at the time 'a prevailing national mania'[33] for fresco painting. Dyce was the first to finish a fresco in the Palace of Westminster, with *The Baptism of King Ethelbert* in June 1846. Daniel Maclise, C. W. Cope and J. C. Horsley followed with *Chivalry*, *Edward the Black Prince* and *Religion* in August 1846. In 1847, Dyce did a series of frescoes based on the Arthurian legends. Albert also commissioned him to decorate the Garden Pavilion at Buckingham Palace with scenes from Milton's *Comus*, and, in 1846, Dyce created one of his finest works, a fresco for the staircase at Osborne House of Neptune resigning his Empire of the Sea to Britannia.

These commissions from Prince Albert did much to encourage the patronage of the arts in Britain. At Osborne, he could provide a showcase of his taste. Central to the conception of this homage to his cultural tour of Italy as a youth was the sculpture gallery in the principal corridor of the house, where modern busts and statues, such as William Theed the Younger's *Psyche Lamenting the Loss of Cupid* (1847), stood side by side with ancient casts. Albert never had the money to be a collector on the grandest scale, which is why the paintings of Dyce provided so acceptable an alternative to buying actual Raphaels. He also commissioned copies of his favourite Italian masters, such as the exquisite reproduction of Raphael's *Colonna Madonna*, which he had painted on Berlin porcelain.

The whole effect of the house, as it reached perfection and completion, was of Enlightenment and airiness. It was a modern palace for a Renaissance prince.

If the tensions over politics and power never entirely went away, and if Victoria's resentment at repeated pregnancy clouded her existence, the early to mid-1840s, when their children were infants, was a time of great harmony between the Queen and the prince. Having engaged Lady Lyttelton to be the governess and teacher to the rising tribe, the parents had plenty of time alone together. On a wet May day in 1842, when the family was at Claremont, Victoria and Albert went for a walk on Oxshott Heath and were caught in a violent shower. They took refuge in a shed next to a cottage.

> An old man, who was working in the garden, begged us to walk into the cottage, which we accordingly did, & went into the kitchen, he insisting on our sitting down near the fire. The kitchen was clean & tidy, though he was greatly distressed at its being so dusty. He said it was 'an humble Cot'; he was very civil, poor old man, but did not in the least know who we were. He told us his whole history, & that he had been 50 years with the Earl of Fingall.[34]

Such encounters were unusual in England. The companionship of those who dwelt in 'an humble Cot' was one of the things which always attracted the Queen to the Celtic fringes. Both she and Albert were very drawn to Ireland, but, even before the devastating famines of 1846–8, which killed a million people and drove over a million to emigrate, the situation in Ireland was so volatile that they were advised it would not be safe to go there.

Scotland was a different matter. In September 1842, they made their first visit to Edinburgh. While staying at Dalkeith with the Duke of Buccleuch, the Queen had her first taste of oatmeal porridge 'which

I thought very good, & also some of the Finham [sic] Haddock'.[35]

She associated Scotland, always, with feelings of freedom, with a casting off of the restraints of court life and of formality. On this first visit, she delighted in the sight of 'the old women in their caps, which they call a "Mutch", & the young girls and children, with flowing hair, many pretty ones amongst them, are so picturesque. One hardly sees a woman with a bonnet.'[36] Apart from being enraptured by the bad weather – 'A thick Scotch mist came out' followed by the occasional 'quite enchanting' view – the Queen loved being away from her children. 'Albert returned at ½ p. 11 having visited the University & various other Institutions. Began reading to him out of Scott's "Tales of My Grandfather".'[37] That tour took in Taymouth, Craigie Beans, and a wonderful evening staying with Lord Breadalbane at which she saw Highland reels being danced and heard the bagpipes played, 'which had a wild & very gay effect'.[38] Two years later, they took the two elder children to enjoy the delights of Scotland. It was at Blair Atholl, where the prince shot a stag, that he guided his eldest child's hand to write her name for the first time: an emblematic gesture – both the name, Victoria, and the fact that Albert's hand guided that of clever little Vicky. When they boarded the royal yacht in choppy waters to leave Scotland, the Queen felt 'it was indescribably melancholy seeing the dear hills gradually disappear'.[39]

At home, life took on a pattern of the Queen continuing to govern within the intervals of pregnancy after pregnancy. In April 1843, 'a healthy girl' (Alice) had been born. The Queen – who, as was the custom in England for those who had just given birth, until the 1950s, was laid up for a month – was pushed around in her bed on casters, or took to a wheelchair, or, as she put it in her vividly Hanoverian turn of phrase, 'was rolled into the Audience Room for my dinner'.[40]

With some of the feeling of Shakespeare's last Romances, as new babies came into the family, the old guard one by one left the stage. Not long after Alice's birth, the Duke of Sussex, the book-loving eccentric uncle who had given away the Queen in marriage, died. 'Albert came in at 8 in the morning,' the Queen wrote, 'in his mourning attire, ready to attend Uncle Sussex's funeral. He wore a long black cloth cloak, over a black coat, with a sword, & an immense hat, with black crepe. He drove off with George C. & Fritz Mecklenburg, &c. Returning at ½ p. 12. All had gone off extremely well, but they had had to wait a very long time.'[41] Ever an odd one out, Sussex had chosen, rather than interment at Windsor, to be buried in the new municipal burying ground at Kensal Green.

They had royal visitors from abroad. The King of Saxony came in June 1844. 'We have given him the Breakfast Room,' she wrote (in Buckingham Palace), '& the one next to it, which are the only ones available, as this house has such wretched accommodation.'[42]

They took the King on to Windsor where they were joined by no less a personage than the Emperor of Russia, who knew how to please the Queen. He said, '*C'est impossible d'être plus joli garçon, que n'est le Prince Albert; il a l'air si noble, si bon*'; 'which,' as she added superfluously, 'is very true.'[43]

By the time the Prime Minister had finally decided to make up his mind to repeal the Corn Laws, in the summer of 1846, he had no stauncher allies than the Queen and the prince. She read the speeches in the House of Commons with mounting disbelief, particularly when Lord George Bentinck called Peel a hypocrite and a turncoat – and 'that dreadful Disraeli followed in the same track'.[44]

Far from being 'above politics', Victoria and Albert were now Free Traders and fervent Peelites. The Tories had come into the election pledging to support Protection, and Bentinck and Disraeli were right to say that he was now going back on his word to the electorate. This meant nothing to the Queen, who thought his speeches 'beautiful and indeed unanswerable'.[45]

On 19 January 1846, Peel told the Commons, 'It is no easy task to ensure the united action of an ancient monarchy, a proud aristocracy and a reformed constituency [i.e. the elected House of Commons post-Reform Act]'.[46] A little over a week later, on 27 January, Prince

Albert himself came to the gallery of the House to watch his hero introduce the proposal: total abolition of the Corn Laws within three years.

Colonel Sibthorp 'trusted that the English people would combine as one man in an effort to make the Prime Minister understand how odious to them were his proceedings'.[47] The House divided, with only 112 Conservatives supporting Peel, and 231 following Bentinck and Disraeli into voting against. The Corn Laws were repealed by Whig and radical votes joining those of the Peelites, and the Government limped on until June.

The Corn Laws were consigned to history, for better or worse. Lord George Bentinck, in an immense speech delivered to the Commons on 27 February, questioned the very economic basis of the argument, pointing out, among an avalanche of statistics, that the price of a four-pound loaf was ten pence in 1842, when Peel had introduced his Canada Corn Bill. Yet Peel now spoke of a ten pence halfpenny loaf as a 'famine price', only four years later. He questioned whether the fluctuating price of bread, controlled by corn merchants, would be much lower than it was when controlled by tariff, and he spoke with grave alarm of the effect on the landed classes, the farmers and the aristocracy of the nation. But his deepest thrust was reserved for the Queen and Prince Albert. He asked:

> If so humble an individual as myself might be permitted to whisper a word in the ear of that illustrious and royal Personage, who, as he stands nearest, so is her justly dearest, to Her who sits upon the throne, I would take leave to say, that I cannot but think he listened to ill advice when, on the first night of this great discussion, he allowed himself to be seduced by the First Minister of the Crown to come down in this House to usher in, to give *éclat*, and as it were, by reflection from the Queen, to give the semblance of the personal sanction of Her Majesty to a measure which, be it for good or evil, a great majority at least of the landed aristocracy of England,

of Scotland, of Ireland, imagine will be fraught with deep injury, if not ruin, to them – a measure which, not confined in its operation to this great class, is calculated to grind down countless smaller interests, engaged in the domestic trades and industry of this Empire, transferring the profits of all these interests – English, Scotch, Irish and Colonial – great and small alike, from Englishmen, from Scotchmen, and from Irishmen to Americans, to Frenchmen, to Russians, to Poles, and to Germans.[48]

It was a devastating speech, implying, without actually stating, by its great rhetorical peroration, that Peel and Victoria had surrendered the Beef and Liberty, or rather the Corn and Liberty, of Old England into German hands. The prince never ventured into the gallery of the House of Commons again.

SEVEN

I PURITANI

THE VISITS TO France, and to Scotland, from 1843 onwards, had been undertaken on board HMY *Victoria and Albert*, the first royal yacht to be steam powered, being fitted with a 320 kW (430 horsepower) engine. Designed by William Symonds, she was a twin-paddle steamer, 1,034 tons in displacement, laid down in Pembroke Dock in 1842 and launched on 25 April 1843.

As the royal children grew, the yacht became an ideal vehicle for taking them on holiday. In 1846, for example, the Queen and the prince decided it was time that the Duke of Cornwall, now aged nearly five, should visit his Duchy. The Royal Family 'were everywhere extremely well received, and so was "The Duke of Cornwall", who in his sailor dress seemed to be a great favourite with the crew of the Yacht.'[1]

Having visited Restormel, Albert wrote, 'I had long wished to see the mines of Cornwall and was very much pleased with all I saw, particularly the population, which seems to be an excellent one. The women are working together under large sheds, pen at the sides, they sort the ores, wash them, pound them and are said to be very moral and well-behaved. They are certainly very healthy and good-looking. A beautiful new machine, worked by the steam engine, by which the miners are let down the shafts and are brought up again.'[2]

The Queen wanted to go down the mine, and wrote in her journal:

It is an iron mine, & one enters on the level. Albert & I got into one of the trucks & were dragged in by miners, Mr Taylor being so good as to walk behind us. The miners wear a curious dress of wool with a cap, like on the accompanying sketch. They generally have a candle stuck in front of the caps. This time candles were fixed along the inside of the mine, & those of the miners who did not drag or push us, carried lights. There was no room for anyone to pass between the truck & the rock & only just room enough to hold up one's head & even that not always. The whole thing had a most weird effect with the lights at intervals. We got out of the truck and scrambled a little way to see the veins of ore & Albert knocked off some pieces, but usually it is blown off with gunpowder, being so hard. The miners seemed so pleased & are intelligent good people. It was so dazzling when we came up again into the daylight.[3]

On this visit, as on similar excursions into different parts of her kingdom, Victoria was extending the function of the monarchy. George IV did not go down mines. This monarch and her husband were visiting not merely the houses of the great, as in royal progresses of the past, but mines, factories, farms, industrial towns; and by taking their children with them, they were demonstrating the Royal Family as interwoven with the new destiny of Britain, with its reformed Parliament and its expanding industrial economy. Victoria, who was by now regularly taking painting lessons with Edward Lear, saw the passing scenes with the eye of a very accomplished draughtswoman and watercolourist. 'We remained on deck till past 10, looking out for all the little fishing boats & it was such a fine night.'[4]

The family was expanding. There were now five children. Helena was born that May, and named after Prince Albert's first cousin Hélène of Orléans.[5] 'Really, when one is so happy & blessed in one's home life, as I am, Politics (provided my Country is safe) must take only a second place,' the Queen wrote.[6] This is precisely the state of things for which Stockmar had been yearning.

So it was that, as Peel stood down as Prime Minister, it was Albert who saw to the incoming replacement. Peel, whom the Queen had so abominated in 1839, was 'much overcome'[7] when he took leave of her, and kissed hands, in 1846. She wept too. But it was Albert who, on 30 June at Osborne, had seen Lord John Russell, the Whig Leader, and ascertained from him that there was no need for a General Election. The Peelites had agreed that they would support the Whigs in the Commons. Russell and his Whig colleagues could carry on the Government without going to the country.

It was Albert who made this constitutional decision. Of course, the Corn Laws would have been repealed, come what may. But it was Albert who expedited the political process. Russell held on in office until the due time of the next election – 1847 – and won by a narrow majority.

So, by the late summer of 1846, Lord John Russell was Prime Minister. A tiny man, with the rather absurd Russell voice – retained and made famous by his grandson the philosopher Bertrand Russell – he was sixty when he took office. When he was asked by the Prince Consort to do so, Lady John (his second wife, who had been Lady Fanny Elliot, a daughter of the Earl of Minto) exclaimed that his would be the most religious and moral Government the country had ever known.[8] By 'most religious', she meant most Protestant.

Protestantism did not blight the potato, but it was one of the elements in the English psyche which enabled the Government to be so slow to cope with a disaster which, in Russell's own words, was 'a famine of the thirteenth century acting upon a population of the nineteenth'.[9] The unhappy marriage between economic liberals, who disapproved of state aid and who felt the economic order must find its own balance, and evangelicals (such as Russell) who believed that the potato blight might be – or actually was – a punishment for popish idolatry, led to a painful slowness of action. The previous year's potato crop had failed. Even as Russell was forming his first Cabinet, the second crop failed too – unexpectedly. Russell continued a scheme of public works for the poor, which had been set up by Peel the previous summer, but it was not until February 1847 that a halfway efficient system of soup kitchens had been established, nor was it until later in the spring of 1847 that the Government passed the Irish Poor Law Extension Act attempting to deal with the matter as a whole. By then, hundreds of thousands of people had starved to death.

Among those absentee landlords who owned estates in Ireland while living in England was the new Foreign Secretary, Viscount Palmerston. Just as it was Albert who had interviewed Russell about his fitness to form an administration after the departure of Peel, it was Albert who saw Palmerston at Osborne in July 1846,[10] and agreed to his taking over the Foreign Office from his old Harrovian contemporary, the gentler, more moderate Lord Aberdeen.

It was Palmerston who was, on the whole successfully, to resist the prince's bid to reclaim royal prerogatives.[11] Palmerston was the last, and the most vigorous, embodiment of the Whig power. Karina Urbach has pointed to the significance of a twenty-five page memorandum in the Staatsarchiv in Coburg, which Ernst wrote some time after becoming duke in 1844, setting out what should be the true Coburg policy, at home and abroad. It is a key document to understanding Albert's political position, especially in foreign policy, where he clashed consistently with Palmerston.

> Since the Family originates from a pure German House, it is essential to direct attention at all times to remaining a pure German. The generality of Family Members [the word used is *Glieder*, which means both 'members' and 'links', as in a chain] will always want to move in a German Element, and never stop contributing to the preservation and wellbeing of Germany. Apart from the Head of the House [that is, Ernst himself, Duke of Coburg], three Members of the Family have been destined through happy circumstances to take part, either directly or indirectly in the powerful control of

Government. Two arrived at this position through marriage and one through being selected [i.e. as King of the Belgians]. The first two, by the very nature of their position, stand as an equal to their Parent House, and almost to the Interests of whichever country they have married. On the contrary, it must be easier for Members of our House (in contrast to other Houses) to form, from outside, a powerful overall Unit, if we remain perpetually conscious that, if we are sometimes isolated, we can nonetheless endlessly aspire to, and reach a connection of all the Members.[12]

Invoking the spirit of the Three Musketeers, Ernst hoped the Coburgers, whether in England, Belgium, Germany or Portugal, would be All for One and One for All. (*Gegen Fremde stehe der eine für den Andern, und Alle für einen.*) It would be impossible to find a less ambiguous proof that Prince Albert and his family consciously sought to influence the realpolitik of Europe.

In Palmerston, he met his match. Stockmar and Albert were no doubt appalled by Palmerston's morals, his breezy manner, his vulgarity, his unashamed populism. They could not, however, dismiss him as a lightweight, as they might have wished to have dismissed Melbourne. 'Pam' was a consummate diplomat – it could be said, the consummate diplomat of the pre-Bismarck times, if one is simply using the word 'diplomat' to mean one conversant with current affairs abroad, rather than one who is in any sense 'diplomatic'. As he told the Prime Minister in January 1849, 'Dispatches received & sent out [from the Foreign Office] in 1848 was upwards of 29,000'.[13] He combined an encyclopaedic knowledge of foreign affairs with a calculated 'recklessness' (Harold Nicolson's word[14]), which he knew would usually increase his vast popularity with the public.

His political career had begun during the Napoleonic Wars, when he became an MP in 1807, aged twenty-three. Within a month of his election, he was made a junior lord of the Admiralty, and by 1809, Prime Minister Spencer Perceval was offering Pam the choice of being

Chancellor of the Exchequer or Secretary of State for War. He chose the latter. He liked war, and he liked the idea of Britain and a fighting country, and he never really lost the joy of feeling, as he had done during the war, that he could send out ships to blast at foreigners. As a proud, clever Whig, he did not really consider himself answerable to anyone. One of his colleagues, Lord Clarendon, recalled Palmerston 'agreeing with me that Vera Cruz ought to be blockaded, and desiring me to write accordingly to the Admiralty. I said – "Surely not without bringing it before the Cabinet?" – "Oh. Ah: the Cabinet", was his answer. "Very well; call one then, if you think it necessary".'[15] Pam was bombastic, patriotic, a showman, and one who, for all his mastery of diplomatic complexities, had an essentially simple foreign policy. He defined it succinctly in 1848 in the House of Commons when he said that Britain had no eternal allies and no perpetual enemies.[16] His foreign policy was popular with the rank and file of provincial Liberals in England because, with increased bellicosity he favoured what later history would call 'Liberal interventionism'. If it was in British interests, or not against British interests, and if it allowed Palmerston the chance to indulge in some heroic defence of the underdog against tyranny, then – in with the gunboats.

While the young Queen Victoria had enjoyed the company of raffish Pam, her young husband found him deplorable. Albert persuaded Victoria to write frequent letters of complaint to Lord John Russell that he did not show her dispatches before they were sent abroad in her name. The truth was that the Court and the Foreign Office were increasingly at odds.

At first, this was not so. In the matter, for example, of finding a suitable bride for the young Spanish Queen Isabella and her sister Luisa the Infanta, Victoria and Palmerston were agreed. He took a non-interventionist view. Louis-Philippe and Guizot, his reactionary premier, had assured him that they would not, without prior British agreement, marry off the French King's son, the Duke of Montpensier, to the Infanta (aged fourteen) while Queen Isabella (aged sixteen) married her cousin the Duke of Cadiz, who was presumed to be incapable of having children. This would mean that Louis-Philippe's grandchildren would inherit the throne of Spain. The Coburg faction had hoped that Prince Leopold of Saxe-Coburg would marry Isabella. Palmerston was 'reckless'. When the letter was drafted, proposing that Prince Leopold marry the Spanish Queen, Palmerston decided, without consulting Victoria, to confide in the French Ambassador, hoping that the Duke of Montpensier would back off. In fact, the French rushed ahead with marrying Montpensier off to Luisa, much to the fury of Victoria and Albert. The Coburgs would have to wait a generation before they saw a *Glied* on the Spanish throne – Ena, daughter of Princess Beatrice and Prince Henry of Battenberg.

Palmerston's blunder appeared to justify Albert in opposing Pam in everything. He nicknamed him 'Pilgerstein', the heavily literal 'joke' being a translation of the name Palmer/Pilgrim-Stone. But in most areas of foreign policy over the next few years, Pilgerstein got the better of the prince. Palmerston supported the aspirations of the Italian nationalists in wishing to drive the Austrians out of Northern Italy. Apart from the embarrassing fact that Albert wanted to be friends with the Emperor of Austria, perhaps one day to see him as the figurehead of a united Germany, there were too many inconsistencies in the policy. If Britain supported the Italians in wishing to wrest their 'lawful possessions' from the Austrians, where was the logic in opposing Irish nationalism? Yet when the German nationalists wished to absorb the Duchies of Schleswig and Holstein into a German federation, Pam illogically (as Victoria and Albert felt) supported the Danish claim to the Duchies.

The Queen openly told her Prime Minister that she feared Palmerston was threatening 'the peace of Europe in general'.[17] Lady Palmerston wrote to her husband, 'I am angry with the Queen for not being more courteous, the little wretch!'[18] Palmerston was breezy, sanguine. His political experience stretched back long enough to see crowns and dukes and princelings tumble, while the Whigs in their great estates and houses seemingly went on forever.

Meanwhile, the little prince in his sailor's suit, who so beguiled the crew of the royal yacht, was lucky enough to be immortalized by Winterhalter, who painted him that very summer, while his father was debating foreign policy with Lord Palmerston. Standing by an unspecified shore – presumably on the Isle of Wight – the child has his hands in his pockets. The sailor's hat is perched jauntily on the back of his head. His stumpy little legs, encased in slightly crumpled nankeen, stand defiantly, and he looks at the painter with a degree of amused self-confidence. Bertie would never be so beautiful again, but Winterhalter had captured some of the impishness, and some of the charm, which would enable him to survive, more or less, a life scarred by illness, scandal and the hostility of his mother.

But she was not hostile to him when this picture was painted, and gave it to Albert as one of his presents that Christmas at Windsor. 'It is such a perfect likeness and such a charming composition,' she commented.[19]

Franz Xaver Winterhalter (1805–73) was the Van Dyck of the Victorian Court. He played a powerful role in promoting the family-loving, virtuous iconography which was central to Victoria and Albert's political purposes. Nor is the Van Dyck parallel fanciful, since it may be seen that, for example in the full-length portrait of Prince Albert in Garter Robes (1843), the pose, the folds of the garments and the background are clearly modelled on Van Dyck's portrait of Charles I (1636). [20] (Both pictures are in the Royal Collection.)

The children were an essential part of the Stockmar–Albertian plan for the conversion of the monarchy into a bulwark of Liberalism. Britain had a parliamentary system which was the envy of European Liberals. It now had Free Trade, and an economy which was growing – bursting – on a scale unprecedented in history. It could not turn into an autocracy on the Prussian or Austrian pattern; but nor must it risk becoming a republic. For this, it was necessary to train up the Royal Family, not only as an example to the nation of domestic rectitude, but also as new potential European monarchs. Dynastic marriage could be made to achieve what revolution or political rhetoric could not. But for this to happen – for Vicky, and Bertie, and their siblings to grow up responsibly, and marry into the European Royal Families and spread abroad their father's Liberal Protestantism, Free Trade Liberalism, care for the working classes and love of arts and science – it was necessary for them to be educated. They must be as well educated as if they had been brought up in Germany.

The children were divided into two classes. The first, a nursery class, took them to the age of five or six.[21] Lady Lyttelton was their governess, and was in charge of instructing them in English, French, German and the elements of religion.

After the age of six, each child would be moved up a class, and the learning would begin in earnest. A Miss Hildyard had been engaged as their governess, with a salary of £200 per annum. The children would continue to sleep in the nursery, where Mrs Thurston the nurse, with two nurserymaids, supervised their physical needs.

The religious instruction of the Princess Royal was undertaken by the Queen, but from an early age, despite her admiration for Winterhalter's depiction of Bertie in the sailor's suit, the Queen felt an aversion to the Prince of Wales, and left his instruction to others.

Punishment was severe. Princess Alice, who had inherited the Hanoverian short temper, was whipped for not speaking the truth and for 'roaring' when aged only four. Prince Alfred was commended at the age of only eighteen months for displaying 'a very good manly temper; much more like that of most children than that of the Princess Royal or the Prince of Wales'.[22]

The Princess Royal was a strikingly intelligent child, and found no difficulty with her lessons. The Prince of Wales, on the other hand, did not learn easily. His parents had his head examined by a phrenological expert. Phrenology – the measurement and classification of different parts of the skull – was the fad of the 1840s, and although to us it seems like mumbo jumbo, many intelligent Victorians believed in it.

Bertie's report stated that, 'In the Prince of Wales, the organs of ostentativeness, destructiveness, self-esteem etc. are all large, intellectual organs only moderately developed.' This last phrase was an understatement. Prince Albert was one of those highly intelligent people who found unintelligence in others bewildering, and in their own children a source of distress. Against any dictate of common sense, the Prince of Wales's parents determined that he must be forced to become a serious, unselfish, scholarly person like Prince Albert. They had named him Albert Edward with the express purpose of turning him into a miniature clone of his industrious, clever father. With the glorious incorrigibility of humanity, the young prince simply would not, could not, be moulded.

Winterhalter, the son of a farmer from Menzenschwand, a small village on the edges of the Black Forest, had had the good fortune to be talent-spotted by the local priest, Father Lieber, who drew the boy's skills to the attention of Baron Eichtal, their local grandee. It was Eichtal who provided Winterhalter with his vital contacts in the early stages of his career, introducing him to the families who would make his name and fortune. Having studied at Freiburg and Munich, Winterhalter's Italianate, glossy manner was perfected at an early age. By the time of the 1830 Revolution in France, he was in a position to execute over thirty royal portraits establishing Louis-Philippe as a stately and august figure. Through Louis-Philippe's daughter, the beloved 'Aunt Louise', Winterhalter was introduced to Queen Victoria and became her court painter, visiting England for several months each summer from the mid-1840s onwards.

The Queen always considered his masterpiece to be the family group which he painted in the summer of 1846. All those who saw the work in progress – Palmerston, the Duchess of Sutherland, the Cambridge family – admired it. When the painting went on show at the Royal Academy in 1847, it was criticized on the grounds, first, that its artist was foreign, and secondly for its lack of 'taste', its 'sensual and fleshy' depiction of the royal couple, in the words of the *Athenæum*.[23]

The very xenophobia of the English criticism is itself bristling with ironies. While the London periodical wonders why the British needed to go all foreign, many liberals of Europe looked to Britain as

a role model. A German picture of a three-quarters German family
was trying to teach Europe to be more like England. Beside the
constitutional politics, it is precisely in what the fastidious saw as
lack of taste that the picture has its appeal. For a start, it is a piece of
magnificence. The couple sit on a gilded sofa. His index finger, both
to control and to tease erotically, is just about to touch her hand.
She is both regal and a sensual wife. Though ten inches shorter than
her husband when standing up, on the sofa she is higher than he
is, presumably plumped up by cushions. The Prince of Wales nestles
near his mother, a sure sign to all of us that the monarchy has a future.
Little Affie (Alfred) toddles independently in the foreground, while
Vicky and Alice (as perhaps befitted the female members of a family
in 1846) are caring for their infant sister. Lenchen, the baby Helena,
looks back and up – straight at us – while her father looks shyly away.
Among the many clever things about this political emblem is that
while placing the prince centre stage, it allows his Queen the position
of absolute dominion.

The painting was made into an engraving, which proved to be
extremely popular. Thus, the iconography of Winterhalter's Happy
Family was disseminated throughout the Empire, an emblem of
'peace, harmony, concord, wealth, fecundity, obedience, happiness'
(to quote from the percipient National Portrait Gallery exhibition
catalogue of 1987).[24]

The world of 1847–8, when this engraving was making its way out
into the world, was a dangerous place, and Victoria and Albert saw it
as their task to make it less dangerous. The Corn Laws were abolished.
Free Trade was to bring peace and prosperity. The future was as bright
and as blue as the Solent on a summer day.

Then, in February 1848, the government in France was overthrown by
Revolution. Public gatherings had been banned by Louis-Philippe
and Guizot, but in 1847, this had given rise to the 'banquet' campaign:
you could ban a public meeting, but you could not ban a 'banquet'.

A huge 'banquet' was planned in the capital. On 22 February, crowds of students and workers swarmed around La Madeleine and there was violence in the Place de la Concorde as the police tried to disperse them. The violence spread. Within two days, there were 1,500 barricades in the streets of Paris. The monarchy had been abolished. The humiliated Louis-Philippe drove to Le Havre in disguise. He was initially refused passage on a boat, until the British Foreign Office sent word to rescue him, his Queen and their family – the Duke and Duchess of Nemours, the Duke of Montpensier and the Duke of Joinville. The Queen and prince, with Lord John Russell's agreement, offered them Claremont as temporary accommodation, but the accursed French royalty were doomed to bad luck. Dissolved lead in a newly installed cistern was poisoning the water supply, and they were all ill. The King's doctor recommended an immediate change of air and they all decamped to the Star and Garter inn at Richmond. The family who, only so recently, had been frustrating the political machinations of Palmerston and Stockmar by their dynastic ambitions in Spain, and who appeared to hold France under their authoritarian sway, were now a poverty-stricken gaggle of refugees, suffering diarrhoea in a pub beside the Thames.

The Queen's journals convey with vivid candour the sense of shock brought by that February to her, and to the Royal Family. The beginning of the month found them a great concourse of Coburgs happily installed at Windsor Castle. Her uncle Leopold was over from Belgium, and after dinner, on 31 January, Victoria sat on the sofa with the Belgian Queen – her 'Aunt Louise', Louis-Philippe's daughter – pasting in 'our prints of the French King & Princes'.[25] Only a fortnight later, when Sir Robert Peel came to dine, he expressed himself 'much alarmed about France'. By 25 February, they got the news that Louis-Philippe had abdicated, though at first they did not know where he was. 'We could talk of nothing else.'[26]

The first royal refugee to fetch up in London was Louis-Philippe's daughter Clémentine, married to another Coburg – Prince Augustus. She described to a horrified Victoria how 'poor Hélène had her children torn from her'[27] – Hélène after whom Victoria and Albert had named their fifth child. 'Poor Clém says she can get no sleep, constantly seeing before her eyes those horrible faces, & hearing these dreadful cries and shrieks.'[28]

When Louis-Philippe eventually came ashore from the fishing boat, Victoria and Albert were at first all sympathy. 'The French are really a very ungrateful nation to forget in <u>one</u> day all the King has done for them these 18 years!'[29] But when the Queen, and Lord Palmerston discovered that Louis-Philippe, without admitting to them what he was doing, had made plans to send the Duke of Montpensier with his Spanish bride to Europe again to lay claim to the Spanish title, her sympathy evaporated. (Montpensier was making matters worse by going first to King Leopold in Brussels.)

'Oh!! <u>They have</u> brought on much of all this,'[30] the Queen reflected in a letter to King Leopold when she contemplated the devious behaviour of Louis Egalité over the years.

Still, the sheer fact of the thing was shocking. 'The news from France is that the Monarchy & Royalty have been abolished & that the people are going on in a disgusting way.'[31] You could not read a more shocking sentence in a diary written by a pregnant Queen. 'I felt as if I could not believe it.'[32] The journals dwell on the physical pathos of it; the fact that these royal personages, many of them cousins or marital connections, had arrived in London with nothing – no clothes to wear, nothing to wash with, nowhere to live. At least Clém, married to a Coburg, could take refuge in Germany, 'whereas the others are homeless'.[33]

As if these upsetting events were not enough to disturb them all, the Coburgs received the sad news from Germany that old Duchess Caroline Amalie had died – without Ernst, Victoire or Leopold by her side. Albert, with tears in his eyes, broke the news to his Queen that the duchess was dead. 'Thousands of recollections of dear Albert's childhood are broken, he clung to her with such love, she was so clever, so good, so beloved & respected & had such a warm heart.'[34] (She was the stepmother of Albert's mother.)

How could they be certain that outrages such as had befallen the Orléanist monarchy could not befall Victoria, and Albert, and their children? It was a terrifying point in their history. As Victoria went into labour for the sixth time, producing Princess Louise on 18 March, the child was brought into an uncertain world.

The Chartist unrest had gained ground. It was the real hope of those who supported them that they could bring in universal suffrage, and parliamentary democracy. One of the leaders of the movement, Ernest Jones, son of an army officer, was godson to the most reactionary of all Queen Victoria's uncles – the King of Hanover![35] Born in Berlin, educated for the first twenty years of his life in Germany, Jones was a close associate of Karl Marx and Friedrich Engels. In the mid-1840s, Jones had joined forces with the charismatic Chartist leader Feargus O'Connor, who had briefly been an MP (representing Cork). The Chartists wanted an annual Parliament, and the vote for every adult in the country. (O'Connor and Jones eventually emended this to every adult male in the country, since they were persuaded that to campaign for female suffrage was a step too far.) They wanted the ballot, to avoid intimidation at the polls. In many respects the Chartists had more in common with Tories than with classic Victorian Liberals (even though it was with the Liberals that Jones would later join forces). They supported Shaftesbury's Factory Acts. They opposed Corn Law repeal, on the grounds that they wanted to buy land for the working classes and hold it as a co-operative, not to boost Free Trade per se. One of their most successful rallies was a demonstration against income tax.

By 1848, Chartism was already running out of steam. Partly this was because of the popularity of Corn Law Reform, and the mainstream parliamentary radicals, as opposed to O'Connor's ideas of land purchase. Partly this was because in some areas, the working classes had a measure of prosperity which inclined them to hope for reform via conventional parliamentary means. Partly, however, it was the overwhelming brute force of the Establishment which overwhelmed the Chartists, only a few of whom believed in an armed struggle, and many of whom were all-but-pacifist in attitude.

When they assembled in Trafalgar Square – 'the foolish meeting'[36], as the Queen called it in her journal – there was panic in Buckingham Palace, 'which alarmed poor Clém very much', the Queen recorded. The next day, 7 March, Prince Albert came into the Queen as she woke and told her that her mother's windows had been broken the previous evening by the mob. A picket had been stationed outside Buckingham Palace with sixty constables posted there. 'After the horrors of Paris, one cannot help being more anxious.'[37] The next day there came news of 'events' in Germany.

Summoning her diminutive Prime Minister, her only premier not to be noticeably taller than herself, the Queen was reassured to discover that plans were in place to defend London against insurgency. It would be truer to say that Russell had placed the capital on a war footing, than that he had merely arranged to defend it by police. This liberal-minded Whig, when it came to the possibility of life and property being threatened, reverted to type: the Russells had held sway in England since the Wars of the Roses and were not going to surrender it to a mob of idealists.

He placed the operation under the ruthless direction of the Duke of Wellington. The victor of Waterloo brought in the Horse Guards (the 'Blues') from Windsor, the 12th Lancers from Hounslow, the Grenadier Guards, the Coldstreams, the 17th Foot from Colchester, Windsor and Dover, and the 62nd and 63rd Foot from Winchester and Chatham. These troops were put on standby, but they were almost all kept in concealment. Strict orders were given that the troops were not to fire on the crowds when the planned Chartist march went forward.[38]

Meanwhile, huge numbers of special constables had been enlisted. The numbers have never accurately been assessed. Certainly there were more than 80,000; *The Times* reported that there were 170,000: and the important thing about this was that it was believed by the Chartists themselves. O'Connor visited the Deputy Chief of Police with the assurance that none of the Chartists would be armed. Their aim was to assemble from various parts of London on Kennington

Common, and then to march on the House of Commons to present their petition, their Charter, demanding universal suffrage. The Special Constables were, on the whole, middle class. They included the chef at the Reform Club, Alexis Soyer, and the head cook at the Athenæum, a Frenchman who shared his beat with Napoleon's nephew – Prince Louis Napoleon, who was following events in Paris with more than a passing interest. Another figure who stood by with his truncheon was none other than William Ewart Gladstone, the Peelite politician; no longer, perhaps, 'a stern unbending Tory', as he had been in his youth, but not yet, evidently, 'the People's William'.

Lord John Russell decided that the Royal Family should not be in London on the day of the march. They were all put on a train at Waterloo on 8 April and reached 'dear Osborne' that afternoon.

When the day dawned, 10 April, the Chartists were met not merely by tens of thousands of special constables, but by a deluge of driving rain. The expected crowds of hundreds of thousands simply did not materialize. Some 20,000 people reached Kennington Common and heard O'Connor address them in the dreadful weather. Five million signatures had been promised. An impressive 1,975,496 was all they mustered, and it was discovered, to the Chartists' profound embarrassment, that when O'Connor had presented his petition, and the signatures were surveyed, some of them were appended by 'Mr Punch', 'No Cheese', 'The Duke of Wellington', 'Sir Robert Peel', and so forth.

'We had our revolution yesterday,' Albert wrote to Stockmar, 'and it ended in smoke.'[39] The relief, if not the smugness, was understandable. The Year of Revolutions had a long way to run on the Continent, but for the Royal Family at home, there were chances to enjoy the private pleasures of peace. Safe in her island home, the Queen, now mother of six children, and monarch of a nation at peace, attended a weekday celebration of Holy Communion at Whippingham Parish Church. As she took the Sacrament, she 'prayed for peace for all the world, for the maintenance of quiet in this country & for our preservation;

also for that of our own great domestic [happiness], which is the one bright spot'.[40]

Only a few days before the Chartist procession, the Queen had admired the pictures which Landseer intended to hang in the Summer Exhibition at the Royal Academy. In common with most of her subjects, she found them 'beautiful'.[41] *Alexander and Diogenes* represented an exquisitely rendered white bulldog visiting a miserable cur in its kennel (Diogenes). Another canvas represented a doe shot on a snowy hillside, *A Random Shot*. Two young men who attended the exhibition, which opened in May, were, however, less impressed. William Holman Hunt and John Everett Millais, who had been witnesses of and sympathizers with the Chartist demonstration, thought the stuffiness of the Academy exhibition so insufferable that they founded their Pre-Raphaelite Brotherhood that very summer.

The old order was passing away. In February, the old Archbishop of Canterbury, William Howley, had died. 'He was so mild and gentle. There was no important event in my life in which he was not interested & did not officiate. He was one of those who examined me when I was 12 years old. He confirmed me, came to me, the morning of the late King's death, crowned me, married me, & christened our 5 children, besides churching me 3 times!'[42] On the very day of Howley's death, the Queen and her Prime Minister had both agreed that his obvious successor was the Bishop of Chester – Sumner, the boy Lord M. remembered as an Eton contemporary nicknamed 'Crumpet'.

In May another link with the past was severed when the Queen Dowager came to tell Victoria that her Aunt Sophia was sinking. She 'passed away almost imperceptibly with her hand in Aunt Cambridge's'.[43] Victoria recollected the period of her childhood when she saw 'poor dear Aunt Sophia' every day, when they were neighbours in Kensington Palace. She was too charitable to dwell in her journal on the money which Sir John Conroy extracted from the princess to buy his Welsh estate.

The summer was spent pleasantly. As often as they could, they attended the opera, hearing the sublime Jenny Lind twice – in Donizetti's *L'Elisir d'Amore* and in Bellini's *I Puritani*. The fact that Lord Palmerston was causing her acute embarrassment by his loud espousal of the Italian nationalist cause could not blight the domestic happiness she felt.

In September, the royal yacht took them all the way up to Aberdeen, a choppy nine-hour voyage. Not only did Victoria not get a wink of sleep, but 'I was dreadfully ill.'[44]

But this was a life-changing summer, for Lord Aberdeen was offering her and the prince the chance to acquire a castle which had belonged to his late brother. The long journey from Aberdeen was painstakingly described in the journal – changing horses after eighteen miles at Banchory, and then again, after another thirteen miles, at Aboyne (where they 'gave the children something to eat'[45]). 'We crossed the Dee about 4 miles before getting to the Castle, & the scenery became prettier and prettier, & there is much agriculture & cultivation which gives a flourishing look to the country. There are very few cottages between Abergeldie & Balmoral, which we reached at ¼ p. 3. It is a pretty little Castle, in the old Scotch style.'[46]

It was surely one of the most momentous days of their lives together. On 18 September, 'another beautiful day', they took a post-chaise, with Bertie, and drove beyond the keeper's house in the Balloch Buie. Here they got out and mounted ponies, and rode on, accompanied by the keepers – Grant and Macdonald – and by the gillies. One of the gillies who also worked in the stables at this time was a young man called John Brown.

In the evening Lord John Russell had arrived, and the next morning the Queen had anxious conversations with him about Ireland, and about the peace of Europe. She told him how little confidence she had in Palmerston, and how little she liked Pam's attitude to Austria. 'Lord John replied he was aware of it & felt the truth of all I had said.'[47]

Balmoral had already become an extension of the Court. Lord John had come as a guest – he must have stayed there before as the guest of the Aberdeens – but he had also come as the Prime Minister to do business. And as if to emphasize that Balmoral was now a place of semi-official royal status, the Queen received the eminent geologist Charles Lyell that evening. After dinner she knighted him, 'with Albert's Claymore'.[48] Albert's veneration for science was bold. Far more than Charles Darwin, Lyell had undermined religious certainties by demonstrating the age of the planet and disturbing some of the simplicities of the Bible faith. Led by Albert's example, Victoria continued to honour science throughout her reign. Darwin himself was given a funeral in Westminster Abbey and his fellow evolutionist Alfred Russel Wallace was awarded an Order of Merit.

As the autumn progressed, they went south and she took the children to Osborne. On the day that an insurrection broke out in Frankfurt, Lord George Bentinck, the Leader of the Conservative Party who had delivered such a withering attack on Prince Albert during the Corn Law debates in the Commons, died of apoplexy. That 'dreadful Disraeli', as the Queen had called him,[49] was nearer the top of his 'greasy pole'.

For the Queen, a much sadder piece of news came in November, but perhaps the saddest thing about it was that she accepted it so calmly. So completely preoccupied by the children at Osborne was she, and by the routines of when they 'came down' to have lessons with their mother in the evenings, that this passing belonged to another time, another sphere. 'The children come down now at 6 little girls, at ½ past 6 Affie, ¼ to 7 Alice & at 20 minutes past 7 Vicky and Bertie.'[50] It was while the lessons were in progress on the Isle of Wight that, far away in Brocket Hall, Hertfordshire, Lord M. died, lonely and sad. The news reached the island the next day, and the mature Queen Victoria, who had left her giggling teenage self so far behind, almost had to address her journal as if it were a public meeting to convey the gravity of the intelligence. 'Truly & seriously do I deplore the loss of one who was a most kind

& disinterested friend... We took another walk again, after Albert had been planting.'[51]

Lord M. had long been dead to her. So had the old world, to which he, and Aunt Sophie and Archbishop Howley had all belonged. After the Year of Revolutions it remained to be seen whether Europe would hurtle towards a republican progress, or draw back into a cautious reaction. Britain, with its Free Trade, its expanding economy, its unsettled Ireland and its burgeoning Royal Family, would do neither, but whatever happened, it could not but be involved.

EIGHT

HALLELUJAH CHORUS

T HE QUEEN AND the prince paid an eight-day visit to Ireland in the royal yacht in August 1849. Victoria was the first English monarch to visit the city of Cork. She was feeling pretty seasick by the time the yacht pulled into Cork harbour. She renamed the Cove of Cork Queenstown, a nomenclature which was changed back after the Irish gained independence. She remarked in the Irish pages appended to *Leaves from the Journal of Our Life in the Highlands* that 'Cork is not at all like an English town, and looks rather foreign. The crowd is a noisy, excitable, but very good-humoured one, running and pushing about, and laughing and talking and shrieking. The beauty of the women is very remarkable, and struck us much; such beautiful dark eyes and hair, and such fine teeth; almost every third woman was pretty, and some remarkably so. They wear no bonnets.'[1]

It is very similar to her first glimpse of the Scots. As in Scotland, she noted beautiful human beings and scenery. The Celtic women, unbonneted, and probably uncorseted and unknickered, represented a prelapsarian species of humanity to Victoria. But Ireland was not like Scotland, and, as they made their progress from Cork to Waterford to Dublin, even in the bland narrative of the *Leaves*, we sense the tension in the muggy summer air ('"muggy", which is the character of the Irish climate'[2]). She emphasized on almost every page that the people were 'well-behaved', acutely conscious as she was that a million hungry Irish men, women and children had emigrated in the previous two years, and that they still had every reason not to be 'well-behaved' given their desperate plight. When the royal party reached Belfast it was with that air of slight surprise and timidity – which has been so evident in English visitors ever since – that she noted the Catholic Bishop Denvir was 'an excellent and modest man'.[3] There was great unfairness in calling her 'the Famine Queen', as the Irish did, since she was one of the greatest single contributors to famine relief, and she was criticized in the rest of Britain for encouraging others to do the same.[4] The royal visit happened only a month after one of the most violent sectarian clashes of the nineteenth century, in County Down – as so often since, the violence flared when the authorities tried to re-route an Orange parade on the Twelfth of July, to prevent the Protestants provocatively marching through a Catholic village, Dolly's Brae. It was in the wake of this outbreak that the Queen made such an effort to meet Catholic dignitaries and to declare her abhorrence of sectarianism.[5] But you sense the relief in the diarist when the royal yacht steamed eastwards to the rain-spattered, Protestant Clyde.

To his brother Ernst, Albert wrote in April 1849, 'At present the democratic and social evils are forcing themselves on the people. The unequal division of property, and the dangers of poverty and envy arising therefrom, is the principal evil. Means must necessarily be found, not for diminishing riches (as the communists want) but to make facilities for the poor. But there's the rub. I believe this question will first be solved here, in England.'[6]

'England' was, for the Victorians, a word used where modern writers would say 'Britain'. It included troubled Ireland; Wales, in which neither the Queen nor the prince ever displayed much interest; and Scotland, which was, for Victoria at least, chiefly a playground, a tartan kingdom of fantasy, more than a place where men and women earned their living. While Albert, when in Scotland, visited institutes, inspected local industry and studied economics – as well as enjoying the deer-stalking and the shooting – the Queen spent most days with her sketchbook and colour-box open. She became an ever-better watercolourist, far above average amateur level, delighting in the picturesque views which opened up on every side, and enjoying the earthy humour of the Highlanders, their whisky and their dancing.[7] (She was never happier than when dancing.)

Prince Albert's sense that the social and economic injustices of the industrial towns of 'England' would lead to communism, meanwhile, were shared by two young German exiles who arrived in England during the same year – Karl Marx and Friedrich Engels. Perhaps the three Germans – Albert, Marx and Engels – were in a better position to get a perspective on the British Isles than some of its longer-standing inhabitants. Certainly they could see more clearly than the Whig aristocrats who were entrenched in their own positions and many of whom were constitutionally unable to see beyond the need to defend their position in narrow party terms.

But one of the paradoxes of the 1850s, as the political consequences of 1846 began to become clear, was that, in the short term at least, the monarchy was more, not less, important to the Constitution. The Corn Laws had been abolished. The British political classes, like the new Poet Laureate, Alfred Tennyson, had 'dipt into the future, far as human eye could see', and now found themselves in a different universe

> In the steamship, in the railway, in the thoughts that
> shake mankind.[8]

The era, and the politics, bristle with paradox. Peel's conversion to Free Trade broke the Conservative Party into two broad factions: Peelites and Protectionists. Neither mustered enough support in Parliament to form a Government on their own: the Tories would not govern outright for decades. This did not, however, give a free hand to their opponents, since the 'left', if it could be so named, was a strange alliance of the Whigs such as Palmerston and the new radicals, ranging from Chartists to Free Traders, from economically aggressive Manchester Liberals to the mildest type of Whiggish squire. The consequence of all this political confusion was that, from the fall of Peel to the late 1860s, Britain was governed by more or less creaky coalitions. The monarchy, in such circumstances, was far from being a mere bit of pageantry or decoration. The letters and journals of Victoria and Albert throughout the 1850s show how closely they were involved with the appointments of ambassadors and Cabinet ministers and in attempting to put into practice the 'good' doctrines of Stockmar – an ever-constant presence, sometimes in person, sometimes writing letters from Germany – King Leopold and Sir Robert Peel.

The vastly complicated scene has too many elements to be summarized glibly; but from 1849 until the late 1850s, we can watch Victoria and Albert attempting to guide their Prime Ministers towards a greater acceptance of Free Trade and its natural political consequence: a gradual extension of the franchise, and the involvement of greater numbers of the electorate in the process of choosing Members of Parliament. In this, one can say that Prince Albert had a decisively positive role to play, in particular with the triumph of the Great Exhibition. In two other great areas of governance, however, matters were more complex. In Ireland, for the next two decades, both in relation to detailed land reforms, and to the much bigger question of whether the Irish felt they were properly represented by the Westminster Government, the royal pair were as adrift and as out of touch as their ministers. In the matter of foreign policy, we find a truly fascinating situation developing, in which the royal pair, especially when Palmerston was Foreign Secretary (less so, paradoxically, when he had at last become Prime Minister), we find a Britain at odds with itself; the Foreign Office and the Crown often completely opposed to one another in their attitudes to France, to Russia, to Germany and the Danish claims over the Schleswig-Holstein Duchies, and to the whole complexity of the Eastern Question – Turkey and the Eastern Mediterranean.

Since it was also a time when the fecund Queen continued to expand her family, with Prince Arthur being born in 1850 and Prince Leopold in 1853, it was inevitable that for at least some of the time

Prince Albert took the primary role as royal arbiter. You see this, for example, in the anguished and punctilious correspondence between Buckingham Palace and the Foreign Office during 1849 and 1850. Over the Schleswig-Holstein Duchies, the Queen wrote, 'the cause of the war [between Denmark and Prussia] having been the unlawful attempt to incorporate Schleswig into Denmark, the peace cannot be lasting unless it contains sufficient guarantees against the resumption of that scheme'.[9] There is a perfect logic in the Queen writing from this point of view in the light of her deep involvement on the side of Germany: her sister was married to the Augustenburg claimant to one of the Duchies; her husband, brother-in-law and many other relations were all deeply committed to the success of German unification and the protection of the Holstein Duchy from Denmark's intrusion. From Palmerston's point of view, however, British interests were best served by forging a strong Scandinavian alliance – especially in view of his increased belligerence towards Russia.

Similarly, when Palmerston, at the beginning of 1851, wanted to move Lord Cowley, a very able diplomat, from Germany to St Petersburg, he did so with the logic of his own position unimpaired. He was warming up to major fisticuffs with Russia and he wanted in place at the Russian Court a diplomat of the first rank. From Victoria and Albert's point of view, however, little as they liked Russia, it was a power to be reckoned with and they had not (as yet) foreseen the extraordinary turn of events which would bring Britain and Russia to war with one another. From their position, the really big 'story' in Europe during those times was not the expanding power of Russia in the East; it was the future of Germany after the Year of Revolutions. After the failure of a left-wing putsch in Frankfurt (hence the arrival of Karl Marx as a refugee in London) the Queen and the prince favoured keeping Cowley in Frankfurt. And the Queen wrote to Palmerston that 'she must insist that the posts of Berlin and Frankfort [sic – it was the common Victorian spelling] which in her opinion are of nearly equal importance, should be filled by men capable of dealing with the complicated and dangerous political questions now in agitation there'.[10] 'She' – the letter bears all the hallmarks of having been written by Albert – links 'the peace of Europe' with the 'welfare of England'. From now onwards, and until the end of her reign, the *tendency* was for the Queen to take a more Eurocentric approach to foreign policy while her ministers, of whatever political complexion, vacillated between various positions of cynicism in what they considered to be 'British interests'. But with none of her ministers was the contrast sharper than with Palmerston in these years of 1849–51.

The Prime Minister, however, was not Palmerston, but Lord John Russell. It is a strange fact that Russell – who in 1832 had been one of the prime architects of the Great Reform Bill, and who could lay claim to being one of the great British legislators – should, as Prime Minister, have been responsible for only one major Act of Parliament: the Ecclesiastical Titles Act of 1851. It was generally agreed, even at the time, to be a mistake; Lord Clarendon was against it – warning that it would cause bad feeling, possibly something rather worse, in Ireland; Gladstone, no doughtier defender of the Church of England than he, was against it; even the Queen had mixed feelings about it, being afraid to upset her Roman Catholic subjects by too open a sympathy with Russell's Bill. Indeed, many of her relations, for one reason or another, such as the King of the Belgians, had embraced Roman Catholicism on variations of the Henri IV principle. (In Leopold's case it was Brussels, rather than Paris, which was worth the Mass.) The Duke of Nemours congratulated her on the 'moderation' of her responses to the 'Papal Aggression'[11] (that is, to the anti-Papal Agression Addresses she had received). She favoured a diplomatic solution – the sending of diplomats to Rome to dissuade the Pope from setting up the new hierarchy, but this scheme 'foundered on the everlasting rock – Lord Palmerston – the obstacle to everything that is good & right'.[12] Prince Albert 'entirely agreed' with Russell's views on Papal Aggression.[13] The more the Queen heard about the antics of Bishop Nicholas Wiseman, the senior English Roman Catholic cleric, the more she agreed too, but she kept her views private. She was torn, as she told her aunt the Duchess of Gloucester, between her 'sincerely Protestant feelings', and 'the unchristian and intolerant spirit exhibited by many people at the public meetings'.[14] Lord John Russell nevertheless persuaded her that Wiseman 'was doing all he could to Romanize this country – to detach the Roman Catholics from their allegiance to me & to bring them entirely under the sway of the Pope. This is very dangerous.'[15]

The 1840s had seen a growth of Irish immigration to England, and a consequent increase in the Roman Catholic population. At the same time, quite unconnectedly, a group of Anglican intellectuals, chiefly from the University of Oxford, and chiefly inspired by the writings and example of John Henry Newman (Vicar of St Mary's, Oxford), had left behind the Church of England and joined that of Rome. They were eminent more than numerous – out of nearly 20,000 Victorian Church of England clergy, only about 400 in the whole nineteenth century followed Newman to Rome, and many of these, like Colonel Sibthorp's clerical brother, hopped back again – some, like the younger Thomas Arnold (brother of Matthew), hopping to and fro more than once.

It nevertheless seemed to both sides of the argument, Catholic and Anglican, as if a great Catholic revival was under way. Newman preached a famous sermon called 'The Second Spring', and the genial leader of the Catholics, Bishop Wiseman, in 1850 made an announcement, writing a letter 'From out of the Flaminian Gate': the Pope had made him a cardinal, and for the first time since the Reformation, there was to be a Roman Catholic hierarchy of bishops, with their own cathedrals and dioceses. He was to be the Archbishop of Westminster; another would be Bishop of Birmingham, another of Liverpool, Salford, Middlesbrough, and so forth. By choosing these unglamorous titles for themselves, and planting their new bishoprics in the working-class Irish heartlands of industrial Britain, they were polite enough not to trespass on Anglican territory, though as one of the Queen's most amusingly mischievous private secretaries was to point out, there was nothing to stop the Pope from creating a Catholic Archbishop of Canterbury – 'and if so, could under the Act of Henry VIII claim precedence as such'.[16] After all, in Ireland, even though there was a Protestant Archbishop of Armagh, the Catholic opposite number, Dr Cullen, styled himself Archbishop of Armagh and Primate of All Ireland.

Lord John Russell perhaps feared some such piece of bravado on the part of the exuberant Cardinal Wiseman. (A stout party who liked his food and wine, Wiseman, it was said, 'had his lobster salad side', but was surely not a mischief-maker, and incapable of upstaging 'the Crumpet' by calling himself the Real Archbishop of Canterbury.) More likely, Russell was simply guided by that gut anti-Catholicism which certainly formed a part of the collective English psyche in the nineteenth century, and perhaps for much longer. As Owen Chadwick, greatest of church historians for this period, wrote, Russell 'clumsily expressed the popular mind'.[17] He who in 1829 had urged the liberty of Roman Catholics to read for the Bar or study at the universities, now felt it was necessary to ban them from having a Bishop of Salford. He laboriously pushed through Parliament the Ecclesiastical Titles Bill, making the new dioceses and bishoprics illegal. There were a few No Popery demonstrations, some of them quite nasty.

Cardinal Wiseman sent an exuberant invitation to all '*les puissances catholiques*' in Europe to attend his enthronement in London. 'This is really rather too much,' commented the Queen, '& would seem to place Wiseman on an equality with myself!'[18] Wiseman was burnt in effigy. In Fleet Street, there were no fewer than fourteen guys burned on 5 November, with a colossal guy sixteen feet high, drawn by a cart, driven by a fat man in a red robe wearing his improvised version of a cardinal's hat. The Roman Catholics defiantly continued to have their bishops and cathedrals, and twenty years later, the legislation was scrapped by Parliament. Lord John Russell had bitterly commented that the Irish famine was a medieval disaster happening in the nineteenth century. By a similar token it could be said that his anti-Catholic legislation provoked an outburst of seventeenth-century prejudice in the middle of the nineteenth. It seems strange to reflect that this esoteric legislation was being pushed through Parliament at the very time when Prince Albert and a Royal Commission were planning the Great Exhibition, as a demonstration of Britain as the most modern and forward-looking nation in the world.

The Queen's strength, high energy levels and general good spirits are demonstrated by the fact that she managed to spend so much of her time, at this period, devoted to discussing political questions with Albert and her ministers; and to music, and sketching and holiday-making in the Isle of Wight and Scotland. For the cycle of pregnancy appeared everlasting. 1850 saw the birth of Arthur, the future Duke of Connaught, named after the Duke of Wellington, who was his godfather. One of Prince Albert's early blunders, when a new arrival, had been to cut a Waterloo Dinner with the Iron Duke. The choice of Wellington as the aged godfather of the new baby was a token of Albert becoming acclimatized to the country of his adoption. Perhaps, too, it reflected the Queen's inclinations more than those of the prince.

Queen Victoria had adored Lord Melbourne, and she respected Sir Robert Peel, but in her heart she was always – unlike her husband – a robust, small-t English Tory. Every instinct made her hero-worship the old victor of Waterloo and Assaye. The soldier's daughter revered the old commander-in-chief, and it was fitting that when he grew up, Prince Arthur should have been a soldier also. He was always her favourite child.

As soon as she was well enough to appear in public again, on 27 June, she took Alice and Affie for a drive in Hyde Park. A large crowd had collected to see her trot past on her way back from Cambridge House. The gate at that point into the park was too narrow for the equerry to ride alongside, so the carriage was compelled to pass within touching distance of the crowds. She had often thought at this point in the drive that it would be a place where an 'attempt' could be made upon her. On this occasion, a particularly unpleasant incident occurred. A fair young man, with a fair moustache, whom she had often noticed on her drives in the park, stepped forward with a small stick in his hand. 'I felt myself violently thrown by a blow to the left of the carriage. My impulse had been to throw myself that way, not knowing what was coming next – till I was raised the moment afterwards by poor Fanny [Frances, Countess of Gainsborough, daughter of the 3rd Earl of Roden, a lady of the bedchamber], who was dreadfully frightened, "saying they have got the man".' The Queen's bonnet was crushed, and she felt 'an immense bruise' on the right side of her head where she had been hit by the stick. She got up in the carriage, 'having quite recovered myself, & telling the good people who anxiously surrounded me, "I am not hurt". I saw him being violently pulled about by the people.'[19] It was the second time that Affie and Alice had witnessed an attack on their mother. She was well enough in the evening to attend the opera – the second act of Meyerbeer's *Le Prophète*.

It was a week of intense drama, in which the attack upon the Queen was only one element. The House of Commons witnessed a debate about Palmerston's handling of a bizarre incident in Athens. Although the matter in question was minor, even farcical, it was really a debate about something much bigger than itself – nothing less was being discussed than Britain's standing in the world, and her attitude to other nations.

A Portuguese Jew called Don Pacifico, resident in Athens, had had his house pillaged. Because he had been born in Gibraltar, he was technically a British subject, and he applied to the Foreign Office in his claim for enormous compensatory damages from the Greek Government.

Palmerston's reaction, even by his own melodramatic standards, was extreme. He ordered the British Fleet in the Mediterranean to blockade the harbour at Piraeus. Greece appealed for help to Russia and France. A ludicrous diplomatic incident could easily have turned into war. The Queen and Prince Albert, despite the fact that she was far gone in her pregnancy when the incident happened and the crisis was brewing, had long talks with Russell about dimissing Palmerston over the incident. But the Prime Minister, little as he liked Palmerston, was afraid of him, pointing out, fairly shamelessly, that both the Protectionists on the right and the extreme radicals on the left of the House of Commons loved Pam. 'Lord John was therefore much anxious to do nothing that could hurt Lord Palmerston's feelings.'[20]

When the matter was aired in the Commons, it was assumed that Palmerston would be severely censured, if not actually defeated in the divisions; and that the matter would be his downfall. By contrast, he used it for one of his stagiest definitions of how he regarded his role, not merely as Foreign Secretary but as what the newspapers called 'the English Minister'. It was Pam, more than Lord John, or sensible Sir Robert Peel, or moderate Lord Aberdeen or Prince Albert, who, in the eyes of the populist press, 'spoke for England'.

He considered himself bound to protect 'our fellow subjects abroad'. He asked whether 'as the Roman, in days of old, held himself free from indignity, when he could say, Civis Romanus sum; so also a British subject, in whatever land he be, shall feel confident that the watchful eye and the strong arm of England, will protect him against injustice and wrong'.[21] The Protectionists opposite – led by Disraeli – could scarcely speak against this patriotic and stirring sentiment. The Government won the vote by 310 to 264 – it was not a triumph for Palmerston but nor was it the disgrace that his enemies had been hoping for.

Among those who spoke against him was Sir Robert Peel. A week after the debate, Peel was riding up Constitution Hill when his horse stumbled, and he fell from the saddle. His injury was serious and on 2 July, to the enormous distress of the Queen and the prince, their political hero died. A week later, her old uncle the Duke of Cambridge also died – 'We live in the midst of sorrow and death!'[22] she exclaimed, though she had never greatly liked the old boy. Her cousin George, however, now the 2nd duke, had always been a friend (even though she recognized that he could be 'disagreeable'). How different public life in England would have been had she married him – though he would always ungallantly say that he had not been tempted to marry 'plain little Victoria'. More or less exactly the Queen's age, George was now a major general, who had done service in Ireland throughout the famine. On the day of his cousin's wedding, he had met the beautiful actress Louisa Fairbrother. They had two children; living a century before the name Adolf became one of dread for the Germans, this Hanover-born soldier called both his sons by the name: George William Adolphus (born 1843) and Adolphus Augustus Frederick (born 1846). In 1847, in defiance of the Royal Marriages Act, George had married Mrs Fairbrother and, although he was not especially faithful to her, the pair lived harmoniously together at 6 Queen Street, Mayfair, until her death in 1890.

Though the Queen was still recovering from her injuries in the park, and though they were both stung by the loss of Peel, Prince Albert was also preoccupied throughout the summer by the future of the Great Exhibition, planned for the following year in the park.

The idea for the Exhibition had been born the previous year, 1849, when Henry Cole and other dignitaries of the Society of Arts visited a large exhibition in Paris. They conceived the idea of a huge exhibition in London, the largest the world had ever seen, as demonstration of industrial design and expertise. Britain was supreme in the economies of the Western world. This exhibition – called from the first the 'Great' Exhibition – would be the outward and visible sign of everything which had been achieved in the nation since the Industrial Revolution began; but it would, more than this, be a celebration of the Free Trade which had been the British privilege since the abolition of the Corn Laws.

Cole – an assistant in the Public Record Office who did much to expand that great institution, and who had also been instrumental in promoting the Penny Post – soon realized that their idea for the Exhibition was too big to be administered by the Society of Arts alone, and needed the backing of a Royal Commission.

As soon as Prince Albert took the chair of this commission, in January 1850, he was taking a bold risk. What Cole and his friends were organizing could turn out to be a financial and propaganda disaster. The commission, which included Lord John Russell, Peel, Henry Labouchere (President of the Board of Trade), architects Barry and Cubitt, and others, quickly found themselves with logistical challenges on a scale unprecedented in the capital. It was possible they would be receiving a million visitors, and as the time raced forward, it became clear that none of the plans had coalesced. Where would the Exhibition be held exactly? Who was to pay for it? In answer to this last question, the members of the commission themselves undertook to come up with the cash, but some of this would have to be raised in the City, and Albert accordingly spoke at a great dinner at the Mansion House in March, setting out their aims.

It was a nerve-wracking experience. Although his English was by now pretty good, it was not perfect, and he rehearsed his speech with the Queen: 'it seemed to make him quite as nervous to repeat it to me as to anyone else'.[23] Albert could surely see, as could the Queen, that the Royal Family were now intimately bound up with the Exhibition in the minds of the public. If this thing failed, it would be a royal failure.

When the site had been fixed in Hyde Park, there remained the question of the architect who would house the exhibits. Designs came in from all over the world, but the commission asked Isambard Kingdom Brunel to come up with something. It was not the great railway engineer's most inspired moment, and by May, the Brunel scheme had been ridiculed in the press – a long, low brick structure which would have been an eyesore in the park, dwarfed by a huge iron dome the size of that of St Paul's.

It was then that Providence appeared to step in to help them. John Ellis, MP and chairman of Midland Railway, had a conversation with Joseph Paxton, the brilliant gardener who had created the Great Stove at Chatsworth. Ellis was so gripped by Paxton's ideas about the acoustics, ventilation and appearance of any ideal exhibition space that he immediately whisked the Derbyshire genius off to the Board of Trade to persuade Lord Granville. Granville was out, but Henry Cole was there. They sent Paxton to Hyde Park to 'step over' the proposed site. That weekend, and the following Monday, Paxton went to see the opening of the railway bridge over the Menai Straits, and as he did so, he began to doodle designs on a piece of blotting paper. The next week, he put them into more detailed shape and by 20 June he was ready with his plans to show the commission. Peel, in his last days, was a great enthusiast.

It was in part the shock at Peel's death, felt in the House, which silenced the objections being raised by Parliament to the use of Hyde Park as an exhibition venue. Colonel Sibthorp brought a motion forbidding the use of the park on 4 July, which was overwhelmingly defeated. The world was now ready for Paxton's giant greenhouse, or, as the comic magazine *Punch* called it, 'the Crystal Palace'.

It was to be 1,848 feet long, 456 feet wide at its broadest point and 108 feet high at the transept. Like many great architectural ideas, it was extremely simple, and, rather than necessitating the destruction of trees – as Sidthorp had feared – it actually incorporated the trees of the park within itself. The commission still dithered, considering other plans and tenders, but on 26 July, it formally recognized Paxton's design.

The entry in the Queen's journal, 1 May 1851, is one of the most celebrated: 'This day is one of the greatest & most glorious days of our lives, with which, to my pride & joy the name of my dearly beloved Albert is for ever associated!'

The Green Park & Hyde Park were one mass of densely crowded human beings, in the highest good & most enthusiastic. I never saw Hyde Park look as it did, being filled with crowds as far as the eye could reach. A little rain fell, just as we started, but before we neared the Crystal Palace, the sun shone & gleamed upon the gigantic edifice, upon which the flags of every nation were flying. We drove up Rotten Roe [sic] & got out of our carriages at the entrance in that side. The glimpse through the iron gates of the Transept, the waving palms & flowers, the myriads of people filling the galleries & seats around, together with the flourish of trumpets, as we entered the building, gave a sensation I shall never forget, & I felt much moved. We went for a moment into a little room where we left our cloaks & found Mama & Mary. Outside all the princes were standing. In a few seconds we proceeded, Albert leading me; having Vicky at his hand, & Bertie holding mine. The sight as we came to the centre where the steps & chair (on which I did not sit) was placed, facing the beautiful crystal fountain was magic & impressive. The tremendous cheering, the joy expressed in every face, the vastness of the building, with all its decorations & exhibits, the sound of the organ (with 200 instruments & 600 voices, which seemed nothing), & my beloved Husband the creator of this great 'Peace Festival', inviting the industry & art of all nations of the earth, all this, was indeed moving, & a day to live forever. God bless my dearest Albert, & my dear Country which has shown itself so great today. One felt so grateful to the great God, whose blessing seemed to pervade the whole great undertaking.

After the National Anthem had been sung, Albert left my side, & at the head of the Commissioners, – a curious assemblage of political & distinguished men, – read the Report to me, which is a long one, & I read a short answer. After this the Archbishop of Canterbury offered up a short & appropriate Prayer, followed by the singing of Handel's Hallelujah Chorus, during which time the Chinese Mandarin came forward & made his obeisance. This concluded, the Procession of great length began which was beautifully arranged, the prescribed order, being exactly adhered to. The Nave was full of people, which had not been intended & deafening cheers & waving of handkerchiefs, continued the whole time of our long walk from one end of the building, to the other. Every face, was bright & smiling, & many even, had tears in their eyes. Many Frenchmen called out 'Vive la Reine'.

It is tantamount to a manifesto. Though Peel was not alive to see it, it was a prodigious demonstration of the alliance which now existed between the monarchy, and the future, as represented by glass and iron, by manufacturers, by economic liberalism, by British expansionism. If European countries wished to compete, they could not hope to do so by asserting the autocratic structures of the past, as in Austria, Russia or Turkey. The only future was the British future. Victoria and Albert had harnessed the Victorian economic success story to make it a political success story. William IV would certainly have agreed with old Colonel Sibthorp; so, too, in all likelihood, did Victoria's cousin George Cambridge, for, though German-born and German-bred, the 2nd Duke of Cambridge was the archetypical English Colonel Blimp. For the time being, however, Victoria and Albert were able to feel justifiably smug.

Charlotte Brontë, whose *Jane Eyre* (anonymously published as *An Autobiography*, edited by Currer Bell) was a favourite with the Queen, was one of the thousands of visitors to the Crystal Palace. 'Its grandeur,' she wrote, 'does not consist in one thing, but in the unique assemblage of all things. Whatever human industry has created you find there… It seems as if only magic could have gathered this mass of wealth from all the ends of the earth'.[24]

The pessimists were all proved wrong. It was said that the mob would march on Hyde Park, that the Exhibition would be used as 'cover' for foreign spies or political agitators, that it would be impossible to police without enlisting police officers from Paris… It was feared that the visitors would be drunken – but alcohol was forbidden in the Crystal Palace; that they would be thirsty – but the contract, won by Schweppes, the Swiss carbonated drinks company, ensured that there was adequate catering. Where would they all relieve themselves? The practical question led to the (slow) adoption by London boroughs of the idea of public lavatories. Meanwhile, 827,000 people made use of the temporary 'retiring rooms' erected in the Exhibition, and countless more males used the urinals.

The range of exhibits was as magical as Charlotte Brontë observed. From India there were hundreds of exhibits – silks, cottons, furniture, rubber, foodstuffs, leather goods, ceramics. Other parts of the Empire demonstrated their distinctive wares: snow shoes and sleighs from Canada, as well as mats fashioned from porcupine quills by Native Americans. The architectural styles on display included Augustus Welby Pugin's medieval court, hard by stands displaying the most up-to-date products of Birmingham: gas fittings, brass bedsteads, buttons, needles, while agricultural machinery signalled a new English countryside. The Northern towns displayed their wares: a giant stainless steel knife from Sheffield, Titus Salt's alpacas and moreens, heavy upholstery fabrics, from Bradford. There was a scale model of Liverpool docks, and a geological model showing 3,000 square miles of Northern England in relief. Photography, ironworks, statues and ceramics (Minton, Copeland, Ridgeway, Wedgwood, Mason, Worcester), steam engines, globes, clocks, all were here in profusion, as well as the madder-seeming modern 'inventions' – a device for tipping people out of bed at a particular hour. Here were French silks, German toys (400 moving dolls taking part in a garden fête in a model of the Castle Florence in Saxe-Coburg); the 'comicalities' of Hermann Plouquet of Stuttgart – a cane-brandishing stoat making baby rabbits learn their lessons, squirrels playing whist; the great silver filigree column from Sardinia; gold ore from the Mariposa mine in California; a model of the Niagara Falls and a mass of zinc from America weighing 16,400 pounds; marble statues (Hiram Powers's *The Greek Slave*); yet more agricultural implements – McCormick's American reaping machine; the four decorated rooms from Vienna, including a neo-Gothic bookcase already donated by the Austrian Emperor to the Queen, a dining table in locust wood and a fountain which spurted eau-de-cologne; the Cuban room, heavy with cigar smoke; the Chinese room with silks, bamboo furniture, lacquered furniture, lanterns, fans, paintings on rice paper, samples of tea. The world had never seen anything like it, for the world was being shown itself: itself, that is to say, at peace, itself purged of bellicosity and angry diplomats, a world only of manufacturers and merchants, to whom the future surely belonged.

The crowds were prodigious. For the first two days, the price of admission was £1, which kept out all but the two or three thousand wealthy; but the admission was lowered to half a crown on Fridays, five shillings on Saturdays and a shilling for the rest of the week. By the time these cheaper rates had been fixed only 200,000 people had attended, but the multitudes soon came – some 6 million visitors before the Exhibition closed.[25]

When it did so, the newspapers, which had been so sceptical about the Exhibition before its opening, were almost universal in their praise. The *Morning Chronicle* saw it as 'an important chapter in the history of the human race... As a people we are not what we were.' Most of the papers congratulated themselves for being British, saluting their own *sang-froid*, *chauvinisme*, *élan* and other English virtues. But what had happened almost imperceptibly was that all these national characteristics – resourceful, steady in a crisis, financially astute, unflappable and rich – were ones which the press, and perhaps the public at large, were now prepared to assign in more or less equal proportions to themselves and to the royal pair. The monarchy was now firmly harnessed to the Victorian success story.

NINE

'GODLIKE MEN'

VICTORIA AND ALBERT believed that 1851, that year of Exhibition-triumph, brought an added bonus in the removal of Lord Palmerston. They mistook a dramatic exit stage left for the final bow of that formidable player on the world stage. Sadly for both of them, Palmerston, a mere sixty-seven, had many years of energy and power left to him, and he would outlive the prince, over thirty-six years his junior, who had become his sworn enemy. Not only would he outlive the prince, but he would, for better or worse, be one of the big figures in the complete shift of European realpolitik. Russia, having been Britain's uneasy rival and ally, would become her enemy in war. France, the old enemy in the Duke of Wellington's heyday, having been viewed askance by the British Royal Family since 1815, would now become the great ally. The German-speaking lands, that is to say the great Central European landmass, would, as usual, be misunderstood and ignored by the British political Establishment.

But that was not how it immediately seemed in the joyous aftermath of the Exhibition. By October 1851, £356,000 had been taken in entrance fees. The profit from the Exhibition had already reached over £200,000. Paxton's palace was demolished, eventually to be rebuilt at Sydenham. The prince wanted to buy a permanent site for educational, scientific and cultural institutions, the land now occupied by the Royal Albert Hall, Imperial College, the Victoria and Albert Museum, the Science Museum, the Natural History Museum, the

Royal College of Music and the Royal College of Art: the so-called Albertopolis.[1] It is not a bad legacy for a foreign prince of whom the British majority were so suspicious when he first arrived on their shores, nor for the Exhibition which he championed, and which pessimists had predicted would be a failure. A Royal Commission was set up to handle the surplus, and it exists to this day, funding fellowships and grants for advanced study.[2] The last financial details concerning the purchase of the site, and the transfer of the funds, was part of the brief, in 1852, of a new Chancellor of the Exchequer. This was none other than 'that dreadful' Benjamin Disraeli. After a long discussion with the prince, Disraeli wrote to his sister that he thought Albert was 'the best educated man I have ever met; most completely trained and not over-educated for his intellect, which is energetic and lively'.[3] How it came about that Sir Robert Peel's destroyer was Chancellor in 1852 was a complicated story. This was the most enmeshed and challenging political period of the Queen's reign, and although, in personal terms, it was marked by the birth of yet another child – Prince Leopold, on 7 April 1853 – and by a very *occupé* family life, with the other children, it is one which found her involved with political events on an almost weekly basis, even when she was separated from London, in Osborne and Balmoral.

Palmerston instinctively understood, and shared, the British public attitude to 'abroad': that is, he had a sense that Britain should get as much advantage as she could from the foreigner, while attempting, where humanely possible, to check and deplore his more barbarous excesses. In Europe, this made Britain 'liberal', since the British tended to side with the 'underdogs' – nationalists, dissidents of various kinds – against old-fashioned, often Catholic, autocracies. (In Asia and Africa, things were slightly different. There, British interests, and the desire to curb the 'barbarism' of the foreigner, led to administrations which, while trying to be fair-minded, were often racist and intrusive.) So it was that, when General von

Haynau, the draconian 'Butcher of Austria', who had put down the attempted Revolution of 1848 with such severity, foolishly visited London in September 1851, he was mobbed when he was recognized at Barclay & Perkins Brewery, being unceremoniously dipped in a watering-trough, and narrowly escaping being lynched. Palmerston wrote a masterly letter of 'apology' to the Austrian Embassy, itemizing Haynau's atrocities and explaining why he was hated in England. When the radical Hungarian leader Lajos Kossuth came to the capital in December, the Russians, anticipating Palmerston's liberal welcome, asked specifically that Kossuth should receive no official recognition. The Queen passed this request on to her Foreign Secretary. Palmerston complied with the letter of his sovereign's request, but he caused glee in all radical quarters, by receiving an English Radical Delegation congratulating him on his support for Kossuth against his Russian oppressors. The loyal address with which they presented Pam contained withering denunciations of the autocracies of Austria and Russia.

How should a Whig with radical sympathies view events in France since the expulsion of the monarchy in 1848? Probably, Pam would have agreed with the minister of public works in the provisional government, Alexandre-Thomas Marie, who was a democrat, but a cautious one, believing that, 'The despotism of a thousand heads is a thousand times more odious than the despotism of a single man.'[4] In some ways, some such idea underpinned the limited constitutional monarchy which the British permitted themselves, together with their reformed Parliament. For that reason, the Queen allowed, and positively favoured, a gradual expansion of the franchise. 'It was better to do it quietly,' she told King Leopold, who had raised his eyebrows at Russell's desire to extend the franchise yet further, 'and not to wait till there was a cry for it.'[5] Many French people felt – as Palmerston did – that 'Bonapartism' was the check on Bourbon tyranny on the one hand, and communism on the other. You could define 'Bonapartism' in any way you liked. Louis Napoleon himself is supposed to have said, after he had styled himself Napoleon III,

'The empress is a legitimist, I am a socialist; the only Bonapartist is Persigny and he is mad.'[6]

It was because he feared 'the despotism of a thousand' that Palmerston shocked his radical supporters and saluted the coup d'état by Napoleon's nephew, Louis Napoleon. Having been elected overwhelmingly as President of the new republic on 10 December 1848, the new Napoleon staged a coup d'état nearly three years later – 2 December 1851 – dismissing both his monarchist and his republican ministers. There was very limited resistance to the coup, and widespread support. The British Ambassador in Paris, Lord Normanby, deplored it, but even the Duke of Wellington had said, that summer, 'France needs a Napoleon'.[7] Palmerston agreed. When the French Ambassador in London, Count Walewski, sought an audience with the Foreign Secretary, Pam saw no need for flannel or discretion. Walewski, the natural son of the first Emperor Napoleon and the Countess Walewska, '*l'épouse polonaise de l'Empereur*', had been married to Caroline Montagu, daughter of the Earl of Sandwich. She had died in childbirth and he had remarried, to an Italian, Marianne Ricci. This did not stop him playing the field and he was a familiar figure to Palmerston in the drawing rooms and country houses. Palmerston openly congratulated Walewksi on the Bonapartist coup.

This time he went too far. Normanby, from Paris, wrote a long letter denouncing Palmerston and his 'cavalier attitude' to his position. This time, Lord John Russell had almost no option but to give Prince Albert the happy Christmas present of Palmerston's dismissal. The prince-president (he had not yet declared himself emperor) was desolated. '*La chute de Lord Palmerston est le coup le plus grave que j'ai reçu; il est le seul ami que je l'avais.*'[8]

Undoubtedly the best joke about Louis Napoleon's coup was made by Karl Marx in his pamphlet on the 18th Brumaire (that is, on the date in the French Revolutionary Calendar when, in 1799, the first Napoleon became the dictator of France, and, on roughly the same date in 1851, the nephew did the same). 'Hegel remarks somewhere that all great world-historic facts and personages appear, so to speak, twice. He forgot to add: the first time as tragedy, the second time as farce.'⁹

There is often far more odium between colleagues inside a political party than between the official opponents sitting opposite one another in either House. So it was with Russell and Palmerston, who cordially detested one another. Far from destroying Pam, his hated old Whig colleague Russell merely brought down his own Government. From the moment of the first Napoleon's elevation, in 1799, his hostility to Britain had been a constant threat. It was by no means clear that his nephew, in 1851–2, would not pose a comparable threat. Or so it was believed in British military and political circles.

Russell, in response to the fear of French invasion, proposed the establishment of local militia. Palmerston, from the back benches, opposed the measure, preferring that there should be a regular militia, rather than an ad hoc 'Home Guard'. Behind this debate stood the unpleasant fact – soon to be revealed on the world stage – of the British Army's total inadequacy to fight a war. But for the time being, the war which mattered was that fought out in the Commons between the two old 'friends', Russell and Pam. Needless to say, Palmerston, in every way the stronger character, rallied support for his idea of a regular militia. Russell's Government was defeated, and he went to kiss hands.

He had not been a successful Prime Minister and neither he nor his wife had ever liked the Queen. His grandson Bertrand Russell 'regretted' to recall, in his amusing memoirs, that Lady John's attitude to Queen Victoria 'was far from respectful. She used to relate with much amusement how one time she was at Windsor and feeling rather ill, the Queen had been graciously pleased to say, "Lady Russell may sit down. Lady So-and-So shall stand in front of her".'¹⁰

What followed was a coalition in which Russell served as Foreign Secretary. The new Prime Minister was the fifty-three-year-old 14th Earl of Derby. Active in politics since the 1820s as Lord Stanley, he had, the previous year, inherited his father's earldom and the palatial house of Knowlsey in Lancashire. Surely one of the cleverest in that clever club of Queen Victoria's Prime Ministers, he was viewed somewhat askance by the puritanical Prince Albert. While Albert might have approved of Lord Derby's translations from Homer, he was made uneasy by his love of the turf, his ownership of racehorses, and his breezy, laughing coterie of racing pals. The Queen, however, who had very different tastes in human beings from those of her husband, noted, 'He certainly is a very cheery companion, though at times perhaps a little fatiguing. But he is extremely good-natured and "sans pretention".'[11]

Forming a Government in the difficult circumstances of Russell's resignation as Prime Minister was not easy. Disraeli was the leader of the Protectionists in the Commons, but this meant that it was next to impossible to persuade any Peelite, still smarting from the wounds of 1844, to serve in a Government with the man who had so effectively knifed their leader at the time of the Corn Law debate. Similarly, there were Whigs, such as Palmerston, who were so opposed to Free Trade that they would not serve in a Government which now appeared, only eight years after the Corn Law debacle, to accept, even to embrace it. The result was a Cabinet which the Queen considered below standard. It became known as the 'Who, Who?' ministry, since the Duke of Wellington, now very deaf and old, and sitting beside Derby in the Lords while one of the new ministers was trying to make a speech, said 'Who? Who?' every time the nonentity named one of his unremarkable Cabinet colleagues. One of them, however, was the far from unremarkable Benjamin Disraeli, who was Chancellor of the Exchequer, which explains how it was he who was responsible for the financing of the 'Albertopolis'. 'Mr Disraeli,' the Queen wrote to her uncle Leopold, '(alias Dizzy) writes very curious reports to me of the House of Commons proceedings – much in the style of his books.'[12] She was beginning to be fascinated. Albert, had he lived another fifty years, would never have seen the point of Disraeli.

In April, Lord Derby went to the country. Disraeli wrote the closest their party had to a manifesto in his election address to the voters of Buckinghamshire. His proposal was 'Conservative progress'. He admitted that the battle against Free Trade was lost. They should embrace 'maintenance of the colonial empire, the investigation of electoral corruption and commitment to the Protestantism of the English Crown'.

With a General Election in prospect, the Queen hoped that the confusion of coalition government might be brought to an end. Writing from Osborne in March – where, as so often, Stockmar was staying – she told the King of the Belgians, 'One thing is pretty certain—that out of the present state of confusion and discordance, a sound state of Parties will be obtained, and two Parties, as of old, will again exist, without which it is impossible to have a strong Government.'[13] There were five parties represented in Parliament – the Whigs and the Protectionist Tories were the old aristocratic parties, with their roots in the political world of pre-1832. The Peelites, headed by Lord Aberdeen, obviously had some aristocrats in their number, but in so far as they had come into existence as defenders of Free Trade, they represented an emergent urban mercantile class, which was just as likely to vote, in different regions, for the radicals or Liberals. The Irish formed a block vote in the Commons of ever-increasing power and importance, demanding that their voice be heard. It was unlikely that the Queen's wish would be granted in the course of just one election, for, of course, these different political interest groups overlapped, and it was possible for individuals to swim in and out of them. Many of the old Whigs, like Palmerston, had their doubts about having supported Free Trade. Some even had their doubts about having extended the franchise. In some aspects they had more in common with the aristocratic Protectionists than with the Peelites. Some Peelites repented of the split in the Conservative ranks and would like to have been back with the Protectionists. Some new Liberals were pro-Irish, and many were not. When the two non-Irish groups later formed parties behind Disraeli and Gladstone, the 'strong Government' for which the Queen, and perhaps many of her subjects, longed was not always very durable. Parties have always been coalitions, which can fracture under sufficient pressure.

Unlike Stockmar and Prince Albert, Queen Victoria was not a cerebral political analyst; yet she was developing, after nearly fifteen years on the throne, a symbiotic sense of her subjects, and what they felt. Sometimes she tried to do this consciously and in those circumstances she often got it wrong. But monarchy is more than a political system. It is a communion between sovereign and people. Victoria sensed the shift which was occurring in Britain, especially in England. While the majority of her ministers were, and would go on being, overwhelmingly aristocratic, the country at large was shifting. The Governing Class, the People who Mattered – what the Victorians called the Upper Ten (meaning the upper 10,000 people in the country) – were no longer all from the landed aristocracy. Many of them were professionals whose backgrounds were in that dreaded word 'trade'. The professional classes themselves had dynasties – of lawyers and doctors and academics and clergy. The commercial classes, at their upper echelons, became landed, and married within the professions and the aristocracy. So, Britain was in a state of creative flux. It was as unlike pre-Revolutionary France as it was possible to imagine – that France where the clever bourgeois never could, by virtue of the rigidity of privilege, ever penetrate the most influential positions in the land. The Victorians were a prodigious mélange of old and new, of inheritance and self-made, as Thackeray's *Book of Snobs* brilliantly pointed out to the readers of *Punch*. There was one profession, however, which remained unbudgeably aristocratic and self-destructively conservative: and that was the army. It would take a disgracefully mismanaged war to expose this fact, and nearly a generation to correct the mismanagement it uncovered.

The election had an inconclusive result. The Conservatives failed to win an overall majority; the Whigs lost heavily in Ireland; and the Independent Irish Party returned fifty-three members. Another coalition was essential. Dizzy knew that it looked ridiculous to have split the party by holding fast to Protectionism in 1844, only to abandon the principle eight years later. 'We built an opposition on Protection and Protestantism,' he told Derby. 'The first, the country has pissed upon,' while the second 'seemed to have worked us harm'. [14]

England was not invaded by France. The Iron Duke, who had not heard the names of so many new Cabinet ministers, and who would not have recognized them if he had, witnessed a country preparing to go to war with his old enemy France, but it was a war which never happened. Then, on 14 September, in his little iron bedstead in Walmer Castle, the Duke of Wellington died, and the old pre-Reform Bill world decisively died with him.

The Queen heard the news at Balmoral. Lords Derby and Aberdeen were both staying with her. 'One cannot think of this country without "the duke", our immortal hero!' she rhapsodized. 'There will be few dry eyes in the country.'[15]

Her neighbour on the Isle of Wight, the new Poet Laureate, decided that his first acknowledged work as Laureate should be an ode on the death of Wellington. Because the old body at Walmer was embalmed, in readiness for a funeral two months hence on 18 November, the poet had time to write his solemn tribute, 10,000 copies of which were put on sale, for two shillings each, on the day of the funeral.[16]

Tennyson's poem saluted Wellington as 'the last great Englishman'. It remembered not only the military victories, but the charm, and

> one about whose patriarchal knee
> Late the little children clung.

Tennyson, the Laureate who more than any other was in tune with his own age, instinctively conscious of its mood, linked the death not only with the political uncertainty of the time, but with the advances in science, especially in geology, which had shaken faith for many during the years of Tennyson's young manhood.

For though the Giant Ages heave the hill
And break the shore, and evermore
Make and break, and work their will;
Though world on world in myriad myriads roll
Round us, each with different powers,
And other forms of life than ours,
What know we greater than the soul?
On God and Godlike men we build our trust.[17]

As Tennyson would eloquently point out, some of this feeling, of needing a figurehead in times of great national change, would focus itself upon the monarchy, which is one of the reasons that Queen Victoria has remained so fascinating a subject for biography. The emergent Victorians did build their trust on her. 'Men make their own history, but they do not make it as they please; they do not make it under self-selected circumstances, but under circumstances existing already, given and transmitted from the past.'[18] These words of Marx, on the 18th Brumaire of Louis Napoleon, have a peculiar aptness for the Queen of that country where the German philosopher had now taken up residence. The Great Duke was buried with full honours next to Nelson in the crypt of St Paul's Cathedral. It was one of the largest funerals the capital had ever seen. These Janus-occasions, when a nation surveys the glories of the past, are always preparations for something new: and the ironies of a grand alliance with a Bonapartist regime, which Britain was about to forge, would not have been lost on the wise old head they laid to rest in London's heart.

One of the ways in which a female monarch can become a figurehead and focus of national self-awareness is by motherhood. Victorian England was a country growing in population at an enormous rate. As the ingenious agricultural machinery moved from its stands in the Crystal Palace to the fields of the shires, and as the cause of

Protectionism was killed in Parliament, agricultural labour became harder to sustain, and workers crowded from the country into the cities. The birth rate soared, even though the mortality rates were still, by the standards of later ages, horrifyingly high, both in mothers and their babies.

On 7 April 1853, Queen Victoria made history by becoming the first royal personage to give birth using an anaesthetic. Dr John Snow (1813–58), a working-class man from York, had trained as a doctor and worked as a colliery surgeon before coming south to train at the Hunterian School of Anatomy in Soho's Great Windmill Street. Rather an oddball, Snow was a bachelor, a vegetarian and a teetotaller, and died of a stroke aged only forty-five. But before then, he was an outstanding pioneer in two spheres. As a witness of the appalling cholera outbreak in Soho in 1849, he was a founder member of the Epidemiological Society of London: it was Snow who was largely responsible for discerning that cholera was a water-borne disease, and this was the breakthrough which led to the eventual elimination of this plague in Victorian London.

He was also a pioneer of anaesthetics. Three of Queen Victoria's regular doctors had worked with him, and had serious reservations about the practice. They had forbidden the Queen to use chloroform during the birth of Prince Arthur in 1850, but in 1853, she insisted upon the attempt. Snow had invented an inhaler for use in labour, but when he came to treat the Queen he used an open-drop approach, probably at her own request.[19] Snow, who anaesthetized seventy-seven obstetric patients with chloroform, waited until the woman had reached the second stage of labour. He limited the dose so that the patient could achieve satisfactory analgesia, but was still capable of obeying the command to push. There were several cases where, far from anaesthesia slowing labour, it actually speeded the process.

Rather poignantly, the Queen noted in her journal a fortnight after the birth, 'the dear little Baby is a nice healthy child'. In fact, Prince Leopold was a haemophiliac. 'He has got as wet nurse, a strong, healthy Highland woman, a Mrs Macintosh, from near Inverness.

She can speak but little English & arrived in a Highland cap and plaid shawl!'²⁰

That year, 1853, was one which saw the total reversal of British foreign policy, in the light of the grave crisis blowing up between Russia and Turkey.

In October 1852, the Queen had hastened to pass on to her uncle Leopold an anecdote sent to her by Lord Cowley from Paris, 'that under one of the Triumphal Arches a Crown was suspended to a string (which is very often the case) over which was written, "*Il y a bien mérité*". Something damaged this crown, and they removed it, <u>leaving</u>, however, the <u>rope</u> and <u>superscription</u>, the effect of which must have been somewhat edifying!'²¹ Although she would always enjoy this sort of joke, her opinion of the Emperor Napoleon III would undergo radical alteration. Just as she began by hating Peel, and came to revere him; loathed 'that dreadful Disraeli', and came to love him; so 'the emperor', as she was perfectly happy to call him, became of all foreign potentates perhaps the one she found most charming. The truth was – as our eyes of hindsight allow us to see – that while loving Albert as a man, she had a fundamentally different political, and personal, temperament. Once she was widowed, she even came to like Palmerston. The harder Albert worked to promote his German federalist view of Europe, the harder she had to struggle to suppress her lack of sympathy with politics. The simplest way of doing this was to adopt the pose that she was only a wife and mother, only a little woman who did not understand male affairs such as politics. Sometimes, quite probably, this really was what she felt.

'Albert becomes really a <u>terrible</u> man of business,' she once complained to her uncle, King of the Belgians. (The English language is ambivalent; by 'terrible', she means he was a 'workaholic', not that he was incompetent.) 'I think it takes a little off from the gentleness of his character, and makes him so preoccupied. I grieve over all this, as I <u>cannot</u> enjoy these things, much as I interest myself in general

European politics; but I am every day more convinced that <u>we women</u>, if we are to be good women, <u>feminine</u> and <u>amiable</u>, and <u>domestic</u>, are <u>not fitted to reign</u>; at least it is <u>contre gré</u> that they drive themselves to the <u>work</u> which it entails.'[22]

Events changed things fast. By December, Louis Napoleon who had deserved the rope, and whom Victoria would never receive when he lived in his London exile, was being addressed by her as 'my good brother, the Emperor of the French'. It was a token that Britain might need France as an ally that she was prepared to sacrifice her loyalty to her Orléanist relations and to acknowledge Napoleon's royalty. The Russian Emperor would not write to Napoleon as '*mon frère*' but only as '*mon cher Ami*'.[23]

One matter which loosened the Queen's somewhat taut attitude to 'the emperor' was his marriage. As anxious as any would-be monarch to continue his line, Louis Napoleon, since his seizure of power as a republican President, had made it clear that he was on the marriage market. One figure whom he had selected for the role of wife was Queen Victoria's niece Ada – the daughter of Feodore of Hohenlohe. She was only seventeen, to his forty-five. During his English exile, Louis Napoleon had moved in a raffish set (which included Disraeli and the Count d'Orsay) and openly kept a mistress – though it would be truer to say that she, Harriet Howard, being very rich, had kept him. (This flame-headed millionairess, whose real name was Elisabeth-Ann-Haryett, inherited her fortune from her father, a Brighton hotelier.) She generously bankrolled Louis Napoleon in his political ambitions. Princess Ada turned him down when the proposal reached her – via her own father, Prince Hohenlohe.

'Now that this terrible affair about our dear Ada has been decided by herself,' the Queen wrote to her sister Feodore, 'I can and will write to you about what I have felt and what mature reflection has made me feel <u>more</u> strongly even than I did at first. I feel that your dear child is <u>saved</u> from ruin of every possible <u>sort</u>. You know what <u>he</u> is, what his moral character is.'[24]

It is always rather difficult to take the temperature of Queen Victoria's expressions of puritanism, especially where sex is in question. As her boys grew up, this was usually, but not always, her tone ('You know what he is...'). But she enjoyed extremely cordial relations with her cousin George Cambridge, while turning a blind eye to his marital irregularities, and if she chose to love a man, such as Lord Melbourne, she would always overlook this side to their nature. Having been brought up by a widow was different from being brought up, as Albert was, in a home broken by adultery; so her distaste for raffishness, though she would loyally echo her husband's strong moral line, lacked the pathological edge which it possessed in his case.

In the event, the Emperor Napoleon III, who clearly favoured redheads like Harriet Howard, selected as his bride Mademoiselle Eugénie de Montijo, who had been settled in the Parisian demi-monde since 1851. Her pedigree was the subject of speculation. Her mother, daughter of the American Consul in Malaga (William Kirkpatrick), had married an illustrious Spanish aristocrat, the Count of Teba, who died in 1839. Whether the count was Eugénie's father was never established to the gossips' satisfaction, some going so far as to imagine that she was the daughter of Lord Palmerston. When Napoleon III himself speculated that she might be the daughter of Lord Clarendon, Eugénie's mother replied, '*Mais, sire, les dates ne correspondent pas.*'[25]

Lady Augusta Bruce, lady-in-waiting to Queen Victoria's mother, and already a great friend of the Queen's, attended the wedding at Notre-Dame, much impressed by the military uniforms, the velvet and ermine and silver of the vestments, the innumerable candles burning, but above all by the beauty of the bride.

> Her beautifully chiselled features & marble complexion, her head so nobly put on, her exquisitely proportioned figure & graceful carriage, were most striking & the whole was like a Poet's vision! I believe she is equally beautiful when seen close

by but at the distance at which we saw her, – the effect was more that of a lovely picture – aerial, ideal. On her classically shaped head she wore a diamond crown or diadem, round her waist a row of magnificent diamonds to correspond, – the same as trimming round the 'basque' of her gown. A sort of cloud or mist of transparent lace enveloped her.

This thirty-year-old Scottish aristocrat – one of the handful of really interesting and intelligent people in Queen Victoria's Court, whose letters are in the Sévigné league – was the daughter of the 7th Earl of Elgin, the man who purchased the Parthenon Marbles. Natural patriotism made her worship Eugénie's beauty, whose 'grace and dignity... came from the blood of *Kirkpatrick*!!'[26]

The ceremonies in Notre-Dame were not the only ecclesiastical rites organized that winter season by Napoleon III. A few weeks before his wedding, he had paid for Franciscan friars to march into the Church of the Nativity in Bethlehem and affix a silver star engraved with the emblem of France on the supposed spot where the Incarnate God had, 1,852 years previously, been laid in a manger.

Although the friars were exercising a privilege established by force in 1099, the Christian Holy Places had, by convention and habit, largely been the possession of the Greek Orthodox Church, whose bishops and monks had traditionally looked to Russia as their protector. What was superficially an ecclesiastical dispute was in fact highly political. The silver star of Bethlehem was a message to the Russians that, if they intended to carve up the Ottoman Empire, and capture the spoils of 'the Sick Man of Europe', they would find a rival imperial power in France. Incidentally, the celebrated Russian description of Turkey as 'the Sick Man of Europe' drew from Queen Victoria the tart observation, 'The mode of proceeding at Constantinople is not such as would be resorted to towards a sick friend for whose life there exists much solicitude.'[27]

Derby's coalition foundered at about the moment the Franciscans were setting out with their silver star and their screwdrivers for the Church of the Nativity. It was supplanted by another coalition led by the Peelite Lord Aberdeen. Disraeli was replaced as Chancellor of the Exchequer by William Ewart Gladstone. Palmerston, rather strangely for one whose entire political career had been in the sphere of foreign affairs, became, at this crucial moment of national history, the Home Secretary. The Foreign Secretary was Lord John Russell.

This was the Cabinet which would eventually take Britain to war in the Crimea: a fact shimmering with paradox, since the Prime Minister, Aberdeen, was probably one of the least bellicose politicians in history, while his old Harrovian contemporary, Pam, as unlike Aberdeen as chalk and cheese, was, notionally at least, involved with domestic matters. Palmerston, as so often in his life, was blessed with a mixture of amazing political luck and nous. As Home Secretary, he could scarcely be held to blame for the blunders which led Britain to war, nor for the maladroit way in which the war was conducted. As Home Secretary, he rightly attracted kudos for putting his weight and dynamism behind such very necessary reforms as forcing through the long-delayed Factory Act, controlling the hours which could be forced on workers. He also was swift to act on the discovery made by the enlightened Dr John Snow that cholera was water-borne, and he was the Home Secretary who began the work of clearing up London's pollution and constructing proper drainage for the capital. He also brought to an end transportation to Tasmania as a criminal punishment, and introduced reform schools, rather than prison, for juvenile offenders. Nevertheless, the flavour of Palmerston's home secretaryship was nicely captured by an anecdote in Greville's diaries. Industrial strikes threatened to paralyse the North of England as workers demanded a 10 per cent increase in their wages. The Queen asked her Home Secretary whether he had heard any news of these strikes. 'No, Madam,' was the reply, 'I have heard nothing, but it seems certain that the Turks have crossed the Danube.'[28]

All the while, of course, the minds of the Cabinet, of the press, of the Royal Family, and of the whole of Europe, were focused on Russia and Turkey.

Alarmed by the aggression represented by the Bethlehem Star, the Russian Emperor, Nicholas I, felt the moment had been reached when his Empire should reassert his traditional role as protector of the Holy Places. One of the many unfortunate circumstances in the whole story was that he chose as his legate an insensitive diplomat called Prince Menshikov. In April 1853, Menshikov went to Constantinople, where he conducted negotiations with the sultan and with representatives of the French and British Governments: the British Ambassador was Stratford Canning, now Viscount Stratford de Redcliffe. Menshikov pulled off what at first sight seemed like a Russian victory. Fuad Pasha, the Grand Vizier who had granted the Latins the privilege of putting the silver star in the Church of the Nativity, was forced to resign. The sultan reasserted the Russian right to protect the Holy Places. Menshikov, however, then pushed things too far by asking the Turks to agree to Nicholas I being the protector of all Orthodox believers within the Ottoman Empire. Negotiations were broken off, and Menshikov returned to Russia towards the end of May.

Following this failure, Russia occupied the Romanian principalities – where the Orthodox felt particularly threatened by the Muslims – on 2 July, and diplomatic relations between Russia and Turkey were broken off. To this day, historians disagree about the part played in events – up to the summer months of 1853 – by Britain. Did Stratford actually want to provoke a war with Russia? Did he yield so readily to Menshikov's demand for the Holy Places in order to make him seem aggressive when he then expressed what he wanted more – namely protection of the Romanian Orthodox? Russian and Turkish politics reverberate with conspiracy theories. It is easy to see why, since the Crimean War was really in no one's interest; and it is hard to see what 'victory' on either or any side would have achieved.

In the second half of 1853, there was an electric tension about the situation. The British Fleet was on alert, though where it should be

1. One of Thomas Sully's portraits of the young Queen Victoria ascending her throne, 1838.

2. Victoria and Albert in their thirties. Already the bloom of Albert's youth has faded, while she retains her girlishness.

3. *Above:* Queen Victoria reading with four of her grandchildren, Prince Albert Victor of Wales (Eddy) (1864–1892), Princess Victoria of Hesse (1863–1950), Prince George, later King George V (1865–1936), and Princess Elizabeth of Hesse (1864–1918).

4. *Left:* Queen Victoria's mother, Victoria, Duchess of Kent, with Prince Alfred and Princess Alice.

5. *Right:* Miniature of William Lamb, 2nd Viscount Melbourne (1779–1848) by William Charles Bell. 'The best-hearted, kindest, and most feeling man in the world.'

6. *Left:* King Leopold I of Belgium, 'Uncle Leopold', one of the key influences on Queen Victoria. Note the wig.

7. Prince Albert's intimate circle – (from left to right): The Hon. Charles Phipps, Mr Frederick. W. Gibbs, the Prince of Wales, Prince Albert, Baron Stockmar, Dr Ernst Becker and Baron Ernst Stockmar.

8. The Prince of Wales, Bertie, before he plumped out.

9. Princess Alice, who looks as if she is in mourning for her life, even before her deepest tragedies began.

10. *Above:* A daguerreotype of the Royal Family on the terrace at Osborne in the 1850s.

11. *Right:* Prince Arthur, Duke of Connaught, dressed as a private in the Grenadier Guards, Princess Helena (Lenchen) as a Chasseur de Vincennes, and Princess Louise as a Vivandière. Costumes for a tableau entitled 'The Allies'.

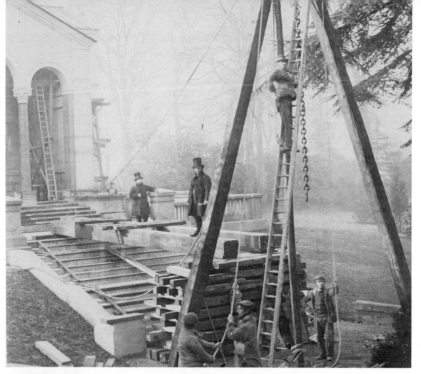

12. *Above:* The mausoleum at Frogmore under construction.

13. *Left:* The children of the Duke of Edinburgh in mourning – Prince Alfred, Princess Marie (on the pony), Princess Victoria and Princess Alexandra.

14. *Above:* Queen Victoria and the Empress Frederick (Vicky) in mourning for the Emperor Frederick III, who died in June, 1888.

15. *Left:* Queen Victoria seated with (from left to right) Princess Louise, Prince Leopold, the Marquis of Lorne and Princess Beatrice.

deployed was a debatable matter. Russia was a vast empire, and as soon as the 'hawks' in Cabinet and the upper military echelons realized that war was a possibility, they saw it as a chance to do much more than simply keep the Russians out of Constantinople. Here was an opportunity to control the Baltic, force Russia to return Åland and Finland to Sweden, to re-establish Poland as a sovereign state, to restore the mouth of the Danube to Turkey, to establish an independent Georgia, and many other aims.[29]

A conference of the Great Powers met in Vienna in July. The ambassadors drew up a form of words suggested partly by Napoleon III, and partly by Lord Clarendon, who had become Foreign Secretary in February. This document came to be known as the Vienna Note. It asked the sultan to promise not to modify any of the existing rules respecting the Christian subjects of his empire without first consulting France and Russia. The Russians accepted the Note; the Turks, obviously, rejected it, since it gave the Russians and the French the right, in effect, to police the Ottoman domains. The sultan said he would be faithful to previous agreements, but rejected the right of the French and the Russians to interfere.

By September, when the Royal Family had gone to Balmoral, the crisis had deepened. The Queen's journal makes clear that conversation was of little else, except for those joyous moments when the prince or one of his guests shot a stag. Late in September, Palmerston spent nine days at the Castle, though the only thing the Queen recorded him doing was playing billiards with the prince. It would have been fascinating to watch these games. Did the two, whose antipathy was strong and mutual, play in silence, or did they talk about the Vienna Note, the Royal Navy, the Russian Emperor, Napoleon – as everyone else in the house was doing? The Queen merely noted how short-sighted and old Palmerston seemed. Another of the guests was Prince Alexander of Württemberg – one day to be the '*Grosspapa*' of Queen Mary. He was stationed in St Petersburg and was probably closer than anyone else in the house party at Balmoral to knowing the situation in Russia. Alexander was convinced that there were 'some Priests and

Confessors... in the background, pushing on the Emperor, for the sake of the Greek Orthodox Church'.[30] While Victoria urged him to get out of St Petersburg, and pursue a military career in Germany,[31] he told them that the Emperor Nicholas had talked to him 'constantly' about the imminent downfall of the Ottoman Empire, and the necessity of settling with the other Great Powers what should be done about it.[32] This conversation occurred two days before an unsuccessful grouse shoot, attended by the gillies Macdonald and John Brown, and during which the first and second drives failed.

The Prime Minister, Lord Aberdeen, was also staying at Balmoral. He had changed his mind so much about the progress of affairs in the previous few weeks that it was difficult to know where he stood. Worse still, he and the Queen were not good at talking directly to one another.

The Queen's political inarticulacy was to be a problem for her later in her reign. With a dithering, indecisive Prime Minister, and a country which either might, or might not, go to war, it was clearly unsatisfactory, to say the least. When the politicians had left to go south to London, the news came that Turkey – on 4 October – had declared war on Russia. Reports reached Europe (some inaccurate, others exaggerated) of street fighting in Constantinople, and it was thought necessary, both in Paris and London, that the French and English needed to stand by.

The Prime Minister had left Balmoral with the impression that his sovereign was a hawk. He was surprised to discover otherwise, when, in the middle of October, she implored him to do anything possible to maintain the peace. After a long and painful audience at Windsor Castle on 16 October, Aberdeen admitted that, 'Had he known what the Queen's opinion exactly was, he might have been more firm, feeling himself supported by the Crown, but he had imagined from her letters that there was more animosity against Russia and leaning to war, in her mind.'[33]

Stratford was instructed by the Cabinet to ask the sultan not to send his fleet into the Black Sea. The British Navy was standing by to protect Constantinople from Russian invasion. The advice was too late to prevent the dispatch of a small flotilla to Sinope, which encountered the Russian Navy. The Turkish ships were destroyed.

Such was the mysterious war fever growing in Britain that Aberdeen was held responsible for this 'massacre' of Turkish war vessels. This point of view overlooked the fact that it was the Turks who had declared war on the Russians, that the two nations were at war, and that the flotilla appeared to be crossing the Black Sea to invade the Caucasus. Palmerston, ever with his eye to the main chance, resigned from the Cabinet. By now, the hawks were having it all their own way. The British Fleet was ordered into the Black Sea, and Aberdeen agreed to allow the French and the British to besiege the Russians at the Black Sea port of Sevastopol, to prevent further aggression against Turkey. Early in February, the Emperor Nicholas withdrew his ambassadors from Paris and London, and on 27 March (France) and the 28th (Britain) 1854, Turkey's two new allies declared war on Russia.

PART THREE

AT WAR

O N 29 JANUARY 1854, crowds assembled outside the Tower of London. They had come to see Prince Albert and the Prime Minister, Lord Aberdeen, being led away to the Bloody Tower in chains. The rumour was the prince and the Prime Minister had been arrested for treason. Effigies of Aberdeen and Albert were set alight. Such is the nature of war fever. Within six weeks, France and Britain, somewhat improbable allies, would be at war with Russia over the relatively obscure question of who controlled the Holy Places of Palestine. The war was in reality a conflict about whether Russia could exercise control over the enfeebled Ottoman Empire, which stretched from the Balkans to what we now term the Middle East, and included large parts of North Africa. Much of the discussion in the British Foreign Office, and between Queen Victoria and her Government, in the run-up to the war, concerned the extent to which Russia had designs on Constantinople itself, the Ottoman imperial capital. This was why the war, when it came, was fought not in Palestine, but in the Crimean highlands adjoining the Black Sea.

It had been nearly forty years since Britain had been engaged in a European war. There existed no officer-training staff college, as in Prussia.[1] No British officer had been trained in the writing or the transmission of orders. The French, Italians and above all the Prussians had a permanent military staff, ready to supply, inform and guide troops in the field. Forces of the Crown had, it is true, been engaged in almost continuous combat since the beginning of the reign, in Afghanistan, in Egypt, in parts of India. As recently as May 1852, the British had finally conquered Burma, having taken Rangoon and Bassein.

But the truth was, there were really two Victorian armies. There was a small, more or less professional, army, which did the fighting – chiefly in and around India, but also, sporadically, in the Cape colony, in Ashanti and in North Africa. The rest of the Queen's army was the one which stayed at home. Its officers, all aristocrats who had bought their commissions, designed more and more elaborate uniforms for themselves, and did very little in the way of active service, unless a magistrate called out the militia to subdue the disgruntled populace.[2] It was this army, the army of lords Cardigan, Raglan and Lucan, which was now to be put to the test. The Queen, and the diplomats, and the politicians, had been so concerned about the acceptability, or not, of the Vienna Note, the likelihood, or not, of the Turks or the Russians taking this or that course of action, in the latter half of 1853, that none of them had been unpatriotic enough to ask whether Her Majesty's troops were in a position to fight a war against another great European army.

Wellington had wanted Prince Albert to succeed him as Commander-in-Chief of the British Army. Though no warrior, the prince would certainly have brought to the task all his customary efficiency, and what in a later age would have been called his management skills would have saved many lives. Viscount (Sir Henry) Hardinge, a clergyman's son, who had proved himself an exemplary staff officer in the early days at Torres Vedras in 1814, and had a second bout of success thirty years later in the Sikh wars of 1845, was now sixty-seven years old. The inadequate preparations for the Crimean War were laid at his door, and though his defenders would say that the deficiencies were not Hardinge's fault alone, he could scarcely be absolved of responsibility.

Lord Raglan was appointed Commander-in-Chief of the British Army, and Marshal Arnaud of the French (Arnaud died in September to be replaced by Canrobert). Although it is called the Crimean War, there were in fact three fronts: the Danube, the Crimea and the Baltic. In March 1854, the Queen, Prince Albert and the four eldest children saw a 'never to be forgotten sight', the fleet sailing from Spithead. 'My prayers will ever attend my great and splendid Navy!' the Queen told her journal,[3] as they sailed off to the Baltic (there was an early thaw that year) on an abortive and ill-prepared naval campaign against Russia. They failed to enlist the help of Sweden, which had been part of the plan, and by summer, this battle-front had been abandoned. Things proceeded with apparently more success in Turkey. Gallipoli and Constantinople were secured, and in July the decision was taken to enter the Black Sea and head for the Crimea, the aim being to hold the Russians in their own territory by a siege of Sevastopol. There were 80,000 Russian troops amassing in the Crimean peninsula. The British force was about 26,000, the French about 30,000 and the Turks 5,000. By the time autumn had set in, the troops, ill-equipped and badly prepared, were beginning to suffer the consequences of poor food and lack of cleanliness. Disease was sweeping through the ranks.

Raglan's initial assault on the Russians on the banks of the River Alma were victorious – though there were setbacks: the French found all their equipment had been left on the wrong side of the river. It was a defeat in the field for the Russians, but Raglan took no prisoners, allowing the Russians to straggle away and take refuge in Sevastopol. The Russians, who had begun to think they would dig in at Sevastopol for the winter, realized that they would be besieged unless they attacked. Early in the morning of 25 October, they made a surprise assault on the British garrison in the port of Balaklava.

Raglan had given orders that, in the event of an attack at Balaklava, two divisions should be moved down from the windswept plateau above the port. Raglan's divisional commander, Lord Lucan, moved the cavalry further inland, to the top of a valley. His brother-in-law, one of the most detested officers in the army, was Lord Cardigan, loathed by his men for many reasons, not least that, rather than endure the hardships of the soldiers on land, he always slept aboard his luxurious yacht in Balaklava harbour. Two remarkable charges took place during the Battle of Balaklava. The first was when the Heavy Brigade charged uphill against 3,000 Russian cavalrymen.

The second charge happened by accident. Raglan told Lucan to send his cavalry to recapture some guns seized by the Russians. Lucan took the order to mean that he should ride a mile and a quarter distant to attack the Russian guns. The order was brought to Lucan by a Captain Nolan. With the absurd courage of the hunting field, Cardigan and his men cantered into the Russian guns. While Nolan desperately gesticulated, trying to stop them, he was shot down. Cardigan's Light Brigade took the Russian guns but at terrible cost. Of the 673 horesemen who began the charge, 113 were killed, 134 wounded; 475 of the horses were killed and 42 wounded.

A little over a week later, the Russians attempted another attack, this time further up the plateau at Inkermann. By now the weather was wintry. There was thick fog, and 12,000 Russians were killed, and some 2,500 British. Ten days later, blizzards more or less blew the British camps away, the hospital marquees were destroyed and the ships in the harbour were all but wrecked by bad weather. By the time the siege of Sevastopol had begun, cholera had swept through the British and French armies, 14,000 men were in Florence Nightingale's hospital at Scutari, back on the other side of the Black Sea in the outskirts of Constantinople, and the situation on both sides was desperate.

The Queen, watching from home, noted how the war began as a prodigiously popular thing; but this was the first war at which photographers, and a good war reporter (William Russell of *The Times*), had been present. When the inefficiency, and the sickness, and the sheer horror of the conflict became known, the public turned their wrath on the politicians.

The Queen's journal conveyed little of this. She wrote always with a consciousness that she was the Queen. When the first news came in of the Battle of Balaklava, she was 'much annoyed'[4] that such setbacks had been reported in the newspapers. Then, when the telegraphic dispatch reached Windsor, during dinner on 11 November, her natural talent as a diarist photographed the scene. 'It was a curious sight to see everyone listening to the Despatch, (which was printed) the Gentlemen all standing in a group round the one of them who was reading & all, listening with such interest and anxiety.'[5] Then, she told the tale to her journal, as Tennyson would immortalize it in his poem on the Charge of the Light Brigade, and as the English have been telling it to themselves ever since: 'All behaved like heroes, & not one better than poor Lord Cardigan, who led them to the murderous fight... I trembled with emotions, as well as pride, in reading the recital of the heroism of these devoted men.'[6]

Ten days after they heard the news of the Charge of the Light Brigade, it was the Princess Royal's fourteenth birthday. Throughout this war, happening so far away, the Queen's domestic life went on undisturbed.

Vicky's birthday ('a clever, warm-hearted child') was spent at Windsor. The Queen spent the day quietly with the children and 'sketched Gouramma'. This was her god-daughter, the Princess Gouramma, now Victoria Gouramma, of Coorg. Her father, the deposed rajah, driven from his lands in Southern India, had for a while resided at Benares. In 1852, the rajah brought Gouramma, then aged eleven, to London and offered her to the Queen for adoption 'if the Queen would take charge of my daughter & treating her with honour and kindness grant her an education complete in every respect & suitable to her rank, and bring her up according to English customs in the Christian faith'.[7] It was a tall order, but the Queen always felt sheepish about the deposed Indian maharajahs whose wealth had been seized by the East India Company. At first she replied to the rajah that 'it would not be in accordance with the usages of this Country that Her Majesty should take the charge of his daughter'.[8] The India Board offered to pay for the upbringing of the child and to pay him a stipend while he was in England. Prince Albert suggested giving the rajah £40 per month for the child,[9] and the rajah's response was that 'your Majesty has been graciously pleased to grant me much more than I prayed for with regard to my little daughter'.[10] It was suggested that the child be made a ward in chancery of Sir James West Hogg, baronet, chairman of the East India Company. This was not quite what the rajah had in mind. He felt that a 'lady of rank' should be found to look after the child. Moreover, the little girl was staying with her father in an hotel. The culture shock was mighty. He complained of 'people lurking in the passages to see her', and threatened that if she were further 'humiliated', he would have no alternative but to put her to death.[11]

The background was as painful as any colonial story could be. On the one hand, the Rajah of Coorg was getting a very poor deal from the East India Company. He had provided the British with 'many thousands' of his own subjects, to act as coolies for the Bombay army; he had supplied 'upwards of 3,000 pack bullocks... 40,000 bottles of rice, 5 elephants, and 3,000 sheep. <u>For all these supplies the Raja received no pecuniary indemnification.</u>'[12]

There could be no doubt that the rajah had been swindled by the Company. On the other hand, he was no saint. Evidence had been collected of atrocities perpetrated under his regime. Lord William Bentinck had decided, as far back as 1834, that 'the interests of humanity' would be served by removing a man who, though open and friendly in his manner and a skilled horseman, performed such cruelties as forcing his subjects to act as human stockades around wild elephants during his hunting expeditions. Any who let the elephants escape were put to death. One witness, Richard Royle, 'himself a half-caste', said that he had been present when twenty-five heads were chopped off in one session at the rajah's command, and he knew of sixty families where daughters had been hastily married off to absolutely anyone to avoid their being recruited into the rajah's overcrowded seraglio.[13]

Little Gouramma had hardly grown up in the sedate atmosphere of Vicky, Bertie and the other royal children at Windsor. The Queen agreed to stand godmother to the child, who was baptized by Sumner, the Crumpet, in the chapel at Buckingham Palace on 1 July 1852. It was no hole-in-corner affair. Lord John Russell's clergyman half-brother, Lord Wriothsley Russell, and Dean Gerald Wellesley, the nephew of the Duke of Wellington, assisted. The princess was, in effect, adopted by an Indian army couple, Major and Mrs Drummond, who took her riding, read her *Gulliver's Travels* and tried to make her have the enthusiasms of an upper-class Scottish aristocrat. To some extent they succeeded, but Princess Victoria Gouramma was neither a demure nor a healthy person. Coquettish from the moment of her arrival in Britain, by the time she was sixteen the Drummonds found her as interested in stable boys as in ponies, more than once finding her wrapped in the arms of a groom. At the Juvenile Ball held at Buckingham Palace in April 1856, Gouramma danced merrily with the boys, and clearly attracted the Prince of Wales, but this was the first time she began to cough blood.

The Queen, who was really only a puritan when it came to considering the behaviour of her own children, never lost her affection for the Indian princess, however much of a scamp she was. For a confirmation present, she gave her a coral and diamond necklace, hoping 'that these ornaments, instead of gratifying the vanity of the young Princess, may serve, when she looks at them, to remind her of the high duties and responsibilities which she has taken upon her'.[14] The hope was a little optimistic. Some time in 1859, her father gave her a bag of jewels, before expiring and being buried in Kensal Green. The Drummonds, slightly unable to cope with the princess's latest attachment (to an under-butler), applied to the Queen, who was entirely unshocked by the girl's amorous propensities and merely recommended that they take her on a continental tour.

Gouramma was not the only Indian child in whom the Queen took an interest. In 1854, the Maharajah Duleep Singh, the Lion of the Punjab, had arrived in England. He was a charming boy, as Hardinge had observed when bringing the Kingdom of the Punjab to an end, at the close of the last Sikh wars in 1850, and appropriating Duleep Singh's greatest treasure, the Koh-i-Noor, which means 'Mountain of Light'. This enormous uncut diamond, the size of a pigeon's egg, had for generations been passed from conqueror to conqueror as a symbol of power in the Punjab. By stealing it for the Queen, Hardinge made a significant gesture, demonstrating – if further demonstration were required – that the British regarded themselves as lords of the Indian subcontinent.

When Duleep Singh was presented to Queen Victoria in July 1854, she felt decidedly embarrassed, and in later years, when the Koh-i-Noor had been recut, she felt shy of letting the maharajah see it. She was instantaneously enchanted by the boy who was as beautiful as he was charming, and it was fortunate that the young maharajah had arrived when Winterhalter was in England. The great painter was immediately commissioned to immortalize Duleep Singh in his youthful beauty. The painting, which hangs in a corridor at Osborne House, is one of Winterhalter's best.

Duleep Singh, who grew up to become a country squire, with a large estate at Elveden, Suffolk, and a shoot much enjoyed by the Prince of Wales, had been baptized already, so there was no need, as in the case of Gouramma, to get bishops into Buckingham Palace to perform that ceremony. Until his 'mid-life-crisis', when he reverted to the Sikh religion, he was a practising member of the Church of England. The Queen's hope was that Gouramma would marry her new protégé, but Duleep, at this stage at any rate, was too strait-laced for her, and when the pair were introduced, at Lord Normanby's seat of Mulgrave Castle, it was not a success. At that house party, however, Singh introduced her to a Thackeravian roué called Colonel John Campbell. Meanwhile, the diligent Drummonds pursued an unsuccessful legal case against the East India Company to restore the maharajah's appropriated property. A child was born to the marriage, but it was not a happy union. Princess Gouramma died of consumption, in not very salubrious lodgings in Jermyn Street.

Colonel Campbell was seen slipping out of the house carrying a bag, presumably of the maharajah's jewels. The Queen kept up with the daughter, whose name was Edith.

But all this was far in the future, and, as she sat sketching the fourteen-year-old Princess Gouramma, the Queen's mind was on the war.

The dispatches in the press told a terrible story, which the public was not slow to grasp. It was not simply that tens of thousands of young men had been killed for no purpose, nor that many of them were languishing with disease in appalling conditions. This news, utterly distressing as it was, could almost have been endured had the accumulation of mistakes and disasters not trumpeted to the world that Britain was no longer capable of fighting a European war. The implications of this would take years to sink in, especially among the military top brass; but the stinging shame was almost immediate. When a radical MP, James Roebuck, put down a motion of censure on the Government's handling of the war, the Foreign Secretary, Lord John Russell, resigned that very evening, and Aberdeen's credibility, never strong, was in tatters. When his ministry fell, the Queen asked Lord Derby if he could come back and form a coalition War Cabinet, but was not able to do so. Little as Prince Albert (and to a lesser extent the Queen) wanted to admit it, there was one man whom the public wanted as Prime Minister, and only one man who could form a Cabinet. With one very short interruption (in 1858), he would be the Prime Minister for the next ten years.

The agitation in the Queen's journal, as in the parliamentary world at large, before this *fait* became *accompli*, reads like one of Trollope's political novels. 'Much overpowered by the state of affairs, which is in the highest degree fatiguing, exciting and worrying,' she wrote on 2 February, when Albert was still hoping against hope that Lord Lansdowne, Russell, anyone, might form a Government rather than his old enemy. The next day, Lord Palmerston came in person to

Buckingham Palace and told Queen Victoria he was 'at my orders'. The reverse was true, and she and the prince, a little oddly in the circumstances, decamped to Windsor. Lord Clarendon had already told them that he would not 'step over the dead bodies of colleagues in order to join the man who had killed them'.[15] The next day, with the blood still dripping from his dagger, Palmerston wrote to the Queen that he was in the position to form a Government. He further informed her that the Peelites were no longer prepared to serve under Aberdeen – a fact which she found 'startling' and 'incomprehensible'.[16] Palmerston was demonstrating to her in no uncertain way that his presentations of humble duty, his attendance upon the sovereign's orders, were a mere form of words. He was the one who now exercised power in Britain. He did so under his sovereign, but there was no resisting that power. He promised her that he would try to negotiate a peaceful end to the war, and that he would not massacre all the Russians in Sevastopol. 'That so good a government has been able to be formed is entirely owing to my dear kind, excellent friend, Lord Aberdeen, but to change <u>him</u> for Lord Palmerston is somewhat of a <u>trial</u>,' she told herself. 'Still, as matters now stand, it was decidedly the right and wise course to take.'[17]

Albert had been urging the Cabinet for months to bring in two measures – the completion of the militia by ballot, and the enlistment of foreign mercenaries. Both ideas were rejected. He then pointed out to them the incredible fact that there was no system of regular returns or statements from the Crimea about the numbers of men available for action, or what supplies they required – horses, clothing, guns, ammunition. Albert urged such a policy upon the Secretary of State for War, the Duke of Newcastle, but with little immediate effect. The message, however, did get through. When the duke resigned in February 1855, Lord Panmure, his replacement in Palmerston's Cabinet, wrote to Lord Raglan in the Crimea in words which echoed the prince's memorandum precisely.

By the time Palmerston became Prime Minister only a little more than half the British troops who had been dispatched to the Crimea still survived. Less than a month after Palmerston kissed his sovereign's hands as premier, the Russian Emperor, hearing the news of yet another setback in the war (the failure of the attack on Eupatoria), succumbed to a minor illness and died. He had lost the will to live. The war, which had been so popular in England twelve months before, was now seen to be the pointless, bloody mess which the peace party had always predicted. The arrival of Palmerston as Prime Minister did not please either Albert or Victoria, but they had no choice in the matter, and relations between the new premier and the Court, at least in the matter of war policy, was unclouded by personal animosity. Now that Pam had what he wanted – unbridled power – he became more amiable to them. In one aspect at least, Palmerston acknowledged Albert's help. When Lord Raglan died in June 1855, it was obvious that the most suitable replacement was General Codrington, but there were three other generals with higher claims of seniority. Albert suggested that the British force be divided into two army corps, and that two of the senior generals be given command of each corps under Codrington's supervision. 'I and all the other members of the Cabinet feel greatly obliged to your Royal Highness,' wrote Palmerston, 'for having suggested an arrangement which had not occurred to any of us.'[18] It was a moment which might have reminded some Cabinet members that the old Duke of Wellington had thought so highly of the prince that he had proposed, in 1850, that Albert should succeed him as Commander-in-Chief.

There was not much which was amusing about the war, but one delightful consequence of the military alliance between France and Britain was the friendship which blossomed between the two Heads of State. The State Visit to Britain of Napoleon III and the Empress Eugénie in April 1855 was, in Victoria's words, 'a most curious page of history'.[19] The night before the imperial pair's arrival, Prince Albert ate 'a small dinner' at Windsor Castle: already, the ominous signs were apparent that moments of stress and tension disrupted his already weak digestion. He went to spend the night in Dover, and the next day, through a thick fog on the Channel, the Emperor and his wife arrived, to be conducted directly to Windsor. Both prince and Queen had gone to immense labour to ensure that the apartments were furnished appropriately. Only on the 13th, they had received a visit from the exiled Queen Marie-Amélie and Clém, and watched them drive away 'in a plain coach with four miserable coach horses'.²⁰ By the 15th, they had put the finishing touches to the room, 'all hung with red satin, with the fine old pictures, handsome furniture, & a really beautiful bed, with feathers at the top of the canopy, the same as it was when it was in George IV's State bedroom'.²¹ However much she had loved her Orléanist relations, Victoria was realistic enough to know that furniture, pictures, gold knives and forks and a state banquet must be used to reflect the political realities, and a profound change had taken place in European politics.

When Prince Albert arrived at the Castle with Napoleon and Eugénie, there was a guard of honour waiting for them. The band could scarcely play the republican anthem, 'La Marseillaise', in such a setting, so they played the old Napoleon's march which had been composed by Napoleon III's mother, 'Partant pour la Syrie'. It is a song about a crusader departing for the Holy Land, so perhaps its pseudo-medieval piety was a bow in the direction of Napoleon's provocative gift of the Silver Star to the Bethlehem shrine.

The Queen felt stage fright before the imperial arrival, and was half-reassured to notice, when the Empress Eugénie arrived at Windsor, that she too was 'evidently very nervous'. The nerves evaporated, however, and certainly as far as Queen Victoria and the imperial pair were concerned, what had begun as an official occasion melted into a personal friendship. It was not just flannel when, in his thank-you letter for the visit, the Emperor spoke of the impossibility of spending a few days in her intimate circle without being overwhelmed by her charm.²² Perhaps one of the reasons biographers return so often to the subject of Queen Victoria is that her extreme diffidence, and stiffness when shy, and abrasiveness when riled could make her seem to many people an unsympathetic figure. When she was engaged with another personality, the charm was total. The Victoria resented by Conroy and the Victoria loved by Lehzen were almost two different girls; the Victorias seen by Melbourne and Peel (in his early days) were, likewise, two different people, one a playful coquette, eager to learn the political game from a flirtatious elder; the other a stubborn, politically stupid person who unsuccessfully stamped her foot and played the tyrant.

The little emperor – even Victoria, at less than five feet in height, considered him 'extremely short' – was a peculiar sight, 'with a head and bust, which ought to belong to a much taller man'.[23] He knew how to be charming, however, and he had the classic, 'come closer' seducer's manner of speaking very quietly to women. The Queen almost had to brush his cheek to hear what he was saying at their first dinner in the Castle, and discovered that 'we got on extremely well… & my agitation soon & easily went off'.[24] Napoleon told her that he had first seen her eighteen years earlier, when she was proroguing Parliament, and it had made a deep impression to watch '*une jeune personne*' exercising that role. He asked tenderly after Queen Marie-Amélie and told Victoria that the exiled Queen was at liberty to cross France unmolested, if she wished to make the journey from her brother-in-law in Belgium to her brother in Spain. Since the Emperor was well read in the works of Scott, he and the Queen could discuss the Waverley novels and Bonnie Prince Charlie. The next day there was a military review in Windsor Great Park of infantry and cavalry who had been serving in the Crimea. Among them were a dozen fine horses which the Emperor had sent from France as a present to Victoria. Himself on horseback, Napoleon was presented to the 'hero' of Balaklava, Lord Cardigan.

Even as the royal personages got to know one another in Windsor, the Great Powers were again assembling in Vienna to negotiate an end to the war. Britain, France and Austria demanded a reduction of Russian naval power, but as long as Sevastopol held out, the

Russians refused to accept this. There continued to be threatening
ship movements in the Baltic throughout the summer.

When Napoleon and Eugénie went into London the next day, the
crowds were immense. The beauty and stylishness of the Empress
were immediately attractive. This was the first time London had seen
a woman in a crinoline dress, grey with black lace and pink bows, and
a wreath of pink chrysanthemums in her red hair.[25]

Victoria and Albert took their guests to the opera – *Fidelio* – where
the orchestra struck up 'Partant pour la Syrie', and where, at the end
of the performance, the chorus sang a specially composed verse of the
National Anthem. *The Times* thought it should have been sung as a
solo by the great Jenny Lind:

> Emperor and Empress
> O Lord, be pleased to bless
> Look on this scene!
> And may we ever find
> With bonds of peace entwined
> England and France combined
> God save the Queen!

It would have been difficult to say, exactly, what the words meant,
but the sentiments of entente cordiale were impossible to mistake.
The Emperor had taken the visit to the opera as an opportunity
to tell the Queen all about his experiences in London as a Special
Constable, perhaps to distract her attention from the distress of the
prisoners in chains. Only one Londoner raised a protest at Napoleon's
autocratic style of government – a bookseller called Truelove in the
Strand displayed the works of Victor Hugo in his window, including
a pamphlet denouncing Napoleon III and his undemocratic style
of politics. He was hardly noticed among the bunting, the flags, the
enthusiastic hordes. *The Times* reckoned that there were more than
100,000 people assembled to see the French ruler. On the day of
Napoleon's forty-seventh birthday, 20 April, little Prince Arthur, aged

five, presented him with a posy of violets, the Napoleonic emblem. Although the Crystal Palace had been reassembled at Sydenham, it was not yet open to the public, but Albert and Victoria took the imperial pair to a preview. Again, huge crowds assembled – over 20,000 on the terraces at Sydenham. Napoleon was wistful about Victoria's many children. He wrote in the album of the Prince of Wales a poem of his own composition in slightly wonky German, which could scarcely have been less appropriate, given the boy's subsequent development:

> *Jüngling mit der reinen Seele,*
> *Mit der Unschuld freiem* [sic] *Gefühle,*
> *Prüf und Wahle,*
> *Aber Lob sei nie dein Ziel!*
> *Ob dir Beifall jauchzt die Menge*
> *Ob sie lästrt, wanke nicht,*
> *Trüglich oft sind Preisgesänge,*
> *Doch des Wahrheit Pfad ist enge,*
> *Zwischen Klüften geht die Pflicht...*

('Young lad with the pure soul innocent and free! Make your choice, but may you never seek simple praise. Whether the crowd shouts applause to you, or whether it insults you, have no fear. Songs of praise are often deceiving, straight is the path of truth, Duty traces a path through narrow gaps.'[26])

There would be many a cuckolded husband, nightclub proprietress and casino croupier in later decades who would have raised an eyebrow at Bertie being described as a pure soul; but the song was right to predict that he would be a man of personal charm, with a gift of appealing to crowds. His inability to tread the path of duty would, however, be the despair of Queen Victoria, and, when he was old enough to have them, also the despair of his advisers.

How very unlike his father the Prince of Wales was growing up to be! The Queen had occasional spats with Prince Albert, and sometimes worse than spats – deep fallings-out. The pattern of her relationship with her husband, however, was docile and submissive. She (nearly always) deferred to him in matters of taste, and usually in matters of public policy. They remained, nevertheless, very different characters, and perhaps this was shown to glaring effect during their return visit to the Emperor Napoleon, who insisted upon repaying their hospitality.

They arrived in Paris in the broiling heat of August, a strange month to visit the French capital, since it is the month when all fashionable French society is out of town. Nevertheless, there were huge crowds. The royal pair were accommodated in the Palais de Saint-Cloud. Pictures had been brought from the Louvre to show that the French could rival the royal collection at Windsor. The Empress Eugénie had had works by Rubens, Van Dyck, Andrea del Sarto and Madame Vigée Le Brun hung on the Queen's bedroom walls.

The Queen immediately gave herself up to the delights of the Parisian visit – the happy crowds, the luxurious foods, the enter-tainments all delighted her. They went to the opera and displayed the difference between a true-born queen and a parvenue empress. When the national anthems had been played, the Empress looked behind her to make sure that her chair was in place. The Queen of England, confident that the chair would be there, sat down without turning. Mary Bulteel, her Maid of Honour who noticed this detail, was also able to reassure Eugénie's baffled entourage that the Queen was always 'badly dressed'. It did not prevent Victoria from being unaffectedly enraptured by Eugénie's range of gorgeous outfits. Victoria adored the Empress and it was a friendship which lasted for life. 'Altogether,' she told her diary, 'I am delighted to see how much my Albert likes and admires her, as it is so seldom I see him do so with any woman.'[27] Perhaps it was so, or perhaps he was being polite. The Queen's dowdiness and (by the exacting standards of Parisian journalists) poor dress sense were more than outshone by the splendour of her jewels.

The high point of the social week in Paris was the grand ball in the Hôtel de Ville, choreographed by the Prefect Baron Haussmann.

As they approached from the Palace of the Tuileries, the royal party came down a rue de Rivoli heavy with banners and dense with crowds cheering '*Vive La Reine!*' Housetops and balconies twinkled with Chinese lanterns and stars of gas. The Tours Saint-Jacques had been lit by electricity. In the square before the Hôtel de Ville were sixteen gigantic pyramids, each illuminated by variegated lamps. 'The air was as luminous and hot as that over a furnace from the blaze of gas,' said *The Times*.[28] No expense had been spared. A special staircase, a copy of that at Fontainebleau, had been erected by Haussmann. Beneath it were splashing fountains and naiads representing the Seine and the Thames. The courtyard, thickly carpeted, had been roofed with glass. All over the carpet, the ill-bred guests had dropped the envelopes from their invitation cards.[29] There were 8,000 guests in the overpowering heat. The dancing, which had begun at eight, paused, when the Emperor and the Queen took the floor to execute a quadrille. The crowds were patronizingly astonished by the delicacy and skill with which she danced.[30]

We know from Victoria's subsequent reflections (written at the time of the Franco-Prussian War of 1870) that Prince Albert had been reminded, on this visit to the French capital, of the worst excesses of Sodom and Gomorrah. Victoria was an owl, Albert was a lark, and he always found late nights wearisome. Moreover, the visit awoke in him melancholy memories of his boyhood. The Emperor and Empress took the Royal Family to see the ruins of Louis-Philippe's favourite summer residence, the Château de Neuilly, which had been destroyed in the Revolution of 1848. Albert had been brought here as a boy by his father. 'Nineteen years ago,' he wrote to his mother-in-law, 'I was in Paris with Ernst and Papa, and I have not been there since. You may imagine what a strange impression so many changes must have produced. Neuilly, where we were then received, now lies in ruins, and the grass grows upon its site. The Duke of Orleans was then alive and unmarried; Marie and Clementine, daughters of the house; Nemours, Aumale and Montpensier were at school; Joinville a naval cadet. All this is vanished as if before the wind, and in its stead, we brought with us two children, almost fully grown.'[31]

Vicky was fourteen, Bertie a year younger.

Three weeks after they returned from Paris, the Royal Family were in Balmoral, awaiting the arrival of the Prussian Crown Prince, Friedrich Wilhelm. The King of Prussia, Friedrich Wilhelm IV, was fully aware of the political dangers of what was intended. Prussia was pro-Russian, anti-French, and completely against the Crimean War. Nevertheless, he knew that his wife, Queen Augusta, had been in correspondence with Prince Albert, and that there would be advantages in a marriage between the Queen of England's eldest child and the heir to the most powerful of the German kingdoms. The Queen added to her own personal reflections and her husband's loftier dynastic dreams: the girl had, she told Queen Augusta, 'developed amazingly of late'. She spelt out that menstruation had begun earlier in the year, and that she 'did not suffer even the slightest indisposition'.[32]

Fritz, the figure who arrived at Balmoral, nine years older than his potential bride, had been reared, in true Hohenzollern style, as a soldier from boyhood. The twenty-three-year-old prince was accompanied by his aide de camp Colonel Helmuth von Moltke, a worldly socialite in his mid-fifties.

Vicky was late for dinner on the first evening. When he looked up at his prospective bride, Fritz saw a child in a white dress, tied with scarlet ribbons. She laughingly excused herself, and chatted merrily to him, sometimes in German, sometimes breaking into French. He noted that 'we looked at each other a great deal'.[33] As well they might. They had a very complicated journey to tread together.

She was an extremely intelligent person, and she was devoted to her father: the only one of the nine children with Albert's range of intellectual and imaginative gifts. The life which Prince Albert, Stockmar and Queen Victoria were plotting for the child was more difficult than they could possibly have foreseen, and much of the reason for this would be connected with the German politician they had met at the ball in Versailles – Otto von Bismarck.

The couple were sent for a walk on their own the next day up the slopes of Craig-na-Ban. Fritz picked her a sprig of white heather and they had their first kiss. That evening, Vicky ran into her mother's room, 'very much agitated', to say, 'I am very fond of the prince.' It did indeed turn out to be an arranged match, like that of Victoria and Albert themselves, which was also a love match. The Queen specified that they must wait until Vicky was seventeen years old.

The Crimean War dragged on much longer than any of the participants would have wanted. Sevastopol eventually fell, but only after the British had suffered an humiliating defeat at the Redan fortress. The British Army was losing between twenty and thirty soldiers a day to cholera; and although Cavour had persuaded Italy's King Victor Emmanuel to declare war on Russia, and send troops from Sardinia, and although Palmerston was trying to enlist some Swiss mercenaries, by the end of 1855, there simply was not the will to continue among the exhausted, disease-ridden troops. Palmerston asked the Archbishop of Canterbury for a National Day of Thanksgiving to be proclaimed on a Sunday in the near future. Sumner refused, rightly pointing out that the fall of Sevastopol was not, like the Battle of Waterloo (the last time such a Thanksgiving had been declared by the National Church), a decisive event, bringing an unambiguous end to the war. The Queen was disappointed that the war should end on a British setback. In the event, the Congress of Paris, which negotiated the terms of the peace, simply reiterated the six points which the supposedly 'wet' Lord Aberdeen had suggested two years earlier. If they had all been able to agree on those when proposed by Aberdeen, tens of thousands of lives would have been saved. But that is not the way that war or politics functions. The British public shared the Queen's disappointment that the war ended so unsatisfactorily. The heralds who proclaimed the peace in the City of London were hissed. It was the last really popular war in the British collective psyche. The cardigan, the Raglan overcoat and the balaclava are all reassuring garments. Most English towns have a street or a square which alludes to it: Alma Street, Inkermann Crescent, and the like. There are no Somme Streets, no Mons Squares.

Another Prime Minister would have been crushed by the humiliation of the Treaty of Paris, but Palmerston bluffed it out, announcing
it as a triumph to anyone who chose to believe him. Because he was
liked, many wanted to believe him. The Duke of Argyll felt that
the cheery manner in which the Prime Minister told the Cabinet
about the peace was a mask. If it was, it was successful, since the
inner doubt, angst or self-reproach, if these things were ever part of
Palmerston's nature, certainly did not show. Cheeriness, the capacity
to move on to the next thing, not too much concern for the truth,
these are wonderful assets in a statesman. There is more than one
way *encourager les autres*. The Queen had entirely come to overlook
Palmerston's defects. In April 1856, she awarded him the Order of the
Garter.

ELEVEN

'SCOLDER AND SCOLDED'

THE ENDING OF the Crimean War was a fudge; a compromise. It was to this extent a minor war. It wasn't like the ending of the 1914–18 War, when the whole world order was palpably changed forever. Nevertheless, the world had changed. France and Britain were now allies, for the first time in centuries, and this would have a powerful influence on the future. Britain had revealed itself as militarily incapable of decisive action in Europe: this too would have enormous consequences. Russia had been bloodied, but not crushed. Austria-Hungary, having stood on the sidelines in the war, was itself about to be sidelined by a more energetic, more modern, German-speaking power. Prussia, increasing monthly in industrial and military prowess, watched askance as her Royal Family allied its crown prince, Fritz, with the English princess (as she would be known in anti-English German newspapers).

Once the hostilities ceased, however, the Powers restored diplomatic relations, and the vital glue of royal familial relations played a large part in restoring normality. It was even possible to watch the Coronation in Moscow of Alexander II with some optimism. He was comparatively young, at thirty-seven years old. He was married to a German – a princess of Hesse-Darmstadt who had been rechristened as an Orthodox and become Maria Alexandrovna: but there was here a window into the West. He had travelled widely not only in Europe, but also in his own Empire – he was the first Russian Emperor of modern times to visit Siberia. He was destined to be known as Alexander the Liberator, for he would liberate the serfs. Fritz, Vicky's betrothed, was sent as the Prussian representative at the splendid Orthodox Coronation ceremony in the Cathedral of the Dormition in Moscow's Kremlin. In Russia, which was literally behind the times and had not yet adopted the sixteenth-century papalist Gregorian Calendar, it was 26 August. At Balmoral, it was 7 September. Prince Albert wrote to his future son-in-law,

> It is impossible to imagine a greater contrast than the way in which you and we are living: you in the Oriental splendour of the Moscow festivities and we in the quiet isolation of the Scottish Highlands... I understand that your future alliance is looked on askance in Russia... The German stands in the centre between England and Russia; his high culture and his philosophic love of truth drive him towards the English conception, his military discipline, his admiration of the asiatic greatness... which is achieved by merging of the individual into the whole, drives him in the other direction.[1]

It is clear from this very revealing letter that Prince Albert, for all his adoration of Vicky, was prepared to lose his most beloved daughter, and send her to live in Germany, in order to forward the Stockmar-inspired Coburg-federalist vision of a Europe in which Germany played the central role. Close as Albert was to the Queen – and no one could doubt their closeness – he was in some ways closer, intellectually, to the Princess Royal. She was his equal in terms of reading, intellectual passion and vision. As a grown-up, she would share his view of Europe blessed by an enlightened, liberal-conservative German centre. This would be based upon the varied states of the German *Vereinigung* coming together to form a single nation, if it could ever be decided whether Prussia or Austria would be the senior partner in such a confederation. Prussia was key, and

Prince Albert was placing the burden of influencing these political movements on a child of fourteen. It was, however, his best throw of the dice. He could scarcely have guessed, while still in his late thirties, how little time he had left to play international politics; but the Prussian match between Fritz and Vicky was by far the biggest catch of which he would be capable – it equalled in significance his grandmother Auguste's legerdemain, in engineering first Leopold's marriage to Princess Charlotte, and then, when that ended in premature death, the marriage of her daughter Victoire to Edward, Duke of Kent, thereby ensuring the Saxe-Coburg place at the head of the most powerful country in the world.

The Prince of Wales, at thirteen, was too young to marry, even by the almost oriental standards of the Royal House. To achieve absolute balance of power he could, perhaps, have been betrothed, in medieval fashion, to the new Russian emperor's most eligible daughter, Maria Alexandrovna: but she was not yet three years old. She must wait to be married to the English Prince Alfred when she grew up.

Queen Victoria, who believed herself to be the loyal wife who left the political thinking to her husband, was, by virtue of who she was, in a rather different position. She was three-quarters German; she looked, as Albert did, to King Leopold and to Stockmar for political guidance in European politics… but. There was always a 'but'. There was always the fact that she was also the Queen of England, working alongside her Prime Ministers, and conscious of Britain's position as an imperial power. This sense of the British dominions beyond Europe was sharpened by the Crimean debacle.

1856 was a dark year for the royal pair. The Queen felt depleted and fussed by having so many children. Naturally, she had help with them: indeed, during the daytime scarcely saw them, and only ate with them when they were almost grown-up. But she felt 'agitated'[2] when separated from them, and exhausted by them when they were present. Profoundly in love as she was with Albert (even when they were not in a state of harmony), she resented the children's intrusion upon her marital intimacy.

'It is indeed a pity,' Albert wrote to her in October 1856, 'that you find no consolation in the company of your children. The root of the difficulty lies in the mistaken notion that the function of a mother is to be always correcting, scolding, ordering them about and organizing their activities. It is not possible to be on friendly terms with people you have just been scolding, for it upsets scolder and scolded alike.'[3] On top of all this, there was the simple fact that being a conscientious Head of State involved a Herculean workload. The civil service and the diplomatic service were, by modern standards, skeletal. Huge quantities of paperwork, which in a modern constitutional monarchy would pass through one of the Government ministries, came to the Queen, at least notionally for her approval or comment. Colonel Phipps, who was doing three jobs – Keeper of the Privy Purse, Treasurer to Prince Albert and Cofferer to the Prince of Wales – was receiving 14,000 letters a year.[4] The prince, who attributed the Queen's short temper and volatile mood swings to pressure of work, told Sir James Clark, her doctor, that although he personally now drafted all the Queen's official correspondence, she had to copy it out, since the letters – to Prime Ministers, ambassadors, the commander-in-chief of the army, and so on – had to bear at least the appearance of having come from her. The prince also retained the fear to the end of his life that he would make mistakes in his written English, and would bring his drafts to the Queen saying, '*Ich habe Dir hier ein Draft gemacht lese es mal… ich dächte es wäre recht so?*' ('I have made a draft here – read it through – is it all right?') 'So few faults were there to be found,'[5] the Queen recalled, which shows us that, even through her rose-tinted spectacles, Albert's written work was noticeably not that of an English-speaker.

The doctor, whom she regarded as 'that kind fatherly old friend',[6] was evidently as worried as all the older generation were by the possibility that the Queen's volatility might be an early-warning signal of her grandfather George III's insanity about to burst out. On 5 February 1856, he noted, 'Queen's health has not improved. She has complained of feeling weaker than usual more especially of late, &

has been at times frequently low & nervous. I have never seen her weaker than this day... I feel at times uneasy regarding the Queen's mind unless she is kept quiet and still amused, the time will come when she will be in danger. She told me today that if she had another child, she would sink under it. I too have my fears, but they are more for the effect on the mind than the health.'[7]

Needless to say, within four months of making this dramatic prediction, the Queen had gone down to Osborne in sweltering weather. On the Isle of Wight, her children – who in Buckingham Palace were only a worry – seemed delightful. Affie was twelve years old. Little Prince Arthur charmed everyone. The weather was tropical, calm and hot. At night they sat out on the terrace, and in the mornings, after late rising, they breakfasted in the Alcove.[8] She became pregnant again – this was the last time – and Princess Beatrice, always called 'Baby' by her mother – was born on 14 April 1857.

A glimpse of the volatile, downright irrational behaviour which troubled the kind old doctor can be seen in one of Albert's many letters to her, written that autumn:

> I don't yet know why my question, while we were slowly and quietly reading the Princess's letter, 'what makes you so bitter?' produced such an outburst. It is my duty to keep calm, and I mean to do so, but unkindness or ingratitude towards others makes me angry, like any other kind of immorality. Fritz is prepared to devote his whole life to our child – whom you are thankful to be rid of – and because of that you turn against him: Stockmar, who has shown us nothing but kindness for as long as we can remember, is suddenly asked, old and ill as he is, to drag himself over here, and his coming is taken as an offence. This is not a question of bickering, but of attitudes of mind, which will agree as little as oil and water, and it is no wonder that our conversations on the subject cannot end harmoniously. I am trying to keep out of your way until your better feelings have returned and you have regained control of yourself.[9]

This was one of the many rows about Vicky. Naturally, in 1856–7, it was the two eldest children who occupied the minds of the parents. Bertie was the despair of his tutor, Mr Gibbs. Idle, and with a poor attention span, he caused his serious-minded parents 'immense anxiety!'[10] For her clever firstborn, Victoria felt no such worries, but her emotions about Vicky were complex, and the fact that they were contradictory did not prevent her feeling them very strongly. First, she felt the classic envy which mothers so often feel for a daughter, on the verge of womanhood, who deeply engages the emotions of her father. There were tensions between the mother and daughter. The Queen complained of Vicky's 'wayward temper, her want of self-control, sharp answers – contradictoriness & dislike of any observation'[11] – which makes one want to ask, 'Yes, but what observations were you making?'

Then again, Victoria was in awe of the princess's cleverness – again, something which bound her more closely to her father than to her mother. In other moods, the Queen felt about Vicky, who was only twenty-one years younger, 'more as if it were my sister rather than my child'.[12] At the same time, she felt the inevitable cluster of emotions which passes through the mind of any parent confronting a daughter's loss of virginity – 'she will no longer be an innocent girl – but a wife – & – perhaps, this time next year already a mother!'[13] and the no less painful realization that, once Vicky was married and living abroad, 'she will return but for a short time, almost as a visitor!'[14]

At the same time, the Queen was capable of realizing that these worries were only a magnified version of what all parents worry about as their children are growing up, and could not be compared with true horrors. There were plenty of those in the world, and in 1857, attention was focused on India. Britain's infiltration into the entire subcontinent had been gradual and piecemeal. The commercial interests of the East India Company; the military need to drive out the French (from the mid-eighteenth century onwards); the zeal of Christian missionaries to convert Hindus, Sikhs and Muslims to membership of the Church of England: all these things coalesced in India in the decades after the Napoleonic Wars. Little by little, India ceased to be a collection of independent princedoms and kingdoms in which the British exercised influence, and became 'British India', with a British Governor-General ruling from Calcutta. A key moment in the history of modern India was in the 1830s when, acting upon the recommendation of Thomas Babington Macaulay, the historian who joined the Council of the East India Company as law member in 1834, the Company decreed that English become the common language of India. It replaced Persian as the language of the Higher Courts, and thereafter, the British felt more entrenched in their positions as the Governors of India.[15]

The ending of the Crimean War did not altogether diminish British paranoia about the possibility of Russia infiltrating India from Afghanistan. Russian influence had been growing in Persia, decade by decade, and it was a fear which would only be fully overridden when, in the early years of the twentieth century, the British began to fear German infiltration, possibly by an extension of the Berlin–Baghdad railroad.

There was never a time in the nineteenth century when matters in India were entirely stable, and in the mid- to late 1850s, many areas were ripe for trouble. The outbreaks of Indian resistance to the British, known for decades afterwards as the Indian Mutiny, did occur, at first, as a piece of simple military insubordination; it was Indian insubordination in reaction to gross insensitivity on the British part. The East India Company had at its disposal an army of 238,000, of whom 38,000 were European. Each presidency or locality had its own army, and the only part affected by the Mutiny was that of Bengal, with 151,000 troops, 23,000 of whom were Europeans. Very many of the sepoy, or Indian, officers in this army were of high caste, Brahmins or Rajputs, down on their luck, and pursuing careers as army officers *faute de mieux* (the British having in many cases appropriated Indian land and property).

Two new measures were brought in at about the time that Dalhousie (a relatively successful Governor-General) was replaced by

Lord Canning (son of the statesman who was briefly Prime Minister in 1827). One of these hated measures was that members of these local armies would no longer be confined to their own areas and might be required for service anywhere in the world, not just in India. The other was the introduction of Enfield rifles. It came to be known that the cartridges for the new guns had been greased with the fat of cows and/or pigs. It was a symptom of the volatility of the times that this story was so widely believed, even though it was not immediately denied or confirmed. In fact, at the Woolwich Arsenal, animal fat had been used to grease the cartridges and, naturally – no Hindus or Muslims living in Woolwich at that date – no one had thought to consider what would happen when a Muslim or Hindu officer was asked to bite off the end of a cartridge, before loading. The casual way in which the British expected a Muslim to let pig-fat touch his lips, or a Hindu beef-dripping, was what caused the outrage, as much as the forbidden meat-substances themselves.

By the beginning of 1857, the authorities realized the danger of the situation. All further orders for cartridges from England were cancelled until it could be made clear that they did not contain forbidden grease. But unrest had begun – first in Barrackpore, near Calcutta, in January, and gradually spreading to Meerut and elsewhere. By May, the 'mutineers' had taken Delhi. At Jahnsi, British men, women and children were butchered by sepoy regiments. At Cawnpore, the British Governor Sir Hugh Wheeler was confident in the loyalty of Nana Sahib, the local Indian bigwig, but the place was surrounded by sepoys. When food supplies ran low, Wheeler accepted the offer from the treacherous Nana of safe conduct down the river for the 400 or so women and children. As soon as they had left, the remaining European men were shot, and the women's boats were then fired on. When brought to shore, many of the women and children were killed with sabres. The rest were imprisoned in hideous conditions, and in spite of the protests of sepoy officers, they were, on the Nana's orders, hacked to pieces and thrown down a well.

It remains a matter of contention between scholars whether the tragic events of 1857 were the first rumblings of Indian nationalism, or merely localized expressions of outrage. Lord Aberdeen himself said, in August 1857, 'The important question which is not yet clearly answered, is whether the revolt is a military mutiny, or a national movement. Should it be the latter, our tenure cannot be very secure.'[16]

When the news of the Mutiny began to filter through to the West, the Queen, along with everyone else in England, read the accounts with mounting disgust.

> Oh! When I think & talk of my own sorrows... & reflect on the fearful appalling horrors wh. have taken place in India, & on the hundreds of families who have lost sons – Husbands – brothers – & what is so infinitely worse had daughters – sisters – wives – (I hope few have survived this [illegible]) & friends murdered, butchered, tortured – with a refinement of fiendish atrocity wh. one couldn't believe – & exposed to every outrage wh. a woman must dread more than death and wh. makes me tremble – how unbearably small does every suffering of ours appear![17]

As the Queen read 'dreadful details in the papers of the horrors committed in India on poor ladies & children',[18] they prepared for an informal visit of the Emperor and Empress of France to Osborne. Eugénie looked 'lovely in a light organdie dress, embroidered all over with violets, a wreath to match, in her hair, and pearls'.[19] Palmerston came to stay for a few days, bringing Clarendon, the Foreign Secretary, while the Empress and Prince Albert were locked in talk with Napoleon about 'Principalities, – difficulties, – rapprochements, alliance, &c.', as the Queen noted rather vaguely. On the Sunday of his visit, Napoleon III went into Newport for Mass at the Roman Catholic church, accompanied by his much more pious wife this time looking 'lovely in simple white embroidered cambric dress, with lilac ribbons'.[20] The wistfulness with which Victoria described

Eugénie's outfits whenever the two met is touching. She was the Queen of England and could have afforded the finest couturier; but she was tiny, increasingly rotund, much of the time depressed or petulant. Her homely dress sense reflected a growing dissatisfaction with her appearance: clothes were for swathing a body which was by any ordinary standards a very peculiar shape, not for adorning it or drawing it to people's attention. Albert was beginning to grow bald and to develop a paunch. Youth was very definitely, and somewhat prematurely, behind them. On 25 August, she told her journal she had 'talked much of its being my adored one's last evening when 37! Every "Lebens Abschnitt" [phase of life] makes one sad, when one is so blessed as I am'.[21] Young as they both were, from now onwards there are strange gusts of cold in the atmosphere, coming from time to time, as if they half sensed the coming of calamity.

Later in the year, the Queen and the Prince Consort, while in Scotland, went to stay as the guests of Lord Aberdeen at Haddo. In true old Highland fashion, he assembled all his tenants on horseback to welcome her: some 600 of them escorted her to the fine Georgian house which struck her, with her more 'baronial' tastes, as 'plain, about 100 years old'.[22] She had recently bestowed on the bony old Scottish peer the Order of the Garter. Although she did the same for Palmerston, it was surely a token of the Prince Consort's misgivings about Pam's swashbuckling foreign policy that they should also have honoured the quieter, more pacific Aberdeen.

While the young Princess Royal spent her last summer and autumn with her family in Britain, the British were fighting for the reclaim of the ancient capital (Muslim and Hindu at different phases) of Delhi. It was a desperate campaign, culminating in six days of heavy street fighting, during which Brigadier-General John Nicholson was killed. Some 30,000 mutineer troops were eventually scattered to surrounding hill villages, and when the British reclaimed Delhi, the danger of the Mutiny was over. What remained was what has sometimes euphemistically been called the 'cleaning up' or 'clearing up' operation.

The Queen felt more nervous on the day of her first daughter's wedding than she had on her own nuptial day.[23] Vicky was now just a few weeks past her seventeenth birthday. She was dressed in a white silk moiré gown over a petticoat flounced in lace and wreathed in sprays of orange blossom and myrtle.[24] Orange blossom symbolizes eternal love and fruitful marriage; myrtle bestows good luck in marriage. Vicky had the good luck to marry a man who loved her and whose love was fervently returned; but there was not much else which was lucky about the marriage – she was going into a country which was hostile to her; her children were to cause her grief; and her beloved Fritz would die hideously.

On the wedding day, however, the message of the flowers was almost convincing. On that brilliantly sunny winter day, the streets between Buckingham Palace and the Chapel Royal in St James's Palace were thronged with crowds. In the chapel itself, there was Lord Palmerston bearing the Sword of State, and a very nervous Archbishop of Canterbury. The young couple spoke their vows clearly, and they were the first British royal pair to leave the altar steps to the air of Mendelssohn's 'Wedding March'. They were also the first, before a wedding breakfast in the Palace, to appear on the balcony to wave to the crowds. In spite of the presence at the breakfast of old Lotharios such as the Prime Minister and Uncle Leopold, the bride's parents must have felt vindicated. Their Respectable Revolution, after the dissipated days of Duke Ernst in Coburg and William IV in London, was now complete. A respectable pair had spawned another respectable pair, and the crowds who cheered them could return to respectable homes, feeling that the monarchy and the decent majority had buried forever the scandalous days of the past. No one needed to know that when Fritz's mother, Princess Augusta of Prussia, had entered the chapel accompanied by two ladies-in-waiting, one of these women, Countess Louise Oriola (dressed garishly in bright orange), was one of the several mistresses of Prince Wilhelm – the groom's father. Later that evening, London lit up, with illuminations twinkling from the major public buildings and fireworks exploding in the parks as the bridal pair took the train to Windsor.

Her last day at home was 1 February. Vicky told her mother, 'I think it will kill me to take leave of Papa!'[25] But Albert was calm. 'Vicky is very reasonable,' he wrote to his brother Ernst, 'she will go well-prepared into the labyrinth of Berlin.'[26] They left in thick snow, and floods of tears, from Gravesend in the Royal Yacht *Victoria and Albert* on 2 February.

Queen Victoria's mother had done it; Queen Adelaide had done it; it was the lot of royal women to be exported, for political purpose, into strange courts and foreign worlds. Vicky at least took with her a husband she loved, and a perfect understanding of his language. (It was indeed the language in which she had habitually spoken to her father.) Posterity, while reserving tender thoughts for the young teenager snatched from home and put into the truly frightening world of Bismarck ('who was never ill, but once lost a tooth biting through the hind leg of a hare'[27]) and the Prussian Court, can nevertheless be grateful, since the separation necessitated the beginning of one of the most fascinating exchanges of letters in history. To Prince Albert, Vicky wrote, 'I thought my heart was going to break when you shut the cabin door and were gone – that cruel moment which I had been dreading even to think of for 2 years and a half were past – it was more painful than I had ever pictured it to myself.'[28]

Prince Albert was now at the zenith of his powers. There did not appear to be any area of life in which he did not have an interest; and scarcely any aspect of public life in which he did not consider it his duty to offer advice. Yet he remained, in many quarters, disliked simply because he was foreign. This in itself was a fairly useful quality, from the point of view of the monarchy's standing with the public. When the public liked something which the monarchy did, it could cheer the Queen. When it disliked a thing, it could blame that German prince. So it was that, at the beginning of 1855, Albert, in seeing what was happening in the Crimea, had begun to draw up the idea of a special award for the highest gallantry, to be called the Victoria Cross. '1. That a small cross of merit for personal deeds of valour be established. 2. That it be open to all ranks. 3. That it be unlimited in number. 4. That an annuity (say of £5) be attached to each cross. 5. That it be claimable by an individual on establishing before a jury of his Peers, subject to confirmation at home, his right to the distinction.'[29] It was in 1856 that the first crosses were awarded, and, despite the complaints by conservative-minded officers that all soldiers were required to be brave, it was an innovation which redounded to the Queen's glory. (In the event, it carried an annuity of £10, twice the prince's original hope.)

It was inaugurated on 26 June 1857, the day on which it was also finally declared, after the Queen's years of waiting and cajoling politicians, that her husband could be known as The Prince Consort. (He was actually awarded the title by Letters Patent four days later.) As well as being the first day of her awarding the Victoria Crosses, it was also the first time she had ever conducted a review on horseback. She was in full uniform, accompanied by Albert, who was also mounted. Little Prince Leopold appeared for the first time in public, and all his elder siblings were present, except Affie who was away on his naval training. Vicky, still unmarried, was accompanied by her fiancé, who appeared in public in London for the first time. As the Queen pinned on forty-seven medals, on a blazing hot day, she had never been more popular. Yet the new Prince Consort remained unpopular. A pamphlet of 1856 called *Prince Albert. Why is he Unpopular?* stated that the unpopularity was 'a feeling shared by almost anyone... The consort... of the most amiable Sovereign that has ever sat on the throne of these seagirt isles, is the most unpopular man in them!'[30]

So it was that he received no credit for inventing the Victoria Cross, but was blamed for the appointment of the Duke of Cambridge as

Commander-in-Chief of the army after the resignation of Lord Hardinge. Again, there was a supreme irony. It was Victoria, 'the most amiable Sovereign', who had insisted that her cousin George take over the position and sit in his office in Horse Guards. But the cartoon in *Punch* showed the Duke of Cambridge riding to Horse Guards on Prince Albert's back, and saying, 'Now then, Albert, Jack in your Tupenny'. In fact, Albert and George Cambridge were not especially fond of one another and Albert was a meritocrat, not a nepotist as his wife was.

His impressiveness remains on so many levels. When Theodore Martin wrote his great multi-volume biography of the Prince Consort (published 1875–80), he received hundreds of letters descanting upon Albert's virtues. A moment typical of the man occurred in Leeds, where he went to open the new Town Hall in 1858. The next day, when the ribbon-cutting and hand-shaking with aldermen had been completed, he went back to the Chamber of Commerce on a private visit. On the table of the President of the Chamber there were some pieces of a wool-combing machine which the prince had been shown the day before. It had been an exhibit in Hyde Park in 1851. The machine had been demonstrated to the prince in another part of the building, but, as the inventor (Mr Donisthorpe) recalled, the prince 'needed, however, no explanation, at once understanding the complex and most valuable invention; but looking closely at the machine, he remarked that there was a wheel or something of the kind wanting, pointing out where it should be introduced – to the great surprise of Mr Donisthorpe, who said it was so, it had been accidentally left out, but that not one man in 10,000 would have noticed the omission'.[31]

When he was dead, Victoria found herself making lists of all the things Albert had been good at – his construction of the beautiful new dairy at Windsor, the laying out of the superb kitchen gardens, the brilliance at the piano, the musical compositions, the building up of the royal art collection, the Great Exhibition of 1851, the creation of the Royal Horticultural Garden, the Kensington Museums, the foundation of Wellington College... And there was all his political involvement, both in Germany and in Britain. This was not to mention his productive work as Chancellor of the University of Cambridge, his programmes of social housing in Kennington, his fascination with scientific discovery, and his wide reading in contemporary literature and in philosophy.

Although courtiers and officials could find Albert a stiff person, he loosened up when mixing with his intellectual peers – whether with an engineer such as Mr Donisthorpe of Leeds, or the historian Thomas Carlyle who found him 'very jolly, and handsome in his loose grey clothes… He was civility itself in a fine simple fashion.'[32]

On the Isle of Wight, he again demonstrated an easy lack of pomposity with his near-neighbours the Tennysons. (Tennyson lived at Freshwater, which the prince liked to visit by boat from Osborne.) 'Prince Albert called on me the other day here,' Tennyson wrote to his aunt Elizabeth Russell, 'and was very kind in manner, shaking hands in quite a friendly way. We were in the midst of packing bustle, things tumbled about here and there… he stood by the drawing room window admiring the view which was not looking its best, and on going away, said, "I shall certainly bring the Queen – it's such a pretty place".'[33] The Tennysons also liked to tell the rather charming story of the Prince Consort visiting when they were out, and saying to the housekeeper, 'Merely say, Prince Albert called.'[34]

NERVE DAMAGE

DURING THAT EXCITING political year of 1848, Prince Albert had written to his brother, 'You cannot imagine how my fingers itch at being separated perforce from Germany at this moment.'[1] A decade on, and he now had his beloved daughter planted in the Heimat. When Vicky visited her uncle Ernst in Coburg in April 1858, his wife Alexandrine wrote ecstatically to the Queen, 'The adorable Vicky brightens everyone with her cheerful being, her lively sympathy, and her bottomless charm… She wins all Hearts.'[2]

It was true that the scattered German states could take hope from the arrival of youth, and that the Kingdom of Prussia in particular was in desperate need of a monarch who displayed health of mind and body. In the year before Fritz married Vicky, his uncle the King – Friedrich Wilhelm IV, who had been displaying signs of mental weakness for some time – became incurably mad, and then suffered a stroke. Fritz's father, Prince Wilhelm, took over as Regent, becoming King Wilhelm I when his brother died in 1861. Neither of the brothers was liberal by the standards of English liberalism, and, egged on by the ultra-reactionary Count Otto von Bismarck, who was coming increasingly to the fore as the greatest power in German politics, the Prussian monarchy had no truck with progressivism. They would have more or less shared the view of Queen Victoria's uncle, the King of Hanover (also Duke of Cumberland, who died in 1851), that Prince Albert was 'a terrible Liberal, almost a radical'.[3] King Friedrich

Wilhelm IV had been contemptuous of anything which smacked of modern democracy. He deplored the fact that the Hohenzollerns had been given back the Crown in 1848 after a conservative coup d'état. He felt he ruled by right, and it was humiliating to think he actually did so on the say-so of a Parliament. He jestingly called his crown 'the sausage roll' and said he ruled, 'by the grace of bakers and butchers'.⁴ During those alarming days in 1848, Wilhelm had fled to England, but when he returned to Germany he had become even more entrenched in his conservatism. He saw the army as serving the Crown, not the nation; he conceived it the monarch's function to determine foreign policy, and to uphold (the Protestant) religion. When he became king his first speech from the throne promised, 'Kingship by the grace of God, adherence to law and constitution, loyalty of the people and of the triumphant army, justice, truth, faith and fear of God'.⁵ Queen Victoria believed in all these things, but she would somehow have trod more gently when proclaiming them in public, and Vicky, who had learned her political wisdom at the knee of Prince Albert, would find Prussia an unsympathetic environment.

During Vicky's first year in Prussia, in which she became pregnant, her native land underwent a change of Government. It was prompted by the very contemporary subject of political assassination. There were no fewer than eight assassination attempts against Queen Victoria during her reign. The two contemporary rulers who may be said to have liberated their slaves – Abraham Lincoln in the United States and Tsar Alexander II – both died at the hands of assassins (in 1865 and 1881 respectively). Being Head of State in the nineteenth century was a dangerous occupation. Ten days before Vicky's wedding in London, Napoleon III and Empress Eugénie were trotting past the Paris Opéra in their carriage when 3 grenades were thrown, killing all their horses and injuring 102 bystanders. The leader of the plot, Felice Orsini, had travelled to France with a British passport under an assumed English name, carrying bombs which had been manufactured in Birmingham. The Foreign Secretary, Lord Clarendon, feared this would lead to an anti-British backlash in France, perhaps even a fracturing of the entente cordiale, and a reforging of the French alliance with Russia.

It was felt necessary to bring in hasty anti-terrorist legislation in order to advertise to the French how seriously the British took this breach in security. Clarendon had a long conversation with the Conservative Leader, Lord Derby, who gave the assurance that he would not oppose a Conspiracy to Murder Bill, increasing the penalties for crimes which were intended as well as for those which had been perpetrated. He warned, however, that there would be difficulty in passing such a Bill through the Commons. Palmerston's old foe Lord John Russell then announced that he would oppose the measure 'to the utmost of his power'.[6] When Palmerston proposed the Bill in the Commons on 5 February, his majority dissolved into anarchy. The radicals denounced the Government for kowtowing to French bullying. One member spoke of Napoleon III himself as the failed assassin of the Duke of Wellington. Russell denounced the measure as contrary to the 'whole course of modern enlightened legislation'. There was even talk of war with France within six weeks.

The next week, the Commons debated the mishandling of the Indian Mutiny by the East India Company, and the question of the Company's abolition, and a Viceregency being established in the subcontinent. This measure was passed. But on the Second Reading of the Conspiracy to Murder Bill, Pam was routed by nineteen votes. Having been defeated roundly, by his own followers in the Commons as well as by the Conservatives, Palmerston had to resign.

As the Queen tartly wrote in her journal, the two possible candidates were Lord Derby and Lord John Russell – 'the one, having no party, & the other, in a minority!'[7] The fifty-eight-year-old Lord Derby made the short journey from his handsome house in St James's Square to Buckingham Palace to kiss hands for his second administration.

In the previous year, Aberdeen had remarked to Gladstone that, 'there is now no such thing as a distinctive Peelite party in existence'.[8] Derby's second administration, therefore, short as it was – a little over a year – possesses an historical significance, since it shows us the emergence of the modern two parties, Liberals and Conservatives. Since the Prince Consort was a more or less confirmed Peelite, this left the monarchy without a party to support, and it was perhaps easier for the prince and the Queen to see themselves as above politics. Derby was never a Peelite: he had resigned from the Cabinet rather than vote for the repeal of the Corn Laws. But his moderate approach wooed some seventy Peelites to support him in the Commons and he thereby reconstituted the Conservative Party as a plausible electoral entity. Other Peelites, such as Gladstone, after some vacillations, allied themselves with the Liberals.

Before the Government left office, there was just time to vote through the Commons a vote of thanks to those who had suppressed the uprisings in India. The Opposition endeavoured to remove the Governor-General, Lord Canning, from those who were thanked by name. His nickname, 'Clemency Canning' – because of his supposed softness towards 'rebellious' Indians – was intended as an insult. Those of a pacific or gentle disposition, such as Lord Aberdeen, read the news of British reprisals against the Indians with horror. 'The exhortations of our [news] papers recommending indiscriminate slaughter, are abominable; but they are also suicidal; for we could never long exist in India, after having taken such means to create the most inveterate spirit of revenge.'[9]

It was not until March 1858 that Lucknow was recaptured, and it was only in July that peace was formally declared. By the end of the year, the East India Company had been wound up, and on 1 November, Queen Victoria's proclamation declared that India was now a British dominion. This declaration was ratified by the Government of India Act in Parliament. The Raj, which many British people believed to be eternal, would last eighty years, a very short interval in the long history of India. To the Queen, though she never visited India, the place, its people and languages were of increasing significance and interest with each passing year.

In this, it could be seen that she was demonstrating that instinctive sympathy with the spirit of the times which was one of her hallmarks as a monarch. But whereas the popular newspapers and many British people, Liberal and Conservative, took a view of India which was racist and patronizing, Victoria's attitude was always different, always one of fascination; she felt a diffident sympathy for the deposed maharajahs, especially when they were as handsome as Maharajah Duleep Singh, and she was devoid of racial prejudice. That there had been atrocities perpetrated on English men, women and children by Indians was not in question. It was the scale of the reprisals which shocked, and which Canning did his best to restrain. Russell, the *Times* correspondent who had covered the Crimean War, witnessed Sikhs and Englishmen looking on while a bayoneted Indian prisoner was turned on a spit and roasted. Rape and pillage in villages which had no direct connection with the Mutiny were openly encouraged by British officers. One officer wrote home cheerfully that 'peppering away at niggers' was a sport which he and his friends 'enjoyed quite amazingly'.[10] The Queen wrote indignantly to Clemency Canning that she shared his 'feelings of sorrow and indignation at the unchristian spirit shown – alas! also to a great extent here – by the public towards Indians in general and <u>towards Sepoys without discrimination!</u>' She emphasized that Indians should be assured 'that there is no hatred to a brown skin'.[11]

While these troubling events unfolded in Asia, the Queen and the Prince Consort, young as they were, witnessed the ending of their elder children's childhood. With Vicky in Germany, they exchanged a deluge of letters. At the end of March, the sixteen-year-old Prince of Wales was confirmed in St George's Chapel, Windsor. He was examined for a full hour by the Archbishop of Canterbury on the

Catechism, the Articles of Faith and the Sacraments. To his parents' enormous relief and surprise 'Bertie really answered very well',[12] so the archbishop told the boy's parents, but they did not need to be told since, alarmingly, they sat in on the viva. Perhaps the old man, knowing how anxious they were to find fault, was a little generous in his assessment of Bertie's theological interests. 'Oh!' exclaimed the Queen, 'how earnestly <u>did</u> I pray to God for <u>help</u> & for blessings on that poor Boy who causes us from his character & position such <u>immense anxiety!</u>'[13]

Bertie proved more than a match for his tutor Mr Gibbs – just as he had been the 'despair' of Gibbs's predecessor Mr Birch.[14] The parents made the sensible decision to supplant Mr Gibbs and to put the boy in charge of a 'governor'. For this role they selected the brother of Lady Augusta Bruce – the much-loved and admired young lady-in-waiting to the Duchess of Kent. Colonel Bruce was ideally suited to the task. He showed 'a clear insight into poor Bertie's difficult character, so full of anomalies! Oh I feel <u>full</u> of anxiety for the future!'[15] 'You will find Bertie grown up and improved,' the Prince Consort told his daughter, who was expecting her brother for a three-week visit to Berlin. 'Do not miss any opportunity of urging him to work hard.'[16] It was a successful visit, as far as his German hosts were concerned. They were able to see the boy's charm, his affability, where his parents only saw idleness, stupidity, interrupted by periodic fits of the Hanoverian rages. It baffled Prince Albert that Bertie made no comment on the buildings or works of art in any of the European cities he visited. 'He takes no interest in anything but clothes and again clothes.'[17] If his father but knew, this was not the case. While abroad, Bertie took the opportunity to write, not a connoisseur's notebook of favourite Old Masters, but letters to one of the Queen's prettiest ladies-in-waiting, Jane Churchill. During that visit to Berlin, he remained his unregenerate self, according to his mother 'playing practical jokes of a shameful nature on his poor valets!' The Queen added, 'He has been unable to vent it on any one else (formerly he had his poor animals) and <u>this</u> is the result.'[18]

His parents did the obvious thing and decided to give the undisciplined young loafer a military training. Although Victoria's soldier-father had trained in Germany, where real military skills and discipline could be forcefully instilled, in the case of the Prince of Wales, it was decided, with very predictable results, that he should merely be enlisted in the British Army in the lazy pre-Crimean fashion. On 9 November, he got his commission as a lieutenant colonel, but he could not be a proper soldier since he had no military training of any kind. They sent him for three months to Edinburgh University, then for a term at Oxford. It was a haphazard existence, and in marked contrast to the way they were training his younger brother Alfred for a professional career in the Royal Navy. The contrast between the way that Affie buckled down to his training as a naval cadet only served to make their mother the more indignant with Bertie's perpetual indolence. 'When I see him and Arthur and look at...! (You know what I mean!) I am in utter despair! The systematic idleness, laziness, disregard of everything is enough to break one's heart, and fills me with indignation. Alice behaved so admirably about it – and has much influence with him – but to you, I own, I am wretched about it!'[19]

The Queen was writing to Vicky in Germany, adding in a letter the following week that she was making Bertie read aloud to her in the mornings (Dr Arnold's Sermons).[20] The letters she wrote to Vicky are a spontaneous stream of consciousness, and we read them as she wrote them – unlike the journals, which were transcribed and censored by Princess Beatrice. For whatever reason, it is in these letters that we find Queen Victoria without any mask or inhibition. The young girl's marriage set off in the mother a candid series of recollections about her own difficulties in the early years of wedlock. Within weeks of the wedding, the Queen checked that Vicky was not pregnant.

I cannot tell you how happy I am that you are not in an unenviable position. I never can rejoice by hearing that a poor young thing is pulled down by this trial. Though I quite admit the comfort and blessing good and amiable children are

– though they are also an awful plague and anxiety for which
they show one so little gratitude very often! What made me so
miserable was – to have the first two years of my married life
utterly spoilt by this occupation! I could enjoy nothing – not
travel or go about with dear Papa and if I had waited a year, as
I hope you will, it would have been different.[21]

Only a month later, however, on 26 May 1858, she wrote, 'The
horrid news contained in Fritz's letter to Papa upset us dreadfully.
The more so as I feel certain almost it will come to nothing.'[22] Many a
mother would have held back from telling a child aged seventeen that
her birth had ruined the first year of marriage; and many a mother,
also, would at least pretend to be pleased when hearing of that child's
first pregnancy. But Queen Victoria was not any mother. As well as
describing the pregnancy as 'horrid news', she predicted a miscarriage, for no clear reason. Later in the pregnancy, when Vicky spoke
of her pride at giving life to an immortal soul, her mother retorted,
'What you say of the pride of giving life to an immortal soul is very
fine, my dear, but I own I cannot enter into that; I think much more
of our being like a cow or a dog at such moments; when our poor
nature becomes so very animal and unecstatic.'[23]

Prince Albert visited his daughter in June on his way to and from
Coburg. In August he came back for an extended visit of two and a
half weeks, but this time, bringing Queen Victoria, Sir James Clark
and – despite their assurances that it was a purely private, family
visit – Lord Malmesbury, the Conservative Foreign Secretary. The
Queen was nearly always happy when abroad. The crowds in Berlin
cheered her in the streets. And they were enchanted by the Schloss
Babelsberg, Prince Wilhelm's neo-Gothic summer palace, set among
rolling lawns which sloped down to the river and conveniently near
the military barracks where Fritz reported most days. (Sir James
Clark, who was less impressed than the Queen by the atmosphere of
the Prussian Court, complained of the 'perpetual uniform... none of
the Royal Family, or princely class, ever appear out of the stiff military

dress, the whole country seems occupied in playing at soldiers'.[24])

Prince Albert had been ill, on and off, throughout the summer, a fact which Sir James attributed to overwork. The death of his old valet Cart – the last link with his Coburg childhood – threw him into a decline, and the visits to Vicky, delightful as they were to him, were tarnished, inevitably, by the stab of parting.

In September 1858, back in the Schloss in Berlin which she found so depressing, Vicky caught her foot in a chair and fell 'with violence on the slippery parquet'. She always afterwards blamed this fall for the baby being in a 'false position' in her womb. She kept the fall from her mother. The Queen continued to bombard Vicky with advice, while keeping the news of their sister's pregnancy a secret from the other children. When Affie, the naval cadet, aged fourteen, visited Vicky, he pointed to her extended stomach, but did not know what this signified. She did not dare to tell him, since the matter had not been cleared with their parents, who were still in Balmoral – 'while Papa was after the stag – and good J. Brown was so attentive to us and so careful – he is now my special servant'.[25] Picnicking among the heather, little Princess Helena (Lenchen) told Brown that it was the birthday of Fritz (Prince Friedrich Wilhelm). Mishearing or misunderstanding, Brown thought she was saying that the birth had already happened, and exclaimed with delight, 'Aye! Has she got a girl or a boy?' The Queen would have been outraged had an English flunkey presumed to suggest that her daughter had given birth seven months after her wedding; but she merely laughed, and was amused at Lenchen's bafflement, since 'she suspects nothing'.[26]

From Windsor, on 27 October, the Queen confided her grief that Affie – still ignorant of the facts of life – had gone off to sea for ten months. She also gave notice that she was interviewing midwives and nurses to care for Vicky and the baby when it came. So amused was she by 'the mistake of good J. Brown' that she repeated it, adding that she still had not told Vicky's siblings – 'those things are not proper to be told to children'.[27] She eventually found a very reliable-seeming maid, Mrs Hobbs; but in common with most of her *Punch*-reading contemporaries, the Queen found Mrs Hobbs's Cockney accent irresistibly funny, calling her a 'Hatcher', that is, someone who misplaced aspirates. A letter from Mrs Hobbs assuring Princess Beatrice's nurse, Mrs Thurston, that 'the princess his[sic] getting on very well' struck the Queen as side-splittingly amusing, and she reported that Mrs Thurston 'is horrified at the prospect of the little individual speaking Cockney English'.[28] Had she been allowed to mix, during her girlhood, with the British aristocracy in the 1820s and 1830s, Victoria would have noticed that many of them spoke Cockney too, as they continued to do into the twentieth century. (Listen to the early radio broadcasts of her grandson King George V for traces of this 'upper-class Cockney', which was very strong, too, in King Edward VIII's diction. Was it attributable to the fact that this class was all reared by nannies?)

Lord Clarendon, now out of office, happened to be in Berlin in October, where he encountered Baron Stockmar. 'I want to talk to you,' said the old doctor, 'on a very important matter and to invoke your aid. It relates to "this poor child here"' – Vicky. Stockmar told Clarendon that the Queen 'wishes to exercise the same authority and control over her that she did before her marriage: and she writes her constant letters full of anger and reproaches, desiring all sorts of things to be done that it is neither right nor desirable that she should do'.[29] Stockmar asked Clarendon, when he returned to England, to pass on their concerns to the Prince Consort.

Roger Fulford, the editor both of the Queen's letters to Vicky, and of the Greville journals in which this incident is recorded, points out the unfairness of Stockmar's confiding in Albert, and putting all the blame for 'interference' on the Queen; for, wrote Fulford, 'if she was "meddling with trivialities" [Stockmar's phrase] the prince was attempting to guide the young couple on political matters'.[30]

Albert continued to be ill as autumn turned to winter. Just before Christmas he took Bertie to the Latin play at Westminster School and, for once, was relieved by the boy's ignorance of the ancient tongues, since the drama was 'very improper'. As Bertie and his siblings moved into their sexual maturity, the still-young parents became ever more fastidious. This pair, who had produced nine children, and enjoyed hymning the delights of connubial love to one another, were prudish even by the standards of that generation of Podsnaps. Does the excessiveness of their disapproval of any hint of bawdry suggest a crisis, or even a cessation, in their carnal relations? It is clear that the Queen had not yet reached the menopause. It is equally clear that she had hated her final two pregnancies and confinements even more than the previous seven; that a line had been drawn. For whatever reason, Victoria and Albert had turned into parodies of hypersensitivity where sex was concerned. Even that arch-puritan Cardinal Newman rehearsed the pupils of the Birmingham Oratory with a Latin comedy each year, usually Terence, though with some of the more flagrant crudities excised.

The Crown Princess's confinement was at the end of January. 'God be praised for all his mercies, and for bringing you safely through this awful time!' wrote the Queen on 29 January, but she did so because Vicky had kept her mother in ignorance of the full nightmare of the experience, described by Cecil Woodham-Smith as 'one of the worst recorded in obstetrical history'.

Labour began shortly after midnight on 26 January 1859. The rest of the night was spent either on the bed, or walking around the room, supported by Fritz, or two of her German ladies, Countess Blücher and Countess Perponcher. When labour began the house physician, Dr Wegner, called for Dr Martin, the specialist. By a series of mischances, the note did not reach Martin until 10 am, and by the time he arrived it was almost too late. After eight or nine hours of screaming and writhing, and begging for everyone's forgiveness, Vicky had consented to have a handkerchief put in her mouth to prevent her from grinding her teeth and biting herself. Countess Blücher and Mrs Innocent, the midwife sent over by Queen Victoria, were in despair. One of the doctors in the room was openly saying that the baby would die. It was a breech birth, and it seems doubtful that the deferential Dr Wegner had conducted the necessary examination to establish this fact. When Martin arrived, he told Sir James Clark to give Vicky chloroform, though she still complained of 'unbearable pain' even after being dosed. Martin gave her a uterine stimulant to increase the frequency and intensity of the pains. He then extracted the child, who appeared to be dead. It took some time to start the child's breathing, which could have resulted in loss of oxygen to the brain. Shortly after the infant began to cry, a 101-gun salute told the Prussian people that a new heir to the throne had been born. It was a boy.

Such was the relief in the room that the child was alive that no one seemed to notice, at first, that the baby's left arm hung useless from its socket. Nerve damage is common in breech deliveries, but it was three or four days after the birth of the boy – named Wilhelm – before Mrs Innocent noticed the lifeless arm. The doctors, anxious not to be blamed, minimized the extent to which the arm was useless.[31] Pascal perhaps exaggerated when he wondered if the course of world history would have been different had Cleopatra's nose been a hint shorter. It would not, however, be an exaggeration to say that the dangerous psycho-history of the future German Emperor Wilhelm II was affected most profoundly by his useless arm, and by the misplaced guilt which would poison his mother's relationship with him.

THIRTEEN

'ARME FRAU'

Thomas Hardy, the architect-turned-novelist who was born three years after Queen Victoria came to the throne, borrowed a phrase from the Greek tragedian Aeschylus to conclude his most celebrated book. 'The President of the Immortals, in the Aeschylean phrase, had finished his sport with Tess.'

Those who follow the life of Queen Victoria must feel, as they approach the year 1861, a comparable sense of doom. The characters in the tragedy step ineluctably towards a dreadful fate. It is a drama in which even the comic elements, such as young Bertie's irresponsible burgeoning erotomania, seem like ingenious plot-devices which can lead only to the cataclysmic unravelling.

The outward events of the story were to be sad by any reckoning. But before they unfolded, the Queen's own state of mind was something which had already caused anxiety to her medical advisers.

When Albert tried, as delicately as he could, to pass on Stockmar's advice to the Queen, about toning down her bossiness in letters to Vicky, there was an explosion of wrath against the baron. It led to a series of rows with Albert himself, who, plainly, found it difficult to restrain his anger with a completely unreasonable Victoria.

'You have again lost your self-control quite unnecessarily,' he wrote to her.

I did not say a word which could wound you, and I did not begin the conversation, but you have followed me about and continued it from room to room. There is no need for <u>me</u> to promise to <u>trust</u> you, for it was not a question of trust, but of your fidgety nature, which makes you insist on entering, with feverish eagerness, into details about orders and wishes which, in the case of a Queen, are commands, to whomsoever they may be given. This is your nature; it is not against Vicky, but it is the same with everyone and has been the cause of much unpleasantness for you. It is the dearest wish of my heart to save you from these and worse consequences, but the only result of my efforts is that I am accused of want of feeling, hard heartedness, injustice, hatred, jealousy, distrust, etc. etc. I do my duty towards you even though it means that life is embittered by 'scenes' when it should be governed by love and harmony. I look upon this with patience as a test which has to be undergone, but you hurt me desperately and at the same time do not help yourself.[1]

Ticking in the background, while they bickered, was another time bomb: Victoria's unexplored emotional history with her mother. Ever since her daughter had married Prince Albert, the Duchess of Kent had been a more or less exemplary royal parent. It is clear from her voluminous correspondence with the Queen (Victoria answering about one letter in three of her mother's) that Victoire of Saxe-Coburg was grovelling in her acknowledgement of the monarch's absolute right to command or dismiss her. From the beginning of the reign, when the teenaged Queen had banished Conroy, there was always the dread, on the mother's part, that she would also be spurned. Not an anniversary was missed by the old lady. Every grandchild's birthday was remembered. Presents were sent, wherever they happened to be. Permission was always sought to visit them. Deferential thanks were always sent when she had so much as been allowed to sit at the

dinner table. It is clear from the many notes and letters which the
duchess sent her daughter that no actual estrangement occurred. The
pair were in the same room together during much of the year, except
for those months of the summer when the duchess tended to return
to Germany to spend time with her son Charles and her daughter
Feodore. At the same time, the notes and letters tell a consistent
story of studied neglect by the Queen. A typical letter, going through
arrangements for the summer of 1853, says, 'As I can never find a quiet
moment to speak to you, I will better put down my plans in writing,
that you and Albert may say if you <u>approve</u> or <u>disapprove</u>.'[2] (There
follows a series of requests, asking permission to have Feodore to
stay, and acquainting the Queen with the comings and goings of the
duchess's ladies-in-waiting.) The letters cannot conceal the fact that,
although she was nearly always accompanied by her ladies – and the
Baroness Späth was a constant presence – the duchess felt intense
loneliness. 'O, Victoria, <u>why</u> are you so cold and indifferent with your
Mother; who loves you so <u>dearly</u>?'[3] She asked the question when
Victoria was a little over twenty years old, but it would have been just
as relevant to ask it when she was turning forty.

Victoria had poured all her emotional energy into her marriage,
and, almost literally, she had no time for her mother. In order to make
this possible to her conscience, Victoria had told herself a story –
that her mother had been cold and unfeeling during an 'unhappy'
childhood. The Queen had chosen to view her childhood through the
screen of those unhappy months and years when, as an adolescent,
she had clashed violently with Conroy, and blamed her mother for
not keeping him under control. By telling herself this story, and then
acting upon it for twenty years, Victoria gave herself the freedom and
time to neglect her mother emotionally, while concentrating upon
Albert, her marriage and her role as Queen.

As her own children passed through adolescence to adulthood,
however, it was impossible to ignore the inaccuracy of this vision
of things. Her kind, sentimental, needy mother had in fact been a
constant supportive presence in her life. From the very beginning, it

had been just the two of them, and much of Victoria's monster-ego, her need to be Queen, not only in a constitutional sense, but in all emotional departments of life, had been allowed free rein by the duchess's self-immolation. In May 1859, Sir James Clark warned Prince Albert that the duchess was suffering from a cancer which would one day prove to be fatal. For most of the month of May 1859, the duchess was ill, sometimes confined to bed in London. Victoria visited her in Clarence House, but she did not postpone her own planned visit to Osborne. The illness, however, began to concentrate the daughter's mind. Her own firstborn child, Vicky, came to join her at Osborne in readiness for her fortieth birthday on 24 May. It was a very happy reunion, and Vicky, 'so *embellie*!',[4] 'only began to cry when she talked of her poor little boy's left arm being so weak, which it has been from his birth'.[5]

Then, the next day, came a telegram from her mother's doctor, Mr Brown, in London, to say that the duchess was weak and unable to eat. Sir James Clark reassured the Queen (always rather an ominous signal, as her biographers, if not the Queen herself, could not help noting). On this occasion, Clark was right, and the duchess began to eat and pulled through. But she was in her seventy-third year, and there had been plenty of examples of mortality to nag at Victoria's conscience. The day after the Queen was forty, she wrote to her uncle Leopold, 'I am thoroughly shaken and upset by this <u>awful</u> shock; for it came on so <u>suddenly</u> – that it came like a thunderbolt upon us, and I think I <u>never</u> suffered as I did those four dreadful hours till we heard she was better! I hardly myself <u>knew how</u> I loved her, or how my <u>whole existence</u> seems bound up with her – till I saw looming in the distance the fearful possibility of <u>what</u> I will <u>not</u> mention.'[6] It is a fascinating and ominous confession; the sort of sentences which in a later generation would emerge from patients undergoing psycho-therapy. For all of a sudden, the most important relationship of her life was seen to be, not her relationship with her Angel, Prince Albert; and not with her children; but that with her poor spurned mother. With that epiphany came a tsunami of emotions – terror at what she was about to lose, tenderness for the vanished days of childhood, love for the mother who had been so constant a part of her life, fear for herself, watching her children and grandchildren emerging from their chrysalises, a phenomenon which is only able to fill a parent's heart with uncomplicated joy in the most perfectly well-balanced personalities: in others, it brings, together with joy in the burgeoning of new lives in the family, a remembrance of past failures, a mental replay of one's own childhood traumas, and a consciousness of mortality.

The children, and Albert, naturally suffered the consequences of the Queen's mental torments. Her tolerance for what she perceived as their faults was never strong, and she was never one to keep discontents or unhappinesses to herself. 'You say no one is perfect but Papa,' the Queen wrote truculently to Vicky, 'but he has his faults too. He is often very trying in his hastiness and over-love of business, and I think you would find it trying if Fritz was as hasty and harsh (momentarily and unintentionally as it is) as he can be!'[7] She was also vexed by Albert's perpetual illnesses – 'dear Papa never allows he is any better or will try to get over it, but makes such a miserable face that people always think he's very ill. It is quite the contrary with me always; I can do anything before others, and never show it, so people never believe I am ill or ever suffer. His nervous system is easily excited and irritated and he's so completely overpowered by everything.'[8]

She who had been so ecstatically happy with Albert in their early years could baldly tell her daughter that 'all marriage is such a lottery – the happiness is always an exchange – though it may be a very happy one – still the poor woman is bodily and morally the husband's slave. That always sticks in my throat.'[9]

Since Vicky was now herself a matriarch in Germany, and the mother of a future King of Prussia, she was well placed to help her mother in what was to be one of the chief preoccupations of her middle age:

namely the marrying off of her children, as they grew to maturity. The Royal Marriages Act (1772) made it impossible for any of the children to be married to Roman Catholics, so the field was limited to the Greek or Russian Orthodox, but preferably to the Protestant royalties of roughly appropriate age. There was not such an enormous pool to draw upon, since until the marriage of her sixth child, Princess Louise, Victoria did not contemplate looking outside the European royal pool for her children's consorts.

Princess Alice, the Queen and Prince Albert's third child, reached her sixteenth birthday 'without any engagement, or even thought of one, and the longer we can keep this off the better'[10] – that was the Queen's view in April 1859. Alice had grown into a beautiful girl, much taller than her mother (which was admittedly not difficult), serious-minded and inclined, even more than most teenaged girls, to melancholy. Although the Queen professed relief that Alice was not yet engaged at sixteen, her father never ceased to see her as merchandise in the marriage market. He deplored a lithograph of her – much liked by other members of the family – because 'it will do Alice harm if it is seen by those who don't know her' – that is, by potential suitors. Victoria, who found Alice 'a very dear companion', was glad that she 'is not at all anxious to marry'.[11] Nevertheless, it was essential to place her in the European Court. Prince William of Orange was considered, but he was quite a bit younger than she was. When they were placed next to one another at dinner in Buckingham Palace, he was 'very dull and positively rude'.[12] Vicky was asked to sound out the suitability of Louis of Hesse-Darmstadt. As well as being extremely plain, the youth was a bore, but when invited to the Palace in June 1860, he made a good impression on the Queen.[13] Alice formed an adolescent crush on this unprepossessing dullard, and she mistook it for love. The pair were engaged. It was a blow to her brother, the Prince of Wales, since Bertie and Alice had always been friends.

It was decided by both parents that, in addition to being made a colonel without any military training, the Prince of Wales too should be married off as soon as possible before he was tainted by the experience of life. The Queen followed the Hanoverian tradition of having the strongest possible antipathy towards her heir; but, being Victoria, she took this to operatic heights, never neglecting the opportunity to denigrate him or to find fault. 'I am glad that Bertie is amiable and companionable towards you,' she told Vicky back in 1858. 'I own I think him very dull; his three other brothers are all so amusing and communicative.'[14] In April 1860, having received the Sacrament with Bertie at St George's Chapel, Windsor, the Queen felt constrained to observe that 'he is not at all in good looks; his nose and mouth are too enormous and he pastes his hair down to his head, and wears his clothes frightfully – he really is anything but good-looking.'[15]

The Queen's language about the Prince of Wales became so intemperate that Vicky, after an extended visit to her mother in England, felt the need to expostulate. 'Only one thing pains me – when I think about it and that is the relation between you and Bertie! In the railway carriage going to Dover I thought so much about it, and wished I could have told you how kindly, nicely and properly and even sensibly he spoke, his heart is very capable of affection, of warmth of feeling and I am sure it will come out with time and by degrees... I know, dear Mama, you will forgive my saying all this and not be offended.'[16] Such remonstrances had little or no effect, and the Queen – with a few rare intervals – would maintain her hostility to Bertie until her dying day.

Prince Albert had made the more general point to the Queen, time and again, that if she persisted in scolding the children, and having only negative thoughts about them, it could only poison her relations with them. 'You are quite mistaken if you think I am not concerned to maintain your maternal authority with the children,' he wrote. 'On the contrary, it is my consistent care to safeguard it and preserve the warmth of the children's feeling for their Mother, and that is just the reason why I have felt it my duty to warn you of the rocks on which all our efforts are wrecked. I admit it was an error of judgement to speak to you yesterday about Alice's weeping, for I ought to have remembered the state of your nerves, but I really did not think they were shaken to the extent they have since shown themselves to be, and there was nothing in what I said to excite a healthy person to such an outburst.'[17]

'Dear Darling', she recollected in bereavement. 'I fear I tried him sadly.'[18]

Sensing that Bertie was likely to find himself in trouble with women, his puritanical parents were keen to see him married very young – as they themselves had been. By the end of December 1860, Vicky thought she had found someone – the daughter of Prince Christian of Denmark – who might be suitable on some levels. That is, 'she was beautiful and healthy, and amiable… though I as a Prussian cannot wish Bertie should ever marry her'.[19] She was referring to the long-standing quarrel between Denmark and Prussia about the status of the Schleswig-Holstein Duchies. It was, indeed, as Vicky warned her parents, a diplomatic hot potato, which for some reason Bertie and his parents conspired to ignore. But many a tempest would blow across the sky before the obviousness of this fact was borne in upon them.

Political events at home and in Europe, which had nothing to do with Schleswig-Holstein, occupied much of this period. In Britain, there was the unfolding story of how far parliamentary reform could be allowed to go. For the Tories, and many of the old Whigs, the matter was a holding operation, attempting, against the tides of time, to resist the movement towards a representative democracy in Parliament. For other Whigs, for Liberals and radicals, it was a matter of urgency to extend the franchise. It was over this issue that Lord Derby's short-lived second premiership foundered. The Liberals came back in, and the Queen was in a dilemma: whom should she ask to form the administration? Both Lord John Russell and Lord Palmerston had been Leaders of the Liberal Party. Both had been Prime Minister. Her instinct was to ask neither, and she turned to Lord Granville. She was 'much shocked' to open her copy of that newspaper she in any event deplored, *The Times*, on 13 June 1859 'to find her whole conversation with Lord Granville yesterday and the day before detailed in this morning's leading article'.[20] The leak, which Granville denied, was a terrible blunder, and by 1 July, Pam was back as Prime Minister, with Russell as Foreign Secretary and Mr Gladstone as the Chancellor of the Exchequer.

The Queen had, as yet, no reason for disliking the tall, clever, eagle-eyed figure of William Ewart Gladstone, who was one of the surviving Peelites – a political position which she – or at any rate the Prince Consort – found sympathetic. She did not know that Gladstone had made it a condition of his joining Palmerston's Cabinet that the Government wished to 'see the Germans turned out of Italy'.[21]

The cause of Italian nationalism was dear to the heart of English Liberals. Henry Cary's translation of Dante into English had made the father of Italian poetry as popular as the English Romantics themselves in the early decades of the nineteenth century. Gladstone, the scion of a rich merchant family of Scottish origin who had made their fortune in Liverpool, had been educated at Eton. It was there, and later at Oxford, that while imbibing the whole of classical, and much modern, literature, he also became an enthusiast for the works of Dante. Gabriele Rossetti, the Italian exile in London and father of, among others, the famous painter Dante Gabriel and poet Christina, saw Dante's medieval works as allegories foreshadowing the political liberalism and freethinking of the nineteenth century. Though Gladstone deplored Rossetti's religious freethinking, he ardently embraced the cause of the unification of the Italian states, the depriving of the Pope of his secular powers, and the expulsion of the Austrians from cities and territories in the Veneto and Northern Italy. In this, he echoed the majority of enlightened English opinion. Gladstone's visit to Naples in the winter of 1850–51 had convinced him that the rule of the Bourbon King Ferdinand was 'the negation of God erected into a system of Government'. The pro-Italianism of the Brownings – Robert and Elizabeth Barrett – was popular with the reading public. Many a middle-class English household possessed a copy of Elizabeth Barrett Browning's *Casa Guidi Windows* of 1851 – 'Life throbs in noble Piedmont!' The Queen had asked Robert Browning to dine at the British Embassy in Rome when the Prince of Wales made a visit in 1858.

Lord John Russell, as Foreign Secretary, received a full account from his nephew, Odo Russell, of an audience he had had with Pope Pius IX. 'Caro mio Russell,' said his Holiness, 'what is to become of us with your uncle and Lord Palmerston at the head of affairs in England?'[22] Russell sent a copy of the memorandum to the Queen. He well knew that, on this single but important issue, the Prince Consort was entirely at one with the Pope. Albert deplored the idea of the Austrians being driven out of Italy, and felt that the cause of Italian nationalism set a dangerous precedent. For whom? Well, for the Irish to start with… Albert was not to survive long enough to see how forcibly the success of Italian nationalists would inspire Bismarck and the Prussians to force forward their own version of German nationalism – a version very different from anything taught to Albert in his youth by Baron Stockmar or Uncle Leopold. The English liberals felt that the best hope for a united, liberal Italy was to be found in the Kingdom of Piedmont, under the kingship of King Victor Emmanuel and the country's leading statesman, Camillo, Count Cavour. But there was many a hazard to overcome before the modern state of Italy as we know it today was achieved. Napoleon III waged war on Austria in the summer of 1850 for a few months, notionally in the cause of Italian nationalism, in fact to emphasize France's claim on Nice and Savoy. He left the Veneto in the hands of the Austrians, despite his promise to Cavour that he would fight until Italy was free from the Alps to the Adriatic. In May 1860, Garibaldi – immensely popular in Britain – landed in Sicily with his 1,000 volunteers and overthrew the Bourbon Government. Cavour sent forces to Rome, and Victor Emmanuel marched down to Naples to meet Garibaldi – half to show solidarity, half to ensure that the old republican did not establish a southern Italian *repubblica*. Whatever the outcome in Italy, it was fairly clear that the era of the Bourbon control of the South was over, and it was only a matter of time before the Austrians were cleared out of the Veneto, and Pius IX surrendered his temporal power over the Papal States. All of this was good news to the Protestant British – and to the Queen when in British mood, though not when attending to Albert's pro-Austrian hopes.

The last Christmas before tragedy broke up the family was that of 1860, and it was a happy one. Even Albert and Victoria, everlastingly on the lookout for faults in the Prince of Wales, were pleased with their eldest son. He had just fulfilled his first major public engagement on his own – a four-month tour of Canada and the United States. The nineteen-year-old young man, who had travelled with a distinguished suite including the Duke of Newcastle, Secretary of State for the Colonies, General Bruce, his governor, Henry Acland, Regius Professor of Medicine at Oxford and the prince's personal physician, and others, had conducted himself with remarkable charm and maturity. Any gaffes had been minor ones – the Roman Catholic bishops at the University of Laval, Quebec, had objected to the prince addressing them merely as '*Messieux*', but others in the audience were delighted by his flawless French. (The Orangemen at Ottawa had then objected to the Duke of Newcastle's apology to the bishops!) At Niagara, the prince had watched Blondin cross the Falls from the American side on a tightrope. In the United States on the verge of Civil War, he was an instant social success, and in Chicago, St Louis, Cincinnati, Pittsburgh, Baltimore and Washington it was the same story – civic dignitaries and crowds found a young man whose jollity and friendliness were instantly appealing. When Bertie had attended the opera at Philadelphia, the whole audience stood up and sang 'God Save the Queen' – a spectacle which might have surprised the ghosts of those who had rung the Liberty Bell in that city, or had so ingeniously crafted the republican Constitution. On the final leg of the trip, General Bruce had written to the Queen, 'The reception at New York has thrown all its predecessors into the shade. I despair of its ever being understood in England... Believe me, however, that exaggeration is impossible.' Bertie had been driven down Broadway in a barouche next to the Mayor, Fernando Wood, 'amid an ocean roar of cheering'.[23]

Thomas Carlyle once said that if it had been possible to unite the two great 'half-men' of the eighteenth century, David Hume and Samuel Johnson, a perfect individual would have been formed. Similarly, in the nineteenth century, had a monarch been found with Victoria's emerging political nous, her peculiar intuitive sense of national mood and feeling, and her punctilious willingness to work hard behind the scenes, and had this figure also been endowed with Bertie's geniality, his friendliness with strangers and his lack of shyness, then an ideal monarch would have been born. As it was, the very workable monarchy which Victoria and her heir handed on to the twentieth century was created not out of such a magical fusion but out of the conflict between the pair. The Queen recognized that the visit to America had revealed qualities in her son which she would never possess herself. She generously acknowledged that much of the credit for this must be given to General Bruce, and she suggested to Lord John Russell and to Palmerston that she should make Bruce a knight commander of the Order of the Bath. They poured cold water on the notion, saying that it was inappropriate to recognize Bruce's private service to the Royal Family by a public honour. At least the Queen made the Duke of Newcastle a Knight of the Garter.[24]

The Prince of Wales was welcomed to Christmas at Windsor, where bright winter sunshine lit up castle windows thick with crystalline hexagons of frost, where the lakes were frozen so thickly that the young could play ice hockey, and where the Prince Consort, always at his happiest during these days of the year, supervised the hanging of giant Christmas trees from the ceilings, festooned with candles and decorations.

The great German Christmas was celebrated, as it happened, for the last time. The presents were arranged, each on a special table for every recipient – though now Alice shared her table with young Louis of Hesse-Darmstadt. The dinner was eaten – though the grown-ups found themselves without much appetite that year, even Victoria, who normally found it difficult to resist good food even when anxious – cold baron of beef, brawn, game pies, stuffed turkey, wild boar's head, always the prince's favourite, with a particular German sauce which Öhm, the chef at Coburg, had invented – mince pies, bonbons of all kinds.

New Year was ushered in, with everyone anxiously looking at the fingers of the clock before it struck midnight. Then they kissed one another. Albert had tears in his eyes this year as he embraced his wife, even before he went to his bed and found that she had kept to her mother's tradition of writing a New Year's letter, this time begging him to forgive her for her faults.[25]

The happiness of the Christmas period made both partners in the marriage resolve to try not to bicker. 'I willingly testify that things have gone much better during the last two years,' Albert said.[26]

Afterwards, in her bleak widowhood, Victoria would remember that Christmas as the last time they had enjoyed thick snow together. She tenderly listed the dates when he had taken her for a ride in a sledge – 'in 45 at Brighton, in Jan and Feb 47, in 55... and then for the last time Dec 27, 1860 at Windsor when Louis was still there. My Angel always drove me from a seat behind, sitting astride with his feet in large boots – he wore a fur coat with fur gloves – and he enjoyed it so much.'[27]

Her Angel. He was always 'my Angel'. She was '*mein liebes Kind*' – 'my dear child'. 1861, that year of disaster, and not 1837, was the date which would mark the end of her childhood. She who had been so dependent upon Albert as a parent-substitute would lose mother and husband within a space of months. It was also a year of painful estrangement. In the Reminiscences which she wrote down at Osborne in January 1862, she recollected that in previous years they had enjoyed playing the piano and singing together. 'Sometimes we sang (not at all last year) but formerly very often.'[28] The last song she remembered Albert singing had been at Balmoral the previous summer – 'Eine Thrane' ('A Tear'), with its question, '*ob sie wohl kommen wird zu beten auf mein Grab*' ('whether she will come to pray at my Grave').[29]

The condition of the Duchess of Kent was clear to the doctors, but although they had explained matters in depth to the Prince Consort, the Queen had not been kept fully informed. Perhaps if she had been observing the illness of any other old lady – unable to eat, increasingly uncomfortable in her movements – she would have begun to fear the worst. But instead, she drugged herself with hope. The letters she wrote to the duchess during March 1861 are addressed to herself as much as to her mother. On 2 March, 'We are truly happy to hear a favourable account: of you, tho' grieved that the poor arm should be so troublesome, but Brown is sure it will soon improve.' Two days later, she wrote of her pleasure in hearing a positive and favourable report, and recommended her to read *Adam Bede* and *The Mill on the Floss*.[30] There was talk of having the duchess to stay at Osborne during that week, but she was too ill to move. When the Royal Family came back to Buckingham Palace, the Queen reported, 'we are all well & prospering but find London very stuffy & close after dear, sweet, <u>Osborne</u>'. She spoke of wanting to have the duchess to stay at the Palace. Clearly, she was referring to what a tongue-tied doctor had told her, when she wrote, 'altogether the report of your precious self is favourable as regards the progress towards decided relief'. Then reality broke in as she wrote, 'but it is terrible to be <u>so</u> plagued, so tired – I can't bear to think of all you have to go through… if only I could be <u>near</u> you… & see you very often and long to beguile away the dull hours when you can't amuse yourself!' Presumably, the sheer business of the Queen's working routine made her believe that she had to postpone devoting herself to a few days at the sickbed. 'Very soon we <u>shall</u> be close at hand, & then later after Easter, we hope you will come here as long as you like and stay here as long as you like. I

wish I cd. <u>send</u> you any thing you might fancy to eat.' But the elder
Victoria was beyond eating, and the Duchess of Kent would not live
till Easter.[31]

She threw herself, literally, on Albert. When she wanted to go
back, the day after her mother's death, to look at the corpse once
more, he dissuaded her, saying that any change in the appearance of
the body could only be distressing. All the painful funerary business
was conducted via the Prince Consort. On the Sunday evening,
he came to ask when the duchess could be placed in her coffin.
Victoria told him that she trusted him to do anything that was
necessary. She cast herself into his arms, and he said, '*Arme Frau*' –
'poor woman'.

When her mother was dead, Victoria collected up all the letters
which the old lady had ever written to her. In the Royal Archives
at Windsor there are six[32] stout volumes, bound in black morocco;
the first two volumes are pricked in gilt: 'LETTERS FROM DEAR
MAMA'. They begin with the little love letters on bright pink paper
which the duchess, still uncertain of the English in which she wrote,
had penned to Victoria as an infant. They ended with pathetic pencilled
scrawls to her ladies-in-waiting: 'Thank you, I slept well, but these
pains torment me very much'[33] and – what is noted by Victoria to be
'Beloved Mama's Last Writing' (the annotation on it reads, 'HRH's
last writing with her dear right hand') – 'Write by Telegram to the
Queen you may write some part out of this note.' The words, like the
life, slither out into incoherence.[34]

It was not possible, as she read these outpourings of maternal
affection which cover four decades, to sustain the personal myth that
she had been an unloved child. On Victoria's eleventh birthday (1830),
the duchess had written, 'Although I am sure you will always mind
what your affectionate Mother tells you: and particularly on such an
occasion as your birthday: I like to write to you these few words, that
when the years pass away, you may read them over and over again:
and that in comparing these notes, you will find, my beloved Victoria,
that your Mother's love never changed.'[35]

It is not an exaggeration that the recognition of her mother's love unhinged the Queen, and that the bereavement precipitated something which was far, far worse than her usual 'nervousness' – to use Prince Albert's tactful word.[36] His remedy – 'You must try to make up by being as loving to others as you can'[37] – might have been good advice for the morally robust, but Victoria was in a state of extreme emotional fragility.

In her widowhood, the Queen would remember how, when he came in, whether from sport or work, she always had something to show the prince. 'I was always so vexed & even nervous if I had any foolish draft or despatch to show him as I knew it wd. distress & irritate him & affect his poor dear stomach.'[38] There is abundant evidence that Albert was suffering for years before his death from 'nervous' stomach attacks. He scarcely ever ate luncheon, and became increasingly 'careful' about what he could eat, cutlets, game, potatoes, but all eaten in tiny quantities (or tiny by the Queen's heartier standards), chicken casseroles, and 'oeufs à l'allemande' which was made with eggs, sugar, wine and biscuits. From the autumn of 1860 onwards, his stomach was frequently 'deranged', as Victoria put it.[39] They increasingly ate their meals separately, leaving Albert 'well-nigh overcome' with work which she felt obliged, through grief, to neglect.[40]

If Albert's stomach was 'deranged', as is now believed, by Crohn's disease, and possibly with abdominal cancer,[41] there was much to exacerbate his nervous system. His teeth and gums were in an appalling condition. 'Poor Papa has been suffering badly with toothache since three days,' the Queen told her eldest child.[42] And the toothache, to which were added the agonies of gumboils, remained a feature for the rest of his life. It left him 'despondent and weak and miserable – I would so willingly have borne it all for him; we women are born to suffer and bear it so much more easily, our nerves don't seem so racked, tortured as men's are!'[43] Victoria, who remained all her life in basically robust health, could simply not appreciate the fact that Albert's constitution was wrecked, that he was fundamentally weak, and that the worries caused by overwork and by the worsening international situation made every symptom seem worse. In Europe, tensions between Prussia and Denmark over the Schleswig-Holstein Duchies was threatening to reach crisis point. In April, the American Civil War broke out, an event calamitous in itself, but with dire effects upon British industry, since the textile mills of Lancashire depended upon cheap cotton from the Southern States. While events in the great world worried Albert, all the old moral anxieties about the Prince of Wales resurfaced.

Bertie had been transferred from Oxford to Cambridge, and during the Long Vacation it was decided to continue his military life – the use of the word 'training' would scarcely be appropriate – by sending him to Ireland. He was there when the Queen and the Prince Consort made an arduous visit to the island. Coming as it did after a painful spell of bereavement, and coinciding with Albert's birthday on 26 August, it felt like an occasion for self-pity. 'Alas! So much is so different this year,' the Queen told her journal, 'nothing festive, – we on a journey & separated from many of our children. I am still in such low spirits.'[44]

Crippled by stomach troubles, Albert was on the verge of collapse when he visited the military encampment at the Curragh, the military grounds near Dublin where Bertie was stationed. Although supposedly a colonel, Bertie merely took command of a company – of the Grenadier Guards – during the march-past in the Queen's honour. The symbolism was noted – his superior officers did not feel that the prince merited a responsibility above that of a captain.

The royal visit to Ireland was stiff and, for both Bertie's parents, unhappy. They would have been even unhappier had they known of a prank played upon a thankfully compliant prince by his fellow bloods. They secreted into his bed a pretty actress called Nellie Clifden.

Victoria and Albert repaired to the healing air of Balmoral. When Bertie returned to England, he was very happy to see Miss Clifden again... and again.

When Victoria and Albert left Balmoral that autumn, John Brown, in his bluff tactless way, wished them well, and hoped 'above all you may have no deaths in the family'.[45]

It had been a period when deaths came thick and fast. Ever since the death in childbirth of Victoire Nemours, Victoria's cousin, at 'unhappy Claremont', there had been a series of shocks. 'Good Cart', a valet from Coburg who had been with Prince Albert since childhood, had died towards the end of 1858. Shortly before the Duchess of Kent died, her secretary and helpmeet of twenty years, Sir George, had died. Their kindly, if incompetent, old doctor Sir James Clark had retired the previous year and been replaced by a clever young physician named William Baly. In February 1861, Baly was killed in a railway accident at Wimbledon in south London. The prince felt it to be 'an incalculable loss'.[46]

When, in November 1861, news came from Portugal that typhoid fever was sweeping through the Court, and that it had killed King Pedro, and Albert's Coburg cousin Dom Ferdinand, aged fifteen, Queen Victoria recalled Brown's prophetic words in Balmoral. Brown 'spoke of having lost (12 years ago) in 6 weeks time [she means in a period of six weeks] of typhus fever three grown up brothers!' Brown's words 'keep returning to my mind – like as if they had been a sort of strange presentiment.'[47] Already, as she contemplated Albert's weak, and weakening, constitution, the Queen was looking to the Highlander with second sight; the sturdy, kilted Brown as a prophet.

Although Albert urged his daughter Vicky – who had also been unwell – to 'spare yourself, nurse yourself, and get completely well. The disaster in Portugal is another proof that we are never safe to refuse Nature her rights',[48] it was not advice which he heeded himself.

The story of the Prince of Wales and Nellie was by now circulating the gentemen's clubs of St James's. That compulsive gossip Lord Torrington was the man who felt constrained to pass on the news to Prince Albert. It was an occasion where some fathers would have smiled indulgently at their foolish son sowing a few wild oats, and where a disciplinarian might have felt the need to remind Bertie of the consequences, in a royal personage, of public indiscretions. For Albert, however, who was in a depleted state of health, exhausted by sleeplessness, perpetual gastric troubles, gumboils and toothache, the escapade of a sensual boy with a pretty woman awoke demons. Twenty years of serious schooling, of filling every minute with botany, grammar and mathematics, twenty years of thrashings and punishments, and verbal admonitions, and readings aloud from the sermons of Dr Arnold, appeared to have been powerless against the Prince of Wales's inheritance. Albert had flogged and talked, and admonished, he had spoken to Bertie till he was hoarse, about the history of Charlemagne, the great masters of the Italian Trecento and the German Gothic cathedrals, about the developments in modern geology and the fascinations of Hegel; and all he got for his pains as a dutiful father was the whole succession of sensualists and vulgarians, on both sides of the family, who now leered at him through Bertie's oyster eyes. Here was old George IV with his collection of erotic prints; here was William IV with his ten illegitimate children; here, oh horror, was Albert's own mother Luise with her lovers, banished from Court by an equally libidinous father – Duke Ernst I, with his foul language, heavy drinking and syphilis.

A modern adviser to Prince Albert might have begged him to keep the affair of Nellie Clifden in perspective. But it was from precisely the perspective of his own family's past, and that of the Queen, that he saw Bertie's escapade with Nellie. He wrote in fury to the prince, who had returned to Cambridge under the supervision of General Bruce. The letters spoke of 'profligacy', and envisaged a future King of England dragged into the courts in paternity suits. He thought of Nellie's ability to plunge the whole Royal Family into embarrassment. 'Oh, horrible prospect, which this person has in her power, any day, to realise! And to break your poor parents' hearts!'[49]

Albert then told the Queen. She confided in her journal that she would never again be able to look at Bertie without 'a shudder'. The Prince Consort's health seemed as if it were going to collapse altogether under the strain. '*Ich hange gar nicht am Leben*', he told her melodramatically; '*du hangst sehr daran.*' ('I do not hang on to life, but you do – very much so.')

It was a completely accurate account of their two natures, but she could not guess that it would be proved correct within a few weeks. Suffering from all his usual symptoms, made much worse by a heavy cold, he nonetheless refused to cancel engagements and went, as scheduled, to the Royal Military Academy at Sandhurst on 22 November, in what he described as 'dreadful rain'. Though this day's work turned his cold into something like influenza, Albert felt it to be his duty to go to Cambridge and to speak to his son man to man. They walked near Madingley Hall. Somehow, in spite of the appalling weather, it was too awkward to face one another indoors, so they paced through the downpour, squelching through muddy puddles, as Bertie penitently promised his father that he had put Nellie aside, that he bitterly repented of the evil, and of the pain he had caused everyone. The talking was so painful, and so all-absorbing, that Bertie, who had believed himself to know the way they were walking, lost his path and they arrived back at Madingley Hall both soaked to the skin. Prince Albert spent the night there, sleepless and shivering, with 'rheumatic' pain in his back and legs. The Queen blamed these pains on 'Bertie's mistaking the road during their walk'. When the Prince Consort returned to Windsor on 26 November, he was a seriously sick man.

The next day, 27 November, a transatlantic British mail packet called the *Trent* docked at Southampton. The captain had a tale to tell. When she left Havana, the *Trent* had on board two envoys of the Confederate Government, James Murray Mason of Virginia, and John Slidell of Louisiana, with their secretaries, who had intended to come to London and to Paris to petition for armed help in the Civil War. Knowing that the two Confederate envoys were on board, the Federals set out in pursuit and fired on the *Trent* on 8 November, claiming that enemy communications were 'contraband of war'. The Federal Captain Wilkes had boarded the *Trent*, threatened violence, and captured the two Confederate envoys with their secretaries.

The reactions of the British premier, Lord Palmerston, can be readily imagined. It was said afterwards that if The Trent Affair had occurred in the era of international telegraph, it would almost certainly have led to war between Britain and the Northern States. As it was, the British had to wait nearly three weeks before the affair was revealed to them. The strength of feeling against the 'Yankees' was in any case strong in England, especially in the Liberal North, where Lancashire was beginning its 'cotton famine' in consequence of the war. Despite the popularity in Britain of *Uncle Tom's Cabin*, and a general revulsion against slavery among a majority of British people, it was felt by most English newspapers, and by the Northern Liberals most affected by the cotton famine, that neither side in America had begun the Civil War with the declared avowal to abolish slavery. To this extent, the North was no more virtuous than the South, and British instincts (quite apart from the cotton famine) sided with the more old-fashioned states of the South and with their desire for the independence of a republic.

It would have taken very little to persuade Palmerston to declare war, and feelings of British outrage against Captain Wilkes's piratical actions were strong. 'Have you seen the news from America?' the fictional Prime Minister asks the young MP Phineas Finn in Trollope's eponymous novel (1867–9). 'I have seen it but I do not believe it,' was the reply.

Albert was too weak to go up to London from Windsor to discuss the matter with Palmerston and Lord John Russell. The Queen went in his stead, returning with draft communiqués. Albert settled down to read the Cabinet papers, but, as he admitted after a few hours, *'Ich bin so schwach, ich habe kaum die Feder halten können.'* ('I am so weak I could hardly hold a pen.') After his death, it was piously believed that it was Albert's moderating influence which persuaded Palmerston to tone down the fire of his dispatches to the Federal Government, and to avert a violent crisis between the two Governments. Whatever the truth of this, Albert's weakly scribbled response to the Cabinet ultimatum on the morning of 1 December 1861 was the last thing he ever wrote.

The Queen's journal gives out, for the year 1861, on 13 December. The first fortnight of the month records the most painful catalogue of her husband's decreasing strength and his doctors' false hopes. Presumably, the hope was so strong that they did not dare to allow themselves to see the obvious. On Monday, 2 December, the Queen recorded, 'My poor Albert had a sad night of shivering, sleeplessness & great distress. Sent for Dr Jenner, who found him extremely uncomfortable, sad & distressed. Dr Jenner assured me there was no reason to be alarmed.' Later that day, the prince sat listlessly on the sofa while the Queen read aloud from Scott's *Peveril of the Peak*.

That night, she dined with Lord Palmerston, who urged her to consult new medical opinion, and the Duke of Newcastle. On 4 December, Albert could take no nourishment, though he could 'sip a little raspberry vinegar in Seltzer water'. On Thursday 5th, they heard the news that the Vicereine of India, Lady Canning, had died in Calcutta. Such was the atmosphere at Windsor, that the news of any death was especially distressing. But on Friday 6th, Sir James Clark came and announced that the prince's 'condition improved'. Jenner agreed.

The next day, the doctors told the Queen that the prince had a fever. They had previously told her that if his fever rose, he would not survive it; but now they said that he would have to let the fever run its course, and that it would last a month. On Sunday, the Queen went to St George's Chapel and heard Charles Kingsley preach. The prince was weaker.

On Monday 9th, Dr Jenner pronounced 'favourably, thank God!' By Tuesday 10th, the prince was wandering in his mind 'but this Sir James said was to be expected… The Doctors were much pleased with his state'. On the 11th, he took a little broth. By now a whole team of medics were assembled, including a cheerful one called Dr Watson, and Mr Brown, who had looked after the Duchess of Kent in her last days. By the 12th, Albert's hands were shaking. Dr Jenner and Sir

James Clark 'thought all was going well'. They gave him ammonia to check his rapid respiration. On the following day, Dr Jenner was expressing the fear that this very quick breathing could lead to congestion of the lungs. Brandy was now being administered every half hour. Dr Watson cheerily told the Queen that he had 'seen many infinitely worse cases' and that 'I never despair with fever.'

That is the last entry for 1861 in Queen Victoria's journal.⁵⁰ The next day, 14 December, would be a date of dread, of solemn horror and misery for the rest of her life.

They had moved Albert into the Blue Room, the room where William IV and George IV had both died. At 6 am, Dr Brown called her, and said he had no hesitation that 'I think there is ground to hope the crisis is over'.⁵¹ When she went in to see him early that morning, the Queen saw a radiant Albert. The weight having dropped off his face, he looked as he had done in youth, when she had first fallen in love with him. She walked out on to the terrace in the cold air with Princess Alice. In the distance, a military band was playing, and Victoria wept copiously.

In the afternoon, they moved the bed away from the wall. The Queen noted that his face now had 'a dusky hue'. He was now speaking in French, worrying over the Orléanist princes who had enlisted in the Federalist forces in America and might find themselves fighting against England.

The doctors asked the Queen if the children could come to see their father. At first, she was worried that the sight of Bertie would agitate him, but one by one they were led through the room to kiss their father's hand. Everyone noticed the Queen's extraordinary calmness. By early evening, he was able to get out of the bed, while they changed the sheets. He could not get back into the bed without assistance. The Queen went to lie next door, but then she heard a change in his breathing, and rushed back in.

'*Es ist das kleine Frauchen*,' she whispered desperately to him. She asked for '*ein Kuss*' and he notionally moved his trembling lips. She ran from the room and threw herself on the ground in anguish.

Princess Alice followed her and begged her to return, for, young as she was, she could see that the end was now very near.

'Oh, this is death,' cried the Queen, taking his left hand and kneeling beside the bed. 'I know it. I have seen this before.'

Princess Alice knelt on the other side of the bed, the Prince of Wales and Princess Helena knelt at the foot of the bed. Prince Ernst of Leiningen, the doctors, Prince Albert's valet Rudolph Loehlein, Colonel Phipps and General Bruce were there, as was the Dean of Windsor, Gerald Wellesley. Lining the corridor were the Gentlemen of the Household in their splendid Windsor uniforms – put on in honour of the dinner they had just eaten, rather than especially to attend a deathbed.

'Two or three long, but perfectly gentle breaths were drawn, the hand clasping mine, & (oh! It turns me sick to write it) all, all was over... I stood up, kissing his dear heavenly forehead & called out in a bitter agonising cry: "Oh, my dear Darling!" & then dropped on my knees in mute, distracted despair, unable to utter a word or shed a tear.'[52]

It was quarter to eleven. Those left in the room heard the Queen's loud sobs as she was carried out by Colonel Phipps. He laid her on a sofa in the Red Room. Her children came to join her. The Prince of Wales ran into her arms. 'Indeed, Mama, I will be all I can to you.' She kissed him again and again. 'I am sure, my dear boy, you will.'

The Household now came in to swear their devotion, to express their sympathy, to promise their loyalty. As she came out of the Red Room, she met the Duchess of Atholl – 'Oh duchess, he is dead! He is dead!'

She took the duchess and the children's governess Miss Hildyard to kiss the prince's hand, which was already cold.

Afterwards, she went to her room, staring wildly at her maids. They got her to bed, and Princess Alice had her own bed moved into the room. It was a repetition of childhood in Kensington Palace, a widowed Queen and a daughter sharing a bedroom. Alice sent for Jenner who gave Queen Victoria a mild opiate, but it was not the knock-out draught she required, and for much of the night she woke and she wept.[53]

When Vicky heard the news in Germany, she wrote, 'Why has the earth not swallowed me up? To be separated from you at this moment is a torture which I can not describe.' On the same day, the Queen had begun a letter to her, with the words, 'My darling Angel's child – Our firstborn. God's will be done.'[54]

PART FOUR

'THE QUEEN'S GRIEF STILL SOBS'

A YEAR ON, in 1862, the Queen prepared herself for her first Christmas as a widow. Special festivals are times which almost all bereaved people find particularly painful. 'Precious one, he loved this festival so much – in all his letters he speaks of "*das liebe Weihnachtsfest*" & he liked it so much as it was "*eine allgemeine Bescherung*", mutual giving and receiving! And those 2 dear ones, who introduced this blessed custom & were so busy & so happy in preparing for others – dear Mama (<u>how</u> kind and busy <u>she</u> was) and my Angel are both no more here!'[1]

Albert's '*liebes Kind*' was a woman of forty-two; but her marriage had – as marriage often can to either sex – infantilized her. She had become so used to his being the one who made the chief political decisions, and drafted the diplomatic and political letters. Intensely shy as she always was, she had gone through the motions of receiving foreign dignitaries, presiding at Drawing Rooms, Investitures, Privy Councils and the like, but always with the prince at her side. Even so simple a thing as knowing when to rise from a State Banquet was dictated by a friendly wink[2] from the Prince Consort. Now she was completely adrift. Nothing could console, but the trappings of grief, the swathing of herself, her children, her household in deepest black, the ordering of thicker and thicker black borders for the writing paper, the keeping as a shrine, a *Todeszimmer*, of the Blue Room at

Windsor, and the planning of mausolea and memorials provided an occupation through her sleepwalk of psychological torture.

The grief-stricken Leopold of Saxe-Coburg-Gotha, upon the death of Princess Charlotte, had built a small Gothic mausoleum in the grounds of Claremont. His gave his nephews, Albert and Ernst, the idea of building a mausoleum at Coburg for their father in 1844. Leopold's sister, Duchess Victoire, had wanted to be buried in this family vault, but in 1859 she decided she wished to be buried at Frogmore. Prince Albert commissioned Ludwig Grüner to design a mausoleum for the Duchess of Kent near her residence in Home Park, Windsor. The building was executed by A. J. Humbert.

When the prince himself died, the Queen lost no time in commissioning another mausoleum, a last resting place for Albert and herself. Grüner was once again approached as the principal architect, and Humbert was employed to execute the great German's designs. Grüner chose to encase Victoria and Albert in a monument of high Italian Renaissance style, embellished with glorious marble and stencilled paintwork of rich reds, dark blues and bright yellow. The walls were decorated with frescoes by contemporary German and Italian artists in the manner of Raphael. And the centrepiece of the whole edifice was to be the marital pair themselves. Albert's love of Scotland and his taste for Italian art were skilfully combined in the huge sarcophagus, which is hewn from dark Aberdeen granite. On top of the massive tomb, however – worthy in size and scope of the great princes of Europe, as magnificent as Charlemagne's tomb at Aachen, or Napoleon's at Les Invalides – lie the pair themselves. Baron Carlo Marochetti carved two exquisite figures in white marble, Albert in the robes of the Garter, and his Queen everlastingly young in a dress which is part ballgown and part shroud. This youthful statue of the Queen was kept in store until her death. Forty years would elapse before the Widow of Windsor was laid to rest beside her lover and prince, but that she already did so in spirit was the unmistakeable message of the architects and the sculptor. Grüner had risen to the emotional-cum-aesthetic challenge with true magnificence. The potent mingling of Love and Death had been the leitmotiv of the Romantic movement – in the poetry of Keats and Novalis, and rising later in the century to its operatic, almost orgasmic musical form in Richard Wagner's Liebestod in *Tristan und Isolde.* There was nothing artificial about the Queen's laceration of spirit, but her expression of grief bore all the hallmarks of her era. 'The Queen's grief still sobs through its interior as though she had left her sorrow on earth to haunt this rich, forbidding temple to her loneliness.'[3]

The site of the Frogmore Mausoleum was chosen by the Queen within four days of the prince's death. The fane was erected with great speed, and a little over a year after Albert's death, the Bishop of Oxford, Samuel Wilberforce, consecrated the mausoleum. The next day, the body was moved from St George's Chapel to its sarcophagus. Thereafter, scarcely a day passed, when the Queen was resident at Windsor Castle, without her visiting Albert's shrine. Nor, of course, would the Frogmore Mausoleum be the only memorial to the Prince Consort. Sir George Gilbert Scott designed the most famous of them – finally unveiled in 1876 – the Albert Memorial, hard by the original site of the Crystal Palace – which was erected in part by public subscription, in part by a parliamentary grant of £50,000.

In our own day, the Albert Memorial, which had begun to show signs of age, has been gloriously restored, so that we can see it in its pristine splendour: the bronze statue of the Prince Consort by J. H. Foley sits enthroned in a Gothic baldachin. The base of this canopy is adorned with a marble frieze with the figures of painters, poets, composers, architects and sculptors. The corners jut out with statues representing the prince's practical concerns: Agriculture, Commerce, Manufacture and Engineering. At the corners of the whole memorial are statues representing the four continents. For once, a piece of extravagant funerary statuary does not exaggerate the significance of its subject. Albert, who had been so little understood in his lifetime by the British Establishment, had possessed a prodigious range of talents, interests and accomplishments. Britain had failed to see his excellence, but he had seen Britain's. The Memorial is therefore both a salute to the only member of the Royal Family in recent history, or perhaps ever, who deserves the name of genius, and to the wonderful age in which he lived. From his Highland home in Balmoral to his birthplace in Coburg, and in many of the new industrial cities of the Midlands and the North, statues of Albert sprang up, and Albert Streets, Albert Squares, Albert Terraces and Albert Crescents rampaged through the road maps of British towns. In Balmoral, in August 1862, 'We went through a sad ceremony. I and my six orphans went up (I – wonderful to say – in my little carriage) to the top of Craig Lowrigan – just opposite Craig Gowan and placed the first stones (at least some stones), in the front of which all our initials will be carved in large letters; and we have placed at the end the initials of you three absent ones, thinking you would like it,' the Queen wrote to the Crown Princess of Prussia. 'It will be 40 feet at the base – and 35 feet high and the following inscription is to be placed on it – in very large letters, "To the beloved memory of Albert the great and good, Prince Consort. Raised by his broken-hearted Widow."'[4] It was inscribed with a quotation from the Book of Wisdom – which, not being part of the canonical Scripture recognized by the Reformation, was criticized by the Free Kirk – 'shamefully'[5] in the Queen's eyes.

It is the conventional belief that, after she was widowed, Queen Victoria sank into a depressive seclusion which led to a withdrawal from political affairs and public life; that after nearly a decade of this seclusion, the monarchy itself was imperilled; and that, had it not been for the near-death of the Prince of Wales, of typhoid fever in 1871, prompting a surge of patriotic love for the institution, the monarchy and the Queen's reputation might never have recovered. Mythologies do not arise out of nothing, and there is plainly some truth in this analysis of the ten years or so which followed the death of the Prince Consort.

It is true, certainly, that Victoria was desolated by Albert's death; that the woman, who loved the theatre and the opera and the ballet, who enjoyed great dinners, was changed into a sable-clad widow who shunned society. It is by no means true, however, that she lost interest in political affairs. At times, the weight of grief and depression were so great that she found it difficult to function as a human being. But there were actually very few months, even at the worst moments of blinding, and almost maddening, desolation, when she was not also politically engaged. This was often how matters appeared to her exasperated ministers, who found her cancelling Privy Council meetings at a moment's notice, and shrinking from public duties such as the State Opening of Parliament.

Another way of viewing the story, however, would be to say that Victoria was, in her extraordinary way, a woman battling with demons, and overcoming them – largely alone. For many years after she was left alone, she was wandering through the valley of the shadow; but she would emerge. That is the triumphant ending which any reader (or author) of a biography of the Queen can expect. It is a story of victory against painful odds. She was not exaggerating when she wrote, '*ich habe Alles verloren!*'[6] ('I have lost everything!') Yet even in the immediate years after she was widowed, although she withdrew from much of public life, she continued to play a daily and active role in the political affairs of Europe. She had no choice. Moreover, as her mental health broke down under the burden of bereavement, she found herself having to struggle with an intractable international situation, one whose outcome would affect the entire future of Europe, one in which her family was intimately involved, and a situation, moreover, where she feared the intemperate attitudes of her Liberal ministers would lead Britain into a futile war. 'Had a bad night. So worried about this terrible Holstein question,' she told her journal, and, to the Duke of Newcastle, 'I urged most strongly the necessity for great caution and no irritating language against Germany being used, for it would produce an everlasting irritation'.[7] Events proved her right about this. The rise of Bismarck, and with it the success of Prussia in its territorial and political ambitions, was relentless. There would have been nothing that Palmerston or Gladstone or Russell or Newcastle, or any of these

Englishmen, could have done about it. Anything they might have tried to do would have been to make matters worse, and expose Britain to a humiliating war against Prussia, which they would undoubtedly have lost. Not for the last time, Victoria, even in her extremity of nervous collapse, saved her male ministers from their own folly.

1861 had taken from her both her mother and her husband. Between them, Duchess Victoire and Prince Albert had sustained for Victoria, from her very earliest years, a world of home which provided her with stability; it was an alternative world to the alarming and quarrelsome British world outside the walls of, at first, Kensington Palace, and subsequently, outside Osborne and Balmoral. As a child, she had been frightened by the dysfunctional, fissiparous feuds among her British uncles and cousins. As a young monarch, she was alarmed by the British courtiers and by the politicians who seemed to be her enemies. Victoire, and then Albert, came from another world, from Coburg. Never having been exposed, as mother and husband had been, to the darker sides of Coburg life – to the dissolute Duke Ernst I's marriages, to the quarrels within the German Court – Victoria was enabled to idealize Coburg, and to find in the world of Germany, its language, music and culture, a comfort blanket which smelt of home. This also happened to be the decade in which modern Germany itself, from dozens of German-speaking duchies, former electorates, free cities, princedoms and kingdoms, was struggling to be born. Seen from the perspective of her British subjects, and biographers, the 1860s could be viewed primarily as the time of seclusion. Seen from the perspective of Victoria's children – three of whom were to be married to Germans by 1870 – and seen from the perspective of the Queen herself, this was the decade in which the Kensington child of a German exile rediscovered her German roots. When Princess Charles of Hesse-Darmstadt came to the Isle of Wight in 1862 to attend the wedding of her son Prince Louis to Princess Alice, she remarked, 'from the moment... I was presented to the Queen, and her kind, almost motherly words in pure German sounded in my ear, a feeling of home came over me.'[8]

There was, therefore, a strange paradox at work in British political life during the 1860s. For largely inner, psychological reasons, Victoria turned towards Germany in this decade, visiting and revisiting the palaces where her mother and Albert had grown up. She became increasingly aware, not least through letters to and from her daughter Vicky, the Prussian Crown Princess, her daughter Alice, Grand Duchess of Hesse-Darmstadt, and her sister-in-law, Duchess Alexandrine of Coburg – with all of whom she engaged in more or less weekly, sometimes daily, correspondence – of the monumental changes which were taking place in Germany, and hence in the world. When many of the senior British statesmen of the age thought that the chief story of these years was to do with electoral reform at home – or with changes in Irish–British relations, or with the effects of the American Civil War on British trade – Victoria was one of only a small handful of people in the British Isles who was aware of the enormous convulsion brought to pass by the strength of Prussia and the career of Otto von Bismarck. The rumbling and complex question of who should rule over the Duchies of Schleswig and Holstein, in Southern Denmark or Northern Germany (depending upon your point of view), concealed the much bigger question of who would control not merely these little bits of territory in the Baltic, but the whole of Germany, and indeed the question of whether there might now actually be a political entity called Germany. Victoria, who by the end of the decade would have one child married to a Dane, and another to a Schleswig-Holsteiner, and several others to Germans from different parts of that land, possessed within her own family living evidence of the huge significance of the Schleswig-Holstein Question. Palmerston's famous joke about it[9] seems as crass, in hindsight, as Neville Chamberlain's view that Czechoslovakia was a faraway country of which we know nothing. As we enter the 1860s, therefore, we need to hold several matters in our head at once: the Queen's deep unhappiness, leading at times to an unbalanced state of mental health; the political changes coming to Britain as the old guard of 'dreadful old men' gave place to the rivalry between Disraeli and Gladstone; but also the new Europe which was coming into being. Seen through the prism of a biography of Queen Victoria, the paradox is that the supposedly 'out of touch' monarch, with her purely personal reasons for clinging to her German husband's beloved memory and her German roots, was sometimes more politically aware than the old and middle-aged men who threw up their hands in despair because she was too weepy, and too far from London, to give what they considered sufficient attention to domestic politics.

In 1848, when the Prussian prince had taken refuge in England, and so many convulsions had shaken the German states, Prince Albert had longed to be in Germany alongside his brother Ernst. To Stockmar, then a member of the Frankfurt Diet, Albert had sent his carefully drawn 'plan for the new Germany'. It proposed a union of the German states with Austria, and an acceptance of the Austrian Emperor as the elected or constitutional head. Albert's proposal was published posthumously as a pamphlet in 1867 – *Zum Verständniss der deutschen Frage*[10] ('Towards an Understanding of the German Question') – but by then, events had moved on. Far from accepting a Habsburg Emperor as the unifying symbol of the German people, Prussia had inflicted upon Austria a military humiliation. Germany was moving towards another type of unification altogether with Prussia as the dominant partner. As for Albert, his influence could only survive from beyond the grave in the persons of his widow, his daughter Vicky, the Prussian Crown Princess, and her husband Fritz – 'this fool of a Crown Prince',[11] as he was regarded by the man who was in fact to dominate German politics for the next decade and beyond – Otto von Bismarck.

The rise of Bismarck was the central event of European political history in 1862. Wilhelm, Vicky's father-in-law, who as the Prussian prince had taken refuge in London with Victoria and Albert during the Year of Revolutions, had been ruling as Regent in Berlin while his brother was mad. In 1861, that brother died, and Wilhelm succeeded as King of the Prussians. 1861, which had been so doleful a succession of bereavements for Queen Victoria, was for King Wilhelm I one of repeated constitutional crises. He was not by nature a democrat and the demands for constitutional reform, army reform and limits on his powers were more than this volatile and frequently tearful sixty-year-old monarch could tolerate. He drew up a deed of abdication in favour of his son Fritz. It was an astute political move by a natural conservative, causing as it did a closing of ranks by the right wing. The last thing required by the *Junkers* and the diehards was a *Dummkopf Kronprinz*, his head stuffed with English liberal ideas, sitting on the throne of Frederick the Great and offering votes to Jews and Poles, or Budget decisions referred to Cabinets. The Prussian Minister in Paris was called home to become the Prime Minister: this was Bismarck aged fifty and at the very height of his political energy. The King did not abdicate. Any dream that Prussia, or a United Germany, would become a liberal State based on British parliamentary principles, was firmly snuffed out. But this was not obvious at first, and for Queen Victoria, as for her daughter the Crown Princess – the very opposite of a *Dummkopf*, she! – there was now a sacred duty to continue Prince Albert's work on earth.

'Heaven forbid,' wrote the Crown Princess to her mother at the beginning of 1862, 'beloved Papa's work of 20 years should be in vain. God requires immense sacrifices of you and has imposed most difficult duties on you but He has given you adored Papa for a pattern. His bright example will be your guide!' This letter makes clear that Vicky expected her mother to play an active role not merely in British but in German politics. 'Who can know his feelings and opinions on all things as well as you, beloved Mama! Who could carry out his plans better?'[12]

The conflict between private heartbreak and public duty was, however, all but intolerable. When the Chancellor of the Exchequer, Gladstone, made a public speech in Manchester in April 1862, the Queen poured out her feelings to him. Their later relations were strained and frozen, but in these bleak months, she could write from 'the depth of a heart which bleeds <u>more</u> and <u>more</u> to tell Mr Gladstone that his speech touched and satisfied her much'. Gladstone, who as a follower of Sir Robert Peel, had been close politically to the Prince Consort, was also, like Albert, a person of relentless seriousness, filling every minute with intellectual research, or good works, or attempts to improve and reform the political system. For him the death of Albert had been a personal and political tragedy. The Queen could therefore write to him that

> He well described the love that bound and binds the poor heartbroken Queen, and that adored and perfect Being who was and is her <u>All</u> but without him, <u>Life</u> is <u>utter darkness</u>. The Queen struggles and works and will devote herself hourly to what her precious Husband wished... and do her duty – to the last hours of her life – but her faithful servants and kind friends must not deceive themselves by thinking her efforts will carry her on – for the continual longing – and pining – the void and suffering! which never ceases [sic] by day or night – accompanied by the amount of work and responsibility weighs alone upon her health and strength – she gets considerably weaker, her health worse, & her nerves terribly shattered... Mrs Gladstone who the Queen knows is a most tender wife – may in a faint measure picture to herself what the Queen suffers.[13]

The old spectre which haunted her ministers was not the late Angel Prince Albert, but the ghost of mad King George III, Victoria's grandfather. She warned Lord Derby that 'three times at Balmoral she had thought she was going mad'. Lord Clarendon noticed that when she spoke of the state of her mind, her eye and manner 'became excited' and that she was 'evidently in a highly nervous state'. More than once, she murmured, 'My reason, my reason' and tapped her forehead.[14]

That March in Windsor, Clarendon was dismayed to note that she repeatedly referred to the prince and his opinions as if he were in the next room. His writing table, with fresh ink in the inkwell and a vase of flowers, was kept as if he were about to sit and pore over dispatches.[15]

After her visit to Coburg in the first year after Albert's death – in September 1862 – she wrote, 'I miss dear, dear Coburg so much! It was full of all precious recollections – in fact I felt it like the home of my childhood (which you know is swept away in England). I miss the dear German language, all which I feel necessary to my very existence. Do you all cherish it, and do so when I am gone – promise me all of you? Tell Bertie how pleased I am to hear he loves our precious Coburg.'[16]

Though her own marriage was over, the Queen could not neglect to attend to the marriage prospects of her growing children. Eighteen-year-old Alice's betrothal to Prince Louis of Hesse-Darmstadt had been arranged by July 1861. A dowry of £30,000 had been voted by Parliament for the girl, as well as an annual allowance of £6,000;[17] wracked by grief as Victoria was, she knew that this was not a marriage which could be passed over. So, on 1 July 1862, the wedding took place in the drawing room at Osborne House. 'The Archbishop of York [Longley] read that fine service (purified from its worst coarsenesses) admirably, and himself had tears running down his cheeks – for he too lost his dear partner not long ago. I sat the whole time in an armchair, with our four boys near me; Bertie and Affie led me down stairs. The latter sobbed all through and afterwards – dreadfully.'[18] The coarsenesses of the Prayer Book to which the Queen objected were those lines in the service suggesting that holy matrimony was ordained 'for a remedy against sin and to avoid fornication', even though it was not to be undertaken merely 'to satisfy men's carnal lusts and appetites, like brute beasts that have no understanding'.[19]

Alice, who had borne the brunt of her mother's wildest grief in the previous seven months, now went to her new life in Germany. Lady Augusta Bruce had noticed that the nineteen-year-old had become 'a different creature'[20] since her father died, wise beyond her years, but also – she had inherited her father's intense seriousness and her mother's sense of tragedy – a solemn creature, plagued with depressions and doubts. It was almost as if she intuited that hers was to be a tragic destiny. In Darmstadt, she was often extremely homesick. Particularly, she missed Bertie, her favourite sibling. A carrier of haemophilia, she would become the mother of seven children, at least three of whom were affected by the cursed gene. Her married life was pitted against the background of German civil war. Two of her daughters, Elisabeth and Alix, had unhappy fates: Elisabeth, as the wife of Sergei, Grand Duke of Russia, saw her husband murdered, and was herself hurled into a lime pit by revolutionaries. Alix, as the Empress Alexandra Fyodorovna, was the last of the tsarinas, massacred at Ekaterinburg. Alice was a woman with a devoted social conscience, and a great promoter of nursing. She was in full correspondence with Octavia Hill, the social reformer, about the condition of the London poor. Royal biographies abound with sycophantic hyperboles about figures who would not attract any notice were they not of illustrious descent. Alice was not one such. She was a genuinely interesting nineteenth-century woman – acutely alive to all the changes in society going on around her, not least in the position of women; a kind and attentive friend and mother and, like her sister Vicky, highly intelligent; but carrying this strange doomed feeling. 14 December, that day of dread when she lost her father, would be a date of doleful significance in her own life too.

It was essential to marry Bertie to a suitable bride, and Victoria continued, somewhat strangely – given her strong views about Schleswig-Holstein – with plans to wed him to the Danish princess. The Queen never entirely shook off the belief that the Prince Consort's death had been Bertie's fault, that the saintly Albert had been forced to an early grave by the lechery of his son. She needed Bertie out of her sight in the immediate aftermath of Albert's death; and she needed to make him respectable. It was therefore decided to dispatch him on an improving tour of the Levant, with General Bruce and that unworldly scholar, Arthur Penrhyn Stanley, the 'Arthur' of *Tom*

Brown's Schooldays, who shamed the rough dormitory at Rugby by kneeling down to pray before getting into his bed. It is hard to think of any three men less different in character than Stanley, an ethereal aristocrat scholar, the bluff General Bruce and Bertie, whose chief interests at this date were women and horse racing. To the credit of all three, they made a fist of it, and the tour was far from disastrous. Bertie recommended the older men to read *East Lynne*, a trashy novel by Mrs Henry Wood, and Stanley, rather as if he were discussing one of the Dialogues of Plato with Benjamin Jowett on a Balliol reading party, gave his great mind to the intricacies of Mrs Wood's sensational tale.

While Bertie was away, Victoria and Vicky set to work to expedite his wedding arrangements: for it was obvious that continence was impossible to him, and they believed – with unfounded optimism, as history would quickly make plain – that if he were happily settled with a good wife, he would stop philandering. Sure enough, when he returned his mother could report, 'He is much improved, and' – what amounted to a synonym – 'is ready to do every thing I wish.'[21]

The victim of the trip was Bruce, who succumbed to liver failure and died shortly after their return, aged only forty-nine. Whether the tedium of Bertie's expositions of *East Lynne* had forced the general to apply himself too liberally to the brandy bottle or whether he picked up 'gippy tummy' from some Levantine swamp will never be known. Victoria, of course, held Bertie responsible. 'Dear, dear General Bruce!' exclaimed the Queen, 'he has sacrificed his valued life for our poor dear child! And Bertie is quite overwhelmed by it. Poor dear child! He is indeed very forlorn. Oh! God! For what purpose is all this?'[22]

After Alice's wedding – 'more like a funeral than a wedding'[23] – the Queen took off for Germany. She was accompanied to Coburg by her sons, twelve-year-old Arthur and the haemophiliac Leopold, aged nine. The journey came to an abrupt halt in Reinhardtsbrunn, the Gothic hunting lodge built for Victoria's uncle and father-in-law

Duke Ernst I on the edge of the Thüringer Wald. Leopold, presumably sucking a sharp steel pen in the carriage out of boredom, pierced the roof of his mouth with the nib. The bleeding could not be controlled. Dr Jenner got to work with his usual remedy – emetics and laxatives – which had no effect on the bleeding. Rudolph Loehlein, Prince Albert's former valet, did his best to keep the child comfortable, and they eventually sent for Professor Wilms, a specialist in Berlin, who painted a strong cauterizing solution on the roof of the child's mouth and ordered finger pressure on the wound, no matter what the difficulty, at the first sign of any bleeding.

'He has not lost near as much blood as frequently before,' the Queen wrote to Alice, 'but the fear was – the bleeding cd. not be stopped & then – you know he cld. not have lived. On Tuesday night I went in at ½ p. 11 & there he was – nursed by Loehlein – very sick – bringing up blood – & it was an anxious sad sight.'²⁴

The prospect of losing her sick son, however, was less terrible to her than the dissolute behaviour of his two elder brothers, Bertie, with his clubs, mistresses, late nights of gambling, and Affie, who, having recovered from typhoid in Malta, seemed hell-bent on pursuing a life of dissipation which was scarcely more edifying. 'But oh!' exclaimed the Queen in a letter to Vicky a year later, as she contemplated another instance of poor little Leopold's painful bleeding, 'the illness of a good child is so far less trying than the sinfulness of one's sons – like your two elder brothers. Oh! Then one feels that death in purity is so far preferable to life in sin and degradation!'²⁵

Professor Wilms's treatment, however, worked and the child lived. The royal party reached Coburg on 3 October.

Queen Victoria was in Germany during one of the most crucial months of its history, the very week when King Wilhelm I of Prussia tried to abdicate in favour of her son-in-law Fritz, and Bismarck, recently installed as Minister President, the most powerful man in Prussia, talked him out of it. Bismarck was from now on, throughout this pivotal decade, in control of events. Albert's vision of Europe and the future of Germany is laid to one side in favour of the policy of the extreme right.

In October 1862, news reached London of the deposition of the unpopular King Otto of Greece. The vacant throne was offered by the army to Nicholas, Duke of Leuchtenberg, a cousin of the Russian Emperor. The mass of the Greeks, however, favoured a constitutional monarchy on the British pattern. A plebiscite was held, and Prince Alfred, Duke of Edinburgh – Affie – was chosen by the Hellenes by a huge majority as their monarch of choice. Greek politics, however, has never been easy, and the three Great Powers had taken a self-denying ordinance that they would not supply a monarch for Greece. Greatly to his relief, therefore, Affie was ineligible. It was offered to his uncle Ernst – Prince Albert's brother – who turned it down. Eventually the Greeks were given Prince Wilhelm of Schleswig-Holstein-Sonderburg-Glücksburg, who was crowned as King of the Hellenes the following year. As an inducement to the Greeks to accept this arrangement, Lord John Russell arranged that the Ionian Islands, which had been a British Protectorate since 1815, should now be ceded to Greece. The new King was seventeen. He ruled as King George for nearly fifty years until his assassination in 1913. He was the grandfather of Philip, Duke of Edinburgh, husband of Queen Elizabeth II.

Meanwhile, in Germany, Vicky kept her mother informed of the machinations of Bismarck and the anti-British policy of the Prussian Court. 'Bismarck makes more mischief every day – party spirit is rising on both sides alarmingly, the King makes the most imprudent and ill-judged speeches and is more deluded than ever. He wanted to go to England but was prevented by his ministers of course. I wish those last-named dear people were at the bottom of the sea with millstones round their necks!'[26] That autumn, Bismarck had made the speech which would be seen to typify the whole of Prussian politics up to and including 1914. 'It is not with speeches or with parliamentary resolutions that the great questions of the day are decided... but with blood and iron.'[27]

The dreadful anniversary, 14 December, passed. A melancholy Christmas ensued. Bertie's marriage to Princess Alexandra of Denmark was fixed – in defiance of canon law – during the penitential season of Lent. The beauty and charm of the princess, and her attractive docility – always a quality which the Queen admired, especially in members of her family – allowed them all to overlook the diplomatic awkwardness of the Danish–Prussian hostilities.

The public were determined to regard the marriage of the Prince of Wales as cause for high celebration. The Royal Yacht *Victoria and Albert* brought the Danish party from Antwerp. Bertie went to greet it at Gravesend. He arrived late, and ran up the gangplank, causing a storm of cheering from the onlookers when he openly kissed the beautiful eighteen-year-old princess. In an open carriage with the princess and her parents, the prince drove over London Bridge and made his way to Paddington Station by way of Temple Bar, Pall Mall, St James's Street, Piccadilly and Hyde Park. Princess Alexandra wore a grey silk dress and a violet jacket trimmed with sable and a white bonnet adorned with red rosebuds. She was by any standards a stunner. In the city, so many office workers came out to see the carriage pass that people were crushed. At one point the Life Guards drew sabres to make them draw back.

When the train reached Slough, another carriage procession formed, passing through Eton where the boys cheered themselves hoarse.[28] Through all the vicissitudes of the monarchy's reputation over the next half century, Alexandra remained a deeply loved figure in England. The Queen shared in the general adoration. 'She is so nice – so sympathetic – quiet, but gay and clever. I cannot thank God enough for having given us such a daughter,' she told her sister-in-law in Coburg.[29]

She was too 'desolate' to have dinner with the Danish party on their arrival; but before dinner, Princess Alix went to the Queen's apartment, 'knocked at the door, peeped in & came & knelt before me with that sweet, loving expression which spoke volumes. I was much moved & kissed her again & again.'[30]

The next day, Princess Alice accompanied the Queen to the mausoleum to receive the blessing of the dear departed Angel. And on 10 March Alix and Bertie were married at St George's Chapel, Windsor. Weeping as she took leave of her mother, Alix said to her, 'You may think that I like marrying Bertie for his position; but if he were a cowboy I would love him just the same, and would marry no one else.'[31]

The choir sang a chorale of Prince Albert's composition, and Jenny Lind sang a solo. The Queen sat in a Gothic box high on the wall of the chapel, looking down on the proceedings – wearing widow's weeds and a cap 'more hideous than any I have yet seen', in the eyes of Lord Clarendon. She also wore the blue sash and star of the Order of the Garter. For the first time since the death of the Prince Consort, the Court, though not the Queen herself, knew an atmosphere of festivity. There was a resumption of court balls and concerts. In London, Disraeli said it felt as if their honeymoon was going on for months, with a 'whirl of fetes and receptions, processions and ceremonies'.[32]

While the young couple went off to their life of enforced idleness, the Queen was still suffering; and she was compelled to work. 'You say that work does me good,' she had written to her uncle Leopold in February, 'but the contrary is the fact with me, as I have to do it alone, and my Doctors are constantly urging upon me rest. My work and my worries are so totally different to any one else's: ordinary mechanical work may be good for people in great distress, but not constant anxiety, responsibility and interruptions of every kind, where at every turn the heart is crushed and the wound is probed! I feel too visibly how much less able for work I am than I was.'[33]

The Schleswig-Holstein Question was a personal one. Vicky supported the Prussian claim to Holstein. Alix and Bertie, obviously, supported Denmark's claim at least to Schleswig. Meanwhile, were it not for the intransigence of the Danish King, Holstein would have been under the jurisdiction of the Duke of Augustenburg, who was the Queen's nephew – the son of Feodore. Anyone in the Queen's position would have been torn by this desperate international situation, even if they were not in the deep troughs of sadness caused by bereavement.

In July, the House of Commons voted by 287 to 121 against purchasing the Exhibition buildings at South Kensington. These were to have been Prince Albert's cultural legacy to the nation – becoming the Science Museum, the Natural History Museum and the Victoria and Albert Museum. So much for their sense of his contribution to the intellectual progress of the nineteenth century. 'A crushing defeat,' Disraeli said to the Queen's private secretary (formerly Albert's) General Grey. 'The House was really mad or drunk.'[34]

The Queen wrote to Palmerston, 'However, we have got the land and we must <u>now not lose</u> a moment in preparing plans and estimates for the necessary buildings to <u>replace</u> the present Exhibition one, for the purposes contemplated. As it is, the <u>folly</u> of last night will by and by be repented of.'[35] One should not underestimate the part played by the Queen herself in getting those museums built.

Stockmar died six days later in Coburg.

> One thought alone sustains me – it is the blessed one of the reunion of those two <u>blessed</u> spirits who loved each other so dearly, and understood each other so well, for dear old Stockmar said to me last year, looking at my darling's picture: 'I shall be so glad to see him again, my dear good Prince.' And <u>now they are together</u> – looking upon us poor mortals struggling on alone in a most imperfect and sad world – 'with larger other eyes than ours, making allowance for us all', as Tennyson says. They see the end of what seems interminable to us![36]

Once again, that summer the Queen visited Germany. The Duke of Edinburgh preceded her, going to spend time with his uncle and aunt in Coburg. He in turn was preceded by ardent letters from the Queen to the Duchess Alexandrine. Her heartbreak was real, but she was not ashamed to use it for moral blackmail, especially in matters about which she felt as strongly as the evils of smoking: 'One request which I direct to Ernst from the bottom of my broken Widow's and Mother's heart! As regards Alfred – that Ernst shouldn't encourage him to smoke, which has been strictly forbidden by his doctor.' She also implored Alexandrine not to allow Ernst to indulge in ribaldry with the lad or to speak to him 'man to man'. Dirty jokes and smoking would be an insult to the Angelic Memory, 'and I know that he holds that memory too sacred, not to follow Our wishes'.[37]

The late summer visit to Germany, however, was not merely a family trip. A great Congress was taking place at Frankfurt, attended by the British Foreign Secretary, Lord Granville, on the future of Germany, and on the European crisis caused by the Schleswig-Holstein affair. Exhausted, grief-stricken, and overpoweringly shy as Victoria was, she found herself at the epicentre of this political maelstrom. On almost every day of the Schleswig-Holstein crisis and the Danish–German war, Victoria, both in Germany and in England, was with her half-sister, 'dear Feodore, who is such a comfort'[38] – that is to say, with the mother-in-law of the Augustenburg claimant. She was, on the other hand, increasingly fond of her Danish daughter-in-law Alix.

It was the Queen herself, before any British diplomats, who, at the end of August, saw first the King of Prussia and then, on 3 September, the Emperor of Austria to discuss Prussian–Austrian rivalry.[39]

It was a nerve-wracking occasion, the first major public event in which she had been centre stage since she was widowed. She found it 'very trying'.[40] The grand staircase of the Schloss Ehrenberg was decorated with flowers. 'Felt so nervous, all being in state and I alone!' She was followed up the stairs by Alice and Lenchen and together these three small women entered the Hall of Giants, the stupendous room where her parents had been married, to meet Franz Josef, the Emperor of Austria.

The two monarchs were shy with one another. He 'talks but little', and such a major diplomatic encounter, without a minister or Prince Albert at her side, was out of her experience. She saw it was necessary, however, and the two bravely went through the motions of a public meeting. In recollecting it, her grasp on the English language seemed to go adrift. 'I then mentioned Mexico, & Max going there, which I discouraged, & which the emperor does not either seem to like.'[41] (Maximilian was married to Charlotte, the daughter of King Leopold of Belgium, and 'very like angelic Louise' – i.e. her mother.) Over the matter of Poland, the Emperor thanked her Government for their support. 'Before & after luncheon I managed to say to the Emperor that I found the King of Prussia much irritated & fearing that Prussia would be passed over, which the Emperor said no one dreamed of. I added that I hoped I might assure the King of this, which he affirmed.'[42] It was a relief, when the formal luncheon was over, to drive back 'to the dear, peaceful Rosenau'. Her wish to sleep in Albert's birth-palace meant that she did not have the chance to sample the modern conveniences of the Schloss Ehrenberg. In readiness for the imperial arrival, Ernst had imitated his brother Albert's modern innovatory approach to domestic hygiene and installed a water closet in the emperor's bedroom. Two wooden chambers, similar in design and proportion to those at Osborne, were erected right next to the pillow-end of the bed. The modern polished mahogany doors of these 'thunderboxes' detract from the baroque splendour of the room. The lavatories themselves, manufactured by Thomas Crapper of Chelsea, had to be ordered direct from London.[43]

The next day, Ernst and Alexandrine drove out in their landau to visit Victoria and her daughters at the Rosenau. Ernst and the Queen discussed how the meeting had gone with the Emperor. Ernst believed that the Emperor would accept the strengthening of the German federation,[44] but perhaps Victoria – in constant touch as she was with Vicky in Berlin – had a closer sense than Ernst of the chill in the air, the change in the political climate. Events were fast moving to the point where what the Austrian Emperor approved or disapproved of would be of less consequence than the will of Chancellor Bismarck.

The Schloss Rosenau is a house of stupendous beauty, and the adjoining parkland was deliberately planted to resemble an English meadow. The whole place was soothing for the royal party. Leopold, who was well on this occasion, acquired a new dog, a dachshund called Waldmann or Waldi.[45]

The period of the Queen's 'seclusion' had begun. This was going to last at least for the duration of this decade. There was no doubt an accumulation of reasons for the seclusion, chief of which was heartbreak for Albert, and the nervous breakdown which it precipitated. Another factor, however, to which neither her ministers nor her biographers were always sensitive, was the sheer amount of time taken up by Prince Leopold's sickliness. It was not that she stopped work altogether but she withdrew from public life: the work of conferring with politicians and diplomats and with other European Heads of State continued as much as before the Prince Consort's death, even though she found this a very great physical and psychological burden. But she did not stop functioning altogether. The routines of life went on. Before she left the Rosenau, she assured Ernst, who was coming up to Balmoral that autumn for the sport, 'The Hunt is something which comes entirely under my jurisdiction, and the children can do nothing about stalking or shooting without my permission.'[46]

Back in England, she was reassured to find Palmerston 'wonderfully fair' in his views of the German situation; and when Gladstone, the Chancellor of the Exchequer, visited Balmoral on 26 September, she found that 'About German Unity, he seems very sensible.'[47]

The Queen deeply and intelligently engaged with her ministers in all the day-by-day developments of the Schleswig-Holstein crisis. Then the King of Denmark died – 'a terrible business', said the Queen.[48]

The new King, Alix's father King Christian, took a much more belligerent attitude towards the Duchies. Fritz and Vicky, too, on the other side, were, noted Victoria, 'very excited about this luckless business, which drives me half wild, for I have no longer my beloved

Albert to guide, cheer, advise & pilot me through the great difficulty.
I know what he would have felt about it. I still cannot help hoping
that the Great Powers will recognize the Treaty, as that is the <u>only</u>
way I can see of avoiding war!'[49]

She spent Christmas at Osborne. Shortly thereafter, the thirty-
four-year-old Professor Max Müller came to give lectures to the
Household on the origins of Indo-European languages. His presence
presumably allowed the Queen to speak in German for a few days,
a fact suggested by the un-English expressions in her journal, such
as when she says that Müller was 'now since 15 years established at
Oxford'.[50] 'He has a very soft voice, and his intonation and train of
thought, as well as beautiful language, reminded me and others of
a voice that is ever sounding in my ears and which is silenced now
forever!'[51]

Another memory of the Prince Consort was stirred by a more
grotesque experience. In 1845, the royal pair had visited Parkhurst
prison on the Isle of Wight (then a prison for juvenile boys, but now
used to incarcerate women) and, nineteen years on, she decided to
repeat the trip. There were 354 female convicts – 'only five for murder.
These are the saddest cases & as far as character goes, not the worst,
for they are poor young girls who from shame, & desertion have
destroyed their newly born children.'[52]

She went through many parts of the prison, but was only allowed
near the prisoners who were well behaved. ('The dress worn by the
women is not unbecoming, a tidy white cap or handkerchief & a not
ill-shaped blue serge dress and apron.') The governor told her that
there was one wing which she should not visit – that in which the
Irish were locked up. The visit during the previous week of a Roman
Catholic priest had left them 'unmanageable & excited'.

Although, naturally, the governor knew the identity of his visitor,
it was in no sense an official visit and the prisoners were not told
the Queen was coming. Then, in the laundry, one of the women

recognized her. 'In an instant many threw themselves on their knees, crying & sobbing, calling on me to pardon them. It was a most painful scene & I hurried up the flight of stairs in the long ward, to where the nursery was.'[53]

This was surely one of the strangest incidents in Victoria's early widowhood. It is also historically revealing, insofar as these women had not all instantly recognized the Queen. Before the days of newspaper photography, let alone films, newsreels or television, public figures were not necessarily recognizable to the population at large. (One remembers the walk in the rain from Claremont, when Victoria and Albert sheltered with a cottager and were not identified.) How many men and women in England in 1864 could have recognized Gladstone or the Prince of Wales? Far fewer, proportionately, than would today be the case with comparable figures. It was partly for this reason that the politicians were so anxious, as Victoria developed habits of private grief and hidden introspection, that she should be encouraged to be on parade, as she had been when she was Sir John Conroy's puppet as a teenager; and as, rather more willingly, she had allowed herself to be in the lifetime of the Angel.

On Wednesday, 27 January 1864, Russell, now Earl Russell, failed to secure agreement to armed assistance for Denmark from Britain in the event of German aggression. This left the Government with no clear policy to recommend to Parliament. The Queen was at one with the majority of the Cabinet, and with public opinion, that Great Britain should not be dragged into a war with Prussia over the question. She wrote to the Prime Minister:

> The Queen has read with the greatest alarm and aston-
> ishment the draft of a despatch to Sir A. Buchanan and Lord
> Bloomfield in which Lord Russell informs them that he
> has stated in conversation to Count Bernstorff that, in the
> event of the occupation of Schleswig by Prussia to obtain a
> guarantee for the withdrawal of the proclamation of the joint
> Constitution, Denmark would resist such an occupation and

that Great Britain would aid her in that resistance. The Queen has never given her sanction to any such threat, nor does it appear to agree with the decision arrived at by the Cabinet upon this question.[54]

For a broken-hearted widow who is written off by so many biographers as a mental 'case' at this period, she was doing rather well at restraining Palmerston and Russell's last gasps at Whiggish gung-ho foreign policy.

Partly as a result, perhaps, of worrying about the hostilities in which her native land was engaged, Princess Alix went into premature labour on 8 January 1864. The prince was born weighing only three pounds and twelve ounces.[55] The parents settled on the name Albert Victor Christian Edward, though confusingly the child was always called Eddy. It would have been impossible not to name the child Albert, and every time one of her grandchildren was born, the parents had to tread carefully if they did not include either the names of Albert or Victor in the case of boys, or Victoria for girls. The Queen recommended to Bertie that she would reserve '*Edward* for a second or third son' – the advice was ignored.[56]

While it would be an insult to omit the name Albert from the child's list of names, it would also, of course, be a delicate matter of whether the sacred name could ever be used. The Queen spelt it out. 'Respecting your own names, and the conversation we had, I wish to repeat, that it was beloved Papa's wish, as well as mine, that you should be called by <u>both</u>, when you became King, and it would be <u>impossible</u> for you to <u>drop</u> your Father's. It would be monstrous and <u>Albert alone</u>, as you truly and amiably say, would not do, as there can be only <u>one</u> ALBERT!'

Bertie replied, 'Regarding the possibility of my ever filling that high position, which God grant may be far, very far distant, I quite understand your wishes about my bearing my two names, although no English Sovereign has ever done so yet, and you will agree with me that it would not be pleasant to be like "Louis Napoleon", "Victor Emmanuel", "Charles Albert" etc.'[57]

Meanwhile, over the Danish crisis, the Queen wrote to Vicky that 'my heart and sympathies are all German'.[58] In February, she wrote to Earl Russell, 'How dreadfully we must all, but above all, the unhappy Queen, miss now the one wise, far-seeing, and impartial head, who would have guided us safely through these difficulties!'[59] With great recklessness, King Christian laid claim to both Duchies, giving Bismarck the excuse he needed to occupy both. He had squared the Russians, and the armies which marched into Schleswig on 1 February were not only Prussian, but Austrian too. Fritz was there at the head of his cavalry regiment. The Queen deplored the war, especially when she realized that Bismarck had no intention of exploring the Augustenburg claims to Holstein. Both Duchies were to come under the heel of Prussia. 'My prayers will be offered up for poor beloved Fritz,' she wrote, but added, 'I still disbelieve in war'.[60] Two weeks later, she exclaimed, 'Oh! If Bertie's wife was only a good German and not a Dane! Not, as regards the influence of the politics but as regards the peace and harmony of the family! It is terrible to have the poor boy on the wrong side.'[61] The bombardment of Sonderburg in March and April caused outrage in the British press, especially in *The Times*, but for Vicky, there was nothing 'inhuman or improper'[62] about it. An armistice was agreed by May, the Danes formally surrendered on 18 July 1864, and on 1 August, the Prussians took over the Duchies.

The war had been a small thing when measured by other conflicts – for example, by comparison with the slaughter in the American Civil War which raged from 1861 to 1865. But as an historian of the crisis pointed out, it was 'one of the important turning-points in the history of British foreign policy. It produced the most emphatic diplomatic defeat suffered by the Victorians and it precipitated their eclipse in Europe during the Bismarckian age'.[63] The Prusso-Danish war had caught old Palmerston and Russell off guard. Palmerston believed that the attempts of minor German states to determine the future of the

Duchies were as uncalled-for 'as the Duke of Devonshire's servants' hall assuming to decide who shall be the owner of a Derbyshire country gentleman's estate'.[64] The words showed that he had entirely missed the significance of what had happened. Bismarck, by winning Schleswig-Holstein for Prussia, had not only established, beyond any question, the German destiny and the German future. He had also advertised to the world British impotence in Europe. Henceforward, Britain's Empire might be expanding in Asia and Africa, but in Europe, the decline of British influence, which had begun with the follies of the Crimean War, would now accelerate.

There was a vacancy for a lady-in-waiting, and in the course of the summer and autumn, the Queen looked about. She had already grown close to Lady Augusta Bruce, the sister of the late general who had been Bertie's governor. In December, however, this much-loved personal friend of the Queen had married none other than Dean Stanley, now the Dean of Westminster – the same man who had accompanied General Bruce and Bertie on their tour of the Levant and made manful efforts to appreciate Mrs Henry Wood.

Lady Augusta would remain close to the Queen, but marriage inevitably took her away, and from now onwards, Victoria found it comforting to surround herself with widows, who both sympathized with her plight and were less likely to abandon her. One very eligible figure was Lady Waterpark (Eliza Jane), recently widowed. (Lady Waterpark was to be the aunt of a future Prime Minister, Lord Rosebery, and the great-grandmother of the celebrated photographer Patrick Lichfield.)

On 10 September 1864, writing to a lady-in-waiting, Lady Fanny Howard, the Queen spelt out the role's duties. She did not mention the very necessary one, an ability to endure the cold. The Queen's loathing of hot rooms, and her indifference to the cold, became unrestrained during her years of widowhood, and those who visited Balmoral, in particular, were always in danger of feeling cold. Lord

Stanley when Foreign Secretary found her breakfasting out of doors on a September day which he considered colder than an October day in England, and he remarked, 'Her love of exposure to the weather and her dislike of heat and close rooms, are almost morbid.'[65] It was open to question whether the Queen even noticed that others around her were shivering. As for Lady Waterpark's suitability as a lady-in-waiting, Victoria wanted to know:

> 1st. Is Lady Waterpark's health good?
>
> 2nd. Can she walk & ride (that is at a fool's pace in the Highlands, which I am ordered to do as I can walk but little).
>
> 3rd. Will she be prepared to take part in society, that is as far as to be able to go to Drawing Rooms, & to appear regularly at the Household dinners etc.
>
> All these things have become doubly necessary since my misfortune, the Lady in waiting constantly representing me at dinner, & having also to chaperone our daughters. – Balls & Theatres she would be asked to go to. –
>
> She speaks French of course – I think it is necessary that Lady Waterpark should know and <u>fully</u> consider all these points <u>before</u> she undertakes the office, as it is unfair by the other ladies, as well as by me, that a new lady should come in, & then prove unable to perform these duties. Augusta Stanley being away, I thought it best to write to you myself. Ever yours affctly and sadly, V.R.[66]

To Lady Waterpark herself, when she had accepted the role, Victoria explained that the dress code was widow's black. 'All those who are waiting on me wear the sable garb, which I think best suits our sad sisterhood.'

Lady Waterpark's husband, a former lord-in-waiting to Prince Albert, died in the previous year, and the Queen was 'hoping that you may find it suitable to you, and not dislike to serve the poor broken-hearted Widow of one whom your dear Husband served as well as

Herself in happy days. I think that we understand one another & feel that <u>Life</u> is ended for us, except in the sense of duty – This House [Balmoral] is a sad and solitary one bereft of its Master, & its joy and sunshine.'[67]

Sad and solitary as Balmoral was, it was a place which always brought consolations. Victoria loved sketching, she found the Highland air refreshing, and the company of the unaffected Highland servants made a stimulating change from the stuffiness of Windsor and Buckingham Palace. In the happy days of marriage, she had already taken a great shine to John Brown, the gillie. By the end of 1864, Princess Alice, who had noticed that rides in the pony cart at Balmoral were almost the only things which made her mother half cheerful, recommended that they brought Brown to England. She put the idea to Dr Jenner and to Colonel Phipps, Keeper of the Privy Purse. They both agreed that it was an admirable idea. So it was, in December 1864, that John Brown came to Osborne House.

From now onwards, Brown would be her constant companion. At Osborne, he brought in her private correspondence at 10 am, and took her for a morning ride. This was repeated in the afternoon. At Balmoral, he stayed with her while she did her correspondence and took it upon himself to post the letters. At Windsor, he would stand guard in the corridor outside her room, 'fending off', as one courtier put it, 'even the highest in the land'.[68]

The very qualities which others found irritating in Brown were ones which made him an ideal companion for Queen Victoria. He was humorous – not since the death of Lord Melbourne had she had a companion who was genuinely funny. He was abrasive with pompous courtiers. Above all, however, he saw her primarily as a human being. He 'protected her as she was, a poor broken-hearted bairn who wanted looking after and taking out of herself'.[69] 'It is a <u>real</u> comfort,' the Queen told her uncle Leopold, 'for [Brown] is devoted to me – <u>so</u> simple, so intelligent, so unlike an <u>ordinary</u> servant.'[70] To Vicky, she could say, 'I feel I have here and always in the House a good devoted <u>Soul</u>... whose only object & interest is my service, &

God knows how much I want <u>so</u> to be taken care of.'[71] There would never be a substsitute for her mother, or for Prince Albert; but Brown filled a gap.

Needless to say, his abrasive manners irritated the regular servants and courtiers. The Queen used Brown to fetch members of the Household, and he often did so in a way which they regarded as ill-mannered. He fell out with General Charles Grey, the Queen's private secretary, very early on. Grey's daughter, the Countess of Antrim, recalled that he refused to accept the message from the Queen in Brown's crude wording, and thereafter 'the two men bore each other a grudge'.[72]

On one occasion, Brown was sent to convey a dinner invitation to the lords-in-waiting who were waiting in the billiard room at Windsor to see whether or not they were to dine with the Queen. Brown merely opened the door and bawled out, 'All what's here dines with the Queen.' Such manners were not liked. Sir Henry Ponsonby, who succeeded Grey and knew how to handle Brown, remembered one occasion when the Mayor of Portsmouth came to Osborne to invite the Queen to inspect a force of volunteers. Her refusal was no doubt couched in polite language, but when Brown returned to the equerries' room, where he sat with Ponsonby, he merely said, 'The Queen says saretenly not.' He was frequently tipsy, and he gave whisky to the Queen. Her indulging his idiosyncracies enraged her servants and embarrassed her courtiers. The pair were soon exchanging gifts. 'On one occasion, he produced a "dozen cheap egg-cups of gay and florid design". To the complete surprise of her ladies, the Queen accepted the garish utensils with the delight she had usually reserved for Prince A's little *Geschenk* [present], which he usually inscribed "*Meiner theuren Victoria von Ihrem treuen Albert*". [To my dear Victoria from her loyal Albert.] The egg-cups were used every Sunday on the Queen's breakfast-table until they were finally all broken years after Brown's death.'[73]

Though Prince Albert had never found much common ground with 'Pilgerstein', Queen Victoria discovered an admiration for the 'dreadful old man' in his latter days. Discussing international affairs with her elderly Prime Minister, she found Palmerston to be 'wonderfully fair, pacific and moderate about Poland and Russia, also Denmark and even Germany'.[74]

Palmerston, the older he grew, advanced in popularity with the electorate and with the public at large. Remaining to the end of his days a Whig aristocrat with eighteenth-century attitudes to his own personal behaviour, private wealth and sexual morality, he was nevertheless able to espouse the mood of the times, and to make his party, the Liberals, the driving force behind improving working conditions with a series of Factory Acts, and supporting progressive causes in a variety of Royal Commissions. The scandal in 1863, when Palmerston, aged seventy-nine, was accused of adultery with Margaret O'Kane, the wife of a radical Irish journalist, only increased his popularity with the public. As one jaunty ballad had it,

> Here's jolly good luck to Palmerston,
> And although near fourscore,
> We hope that he may live in health,
> For twenty years or more[75]

In the election during the summer of 1865, Palmerston won a comfortable majority for the Liberals. Then, on 18 October 1865, the inevitable news reached Balmoral. The Queen was spared the scurrilous rumour that her Prime Minister had died in flagrante, having one final fling with a maid on the billiard table at Brocket Hall. As a matter of fact, his end was seemly. Having suffered from cold and gout and a bladder and kidney infection, Pam sank into a calm silence, allowing himself to be nagged by an evangelical doctor, of the name of Smith, and by his nephew Lord Shaftesbury, into accepting Christ as his personal saviour. As they prayed by Pam's bedside, they took his silence to be assent, and the Victorian statesman breathed his last surrounded by prayer. It was hardly surprising that an eighty-one-year-old man should have reached the end, but everyone recognized that with the old roué's carcass was borne away an old way of doing politics which would never be replaced. A few months earlier, he had remarked to Shaftesbury that when he died, 'Gladstone will soon have it all his own way, and whenever he gets my place, we shall have strange doings'.[76] No one, when it happened, would be more aware of this than Queen Victoria.

FIFTEEN

'I COULD DIE FOR YE'

IN THE LITTLE over three years which followed Palmerston's death, there were four Prime Ministers – the Liberal Earl Russell (from October 1865 to June 1866); the Conservative Earl of Derby, who resigned through ill health in 1868, dying the following year; and then the two figures who would dominate the political life of Britain for the next decade – the Conservative Benjamin Disraeli, who was Prime Minister for most of 1868 (February to December), followed by the Liberal W. E. Gladstone.

This rapid turnover of Prime Ministers was chiefly the result of the advanced age of the political top brass, but also because Britain was passing through a period of political turbulence. We speak of 1832, and the Great Reform Act, as the turning point of nineteenth-century politics. But in its way, 1867 was more revolutionary, for it was the Reform Act of that year which extended the franchise to the big industrial cities and paved the way for modern British politics. In addition to questions of the franchise, the political classes were faced with the cotton famine, the economic privations which overtook Lancashire during the American Civil War, when the production of cotton goods in Britain came to a virtual standstill; and with the beginnings of the Irish Fenian convulsions which would lead, within half a century, to Ireland leaving the United Kingdom altogether. So, much was going on during these years, and it was not surprising that the monarchy itself came under critical scrutiny. Nor, perhaps, was it surprising that, as far as European politics was concerned, British politicians found themselves out of their depth, nor that the Queen should sometimes have been in closer touch with the European situation than her politicians, with their English and Irish estates, and their parliamentary distractions.

Palmerston had been just short of eighty-one when he died in office as Prime Minister; Russell was seventy-four when he took over, and admitted he was too weak to do the job; Derby nearly seventy. 1867, then, signalled a radical change in the political climate in Britain. Derby, arguably the cleverest man who has ever been Prime Minister, was the last great survivor from the reign of privilege. He saw Parliament as a representative body. He had been acutely conscious of the change in climate ever since the First Reform Bill of 1832, and he was largely responsible, with Disraeli, for making the Conservative Party electable after its years of dissolution, following the disastrous split over the repeal of the Corn Laws. Conservatism had to come to terms with the popular will, but Derby remained, to the end of his days, a man who had been fundamentally happy with government remaining in the hands of the governing classes, and with the voting at election time being restricted. Gladstone observed that Derby was 'too much of a parliamentary politician to seek "the strength of public opinion"'.[1]

It was Derby's Government which oversaw the 1867 Reform Act. Before this Act, in a country whose adult male population numbered some 5 million, there were some 1 million voters. The Reform Act added 938,000 to the electorate. In most constituencies there was still some form of 'rate' determining that the voter should be a property-owner, or a taxpayer of, say, a minimum of £1 per annum. Yet, despite the objections of Tories such as Disraeli, the Government of Derby extended the franchise to include some working-class voters in the big industrial cities. Liverpool, Manchester, Birmingham and Leeds now had MPs to add to those of the Tory shires.

It meant that there was going to be an inevitable shift of political emphasis. Instead of the political classes confidently knowing what was good for the electorate, they were now in a position of having at least to give the impression that they cared about public opinion. The rabble-rousing jingoism of Disraeli on the political right and the ever more radical populism of Gladstone grew out of the new electoral circumstances. The acerbic historian and disciple of Carlyle, J. A. Froude, remarked in 1874 that it was becoming assumed that the nation was wiser than its leaders.[2] It was a radical shift. Diehards did not like it. True Blue figures such as Lord Cranborne, who resigned from the Cabinet in protest at the Reform Act, would do everything possible in later years to behave as if the old world was still in place, but Cranborne (who as 3rd Marquess of Salisbury rivalled Derby for title of cleverest Victorian Prime Minister) knew perfectly well what had happened.

Lenin's deep question – Who? Whom? – had slightly different answers in Britain after 1867. Only slightly different. The governing class went on governing until the First World War. The Duke of Omnium (the grandee at the centre of Anthony Trollope's sequence of political fictions) was still in his castle. The Archbishops of Canterbury and York still lived with vast emoluments in three separate residences, as if they were dukes. But the wind had changed. All those with sensitive political antennae were aware of it, and it was their earnest wish that the Queen should become aware of it too.

In Albert's lifetime, Victoria had been persuaded to turn away from her partisan love of Lord Melbourne and the eighteenth-century Whigs, to a belief in the progressive conservatism of Robert Peel. Such a creed did not suit her temperament. She was an impulsive romantic, not a moderate; she was by nature an autocrat. And a world in which journalists or pamphleteers or Members of Parliament could tell the Royal Family how to behave was not one to which she ever recognized herself as belonging.

Unfortunately for those who felt themselves responsible for advising the Queen about what would now be called her 'public image', Victoria had no coyness in the face of popular opinion. She continued to micromanage political affairs, commenting in detail upon every

Cabinet appointment, and every vacant bishopric, while following international affairs with anguished and close attention. But she refused to be paraded in person on the public stage, and in so far as the public were becoming aware of her private behaviour, she retained a haughty indifference to this fact which reduced courtiers and politicians to despair. When one uses the word 'haughty', however, it is not to suggest that she dismissed the advice of her private secretary or her Prime Minister from a position of strength. For much of this period, she was deeply ill – mentally ill, and plagued by psychosomatic pains, neuralgia, sleeplessness and fear. The last years of the 1860s constitute the shadowiest and most impenetrable period of Victoria's life.

Yet, though reduced to panic by public ceremonials, and resistant to the bossy advice of Government ministers, the Queen was not unaware of the public. Far from it. Victoria was an historical figure of profound paradox. On the one hand, she could be viewed as someone who was deeply resistant to the political progressivism of her times. She viewed political radicalism with horror, and came to feel that Gladstone, by embracing it, or using it for his own political ends, was actually insane. She stubbornly resisted the attempts by politicians to make her into a modern 'constitutional monarch'. Indeed, the more time elapsed from the deaths of Peel, Prince Albert and Baron Stockmar, the more she seemed to lay aside their lessons. Some of her retorts to Prime Ministers about such varied matters as the Civil List, army reform and foreign policy could have been made by Charles I before the First Civil War. She was at her happiest with large-C Conservative Prime Ministers, and in many ways her happiest political collaboration was not with Disraeli – the most famous of her political flirtations – but with that highest of high Tories, Lord Salisbury, at the end of her reign.

But there was another side to her mercurial personality which is curiously modern. Resistant to opening Parliament, or new bridges, or being 'on parade', she might have been. But she was not at all reluctant to come forward as an author. In an age when the printed word was the only means of popular communication, the published word was the most immediate and intimate means of communication. Victoria, who was shy of appearing in the House of Lords with a crown on her head, was prepared to have her journals put up for sale in bookshops alongside the popular novels of the day.

In the last ten years of the life of Diana Princess of Wales, and in the aftermath of her untimely death, it was said by conservative-minded commentators that Diana had introduced a new and rather un-British element into the formula of modern monarchy. As well as being a star performer on the public stage, which Victoria never was, Diana was also someone who hugely increased her personal popularity, not by hiding, but by displaying her emotions. 'Feel my pain' was a motto which had not been part of the royal vocabulary in the twentieth century. After the abdication of Edward VIII, Queen Mary, his mother, broke with protocol. It used to be the case that the widowed consorts of previous sovereigns did not attend Coronations. But, since the monarchy had just passed through so appalling a crisis, Queen Mary did attend the Coronation of George VI, who, with his wife Elizabeth, was faced with the task of rebuilding the monarchy after the debacle. At that ceremony, Queen Mary openly wept: it was a fact which was officially censored in all accounts of the ceremony, but in her diary, she wrote, 'We were all much moved... A wonderful day.'[3]

'Feel my pain' was not the invention of Diana Princess of Wales as a royal message to the public. Queen Victoria chose to convey that message to her public in the most modern method available to her: through publication. In 1867, she made a private publication of *Leaves from the Journal of Our Life in the Highlands, from 1848 to 1861.* It was dedicated to the beloved memory of Prince Albert, and circulated among courtiers and close friends.

The contents were indeed written by the Queen's own hand, but the book had been compiled from her journals by Arthur Helps, Clerk to the Privy Council. Helps had already prepared *The Principal Speeches and Addresses of His Royal Highness the Prince Consort* for publication

in 1862, and by assembling selections of her journals he excluded the
many references to 'political questions and affairs of government' with
which she peppered her writings.

She did not actually decide to go public with the journals until
the summer of 1867, when she visited Abbotsford, the former home
of Scotland's grandest man of letters. She was staying with the Duke
and Duchess of Roxburghe at Floors Castle, near Kelso, in the
Scottish borders, and it was suggested that the Queen would like
to visit the treasure-house on the banks of the Tweed built by Sir
Walter Scott. The present inhabitant was Scott's grandson-in-law,
James Hope-Scott, who had converted to Rome and built a Catholic
chapel in which John Henry Newman, another avid reader of the
Waverley novels, had offered Mass. Hope-Scott had married, *en
secondes noces*, in 1861, one of Queen Victoria's god-daughters, Lady
Victoria Fitzalan-Howard (daughter of the 14th Duke of Norfolk).

It will be remembered that the great Sir Walter had met Victoria
on 19 May 1828, during the festivities for Victoria's ninth birthday,
and dined at Kensington Palace. The Library at the Schloss Rosenau
was largely inspired by Duke Ernst I's mania for Scott. And as a child
Victoria had enjoyed dressing some of her large collection of dolls as
characters from Scott's Elizabethan fiction *Kenilworth*. 'Walter Scott
is my beau ideal of a poet,' the Queen once said.[4]

Abbotsford has been described as a Waverley novel in stone. Here
may be seen the study where Scott wrote many of the novels. Here
is to be found his unsurpassed library of Scottish lore and history,
and his collection of mementoes – Archbishop Sharp of St Andrew's
grate, the rosary of Mary Queen of Scots, Rob Roy's dirk, and so
forth. And here too was that, in some ways, most remarkable of all
treasures, Scott's journals, the record of his bankruptcy following the
crash of London banks in 1826, and his heroic decision to save his
estates, and his creditors, by a fervid five years of writing, an act of
scribal hyper-energy which led to his premature death in 1832.

The Queen was asked to sign her name in Scott's journal, 'which I
thought hardly right'.[5] The royal party then entered the dining room,

with its pretty Coalport china and its view of the babbling Tweed, where fruits, ices and other refreshments had been prepared. 'Her Majesty partook only of a cup of tea and "Selkirk bannock"'.[6] (For the uninitiated, the Selkirk bannock is a deliciously fruity flat bun, crammed with currants and raisins.)

Scott, who was a Sheriff-Depute for Selkirk, and an Edinburgh lawyer of distinction, had initially kept his identity as a novelist quite secret. The publication of his biography in 1837, by his son-in-law Lockhart, contained copious extracts from the journal; this made him the reverse of an anonymous Enlightenment lawyer. Instead, he became, in the pages of his incomparable[7] journals, a character as vivid as any he drew in his fiction. Classicist and son of the Enlightenment as he was, he was now, like any of his Romantic heroes, a man whose own struggles and pains and inner thoughts had become the most fascinating thing about him.

The Queen was to follow this pattern. She was not only the Head of State. She was also a woman screaming inside the royal straitjacket and sometimes longing for release.

Of course, *Leaves from the Journal of Our Life in the Highlands* was very mild, being a chronicle of picnics and sketching parties among mountainous scenery. Their excitement was not in what they revealed, but in the fact that they had been published at all. Not since Royalist propagandists published Charles I's pious reflections on the eve of his execution, the *Eikon Basilike*, had there ever been published in Britain a book purporting to be the work of a monarch. And the *Leaves* was a good deal more intimate than the *Eikon Basilike*.

Bound in embossed, moss-green covers, decorated with antler motifs in gold, the book was first published in January 1868. It sold 20,000 copies almost immediately. It was soon to sell 100,000 and to be translated into several languages. The royalties accrued were all given to charities. Theodore Martin, the biographer of the Prince Consort, was responsible for administering the royalties, but it was typical of Victoria that she micromanaged the sums involved:

The Queen thanks Mr Martin very much for his two letters and for the cheque which she has sent this day to Mr Helps. She quite approves of what he intends doing with the remaining £4,016 6s. Of this the Queen would wish him to send her a cheque for £50 which she wishes to give away. £2,516 she wishes absolutely to devote to a charity such as she spoke of, and the remaining £1,450 she wishes to keep for other gifts of a charitable nature, at least to people who are not rich. Would Mr Martin just keep an account of sums he sends her so that we may know how and at what time the money has been disposed of? The Queen will keep a copy of the names which she does not wish others to know.[8]

Like Sir Walter Scott's journals, the Queen's abound in reflections on the sturdy, earthy and amusing nature of the Scottish character. And it might be said that the hero of the *Leaves* is the man who, next to that of the Prince Consort, is forever associated with her memory. There are twenty-one separate references in the book to John Brown. When the Prince of Wales received his copy, he complained that, while Brown was so frequently mentioned, he, her firstborn son, was not. She tersely replied listing the pages in which the prince was in fact mentioned. The frosty exchange demonstrated the painfulness of the subject. Bertie had not properly read the book (does evidence exist that he ever read *any* book *through*, except *East Lynne* by Mrs Henry Wood?). The royal children all felt excluded by their mother's adoration of Brown, and embarrassment at the innocence, or brazenness, with which she flaunted it.

Victoria and Albert had both found enormous refreshment, when at Balmoral, in escaping the stultifying formality of court life. She loved the Highlanders' lack of side. 'I'm happy tae see ye lookin sae nice,' said old Mrs Grant – the mother of one of the gillies – to the Queen one day. It made Victoria glow with pleasure. Many people, including Victoria herself, feared at times for her sanity. It could be fairly said that without Balmoral, and the friendship of Brown during the 1860s, Victoria probably would have gone mad – or even madder than she actually was.

'Remember Brown? Aye that I do; and a very good fellow he was too. Sometimes when I was a' mowin' the lawns – it used to take me fourteen days to go right over all of 'em – anywhere near the house if he seed me, he'd put up his hand in the air and call, "Hi, Jackman!" and he'd say when I come up: "Don't stay thirsty out in the sun an' heat; you just go in the hall and say I sent you in for a good draught"'. So remembered William Jackman, one of the Balmoral estate workers.[9]

Brown took a similarly protective attitude towards his Queen, and his own dependence upon alcohol would lead him to apply similar counsel to her in her troubles. 'Don't stay thirsty.' It is an essential part of the story. Without recognizing the presence of the whisky bottle, there is much about the behaviour of both Brown and Victoria which is difficult to fathom. (Much is difficult to fathom even with the whisky bottle, but of this, more later.)

It was during that summer of 1864 that Princess Alice had the discussion with Dr Jenner and Colonel Phipps, and Brown became a permanent fixture at Court.

His arrival brought back a vital element of stability to the Queen's life. No one could replace Albert. That was a given. But at last she had what she had always so very much felt she needed: a man at her side. Though it would have been a blasphemy to whisper it, a blasphemy, that is, against the Religion of Albert which was her professed creed, history can also see that Brown represented a refreshing change. Albert, for all his greatness, was a fussy man, a stickler, a pedant, a sickly man who could not overindulge in food or drink. Prince Albert's most ardent admirer[10] would not look to him for laughs. Victoria saw in Brown one of the bluff, honest sons of the earth depicted so humorously by Sir Walter Scott. She was surely right to do so. Here was a man with the no-nonsense common sense of Edie Ochiltree, the passionate integrity of Jeanie Deans, the common sense of the Bailie Nichol Jarvie. The English Establishment protects itself by two weapons: pomposity and facetiousness. Victoria was entirely lacking in both qualities; Brown was proof against both. He also possessed, or appeared to possess, a quality which was extremely rare. He was unafraid of the Queen. From early childhood, Victoria had her mother cowering before her. The duchess had only dared to remonstrate in writing when the adolescent Victoria had been foul to servants. And even intimates like Lord M. had minded their Ps and Qs. There was an aura of impressiveness about her which made her more than a little frightening, even when she was in a good humour. It must have been lonely to produce this effect in everyone, including her children and her closest ladies-in-waiting. Brown simply treated her as another human being. Once a young footman came into the room and nervously dropped a silver salver. With her characteristic Hanoverian petulance, the Queen ordered that he be demoted to the kitchens. Brown remonstrated. 'What are ye daein' tae that puir laddie? Hiv' ye never drappit onything yersel'?' The footman was reinstated.[11] His directness of approach was all part of his power of sympathy. On the fourth anniversary of Prince Albert's death, the Queen took her children to pay their respects at the Frogmore Mausoleum. Brown came too – for the first time.

> When he came to my room later, he was so much affected; he said, in his simple expressive way, with such a tender look of pity while the tears rolled down his cheeks; 'I didn't like to see ye at Frogmore this morning; I felt for ye; to see ye coming there with your daughters and your husband lying there – marriage on one side and death on the other; no I didn't like to see it; I felt for ye; I know so well what your feeling must be – ye who had been so happy. There is no more pleasure for you, poor Queen, and I feel for ye but what can I do though for ye? I could die for ye.'[12]

When she became queen, Victoria had thought solitude a luxury. After eighteen years in which she had shared a bedroom with her mother and never been out of another human being's sight, she took pleasure in independence. Such feelings did not last. Solitude cast her adrift and she was not good at it. Her years of marriage had been ones in which she scarcely let her husband out of her sight. Her widowhood placed intolerable burdens on her younger daughters, since Victoria needed companionship which was literally constant, night and day.

The arrival of the faithful Brown as a permanent feature in the Court caused intense irritation to the Queen's elder children, and ruffled the pomposity of the courtiers. But it supplied a deep need. Russell had been Prime Minister eight months when she reminded him of her frail condition, and her need for the safety valves provided by Balmoral and Osborne:

> She _must_ say that she feels she COULD not go on working as she does, _without any real_ relaxation (for she _never is_ without her boxes and despatches etc., which her Ministers _often_ are, for a few weeks at least) IF she did _not_ get that change of scene and that pure air, which always gives her a little strength, _twice_ a year. Nine or ten days are very short, but they will _still_ do her some good, and she will have _more courage_ to struggle onwards, though every year which adds to her age, finds her nervous system and general strength _more and more_ shaken. She always fears some complete breakdown some day; and she is just now greatly in _want_ of _something_ to revive her after an autumn, winter, and spring of great anxiety, and many sorrows of a domestic nature, which shake her very nervous temperament very severely.[13]

When she penned this letter to her Prime Minister, the Liberal Government was being assailed by the Conservatives about the Distribution of Seats Bill – the important matter of how the new constituencies would be divided after the franchise was extended to the industrial cities – and Europe had erupted into the second war of the decade. It was one Russell could do nothing to avert. The Danish–German war of 1862–4 had demonstrated British impotence. The war of 1866, in which Prussia took on Austria, was one in which that impotence was now a fact of life.

Lord Clarendon was the Foreign Secretary when Bismarck pushed Prussia forward in her war against Austria. Clarendon wrote to the Queen's secretary, General Grey, 'I cannot believe that there would be the slightest use in the Queen's again writing to the King of Prussia. I wish I did. Her Majesty could not express herself more strongly than she has already done and she would only again be told that it is all the fault of Austria and that Prussia is always innocent and always in the right.'[14]

The Austrian War was the second act in Bismarck's successful campaign to unite Germany behind a dominant Prussia, and to exclude Austria altogether from the loose union of German-speaking peoples. It brought to a decisive end the vision of German unity envisaged by Prince Albert and Baron Stockmar in earlier days. Clarendon was right to say that the Queen could have done nothing to stop it. The Queen probably shared Vicky's view of Clarendon: 'touchy, irritable and cross'.[15] Stanley noted, after a conversation with Victoria about Germany, that 'she cannot endure the idea of her country (for she feels it as such) being threatened'.[16]

With these dreadful events unfolding, the Queen felt isolated on the European stage. Without Albert at her side, 'we are as sheep without a shepherd',[17] as she wrote in May 1866; and her other great political mentor, King Leopold of the Belgians, was also dead – he died on 10 December 1865.

She and Clarendon, however, were among the very few people in British politics who appeared much concerned with what was happening in Europe. Stanley noted that the Queen 'interferes little' in his work as Foreign Secretary, 'and only where Germany is concerned'.[18] Cut off from London as she might have been during her sojourns at Balmoral and Osborne, she was in thrice-weekly touch with Vicky, who tartly and accurately commented to her mother that the British politicians and diplomats 'are not so perfectly informed of European affairs as they ought to be'.[19]

A charming illustration of this was provided for Clarendon later that year, in November, when he came across the Chancellor of the Exchequer, W. E. Gladstone, having a holiday in Rome at the same time as the Duke of Argyll and the Cardwells – Cardwell was Chief Secretary of State for Ireland at the time and Argyll (soon to become father-in-law of Victoria's daughter Princess Louise) was Lord Privy Seal.

'Italian art, archaeology and literature are Gladstone's sole preoccupation,' wrote Clarendon. 'Every morning at 8, he lectures his wife and daughters upon Dante and requires them to parse and give the root of every word. He runs about all day to shops, galleries and persons, and only last night told me that he hadn't time for the reading room and had not seen an English paper for three or four days!'[20]

For the British governing classes, and for the Establishment generally, Europe was a series of landscapes to be captured in watercolour, an architectural background to their great works of literature, just as much as it was a living political reality. Gladstone and his fellow Liberals supported the aspirations of Mazzini, Garibaldi and the Italian nationalists largely because they had persuaded themselves that it was in accordance with Dante's *De vulgari eloquentia*, just as Byron in an earlier generation had supported Greek independence as an extension of his classical education at Harrow and Cambridge. The machinations of Bismarck were not quite overlooked, but they were secondary to the cultural echoes of times past. To the Queen, the future of Germany was being fought out, quite literally, by members of her own family. Fritz, her Prussian son-in-law, was a cavalry officer in the war of 1866. Her other German son-in-law, Duke Louis of Hesse-Darmstadt, was a cavalry officer fighting for Austria on the opposite side. She rightly summed up Bismarck's action as 'a war – which is in fact a civil one'. The experts, including Friedrich Engels and Louis Napoleon, predicted that it would be a long war, and that Austria would win it. In fact, it was settled by one battle. The Prussian troops triumphed over the Austrians at Sadowa/Königgrätz on 3 July. 'I fear this great victory, which I think of doubtful happiness to you all, has been most dearly bought,' she wrote to Vicky.[21] She was referring not only to the losses – 9,000 Prussian dead – but to the political consequences for the future of German-speaking peoples. Fritz had been marginalized by Bismarck, and the Prussian Court, in the run-up to the war, because he was married to 'die Engländerin', that liberal enemy of so much that Bismarck stood for. But in the war, he had acquitted himself as a gallant officer in the field.

In the midst of that turbulent summer, Victoria's family had also extended itself into European life. Vicky herself gave birth to a daughter on 12 April ('Though it is very naughty of me,' the Queen had written, 'to show dearest Fritz's English up to you, I must tell you as you will laugh so, he telegraphed you were "happily delivered <u>from</u> a strong and healthy daughter!"'[22]), and Francis, Duke of Teck – 'thoroughly unassuming and very gentlemanlike'[23] in the Queen's view – had become engaged to Princess Mary of Cambridge. They were destined to become the parents, on 26 May 1867, of Princess May, future Queen of England and grandmother of Queen Elizabeth II.

Princess Mary of Cambridge's brother George had, like their cousin the Queen, viewed events in Germany since the rise of Bismarck with alarm and dismay. 'To see all our old German associations knocked on the head, and our friends and relatives, I may say, scattered to the winds, is indeed a state of things which may make the stoutest heart shudder at the bare thought,'[24] he wrote to Victoria. The Schleswig-Holstein war had seen humiliation for the Augustenburg claimant and military defeat for the Danes – with both of whom Victoria had marital connections. But the 1866 'civil war', in which Austria was defeated, saw more widespread humiliations and political defeats for her blood-relatives. George V, the blind King of Hanover, and a grandson of the English George III, had, as the Duke of Cambridge put it, been 'driven from his Kingdom by his neighbour the King of Prussia. Frankfurt had been invaded by the Prussia army. The citizens were told that they must pay six million guilders on the spot and a further twenty-five million guilders within a day. Unable to comply with the request, the mayor of Frankfurt hanged himself.'[25]

Alice, Grand Duchess of Hesse, had during the previous five years of childbearing, suffered from headaches, rheumatism, depressions and nervous strain. While her husband had ridden into battle for Austria, she had watched appalled as not only her brother-in-law Fritz, but also her uncle Ernst (Prince Albert's own brother) had put himself forward, and taken a command to fight for the Prussians. Hesse had suffered particularly badly in the war and was full of wounded soldiers. Many philanthropists are those with particular inner demons to conquer. Alice, clearly an extremely unhappy person, established a network of women's groups across the whole of Germany. They were committed to nursing in times of war, and in peacetime to medical training. She was in correspondence with Florence Nightingale. The Germans found difficulty in pronouncing her name, but soon the Alice-Frauenverein für Krankenpflege – the Princess Alice Women's Nursing Association – had spread across wide areas. There were over seventy of its hospitals before it merged with the German Red Cross in 1867.

Hesse also suffered extreme financial hardship because of the war. There could now be no doubt of who was boss in Germany, and Prussia exacted painful financial reparations from those German states that had stood against her. By far the smallest of the remaining independent states, with its own grand duke and duchess, Hesse could only survive by paying Prussia money which it simply could not afford. It meant that Alice's good causes, above all the Alice-Frauenverein, suffered as a consequence. She begged her mother for help, requests which caused Queen Victoria 'horror'.[26] By 1871, Victoria had decided that 'Alice's greediness for money was terrible'.[27]

Queen Victoria and the Royal Family could see nevertheless that Prince Albert's plan, for a benign Germanic federalism held together under Austrian control, now lay in ruins. Prussia ruled, with her vast, well-trained army and booming economy. Even the British politicians could see it – some of them, at least – when, in the following year, 1867, France and Prussia began sabre-rattling: Emperor Napoleon III began negotiations to purchase the Grand

Duchy of Luxembourg from the Dutch Government, even though it was part of the German *Bund*, and garrisoned with Prussian troops. He was providing himself with an excuse for a war against Prussia, which he foolishly thought he could win. The Foreign Secretary, Lord Stanley, airily, and very wrongly, supposed that 'neither party, I believe, wants a war, and they are glad on both sides to have a decent excuse for remaining at peace'.[28] He thought that in April 1867. By the end of the year, he had cynically decided that he was indifferent to the question which so agitated the Queen. 'A war between France and Germany, though disagreeable, would not for us be dangerous,' he confided to his journal.[29]

Besides, in that year, there was much else in the world to distract attention from Luxembourg and its future. Napoleon III had dispatched troops to Rome to help the Pope resist the Italian nationalists and the volunteers who had massed behind Garibaldi. In Mexico, the French forces had withdrawn, leaving the Emperor Maximilian (the brother of the Austrian Emperor Franz Joseph, and son-in-law to the late King Leopold – he was married to Leopold's daughter Charlotte) to fight on his own against the republicans. He was condemned to death by a Council of War and shot at Querétaro, the subject of famous canvases by Manet. Irish Fenians invaded Canadian territory in 1866, and these convulsions were partially responsible for the British Government's decision to bring all the North American colonies of Great Britain into one 'Dominion of Canada'.

At home, the two most urgent concerns of the political classes were the future of the proposals for electoral reform, and the future of Ireland. Reform was a complicated business, taking hours of parliamentary time, as they debated not only the extent of the franchise, but also such crucially decisive questions as the boundaries of the constituencies.

Reform of the voting system had been long overdue in Liberal eyes, but it was a slow process. The problems concerned less the diehard opponents who seemed to have history, as well as the Liberal Party, against them as in the fine points. It was less a question of when, than of how, reform would happen.

Ireland was different. The Irish Question did not creep up; it exploded. It did not quietly nag; it forced itself upon the attention of the Westminster politicians. The ending of the American Civil War released from the Federal Army many Irish Americans who did not feel tempted to return to a peaceful civilian life. The Italians had formed themselves into armed bands behind Garibaldi to fight for their national freedom from Austria. The Polish nationalists were resisting the Russians. Why should Irishmen hold back, particularly since the Fenian Brotherhood was started in the United States in 1858 with a mission to fight for the home country?

Throughout the 1860s, there had been outbreaks of violence in rural Ireland, in protest against the tenancy arrangements. There was still a tithe; that is, the Irish were still obliged to pay a tax towards the Protestant Church, regardless of the fact that the majority of them were in fact Catholic. Perceived injustices of this sort fuelled the feelings of those Irish Americans who had escaped the famine of twenty years earlier.

As would so often happen in the unfolding century, it was outbursts of violence by Irish nationalists which triggered the liberal English conscience into thinking something must be done about Ireland. Two Fenian prisoners, being conducted through Manchester by the police, were rescued, and one policeman, Sergeant Brett, was killed on 18 September. Three men – Allen, Larkin and O'Brien by name – were executed for the crime, instantaneously joining the Irish Republican martyrology. Then, on 13 December, a bomb was placed in Clerkenwell Prison in an attempt to rescue more Fenian prisoners.

Luckily for the Irish, one English politician felt it was his 'mission' 'to pacify Ireland'. Even more fortunately, he was also at the vanguard of the English Liberal Party, in favour of reform at home, the promotion of liberalism abroad, and in Ireland, in favour of allowing the Irish a greater say in the running of their own affairs. This was William Ewart Gladstone. He had begun his political life as a 'stern unbending Tory', whose chief interests, beyond Homer and Dante, were Church politics. But he was also the son of a go-getting merchant, and he had intense political ambitions. The combination of contrarieties in his character makes him one of the most fascinating figures in British political history. He resigned from Peel's Cabinet over the – to us – esoteric question of whether the Government would give a grant towards the training of Catholic clergy at Maynooth, near Dublin. Esoteric, because of Gladstone's motives: the point of his resignation was to emphasize his High Church belief that the Church of England was the rightful branch of the Catholic Church in Britain, and that for the Queen's Government to give money to a Roman Catholic seminary was to undermine the National Church. So he abandoned his position as President of the Board of Trade in 1845, and went to Buckingham Palace for an audience with the Queen.

She was gracious enough to express regret at Mr Gladstone's decision, though it is rather doubtful whether she understood it, having a detestation of the High Church position which was his lodestar and raison d'être. ('I am very nearly a Dissenter – or rather more a Presbyterian – in my feelings, so very Catholic do I feel we [i.e. the Church of England] are,' as she once confessed to one of her daughters.[30]) Even in that 1845 interview between Gladstone and the Queen, we can see the beginnings of their famous estrangement twenty years later. 'I have had the boldness to request an audience, madam, that I might say with how much pain it is that I find myself separated from Your Majesty's Service...'[31] This tall, fanatical, verbose man was the reverse of anything she found charming. He made no effort to flatter her, nor did he speak directly. When she tried to draw him out on the subject of the Chartists, he said he believed 'the main feeder was want of employment'. Before Gladstone left the audience, she asked him about his friend Henry Edward Manning – then a High Church Archdeacon, but about to defect to Rome. Within a short space, Gladstone was back in Peel's Cabinet, as Secretary for War and Colonies, a move which allowed cynics to wonder what had happened to the conscience which, only months before, had made him resign over Maynooth.

All this was decades back in the past. Gladstone, and his great political rival Disraeli, had been obliged to wait for the political bigwigs to grow older and older before they could take power themselves as party leaders. Gladstone was in his late fifties before leadership of the Liberal Party was within his grasp.

Had she been able to read Gladstone's assessments of her, the Queen might have been flattered by the occasional phrase, but she would surely have been repelled by his constant need to pass pompous judgements on her, as though he were entitled to read her soul. Many of these judgements were made to the Duchess of Sutherland – Mistress of the Robes. In 1862, he expressed the hope that the Queen's refreshment from a Scottish holiday would be morally improving: 'Such contact with Nature's own very undisguised and noble self, in such forms of mountain, wood, breeze and water! These are continual preachers.' In 1863, when he was Chancellor of the Exchequer, he pronounced the Queen's tone 'delightful' and her physical strength 'satisfactory'. The next year, at the height of the Danish war, he again gave her high marks. 'Often as I have been struck by the Queen's extraordinary integrity of mind – I know of no better expression – I never felt it more than on hearing and reading a letter of hers on Saturday (at the Cabinet) about the Danish question.'[32] Gladstone himself clearly felt fully entitled to make such judgements, but they all read as if he were marking his monarch out of ten. His manner would grow no less awkward with the passage of the years, and by the time he took office as Prime Minister he was on a collision course with the Queen.

Before the Gladstonian tragi-comedy began in earnest, however, the Queen had a foretaste of political happiness of a kind undreamed-of since the demise of Lord M. The Reform Bill passed. Lord Derby resigned through ill health, and he was succeeded as Prime Minister and as Conservative Leader by the bizarre, pomaded figure of Benjamin Disraeli. 'Mr Disraeli is Prime Minister! A proud thing for a man "risen from the people" to have obtained!' commented the Queen. 'And I must say – really most legally; it is his real talent, his good temper and the way in which he managed the Reform Bill last year which have brought this about.'[33]

Vicky shared her mother's feeling that 'it is absurd to have an aristocratic prejudice against Mr Disraeli – on account of his being a Jew and an adventurer... My fear was that his other qualities were not such as to enable him to fill the place well.'[34] The Queen saw no reason to fear. Disraeli had one quality which covered a multitude of sins. He was 'certainly... loyal... to me'.

Gladstone, meanwhile, as Leader of the Liberal Party, had come out in favour of disestablishing the Irish Church. He, who a quarter of a century before had wanted to deprive the Irish of the Maynooth grant, now felt the position of Established bishops (Anglicans) in Ireland to be untenable. The Queen felt his position would do 'immense mischief'.[35] Disraeli's religious views were eccentric. He was a baptized member of the Church of England who used to take the Sacrament at Easter, but he once rather bafflingly told the Queen, 'I am the blank page between the Old and the New Testament.'[36] Whatever this meant, he could see that the natural Tory position on the Irish Church was to oppose any attempts to undermine it, or to remove the Queen's power to appoint the Irish bishops. The Queen's dislike of Fenians was intensified, meanwhile, by an Irishman named O'Farrell shooting the Duke of Edinburgh in the back in Sydney. 'I fear the wound must be a severe one, though please God it will leave no permanent effect on his health.'[37]

Disraeli considered that there was a chance of easing the Irish crisis through the mediation of Manning – now Cardinal Manning – but once Gladstone had proposed disestablishing the Irish Church, an idea which had been encouraged by the cardinal, the Tory Leader dropped the Roman Catholic cleric like a stone. He made good use of his acquaintanceship with Manning, however, in his most amusing political novel, *Lothair*, in which the figure of Cardinal Grandison swans about the drawing rooms of London in a watered-silk scarlet ferraiolo, scheming to convert duchesses to his creed.

Sadly for the Queen, who had taken a great shine to Disraeli, his Government was short-lived. His own party contained many who disliked him. Lord Cranborne, who had now succeeded as the 3rd Marquess of Salisbury, was only the most feline, intelligent and politically astute of those who winced at the idea of the English Tories being led by that Blank Page. The question of the Irish Church led to the Tories' defeat in the Commons. There was a General Election, after which, with what one imagines to be very gritted teeth, the Queen was obliged to send General Grey to Hawarden, Gladstone's house in North Wales, with this letter: 'December 1st 1868 – Mr Disraeli has tendered his resignation to the Queen. The result of the appeal to the country is too evident to require its being proved by a vote in Parliament and the Queen entirely agrees with Mr Disraeli and his colleagues in thinking that the most dignified course for them to pursue, as also the best for the public interests, was immediate resignation. Under these circumstances, the Queen must ask Mr Gladstone, as the acknowledged leader of the liberal party, to undertake the formation of a new administration.'[38]

SIXTEEN

'MEIN GUTER TREUER BROWN'

SOME ACCOUNTS OF the relationship between Gladstone and Queen Victoria speak as if the animosity between them was of a purely personal nature. Victoria made everything personal, and so, of course, she came to make her resentment of Gladstone into one of the most notorious battles of wills in English political history. As in the case of her unwillingness during her girlhood to come to terms with the resignation of Melbourne and the arrival of Peel, there was a strong element here of disappointment at losing a Prime Minister whom she was coming to like enormously – Disraeli – to be replaced by one whom she found uncongenial. But the fifty-year-old Victoria, when she was allowing her mind to operate politically, was a much more astute figure than her girlhood self; and she used every weapon, including her psychological and physical illnesses, to stall what she believed to be attacks on the monarchy itself. Little by little, however, though she never grew to like Gladstone, she recognized the direction of the political wind, and she did usually have the common sense (often after many hysterical displays, and dozens of ink-splodged exclamation marks on black-bordered writing paper) to do as he suggested – just as she had conceded in the earlier part of her reign to the quiet reforms of Peel.

The primary problem for Gladstone, in his relationship with the Queen when he first became her Prime Minister, was, however, the

Queen herself: whether she was any longer willing or capable of doing the work of a constitutional monarch.

It was not particularly surprising, when the new Liberal Government's suggested army reforms were laid before Her Majesty, that she should have used her weapon of first resort, the explosion. G. O. Trevelyan, nephew of Lord Macaulay and a Liberal MP of the radical persuasion, had risen in the House of Commons to state the obvious: namely that the 'tremendous influence of the Court' was one of the obstacles to be overcome by anyone who desired a reform of the War Department.

'Mr Trevelyan simply states what is not true,' she spluttered. It was 'a most outrageous speech to have been made by any member of the Government... Though he may have a perfect right to entertain the opinion he expresses, he has no right as a subordinate member of the Govt. to make such a public declaration of it without knowing what the views of his official superiors may be upon the subject.' She insisted to Gladstone that Trevelyan be made to resign for his impertinent suggestion that it appeared that 'a Royal Duke' must be in permanent command of the army.[1]

The army reforms were the responsibility of the Secretary of State for War, Edward Cardwell. It was impossible to look at the success of the Prussian Army, during its two recent wars, and not to see that triumph had not come by accident. There was no question of Cardwell introducing conscription, as the Prussians had done, thereby building up a huge army; but there was a case for building up reservists. Cardwell reduced the length of service 'with the colours', but introduced a corresponding period of service on reserve, with a payment of 4d per day. He also transferred more and more men from the militia to the regulars.

Cardwell's particular innovation was the so-called linked battalions. Rather than being sent to any part of the army which the War Office required, a new recruit would now be trained at local depot barracks, thereby linking the army to different areas of Britain. Different regiments would find themselves sharing more or less local fortresses: for example, the 34th (Cumberland) regiment and the 55th (Westmoreland) were linked, with a depot in Carlisle Castle.[2] The huge fortresses used to house these Victorian army depots are a feature of the landscape to this day. The reform was disliked by the War Office, and in particular by the commander-in-chief. Since the resignation of Lord Hardinge in 1856, this role had been occupied by Queen Victoria's cousin George.

As far as army reform went, the diehards would accept the abolition of the sale of commissions and the more barbarically eighteenth-century features of the Victorian army such as flogging. But the reformers would lose their case when it came to getting rid of the 'tremendous influence of the Court'. It was no mere figure of speech when the Queen liked to say she was a soldier's daughter. She took a deep interest in her armed forces, regarding them as her army and her navy. Moreover, she had always enjoyed a cordial relationship with her cousin George William Frederick Charles, 2nd Duke of Cambridge (1819–1904). Far from giving his job to a commoner as the Liberals thought he should, the duke did not resign until he was seventy-six years old – in 1895. Even then, he did so reluctantly.[3] His name and features survive on many an inn sign to this day.[4] One senses his tone, as well as his views, coming through many of the Queen's letters on the subject of army reform. He remained a man of legendarily bluff opinions, expressed with vigour. He used to say that he saw no reason why one gentleman should not command a regiment as well as another. It was once brought to his attention that there had been an outbreak of venereal disease at the Royal Military College at Sandhurst. He set off at once 'en civil', carrying as ever a rolled umbrella, to deliver a rebuke. When the cadets were all assembled, the Duke of Cambridge waved the umbrella above his head. He thundered, "I hear you boys have been putting your private parts where I wouldn't put this umbrella!"'[5]

Nevertheless, there was some justice in his resentment of inter-ference in military affairs by civilian politicians and civil servants. Cardwell (Winchester and Balliol) was, like Gladstone, the son of a rich Liverpool merchant, a Peelite, a cerebral, decent man for whom administration was a calling, an opportunity to improve the world. While President of the Board of Trade, he had collated – an intricate and massive task – all 548 pieces of legislation relating to the Merchant Navy, thereby greatly increasing the welfare of ordinary merchant seamen, as well as making trade more efficient. He had also introduced – in that era of many railway fatalities, and chaos as all the different railroad companies expanded all over the kingdom – a rationalization of the railways. With the armed forces, he would find reform less easy. The two measures which were immediately recognized were the abolition of flogging and of purchase. Henceforth, the British Tommy could serve without being thrashed; and the officer could be promoted on merit, rather than simply by producing great sums of money. But it would be unfair to represent the Duke of Cambridge as a purely obscurantist reactionary. It was he, and not Cardwell, who, guided by the tremendous success of German staff colleges, helped found the Staff College at Camberley, and he introduced modern German training at Sandhurst. He had, after all, been a colonel in the Jäger division of the Hanoverian Guards since he was nine years old.[6]

Judging from the journals, I should say that the Queen and the Duke of Cambridge met every two or three weeks of their grown-up life, except when she was in Scotland. They were close. Trevelyan was absolutely right to discern that there was a 'tremendous' influence from the Queen personally, and from her cousin, on the day-to-day management of the army, as well as such questions, always of interest to the Queen, as who should become colonel-in-chief of which regiments. The correspondence between the two, preserved in the Royal Archives, is copious and businesslike.

The death of Albert had created vacancies at the head of several of the grander regiments. It was a delicate matter for the duke, getting the Queen to sign the necessary papers appointing to Albert's colonelcies, since the usual formula on such occasions was to refer to the appointee's predecessor. She did not object to the appointments, but 'would wish it done... without allusion to whom they belonged before – that the Queen <u>could</u> not sign – as in her bitter agony (which only seems to increase every day) she can't allude even to such things which she tries to ignore'.[7] (This, from a letter to General Grey by the Duke of Cambridge, explaining, in 1867, why the Queen found the whole matter so painful.) In the event the Duke of Cambridge took over the colonelcy of the Grenadier Guards, in succession to the Prince Consort, only without the usual formula of 'vice etc etc'.[8]

At the Queen's request, in March 1869, as Cardwell's reforms began to take shape, General Grey was instructed to tell Cardwell how little his sovereign liked them. She disliked, and considered unwise, the reduction of troops in the colonies, many of whom were brought back to serve at home. She deplored, as did the Duke of Cambridge, the moving of the duke's offices from the Horse Guards, and his being forced to work under the umbrella of the War Office. Above all, she deplored the low esteem in which the sneering Liberals regarded her cousin.

'A disposition exists in some quarters (she fears even among some of the subordinate members of the Government, as for instance Mr Trevelyan) to run down the commander-in-chief and generally to disparage the Military Authorities, as obstacles to all improvement in our Army Administration... Ever since he has been at the head of the Army, HRH has deserved the Queen's entire confidence & is entitled to her best support.'[9] He certainly got it – and without fail.

In the case of the Irish reforms, Victoria knew herself to be powerless, and so, as she usually did, she conceded to Gladstone's wishes, though not without a fight. 'Regret, however, is now useless.'[10] In the same spring that she was expressing herself so strongly about Cardwell's army reforms, she was fuming about the proposal to disestablish the Irish Church, and wrote, 'Mr Gladstone knows that the Queen has always regretted that he should have thought himself compelled to raise this question as he has done and still more that he should have committed himself to so sweeping a reform.'[11]

The question which she was avoiding was the more troubling one of what the incoming Liberal Government expected of her as their Head of State. Victoria, who was still in a rocky state emotionally, was torn between two contradictory positions, equally strong. On the one hand, a deep distrust of the radicals made her wish to emphasize the vital role of the monarch in constitutional life, and to interfere with and question almost every measure Gladstone undertook. On the other hand, her loathing of business and her desire to lead a quiet life had led her to withdraw from the centre of Government, and to spend months of each year at Osborne and Balmoral.

The press, the Queen's own children, monarchists and republicans were all finding themselves beginning to ask the same sort of questions. If it was possible for a country to function when its Head of State spent half the year in her Scottish retreat or on the Isle of Wight, was this not a sign that it could function without a monarch at all? If she refused to undertake even such rudimentary duties as taking part in the State Opening of Parliament, were they not entitled to wonder why she was paid huge sums by the Civil List?

Her private secretary, General Grey, used the arrival of a new Prime Minister to utter what began as a series of frank inquiries, man to man, and ended as a doleful *cri-de-coeur* from one who had reached the end of his tether.

In June 1869, Grey copied out one of the Queen's 'stinkers' to the Prince of Wales, accusing him of self-indulgence and failure to do his duty. As he did so, the patient Grey realized that this 'excellent good advice... would have been more applicable here'.[12] Grey was convinced that claims to be too ill to perform her duties were totally without foundation. 'In spite of Sir William Jenner [the doctor], I believe that neither health nor strength are wanting, were the inclination what it should be. It is simply the long, unchecked habit of self-indulgence – that now makes it impossible for her without some degree of nervous agitation to give up even for 10 minutes, the gratification of a single inclination or <u>whim</u>.'[13]

It was Grey's view that Victoria was simply Bertie without the beard and cigars – a totally selfish, childish person without any of the sense of the duty which motivated her courtiers and statesmen. He had discovered that the Lord Mayor of London had asked the Queen if she would come to open the new Blackfriars Bridge when it was completed. Determined to wriggle out of such an odious appointment if she were able, the Queen had 'told no one in the house but the Duchess of Atholl'.[14]

This drama would drag on throughout the summer and autumn, with various figures – Gladstone, the royal children, Grey – all imploring the Queen to consent to open the bridge. She responded as if every such request was a stabbing. 'She thought she had clearly expressed that it was impossible for her to open Blackfriars Bridge – but as Mr Gladstone seems still in doubt – she will repeat her sincere regret that it is <u>quite out of the question</u> for her to do anything of the kind in the heat of the summer.'[15] (An objection to attending the State Opening of Parliament in November was that it was too cold for her to appear wearing the ceremonial clothes.) In July, when more and more pressure was being put upon her, she protested, 'The Queen is much surprised at being <u>again</u> teazed [sic] & tormented about this Bridge – having – 3 weeks ago – nearly – been asked by Mr Gladstone that as the Queen cld not open the Bridge & Viaduct the fatigue of the whole thing being <u>much too gt & a day [sic] commencing in the HEAT</u>.'[16] In the event, when November came, she opened the bridge.

Yet, even in this tormenting matter of whether she would open the bridge, one senses that Grey – whose exasperation with her moods and whims is more than understandable – was being insensitive to what exactly was going on. True, by the standards to be expected of public-spirited Victorians such as Grey, Gladstone and all the males around her, she was behaving deplorably. But there is also more than a hint in Grey's realization that she and her dissolute rake of a son Bertie were the same character, that her idleness was attributable to the self-same vice. While Bertie amused himself with chorus girls, or the wives of his clubland aristocratic friends, the Queen spent hours of every day with John Brown.

Whatever the truth of Grey's suspicions – and we can be sure that any hint of it which survives in written sources will, wherever possible, have been hidden or destroyed – there *is* written evidence that Grey, the Queen's children and the politicians were being somehow unfair to Victoria. If you go to the actual written records and see the letters she was writing throughout this period, there is undoubted evidence of a woman who was on some occasions perfectly rational, and then quite out of control. Out of her mind.

It is perhaps not possible at this distance to imagine, or to explain, exactly what was happening on the days when this was the case. But the paper evidence is there before us. In the Gladstone Papers, for example, in the British Museum, we see, in the letters of 1869, a vast disparity between the letters in which Victoria, however strong-willed and contradictory, was in control of herself and commenting upon affairs, and those in which she is hardly able to wield a pen. Indeed, some of the letters, roughly scrawled in pencil or blue crayon and barely legible, consisting of only a few words, are evidence of complete loss of control. Whether the reasons for this are purely psychological or hormonal, or whether she had been prescribed too much laudanum or some other opiate by Jenner (a doctor who, Gladstone said, he would not have let loose on his cat), or whether the Queen reached for the whisky bottle, or whether all these things were the case at once, these strange scrawls are disturbing evidence that the Queen was, for much of the time, 'not herself'. One of the notes scrawled to Gladstone in blue crayon while he was staying at Balmoral reads, 'It is not to Tahiti but to Honolulu that the complaints relative to Prince Alfred refer.' That is *all* the note says. Another scrawl, written on the same day, says, 'It is very wicked to have again attacked Prince Alfred for it is quite false. But it shd not be heeded.'[17]

These weird scrawls are in a quite different idiom from the admittedly semi-legible, brisk commentaries which her letters to courtiers and politicians offered when she was in a more composed frame of mind, as, for example, on 1 November in the same year, 1869. She 'thanks Mr Gladstone not to press the subject of Sir L. Rothschild's peerage. The Queen really cannot make up her mind to it. It is not only the feeling, of which she cannot divest herself, against making a person of the Jewish religion, a Peer; but she cannot think that one who owes his great wealth to contracts with Foreign Govts for Loans, or to successful speculations on the Stock Exchange can fairly claim a British Peerage.'[18]

This letter, however distasteful to modern sensibilities, is scarcely deranged, as were the notes scribbled in the summer. In a political history of the period, it would be right to sympathize with the male Establishment in wishing this woman, with her whims and self-indulgence, would be more assiduous in the exercise of public duty.

Clearly, what was causing General Grey so much anxiety was something much more serious than simple laziness, or unwillingness, on the Queen's part, to take part in public ceremonials. In fact, the Queen was right to insist that, in her own fashion, she worked hard – though with lapses, and always with the proviso that she was allowed to do so for much of the year at Balmoral or Osborne. Twenty-first-century monarchs would probably feel it to be a duty to be on parade, to cut ribbons, open hospitals and shake the hands of subjects. But, then, a twenty-first-century monarch would probably be less intimately involved in the political decision-making processes. A survey of the Queen's correspondence with her Prime Minister during this difficult year for her private secretary shows that Victoria was very far from taking no interest in politics or affairs of State. It was public duties from which she shrank; and it was the demands of the Government and her secretary that she should leave those places where she could lead her life in private – Balmoral and Osborne. This by no means diminished her daily interest in the measures of the Liberal Government, many of which she deplored. As well as going through legislation about army reform and Ireland with a fine-tooth comb, she scrutinized all senior Church appointments and she kept a close eye on those proposed for honours. Equally, she watched the international scene, and monitored the situations in India, Afghanistan and Egypt.

There was, moreover, a perfectly respectable reason why this single mother of a haemophiliac son might not have the time or inclination to be performing public duties when she had the prime care of Prince Leopold. On her German tours, she had watched him nearly bleed to death. He was now fifteen, and she must have known that it was touch-and-go whether he would survive to adulthood; or, if he did so, whether he would be able to lead a normal life. In one of her strange mixtures of German and English she wrote to Alexandrine, '*Er wird für die Zukunft mein first object in life sein, und ich werde ihn nie verlassen oder mich von ihm trennen ausser wenn es absolut nöthig sein müsste.*'[19] ('For the future, he will be my first object in life, and unless it is absolutely necessary, I will never be separated from him.')

It was typical of Victoria's approach to any family problem from now on that she saw the best possible solution was to turn to John Brown. In July 1865, she engaged Brown's younger brother Archie as a 'brusher', or junior valet, to Prince Leopold. It was Archie's task to carry the prince if he ever suffered a collapse or found himself in difficulties. Leopold detested Archie – indeed, loathed John Brown too. 'J. B. is fearfully insolent to me, so is his brother [Archie] hitting me on the face with spoons for fun, etc.' Not the best treatment for a haemophiliac. 'You may laugh at me for all this; but you know I am sensitive. I know you will feel for me – their impudence increases daily towards everyone.'[20] The poor boy was writing sorrowfully to Walter George Stirling, a young adjutant of the Royal Horse Artillery, who had been appointed Leopold's governor. Stirling and Leopold developed a real rapport, as did Leopold and a servant named Sutherland, but when both fell foul of Archie Brown, it was Stirling and Sutherland who were dismissed and the hated Archie who remained.

Moreover, family, Court and friends were all expected to share the Queen's love of the Browns. When Brown's sister died, for example, it was no doubt very sad for him. But even the Court at Coburg was expected to enter into the spirit of bereavement over the matter, and Duchess Alexandrine was thanked for her polite expressions of sympathy for '*mein guter treuer Brown*' ('my good, loyal Brown'). The hatred felt by her courtiers for the Brown family seemed to act as an incentive for the Queen to give the Browns more and more power and influence. Victoria, with one side of her nature, loved defying the Establishment. Besides, it was questionable whether she ever realized just how bizarre her devotion to Brown appeared to the outside world. The longer she stayed away from public view, moreover, the harder the Queen herself found it to contemplate engagements which made her into a public spectacle. When she did make one of her rare public appearances, she scandalized the politicians by invariably having Brown in tow. Lord Stanley had plaintively written in 1867, 'The Queen parades this man about London behind her carriage, in his Highland dress, so that every street boy knows him.'[21]

If all the Queen's circumstances are considered, the clearer it seems that the Establishment and the Court were alarmed, not by the Queen's general slackness, as General Grey claimed to be, but by the figure of Brown and the amount of time she spent with him. True, she missed the State Opening of Parliament in 1867, but she attended it on other years – and she never had been brave enough to read the Queen's Speech – it was always read for her, usually by the Lord Chancellor of the day. She took a close interest in procedures in Parliament, in diplomatic endeavours in Europe, and in the colonies. It would be perfectly reasonable, in these circumstances, for her politicians to have seen, given her nervous disposition and her son Leopold's illness, that allowances had to be made. And this, surely, is what they would have done had they not in fact been chiefly worried by Brown. All the things which made Brown attractive to Victoria – his lack of side, his directness, his breeziness – offended their sense of decorum. And of course they suspected him of sleeping with her. Lord Stanley, Foreign Secretary in his father Lord Derby's Third Cabinet, asked in his journal, 'Why is the Queen penny wise and pound foolish? Because she looks after the browns and lets the sovereigns take care of themselves.'[22]

If she had been a widowed King who had bedded one of his servants, the Court would have politely turned a blind eye and even affected a certain manly amusement. But she was a woman, and so the fact that she was behaving just like her reprobate son Bertie made her 'self-indulgence' intolerable. Grey, as a responsible and loyal royal servant, would never have been so incautious as to spell out in writing what he meant. But he was as blunt as can be in his language that nothing less than the future of the monarchy was under threat. He would not have supposed this to be the case if the Queen were simply work-shy. Monarchies do not fall merely because a sad, sick Queen is unwilling to open a bridge. Grey had discussed 'the evils of the present state of things' with two of Victoria's daughters. 'They both, Princess Louise in the strongest language, expressed their entire concurrence in every word I said to them – and also in my belief of the Government alone having the power to put a stop to a system of running away from her duties, which may at last terminally affect the safety of the Monarchy itself if it goes on.'[23]

If *what* goes on? Clearly, the supposed affair with Brown is meant. If a prize were to be awarded to the courtier or Royal Family member who most hated Brown, that hotly contested award would probably have been given to General Charles Grey. The Queen once conveyed a message to him via her Highland servant; it was delivered in such an offhand manner that Grey, no doubt pompously, 'refused to accept the message in this rude form', as his daughter recalled.[24] Naturally, General Grey could not commit to paper, when writing to the Prime Minister, his fear that the rumours were true. But by comparing his monarch to the notorious womanizer the Prince of Wales, and saying that they both displayed the same levels of selfish self-gratification, it is clear what the old soldier feared.

A quarter of a century later, in June 1894, the Marquess of Queensberry would say to Oscar Wilde, whom he suspected of having a sexual relationship with his son, Lord Alfred Douglas, 'I do not say you are it, but you look it and you pose at it, which is just as bad.' Although no one would ever use the word 'pose' in connection with such a creature of impulse and passion as Queen Victoria, the rest of the sentence would neatly summarize the fears felt by the political classes when contemplating the relationship between their monarch and this drunken, loud-mouthed Highlander, John Brown. In some senses, whether she was actually sleeping with him was irrelevant. The Queen's infatuation with her servant and the man's unruly behaviour at Court were enough to cause the scandal. 'Servants are often the best friends to have,' she told her sister-in-law Alexandrine. She wrote these words in German, and then broke into the weird macaronic '*was die Highlanders von allen anderen Dienen auszeichnet* ['what distinguishes the Highlanders from all other servants'] – their great independence of character, and feelings of a gentleman, often far more as, than [sic] gentlemen of the highest rank. *Sie sind geborene Gentleman* ['They are born Gentleman'].'[25]

'It was the talk of all the Household,' said that notoriously unreliable tittle-tattler Wilfrid Scawen Blunt, 'that he was "the Queen's stallion"... He was a fine man physically, though coarsely made, and had fine eyes (like the late Prince Consort's, it was said) and the Queen, who had been passionately in love with her husband, got it into her head that somehow the prince's Spirit had passed into Brown, and four years after her widowhood, being very unhappy, allowed him all privileges... She used to go away with him to a little house in the hills where, on the pretence that it was for protection and to "look after the dogs", he had a bedroom next to hers, ladies in waiting being put at the other end of the building... [There could be] no doubt of his being allowed every conjugal privilege.'[26]

If Blunt wants us to believe this, we must test his words as stringently as possible. Victoria's letters and journals supply abundant evidence, in the years 1862–6, of her need for love, her sense of being bereft. Of that there is no doubt. Nor can it be questioned that in the companionship of Brown, she found something approaching consolation for her intolerable bereavement and sense of loss.

Yet, consider the letter, quoted in the last chapter, in which she told Vicky of her walk to the Frogmore Mausoleum with the other children and Brown, and of Brown's tearful expressions of sympathy. ('I felt for ye; to see ye coming there with your daughters and your husband lying there – marriage on one side and death on the other.')

Only a dissembler, which Victoria never was, could have penned such a letter if Brown had not been, at this date, purely and simply what she claimed: her friend, a man who was able to sympathize with her inmost sorrows and to weep with her. Vicky, together with the other children, might cringe at the intimacy which had sprung up between Brown and their mother, but Victoria made absolutely no attempt to cloak it. He was 'so simple, so intelligent, <u>so unlike</u> an <u>ordinary</u> servant and so cheerful and attentive'.

He was cheerful and attentive to her, but he did not extend such courtesies widely. Her nature was a mixture of tenderness and shrillness; with Brown, as whisky was imbibed (and whisky does increase hot-temperedness and lack of charity), she came to catch some of his abrasive spirit. His violent Presbyterianism helped fuel her own prejudice against bishops. 'I'm sure the dear Bishop will go straight to heaven when he dies,' she remarked of a missionary, John Coleridge Patterson, first Bishop of Melanesia. 'Weel, God help him when he meets John Knox,' was Brown's answer. The Queen was a timid railway passenger, terrified by newspaper reports of crashes and accidents. She commanded that no royal train should travel faster than fifty miles per hour. She once sent him down the platform when the train stopped at Wigan with a message for the driver to go slower, to which Brown added, 'Her Maa-dj-esty says the carriage was shaking like the Devil.'[27] It is not difficult to see how ill the courtiers, diplomats and politicians would take such amusing translations of royal injunctions. When 'The Queen requests that the train should travel more slowly' is translated into the sentence just quoted, it was comic. But when she herself began to share some of Brown's abrasiveness and to discard her habitual courtesy, it is not surprising that feathers were ruffled.

As early as July 1866, *Punch* printed a mock Court Circular: 'Balmoral, Tuesday. Mr John Brown walked on the slopes. He subsequently partook of haggis. In the evening Mr John Brown was pleased to listen to a bagpipe. Mr John Brown retired early.' At the Royal Academy Spring Exhibition on 6 May 1867, crowds flocked to see *Her Majesty at Osborne in 1866*, a huge oil painting by Sir Edwin Landseer, in which Brown takes pride of place holding the head of the Queen's pony. One critic wrote, 'If anyone will stand by this picture for a quarter of an hour and listen to the comments of the visitors he will learn how great an imprudence has been committed.'[28]

The horrified inference of Sir Charles Grey and the other courtiers was that the pair were sleeping together. They were certainly drinking together – which is surely the simplest explanation for the collapse of either legibility or sense in her blue-pencilled scrawls.

If – and it is a very big if – Victoria and Brown entered into some indiscreet pact or union, it was surely during this strange phase of what seems likely to have been the Queen's menopause.

When it is known that a biographer is at work on Queen Victoria, there is one question which friends and strangers alike will be sure to ask. What was the nature of the Queen's relationship with Brown? Having worked on the subject of Queen Victoria for many years, I have to confess to the rather unsatisfactory answer that I still feel unable to make up my mind. My instinct is to believe that it was what it appears to be in her letters to Vicky: namely an embarrassingly close monarch-and-servant relationship. Brown meant it when he said he would die for her, and the Queen meant it when she called him her '*treuer*' Brown. If I were forced to say what did or did not happen, I would point out the impossibility of carnal relations between them in the early years of her widowhood, when she was plainly fixated on the memory of Albert, and he was plainly no more than her Highland servant.

Nothing can be proved about the later period – say, from 1868 onwards. Scawen Blunt's tittle-tattle was not proven – that Brown was the Queen's stallion. But there is a much soberer witness in the person of Lewis Harcourt, son of Gladstone's Home Secretary and Chancellor of the Exchequer. Harcourt, known as Loulou, died in 1922, aged fifty-three, while implicated in a case of child-molestation. (The child was the twelve-year-old Edward James of West Dean Park, the aesthete and wit whose mother, in a scurrilous rhyme, 'will entertain the King' – that is, Edward VII.) Loulou's sad end should not cloud our judgement of his journals, which paint a vivid and realistic picture of the mid- to late Victorian political world.

On 17 February 1885, Harcourt wrote that Lady Ponsonby – wife of the Queen's private secretary – 'told the Home Secretary a few days ago that Miss Macleod declares that her brother Norman Macleod confessed to her on his deathbed that he had married the Queen to John Brown and... had always bitterly regretted it. Miss Macleod could have no object in inventing such a story, so that one is almost inclined to believe it, improbable as it sounds.'[29]

All these urgent requirements pressed upon the new Prime Minister and his Liberal Government, which consisted in a coalition of old-fashioned Whigs and new radicals. As Gladstone, a hyper-energetic fifty-eight-year-old, began his task, it soon became clear that while some of the reforms dear to his heart could be effected purely by parliamentary measures, there were others which involved at the deepest level a consideration of the monarch and her role in the new order.

Two of the most fundamental changes which his Government wanted to bring about were a reform of the army and a change to the position of Ireland. Everyone (except the military top brass) had known since the disasters of the Crimean War that the army needed root and branch reform. By the end of the 1870s, it would be required to fight wars in North and South Africa, and in Asia, as well as to be on standby if the inflammatory situation in Ireland grew worse. The expansion of the Empire made it necessary for a vast military expansion and reorganization. This was all now in the hands of the new Secretary of State for War, Edward Cardwell – and he would have his work cut out.

In Ireland, Gladstone believed in the urgency of land reform to assuage the discontents which had led to small tenants being driven from their land. He intended a twofold approach: on the one hand the introduction of a new Land Act to guarantee tenants' rights, and also, in recognition of the fact that most Irish people were not Anglicans, he wanted to bring in a Bill which disestablished the Irish Church and put the Church of Ireland bishops on the same footing as the Roman Catholics or the ministers of the Protestant Churches – namely merely religious leaders of their own community, rather than bishops of an Established Church appointed by the Crown and allowed to collect, as were bishops in the largely Nonconformist Wales, the hated tithe, or tax, to pay for Church expenses.

Here, as in the case of army reform, Gladstone would come up against formidable opposition from the Establishment. The Archbishops of Canterbury and York were furiously opposed to the idea of losing the Irish Church, and they had no difficulty in enlisting to their viewpoint the centre of the Establishment spider's web herself, Queen Victoria.

So, in two of the most fundamental parts of his reforming programme, Gladstone, though a loyal monarchist, knew himself from the first to be facing a formidable problem. The whole complex structure of the British Establishment, with its unwritten Constitution, was an organic thing, which changed as it grew. Would it be possible to bring about these radical reforms – a modern efficient army, an Ireland shorn of an Establishment Church – without in turn bringing about some reform to the monarchy itself? And, indeed, in a world where democracy was on the march, what was the function of the British monarch?

PART FIVE

SEVENTEEN

A PEOPLE
DETACHED FROM
THEIR SOVEREIGN

O N 5 JULY, taking up his duties as the Foreign Secretary after
the death of Lord Clarendon, Lord Granville was informed
by the Permanent Under-Secretary at the Foreign Office that 'he
had never had during his long experience known so great a lull in
foreign affairs'.[1] It was a remarkable misjudgement: not one that
Lord Clarendon himself would have made – his journals of the 1860s
are full of foreboding about the machinations of Bismarck and the
advancement of Prussian military power. Nor would the Queen,
ever-conscious of the tensions between Prussia, Russia, Denmark,
Austria and France (both as political events and as rifts within her
own family), have considered the late 1860s to have been a 'lull'.

Gladstone, in one of the strangest manifestations of detachment
ever perpetrated by a Prime Minister, wrote an anonymous article
in the *Edinburgh Review* denouncing the foreign policy of his own
Government. That oddly divided personality was a different person,
as he sat in his 'Temple of Peace', the study at Hawarden Castle,
from the devious politician of Westminster. Scratching with his
steel-nibbed pen on the page, and looking like a mad clergyman,
this scholarly recluse could attack the very Government of which the
politician Gladstone was the leader. He described France as 'motivated
by a spirit of perverse and constant error', he questioned Bismarck's

'scrupulousness and integrity', and concluded by talking of 'Happy England' endowed by God with 'a streak of silver sea to separate it from the conflicts of less fortunate peoples'. Lord Kimberley confided to his diary when he read the article that Gladstone 'could not guide safely the foreign relations of this country'.[2]

When Gladstone had formed his First Cabinet in December 1868, a new world, beyond the shores of the United Kingdom, was waiting to be born. The war between France and Prussia, which broke out in 1870, would result in the abject defeat of France, a period of appalling civil violence and the arrival of the Paris Commune. The spectre of communism, which had been 'haunting' Europe, according to Marx and Engels in 1848, would be a living political reality in Paris by 1871. Prussia, triumphant, militarized and led by Bismarck, pushed onwards to the creation of the new nation of Germany, which absorbed all the former princedoms, duchies and kingdoms of Victoria and Albert's youth, including Saxe-Coburg. By September 1870, the troops of Victor Emmanuel would enter Rome and the new united nation of Italy would be a reality, after the long dreams of Italian patriots.

So, it was a changing world to which a radically altered Britain, now with an extended franchise, must respond. Not least of the new Government's worries were the precarious situation in Ireland and an uncertain peace in Afghanistan, with a worry that Russia was extending its power following the fall of Tashkent (1865) and Samarkand (1868) into Russian hands. At home the expansion of the urban population in the previous two decades had led to acute housing shortages, the spread of epidemics and the urgent need for programmes of education. The Franco-Prussian War dominated the summer of 1870, and it is against the background of that conflict, and of the convulsions in Italy, that the Queen's personal life story during this year must be seen.

For some years now, General Grey had been looking for a way to resign as the Queen's private secretary. Although relations between the wise old soldier and his monarch had deteriorated – she found him 'often very irritable and excited'[3] – she would not hear of his resignation. The burden of work was heavy. Grey kept to Prince Albert's system of filing, which required multiple copies being made of important documents. Clerks were kept on hand at Buckingham Palace and at Osborne for the purpose, but anything of a confidential character needed to be copied by Grey himself. As noted in the previous chapter, the Queen was indignantly resistant to Grey's suggestion that she play a more public role. He in turn was exasperated by what he considered to be her selfishness and sensuality. It was particularly frustrating to Grey, during this period of political change and turmoil, that she forbade any political discussions at dinner – even though contemporary politics had been the stuff of the late Prince Consort's table talk. So, while the Government of Gladstone came to terms with the convulsions in Europe, and such crises at home as the threatened peace and stability of Ireland, with educational and army reform, Grey was obliged, during his many dinners with the Queen, to keep off all these subjects. As the nephew of the author of the 1832 Reform Bill, Grey must have found this worse than exasperating.

On 26 March, Grey suffered a stroke. He was paralysed down one side, was unable to recognize anyone and on 31 March he died. The next day, accompanied by Princess Louise, Colonel Henry Ponsonby and Jane Churchill, a lady-in-waiting, the Queen went up to town from Windsor. The party went at once to Grey's house. The Queen found his widow 'wonderfully resigned and patient in her grief. How I feel for her, having gone through the same terrible misfortune myself!'[4]

It is not recorded how Mrs Grey felt to be visited by the Queen on the very day after her husband's death. 'After talking for a little while, she took me into the room where the dear General lay, looking so peaceful, nice and unaltered, without that dreadful pallor one generally sees after death. His bed was covered with flowers, of which he was so fond. Poor dear General, I could not bear to think I should never look again on his face in this world.'[5]

Grey's departure, or merciful release, had been something which the Queen had anticipated; and she does not appear to have had any doubt about who should succeed him. This was Colonel Henry Ponsonby, who had been at Court since 1857. Ponsonby, himself from an aristocratic Whig family, was married to Mary Bulteel, a niece of General Grey.

The Ponsonbys were, on superficial levels, surprising choices for the Queen. While she was increasingly Tory, they were unabashed Gladstonian Liberals. In religion, they were High Church, like Gladstone, whereas the Queen was her own distinctive brand of Broad Church Pantheist/Presbyterian. Mary Ponsonby was highly educated, and a feminist; Queen Victoria deplored feminism.

Only in January 1870, the Queen had told Gladstone that she had 'the strongest aversion for the so-called & most erroneous "Rights of Women"'.[6] Later in the year, she would make clear her disgust at the idea of female medical students. She hated 'the <u>awful</u> idea of allowing young girls & young men to <u>enter</u> the dissecting room together'.[7]

The Ponsonbys would probably have smiled, as would those who love Queen Victoria to this day, at the vehemence of this viewpoint. (Connoisseurs such as they would surely have savoured the underlining of the word 'enter' – why that word, rather than, say, 'together'?) Although the Queen would cause both of them years of slightly disloyal amusement, and a great deal of embarrassment, nevertheless it was a triumphantly successful relationship. It is, indeed, difficult to imagine the Queen having a better private secretary than Henry Ponsonby, and much of the reason for his success in the role, which he exercised for the next quarter of a century, was because of his happy partnership with his wife.

Both Ponsonbys were loyal, in all important respects, to Queen Victoria, and they both warmed to her spontaneity. Victoria was a difficult woman to like, but an easy woman to love. Speaking of Prince Albert, Mary once said, 'There was a complete absence of that frankness which was such a charm in the Queen's manner.'[8] And this, surely, is the clue to why Ponsonby and the Queen worked so well together. Neither had any 'side'. Rather like a master angler, who knew when to give the salmon plenty of line and when to reel her in, Ponsonby was able to manage the Queen's moods without being reduced, as Grey so often had been, to exasperation, and finally to apoplexy. Unlike Grey, Ponsonby got on well with Brown, and found his antics and brusqueness amusing. Above all, the Ponsonbys both possessed that essential quality in a courtier: a finely developed sense of humour. They loved the Queen, and they would not betray her. But they knew when laughter behind her back, and apologies to politicians to whom she had been spectacularly unpleasant, were among the weapons they needed to deploy to save the Queen from herself.

Henry Ponsonby became her private secretary immediately upon Grey's demise. At once, much of the tension was taken out of the atmosphere at Court. A small example occurred in the autumn of 1870 when the Duke of Westminster became a Knight of the Garter. This is the sort of matter where Grey would have nagged and nagged the Queen – probably to no effect – to hold a formal ceremony of Investiture. This was precisely the sort of ritual which made the Queen shy, and about which she was lazy. Ponsonby accepted this. After a few attempts to make the Queen perform the ceremony, he shrugged, remarking to Gladstone, 'So, Westminster must put on his Garter in his bedroom.'[9]

The monarchy survived the turbulent and difficult years of the early 1870s. That it did so was chiefly because the public and the politicians wanted it to do so, in spite of the obvious faults of the Queen and the Prince of Wales. But it was in no small measure owing to Ponsonby that it survived so triumphantly, and that the Queen moved from being deeply unpopular in some quarters, at the time of his appointment, to being the beloved idol of an entire Empire of nations.

∽

The Franco-Prussian War and its revolutionary aftermath in France were stark reminders of how easily thrones could be toppled, how quickly monarchs could find themselves to be vulnerable human beings. At one moment, the Empress Eugénie was in the royal palace in the Tuileries. The next, the imperial standard was pulled from the flagpole and she was told that the mob was at the door. Hurrying to the back entrance, they found it locked, and it was a long time before they could find the key. Then, quite suddenly, Prince Metternich, who had been accompanying her, had gone, and she was alone on a Parisian pavement with a companion, Madame de Breton.

They found their way on foot, without being recognized, to the surgery of their American dentist, Dr Evans, who took them on a train to Trouville. At one point, when they had changed trains and were travelling by fiacre, the driver asked if they had come from Paris. When they said yes, the driver clenched his fists and said, 'Oh! If I could but catch the Empress!' It was only because of the courage of her dentist that she eventually reached Trouville, where Dr Evans got her on to a yacht belonging to Sir John Burgoyne.[10] Her husband, who had surrendered at Sedan with 80,000 French soldiers, spent six and a half months as a prisoner of war at Wilhelmshöhe in Germany. He was eventually allowed to join his wife and son in England, and they settled in Chislehurst. (He died on 9 January 1873.) As Dr Evans remarked in his memoirs, 'There is no country in the world where the distance between the sublime and the ridiculous is so short as in France!'[11]

So it might have seemed to the American dentist. But was it true? Charles I had been put on trial and beheaded in Whitehall, even though he questioned the legitimacy of the proceedings. James II had been in effect[12] dismissed from government in 1688. Following the defeat of Louis Napoleon at Sedan, Paris had fallen into a state of civil war, and the communists had set up a Revolutionary Government by spring 1871. The Queen watched these developments with horror. 'The Commune have everything their own way, and they go on quite as in the days of the old Revolution in the last century, though they have not yet proceeded to commit all the same horrors. They have, however, thrown priests into prison etc.' By June, she was reading, 'Most dreadful news from Paris. The wretched Archbishop, another Bishop, a Curé, and sixty-four other prisoners have been shot by these horrid Communists'.[13] The governing classes of Europe have all thought alike on one question since 1789, and that is that revolutionary fervour is virulent, it is catching. No one had yet tested the political views of the ever-expanding proletarian populations of the British manufacturing towns. Nor was there any way of testing, in Ireland, whether the Fenians represented a majority opinion or whether they were representatives of the hothead extremes. There could be few more nervous times to be extending the franchise, nor a more troubling era for the Queen to be, as Gladstone and his colleagues feared, making the monarchy unpopular. Victoria, who was personally very fond of the Empress Eugénie, could not fail to find the story alarming. On what, after all, did her own authority rest?

The political triumph of Prussia, and the creation of the German Reich, was made possible by the size, efficiency and professionalism of its army. The Prussians used the most up-to-date methods of armament – and, vitally important, of transport. They were the first people in the world to make use of the railway to transport troops – most notably and triumphantly in 1870, but they had been doing it since 1846.[14] The Prussians had a system of conscription which helped to swell their unconquerable army of a quarter of a million men. But they also had a system of officer training which was without compare, and officers were promoted on merit. The British Army, by contrast, in the early years of Mr Gladstone's administration, was in effect unchanged since Waterloo – in terms of its administration and discipline.

Some time in the early 1880s, the Prince of Wales and Prince Leopold asked Ponsonby who should command the army – the Royal Family or the Government? 'They seem to ignore the fact that this was settled by the late Charles I,'[15] observed Ponsonby wrily. Although this matter was, indeed, settled in 1649, with grisly consequences for Charles I, it was not always easy for Queen Victoria to know where her authority began and ended. Clearly, since 1689, no British monarch had been an absolute autocrat. On the other hand, the army and navy were, technically, in the service of the Crown, and this was something which she regarded as rather more than a technicality.

When Cardwell began his sweeping reforms of the army, she became incensed with rage that he should do so without consulting her. So sensitive was this matter, that when Philip Guedalla published his edition in 1933 of the correspondence between the Queen and Mr Gladstone, the more intemperate of her letters were censored from the printed version. As with the army, so in the case of naval appointments; it enraged her that G. J. Goschen, as First Lord of the Admiralty, should oversee the appointment of senior naval personnel.

'You consider...' Goschen wrote to Ponsonby in August 1871, 'that Admirals are appointed by the Queen, but that is not so. If that were the case, it would, of course, be incumbent on a First Lord to take the pleasure of Her Majesty as to cancelling an appointment made by Her Majesty. But flag officers are not appointed by Her Majesty either in fact or in name, as in the case of other departments to which you allude, and the appointments under which are gazetted as having been made by the Queen. All naval appointments are made by the Lord Commander of the Admiralty in virtue of the powers delegated to them by the Patent under which they execute the office of Lord High Admiral of the United Kingdom.'[16]

As late as 1880, the Queen was still writing to her ministers as if she had direct control over what happened in the armed forces. 'The Queen was surprised,' she wrote from Balmoral, 'to see the announcement of the abolition of flogging in the Navy. Perhaps a few words from the Admiralty would explain this to the Queen.'[17]

The clash between the War Office and the army, whose commander-in-chief was stationed in Horse Guards, was a perennial one. What needled the Queen – as well as her cousin the Duke of Cambridge – was the insistence of Liberal ministers that they, as elected representatives, rather than the sovereign, were ultimately in charge of the armed services. 'The superior control of the Queen, exercised through her Minister, and the responsibility of that Minister have never <u>been denied</u>,' she said, 'and no man admitted this more cordially that the Duke of Wellington.' It was a sentence which was crying out for an almighty 'but', or 'however', and she let rip at Gladstone:

> The Queen must, however, record her opinion that if Doubt and uncertainty have been thrown of late years over the system of military Administration, the fault seems to be chiefly with the War Office [i.e. with Cardwell] when there has been a constant succession of changes – old offices abandoned – & again restored – amalgamated – & again replaced – new offices created and modified & again abolished, till it is very difficult to define or understand what the existing system is. One thing <u>only</u> is <u>clear</u>, viz. that the <u>fault does not</u> lie with <u>the Horse Guards</u> [i.e. the Duke of Cambridge], where the duties purely military are well defined and efficiently executed.

Gladstone robustly replied, finding himself 'surprised at Your Majesty's language'.[18]

If Trevelyan's views on army reform had upset the Queen, his intrusive interest in her personal finances was even more troubling. The Queen was voted £385,000 annually from the Civil List. Trevelyan, writing under the pseudonym 'Solomon Temple, Builder', penned a pamphlet entitled *What Does She Do with It?*

The Gladstone Papers are full of letters, none of which found their way into the official, printed edition, in which the Queen wheedled, pleaded, cajoled, begged and squirmed, to get her Chancellor of the Exchequer and her Prime Minister to provide more money for her children from the Civil List. The parsimonious Gladstone knew that money was her weak point, and he deliberately allowed his radicals a free rein in asking awkward questions about the royal finances which he could never ask himself.

For example, in 1862, Lord Derby's Cabinet proposed an annual allowance for all the Queen's younger children, in the event of their not marrying, of £20,000. At the time of the proposal there were six unmarried children, and this allowance was intended to cover the expenses for all of them. Disraeli endorsed this arrangement in 1868, making the assurance that although the allowance could be diminished, as more and more of the children married, it would never sink below £10,000. The Queen had beadily spotted that Sir Charles Dilke, a noted radical, had abstained when this measure was passed through the Commons, and indeed was still recalling Gladstone's mind to Dilke's abstention in a letter she wrote to Gladstone fourteen years later in April 1882![19]

What, indeed, did she do with it? From the relative poverty of her upbringing in Kensington Palace, when her mother had been kept on tight purse strings by George IV and William IV, Victoria had seemingly squirrelled away what was in effect public money, voted to her by Parliament for the exercise of her monarchical duties, and appropriated it as her private fortune. She had built up Osborne House and Balmoral as her private domains and supplied Bertie with his house and substantial estates at Sandringham. The distinction between the sovereign's private wealth and the wealth of the Crown had been blurred by the way that Victoria had chosen to live. Clearly, as far as she was concerned, there was no distinction between her private wealth and that of the State she held as sovereign. She was the Queen, and that was the end of the matter. Although her private fortune gave her a measure of independence from the whims of her politicians, it also made her more vulnerable to the charge, from radical quarters, of being insensitively rich. She had perhaps not given as much thought as a sovereign should to the memory of the affair of Marie Antoinette's Diamond Necklace.

When the pamphlet reached Balmoral in the autumn of 1870, Ponsonby spent several weeks considering it before writing to Gladstone. The Prime Minister was much too wily to admit that he had known Trevelyan was writing it. Instead, he consulted with Ponsonby how they might best limit the public damage of 'Solomon Temple's' investigations. And, no doubt to Gladstone's satisfaction,

Ponsonby disclosed to the Prime Minister the extent of the Queen's actual fortune.

In 1852, she had been left £250,000 by a miser named Nield. ('Solomon Temple' had exaggerated the sum.) Nor was Trevelyan right in suggesting that he knew what the Prince Consort had left, since 'Prince's wills are never proved'. But it was grossly exaggerated, said Ponsonby, to suggest that Albert had been able to save £1 million from his annual allowance. He had in fact left the Queen £25,000, with a charge on it of about £2,000 or £3,000 for pensions – presumably to dependents. Meditating upon the question years later, Ponsonby said to his wife that most of the Civil List was spent on upkeep – out of the £384,000 or so which Parliament granted to the Civil List 'the Lord Chamberlain saves very little. [The Lord Chamberlain, in charge of the Household, would have paid for upkeep of the fabric, wages and stipends, etc.] The Lord Steward does, but not above 3 or 4 thousand and the Master of the Horse exceeds his allowance.'[20]

The money received by the Queen from the Treasury, however, was only a small part of her actual income. True, Prince Albert had managed very efficiently with what assets and incomes they possessed. True, Victoria's parsimony in such matters as heating and wardrobe helped. But 'Solomon Temple, Builder', and critics since, missed a trick by suggesting that the Queen was squirrelling away the Civil List. As anyone could tell from considering the expense of running the horses and households and palaces, such a squirrelling exercise would be profitless. The real source of Queen Victoria's wealth, and what made her so much richer than any monarch in previous British history, was the Duchy of Lancaster, whose assets and incomes the Queen took over upon her accession. John of Gaunt – 'time-honoured Lancaster' – bequeathed the Duchy with its vast holdings to Henry IV, and ever since they had been the possession of the Crown. Until the reign of Queen Victoria, the wealth from the Duchy came largely from the rents in agricultural land, but with industrialization and the growth of the cities, these incomes rocketed. The Duchy owned – and still owns – huge tracts of London, including the Savoy district (though not the hotel!) as well as much of south London. The Duchy held land in the Midlands and the North. Most of the foreshore of the Mersey belonged to it as did the Mersey Docks, with all their warehouses and valuable moorings for export vessels. As did, in that era of increased leisure and holidaying, the Blackpool Promenade. The Duchy owned Kidwelly in South Wales – in George IV's time a sleepy market town with a picturesque ruined castle painted by Turner – but in the era of Albert and Victoria a coal-mining district. The Duchy owned coal mines throughout South Wales, Derbyshire, Yorkshire, Staffordshire and Lancashire.

At the Queen's accession, the Exchequer had considered absorbing the Duchy's income into the public purse. The Duchy's Council argued forcibly against this, and it was this happy chance which was the foundation of Victoria's immense wealth. Cockfosters and Handley Wood, and other acres of cheap grazing land north of London in 1837, became urban real estate in the following decades. In Birmingham, Manchester and Staffordshire many of the new industrial estates, mines and factories were now enriching the Royal Family. The two Yorkshire spa towns of High and Low Harrogate were 'developed'. The Duchy was the direct beneficiary of Harrogate's expansion into the principal spa town of health- and leisure-obsessed Victorian Britain. Though the Queen never visited the town which she in effect owned, by 1861 its rateable value soared to £30,000, having been worth very little when she came to the throne. The expansion of the nation's population, its industry and its leisure facilities all enormously enriched the sovereign. And these assets were indeed stored away for the personal enrichment of herself and her successors. By the 1880s, Victoria would have a personal annual income in excess of £300,000 (on top of the Civil List), making her easily the richest person in Britain, with only the dukes of Westminster (on £290,000) and Bedford (£225,000), with their huge estates in London and the country, even approaching her levels.[21]

Ponsonby in 1870 had been playing a slightly duplicitous game in revealing the details of the Privy Purse to the indiscreet Gladstone, but if there was an extenuating circumstance, it was that the Prime Minister had just visited Balmoral and had taken a battering. Ponsonby felt Gladstone deserved a little compensatory reward. Both Gladstone and the Queen dreaded the annual ritual of the Prime Minister's visit to Balmoral. When Gladstone arrived at the Castle, it was six weeks since he had seen his sovereign, and it was noted that she was too ill to see him. Leaping perhaps a little too eagerly at the chance of not having to see her at all, Gladstone wrote to her, 'Mr Gladstone, in announcing with his humble duty his arrival at the Castle, aware of Your Majesty's habitual condescension and courtesy intreats [sic] Your Majesty, after so serious a derangement of health on no account to make any effort for the purpose of seeing him during his stay.'[22] Ludicrously, nearly all the communications between the two, while he was staying under her roof, were conducted in writing, and this was to be the pattern of future visits. What was the point of his being there at all?

When she did surface, it was to excoriate Gladstone about the reforms of the army. When the Prime Minister left, and wrote a note to Ponsonby while sitting on the platform at Ballater Station, the Queen's secretary thanked Gladstone for 'a tone and temper which few would be able to boast of under such trying circumstances'.[23]

Psychosomatic illness was a weapon which the Queen unashamedly used whenever she felt Gladstone was bullying her or fighting her into a corner. She had by then been suffering for months with attacks of rheumatism, and with a mysterious sore throat, which apparently made it impossible to undertake any duties or attend any public functions. She spent much of the summer in bed being attended by the useless Jenner and by the distinguished Dr Joseph Lister, the pioneer of antisepsis. Jenner blamed the 'advancing democracy of the age' for all the complaints about the Queen's withdrawal. (Over fifty republican clubs or organizations grew up in England during this period.) But it was not only the democrats in Parliament who found her behaviour verged on the indefensible. 'Yesterday...' wrote Colonel Ponsonby to Gladstone, 'I saw a strong man, Lord Essex, rolling about in the extremest agony. He fought bravely against it, and a little while after, still in much pain, he was discharging the duties of courtesy to his guests. What strange contrasts does this world afford!'[24] This was when she had not even warned the Lord Chancellor that she was too 'ill' to prorogue Parliament or to summon the necessary Privy Council meeting. It meant that the entire Establishment of Great Britian was awaiting Her Majesty's pleasure – Parliament could not be prorogued while the Queen remained in bed in Balmoral. 'Worse things may easily be imagined,' wrote Gladstone, 'but smaller and meaner cause for the decay of Thrones cannot be conceived. It is like the worm which bores the bark of a noble tree and so breaks the channels of its life.'[25]

In 1871, she managed to open the Royal Albert Hall on 29 March, but limited herself to speaking just one sentence, and felt 'quite giddy', confronting the huge crowds. She also mysteriously felt well enough to open Parliament; but then Prince Arthur, her favourite child, had just turned twenty-one, and she wanted Gladstone to vote him an annuity of £15,000. The vote for the annuity was passed on 3 August but with an unprecedented fifty-four votes cast against it. On the day of the first vote in the Commons, there was a demonstration in Hyde Park against Prince Arthur receiving his grant, and the meeting moved to Trafalgar Square. In the Commons, there were speeches which could only embarrass the royalist cause. Tories tried to justify the Queen receiving £385,000 per annum by saying that she had surrendered the Crown Lands upon her accession, and that had she held on to them, she would now be receiving rents of over £1 million per year. But this was beside the point. As Mr Dixon of Birmingham told the House, 'there was growing up in the minds of the people in large towns an increasing feeling in favour of Republicanism'. Mr Disraeli had told them that the money paid to royalties was in order to 'keep up the pageantry of the Crown'. But, a rueful Sir William Lawson 'was not in a position himself to say whether that pageantry had been kept up to the satisfaction of the country or not'. Ominously, Sir William said that the Crown was now 'in a different position from that which it occupied 30 years ago'. And an even more sympathetic MP believed he spoke for 'many who, Englishmen as they were, loyal as they were, most anxious in every way to support the Sovereign of this country in that high position in which she was placed, were yet particularly anxious that the Sovereign should come more among her people'. He pointed to 'what was going on in Dublin at the present moment' as evidence of what happened when a people felt detached from their sovereign ruler.[26]

The MP who mentioned what was happening in Dublin had put his finger on one of the sorest points in the body politic. The whole question of Ireland, which had dominated British politics since the famine, could not but make an impact on the position of the Royal Family.

It was a period of extreme personal embarrassment and difficulty for the Royal Family. The British public, on the whole, had been pro-French in the war, and the Queen's firstborn daughter was the Crown Princess of Prussia. The Queen's pro-Germanism was no secret, though it was perhaps as well that some of the sentiments she expressed in her private correspondence to Vicky were not read by the public: 'My whole heart and my fervent prayers are with beloved Germany', for example.[27] Though she was desperately sorry for Napoleon and Eugénie having to escape Paris, she could not restrain herself from feeling that 'it is quite marvellous how the Germans carry everything before them and how wonderfully well the campaign is being conducted'.[28] The invasion of Paris by Prussian troops was surely 'a just judgement – a just retribution on a very guilty government and a very frivolous vain-glorious people, and the fulfilment of beloved Papa's most earnest wishes'.[29]

Meanwhile, as she contemplated the 'fearful extravagance and luxury, the utter want of seriousness and principle in everything'[30] in the Parisians, Bertie was summoned as a witness in court in the sordid 'Warwickshire Scandal'. Sir Charles Mordaunt had married an eighteen-year-old girl named Harriet Moncreiffe. A year later, she gave birth to a premature child – Violet, who grew up to marry the 5th Marquess of Bath. Harriet confessed to Mordaunt that the father was Lord Cole, and she also confessed to having had affairs with several other eminent figures, including the Prince of Wales. When Mordaunt broke into her desk, he found letters in Bertie's hand. Bertie denied any wrongdoing, and his mother, superficially at least, accepted his word. But it was not a good time to be a royal private secretary.

At Sandringham, in the cold spring of 1871, Alix, pregnant for the sixth time, went into premature labour, and produced a son, Prince John, who died after twenty-four hours. The distracted mother lay with the dead baby all day. A sobbing, kilt-clad Bertie, walking hand in hand with his sons Eddy and Georgie, buried the child in the Norfolk earth. The doctor afterwards gave him the news that his twenty-six-year-old wife, who was coughing blood, could not stand the strain of another birth, and that they should have a celibate marriage.

The republican press were totally callous about Bertie and Alix's loss. *Reynolds's Newspaper* wrote, 'We have much satisfaction in announcing that the newly born child of the Prince and Princess of Wales died shortly after its birth, thus relieving the working men of England from having to support hereafter another addition to the long roll of State beggars they at present maintain.'[31]

The Queen recommended a long period of mourning for the child, but Bertie snapped back, 'Want of feeling I never could show, but I think it's one's duty not to nurse one's sorrow however much one may feel it.'[32] He knew that for the Prince of Wales, as well as the Queen, to become recluses, shut away from public gaze, would be potentially catastrophic for the monarchy. His private life that year remained as messy as ever. Shortly before the death of his son, Bertie had impregnated a mistress, Lady Susan Vane-Tempest, daughter of the Duke of Newcastle, and the estranged wife of Lord Adolphus Vane-Tempest, who had been imprisoned in a lunatic asylum with delirium tremens. She was five or six months pregnant in September when she confessed her condition to Bertie, and he behaved heartlessly, insisting she see his doctor, Oscar Clayton. Christmas 1871 found her in Ramsgate living in a large terraced house overlooking the sea. She was complaining to the doctor of 'white discharge... backache... I am a cripple on two sticks and cannot move about!!!' There is no mention of the baby. Had it died or, late as she was in her pregnancy, had Dr Clayton terminated it? She appeared to be showing the symptoms of tertiary syphilis, with leg ulcers and discharge. Four years later she was dead.[33]

In the event, however, it was not his mistress's ill health, nor his wife's, but the Prince of Wales's own which prompted a crisis that year. At a shooting party in Scarborough held for his thirtieth birthday, Bertie complained of a chill and called for cherry brandy and a hot bath. Dr Clayton was summoned – he was seeing a lot of seaside resorts that year – by which time Bertie had developed rose-coloured spots and a severe headache. Sir William Jenner was brought for a second opinion, and there could be no doubt. The prince was suffering from the disease they believed to have killed his father, typhoid fever.

Once they had brought him back to Sandringham, the symptoms became more acute: vomiting, diarrhoea, headaches, delirium. The Queen had never visited Sandringham before, but, as the tenth anniversary of Prince Albert's death approached, she went to her son's bedside. All the royal children who were in England were summoned. Alice, who with her husband Louis had been staying with the Queen at Balmoral, had already arrived at Sandringham, at the stage when the prince's 'chill' had developed more worrying symptoms.

The atmosphere provoked friction among the anxious onlookers. Highly strung, dreading the death of her favourite brother, was the one member of the family with practical nursing experience. She sat with her sister-in-law Alix at Bertie's side for longer than any of them. She gave vivid accounts to Louis of Bertie's delirium:

When Bertie was delirious the other day he said to Alix, 'I have had a terrible scene, but I gave it one of them well'

– whereupon he hit Mrs Jones – then said, 'that mad woman, I can't stand her any longer'... today he said to Mrs Jones... 'Do you know who that is – he is a Swedish gentleman I know'. Then he gives orders that all gentlemen are to come in tights 'because I am very particular about dress – and Gen. Knollys must kneel down and give me a glass of water, it was always done in former days'. Sometimes we can't help laughing to see him like that in spite of all our worry and distress. This morning he asked me – 'What does Louis do without you? Does he know you are here – he'll never see you any more – sad state of affairs'. He doesn't know Alix he calls her 'waiter' and says to her, 'You were my wife, you are no more – you have broken your vows'.[34]

Writing from Sandringham to the Prime Minister a week later, on 8 December, Ponsonby related that, 'The bad symptoms came on last night and today he showed so much weakness that they feared it would not last long. The Princess [Alix] is wonderfully calm though tears sometimes force themselves out; yet she seems determined not to give way but to be with him, and he looks up with pleasure whenever she is near him. He is sometimes conscious. The Queen saw him as soon as she arrived, but I believe he did not see her.'[35]

Three days later, the outcome was still uncertain. Sometimes a doctor expressed hope, which then evaporated. On 11 December, Ponsonby wrote:

... every minute brings a change. The Queen up much of the night. It seems the lungs are not affected but the bronchial tubes are and the formation of phlegm which they tell me is one of the symptoms of the disorder increases while nervous strength is wanting, to enable him to cough up the obstruction. And the bronchial irritation swells the pipes and renders choking possible. This it is, if I understand the case, which now causes the danger, a danger which exhibits itself in painful paroxysms and the termination of which it is impossible to foresee. At six or seven this morning, he had one of these and all the family were summoned to the adjoining room but after a time, it passed off.[36]

Lady Macclesfield, one of Alix's ladies-in-waiting, was one of those who felt excluded by Alice's constant attentions to the Princess of Wales. She piously expressed the hope that Divine Providence would rescue the prince. 'Providence! There is no Providence, no nothing, and I can't think how anyone can talk such rubbish', was Alice's outburst. Lady Macclesfield considered Alice to be 'the most awful story-teller I have ever encountered, meddling, jealous and mischief-making'. Presumably, Lady Macclesfield resented Alice repeating what the prince had said in delirium. Given the state of the Waleses' marriage, it must have seemed particularly tactless to laugh at his telling Alix she was no longer his wife. And Lady Macclesfield was appalled by the blasphemous tenor of Alice's outburst about Providence. But the Queen was gracious enough to acknowledge publicly, when the crisis was passed, that it was Alice's nursing skill which had helped the prince turn the corner.

On 13 December, the Queen was by her son's bedside and for the first time he acknowledged her. Then he sank into delirium again. But her worst fear was not realized. The dreaded day 14 December came and went, and Bertie survived it. Although thereafter, he had days on which his temperature was high, he was past the crisis.

Whether the monarchy was past its crisis was another question entirely. Colonel Ponsonby, Sir Thomas Biddulph, Keeper of the Privy Purse, and the Prime Minister held discussions and correspondence, even as the prince convalesced, about ways to improve public perceptions of the Royal Family. Ponsonby thought that he should give dinners at Buckingham Palace. 'But this of course would be nothing unless he really took a lead. Would it not be difficult for any young man to do much in such a position and will it not be still more difficult for <u>him</u> to suddenly dismiss his Falstaffs?'[37]

In a long letter to Colonel Ponsonby, Gladstone spelt out his gravest misgivings about the current position of the Royal Family. On the one hand, he regretted – quite apart from all their unspoken feelings about the Queen's idleness – a grave concern about the position of the Prince of Wales. Surely Parliament should urge him to undertake philanthropic pursuits? Should he not imitate the example of the Earl of Shaftesbury? 'Shaftesbury himself could not have done it had he not had the means by a seat first in the Commons and afterwards the Lords of giving a practical turn to his efforts and impressing them with a character of responsibility which has so to speak bridled them & checked a tendency to excess rarely separated in the imperfection of human nature from genuine enthusiasm.'[38] It is hard to translate Gladstone's verbosity, but what he appeared to be suggesting was that Bertie's gross manner of life concealed an enthusiastic spirit which could be channelled into some great charitable purpose or some scheme of public improvement.

Even if this were unrealistic, Gladstone also felt that 'society has suffered fearfully in moral tone from the absence of a pure Court. [In the days of Prince Albert, he suggested…] It was like Arthur's Round Table in its moral effect. It did not directly influence many, but it influenced the highest – those who most need it – their influence acted upon others, and so onwards in widening circles. It is a great and important question whether and how this want can be supplied.'

There is little doubt that Gladstone's letter does reflect the sort of thinking which Prince Albert himself would have approved of and developed.

The Prince of Wales's illness undoubtedly made some newspapers feel they had gone too far in their criticisms of the monarch. On 27 February, the Queen, accompanied by the Prince and Princess of Wales, were paraded through the streets of London to attend a service of thanksgiving for his recovery. Gladstone certainly did not share Princess Alice's view that there was 'no Providence, no nothing'.

Even if he had done so, the service was the first step in teaching the Royal Family that they must put on public displays to remain plausible. Queen Elizabeth II is supposed to have remarked, 'I have to be seen to be believed.' Queen Victoria was loth to learn this lesson, and had, as usual when asked to do anything in public, vigorously resisted the idea of 'public religious displays'.[39] A triumphal arch was, however, erected at Oxford Circus, festooned with banners and with the legend 'ENGLAND REJOICES WITH HER QUEEN', as Victoria and the ill-matched Bertie and Alix trotted beneath it in the open landau.

The rejoicing at Bertie's recovery, if not as universal as might be supposed from such carefully manipulated propaganda, was nonetheless widespread and heartfelt. 'From the highest to the poorest "rags"', said Victoria, 'there was but one and the same feeling! It was, of course very fatiguing – bowing all this time.'[40] But, once Bertie was better, the question remained – what should he do?

One suggestion, emanating from Gladstone himself, was that the prince should be sent to Ireland. Victoria's initial reaction was disapproval. 'It does not seem desirable to introduce violent changes into the Government of Ireland at a moment when that country appears to be in a state of fermentation and requires a steady, firm and quiet administration to enable it to settle down.'[41] She had either never read, or chose to ignore, the speech in the House of Commons by Sir William Lawson suggesting that the presence of royalty on Irish soil would help to 'settle' things, and give to moderate Irishmen and women the sense that the Government was aware of their concerns. Eventually, Victoria, having discussed the matter with Bertie, was candid enough to turn it down flat. The prince, she told the Prime Minister, could scarcely go to Dublin and perform the function, in some sense, of the viceroy, 'for it would be impossible to pay to the Pce [sic] of Wales the Salary voted for the Vice Roy'. Besides, the pleasure-loving prince could scarcely be expected to forgo the pleasures of trips to Paris, membership of the Jockey Club, to the great English houses, to the London clubs, in favour of a post which 'compels him to reside in a second-rate Town where his sole duty wd. seem to be to entertain a second-rate Society & to attract the people who will know that he has no real power whatsoever, and that his position is inferior to that of the Lord Lieutenant!'[42] It is easy to see why Philip Guedalla, in his 1933 edition of the Queen's correspondence with her Prime Minister, felt constrained to censor this observation by omitting it from the printed text.

The Irish situation was not going to solve itself. It needed new initiatives and ideas, promoted by British politicians to answer the grievances felt by Irish tenant farmers, and Irish politicians who did not feel they had a voice. Even as she was preparing to go to St Paul's for the service of thanksgiving, Victoria received long memoranda from the Lord Lieutenant of Ireland, Earl Spencer – about the trial of one Kelly, who had shot a policeman and was sentenced to fifteen years' penal servitude; about more shootings in the streets of Dublin; about two elections, one in Galway and another in Kerry, both of which returned candidates in favour of Home Rule for Ireland. Spencer was desperate for the introduction of the secret ballot in Ireland, since both the Kerry and the Galway elections were already being contested on the grounds of alleged intimidation of voters.[43] (It was introduced that year, 1872.)

Two days after the thanksgiving service, there was another attempt on the Queen's life. She set out for a drive in Regent's Park, accompanied by Lady Jane Churchill, Prince Arthur and Prince Leopold. General Arthur Hardinge and Lord Charles Fitzroy were her outriders and John Brown was on the box of the open landau. Watching their departure was an eighteen-year-old youth called Arthur O'Connor of Houndsditch. He worked for an oil and colour manufacturer in that district noted, by Henry Mayhew, for its 'Jewish shopkeepers, warehousemen, manufacturers and inferior jewellers'. O'Connor had attempted to get a petition to the Queen during the St Paul's service but he had been removed by the cathedral vergers. Now, armed with a flintlock pistol, he climbed the ten-foot-high railings around the Palace and without being noticed, he sprinted across the courtyard, and waited beside the Garden Entrance.

When the landau returned from the park, the equerries dismounted, Jane Churchill got out of the carriage, and Brown was coming round to let down the steps, when O'Connor appeared at the Queen's side, with an 'uplifted hand... It is to good Brown & to his wonderful presence of mind that I greatly owe my safety, for he alone saw the boy rush round and followed him!'[44] Brown kept hold of him until the police arrived. When the youth had been taken away, it was discovered that he had a history of mental derangement, that he had bought the pistol in a pawnshop and stuffed its barrel with wads of blue paper. He was given twenty strokes of the birch and a year's hard labour.

Bertie resented the fact that Brown had been made the hero of the hour. Had not Prince Arthur also behaved gallantly in the landau? Yet the Queen, who gave Arthur a mere tiepin as a reward, made a public announcement that she would give Brown a gold medal, with an annuity of £25 attached to it. Brown was the chief witness in O'Connor's trial at the Central Criminal Court, and it was the first chance the public had to hear his distinctive voice as he related the alarming incident: 'The carriage stopped at the entrance for the purpose of allowing Her Maa-dj-esty to alight... The prisoner... placed his hand upon the carriage and I seized his neck.'[45]

The Queen was peeved about the birching of the 'wretched boy'. Much too lenient. She deemed the judge to have 'behaved very stupidly'[46] and took herself on a restorative holiday in Baden-Baden and a comforting round of visits to German relations. She also saw her half-sister Feodore, who appeared to be dying. (Poor O'Connor, who emigrated to Australia, and then came back to London, was finally committed to Hanwell Lunatic Asylum in 1874.) She took no notice of the pathetic piece of paper which O'Connor had left in the hands of Sir Thomas Biddulph at the time of his arrest: a document which he expected the Queen to sign, offering release to the Fenian prisoners.

All this was disturbing evidence that Ireland was the most pressing problem on the political agenda. Earl Spencer felt that the

Fenian press was 'very poisonous, leading the people on to dislike to England and the British Government'. He did his best to censor and prevent the distribution of American newspapers in Ireland. But, even when this allowance had been made, he was clear in his mind. 'The mainspring of all Irish discontent is the long-standing feeling of oppression and injustice, of which Lord Spencer feels that England in many cases was guilty towards Ireland in former days.'[47]

Governments run out of steam. Small blunders and scandals which would inflict no great damage upon a buoyant administration can be bruising to one which is tired. The Lords threw out Cardwell's proposals for army reform, and Gladstone responded by imposing the royal prerogative to by-pass the Upper House. To many, this seemed high-handed. Two very minor cases revealed Gladstone's tiredness. One was where he offered the living of Ewelme to a Cambridge man when by special Act of Parliament (1871) it had been decreed that the Queen could only present an Oxford man to the rectory. Gladstone's enforcement of his own candidate was seen as high-handed, as was the rather different one – where Gladstone appointed Sir John Collier as one of the Judges in Privy Council without following the correct procedures.

Small matters, but they caused storms in Westminster and the Tory opposition began to scent blood. Gladstone's attempts to create a Catholic university in Dublin provided Disraeli and his backbenchers many opportunities to stir up anti-Irish and anti-Catholic prejudice.

The Queen could look forward to an end to what was for her the nightmare of having Gladstone as her Prime Minister. But the year was clouded by personal more than by political matters. In June, she observed the thirty-fifth anniversary of her accession. But what should have been an occasion of some joy was entirely overshadowed by the death of Norman Macleod, the Minister at Crathie. 'Many bitter tears has she shed over his loss, and she feels she is <u>poorer</u> again in this weary world without him! She saw him generally only twice a year, at dear Balmoral, sometimes even only once, but she looked eagerly forward to those meetings, for those words of love and truth and wisdom which remained in her heart to strengthen and comfort and cheer her.'[48]

Inevitably, we pause and remember the truly extraordinary statement, by Lady Ponsonby to the Home Secretary, that Norman Macleod had actually married Victoria to John Brown. 'His truly,' Victoria mused, 'was the religion of Love. He wished to impress all with the feeling that God was our loving father and not a hard judge.'[49] She never spoke with such warmth of any Church of England clergymen, even of the few she liked. Does not the phrase 'the religion of Love' suggest a particular bond, a particular role which Macleod and no other had played in her life?

By the end of the year, she had sustained another loss. It was the final severing of the link with her childhood. Feodore died at the beginning of October. 'Her loss is quite irreparable,' she told Gladstone. 'Her only and most admirable Sister and the vy. last Link (for no one is left now) with her Childhood and Youth gone. Life becomes more and more dreary.'[50]

We are all of us different people when there is no one left on earth who can remember us as children. Victoria was now in that bleak position. No one was left who would address her by her first name. There was no one who could remember the nursery at Kensington, or the dolls, or the funny old uncles. She had lost the woman with whom she shared a mother. From now on, she was a matriarch, though one who had, for all the unsatisfactoriness of her children, at least one faithful companion – 'Brown, in his very fullest and very handsome full dress'. She remembered him in his splendour as they rode to the thanksgiving service that spring, and that brought comfort.

EIGHTEEN

'YOU HAVE IT, MADAM'

QUEEN VICTORIA'S SUPPLY of maternal affection was small. There was not enough to stretch to all nine children. If one child was in especial favour, this had the consequence of increasing her distaste for the non-favourites all the more. Other monarchs in Europe, dysfunctional as their marriages and families might be, looked on aghast at the British Royal Family's failure to conceal their rifts and rows. 'What a tender relationship!' exclaimed the Tsarina of Russia sarcastically after a meeting with Bertie. She noticed that the Prince of Wales took no notice of his mother 'even on the anniversary of his father's death'.[1]

Bertie, naturally, was a constant source of worry. The latest embarrassment for his family at home was his dalliance with the nineteen-year-old Patsy Cornwallis-West – known as the Irish Savage – who would bear a child by the end of 1874 wrongly,[2] but widely, believed to be his.

Lenchen, living blamelessly at Cumberland Lodge in Windsor Great Park with her thunderingly boring husband Christian of Schleswig-Holstein, was a constant irritant to the Queen. She once saw Christian lolling dreamily under a tree while staying at Osborne, and took the trouble to write him a note to say he should find something better to do with his time. She considered that he 'pampered' Lenchen and 'did not understand in the least how to manage her'. (The 15th Earl of Derby neatly summed up Christian as 'an honest, quiet gentleman, who will not set the Thames on fire'.³) As for their children, who were 'excessively plain', the Queen was irritated by their 'cold upon cold and unbecoming stoutness'; a ripe case of the pot calling the kettle black, since the Queen was by now a positive balloon of bombazine. It astounded Victoria that Lenchen was so 'touchy and offended' by her mother's remarks, and felt that her touchiness '(partly from health and partly from Christian's inordinate spoiling and the absence of all actual troubles and duties)… makes it very difficult to live with her'.⁴

Leopold, an undergraduate at Oxford, was still in disgrace because he had refused to take Presbyterian Communion with his mother at Crathie during the previous autumn. She suspected him of having picked up High Church views at Oxford. 'Indeed I have <u>never</u> known <u>any one refuse</u> to take the Sacrament with a Parent – and especially the Head of the Country – if asked to do so.'⁵ As the New Year began, he wanted to return to Oxford. The Queen had developed a dislike of the Dean of Christ Church – Liddell – with whose daughter Alice Leopold had enjoyed dancing and flirting. (Lewis Carroll had written a satirical squib about Mrs Liddell nicknaming her the 'King-fisher'.⁶) And Leopold's health continued to give cause for alarm. His sister – the other Alice in his life – had sent him a bust of her son Frittie, who had died the previous year, aged three, of the same haemophilia which had plagued Leopold's life. 'Oh dear Alice,' he wrote with clumsy candour to the broken-hearted woman, 'I know too well what it is to suffer as he would have suffered, & the great trial of not being able to enjoy life, or to know what happiness is, like others.'⁷ Presumably, the domestic happiness of Lenchen and Christian, visible on the Queen's very doorstep at Windsor, was what helped to make them so irritating to the mother; but also their independence. Victoria really got on best with servants, or friends and relations who were prepared to behave like her servants – such as Princess Beatrice, 'my beloved Baby – who really is the apple of my eye'.⁸

Princess Louise, too, was causing anxiety. Her marriage to the Marquis of Lorne was childless. Louise blamed her mother for forcing her into the match.[9] Society gossips claimed that Lorne was leading a secret homosexual life, and this was the reason for the princess bearing no child. Lorne's father, the Duke of Argyll, had come to suspect that the Queen knew Louise to be barren when she married – because of her having contracted mumps as a child.

As for the Duke of Edinburgh, Affie, who as a youth had been (in Louise's eyes at least) 'clever, bright and beautiful',[10] he was becoming a difficult person. He was short-tempered, and after several years of naval service, he had developed peremptory manners, rudeness to servants and irascibility. His mother, who had never cared much for him, now felt free to say she found Affie 'not a pleasant inmate in a house and I am always on thorns and gêne [discomfort] when he is at dinner'.[11] (He met his match in Brown and the pair had many quarrels, which did not endear him to his mother.) Affie did not cause quite so many scandals as Bertie did with women, but this widely travelled naval officer ran the Prince of Wales a close second and, when in London together, they haunted the same disreputable parties, and chased a similar brand of actresses and tarts. Affie was a much cleverer man than Bertie, however, with a real eye, and an impressive collection of oriental and European ceramics and Venetian glass, which is now on public display in Coburg.

Thickly bearded, as befitted a sailor, Affie had a plausible naval career, reaching the rank of captain by the age of thirty, and sailing the world. But he was in need of a wife. His first choice had been Frederika, daughter of the blind King of Hanover, but the blindness had been hereditary for three generations, and on these grounds Queen Victoria forebade the match. There were other women whom he had loved, but he eventually fell for the Grand Duchess Maria Alexandrovna, daughter of the Emperor Alexander II of Russia.

It was a match which had been vigorously promoted by Alix and her sister Dagmar, who had married Marie's brother Alexander (the Emperor Alexander III from 1881) in 1866. The Tsarina – the one who exclaimed 'What a tender relationship!' about Bertie and Victoria – was another Marie – the daughter of the Grand Duke of Hesse-Darmstadt.[12] Since the Prussian triumph in 1870, European politics was now governed less by the rivalry between France and the Germans, and more by the domination of Europe by the Triple Alliance, the *Dreikaiserbund* of Russia, Prussia and Austria. It was upon the strength of this alliance that the future peace of Europe depended. When the alliance was threatened with fissure, the peace of Europe itself was at stake: indeed, Europe in these few years of Disraeli's premiership came as close to world war as at any time before 1914, and for the same broad reasons: the almost capricious forming and severing of alliances in the *Bund*, and an inability to agree about the future of the Balkans.

When Russia, with its territorial ambitions fixed on the Balkan and Eastern European satellites of the decaying Turkish Empire, clashed with Austria over the question, that peace was threatened. It was to be in the Balkans, one August day in 1914, that all that fragile peace would be destroyed by a Serbian assassin. For Queen Victoria and her children, in 1874, the rivalries between Austria and Russia would have as personal, as familial, a quality as had the Danish–Prussian rivalries of the 1860s. Vicky, the firstborn, was Crown Princess of Prussia. Alice, of Hesse-Darmstadt, had drifted away from her Austrian allegiances since 1866 and was more inclined to side with Prussia against Austria and Russia. Alix's sister Dagmar was about to become the Tsarina of Russia, and Affie was about to marry Dagmar's sister-in-law, so the family could not have been more divided.

When he announced his betrothal to the daughter of the Emperor of Russia, Victoria's response was to say, 'The murder is out!'[13] She felt 'painfully'[14] the fact that the Romanovs were not Protestants. 'It is the first departure since 200 years nearly from the practice of our family since the Revolution of '88!' Vicky tried to reassure her mother that 'the Greeks' – that is, the Russian Orthodox – 'are very much more harmless than Catholics'. Victoria was able to extract some comfort from this, and when ignorant backbenchers in the House

of Commons wondered whether English royalties could marry
Russian Orthodox without infringing the Royal Marriages Act, she
asked Mr Gladstone to make it clear to them that 'a marriage with a
princess of the Greek faith is strictly within the Law and will in no
way affect the succession to the Crown'.[15] Privately,[16] Victoria worried
that Affie would 'be ready to be quite a humble servant of Russia'.
For these were interesting times for an Anglo-Russian alliance. All
Victoria's instincts, and all Disraeli's, were anti-Russian in the international diplomatic game. Even as Affie began his life with Maria
Alexandrovna, British and Russian diplomats were entering a phase
of mutual suspicion over the so-called Eastern Question.

The wedding was fixed for 23 January 1874 – in the Queen's
opinion crashingly tactless of the Russian Royal Family, who could
surely have remembered that it was the anniversary of the death of
her father, the Duke of Kent, at Woolbrook Cottage in Sidmouth in
1820. The full ceremonies of the Orthodox Church were performed in
the Imperial Chapel of the Winter Palace at St Petersburg, the blind
Metropolitan of Moscow, Innocent, being led around in his brocaded
cope by bearded acolytes. Affie and Marie, attended by three of her
brothers and young Arthur, Duke of Connaught, processed round
the altar carrying lighted tapers. After this, the pair were led out to
the Salle d'Alexandre, a drawing room in the Winter Palace, where
Dean Stanley read the reassuring words of the marriage service from
the English Prayer Book. The bride carried a bouquet of white myrtle,
sent by Queen Victoria from Osborne. Alix was there, and Vicky
had come from Berlin. A few days later, the Duke and Duchess of
Cambridge and the royal parties travelled to Moscow, where a solemn
Te Deum was sung in the Kremlin, and the Imperial Family moved
in procession, kissing icons as they went.

It all made an exotic change from the simplicities of divine worship
at Crathie and Whippingham. No doubt Arthur Penrhyn Stanley,
with his expert knowledge of the monasteries of the Levant – consol-
idated while on tour with Bertie in 1861 – viewed the ceremonial with
the interested eye of an anthropologist, even though both he and his

wife, Lady Augusta, who accompanied him, must have been aware how such clanking of censers, such bowings before sacred art, such chants and such repetitions, would have disgusted their royal mistress and her faithful Calvinist Highland servant.

Indeed, in that January of 1874, in very wet weather, the Archbishop of Canterbury went down to Osborne to conduct the confirmation of the youngest of the Queen's daughters, Princess Beatrice (Baby). The service took place in Whippingham Parish Church, which had been 'very prettily decorated with flowers',[17] for the occasion. Archibald Campbell Tait had been the archbishop for five years. An Arnoldian theological liberal, he was precisely the sort of man Prince Albert would have approved as archbishop – a former headmaster of Rugby (Lewis Carroll was a pupil), before that a fellow of Balliol, a Broad Churchman with a social conscience. As Bishop of London, he had preached to the postmen at Mount Pleasant, and he had insisted on free places for the poor being assigned at Westminster Abbey. (Before Tait's reform, one had to pay to attend divine service there.) In 1856, five of his seven children, daughters between the ages of two and ten, died of scarlet fever. (His brother, during childhood, had died of the same illness.[18])

He looked like a man who had been battered by life – a huge, fleshy face, pitted with lines and scarred with grief. He was not close to the Queen, although she had been fascinatedly appalled by the scale of his family loss – as had everyone who heard of it. On the Isle of Wight, the Queen decreed his confirmation sermon to be 'admirable'.

Tait had inevitable feelings of nervousness when he visited the island for the ceremony. He was not by nature a courtier. He thought the princess looked 'very sweet'.[19] He dined at Osborne House, and it was apparently the first time since the death of Prince Albert that the Queen went to the drawing room after dinner. The archbishop was taken aback to discover that the family spoke German to one another. One prince said to him, as they stood back to watch the Queen's arrival in the drawing room, *'Das ist viel besser!'*[20] ('That is much better!')

The Queen told Tait that she wanted to have a long talk with him about the state of the Church, and this happened the next day, in the same drawing room. 'She talked long and very earnestly about the state of the Church urging that something vigorous should be done to preserve its Protestant character... She urged that the Bishops ought to have more power given to them by legislation.'[21]

To Dean Stanley, who had been a boy at the same Rugby School of which Tait would become headmaster, the Queen had expressed herself in similar terms in November 1873: 'As regards the English Church, which she perceives is being greatly threatened with disestablishment, action seems becoming necessary. This disestablishment the Queen would regret. She thinks <u>a complete Reformation</u> is what we want. But if <u>that is impossible</u>, the Archbishop should have the <u>power</u> given him, by <u>Parliament</u>, to <u>stop</u> all these Ritualistic practices, dressings, bowings, etc. And everything of that kind, and <u>above all, all</u> attempts at <u>confession</u>.'[22]

In the year that the Queen came to the throne, the High and Low parties in the Church of England had differed over matters of doctrine, but in liturgical practice they would have been indistinguishable. John Henry Newman or John Keble, as leaders of the High Church faction in Oxford in the 1830s, would have worn the same simple surplices, for celebration of the Communion, as Low Churchmen, and preached in the same gown and bands. They had merely differed in ideas of what the Church was, and they would all have agreed that for them to adopt the Mass vestments of a Catholic priest would have been something like a sham. When, in 1845, Newman had decided that the logic of the High Church position led him to become a Roman Catholic, it had a shattering emotional effect on those he left behind, even though, in terms of numbers, very few actually followed him into communion with the Pope. (In the nineteenth century there were some 18,000 Church of England clergy of whom only a little more than 400 became Catholics.)

But Newman's conversion had, if anything, a greater effect on the Church of England than it had on the Catholic Church he joined. If today Church of England services have incense, vestments, devotions to the Blessed Virgin, and so forth, it is directly the consequence of Newman having left his Church (which in 1845 had none of these things) to join another. Some of Newman's friends who stayed behind in the Church of England began to copy rituals and practices of the Catholics: Eucharistic vestments, rather than a simple surplice, to celebrate the Communion, candles – first two, then perhaps as many as six or more – on the holy table, and so forth. The custom of making a personal confession to a priest, which had always been an option in the Church of England, became more widespread. It was such practices as these which filled the Queen with alarm.

Thwarted in her attempts to hold back Gladstone from his changes in Ireland, and impotent before Cardwell's sweeping reforms of the military, she was determined to save the Church of England for the simple Protestant forms she had known in her girlhood. There was no hope of enlisting Gladstone to her cause. He was a High Churchman himself (though his High Churchmanship, which went back in time to the era before Newman's conversion to Catholicism, was never especially ritualistic). Her dislike of Gladstone was not caused by his High Churchmanship, but the religious difference fuelled the dislike, and she no doubt echoed that great arbiter of theological opinion John Brown, who opined that Gladstone was 'Half a Roman we canna have a worse lot'.[23] Guided by the Calvinistic simplicities of John Brown, who loved the kirk at Crathie, Victoria developed a mania of hatred for the clergy in England who appeared, by their love of rituals and special liturgical clothing, to be aping Rome.

Benjamin Disraeli was before all else a politician. When he became Prime Minister for the second time in February 1874, he knew that it would be impossible to satisfy the Queen by turning back army reform, or by solving the insoluble problems of Ireland. He did see, however, as no previous Prime Minister of her reign had done, the possibilities of uniting the monarchy and the idea of Empire in a truly fantastical manner. And in the meantime, before he pulled this particular rabbit out of his magician's hat, Disraeli knew that the Church issue was one which could be passed through Parliament with apparent ease, and which would satisfy the Widow of Windsor. When he came to see all the complicated consequences of making it illegal to be High Church, Disraeli came to regret his decision. But, although in his way he was religious, church was never especially his kind of thing – unlike Gladstone who attended church every day of his life, often twice.

By pure coincidence, Disraeli's first, short premiership had coincided with five sees, including Canterbury and London, becoming vacant, and four deaneries. The Dean of Windsor, Gerald Wellesley, was the man who advised the Queen about Church affairs, and pointed out to her that Gladstone 'understood who were the distinguished men in each [Church] party much better' than Disraeli. Indeed, on the second of only two visits to Balmoral, Disraeli desperately wrote to his private secretary and confidant Monty Corry, 'Ecclesiastical affairs rage here. Send me Crockford's directory; I must be armed.'[24]

The High churches in Victorian England – that is, churches which burned candles on the holy table, or where the celebrant at Communion faced east, rather than standing at the north of the table – were small. A survey conducted in 1879 found that of the 864 churches in London, only 33 had clergy in vestments, and only 43 had candles. There were thirteen with incense, which was an irritant to Protestants, and probably far fewer had regular times when the congregation could go to Confession. Nevertheless, these ritualistic advances, within the body of the National Church, did cause outrage, not least because the higher, or Anglo-Catholic, churches tended to be in the poorer parts of cities where there were also Irish people. The Roman Catholics disliked the Anglicans imitating the Holy See. The simpler-minded near these High Church shrines possibly believed that the vicars actually were Roman Catholics, infiltrating their Protestant C of E. In some of the slum areas, where the ritualist priests worked so tirelessly, there was more rigorous opposition, for example from the local pimps and gin-shops, who felt their trade undermined by the clergy, who had great success in turning poor men, women and children to Christ. There were also the hard-line Protestants who came to make trouble. In and around the church of St George's in the east in Wapping, for example, there had been riots from the late 1850s onwards. Crowds of over 1,000 protesters, most of them brought in from outside the parish, burst into the church. In spite of their leaders' injunction – 'Do not groan; do not hiss; do not pull the popish rags off his back'[25] – the clergy were attacked physically, and there were attempts, in this parish and others, such as the newly formed slum-church of St Alban's Holborn, to bring legal proceedings against them for such infringements of the canon law as standing to the east of the holy table.

Queen Victoria, when she heard of these High Churches, was horrified to think that such practices could take place in *her* Church. In December 1873, she had written to Gladstone that, 'The Queen has had conversations with the Archbishop of Canterbury, the Bishop of Winchester & other clergymen & all speak of alarm at the state of the Church – which the Archbishop thinks in great danger of being upset if things go on as they do now.'[26]

The First Vatican Council had wound up in 1870, with Garibaldi arriving at the very gates of Rome, and the Pope being forced to give up his dominions and lands and all his temporal power. Pius IX had responded to this diminution in political power by the formal declaration of Himself to be Infallible. It was partly against this background that the Queen found the advancement, both of Roman Catholicism in England, and of High Church rituals within the Church of England, so alarming. She was 'Protestant to the very heart's core', she said.[27] She believed that a bishop 'should have the power of checking practices which are most dangerous & objectionable & totally foreign to the spirit & former usages of the English Church'.[28] If these views seem a little outré to some readers of the twenty-first century, it should be emphasized that Archbishop Tait endorsed them completely, and had for some years been presiding over a committee looking into ways in which the existing laws in ecclesiastical courts could be tightened, to prevent Protestant clergy from wearing 'popish rags'. Although it was now thirty-five years since Roman Catholics had been allowed to sit as peers and MPs in the Commons, the Queen still felt misgivings about it: 'she does object to the principle of treating them on an equality with the Protestants. The Government and many people in this country seem to the Queen to be totally blind to the alarming encroachments and increase of the R. Catholics in England and indeed all over the world. The Pope was never so powerful,' she wrote to Lord Granville in 1869. It is a view which would have been interesting to the contemporaries of the great Hildebrand in the 1070s or to Dante, being punished with exile and the threat of death by Pope Boniface VIII in 1300. 'The Queen is quite determined to do all in her power to prevent this. Every favour granted to the R. Catholics does not conciliate them, but leads them to be more & more grasping and encroaching & the danger of this to Protestant England cannot be over-rated.'[29]

Therefore, when the more sympathetic figure of Disraeli came to power, he found that one of the first pieces of legislation which he was required to enact, to appease the religious prejudices of his sovereign, was the Public Worship Regulation Act. It was the last Act in which Parliament legislated for the Church without reference to Convocation,[30] the Church's own assembly of bishops and clergy. It was largely the inefficacy of the Act which led to the unravelling of parliamentary authority in Church affairs. (In 1882, 336 churches in England and Wales used vestments, and 2,158 churches did so 20 years later.[31]) Five clergymen were imprisoned as 'Anglo-Catholic martyrs', having committed what were now not merely infringements of canon law but of the Law of England – such esoteric offences as mixing a little water in the chalice of wine at Communion (as a symbol of the mingling of water and blood in the dying body of Christ) was now a matter for which a clergyman could come before the beak.

As has been stated, this was a matter about which the senior clergy cared as deeply as did the Queen. But the passage of the Act – even though Disraeli came to rue it – was really a sign of the Queen's lack of power, not a demonstration of her absolute control over her Prime Minister. Much was made at the time of the Queen's crush on Disraeli, and of his shameless, camp, manipulation of this – his dubbing her 'the Faery Queen', her sending him primroses which she had discerned, possibly inaccurately, to be his favourite flower. What was actually going on politically was that Disraeli, that consummate wheeler-dealer, was harnessing the monarchy for the uses of popular, revivified Conservatism. By flattering the Faery Queen by allowing her to imprison a few clergymen in lace, he could get her in the mood for political work. Gladstone's lack of charm met with everlasting royal stonewalling. Disraeli could see that the Queen, for all her caprices and whims, was, at heart, at one with the suburban Tory majority of England. But she did not know it until Disraeli showed it to be the case. Thus, at a stroke, he made the monarchy popular, and he used the monarchy to enhance and strengthen the Tory political position. The monarchy from the late 1870s became riotously more popular in Britain. Was it because the Royal Family became less quarrelsome, less scandal-prone, more charming, more given to public appearances and good works? No. It was because of the rise of popular Toryism.

The Reform Act of 1867 had been a source of terror to High Tories: for what if the big cities turned out to be populated by communists? Every election between 1867 and the First World War showed the opposite to be the case. True, there was a small, growing socialist movement, and Liberalism went on being a vibrant force. But the expansion of the franchise revealed also the huge extent of working-class Toryism, and the popular Toryism of the suburbs. Even Lord Salisbury came to see this, and it was the foundation on which that high aristocrat intellectual built his own power base, though he had to hold his nose before doing so.

1867 had spelt the end, once and for all, not of the power of the political classes, but of the power of the monarchy. That is, in the sense that the monarch of Great Britain, whose power had been held in firm check one way or another since 1689, was now very definitely under the thumb of elected administrations. This was the fact to which both Gladstone and Disraeli were alive, and of which Victoria and her family were really only vaguely aware. Over seventy years ago, R. C. K. Ensor wrote an analysis of what had happened to the monarchy at this point, and his paragraphs remain unsurpassed: 'A constitutional sovereign, while able to stand up against the ministers of an oligarchic parliament in the name of the unrepresented democracy, becomes powerless against men carrying the credentials of democracy itself.'[32]

Gladstone's idea for the future of the monarchy was that it should radiate moral influence. The Prince of Wales, instead of mixing with a raffish world of adultery and champagne, should espouse good causes, and his mother's Court, rather than being a small table of semi-silent courtiers, suppressing their fury at Brown's latest impertinence, should become a Camelot of high thinking. Disraeli was a cannier man than Gladstone. He had seen the popularity of Palmerston, totally undiminished by the old man's lack of sexual continency. He was cynical enough to divine that no British army could withstand the well-trained Prussians in the field, though the Royal Navy was still supreme in the world. The power of the new Toryism was based on the Empire, and on the Tories' belief that the Empire was making Britain richer (which, for a few decades more, it would). With a flourish which combined his political flair and his fantastical inventiveness as a writer of fiction, Benjamin Disraeli came up with the idea that Victoria should become the Empress of India. It is a title which many people would consider more appropriate for a railway engine, or possibly a pig, but it was the consummate cupola on the Victorian political endeavour. The Victorians were now an Empire. And the extremely eccentric, reclusive figure who had shrunk not merely from the public gaze, but from the whole political drift of Gladstonian politics in the previous years, could now come out into the sunlight in a state coach as the figurehead of their military and economic world domination.

❧

Rather than sending Bertie to Ireland – which had been Gladstone's much-derided idea – Disraeli had the inspired notion of colluding in the prince's wish to visit India. The Prince of Wales had squared the idea with Disraeli before asking the Queen's permission. It was undoubtedly Disraeli's influence which made her give it, though she immediately began to question the wisdom of her choice. Could his health stand it? And, if it were a success, would she not feel the most intolerable envy?

She objected to his choice of travelling companions – Lord Carrington and Lord Charles Beresford – and she wrote an angry letter to Disraeli upon the subject to be read out in Cabinet. There was sniggering as the Prime Minister read the epistle, since it was written, said the Foreign Secretary, Lord Derby, 'with so much violence and so little dignity that to hear it read with gravity was impossible'.[33]

He went with an all-male entourage – many of them louche members of the Marlborough House set, such as 'Sporting' Joe Aylesford, but led by the distinguished old India hand Bartle Frere, Lord Alfred Paget and W. H. Russell of *The Times*, showing that this was a stage-managed piece of political theatre. Lord Northbrook (the viceroy, who had been Sir Francis Baring) gave a positive account to the Queen of the prince's arrival in Bombay.

Bertie had many of the monarchical qualities which his mother lacked. He loved public ceremonies, and he was easy with people, he was sexy and the Indians liked him. Queen Victoria had worried visions of Bertie escalading 'zenanas [harems] on ladders of ropes',[34] but no one would have batted an eyelid had he done so. Russell believed that Bertie had elevated a royal visit into an historic event.[35] As so often, a journalistic cliché was true. The chiefs and princes and maharajahs who lined up to clasp the royal hand were colluding in an extraordinary phenomenon. From the foundation of the East India Company until the events known as the Indian Mutiny in 1857–9, the British commercial relationship with India, enforced by military might, had been a confused mixture of mutual admiration, resentment, love and exploitation. Once the government of India itself had become officially a matter for the viceroy, under the British Crown, it was obvious that the relationship had differed. India was in many senses debased by the arrangement. But only in some senses. The Indians maintained their own religious traditions, their own local rulers and their own languages, though English, since Macaulay in Calcutta in the 1830s, was the lingua franca for administration throughout the subcontinent. But Bertie's visit reminded the British of how much they themselves had to gain by their association with India. The sheer size of the subcontinent, its wealth, not only of substances but of history and culture, all added supremely to the status of the small North European trading archipelago known as Britain. Bertie was paraded through six miles of illuminated streets in Bombay. Although on his arrival he had been received by silent crowds, by the evening of the illuminations, the crowds were cheering. Northbrook wrote to the Queen:

> There is certainly a greater appearance of cordiality towards British rule among the people of Bombay than Lord Northbrook has seen in other parts of India, and these processions were more remarkable than the former ones which Lord Northbrook saw in Bombay three years ago. There were, as was to be expected, more people in the streets, and the cheering was more general.
>
> Among the devices at the illuminations there were many expressive of loyalty to your Majesty, and occasionally there was one which was somewhat quaint; for instance, Lord Northbrook noticed one, 'How is your Royal Mother?' and another purely native in one of the picturesque narrow streets of the Fort, 'Tell Mama we're happy'.[36]

Victoria could not but be pleased that those who made these banners had the sense that Bertie was only there as her representative. She soon wearied, however, of reading about her hated son's triumphs – 'Bertie's progresses lose a little interest and are very wearing – as there is such a constant repetition of elephants – trappings – jewels – illuminations – and fireworks'.[37] Disraeli moved quickly to capitalize on the success of the Prince of Wales's Indian visit. If the Public Worship Regulation Act of 1874 was in effect like something out of *Gulliver's Travels*, the Royal Titles Act of 1876 had something of the quality of *Alice in Wonderland*. Long ago, in 1830, *The Times* had carried a flattering review of one of Disraeli's outrageous jeux d'esprit. 'Mr D'Israeli's chapters on Royal Titles supply some amusing extracts,' it said, citing the Court of the Great Mogul, where courtiers lifted up their hands, crying, 'Wonder! Wonder! Wonder!' whenever their sovereign appeared. He noted that 'in England, Henry VIII had been the first royal personage to assume the title of "Highness", and at length "Majesty"'. But he reserved his most satirical observations for the sovereign of Arracan, who 'assumes the title of "Emperor of Arracan, possessor of the white elephant and the two earrings, and in virtue of this possession, legitimate heir of Pegu and Brama: lord of the twelve portions of Bengal, and the twelve kings who place their heads under his feet"'.[38] Perhaps some dim memory of this early joke lingered in the wise old head of the Prime Minister when he proposed her Indian title. Disraeli was ill towards the end of 1875, and, with much else happening at home and abroad, there were those who thought it in an inopportune moment for this gesture. But, 'The Empress-Queen demands her Imperial Crown', said Disraeli. And he instructed Salisbury, the Secretary of State for India, to put the announcement in the Queen's Speech after the paragraph referring to the prince's visit: 'What might have been looked upon as an ebullition of individual vanity may bear the semblance of deep and organised policy.'[39]

The late lamented Louis Napoleon had declared himself an emperor. So had Vicky's father-in-law the King of Prussia. Russia was ruled over by an emperor. It was surely only fitting that Victoria should place herself on the same footing as they. Vicky, herself destined for imperial greatness when her husband Fritz became the Emperor of Germany, wondered whether the other colonies ought to be named in the title.[40]

Apart from the preposterousness of this idea (where would it stop? Empress of Gibraltar, the Falkland Islands, Canada, New Zealand, St Helena…) it lacked the poetic simplicity of 'Empress of India'. By claiming this title, Victoria and the Victorians, like the possessor of the white elephant and the two earrings, were making not merely an extra-territorial statement, but almost a metaphysical one. The Tsar was Emperor merely of Russia, as Louis Napoleon had merely laid claim to imperial France. India, in all its exotic, multicultural size and splendour, now came under the royal dominion of Windsor Castle, and by extension and metaphor, the British laid claim to the whole earth. Of course there were howls of derision in the Liberal press. Disraeli, moreover, made an extraordinary blunder in failing to inform either the Prince of Wales or the Opposition that the Queen was to take this title.[41] Robert Lowe, 1st Viscount Sherbrooke, one of Disraeli's most implacable enemies, made a public speech at East Retford, claiming that the previous two Prime Ministers had been less 'pliant' than Disraeli, and resisted the Queen's vanity in wishing for such a title. (Gladstone gallantly and instantly denied that this was the case.) But by introducing the measure so casually, Disraeli risked his royal mistress being ridiculed in Parliament, and abroad. (The Russian Ambassador in London, Shuvalov, opined that the discussion of the new title 'has given the Queen's prestige a blow from which it will not recover'.[42]) Had the resistance been much stronger, it would have been damaging to Victoria, but she was able to ignore the objections, and tell her journal that 'there is no feeling whatever in the country against it, but the press took it up'.[43] Not for the first, or last, time, royalty blamed the press for having the temerity to disapprove of its own bizarre behaviour.

As she well knew, and as Disraeli knew, there were many much closer to home than the journalists, who took a quizzical view of 'the Empress'. A diplomat dining at Windsor attended a reception before the meal, and met Disraeli there. He was surprised to see the Prime Minister cowering and looking about him anxiously. When the Queen Empress entered the Long Gallery, Disraeli, far from rushing forward to greet her, shrank behind his acquaintance. But there was no escape. In high dudgeon, Victoria advanced on Disraeli and denounced the Duke of Argyll – Princess Louise's father-in-law no less – for mocking her new title, and for his gross disloyalty. It was not an occasion for soft soap, and those who overheard the conversation were struck by Disraeli laying aside his usually courtly manner. He let the Queen have it. He told her that she was entirely mistaken in believing this story, and that she had no more loyal subject than the duke. 'Nor did he cease,' said the onlooker, 'till he had quite silenced Her Majesty.'[44]

Whereas educated, or enlightened, opinion, might have flinched at Victoria's new title, just as they might wince at the imperialistic pretension which it enshrined, Disraeli and Victoria were in tune with the feelings of a large proportion of the British people. For the next fifty to eighty years, the British Empire was the pride of British conservatives, and the envy of many beyond its borders.

Disraeli's great triumph in his relationship with the Queen was to harness royalty with British foreign policy. He wanted – and so did she – to return Britain to a position of dominance in European politics; and he wanted to strengthen India and the Empire. The overwhelming matter which dominated his premiership was the so-called Eastern Question. The Question was the future of the apparently moribund Ottoman Empire, the 'Sick Man of Europe'. What was going to happen to the Turkish Empire which, since the time of the Renaissance, had dominated so much of Eastern Europe, and the Balkans, and the Eastern Mediterranean, and North Africa? What would happen if it actually unravelled as the Greek, Persian and Roman Empires had done in history? Who would dominate Constantinople? Who would control Egypt? Would the Balkans come under a Russian umbrella or would some of its nations, such as Bulgaria, become independent countries? All these questions were knotted together into the Eastern Question.

The future of Egypt and North Africa was vitally connected with this. Turkey had conquered Egypt in the sixteenth century and incorporated it into its Empire. Since the 1840s, however, Egypt had been in the control of the Albanian dynasty of Mehemet Ali, who ruled the country as a sort of Ottoman Protectorate. In 1856 Mehemet Ali's son Said Pasha, the then Khedive of Egypt, granted a concession to the French to construct the Suez Canal – against the furious opposition of Lord Palmerston and the British, for this was a shortcut to India and, if the French controlled it, who knew what would happen? The canal opened in 1869. By now the khedive was Ismail, and he owned controlling shares in the canal. Partly because he waged constant, and expensive, war in the Sudan, partly because he was extravagant and incompetent, Ismail was seriously in debt. Disraeli saw his chance: to buy the khedive's share in the canal, and thereby ensure that the British had control of the short cut to India, and dominated Egypt into the bargain.

As Disraeli's great biographer Robert Blake reminded us, Disraeli and his friend Monty Corry both loved a good story. Their version of events has the excitement of a novel, but it must in substance be true, even if they embellished the details. The khedive owned 176,602 ordinary shares – out of a total of 400,000 – in the Suez Canal Company. Disraeli needed to persuade the Cabinet to buy the shares for £4 million. There was no time to lose since the French dearly longed to buy the shares.

Here is where the novelist Disraeli and his friend Corry perhaps improved the story. Corry was supposedly standing at the door of the Cabinet room. The Prime Minister simply came to him and said the word, 'Yes'. Corry then sped to New Court in the Temple and told Baron Lionel de Rothschild, who had been primed by Disraeli, that they needed the money fast. The Rothschilds had agreed to lend the money at two and a half per cent, that is, for some £100,000. 'When?' asked Rothschild. 'Tomorrow,' said Corry. 'What is your security?' 'The British Government.' 'You shall have it.' On 26 November 1875, the shares were deposited in the British Consulate at Cairo. Two days before, the Prime Minister had written, with the brio of a character in one of his own fictions, 'It is just settled; you have it, Madam. The French Government has been out-generaled. They tried too much, offering loans at an usurious rate, and with conditions which would have virtually given them the government of Egypt. The Khedive, in despair and disgust, offered Your Majesty's Government to purchase the shares outright... The entire interest of the Khedive is now yours, Madam.'[45]

The triumph abroad did something to mitigate the terrible 'own goal' which the Royal Family had perpetrated at home that year. On a clear, bright August afternoon at the Isle of Wight, the Queen embarked on the *Alberta*, the 350-ton steamer which was being captained by her nephew Prince Victor of Leiningen, with Prince Leopold and Princess Beatrice as passengers. The Royal Yacht *Victoria and Albert* was following them into the Solent. The waters were crowded with boats and they were doing 14 knots. An Admiralty Board inquest decided that Staff Captain Welch, who was in charge of the vessel, was not showing enough 'care and attention'. Beatrice said calmly to the Queen, 'Mama, there is a yacht coming against us.' 'And,' recalled Victoria, 'I saw the tall masts and large sails of a schooner looming over us. In an instant came an awful, very terrifying crash, accompanied by a very severe shake and reel.'[46]

The *Alberta* had chugged across the path of a large yacht called the *Mistletoe*. 'In great distress, I said, "Take everyone, take everyone on board."' As the Queen ordered, it did seem at first as if the injured crew and passengers of the *Mistletoe* could be rescued, but within seconds, the yacht had sunk. The captain or master of the *Mistletoe*, 'a big man of at least seventy', was one of those lost. Another seaman drowned, as did the sister-in-law of the vessel's owner.

The public inquest took a more charitable view than the Admiralty Board and exonerated the prince. Nevertheless, the Queen did not help matters by publicly praising his seamanship,[47] and Prince Victor was hissed in the streets of Portsmouth. While Victoria satisfied herself that this was the fault of the 'low Portsmouth people',[48] there were others who felt that the Royal Family could have demonstrated at least more embarrassment, if not penitence, at the unfortunate accident. You did not have to be a communist or a republican to consider it tactless, a mere six years later, to promote Prince Victor to vice admiral.

Meanwhile, it was another royal sailor, our young friend Affie, Duke of Edinburgh, who found himself at the centre of the latest episode of the Eastern Question.

Throughout 1875 and 1876, the eyes of Europe were on the Balkans. The harvests of 1874 had been poor, and by 1875 the Serbs were hungry. When their Turkish masters tried to impose taxes upon them, they rose in revolt, and there was a big summit meeting of the *Dreikaiserbund* – Austria, Germany and Russia – held in Berlin. Very conspicuously, the British were not asked to this meeting. As a result of the conference, the sultan in Constantinople promised 'reforms', but for the Russians this was not good enough. On one level they were playing politics, but on another they were in deadly earnest about their feeling that the Russian Tsar was the defender of the Orthodox faith. Ever since Napoleon III had preposterously claimed the Holy Places in Palestine as his Protectorate, and ever since the humiliations of the Crimean War, the Russians had wanted to establish what was a deeply held belief by many Russian conservatives, that Christian Orthodoxy should be the ideology governing world realpolitik. The Muslim Caliphate was in decay. The rise of the Communist International was apparent in Italy, Germany and Russia. It was conservative Orthodoxy which could put a halt to all this. And the Russian tsars felt that they should be allowed into Turkey to protect the often-persecuted Christian minority. For the Christians of the Orthodox East, Constantinople, and not Rome, was the spiritual capital. There, living as a virtual hostage, was their

Ecumenical Patriarch. The first truly grand church of Christendom, the Church of the Holy Wisdom (Hagia Sophia) had been, since 1453, converted into a mosque. It was the dream of many Christians that all this could be reversed if only the Russians could conquer Turkey.

Clearly, it would be diplomatically impossible for a Russian simply to take over Constantinople. But what if it were to become an international zone, with a Christian, European figure at its head, to keep the peace and ensure fair play between the Orthodox Christians and the Muslims? Who, wondered King Leopold II of the Belgians, could be more suitable than the English prince who had married the Russian princess – Affie, Duke of Edinburgh?

When Affie discovered that this idea was being proposed in the highest diplomatic circles, he was understandably horrified. The news of the scheme reached him when he was serving on board the perhaps appropriately named ironclad HMS *Sultan*. 'I would sooner end the remainder of my days in China to such a fearful prospect,'[49] he said. (He knew whereof he spoke, having visited China ten years before.) It was not to be Affie's last direct involvement in the Eastern Question, since HMS *Sultan* was in Mediterranean waters, and, as the international crisis warmed to boiling point, the steam-propelled warship was in the Dardanelles.

For the Russians, the crisis was an occasion 'to awaken Europe to its duty as a Christian Power'.[50] For Victoria and Disraeli, it was a cynical piece of power politics. She even suspected the Russians of having 'instigated the insurrection in the Balkans'. From now onwards, the Queen's obsession with the matter became so intense that she wrote to Disraeli about it every day, and at high points of crisis, she telegraphed him every hour.

By May, Muslim–Christian conflict had spread way beyond the bounds of Serbia. The French and the German Consuls were murdered by Muslim mobs in Salonika. The Powers, in a draft known as the Berlin Memorandum, insisted that the sultan make peace with the Christian rebels. On 30 May, Sultan Abdul Aziz was deposed in Constantinople and committed suicide with a pair of scissors. He was succeeded by Sultan Murad V, who was himself deposed three months later, and also committed suicide. Abdul Hamid II took power, and was to rule for the next thirty-three years.

By July, Serbia had declared war on Turkey, and Russian troops joined forces with the Serbs, even though Russia was not officially (yet) at war with Turkey. Queen Victoria had formed the impression from Alice that Affie now had the ear of the Russian Royal Family. After all, the Tsarina was a German, of the House of Hesse-Darmstadt, and perhaps the Russians could be persuaded to make peace? For the Tsarina's part, nothing could have been further from the truth. German by both parents she may have been. In this conflict, however, she was wholly Russian. She found the English attitude puzzling, and in this she was not alone, either at the time or in the eyes of history. The Tsar himself asked Affie to intervene with Queen Victoria to tone down her anti-Russian utterances.[51]

Among historians, the verdict is still out as to why Disraeli rejected the Berlin Memorandum for peace. On the contrary, he ordered the British Fleet to Besika Bay. But on 9–10 June he made a secret attempt, via Ambassador Shuvalov in London, for a peace accord with Russia. The Queen was in Balmoral at the time, and it is not clear from the existing, published correspondence between them whether Disraeli kept her fully abreast of his conversations with Shuvalov. Victoria's very undiplomatic contribution was to ask Affie to tell the Tsar Alexander 'how hated' was Ignatiev, the Russian Ambassador in Constantinople. Alexander, with the height of diplomatic courtesy, asked his brother-in-law Louis of Hesse to tell Victoria how he rejoiced to know that she clung to peace.[52] The situation was now highly critical. No one in Britain wanted a repetition of the Crimean War fiasco, but there was the gravest danger that if the Queen's policy were followed to its conclusion, hostilities could break out between the Russian and the British fleets. Hence, Disraeli's cautious stepping back from the brink in his conversations with Shuvalov. As Bismarck shrewdly remarked at the time, 'mistakes on the part of the Great Powers do not bring their own retribution immediately... but they never go unpunished'.[53]

Events were anyway taken out of the hands of the diplomatists. In May and June 1876, while the Great Powers were deliberating about Serbia, about Constantinople, and about the general future of the Ottoman Empire, Bulgarian Christians had decided to imitate their Serbian co-religionists and rise against the Turks. Turkish irregulars, known as Bashi-Bazouks, moved into their villages and began to massacre Christian men, women and children.

The atrocities were to have wide-ranging consequences, and not just in Bulgaria. As far as British foreign policy was concerned, the Queen and Disraeli now appeared to be on the side of a decayed, moribund, corrupt Islamic regime against Christians struggling for their religious and national freedoms. Before the Bulgarian atrocities, the cynical attempt to curb Russian power, by cautiously propping up the sultans, might have looked like hard-nosed realism. After the outrages, it was a position much harder to sustain. The more Turcophobic ministers in Disraeli's own Cabinet – figures such as Lord Carnarvon or Lord Salisbury, and indeed the Foreign Secretary himself, Lord Derby – were all very uneasy about the Government's position. But their unease was as nothing to the public outcry against the Bulgarian Horrors, which first came to light in July in articles in the Liberal paper the *Daily News*. Disraeli badly misjudged the impact of these articles, even making the catastrophic mistake of attempting a joke in the House of Commons. True, he admitted, the Bulgarians had been subject to 'proceedings of an atrocious character', but he denied the allegation that they had been tortured. 'Oriental people seldom resort to torture but generally terminate their connexion with culprits in a more expeditious manner.'[54]

He had completely misread the mood of the country, and of Parliament. He had also misread his greatest political opponent, W. E. Gladstone. By this stage of things, Gladstone had resigned the leadership of the Liberal Party, and was not much seen in the House of Commons. He was hard at work on his third book about Homer – *Homeric Synchronism* – and at sixty-seven years old, he appeared to offer no particular threat to Disraeli. It was surely safe, then, for the

Prime Minister to accept a peerage from his monarch and to sit in the House of Lords as Lord Beaconsfield, since there was no danger of Gladstone arising on the back benches of the Commons to make life difficult for the Government.

Disraeli could not possibly have guessed, as he made his very ill-judged remark, that Gladstone was lying in bed with lumbago and dashing off, in a fervid three days, a pamphlet which was one of the most celebrated and inflammatory pieces of political writing ever circulated in Britain. By 6 September, Disraeli had been sent an advance copy of the work which would eventually seal his fate, and make Gladstone a popular hero: *The Bulgarian Horrors and the Question of the East*.

'The Queen understands Lord Beaconsfield's motive for <u>not</u> expressing "horror" at the "Bulgarian atrocities".' But she gently tried to warn him that 'a word of *sympathy*, if an occasion offered'[55] might not come amiss. Beaconsfield, as we shall now call him, was not simply unwilling to 'emote' for the sake of impressing readers of the *Daily News*. He saw no reason to change his broadly anti-Russian foreign policy.

As far as British politics was concerned, however, an extraordinary hurricane was blowing. In one week 40,000 copies of Gladstone's pamphlet had been sold, and by the end of the month, 200,000. The mad clergyman of Hawarden Castle and the wily Westminster politician had once seemed like two persons. Now they coalesced at last into the People's William. He had made politics a secular version of those Nonconformist chapels to which so many Liberal supporters were attached. Politics was a mission, and the politics of the left in Britain, for as long as its heyday lasted, never lost this quality.

There was now an absolute political division, which would be played out in epic scale for the rest of Gladstone's life. From now onwards, he was to stand for ideas and values, almost regardless of whether they had any hope of success. The electorate could choose between a man who had taken upon himself the mantle of the prophets versus political expediency. Those who espoused the Conservative side of the argument – whether it was about the Eastern Question, or the Irish Question, or affairs at home – had to play a delicate balancing trick. On the one hand, for Beaconsfield, as for Salisbury his successor, politics was very largely a matter of what is practical. To that extent, they seemed like cynics, even if, in religious matters, Salisbury and Gladstone were so close. But on the other hand, the Tories themselves would be anxious to demonstrate that the left in politics did not have the monopoly of ideals.

The soaring rhetoric of Gladstone's pamphlet was deliberately rabble-rousing. Beaconsfield and, later, Salisbury had to rouse their own rabbles. They would do so by the means of cloaking themselves in the flag and supporting the monarchy. From now onwards, it would be clear that when they spoke of the monarch being 'above politics', they meant she was above Liberal politics. In all central respects, Victoria was a Tory populist and she was happy to allow herself to be used as the figurehead for popular Toryism. The resurrection of Gladstone was for her a nightmare. Any liberalism, whether formal Liberalism with a capital 'L' or mere sympathy with liberal points of view, was from now onwards openly suspect for Victoria. 'We must and will take some marked line to show that Russia is not to have all her own way,' she wrote to Vicky in spring 1877, 'which thanks to the most unfortunate and ill-judged agitation of last autumn' – the Bulgarian pamphlet and its aftermath – 'has led Russia on to think she may do anything, and they are the cause of what is happening now!' The Russians had declared war on Turkey on 24 April. This was all Gladstone's fault. 'You never answer when I tell you this,' the Queen went on, 'as if you thought the Liberals and that madman Gladstone must be right and the Government wrong!'[56]

The Russo-Turkish War lasted less than a year. It excited in Queen Victoria the strongest emotions. While Russia and Turkey fought it out, the Great Powers, including Britain, stood back. When the Prime Minister, eagerly encouraged by the Queen, moved the British Fleet closer to the scene of conflict, Lord Derby resigned as Foreign Secretary, to be replaced by Lord Salisbury. In addition, Lord Carnarvon resigned as Colonial Secretary. A High Churchman, he deplored the notion that Britain should side with a Muslim country, Turkey, against the Christian Russia and he said that Britain should not sanction a repetition of the Crimean War. The Queen, in accepting the resignation, 'regrets he should persist in views which she must consider so detrimental to the interests of the Country and Sovereign'. She further pointed out to Lord Carnarvon that the Prime Minister was performing the 'arduous task of maintaining the honour and interests of this country as well as the balance of power in Europe which is so seriously endangered by Russia's duplicity and aggressive policy'.[57] The Foreign Secretary cautiously warned the Queen of the 'evident and scarcely disguised wish of Prince Bismarck to push England into a quarrel with Russia'.[58] Vicky, writing from Berlin, thought Bismarck blatantly pro-Russian. 'How I do long for one good roar of the British lion from the housetops and for the thunder of a British broadside!'[59] she wrote, sentiments which her mother heartily echoed. How much things had changed since Prince Albert's support for the anxious Aberdeen, and the royal contempt for Palmerston's gunboat diplomacy. Affie, by contrast, told the German Ambassador to the Sublime Porte that he feared his mother would 'drive the country [Britain] into war by a false view of what constituted British interests'.[60] The closest the British came to war was when they warned the Russians that their entry into Constantinople would be a *casus belli*. Affie waited anxiously on board HMS *Sultan* in the Dardanelles to see whether he would be required to open fire on ships obedient to his father-in-law.

At first the war went well for the Russians. Their troops crossed the Danube. Sandro, son of Alexander of Hesse-Darmstadt, was the only German officer who was permitted by his emperor to join the Russians, by virtue of his being the nephew of the Tsarina.

This lieutenant in the Hessian Dragoons took part in the siege of Trnova and concluded that 'the country is simply magnificent but the Bulgars are just as fiendish as the Turks… We live among blood and corpses and see such horrible things that all our officers are disgusted with war and would much rather go home again.'[61] After their initial successes, however, the Russians found themselves confronted by the brilliant Turkish General, Osman Pasha, who defeated the Russian advance into the Balkans, cut them off on three sides and inflicted very heavy casualties in a number of decisive battles. By the end of the year, the Tsar was proposing peace at San Stefano, on the shores of the Sea of Marmara. His terms for peace included the request for an independent Bulgaria, with his nephew by marriage, Sandro, as the head of the new country; he also wanted the reintegration into Russia of Bessarabia, lost after the Crimean War.

There was no certainty that these peace proposals by Russia would be acceptable, either to Turkey, or to the other Great Powers. 'We are in an awkward position just now,' said Ponsonby, now a lieutenant general, 'with our fleet at the entrance to the Dardanelles, sniffing like a dog for fear he may find a badger instead of a rabbit inside'.[62]

The fleet then moved further up the coast, and entered the Sea of Marmara. Docked at one of the Prince's Islands, a mile or so out to sea from Constantinople, Affie entertained Sandro to luncheon on board the *Sultan*. It is true that Sandro had fought for Russia, but Britain was not actually at war with Russia, and he was family. His uncle was married to Affie's favourite sister Alice.

When she heard about this family luncheon, Queen Victoria was 'beside herself with rage'. Affie had been entertaining 'a Russian spy'. She was 'furious' with him for his 'anti-natural' behaviour. Although the Russian Royal Family absorbed the explosion, dismissing the Queen's outburst as that of a 'crazy old hag', it was a bruising rebuke, even for one who was used to Victoria's rants. HMS *Sultan* found itself being transferred to the Channel fleet.[63]

In fact, if anyone was the 'Russian spy' in the family, it was not Sandro, but Affie himself, who showed his mother's letters to his wife, who in turn passed them on to her mother and father. 'The insulting things the Queen says in her letters to Alfred,' confided the Tsarina, 'about the Tsar and the Russian people are worthy of a fish-wife. Added to this is her grief that "our dear Marie" should belong to a nation from whose vocabulary the words truth, justice and humanity are lacking. Silly old fool.'[64]

The Treaty of San Stefano, which had been engineered by Ambassador Ignatiev, was not approved internationally. Lord Derby, who had resigned as Foreign Secretary in April 1878, was replaced by Lord Salisbury. It was clear that Britain, having been excluded from earlier international conversations, would insist upon playing a role at the Congress of Berlin which was summoned to decide, narrowly, the outcome of the war and, more broadly, some future answers to the Eastern Question.

Beaconsfield was by now a wheezy old man, his sad eyes like those of a hooded hawk, and seriously ill for much of the Congress. His doctor was just able to get his patient upright in order to attend the formal ratification of the Treaty. Nevertheless, Beaconsfield's contribution to the Congress was generally considered masterly,[65] and he brought home some prizes which cheered the Queen's heart. The Russian demand for an independent Bulgaria was curtailed. The young Alexander of Hesse-Darmstadt, Sandro, became the ad hoc ruler of Bulgaria, of the people he had initially supposed as 'fiendish as the Turks'. It might have been supposed that Queen Victoria would have viewed this promotion – of a man she had so recently believed to be a 'Russian spy'– with dismay. But when Sandro went to London, he found the Queen to be friendly. She was almost roguish in the way she ribbed him about being too Russian. It transpired that John Brown approved of the independence of Bulgaria, a rocky, mountainous, stubborn nation which he believed to have spiritual kinship with Aberdeenshire. Guided by the great expertise of Brown in Balkan affairs, she was able to assure her new Foreign Secretary, 'The Queen is convinced that Prince Alexander has no Russian proclivities and only asks to be left alone. But if he is worried from

Constantinople, he will seek refuge in the support of St Petersburg.'[66] 'It appears that Brown has deigned to approve of the new Bulgaria,' wrote the Tsarina. 'I should have liked to see the two boys [Sandro and his brother Louis of Battenberg – the nephews of Alice's husband Louis] while they were in her toils.'[67] The Russians got Bessarabia. Britain took control of Cyprus, an 'insane covenant' in Gladstone's view. It added to British security in the Mediterranean, but taking over an island as violently divided as Cyprus would perhaps prove, in the long run, to be confirmation of the Bismarck rule that 'mistakes on the part of great powers... never go unpunished'. As far as the Queen was concerned, Beaconsfield came back from Berlin covered in glory. 'High and low are delighted, excepting Mr Gladstone who is frantic.'[68]

News of the Armistice between Turkey and Russia and developments from Berlin reached the Queen by telegram. While such intelligence was being received, however, she was an early witness to an invention which would make telegrams a secondary, if not redundant, means of communicating. 'After dinner,' she told her journal on 14 January 1878, 'we went to the Council Room & saw the Telephone. A Professor Bell explained the whole process, which is most extraordinary. It had been put in communication with Osborne Cottage, & we talked with Sir Thomas & Mary Biddulph, also heard some singing quite plainly. But it is rather faint, & one must hold the tube close to one's ear.' The nervous inventor, Alexander Graham Bell, did not impress her, however. 'The man, who was very pompous, kept calling Arthur Lord Connaught! [her son the Duke of Connaught] which amused us very much.' A telephone line from Cowes to the post room at Osborne was installed in 1885.

NINETEEN

'PROSTRATE
THOUGH DEVOTED'

Alas, the Queen's happiness about the Congress of Berlin was soon to be overshadowed by personal tragedy. No year passed without a great catalogue of deaths, very many of which either fascinated or moved the Queen, sometimes both. She was obsessed not merely by death itself, but, as Lady Ely, now her favourite lady-in-waiting, shrewdly noticed, 'She likes every detail.'[1]

Nothing she had hitherto said or written suggested much sympathy for the Roman Pontiff. Yet when Pius IX died in February, she fired off a telegram to Sir Augustus Paget, the British Ambassador in Rome: 'HAVE JUST HEARD BY REUTER OF THE POOR OLD POPE'S DEATH ANXIOUS TO HEAR SOME PARTICULARS AND IF ALL IS QUIET. THE QUEEN.'

Twenty-three years had elapsed since she had met the King of Italy, and she had never in reality been at all close to him, but when old Victor Emmanuel died in June, she wrote that 'the Queen has felt the death of King Victor Emmanuele deeply. He was so consistently kind to her… when he was in England in '55.'[2] She was avid for the details in this case, wondering whether the new Pope, Leo XIII, had visited the King – there had been estrangement between Victor Emmanuel and the Vatican – and also, slightly salaciously, whether the new King had brought the old King's bastard, his son by the Contessa de Mellefleur, to the bedside. And – could she have a souvenir, perhaps a lock of the King's hair? Clearly, the ambassador did not know how to respond to this strange request, since it was met by silence. Lady Ely telegraphed Sir Augustus the next day: 'The Queen desires me to say she would much like a little bit of the late King of Italy's hair; could you mention this and say how much Her Majesty will value it? If the answer is, yes, will you telegraph it, as the Queen is very anxious about it.' The request for hair was 'gratefully acceded to', but as for the Queen's other intimate questions, the Pope had 'removed all difficulties in regard to the Administration of the Sacrament but His Majesty [the new King, Humbert] did not enter into further details'. He added that he had heard so many rumours that the contessa had indeed been brought to the late King's bedside that he 'cannot help thinking it is true, but is unable to affirm it positively'.[3]

Was she thinking of what would happen when her own moment came to die? On 6 December 1875, she had written a memorandum for Sir William Jenner at Windsor Castle, 'that in the case of serious illness she should only be attended by her own doctors'. With what difficulty the King of Italy had been allowed to die in the company of the woman he loved. Was Queen Victoria thinking, as she mulled over his death scene, of how her sons would try to exclude Brown from the room as she lay on her deathbed? 'She absolutely forbids anyone but her own four female attendants to nurse her,' she had written, 'as well as her faithful Personal Attendant, John Brown, whose strength, care, handiness and gentleness make him invaluable at all times, and most peculiarly so in illness, and who was of such use and comfort to her during her long illness in 1871, in lifting and leading her, and who knows how to suggest anything for her comfort and convenience.'[4]

The nineteenth-century Cult of Death had no more operatic votary than Queen Victoria. The experiences of dreadful bereavement, rather than making her shy away from the horror of deathbeds, invariably awoke in her a fascination. The distant deaths of foreign prelates and potentates, however, aroused something which was in reality little more than necrophiliac curiosity. Meanwhile, the hammer blows of the real thing continued to pound against her family's doors.

In November 1878, diphtheria struck the Grand Ducal palace at Hesse-Darmstadt. At first, the fifteen-year-old Princess Victoria complained of a stiff neck. Her mother Alice thought initially it might be mumps, but the next day, her daughter was pronounced to have diphtheria: a disease which Alice knew, from her nursing experience, to be highly infectious and potentially deadly. Young Victoria was strong enough to survive the disease but within a few days her six-year-old sister Alix showed the deadly patches of white membrane on her throat. In the worst form of the disease, these membranes swell to the point when breathing becomes impossible and the patient chokes to death. While Alice was nursing Alix, little May toddled into the room, and climbed upon her sister's bed to kiss her. Only a few hours later, the deadly spots appeared on her throat too. Irene and Ernie also caught the disease. Only Ella appeared to have escaped among the children. Then Louis, Alice's husband, went down with the disease. 'Well Katie,' said Alice to Miss Macbean, the children's governess, 'you and I are the only ones who are not ill, and we must not be ill, there is so much to be done and seen after.' 'Husband and four children between life and death,' Alice wrote to her mother, and then – the cynicism forgotten, which she had displayed in Bertie's near-death-chamber when she said there was no Providence, she added, 'May God protect them and teach us to say, Thy Will Be Done.'[5]

Exhausted, she went to bed, but was woken in the night to be told the news that the membrane had crossed little May's windpipe and that she had choked to death. In the next two weeks, Alice had the double burden of scalding grief, and the felt need to conceal May's death from the other children. From their beds of recovery, the others kept asking for May and trying to send her books and toys. When she at last broke the news to ten-year-old Ernie, he sat up in bed with tears streaming.[6]

What happened next was so like a scene in the most painful Victorian novel, that it is perhaps best to leave the description of it to the novelist-Prime Minister. Two weeks later, Beaconsfield told the House of Lords:

The Princess Alice – for I will venture to call her by that name, though she wore a Crown – afforded one of the most striking instances that I can remember of richness of culture and rare intelligence combined with the most pure and refined domestic sentiments... My Lords, there is something wonderfully piteous in the immediate cause of her death. The physicians who permitted her to watch over her family enjoined her under no circumstances whatever to be tempted into an embrace. Her admirable self-restraint guarded her through the crises of this terrible complaint in safety. She remembered and observed the injunctions of her physicians. But it became her lot to break to her son, quite a youth, the death of his youngest sister, to whom he was devotedly attached. The boy was so overcome with misery that the agitated mother to console him clasped him in her arms – and thus received the kiss of death. My Lords, I hardly know an incident more pathetic. It is one by which poets might be inspired and in which the artist in every class, whether in picture, in statue or in gem, might find a fitting subject of commemoration.[7]

What was even more like fiction was the baleful fact: Princess Alice, who had been so devoted a daughter to Prince Albert, died on 14 December, the very day on which her father had died seventeen years earlier.

Alice had been popular in England and in Germany and her death could not but cause widespread grief and shock. The Royal Family had been summoned to Windsor, as was usual, to observe the anniversary of their father's demise, so they were all together when the telegram came from Darmstadt. Bertie was hurried out of his room to be told the news by Sir William Jenner. He was still in his dressing gown as Queen Victoria kissed him; he said, 'The good are always taken and the bad remain.'[8]

The German Emperor forbade anyone to attend the funeral in Darmstadt, for fear of further infections, but Bertie, Leopold and

Prince Christian, Lenchen's husband, defied the ban, crossing to Flushing and spending the next day in a train. The Prince of Wales, as chief mourner, followed her coffin, draped in the Union Jack, to its last resting place in the mausoleum at Rosenhöhe.

Her husband, the Grand Duke Louis, lived on until 1892. Of her surviving children, Victoria, the first to go down with diphtheria, survived until 1950. She married Prince Louis of Battenberg, elder brother of Sandro of Bulgaria. If, on paper, their consanguinity looked close – this Louis (Ludwig) was her first cousin – no fears were felt or expressed. Prince Louis was the son of Alexander of Hesse by Rhine, who had morganatically married Countess Julia von Hauke. He grew up trilingual – his mother speaking French to him, his father German, and his English nanny her own tongue. In 1917, the Battenbergs, who took their name from a small town in Hesse, changed their name to Mountbatten, to appear less German. Battenberg became Louis Mountbatten, Marquess of Milford Haven. Their daughter Alice was the mother of Prince Philip of Greece who married Elizabeth II.

Elizabeth, the only child not to contract diphtheria, married the Grand Duke Sergei of Russia, who was murdered in Red Square in Moscow during the Russo-Japanese War of 1904–5. Ella, as she was always known in the family, became a very pious Orthodox, founding an order of nuns. When the Bolsheviks threw her down a mineshaft in 1918, they could still hear her singing hymns when she reached the bottom. She is today revered as a saint in the Orthodox Church. Ernie, whose tears tempted his mother to receive the Kiss of Death, lived on until 1937. A month after his death, his widow, son, daughter-in-law and two grandsons were killed in a plane crash. Alicky, the most celebrated of the siblings, became the Tsarina of Russia. She and her husband Tsar Nicholas II produced the haemophiliac son Alexei, and it was largely through her distress at this fact that she fell under the bewitching spell of Rasputin. By any standards, the inheritance of the House of Hesse was what Lady Bracknell would call crowded with incident.

∽

24 May 1879 found the Queen at Balmoral, where she recorded it was 'My poor old 60th birthday'. She made a long list of her presents, and rounded off the three-page journal entry with the thought, 'It was a sad birthday, but I feel much and am cheered by the kindness of those left on earth. The other dear ones, my beloved Husband & our darling child, surely bless me.'[9]

Although she felt that the experience of losing Alice had 'aged and shaken the elasticity out of me',[10] she was in fact one of those fortunate human beings who are good at being old. Whereas her middle age had been scarred by mental illness and overwhelming depression, she was visibly a new woman by the time she was sixty; much more robust than she had been at forty-five. In spite of, or perhaps because of, the political challenges which faced her – above all the revival of Mr Gladstone as a force in British politics – she was in a buoyant, or, what was for her indistinguishable, a belligerent mood.

'If we are to maintain our position as a first-rate Power – and that no one (but people of the [radical] Bright or rather Anderson Jenkins etc. School) can doubt – we must, with our Indian Empire and large Colonies, be prepared for attacks and wars somewhere or other CONTINUALLY. And the true economy will be to be always ready.'[11]

This was what she dictated to Lady Ely on 28 July 1879 and had posted to Beaconsfield, as a sort of manifesto, in the painful event of the Liberals returning to power. It is one of the most perceptive things ever written about the British Empire. As a military historian has written, 'there was not a single year in Queen Victoria's long reign in which somewhere in the world, her soldiers were not fighting for her and for her Empire'.[12] Victoria had no illusions. The Empire depended upon the willingness to use force. It depended upon violence. In this, she eagerly supported Beaconsfield in all his jingoistic adventures, and deplored the shilly-shallying and dithering and lily-livered men in her Cabinet or in her far-flung dominions who shrank from acts of warfare.

In foreign policy, Beaconsfield was almost Palmerston by another name. Nothing more vividly reveals the difference between Albert's wife of the 1850s and the independent widow of the 1870s than in her 'jingoism'. Whereas Palmerston was content to be a sort of buccaneer policeman to the world, Beaconsfield had developed into an imperialist, and the Empress of India watched with some satisfaction as her domains extended across the globe.

In the matter of South Africa, for example, whereas even the Conservative Cabinet was critical of Beaconsfield's policy, and his Foreign Secretary, Lord Carnarvon, actually resigned because of it, the Queen never abandoned her loyalty to Dizzy. The British had taken it upon themselves to intervene in the fighting between the Dutch – Boer – settlers in the Transvaal and the indigenous Zulus. The Boers had performed appalling acts of violence on the Africans, using German mercenaries to attack black women and children. The Africans had reciprocated, and it was decided in London that the border disputes between the Europeans and the natives could only be solved by Britain annexing Natal. The Indian civil servant Sir Bartle Frere, who had accompanied the Prince of Wales on his Indian adventure, was put in charge.

Frere issued the Zulus with an ultimatum, that unless they agreed to the boundary drawn up by the British, dividing Zulus and Boers, the British would enter the territory and impose the arrangement by force. General Thesiger (Lord Chelmsford) was in command, with a force of 5,000 Europeans and 8,200 Africans. He grossly underestimated the tactical brilliance of his opponent the Zulu King Cetshwayo, with his well-trained army of 40,000 men. Above all, Chelmsford had ignored all advice, that when fighting the Zulu it was necessary to laager the wagons. He led an expeditionary force out of his camp at Isandhlwana in the first ten days of the war, and when he returned, he found that almost every person left behind had been slaughtered, and all his equipment destroyed. All the slain had been disembowelled. Face was saved on the same night a little way away in Rorke's Drift when 103 British soldiers, 35 of them sick, had created a laager. They held out successfully against a massive Zulu force and effected heavy casualties upon them. But the news of the massacre reached Britain and it went down badly in the press, and in the Liberal Party. Huge reinforcements were sent in – five battalions of infantry. Sir Garnet Wolseley, first as Commander-in-Chief, then as Governor-General of Natal, broke Zululand into eight parts, each under the control of a separate chief. But yet another hostage to fortune had been taken, with the British landing themselves with the task of policing and keeping the peace in South Africa. This mistake would come home to haunt the Victorians before the end of the reign.

Among the casualties of the war was the Prince Imperial, the son of Napoleon III and the Queen's great friend the Empress Eugénie. He was speared by Zulu assegais. Beaconsfield had not even been aware that the prince had taken part in the war. 'I am quite mystified by that little abortion the Prince Imperial,' he wrote to Salisbury, admitting that 'H.M. knows my little sympathy with the Buonapartes'.[13] Ernst of Coburg, Prince Albert's brother, tactlessly said it was probably a happy thing for France. Victoria responded with her characteristic vigour that he could not be more wrong. 'He was so clever, so peace-loving, and thanks to his English education, so mature.'[14]

The prince's body was brought back to England for burial at Chislehurst. Protocol decrees that royal personages do not attend the funerals of commoners. This was a sad deprivation for Queen Victoria, who would clearly have loved to do so. Luckily for her, she regarded the Bonapartes as of imperial status. This enabled her to revel in the obsequies of the young man. Her journal entry for the day covered pages of description, of the coffin, attended by the band of the Royal Artillery playing the 'Dead March' in *Saul*, and of the richly robed clergy. Whereas the thought of her own clergy dressing ceremonially filled her with abhorrence, she thought the Bishop of Constantine's mitre 'had a very fine effect'. Mitres were clearly in order if worn by foreigners.

The imperialist adventure of the Zulu War, from which Britain had only just managed to emerge without humiliation, highlighted the vast canyon of difference which had now opened up between the two great political players on the English stage. (Similar disaster occurred at the same period when Afghan soldiers stormed the British residency at Kabul and the unwinnable war against the Afghans broke out once more.) Whereas Beaconsfield, in whatever spirit of cynicism, supported the Empire, and jingoism, and maintenance of the status quo in Ireland, Gladstone had moved radically to the left in his political thinking, and now supported self-government for the Irish (even if he had not yet quite come round to open support for Home Rule); a cautious attitude to colonial adventure; and, with regard to the Eastern Question, an anti-Turkish, pro-Russian Orthodox line. There had probably never been a time in the history of British politics when the division between the chief protagonists was so strong. But even if the divisions between Pitt and Fox in an earlier generation had been of comparable seriousness, what there had not been was an appeal to modern-style electioneering, with a major political figure storming around the country making speeches to his followers, regardless of whether he was speaking in their constituency or not.

This is what Gladstone had been doing ever since the tearaway success of his Bulgarian atrocities pamphlet. If Victoria thought that the 'mad' old man had been safely put out to grass, studying Homer in North Wales, she was sadly mistaken. Although he had made it clear that he would not stand at the next election for his old constituency in Greenwich, he was prevailed upon by Lord Rosebery and others to contest the seat of the county of Midlothian against the Tory Lord Dalkeith (son of the Duke of Buccleuch). Between 24 November and 9 December 1879, he moved in a great progress from Liverpool, to Glasgow, and finally to Edinburgh. He drew huge crowds. At seventy years old, his orotund voice, with its depth and varied tone, and its very faint hint of a Liverpool accent, was as strong as ever. He denounced the Zulu War and contended that the British people had been misled into supposing that the Boers wished to become

British subjects. He denounced the British presence in Afghanistan. He denounced British policy in Ireland. He deplored the conduct of the Government in its relations with Turkey and Russia. With every subject, he was denouncing not merely the views of Beaconsfield but also of the Queen. Nor could Beaconsfield, half choked with asthma and seeming even older than his seventy-five years, possibly compete with this performance, even if there had not been an ingrained Conservative tradition which deplored 'stump oratory'. How did the crowds, often of thousands, hear Gladstone's voice? They did not, but punctuated through the multitudes were speakers who repeated what was being said by the chief speaker on his podium.

When the tour was over, Gladstone returned home to North Wales and awaited events. The Queen and Beaconsfield read of 'Mr Gladstone's mad unpatriotic ravings',[15] as she called them, without being able to believe that they could attract a greater following than the flag-waving of Beaconsfield. On 5 February, Victoria attended a State Opening of Parliament. The woman who wrote of it in her journal is scarcely recognizable as the unhappy creature of the 1860s who could not contemplate public displays of herself. This was what Beaconsfield had done for her. 'I wore the same dress, black velvet, trimmed with minniver, my small diamond crown & long veil. Got in, at the Great Entrance, & went in the new state coach which is very handsome with much gilding, a crown at the top, & a great deal of glass, which enables the people to see me.' There was a good family turnout. 'Beatrice stood to my right, Leopold to my left. Bertie, Affie & Arthur were all there.'[16]

It was surely inconceivable that, if given the choice between the Queen and the mad ravings of Gladstone, the electors would vote Liberal? The Queen did not, in any event, imagine that Lord Beaconsfield would have asked her to parade through the streets in a state coach, and undertake a State Opening if he were contemplating almost instantaneous dissolution.

But this, mysteriously, is what he did do. Parliament was dissolved on 24 March, and an election was called. Seizing upon the Liberal support for Irish Home Rule, Beaconsfield wrote an open letter to the Duke of Marlborough on the subject of Ireland. He guessed, quite wrongly, that this would be a subject to rally the instinctive conservatism of the British people. Queen Victoria felt so confident that the Conservatives would be returned 'stronger than ever' that she set off for Germany as soon as Parliament had risen. While there she was able to see Vicky's son Willy – at twenty, still sprouting adolescent acne. 'His complexion was rather in a distressing state,' his unsparing grandmother told his mother.[17] Vicky managed a quick dash to Rome, where she visited the new King and Queen before returning to her mother at Baden. The election results reached her while she was there, staying at the Villa Hohenlohe. She considered the Liberal majorities small, and the Conservative majorities 'in the City and other important places – so overwhelming that I hardly know how they will form a Government'.[18] It was true that the Conservatives held three out of four seats in the City of London, and that they held nearly every constituency in Kent, but for the most part, they had done very badly indeed. In Wales, they held on to a mere two seats. In Lancashire, where there was a strong Orange vote which might have responded to Disraeli's anti-Irish rhetoric, they suffered heavy losses. Commerce had not been strong in the later years of Beaconsfield. There had been many bankruptcies. A couple of wet summers had destroyed crops, making imported grain much cheaper than home-grown cereals, which had all the inevitable consequences of agrarian depression. There could be no doubt about it, large parts of the electorate had rejected 'Beaconsfieldism'. Moreover, the strong point of Beaconsfieldism – namely its foreign policy – seemed to have come unstuck, with the Russians not seriously weakened by the Congress of Berlin, and with British troops all but trounced by the Zulus.

The Queen saw no immediate reason to return to England, and she enjoyed her visit to the Continent, in spite of the harrowing need to see Darmstadt and the tomb of her daughter Alice.

Gladstone had forsaken the leadership of the Liberal Party in 1874. His triumph in the Midlothian campaign was a personal one. No one could have any doubt, from the moment that he began his tour of the North, that he was the dominant political figure of the age, nor that, if victorious, he would once more resume leadership of the party. But the Queen was technically within her rights to ask lords Hartington (Leader in the Commons) and Grenville (Leader in the Lords) if either of them would form an administration. Hartington ('Harty Tarty') went through the motions of offering Gladstone a place in Government. The Grand Old Man replied that he could not serve in a subordinate position. This message went back to the Queen. It was by way of being a sort of revolution by electoral means. 'Mr Gladstone, too, as Prime Minister seems hardly possible to believe. I had felt so sure he could not return and it is a bitter trial for there is no more disagreeable Minister to have to deal with.'[19]

Fuelling her intense personal dislike of Gladstone was the knowledge that many in his party were republicans and radicals. For Victoria, as for many other conservative-minded people, radicalism was merely the respectable face of dangerous revolution.

No monarch in Europe could be indifferent to the growth of revolutionary communism, terrorism called by whatever name. The war had radicalized many young Russians who had volunteered to fight for the independence of Bulgaria, Bosnia and Serbia, and they now wanted greater political freedom in their own land. The movement *Zemlya i volya* – Earth and Will – wanted to give more power to the peasantry; the mere liberation of the serfs was not enough; as in Ireland, they wanted to be able to farm land and make a decent living. Various other dissident groups, whom the Church and the Government in Russia were trying to suppress with the utmost brutality, fought back, and many were committed to assassinating the Tsar.[20] In February 1880, while Affie and Marie were staying there, nihilists planted bombs in the Winter Palace, causing huge explosions – eleven dead and forty-four seriously injured.[21] 'We are so much occupied with Irish affairs at home,' wrote General Ponsonby, 'that we do not pay proper attention to the Mediterranean where there are so many explosive materials constantly fizzing.'[22] Many Europeans believed that Italy was the nurse of revolutionary internationalism – and Queen Victoria was among them: 'Does Sir Augustus,' she asked Paget, her ambassador in Rome, 'think that Italy is more <u>infested</u> with Internationalists than any other foreign [sic] country? There is, she fancies, much discontent, especially at Naples and Florence, & much distress.'[23]

Having passed her 'poor old' sixtieth birthday, the Queen was gradually finding herself in a new position. She herself had become more self-confident and robust. She was not an intellectual, like Gladstone or Salisbury, but she now had a lifetime of experience of the international political stage and, as her children and grandchildren grew up, she had an ever-widening network of connections with the European dynasties. Was mere anarchy to be loosed upon the world; or would it be possible for moderate, traditionalist governments, respectful of the old hierarchies, to continue? The actual executive power of the British monarchy had been slowly but definitely curtailed, especially by the Reform Act of 1867. But the influence of Queen Victoria, and what she stood for, remained one of the ingredients in the British political story, and that is what makes the latter part of the reign politically so much more interesting than its inception. In her early days, she was little more than a pawn of Melbourne, Stockmar and Albert. Now, she was her own woman, and her capricious, but not entirely unthought, decision to hitch the monarchy's destiny so firmly to one political vision – that of Beaconsfield and the Tories – determined the direction in which it was to move. The quiet lessons of moderate Stockmar were ignored or forgotten; the pretence that the monarchy was politically neutral had now been set to one side.

As someone who had been shot at several times, albeit most recently by a deranged boy with a dummy pistol, she was aware of the perils into which political extremism could take a country. Even when the revolutionaries became respectable and formed governments, she continued to view them with undiluted suspicion. Ponsonby wrote on the Queen's behalf to Sir Charles Dilke, then one of Her Majesty's ministers, that he should have nothing to do with Clemenceau because of his part in the Paris Commune of 1870. ('I abominate people who shoot Generals.'[24]) She let it be known that there was 'astonishment' at the Court of St James's when Monsieur Paul-Armand Challemel-Lacour was appointed as French Ambassador: 'It is repeated of him that he holds communistic opinions, that he was the Communist Prefet at Lyons, and you may remember that there was a Debate in the French chambers as to his conduct when there, and as to a charge which was brought against him, that while acting in that capacity, he ordered a large number of prisoners to be shot.'[25]

On 13 March (Old Style) 1881, a bomb was thrown at Tsar Alexander II's carriage as he returned from a military parade. He was not hurt, and he got out of the carriage, asking after anyone who might have been injured by the explosions. A second bomb was then thrown, which killed him.

'A sense of horror thrills me through and through! Where such a criminal succeeds the effect is dreadful,' the Queen wrote to Vicky. 'The details are too terrible... Poor darling Marie [Affie's wife] on whom her poor father doted, it is too much almost to bear. But she is very courageous.'[26]

If the murder of the Russian Emperor was horrifying, there was an almost equal horror in reading that many revolutionaries actively supported it. 'Have you seen that monstrous paper published here called "Freiheit" [Freedom]?' the Queen asked the Crown Princess. 'It is to be prosecuted for it openly preaches assassination and the language is beyond anything I ever saw.'[27] Johann Most, the German editor of this magazine, was in fact prosecuted, and sentenced to sixteen months' imprisonment with hard labour. The twenty-first-century reader perhaps differs from that of the twentieth or the nineteenth century. Our perspective is enabled to see the whole appalling drama of European history about to unfold – the struggle of the revolutionaries for justice leading to the revolutions of 1917 and beyond, the subsequent rise of the fascist states, the Gulags spread all over Eastern Europe, the massacres and destructions engulfing first an entire continent and then a world. In embryo, we see horrors beginning, and it would be an unimaginative reader of these events who did not recognize both sides as having its victims – the idealist revolutionaries, horrific as their violent deeds might be, representing millions of people whose rights were oppressed, whose poverty was enforced, whose voices were silenced. At the same time, the crowned heads at the tops of these edifices began to look and speak like victims. Victoria was surely right to speak of 'poor, kind Emperor Alexander'.[28]

At home, as the British absorbed the extraordinary news from Russia, they also witnessed not merely the routing of Beaconsfield in the polls, but the death of old Dizzy himself. For forty years, this mysterious man had been one of the giants of the political scene. Whereas Gladstone was a natural Tory who had somehow responded to events in such a way as to make himself into the wildest of radicals, Disraeli was a natural radical who had somehow found himself refashioning the Tories; a cynic who had willy-nilly become the most eloquent defender of altar and throne; a unique novelist whose books, combining political wisdom and social satire, still stand up and are well worth reading[29] – and the most skilful of backroom political fixers. By any standards, he was one of the most fascinating Prime Ministers in British history. The septuagenarian had been for many years – certainly since the loss of his wife – a physically weak man, prone to asthma, unable to lift heavy objects. It had seemed to many sadly apt, having paraded his Faery Queen through the streets of London in a new state coach and persuaded her to open Parliament in a fanfare of pageantry, that Lord Beaconsfield was unable to carry the heavy Sword of State in the House of Lords.

He remained his sovereign's dining companion, even after he had been voted from office. The last time he saw Victoria was on 1 March 1881. Three days later, in the House of Lords, he delivered one of his most powerful speeches, attacking Gladstone's Government for authorizing the withdrawal of British troops from Afghanistan.

When a contingent of British troops were besieged in Kandahar they were relieved by Lord Roberts, who escorted 10,000 fighting men and 8,000 camp followers, marching a distance of 313 miles in 23 days. Roberts dined with the Queen when he came back to England and, as Ponsonby told the new Viceroy of India, Lord Ripon, 'the Queen was much pleased with him – the more so, perhaps, as he strongly supported her views as to the retention of Candahar… Her Majesty believes you think so too in your inner mind.'[30] Ripon, whatever was in his inner mind, authorized the withdrawal from Kandahar.

Denouncing the decision in the Lords, Beaconsfield's speech contained the phrase, in fact borrowed from a conversation with the Russian Ambassador, 'the key of India is London'. The key of London, it could be added, was not merely the political Establishment and Parliament, but also the monarch – and the Queen's love of the Empire, and in particular her obsession with India, was a vital part of the late Victorian political structure. Her sympathy with Indian people, her love of their languages and culture, was perhaps only matched by her love of Scottish Highlanders. If John Brown had been Irish, how different history might have been.

Beaconsfield's last speech in the House, on 15 March, was in support of a vote of condolence to the Queen on the assassination of the Tsar. A week later, a chill from which he was suffering developed into bronchitis, and he slowly declined. On 28 March, he wrote a shaky letter in pencil to the Queen: 'At present I am prostrate though devoted – B.'[31]

As he lay dying, the Russian police were using torture to extract confessions from the nihilist associates of the Tsar's murderer. As poor Dizzy coughed and coughed, he said, 'I have suffered much. Had I been a Nihilist I would have confessed all.'[32]

One of Beaconsfield's last acts as Prime Minister had been to raise his friend Monty Corry to the peerage as Lord Rowton. A few eyebrows were raised, not because Monty had not been a faithful friend, and not because he was not already a member of the aristocracy; but because, like so much about Disraeli, it was enigmatic. The intensity of their friendship was obvious to all, yet, like many obvious things about Disraeli, it was also swathed in veils, questions, paradoxes.

Hearing that his friend and mentor was dying, Monty rushed home from Algiers. At first, Dizzy felt too ill or too weak to see him, perhaps fearful of the emotionalism of the parting. But Monty was eventually admitted and spent the last few days of his friend's life at his side. The last recorded words Beaconsfield spoke were, 'I had rather live, but I am not afraid to die.'[33]

He did so at half past four in the morning of 19 April – Easter Tuesday. Corry was desolate, and he was not the only one. 'Dear Lord Rowton, I cannot write in the 3rd person at this terrible moment when I can scarcely see for my fast falling tears,' wrote the Queen.[34]

To Lady Waterpark, she wrote, 'I know you will feel for me in my very great and irreplaceable loss – I have lost so many, but none whose loss will be more heavily felt than this of dear Lord Beaconsfield.'

It was an extraordinary confession, coming from one who had quite recently lost a beloved daughter, and whose grief for her husband was demonstrated by the Frogmore Mausoleum and Albert memorials galore. But love and grief can never be measured and the hyperbole reflected how very close she had become, both in heart and in politics, to the great charmer. 'He was so wise, so kind & sympathetic,' she added.[35] That was the clue. Although she was able to feel reciprocal love for some of her children, and although she enjoyed an epistolary friendship with Vicky, Victoria had an avid appetite for friendship. It is perhaps the hardest of all the loves for a potentate to sustain. Friendship is a union between equals, which makes it all but impossible for popes, kings and queens to have friends as others have them. Victoria did, and this is one of the things which both enraged her jealous children and baffled those in her Court. Much as she was sometimes mocked for her choice of friends, it was friendship which gave her some of the enormous strength which she possessed as a constitutional monarch. Dizzy had amused her, flirted with her, and – in so far as it was possible to see what he believed – encouraged her political convictions. They had been on the same side in the battle of Life. Alas, because Bertie destroyed as much of their correspondence as he could get his hands upon when he became king, we shall never know all that the two friends shared, but we can be sure that in that particular bonfire, many hilarious asides by Disraeli will have been lost to posterity. The twenty or so volumes of 'correspondence' between the Queen and Disraeli kept in the Royal Archives contain almost nothing written by Victoria. Someone has done a thorough job of removing the evidence.

For reasons of protocol, she could not attend the funeral, at which she was represented by Bertie, Arthur and Leopold. The obvious place for it had been Westminster Abbey, but Disraeli had given firm instructions that it should be held at the parish church at his home, Hughenden Manor in Buckinghamshire, that he should be buried with his wife, 'and that my Funeral may be conducted with the same simplicity as hers was'.

Victoria visited Hughenden when he was safely interred. They reopened the vault, so that she was able to lay a china wreath of flowers on his coffin. She later paid for a marble monument to be erected in the church, inscribed with the text from the Book of Proverbs, 'Kings love him that speaketh right.'

PART SIX

TWENTY

'GRACIOUS CONFIDENCES SO FRANKLY GIVEN'

WHILE SHE SANG an endless requiem in her journals and letters for those who had gone before, Victoria had a robust and recurring capacity to fill up the gaps left by bereavement. No one could ever replace Prince Albert, but Brown was a constant and much-adored companion. Disraeli's loss was a cause of acute grief, but in 1882, she made a new friend, and a lasting one: Randall Davidson. It was all the more striking, since, apart from her dependence on old Dean Wellesley, her devotion to Norman Macleod, whom she scarcely ever saw from one year's end to the next, and her admiration for Dean Stanley, she tended to be impatient with the clergy, fearing that they would be too High Church, too Low Church, too bigoted, or, as preachers, too boring.

Randall Davidson, the son of a Leith merchant, had the advantage of being wholly Scottish, and, until he was sent to Harrow and Oxford, a Presbyterian. There was nothing intimidating about his levels of academic attainment (he got a third class degree in law and modern history) but he had acute antennae for the ways of the world, an instinctive feel for the Establishment, and a kindly temperament. He was an ideal clerical-courtier, who first came to the Queen's attention when he was the young chaplain to Archbishop Tait, whose daughter Edith he had married. (It was one of those classic Victorian courtships, since he married the sister of his best friend at Oxford – Crauford Tait, who died young.)

When Tait died in December 1882, the Queen was of course anxious for 'every detail' of the deathbed, and this Davidson was able to supply. General Ponsonby, hovering by the door of the Queen's drawing room, commented, 'What on earth is happening? I don't know when the Queen has had such a long interview with anybody.' 'I feel,' she wrote in her journal, 'that Mr Davidson is a man who may be of great use to me for which I am truly thankful.'[1] This was indeed to be one of the closest friendships of her later life. Although not brought up in the Church of England – or perhaps, because of this fact – Davidson, while Tait's chaplain, had built up an obsessive and detailed knowledge of Who was Who in the Established Church; he was a fund, among other things, of information and gossip about likely candidates, whenever deaneries and bishoprics fell vacant.

The immediate consequence of Tait's death, of course, was that a successor must be found for the see of Canterbury. Edward White Benson, bishop of the new diocese of Truro, was chosen. Gladstone had approached that old Tractarian R. W. Church, the Dean of St Paul's, who refused the post; and he also asked Browne of Winchester, who was dismissed by the Queen as being much too old. She favoured Benson, partly because he had been the first Master of Wellington College, the school near Aldershot founded by Prince Albert in memory of the Iron Duke for the education of officers' sons, and partly because she had a natural sympathy with those who were not of the Establishment. Benson, like Davidson, came from a comparatively modest background, and his family life was the reverse of conventional. (His wife, who liked to be known as Ben, was in love with Lucy, one of Archbishop Tait's surviving daughters, and their children included Fred, who grew up to be the amusing chronicler of Mapp and Lucia, melancholy Eton beak Arthur, who wrote 'Land of Hope and Glory' and edited Queen Victoria's letters, and Hugh, who became a Catholic monsignor and in his day also a famous historical novelist.)

Victoria found Benson a charming man – not everyone did – perhaps empathizing with his profound heartbreak. (Shortly after he accepted the see of Truro, he lost Martin, his favourite son.) She asked that Davidson should stay on as archbishop's chaplain, so that she could have a close sense of what was going on at Lambeth Palace.[2]

Ponsonby observed to his wife that the Queen 'always laughs at Episcopal garments and dislikes Bishops'. He was writing from Presbyterian Balmoral, where the new Bishop of Salisbury had arrived in late October to kiss hands. Until they swore fealty to their sovereign, new bishops could not begin to receive their enormous emoluments, so there had been strong inducement for the bishop to make the long journey north. The bishop decided to take a walk. 'Rather a clamber,' Ponsonby reported, 'but he was quite up to it. In the evening, H.M. asked the Duke of Richmond about the walk & he told her of the Bishop struggling thro' the brushwood in his shovel hat. She laughed & said, "But I hope not his apron too – that would be too ridiculous".'[3] If her Anglican Orthodoxy was questionable, and if, as she once admitted, she did not like bishops, she had a growing sense that the Church of England by law established was something in which she needed, as sovereign, to be involved. From the time of Gladstone's second administration, formed in April 1880, she had a clear sense, which would not leave her for the remaining twenty years of her reign, of the values and ideas which it was her place to sustain. Throne and altar were allies.

If proof were needed of this, and if the menace of international terrorism had shown its hand in Russia, Italy, Ireland and even in London, she had the profoundest distrust of Gladstone and his radical agenda.

Gladstone himself, an old-fashioned High Churchman, a Free Trader who yearned to do away with income tax, a landed gentleman, or would-be gentleman living on his wife's estates at Hawarden in North Wales, was in many ways the same man in old age that he had been in youth. In other respects, however, he was completely different. His foreign policy and his Irish policy could not have been more different from that of Beaconsfield and the Tories. And, moreover, in order to achieve his aims of promoting Irish Home Rule, he needed the votes of radical backbenchers. His tour of the North, culminating in the Midlothian campaign, had been the triumph of the People's William. Any natural Tory, like the Queen, must have dreaded what was going to fly out of the Pandora's box opened by this election victory.

One of the first manifestations of revolution in the new House of Commons was the appearance of the newly elected radical member for Northampton, Charles Bradlaugh. Each MP has to profess loyalty to the Crown, and this usually takes the form of a religious oath. Bradlaugh was well known as an atheist lecturer and campaigner, and he asked, which he was legally entitled to do (even at this date), to make an affirmation of allegiance (that is, a solemn declaration without invoking the name of God), and the Speaker, Sir Henry Brand, bungled the matter. He referred Bradlaugh to a committee of the House. The matter was to rumble on for years, and Bradlaugh, who kept being re-elected by the people of Northampton, ended his days in 1891 as their MP, but he did not actually take his seat until 1886. 'The Queen has read with interest the discussion of that dreadful Mr Bradlaugh,' she told the Prime Minister, 'and she cannot help rejoicing at the feeling of indignation exhibited agt. [against] such a man sitting in the House. It is not only his known Atheism but his other horrible Principles which make him a disgrace to an assembly like the House of Commons.'[4]

She watched with intense interest as Gladstone chose the members of his Government and took personal exception to each and every appointment which smacked of radicalism. 'The Queen regrets to see the names of such very advanced radicals as Mr Chamberlain and Sir Charles Dilke,' she told Gladstone, when he had advanced Joe Chamberlain to the presidency of the Board of Trade and given Dilke the chairmanship of the Royal Commission on Honours.[5] Much would be heard of both these men in the coming years. Chamberlain, who had been the Mayor of Birmingham and a pioneer of radical local government, providing housing and schools of a much higher standard than in other parts of the country for the citizens, was also, like Bradlaugh, an unbeliever, an anti-aristocratic modern man. By great paradox, Chamberlain actually emerged as a champion, later in life, of many of the Queen's favourite causes. Time would usher him onwards as an imperialist and an opponent of Irish independence. Dilke was a more complicated case, as far as the Queen was concerned. He was a friend of Bertie's, and he and Lady Dilke stayed at Sandringham.[6] Apart from the fact that he mixed in the same fast-living set as the Prince of Wales (though Victoria was not fully aware of Dilke's scandalous way of life at this juncture), he was seen by the Queen as a Judas. His father had been one of those few who gave support to Prince Albert when a majority were pouring scorn on the idea of a Great Exhibition. But young Dilke (he was the grandson of Charles Wentworth Dilke, the antiquary and man of letters who had been a friend of Keats and Shelley) had developed ideas which were openly republican. Keats, probably, and Shelley, certainly, would have approved. The Queen, however, questioned whether such a person should not in all honesty serve in the administration of a constitutional monarchy. Shortly after taking office as an Under-Secretary at the Foreign Office in 1880, Dilke had written to the Foreign Secretary, Lord Granville, to say that 'he thought the Republican Government best for France'. He stubbornly refused to budge from the position, and three years later[7] the Queen was still asking for his resignation on the grounds that the republican French Government was composed of violent revolutionaries who had threatened with murder her friend the Empress Eugénie.

The tide of violence was not a figment of the Queen's imagination. Returning from London by train, she was met at Windsor Station by a carriage and driven off in the direction of the Castle. 'Just as we were driving off from the station there, the people, or rather the Eton boys cheered, & at the same time there was the sound of what

I thought was an explosion from the engine, but in another moment, I saw people rushing about, & a man being violently hustled, rushing down the street.' Princess Beatrice, who was sitting beside her mother in the carriage, had actually seen the man take aim and fire with a revolver, but she had remained calm, so as not to scare the Queen. The Duchess of Roxburghe, also in the carriage, assumed at first that it was all a joke. But the man, a lunatic called Roderick Maclean, was set upon by Eton boys with umbrellas and taken to the police station. It was John Brown, 'with a greatly perturbed face, though quite calm', who told Victoria that the man had fired at her. While she was having her tea at the Castle, and telegraphing 'all my children and near relations', Brown came in to tell her that the revolver had been found loaded, with one chamber discharged; and the next day he brought the gun to show her. Two days later, the Judge Advocate came to the Castle and 'was most warm in his congratulations, & said I could have no conception of the intense feeling for me, the cabmen, & sweepers at the crossings in London, enquiring after me. He thinks the state of Ireland still very bad.'[8]

Even allowing for the pardonable sycophancy which must form part of conversation with royalty, what the Judge Advocate said about the people's love was true. Victoria had – you might almost say in spite of everything – become intensely popular, and would continue to be so. 'It is worth being shot at,' she wrote to Vicky, 'to see how much one is loved.'[9]

The Judge Advocate was wrong to imply that the lunatic Maclean with his revolver was an Irish Fenian, but right to say that the state of Ireland was very bad. On 3 May, Gladstone wrote what looks like one of the thousand routine letters any Prime Minister might have written to a monarch. 'Lord Frederick Cavendish is humbly recommended to Your Majesty by Mr Gladstone to be Chief Secretary to the Lord Lieutenant of Ireland.'[10] Lord Frederick, now aged forty-five, Liberal MP for the northern division of the West Riding of Yorkshire, was married to the Queen's Maid of Honour Lucy Lyttelton. Such was the tight-knit world of the Victorian governing classes, Lucy was the niece of Mrs Gladstone. Lord Frederick's elder brother, Harty Tarty, was that Leader of the Liberal Party who had stood down to make way for the Grand Old Man, and Lord Frederick in his young manhood had been Gladstone's private secretary. The letter to appoint him as Chief Secretary to the Lord Lieutenant of Ireland was actually, though neither Gladstone nor the Queen could have guessed as much, a death warrant.

Four days after it was signed, he was walking in Phoenix Park in Dublin with the Under-Secretary, Thomas Burke. Several men burst out from the bushes behind them and stabbed and hacked them to death with long surgical knives. A group calling themselves the Irish National Invincibles were responsible. They had wanted to kill Burke, but they did not even know of Lord Frederick's identity. Such was the confused, violent state of Ireland and Irish politics.

Inevitably, those who wanted Irish independence by peaceful means felt tainted by the murders. Charles Stewart Parnell, a Protestant landowner from County Wicklow, was now the leader of the Irish nationalist cause, having entered Parliament in 1875. He was quick to make a speech condemning the Phoenix Park murders, which increased his popularity, both among Irish nationalists and among English Liberal voters. But Parnell had Fenians, and men of violence, among his followers in the Irish Land League. The Queen's Speech of 1880 had resolved to abolish the Conservative coercion measure, which suspended Habeas Corpus in Ireland. In the event, the Liberals kept coercion, and the situation was permanently on the verge of anarchy. The economic depression in the agrarian world meant, inevitably, that many Irish tenants were unable to afford the rent, and were driven off their land. Parnell and the Land League introduced a system of protest by which anyone taking a farm from which a tenant had been evicted should be 'isolated from his kind as if he were a leper of old'. Captain Boycott, the agent of a rich landowner in County Mayo was one such, and thereby gave his name to the English vocabulary.

The Irish countryside was in chaos. Hayricks were burnt, cattle maimed, houses looted. Parnell himself was for a while imprisoned under the draconian Coercion laws. Every time a Fenian was released from prison – such as the collectivist Michael Davitt, who campaigned for the nationalization of land – the Queen expressed dismay. 'She does not like to see her law defied and peaceable persons frightened by the terror exercised by the Land League,' Ponsonby told Dilke.[11]

The open republicanism and violence displayed in some quarters by the Irish was matched, in a more minor key, by lack of deference among radical MPs, and the Queen monitored their remarks with close, and disapproving, attention. The paradox of the Queen's position in life was that she cherished John Brown precisely because he showed her affection, without sycophancy; but that she considered it necessary, for the maintenance of the monarchical idea, for royalty to be respected. A comparatively trivial matter, such as the raising of a memorial for the Prince Imperial, killed in the Zulu War, threw up a despicable willingness on the part of backbench MPs not to take royalty seriously.

It was initially suggested that a statue which had already been executed of the Prince Imperial should be erected at his old Army College at Woolwich. He had, after all, died wearing British uniform in a British war against the Zulus. It was perhaps more gallant than prudent for the Queen to get involved with this matter, on behalf of the Empress Eugénie. But when no better place could be found for the memorial, the Queen impulsively decided that it could go in Westminster Abbey. Whether her lady-in-waiting Lady Augusta Stanley, or Lady Augusta's husband the Dean of Westminster viewed the matter in so favourable a light, is not recorded. The proposal lit a touch-paper of anti-French and anti-royal prejudice in the Commons, with William Briggs, the Liberal MP for Blackburn, rising to complain that 'the people of this country were now paying millions of money, the legacy of the Napoleonic Wars between France and England. If there must be a statue, let them put one up to a great and glorious Englishman, the man who armed in a nation's authority, overturned a corrupt throne; the soldier who stayed a civil war at home, and made England respected abroad, the patriot who handed down to us as a precious heirloom our civil and religious freedom – Oliver Cromwell.' These were fighting words, and they made the Queen 'shocked and disgusted'. She pointed out that the young prince had died 'because of the <u>cowardly decision</u> of a <u>British</u> officer... But where is chivalry and delicacy to be found these days among many of the Members of Parliament?'[12] Gladstone's reply to Mr Briggs in the Commons was so inadequate that one is forced to wonder whether the clumsiness was deliberate. He hastened to deny 'the question of court influence in this matter' – thereby making it clear to everyone that the guiding force behind the idea of a Napoleonic memorial was indeed the Queen. 'But I must observe,' he went on, 'that if I am correctly informed, with respect to the burial of a person in the Abbey, the prerogative of the Dean is absolute.'[13] Gladstone had muddied the water. No one was suggesting at this point that the young man should be buried in the Abbey, and everyone knew that the Dean of Westminster was married to one of the Queen's closest friends. It is a trivial but typical example of how Gladstone carried on his everlasting warfare with the Queen, appearing to defend her in public, while actually sowing difficulties for her in the minds of would-be, and actual, republicans. In the event, the Prince Imperial's statue was erected at the Royal Military Academy at Sandhurst.

The second Gladstone administration was, to date, the Government with which Victoria had the most abrasive relations. In 1881, she had, for the first time in her reign, vetoed a Queen's Speech, announcing in advance the decision to withdraw from Kandahar. Hartington, knowing her strong views on the war in Afghanistan, had tried to conceal the speech from her. When the constitutional impropriety was laid bare, the Home Secretary, Sir William Harcourt, bluntly asserted that the Queen's Speech was merely the speech of her ministers, and the sovereign was obliged to approve it. 'Harcourt showed his customary tact (?)'¹⁴ was Prince Leopold's comment. The following year, she refused even to attend the State Opening of Parliament. She was reverting to her pattern of behaviour during Gladstone's first administration.

It was partly because of Prince Leopold, however, that the Queen had to keep lines of communication open between herself and the Liberals. Gladstone continued to keep her informed of all Cabinet meetings, and sent to her every day Parliament was in session a summary of its proceedings in his own hand.

Leopold – who had been granted the dukedom of Albany on the Queen's birthday, 24 May 1881 – was married, on 27 April 1882, to Princess Helen of Waldeck and Pyrmont. It was essential, in his eyes, and those of his mother, before this event, that Parliament should increase his allowance. Gladstone would not have been human had he taken no pleasure at all in the parliamentary debate on this matter, during which robust republican views were aired by the 'usual suspects', such as the Irish nationalist T. H. Healy and Henry Labouchere. 'She must own,' the Queen wrote, 'that she thinks Messrs Strong and Healy were atrocious – truly vulgar and ignorant as well as <u>republican</u>... Mr Labouchere showed great ignorance as to facts – but was far less offensive.' Writing from the safety of an hotel in Menton, she resurrected the question of whether royal finances needed to be debated openly at all. She believed that these 'offensive and humiliating discussions only went upon each occasion to enable people to say things which are unfortunately but too often believed by the poorer classes'.

If Gladstone had hoped that the embarrassing parliamentary debate would have made the Queen shy of broaching the question of money and the Royal Family, he was to be sadly disappointed. Warming to her theme, in the mild sunshine of southern France, and with the leisure of a holiday-morning giving her time to expand herself, she went on to point out that 'these ignorant and ill-conditioned radicals' could not distinguish between the position of the very rich landed proprietors and the Royal Family. The former inherit huge fortunes – 'and yet have no status or Court to maintain. Whereas we have no property – Nothing of our own – & must maintain this status; & and are expected to give largely to Charities &c &c.' The Queen omitted any mention of the income she personally received from the Duchy of Lancaster.

Having begun the subject, she really spread herself, pointing out that grants should be given to the children of the Prince of Wales. She spelt out the sums she considered should be set aside for various minor members of the Royal Family. She tried to remember and thought that the Duke of Cambridge received £12,000 a year and Princess Mary £3,000 a year when their father died.

The next matter she asked the Prime Minister to consider was her youngest daughter, Beatrice. As it was 'most likely' that Baby would not marry 'or leave her Mother during her declining years', the Queen was 'extremely anxious' that money should be forthcoming for her too. She suggested £6,000 a year as a satisfactory sum. Whichever method is used to convert this into modern currency – using the retail price index, it comes to £471,000; using the criterion of comparison with average earnings, it rises to something much higher – the Queen was expecting Parliament to devote quite a lot of public money to supply the income for someone who was, in effect, a lady's companion. The annual going rate for such a role in Cheltenham or Eastbourne at the period would probably have been around thirty guineas.

'Of course the Queen will do all she can for her – but this would not be enough to secure her a <u>position</u> fitting her status [?illegible], and the place she holds as the Queen's <u>constant companion</u>.' She closed this long epistle with an account of how well she felt, how beautiful were the scenery and vegetation of Menton and how clear the air. She then added an abrupt PS: 'Is it true that Sir C. Dilke [Under-Secretary for Foreign Affairs] and Mr Fawcett [postmaster general] did not vote for Pce Leopold's annuity? If so, the Queen thinks it vy unfortunate that such people shd be in the Govt & it must put an effectual bar to their ever being Cabinet Ministers.'[15] Gladstone was either too busy – with the affairs of Ireland, Afghanistan and Egypt, and the extension of the British franchise – or too charitable – to repeat the arguments of G. O. Trevelyan's notorious pamphlet *What Does She Do with It?* that, whereas the Queen's arguments might have been applicable to her father's generation when the politicians really did hold the purse strings of the Royal Family, it was no longer the case that the outright owners of Osborne, Balmoral and Sandringham, with all their estates and rents, could truthfully say, 'we have no property'. It was also the case, which was not true even for the very richest of the landed proprietors, that the Royal Families of Europe could expect, when they married, or marked important anniversaries, to collect very substantial capital in terms of gifts – 'particularly', as David Duff memorably pointed out in his book *Hessian Tapestry*, when 'such royalty were on friendly terms with the imperial House of Russia or the potentates of the East'.[16] Huge amounts of loot, in gold, diamonds and other precious stones, were accumulated on such occasions. 'In one day,' Duff wrote, 'more capital gain could be accrued than many worthy citizens accumulated in a life-time.'[17] Just as her physical greed, her need to guzzle grossly, became almost a pathology for Queen Victoria, she never showed any consciousness of how dangerous it might seem, in republican times, for royal personages to shovel away so much of the world's goods. Whether this aspect of her character was to be explained in terms of her mother, a stranger in a foreign land, having been genuinely strapped for cash, who can say?

Given the condition of Leopold's health, it was in some ways surprising that he had chosen to marry; but he craved to be as the healthy are, and he was everlastingly looking out for useful appointments. In April 1877, when Leopold was twenty-four, Beaconsfield – quite improperly – had given him a key for opening the Government Red Boxes; the surreptitious gift being necessary to avoid trouble with Leopold's brothers. From then onwards, the Queen used Leopold as an extra secretary, but he had no constitutional right to such a position, and his avowed, open support for the Conservatives raised more than a few eyebrows.

He had fallen for several girls, with varying degrees of seriousness. People spoke of him, when he was an undergraduate, as a possible beau for Alice Liddell, but it was really with Alice's sister Edith, one year his junior, that he had enjoyed a mild flirtation. He had been in love with Mary Baring, daughter of Lord and Lady Ashburton, the great bankers. The woman with whom he fell most conspicuously in love was a beautiful Highlander called the Countess of Breadalbane, a country-house crush which came to nothing. And there was a moment when his mother had tried to marry him off to Princess Caroline Mathilde of Schleswig-Holstein ('Calma') – an idea which seemed to annoy everyone else in the extended family: Affie and Marie, because Calma had been promised to Marie's brother Sergei; the Schleswig-Holstein parents, because they did not want their daughter married to a haemophiliac. His actual choice was an acceptably round-faced German, Princess Helen of Waldeck and Pyrmont. Princess Helen came from a little principality near Darmstadt, and if the frail English prince was not an obviously alluring prospect as a husband, he was at least young; her sister Emma, aged twenty-two, had been married off to King Willem II of the Netherlands, who was sixty-four. Leopold and Helen had two babies, Alice and Charlie, and Queen ('We have no property') Victoria gave them as a wedding present the beautiful house and small estate of Claremont in Surrey, where she herself had spent happy childhood months, and which she purchased from her uncle King Leopold.

In 1883, the Queen had a slight fall. As she told Gladstone, 'she slipped her foot going down stairs on Saturday after luncheon, and in saving herself strained the other leg near the knee but without injury to the joint'. She trusted 'that it will soon be cleared up'.[18] At sixty-four, it was perhaps not surprising that the increasingly obese Queen should have fallen, especially if she had been applying herself to her heroic admixtures, at the table, of whisky poured into the claret. Her doctor,

James Reid, was clearly the man who had advised her that there was no cause for alarm.

Reid had been appointed as Resident Medical Attendant upon Her Majesty in July 1881, at the age of thirty-one. It was one of her shrewdest appointments, since Reid was an excellent doctor – indeed, almost ludicrously overqualified for his role – the soul of discretion, and an affectionate man who quickly saw what was undoubtedly always there, the loveable side of his royal employer's character.

In looking for such a figure, Victoria had a list of requirements which would not, at first sight, seem easy to satisfy. First, she wanted a Scotsman – no difficulty there, since the medical training in Aberdeen, Edinburgh and Glasgow was legendarily good. Preferably, the second point, she wanted the man to be from Aberdeenshire. Thirdly, he must be conversant in German. This was a revealing requirement. When she had spelt out to Lady Waterpark, in 1864, the qualifications for a lady-in-waiting, she had merely needed someone who spoke French. But the family had now grown prodigiously, and nearly all the in-laws and foreign visitors to the royal houses and palaces were German-speaking. Reid, a man of relatively humble beginnings and high intellectual accomplishment, had begun his studies at Aberdeen University and the Infirmary in that city and, upon specializing in ear, nose and throat medicine, had taken himself off to Vienna. There he had become an expert in the field, and acquired fluency in German. He also studied pathology.

When Reid was appointed, he was offered £400 per annum to be in constant attendance, with six weeks' leave of absence a year. He was not a part of the Royal Household. He was to take medical and surgical charge not only of the Queen, but also of all her attendants, her dressers and maids, the Royal Family, the Household servants and any visitors. He did not form any part of the medical hierarchy, Physicians and Surgeons Extraordinary, and so forth, who, like Sir William Jenner, were rich and distinguished doctors brought in from their own practices to attend royal emergencies.[19]

So, Reid was a new character in the day-to-day life of the Queen, and in 1883, following the slight fall of his employer on the stairs at Windsor Castle, he was about to witness one of the most conspicuous dramas of her later years.

Reid was a fairly strait-laced man, and he could hardly fail to be struck by the position in the Household of his fellow Scotsman, the fifty-six-year-old John Brown. Reid was to be the Queen's closest medical adviser for the rest of her life, but in all the years he served her, he never once saw her undressed, and he was barely allowed to touch her: all the information he gleaned from her about her physical condition was gathered from question and answer – much of it written. The physical ease and intimacy of the monarch and Brown was clear for all to see, especially after she had slipped on the stairs. He carried her everywhere, as Reid noted laconically in his tiny handwriting. On 21 March, she was a little better, and the Queen took his arm as she came into the room. But then Brown lifted her up. 'Oh, I thought it was here,' she said, obviously alluding to a bruise on her upper thigh, because she lifted up her dress, and moved Brown's hand as she did so – 'No it is here.'[20]

Reid, after the Queen's death, was probably one of the very few people in the world who ever knew the full truth about her relationship with Brown. It was the faithful Reid who was entrusted by King Edward VII to track down and purchase letters which were being used as blackmail by George Profeit, the son of Dr Alexander Profeit, the resident doctor at Balmoral from 1874 onwards. Reid noted in his diary on 11 May 1905, 'At 6.30 went to Buckingham Palace and had an audience of the King and delivered to him the box with over 300 letters of the late Queen to Profeit which after 6 months of negotiations I have got from George Profeit, many of them most compromising. Thanked by the King and also Lord Knollys.'

We must assume that King Edward VII destroyed these documents, and that the mysterious relationship between Queen Victoria and her Highland servant will therefore forever remain mysterious. Whether it was a marriage, as the Ponsonbys, other courtiers and the Home Secretary evidently believed, or whether it was merely an intense intimacy which embarrassed her children, will never fully be known. We do know that George Profeit had written evidence, in the form of those letters which Victoria's son wanted to be destroyed. In November 1990, the diarist James Lees-Milne had a 'delicious nursery lunch of soup, ragout and creamy pudding', with Reid's daughter, Victoria Ingrams. 'Talked of her doctor father who was sixty when she was born and died in 1923. She remembers as a child seeing the green file in which reposed all the letters from John Brown to Queen Victoria. Its contents were eventually destroyed. She is confident that the Queen slept with Brown, and thinks it possible they were married.'[21]

Brown was not to survive that cold March of 1883. A puzzling incident, worthy of the attention of Sherlock Holmes, had occurred in Windsor Great Park at the beginning of the month. Lady Florence Dixie, a celebrated explorer and author, resided at a house called the Fishery in Windsor. She was the daughter of the Marquess of Queensberry (and sister of the later celebrated Lord Alfred Douglas). She was often to be seen in the Great Park, exercising her jaguar, which she had captured on a hunting trip to Patagonia. An absentee landlady of Irish lands herself, the twenty-six-year-old Lady Florence had written to the Queen warning her that the Irish peasantry were starving.

At about the time that the Queen had her slight fall, Lady Florence was walking her St Bernard dog Hubert when she believed herself to have been waylaid by two transvestites, men who 'pushed me backwards and threw me to the ground with great violence'. One had a knife, and she believed them to be Fenians. She claimed that they had slashed her clothing with a dagger, and it was only the dog which had saved her.

The case aroused obvious interest, not least because of the claim that Irish terrorists might be prowling so near the Castle. On the other hand, witnesses, who had seen Lady Florence walking her dog that day, reported that they had seen no assailants, and the more cynical of the courtiers recalled that they nicknamed the Dixies 'Sir Sometimes and Lady Always Tipsy'.

The Queen asked Brown to investigate, and although he was suffering from a cold, he set off across the park on a very cold day. He made a great fuss of Hubert, and asked for a photograph of the dog. Lady Florence allowed him to examine the torn clothing, and he noted that there were slashes on the outer garments, none on the under garments. Also, if she had been thrown to the ground, Brown thought it strange that there was no mud on the back of her dress, only on the front. He returned to the Queen no wiser than the police.

Wrapped in a 'huge assortment of wraps, known to her ladies as the White Knight's paraphernalia', the Queen still wanted her walk on Saturday, 24 March; and even though Brown's cold was by now much worse, he carried her down to the pony chair and accompanied her down the raw, windy Long Walk. By the next day, which was Easter Sunday, erysipelas had extended over the right side of Brown's face and he had developed a raging fever.

He drifted into delirium tremens. Brown's brother Archie insisted upon sending for Sir William Jenner, but the Queen still showed no suspicion that anything was seriously amiss. By Tuesday afternoon, he sank into a deep coma and at 10.40 pm, 27 March 1883, John Brown died. Prince Leopold was given the unenviable task of going to his mother's dressing room and telling her the news. Later, he wrote to his brother-in-law the Grand Duke of Hesse-Darmstadt, 'I have deep sympathy [with the Queen]. We can feel for her, & her sorrow, without being sorry for the cause. At least I can't be a hypocrit [sic].'[22]

The Queen must have noticed, a little, that her children and her courtiers took this attitude, but it is the mark of the true eccentric that she does not see the world as others do; and since her heart had once again been broken, she was unselfconscious in her expressions of grief. She poured out her sorrow for Brown to anyone who would give a sympathetic ear, and often to those who did not. The strength of her expressions were just as vivid as when she had spoken in the past of Prince Albert. Two months after Brown's death, while staying at Balmoral, Lord Carlingford,[23] the Lord Privy Seal, remarked, 'This infatuation is wonderful. It is painfully absurd to hear his [Brown's] name pronounced when one would expect another.'[24] If she sensed such supercilious *snobbisme* among the Establishment class, she cared not a fig. Her Maid of Honour Marie Mallet noted, a good dozen years after Brown's death, that the Queen defied all royal protocols while in Scotland and attended a family funeral of one of Brown's relations.[25]

Her new friend of this period, Randall Davidson, was perhaps professionally qualified to offer consolations. But the young clergyman was no substitute for Brown, with his rough humour, his strong arms, his lack of side and his consoling fondness for the whisky bottle. Indeed, Davidson had not been her friend for long before the two came into conflict over the matter of Brown.

The Deanery at Windsor became vacant again in 1883. Old Dean Wellesley had been the Queen's closest ecclesiastical confidant and adviser until his death the previous year. His successor, a man named Connor, was too old for the job and died after only six months. Who should the new dean be?

Gladstone, an old Christ Church man, suggested his dean, the lexicographer Dean Liddell; but the Queen would not hear of it. Perhaps recalling her fury when Prince Leopold cut up rough, and refused to take Presbyterian Communion, she dismissed Liddell's name with 'Oh, no, he is quite out of the question and too old.'[26] A few other candidates were touted around, but there was no doubt on whose head the Queen's blessing would be bestowed. She wrote from the Isle of Wight that there was 'no other clergyman better fitted for the combined appointment of Dean of Windsor and Resident Chaplain to the Queen' than Randall Davidson. She wrote this on 8 May, and by 9 May was impatient for a reply, so followed it up with a telegram in cipher: 'Her Majesty will be much obliged if

you will make formal offer at once.' Perhaps to keep her on tenter-
hooks a little longer, Gladstone did not make the formal offer to
Davidson until 10 May.[27]

It was a good appointment, and with young Reid as her Scottish
doctor, young Davidson as her Scottish dean, young Baby as her
surely irremoveable companion and dogsbody, and the indispensable
Ponsonby, she was, however heartbroken by the death of Brown, now
laying down a stalwart circle of young friends for her old age. The
less satisfactory she found her older children, the more she could rely
upon these younger friends. When asked for his advice about the
advisability of appointing Davidson, Archbishop Benson gave the
memorable counsel: 'His youth has all the advantage of spring and
freshness... besides, it is a shortcoming of which he is daily being
cured, as Your Majesty says.'[28]

Davidson and she hit it off almost from the first. 'It was her common
sense which welded together the other attributes and enabled her
(though not in the ordinary sense of the words a really clever woman)
to do far more than most clever women could have accomplished.'
He came to believe that her charm stemmed from her 'absolute
truthfulness and simplicity... I have known many prominent people,'
he said when he looked back from a position of high eminence as
Archbishop of Canterbury, 'but I have never known one of them
with whom it is so easy and so natural to speak freely and frankly
after even a very short acquaintance. I imagine it would be difficult to
name any attribute more valuable to a sovereign than the possession
of this particular power.'[29]

Those who realized this always got the best out of Queen Victoria,
even if it meant that sparks flew along the way. Those who did not
realize it, or who shrank into sycophancy or cold hostility, could
only watch her shrink into shyness or stubborn silence. Those who
knew how to deal with her – Melbourne, Disraeli, Brown, Davidson,
Ponsonby – could duck when the sparks flew but gave her trust. She
could be haughtily conscious of the dignity of her office, but paradoxically, she was not pompous or proud.

In one of their long talks, Victoria complained to Davidson about the lack of sympathy which she had encountered for her past sorrows. Davidson, who had clearly seen the smirks and suppressed grins of politicians and visiting dignitaries as she expounded the simple virtues of John Brown, decided 'to speak with freedom and very strongly as to the risk of laying bare the heart to those who don't understand'.[30] He had put his finger on one of her besetting, though rather endearing, faults, and it was never one which she quite saw the necessity to correct. All that was interesting about her was brought out by sympathy, but, such was her combative and difficult nature, such sympathy needed to be combined with the skill and courage of knowing how to stand up to her.

Within a very short time of becoming Dean of Windsor, Davidson was confronted with just such a difficulty. In Lambeth Palace Library, wedged among the copious papers of the great archbishop which Davidson was to become, is a scurrilous pamphlet, published in New York by Norman L. Munro, entitled *John Brown's Legs, or Leaves from a Journal in the Lowlands* by Kenward Philip.

It bears the dedicatory inscription, 'To the memory of those extraordinary Legs – poor bruised and scratched darlings – the writer dedicates this little volume, in the full belief that while John Brown's body undoubtedly lies mouldering in the grave, his Legs go marching on. WINSORAL, March 1884.'

The pamphlet is slapstick, rather than biting satire: 'A dreadful calamity has happened to disturb the serenity of our Life to the Highlands. My servant, John Brown, while attending me yesterday in a walk to Kshruballanachtwister stubbed his toe' is the opening sentence. As well as mocking Victoria's Brown obsession ('Have written a note to Tennyson commanding him to write a sonnet on Brown's legs') it also notes her notorious greed. The spoof-Queen feels sorry for her son Arthur, serving in the army: 'it is dreadful to think of his privations,' she wrote, listing a Sunday dinner eaten by the prince which starts with oysters and mock turtle soup, and includes lark puddings, saddle of mutton, roast pheasants and ice cream. There is a scene which is perhaps a little too knowing, in which Bertie punches Brown in the face.

It is interesting that the (on the whole) serious-minded Davidson kept this squib among his papers. He was certainly acutely aware of the Queen's unawareness of how the public regarded her relationship with Brown: that is, as simply ridiculous – 'painfully absurd', to use Lord Carlingford's phrase. Since Davidson was the man who seemed to have the Queen's ear at that moment, he was delegated by the courtiers to tell her what was generally thought of her latest literary scheme. For she did actually intend to publish a volume, if not entitled *John Brown's Legs*, then a third volume of her *Leaves* from her Highland journals. The book was to be, in effect, a biography of Brown.

Most of the politicians during her long reign had been anxious for the Queen to play a more conspicuously ceremonial part in public life. They wanted more opening of bridges and railway stations, more visits to hospitals, as they extended their own executive power. The correspondence, stretching over thirty years, between Victoria and Gladstone enables its readers to watch the Queen trying to control her own purse strings and exercise influence over Cabinet appointments, while her Prime Minister urges her to attend a State Opening of Parliament.

Her more confiding and intimate tone with Dean Davidson, however, suggests an altogether different monarchical function: one which really only came into its own during the era of the television interview in the late twentieth century, and one which many monarchists deplore. This was for the royal person to come before the public as a human being and ask them to 'share my pain'.

The Queen showed Davidson the manuscript of her John Brown book, and he had clearly been left more or less speechless. She wrote to him from Osborne in June 1884, promising to send him finished copies and thanking him for his advice about omitting 'a few trifling things'.[31] 'The Queen feels that the sacredness of deep grief should never be desecrated by unholy hands.' She emphasized to her young dean that she had found widespread sympathy, however, among those who 'quite understand and know what she suffers'.[32]

Davidson had in fact been trying to dissuade his monarch from 'sharing her pain' with the general populace. 'Such a spirit of ready response to the gracious confidences so frankly given, is not always to be found, and I should be deceiving Your Majesty were I not to admit that there are, especially among the humbler classes, some (perhaps it would be true to say many) who do not show themselves worthy of these confidences, and whose spirit, judging by their published periodicals, is one of such unappreciative criticism as I should not desire...'[33] He had clearly already seen *John Brown's Legs*, and must have been wondering what would happen if a copy of the scurrilous spoof ever found its way into Windsor Castle.

Clearly, Davidson's weak attempts at dissuasion had no effect whatsoever. When she went to Balmoral in June, the Queen summoned Dr Hamilton Lees of Edinburgh to help her put the leaves she had written into publishable order. He wrote to Davidson, 'Miss Stoppard has told that you and she have tried your best to stop this publication of a memoir of John Brown. The Queen, however, is determined that it shall be done.' Lees concluded, 'It is a sad business altogether but we must make the best of it.' In August, Lees wrote to Davidson that if the book were ever published 'it will make a greater sensation' than *John Brown's Legs*. 'Her Majesty has a firm belief that John Brown was popular, with all the classes, and offered, when I ventured to doubt this, to lend me a volume of letters received at his death from the "highest in the land"... It is a most absurd fancy altogether, and I wish it would pass away. Her last message to me before I left Balmoral was "Tell Dr Lees that whether he likes it or not I am determined it shall be done!"' He added, rather ominously, that from the material already put into his hands by the Queen, he could have produced a more amusing brochure than *John Brown's Legs*. She was still 'determined' in November, though she was beginning to concede that there would be some advantage in keeping the memoir short.

Davidson had one last, brave try. He told the Queen that the *Leaves* from the journal already published had a good effect. 'To feel sympathy with human sorrow is good. To be the means of evoking such sympathy is a privilege which for more than twenty years has been Your Majesty's in no common measure, and the privilege, however sad a one, is a sacred power for good.' He warned her, however, that her grief for a husband, while being widely shared, was something different, in the eyes of 'the ordinary upper class newspapers', from her grief for Brown. 'I feel I should be wanting in my honest duty to Your Majesty who has honoured me with some measure of confidence were I not to refer to this, for Your Majesty's consideration, in connection with what Your Majesty in the same letter was good enough to tell me as to some further publication which Your Majesty has in contemplation.'

The Queen eventually snapped. She took offence at the dean's tone, and she ordered him through one of her ladies-in-waiting, Lady Ely, to withdraw his remarks and to apologize. Instead, Davidson offered his immediate resignation as dean.

A long silence followed. Then, he was sent for. He was received by his old friend. All was smiles, and the memoir was never mentioned again. It was, according to the son of Henry Ponsonby, quietly destroyed.[34]

This strange episode revealed, among other things, the Queen's resilient capacity to forgive, and even seemingly to forget, old grievances. Sandro Battenberg noted how warmly she received him – having believed him to be a Russian spy. Lord Carnarvon was in disgrace for resigning from the Cabinet over the Russo-Turkish War. Yet in 1884, the Queen asked him and his wife to dinner – 'just as if all the last six years had gone by and as if all cause for offence with me was entirely blotted out. She talked to Elsie [Lady Carnarvon] after dinner for a considerable time, & evidently with great kindness: about the children, and herself, and all kinds of people and things... It was a real personal pleasure to myself to feel that the Queen was completely reconciled to me: for the alienation of so much kindness to me in former years pained me. However the reconciliation was complete.'³⁵ In 1881, Ponsonby kept a score card of the rows between Gladstone and the Queen over events, some of which we remember, some of which are forgotten. '1. Candahar speech. She gave in. 2. Peers at Easter. He gave in. 3. Wolseley peerage. She will give in… IF 4. He will give in over the question of Wolseley continuing to serve as Quarter-Master General.'³⁶ Davidson was perhaps painting too rosy a picture when he wrote that she 'never' bore a grudge, but he was on the whole fair to say that she preferred those who, for the highest motives, 'occasionally incurred her wrath'.

No one, of course, incurred her wrath in quite the withering, scorching doses which she dished out to her children. Prince Leopold had recovered some points after his marriage to the charmingly dull Princess Helen, and produced a child – a healthy baby girl called Alice – whether after his late sister, or after his celebrated Oxford dancing-partner, Alice Liddell, who could say? Leopold had then slipped down a few notches in the League Table of royal favour when his mother had discovered that he had been making independent approaches to politicians for help in finding a useful occupation. Surely he was contented working as her secretary, writing letters, and doing light, ceremonial duties, such as laying the foundation stone of the Oxford High School for Girls?

Evidently, he was not. When rumours reached him that his brother-in-law Lord Lorne was thinking of resigning as Governor-General of Canada, Leopold wrote to the Colonial Secretary 'to implore you to appoint me as his successor'.³⁷ It was impossible to discuss the matter with his mother that year since she was entirely taken up with grief for Brown, and with her plans to write her Brown memoirs. Leopold's ambition to go to Canada was, nevertheless, somehow 'leaked', and became a subject of public debate in the press. Gladstone, in the House of Commons, pronounced the dictum that princes should be content to 'perform great decorative offices', leaving the real jobs to Government appointees. The radical *Reynolds's Newspaper* described

Leopold as a feeble-minded invalid who would not even be able to find Canada on a map.[38]

The next year, Leopold lowered his sights a little. He had formed what Queen Victoria would no doubt have considered a very undesirable friendship with Sir Charles Dilke, whom he had invited to Claremont. There he poured out his ambitions to do something useful, and told Dilke he had been writing to Lord Derby, Lord Granville and to Mr Gladstone, asking for some position in the colonies. His brother Arthur was serving in the army, Affie was in the navy, Bertie, sidelined as he was by the Queen, at least enjoyed the status of Prince of Wales; Leopold could surely be given something to do. He had heard that they were looking for a Governor of Victoria in Australia, and he asked Dilke if he could help. 'I believe you have been in Australia and are therefore a more competent judge than some others of the ministers as to the adviseability [sic] of my appointment.'[39]

Poor Leopold. He had not yet learned how the world worked. Charles Dilke mentioned it to Lord Derby, Lord Derby spoke to the Foreign Secretary, Lord Granville, who told the Prime Minister, who in turn told the Queen at their next audience. Leopold had not warned his royal mother, and there was, naturally, an eruption.

'Please, dear Mamma,' wrote Helen from Claremont, 'don't be angry with him!!! & do remember how very much he wishes for that post!'[40]

No doubt behind the Queen's wrath was the everlasting gnaw of worry about Leopold's condition. It was obvious to her, though not to him, why he would not have been suited to arduous administrative tasks. In fact, as spring advanced in 1884, he was feeling ill, with painful swelling in his joints, and the doctors advised a break from a fairly strenuous routine of royal duties – distributing certificates in Liverpool schools, presiding over the Windsor Tapestry Works, which had financial problems, and doing quite long hours with his mother's correspondence. He decided to go to the South of France, even though they said that Helen, pregnant again, could not accompany him, having suffered a previous miscarriage.

Cannes was one of his favourite places, and he wrote home excitedly to tell his wife he had decided to buy a plot of land at Golfe Juan, a little way along the coast, and there build a house for his family. On 24 March, he went to Nice for the Bachelors' Ball at the Club Méditerranée, planning to return to his wife and baby in Esher at the end of the week. There was to be a 'Battle of the Flowers' procession along the Promenade, and he rushed back to his room at the Cercle Nautique to change. He slipped on the stairs and knocked his right knee against the bottom step. 'Such pain it was!'[41] he wrote to Helen.

He died of a slow, painful haemorrhage. It was baffling to the press, and to almost everyone, who did not know of his condition. Bertie, who heard the news on Aintree racecourse, immediately wired his mother for permission to go to Cannes and bring the body home.

'The Queen is wonderfully calm,' wired Leopold's old governess. 'Her Majesty is gone to Claremont. It is too terrible.'[42] Victoria, at sixty-five, had now outlived two of her children.

When Sir Charles Dilke wrote a letter of condolence to the Queen, she responded with complete courtesy. 'She knows that you were a personal friend of the Duke of Albany who will feel his death.'[43] Except for moments during the period in the 1860s when she was mentally ill, and with the exception of the case of Gladstone, the Queen hardly ever displayed bad manners.

The calmness is so different from the operatic grief of 1861, yet more testimony of the fact that Victoria was, truly, an almost completely different woman from the person who had been married to Prince Albert. These years, which saw such extraordinary personal turmoil, with the loss of Brown and of her son, also witnessed some of her closest, and deftest, political involvement. If there was something a little icy in her immediate response to Dilke's expressions of sympathy, it perhaps had less to do with his raffish way of life and his friendship with Bertie, and more to do with his political radicalism.

1884 was another milestone in the journey Britain was making from the aristocratic oligarchy of pre-1832 to the parliamentary democracy and universal suffrage extended by the Representation of the People Act of 1928. The 1884 Franchise Act did not pass, however, without a major clash between the House of Commons and the House of Lords and here, as in the controversy over the disestablishment of the Irish Church, the Queen played a vital role in defusing the political heat.

The 1867 Reform Act had created a two-tier voting system. Those urban voters who lived in boroughs now had the vote, if they were householders. Rural voters, however, remained in effect feudalized; they had to accept the candidates imposed upon them by their landlords, invariably aristocratic, though not always Tory. The radicals had been campaigning for at least a decade to remove this anomaly, and the Whiggish Lord Hartington had, in principle, accepted their point.

By 1884, the unquestioned leader of the radicals in the House of Commons was the Birmingham firebrand Joseph Chamberlain, who was not some wild-eyed backbencher, but President of the Board of Trade in Gladstone's Cabinet. He wanted to fight a class war, not a merely technical point of voting procedure. There were plenty of peers, Whig and Tory, would have agreed with Chamberlain that there was indeed a class war in progress. If the lower and middle orders of society were given voting power, and executive power, this could only have the effect of diminishing the inherited power of the peers. Lord Salisbury, the Leader of the Conservatives, moved that the Commons should be asked to accept a Redistribution Bill, by which the boundaries of the constituencies should be redrawn. He reckoned that there would be so many squabbles at local level about the exact make-up of the constituencies that both the Redistribution Bill and the Franchise Bill would founder. Gladstone would not hear of this, and insisted that the Lords pass a Bill which had been unambiguously passed through the Commons.

Salisbury knew that he was only playing for time. He was a man of prodigious intelligence and political skill. The fact that he knew his viewpoint was doomed to defeat, however, did not make him adopt a different opinion. He still believed, as he had written a quarter of a century earlier in *Bentley's Quarterly Review*, that 'The classes that represent civilisation... have a right to require securities to protect them from being overwhelmed by hordes who have neither knowledge to guide them nor stake in the Commonwealth to control them'.

Chamberlain had eloquently put the other side of the argument, not only in his parliamentary speeches, but to rallies in Birmingham which drew thousands. 'Lord Salisbury constitutes himself the spokesman of a class – of the class to which he himself belongs, who toil not neither do they spin; whose fortunes – as in his case – have originated by grants made in times gone by for the services which courtiers rendered kings, and have since grown and increased, while they have slept, by levying an increased share on all that other men have done by toil and labour to add to the general wealth and prosperity of the country.'[44] One of the things which makes the next fifteen years some of the most interesting in the entire history of British politics is that these two men, Salisbury and Chamberlain, would find themselves in the same party, with Chamberlain serving in Salisbury's Cabinet as Colonial Secretary. They came together over the great issues of Ireland and the Empire. Salisbury, whose family had been exercising power since his great ancestor William Cecil was the secretary (in effect Prime Minister) to Queen Elizabeth I, was past master at the manipulation of power. He had no doubts, however, about the direction in which the Franchise Act of 1884 was leading. As he wrote to the Queen, Gladstone and Chamberlain 'insist that the House of Lords has no right to say that it will not pass the Franchise Bill till a Redistribution Bill accompanies it, and they do so on the ground that the Franchise Bill has been sanctioned by certain popular demonstrations. This doctrine, if accepted, would reduce the House of Lords to impotence.'[45] He was of course right, and almost all subsequent history of the hereditary peerage in power, including the Peerage Act of 1911–2, and concluding with the virtual exclusion of hereditary peers from the Second Chamber by Tony

Blair, has been a series of footnotes to this observation. But in 1884, the peers were still technically entitled to block legislation coming up from the Commons, even if it had overwhelming popular backing.

The Queen intervened in this crisis, begging the Liberals to offer the Conservatives some room for manoeuvre, some compromise. Ponsonby, his sympathies with the radicals, looked on with some excitement. The whole incident put him in mind of the moment in Livy's Roman Histories when the Samnites lured the Romans into a mountain pass called the Caudine Forks. They had the chance of massacring the Romans, but honour made them magnanimous. The release of the Romans was, if anything, more humiliating. 'Who now holds the Caudine Forks?' asked Ponsonby excitedly. 'Will they make the same mistake as the Samnites and take a middle course? Those who passed the Caudine Forks won, but not with honor [sic]. I hope neither party will break their faith as the Romans did.'[46] In a sense, it was the Tories who were humiliated by the experience. The Queen persuaded Gladstone to accept a Redistribution Bill at the same time as the Franchise Bill. (Gladstone was happy with that, reckoning it would give him eighty Home Rulers at the next election.) But when Salisbury went to the panting heart of Conservative London, the Carlton Club, to announce the settlement, Lord John Manners, a High Tory of High Tories, merely rolled his eyes in disbelief.

Gladstone told the Queen that many Liberals objected to the party leaders quietly settling so grave a dispute in secret. It was a bad precedent. Victoria, by contrast, believed it was 'a good precedent to avert serious dangers so much desired by Radicals and Republicans'.[47] Salisbury felt he could have achieved greater things if the Queen had allowed him to fight. She retorted, 'But at what a price!'[48] She was keenly aware of what lay behind Lord Salisbury's argument. If the aristocracy were rejected, then the hereditary principle was rejected; and if that was the case, where did it leave the hereditary monarchy?

TWENTY ONE

'AN INFLAMMATORY ATMOSPHERE'

L OVE WAS IN the air, and the Queen's grandchildren were reaching an age when they could be married. Only a month after the death of Prince Leopold, the daughter of Princess Alice – Victoria of Hesse – was to be married to Prince Louis of Battenberg. Though the Queen regarded herself as 'a poor desolate old woman' whose 'cup of sorrow overflows',[1] she was not willing to pass up what promised to be a gala-gathering of her descendants and German cousins. Far-flung relations from all over Germany and Russia were converging on Darmstadt. The little town was adorned with bunting. A substantial contingent of the Prussian Royal Family came over from Berlin – Vicky, Fritz and Willy were the star turns here, even though Willy was feeling estranged from his liberal parents, and furious with the House of Hesse for allowing Ella to marry the Grand Duke Sergei of Russia. Sergei was himself at the wedding, with several other Russian royalties. The Prince of Wales came, and the Grand Duke, Louis, his brother-in-law, Alice's widower, was waiting at the railway station to greet them all.

None was grander or more powerful, perhaps, than the matriarch herself, the little Queen Empress, who strode down the red carpet, her limp more or less cured, accompanied by her entourage of ladies – Lady Ely and the faithful Baby among them.

The presence of so many illustrious royalties in the town at once enabled the grand duke to put on a magnificent few days of ceremonial. There was a confirmation in the church, a royal baptism and several military parades. After his daughter had been married to Louis Battenberg, they all crowded into the glorious Kaisersaal for the wedding banquet. The Crown Prince of Prussia proposed the health of the bridal pair, and the grand duke mysteriously slipped away.

He had a most dramatic secret. Having informed his children and sworn them all to total secrecy, he went to a room in the Schloss where there was waiting for him his Prime Minister, Starck, and the divorced spouse of a fomer Russian Chargé d'Affaires, the Countess Alexandrine Hutten-Czapska, usually known by her maiden name of Madame de Kolémine.

Starck now married the grand duke to Madame de Kolémine before two witnesses.

It is difficult to imagine worse timing, and no one ever quite understood what the grand duke thought he was playing at. Madame de Kolémine, as a divorcee and a commoner, could not be the grand duchess; it was a morganatic marriage. Even so, the choice of his own daughter's wedding day to ratify his union was about as tactless as possible. Rather pathetically, he said that he 'could hardly bear the thought of further loneliness in his life' when his daughter married and 'left him'.[2] He had not reckoned on the near-absolute power – at any rate in the family, if not in her own kingdom – exercised by his former mother-in-law, the Queen Empress.

Naturally, the secret was out within hours. Vicky told Bertie and they were then confronted with the appalling dilemma: who was to break the news to Queen Victoria that, on the day of her granddaughter's wedding, her beloved daughter's clumsy husband had contracted this ridiculous liaison?

With conspicuous lack of gallantry, Vicky and Bertie asked Lady Ely to be the bearer of the bad news. The Queen took it calmly. There was no explosion, but there was a demonstration of her steel. She summoned Bertie and told him to interview the lady at once. Madame de Kolémine was to be told that her marriage was to be annulled. The Prussian royals were sent back to Berlin that day and the Russians left very soon thereafter. The bunting hung limply from the lamp posts of the deserted Darmstadt streets. The party ended, and Victoria and her group returned to Britain. Within a month, her former librarian and German secretary at Osborne, Hermann Sahl, was writing to her, 'You will be glad to hear that <u>substantially</u> the untieing of the morganatic knot is now accomplished, and by degrees the formal severance will be pronounced by a Court of Law convened for this purpose. Diplomatists and Lawyers are never embarrassed about finding a suitable <u>form</u> – as soon as they have secured a convergence of views and aims in <u>substance</u>.'[3] The unfortunate lady, Madame de Kolémine, or whatever you choose to call her, lived deep into the twentieth century; she was last heard of in Paris in 1930 but was thought to have died in 1941.[4] The *Daily News* described her as 'one of the most beautiful and highly-accomplished women of her time' and Lady Ely concluded that she was 'depraved and scheming'.[5] She could, of course, have been all these things.

One surprising development, after the Hessian wedding farce, was that Princess Beatrice, Baby, decided that she did not want to spend the rest of her days as the celibate companion of a widowed, ageing Queen. The lucky man was Prince Heinrich von Battenberg, as he continued to print his name on his visiting card.[6] He was the brother of the bridegroom at that wedding, Louis of Battenberg. 'The young people fell in love at Darmstadt,' reported the satirical Lord Carlingford, 'an inflammatory atmosphere, it seems.'[7] Queen Victoria was enraged by what she considered to be Baby's selfishness. For seven months, though the two women lived side by side, she addressed no word to her youngest daughter. Communication was by note, pushed across the table, with eyes averted. In December, however, the mother relented, provided the young people accepted her terms. 'Liko', Prince Heinrich – from now on to be known as Prince Henry of Battenberg – must give up his career in the German Army and come to live in England.[8] Baby must continue to be in constant attendance on the Queen. These terms were accepted. The young couple had no choice, since Beatrice's mother held the purse strings. 'And now [the Queen] seems very happy about the thing. They are to live entirely with her...' Perhaps unkindly, for few would have regarded the boring Henry of Battenberg as much of a catch, Carlingford added, 'the princess seems to have done pretty well'.[9]

The Prussian Royal Family were snobs about the marriage, and the Empress wrote a fussy letter to Queen Victoria, pointing out that the Battenbergs were only the product of a morganatic union, their father Prince Alexander having married the Countess von Hauke. (For this reason, although Queen Victoria granted Prince Henry the title of HRH there were many German royalties who refused to use it.[10]) With robust common sense, Queen Victoria told the German Empress that 'morganatic marriages were unknown in England and if a King chose to marry a peasant girl she would be Queen just as much as any princess'.[11] The pair were to produce four children – Drino, or Alexander, Marquess of Carisbrooke, who lived until 1960; Queen Ena of Spain, the grandmother of King Juan Carlos, who lived until 1969; Leopold, who volunteered for service in the King's Royal Rifle Corps and died in 1922; and Maurice, who gallantly joined the King's Royal Fusiliers and died at Ypres in 1914. The latter two brothers were both haemophiliacs, Beatrice being a carrier, as was her daughter Queen Ena, who passed on the condition to two of her sons, Alfonso and Gonzalo.

Tennyson was commissioned to pen a nuptial ode for the pair, who were married at Whippingham Parish Church in July 1885. The Queen explained that 'Dear Beatrice will live with me as heretofore, without which I never could have allowed the marriage.'[12] Tennyson incorporated this unusual theme into his ode:

> The Mother weeps
> At that white funeral of the single life...
> but Thou,
> True daughter, whose all-faithful filial eyes
> Have seen the loneliness of earthly thrones,

> Wilt neither quit the widow'd Crown, nor let
> This later light of Love have risen in vain...[13]

As she began her married life, Princess Beatrice must have regretted the demise of Brown. The marriage would appear to have been a success and her mother showed none of the snobbery felt about the Battenbergs by the German Emperor and his family. When Vicky's daughter Victoria of Prussia became attached to Prince Sandro of Bulgaria, Henry of Battenberg's brother, there was great curling of lips among the Hohenzollerns. In the event, it was Sandro who broke this betrothal, when he fell in love with an opera singer, Johanna Loisinger. He gave up public life, retired from his position as the ruler of Bulgaria and was granted the title 'Count Hartenau'. The occasion provided a nice example of Queen Victoria's complete unpredictability. Rather than expressing shock at Sandro's behaviour, she said, 'Perhaps they love one another.'[14]

Much as her domestic happiness depended upon the companionship of Princess Beatrice, however, and fascinated as she was by the continuing soap opera of European royalties, their amours and demises, the Queen was deeply preoccupied by events in North Africa and in Ireland.

The situation in Egypt and in the Sudan had reached a crisis point. When Gladstone and the Liberals took office, they found themselves responsible for implementing a foreign policy with which they completely disagreed. In South Africa, for instance, the Conservative Government had pursued an aggressive anti-Boer policy, in an attempt to annex the Transvaal. Gladstone did not believe in the annexation, and made every effort to withdraw. In the event, they were left with the precarious compromise of an independent Transvaal, subject to British suzerainty. In Afghanistan, the Liberals decided upon an instant withdrawal (this was what had provoked Beaconsfield's last speech denouncing the withdrawal from Kandahar). In Egypt, things were less simple, not least because the khedives had run up such colossal debts to European creditors. When Khedive Ismail suspended payment, the Four Powers – France, Britain, Italy and Austria-Hungary – put pressure on the sultan to withdraw the khedive and replace him with his son Tewfik. The new khedive's difficulties spiralled out of control after only a few years. He was unable to pay his army, which led to a mutiny. Colonel Arabi Pasha, an Egyptian, not a Turk, roused nationalist feeling both against the Turkish control of Egypt and against European, especially British, interference in Egyptian affairs. In 1881, Arabi had surrounded the royal palace and demanded the dismissal of all the Cabinet, and an increase in the army from 4,000 to 18,000 men.

Many members of the Liberal Party in Britain sympathized with Arabi and thought of his nationalist aspirations as on a par with those of the Bulgarians or the Irish, but the unrest was turning into anarchy, and in 1882, Gladstone, a third of whose personal share portfolio consisted of Egyptian stock, had taken the decision to send in British troops, headed by Sir Garnet Wolseley to keep order, to maintain Khedive Tewfik on his throne, and, if necessary, to keep down both mutinies in the army in and around Cairo, and Islamist uprisings in other parts of North Africa. The poor tenements of Alexandria were bombarded by the Royal Navy. Charles Dilke, Colonial Secretary, remarked, 'The bombardment of Alexandria, like all butchery, is popular...'

By 1883, the Government had decided that it wished to withdraw British troops. Sir Evelyn Baring, who was working as an assistant to Lord Ripon, Viceroy of India, was ordered to Cairo, with the rather nebulous rank of consul general. His task was to reorganize the Egyptian administration, and British withdrawal. The financial expertise of this scion of the famous banking family was also thought to have been useful in what remained, *au fond*, a financial crisis. Baring believed that 'there remains nothing in the area of fiscal reform that can't be done by the Egyptians themselves'.[15] The mutinies and rebellions were, patently, all directly the consequence of the khedive's being on the edge of bankruptcy. Far from being able to settle the matter in a few months and then return to London, Baring was to stay for twenty-three years, and the British presence in Egypt lasted until 1956.

Baring recognized, after a very short time in Egypt, that the British were more deeply embedded than the London Government had allowed themselves to realize. In one area, however, he saw the chance for the British to loosen their hold: in the Sudan.

A rebellion against Egyptian rule had been raised by the religious leader Muhammad Ahmad, known as the Mahdi, a charismatic figure who wished to establish the rule of sharia law against the secularism of the invader. The Egyptians had sent a well-trained army out against him, under the command of a retired British officer, Colonel Hicks. Despite being a smaller army with less armament or equipment, Ahmad was able to defeat – entirely to wipe out – Colonel Hicks's army. The Islamists had now occupied the town of Berber, some 250 miles to the west of Cairo, and they had spread their strength to the Red Sea coast – it looked as if there was nothing to stop them marching on Cairo. Baring saw trouble, and warned the Government at home to get out of the Sudan rather than suffer humiliation. He recommended that the Egyptians abandon their claim to territory south of Aswan and for British troops to withdraw completely from the Sudan. It would be a vast undertaking. Over 21,000 troops were occupying the Egyptian garrisons in the Sudan, and they were accompanied by 11,000 civilians. Baring's inclination was to send Egyptians to carry out the withdrawal, but the new Egyptian Government believed there was a danger, if this happened, of the Egyptian Army being carried away by the Mahdi's rhetoric. It would be better, they argued, for the evacuation to be conducted by a British officer.

The name which emerged, much to Baring's distaste, was that of General Charles Gordon. He felt forced into accepting Gordon because 'English public opinion seemed to be unanimous on the subject'.[16] Baring's worries about Gordon were understandable.

His private notes reveal that he believed Gordon to be a drunken fanatic, hovering 'between sanity and insanity'. One manifestation of his unbalanced state of mind was his habit of speeding round London by taxi on Sunday mornings, taking Holy Communion over and over again at different churches. His religious interests had led him to discover what he believed to be the authentic tomb of Christ in Jerusalem, just underneath a rock whose features do indeed remarkably resemble a skull. He rose to fame in China for his part in suppressing the Taiping rebels against the forces of their emperor. He accomplished his Chinese triumphs when he was barely thirty years old. Thereafter, he had very grand ideas of himself. It was Gordon who had established British dominance in the Sudan in the late 1870s – hence his sobriquet, Gordon of Khartoum. By the time he left Khartoum, he had covered 8,500 miles by camel. He had subsequently offered his services to the King of the Belgians, suggesting the King should place him in charge of the Congo Free State. And now he was chosen by the Government to solve the crisis in the Sudan. He was seen off by a deferential Foreign Secretary, Lord Granville, who actually bought his ticket for him at Charing Cross Station, with the Duke of Cambridge in attendance. Queen Victoria followed all subsequent events with the closest interest. Like the Great British public, she idolized the hero of Shanghai and Khartoum, and believed that 'General Gordon is a most extraordinary man and certainly has a wonderful power over these half savages'.[17]

Gordon stopped off at Cairo to discuss his brief with the khedive, with Nubar, the Egyptian Prime Minister, and with Baring. He asked them for two firmans, which he carried away with him: one confirmed his position as Governor-General of Sudan, the other announced the policy of total evacuation. He believed that it would be possible to persuade the Mahdi to help him in his plans, and that he would leave the Sudan in the hands of the Sudanese. He reached Berber by steamer in February 1884, and there he dismissed all his Egyptian troops and officials. In doing so, he also made public the firman stating that he had come to arrange the evacuation of troops from the Sudan.

Most historians now agree that this was Gordon's fatal error. Far from rallying to him as to a saviour, the Islamist rebels and the Mahdi himself now believed that there was nothing to stop them taking over the Sudan. By the time Gordon reached Khartoum, far from greeting him with enthusiasm, the local sheikhs were all dithering about whether to accept him at all, or whether to join forces with the Mahdi. Moreover, when he wired London to tell them to accept Abd-al-Rahman Munir Zubayr as the new Governor of Sudan, they refused to accept this. Many of Gordon's telegrams, either to Baring in Cairo or to London, were self-contradictory.

The Government told Gordon to hang on in the Sudan until the summer, when they would send in military reinforcements. It now became apparent, however, that this might be extremely difficult. Baring begged the Government not to wait, and the Queen added her voice to his: 'Sir E. Baring is evidently <u>not</u> pleased at what the Queen must call the miserable, weak and too late action of the government.'[18]

Gordon was now trapped in Khartoum, in an extremely volatile situation, without Egyptian troops, without British troops, and without the native Sudanese support which he had arrogantly assumed would be the natural consequence of his reappearance in that city. Baring, who was ill, was summoned back to London to give Gladstone and the Foreign Secretary advice. He took the chance, while there, to spell out to them the dire financial straits of the Egyptian Government, and to urge them to join forces with the French in securing further international loans.

They had a short conference with the French during July and decided they should try to force the Egyptians to accept international financiers as the controllers of Egypt's exchequer. The sums involved were enormous, and the British Government was appalled to discover that Baring had all but committed them to lending the Egyptians £8.7 million to pay off current debts and to invest in new irrigation schemes.[19]

Gordon, meanwhile, was still in Khartoum. Far too late, the Government and Baring realized they needed to rescue him, and they dispatched a relief expedition, headed by Sir Garnet Wolseley. The Nile floods had crested and water levels were beginning to fall. The Mahdi had reached Khartoum. On New Year's Day 1885, Baring received a message, dated 14 December, which was written on a piece of paper the size of a postage stamp. It read: 'Khartoum all right. G. C. Gordon.' Baring telegraphed Gordon telling him to abandon the city and make a dash for it across the desert from Suakin. Gordon refused. He had already written, 'Now MARK THIS, if the expedition… does not come in ten days, the Town Hall May Fall and I have done my best for the honour of our country. Goodbye. G. C. Gordon.' On 26 January 1885, the Mahdi's soldiers burst into the palace in Khartoum and speared Gordon to death. The rescue party began to arrive a few days later. On the night that this modern hero suffered martyrdom, when rumours were already flying round that Gordon might be dead, Gladstone had gone to the theatre in London to watch a play called *The Candidate* – 'capitally acted', as he told his journal.

The Queen was understandably angry. It did, apart from the tragedy of the thing, make the British look so incompetent. Before the fate of Gordon had become clear, she sent telegrams to Gladstone, Granville and Hartington, and she sent them *en clair*, that is uncoded and open for any village postmistress to read. Gladstone was handed his stinker by the station master at Carnforth, the Lancastrian railway station later to be made famous as the setting for Noël Coward's film, *Brief Encounter*. 'These news from Khartoum are frightful and to think that all this might have been prevented and many precious lives saved by earlier action is too frightful.'²⁰

It was a calculated insult and one which openly and deliberately lined up the monarchy with the public against the Government. 'The country will be furious,' she told Ponsonby, 'and we are bound to show a bold front.'²¹

Gladstone was indignant and humiliated, knowing himself to be so deeply in the wrong, and considered resignation on the spot. He might well have resigned, would such an action not have scuppered all his aspirations for Ireland. He wrote the Queen a very long letter, dated

5 February 1885, which missed the point entirely. Huffing and puffing, and weighing up General Wolseley's chances of relieving Khartoum, Gladstone failed to address the nub of the question: namely his personal responsibility for the fate of Gordon. He and his Foreign Secretary had reacted too late to the situation and failed to send the relief in time. These exchanges, between the sovereign and her Prime Minister, took place at a time when they were all still hoping against hope that Gordon might be rescued. By the time the truth was known, that Gordon was dead, and that Wolseley was asking to be made Governor-General of the Sudan until the situation was brought under control, the Government was still dithering, and still unable to decide whether Wolseley was the right man for the job. 'The Queen laments this want of decision and firmness in the Government,' she told Gladstone, 'which gives her the greatest anxiety for the future.'[22]

Something extraordinary had happened. The monarchy had not gained in executive power. But it had naturally associated itself with 'popular opinion' against the political class. The Queen hammered home what she perceived to be an advantage. Moreover, Victoria herself had changed very much indeed. Whereas in Gladstone's first administration, in 1868 onwards, the problem for the Prime Minister had been how to coax the hermit-constitutional monarch out of her seclusion to play a part in national affairs, now in his second administration, the problem seemed to be how to shut her up. Whereas during his first Government, private grief seemed to overwhelm any sense of her public duty, in this period of life worry about public affairs appeared to overshadow private grief. At a dinner in Windsor Castle, Mrs Gladstone lamented to the Queen 'over all the trouble and anxiety' Victoria had had. Mrs Gladstone was referring, surely, not only to events in the Sudan, but also to such things as the deaths of the Queen's favourite servant and of her son so comparatively recently. 'I told Mrs Gladstone... that I should have been far less distressed had I felt that the right thing had been done, which would have prevented all this, and she shook her head, saying she hoped not, whereon I told her I was sure of it.'[23]

Granville and Gladstone found the Queen's attitude so tiresome that they simply ignored her, and failed to tell her what was going on over the next couple of months. While Wolseley was waiting at Suakin to hear from them whether he should reconquer Khartoum, news came from Afghanistan. The Russians had attacked and defeated an Afghan force on the Afghan–Turcoman border at Penjdeh.

The Queen was holidaying at the time in Aix-les-Bains, but as 'Countess of Balmoral', she sent a telegram to Gladstone from her hotel: 'IS IT DIGNIFIED THAT BRITISH COMMISSION SHOULD REMAIN IN THE AFGHAN BOUNDARY ANY LONGER?'[24] For some days it looked possible that there might be war over the matter. Granville, with Gladstone's backing, made a double decision – to withdraw any commitments in the Sudan, and to commit £11 million to the defence of the Zulfikar Pass and access to British India. Neither of these decisions were reported to the Queen until they were *faits accomplis*. 'I hope you will not give way to pressure from St Petersburgh,' she wrote to Gladstone,[25] and she professed herself 'greatly agitated. Directly after breakfast saw Major Edwards & asked him to go & tell Bertie to remonstrate with Lord Hartington for his neglect of duty, which has been repeated again & again.'[26] Writing to Wolseley direct, she said, 'Altogether the Queen's heart is sorely troubled for her brave soldiers… Our soldiers <u>fight</u> and have on every single occasion in this exceptionally trying campaign <u>fought like heroes</u> individually, and she hopes <u>he</u> will tell them so from the highest to the lowest from her.'[27] In the event, the problem of the Mahdi was solved by unforeseen means. He died in June 1885, and his successor, lacking his hypnotic power over the masses or his military panache, was easily defeated at Ginnis by a mixture of Egyptian and English forces. The threat of an invasion of Egypt by religious fundamentalists was averted.

But if the wars and rumours of war in the Sudan and in Afghanistan revealed a gulf between the Liberal Government and the monarch, this was nothing compared with their difference over the Irish Question. It was Ireland and its future which dominated the political life of the nation for the next year, a period which has been described as the most dramatic in English party history. What was being debated was nothing less than the future of Britain – whether Ireland would be able to break away from the dominance of the Westminster Parliament. Home Rule was not total independence, but it would have satisfied the majority of the Irish. History would have been very different had Gladstone and Parnell successfully passed it through Parliament. Probably, there was never a chance of doing so, partly because of the entrenched views of the Ulster Protestants, and partly because these views were so forcefully echoed, not only by Lord Salisbury and the Conservatives, but also by a substantial number of Gladstone's own political allies.

In June, at about the time that the Mahdi was dying in the Sudan, and about a month before Princess Beatrice married Prince Henry on the Isle of Wight, the Government suffered an unexpected defeat. They proposed to increase beer and spirit duties. The vote divided 264 to 252, Gladstone resigned as Prime Minister, and the Queen summoned Lord Salisbury to Balmoral, and asked him to form a minority administration. (Minority, because the House also contained all the Parnellite Irish members.) He was the first Prime Minister for seventeen years not to have been called either Disraeli or Gladstone. Fifty-five years old, compared with Gladstone's now seventy-seven, Salisbury was a huge man, eighteen stone in weight, well over six feet tall, with a high domed bald head bursting with knowledge and a thick bushy beard. He was a natural pessimist, and he was also extraordinarily astute politically. He had hesitated for a long time before he accepted the Queen's request; and while he was staying with her at Balmoral, they had actually sent Gladstone a wire, which was refused, begging him to reconsider his resignation. One reason for this was that the Queen was very anxious not to disrupt her holiday; Deeside is at its most beautiful in June. Salisbury, for his part, had mixed feelings about presiding over a Britain which was in political chaos. As the Queen put it in a letter to Gladstone from Balmoral, 'We are near the middle of the stream at the moment – and a change of horses would be a very difficult operation.'[28] He and most of his new Cabinet (the largest in British history, with sixteen members) went to Windsor and kissed hands on 24 June. They were to exercise what was, in effect, a 'caretaker' ministry.

For all his appearance of aristocratic disdain for what was going on around him, Salisbury worked hard, often a fourteen-hour day.[29] Much of his time was spent trying to disentangle the mess left by the Liberals in foreign affairs. He said that the Liberal Government had 'achieved their desired Concert of Europe, they have succeeded in uniting the continent of Europe – against England'.[30] The principal crisis of this short period in office was in Bulgaria. There was a revolution in Philippopolis (now Plovdiv), the capital of Eastern Roumelia. The Turkish Governor-General was expelled and the Bulgarian populace asked Alexander Battenberg – Sandro, Princess Beatrice's brother-in-law – to be ruler of both the formally divided halves of Bulgaria.

Serbia then mobilized against Bulgaria, and it looked as if there was going to be another outbreak of war in the Balkans, with the Russians threatening Sandro, and the British in danger of being drawn into a war, which Salisbury definitely did not want, with Russia.

Sandro, who had fought alongside the Russians in the last Russo-Turkish War, detested his cousin Tsar Alexander III and looked to Britain to defend a 'Big Bulgaria' against the partitioned, truncated Bulgaria favoured by the Russians. Queen Victoria, who had regarded Sandro as a Russian spy when he had lunch with Affie back in 1878, during the Treaty of San Stefano, now saw him as 'poor Sandro', 'dear Sandro', a Sandro and a Bulgaria to be defended at all costs. Salisbury complained to Henry Manners, 'Balmoral has got a telegraphing fit on just now, which is a great aggravation to the trials of life.'[31] The Serbs invaded Bulgaria on 13 November and were roundly defeated in battle by Sandro and his troops a week later at Slivinitza: news, which in the Queen's view, would rejoice the hearts of 'all right-minded people and all who are not under the influence of Russia'.[32]

But the Bulgarian crisis would last longer than Salisbury's caretaker ministry. He stayed in office until January 1886 to oversee the next stage of events in Bulgaria, but he had already been defeated in a General Election, having held office for only five months.

The election had been called in November, and it was the first since the Franchise Act of 1884. There were therefore 2 million extra voters, and Gladstone had been sure that this would work to his advantage. But this was a truth much complicated by the Irish Question, which now dominated both the large islands facing one another across St George's Channel.

The dominant Irish politician was Charles Stewart Parnell, campaigning for Home Rule. This was nothing so radical as wishing for a Republic of Ireland or a complete severance between Ireland and the rest of Britain. What Parnell proposed was a Parliament for the Irish, in which they could largely determine their own affairs; over the question of foreign policy, there was room for manoeuvre and discussion with the politicians of Westminster. One of the first converts to the idea of Home Rule among English politicians was the Tory viceroy, Lord Carnarvon. He was a great resigner, and realizing that he was out of kilter with Lord Salisbury over this issue, he resigned. He had come to the conclusion that Parnell was 'singularly moderate'.[33]

The real political bombshell, however, was Gladstone's overt espousal of the cause of Irish Home Rule. Carnarvon's views were expressed privately to the Prime Minister, and there was no possibility that the Conservative Party would ever, at this juncture, have adopted them. They went against all Salisbury's Unionist notions, besides which Salisbury could see, as a pragmatist, that it would be impossible to persuade the Orange Lodges and the Ulster Unionists to accept the idea. For them, 'Home Rule is Rome Rule'.

16. *Above:* Princess Beatrice (Baby) and her mother in the library.

17. *Left:* The Queen with her grandchildren Prince Arthur and Princess Margaret of Connaught.

18. 19th April 1894 at the marriage of Ernest Louis, Grand Duke of Hesse and Victoria Melita of Saxe-Coburg. Five of the Queen's children, ten grandchildren and one great grandchild may be seen. The German Emperor (Wilhelm II) sits in the foreground in front of the Russian Emperor.

19. Four great Prime Ministers (clockwise, from top left): Palmerston, Disraeli –
perhaps her favourite, Salisbury, and her bête noir W. E. Gladstone pictured with
his axe at the root of the old order.

20. Victoria resplendent with a fur stole.

21. George Duke of Cambridge, always a trusted friend and cousin.

22. Her brilliant secretary, Sir Henry Ponsonby.

23. Her last doctor, Sir James Reid.

24. Dr Norman Macleod – did he perform a marriage service at Balmoral for the Queen and John Brown?

25. Four generations – Queen Victoria, Edward VII, George V and Edward VIII.

26. *Below:* Always a keen dog-lover, Victoria is here pictured with her Pomeranian, Turi, outside one of the continental hotels where she liked to stay.

27. *Above:* John Brown with another of the Queen's dogs.

28. The Queen with Abdul Karim, the 'Munshi', her last favourite.

29. Ponsonby, the 'Munshi', Princess Beatrice and others enacting a tableau of 'The Queen of Sheba'.

30. The Queen's bedroom at Osborne, where she died, being held by the German Emperor. The room still possesses an electrifying atmosphere of her presence.

31. In this late photograph may be seen the passion, caprice, vulnerability and humour that Queen Victoria retained from early childhood.

The General Election was fought in the closing weeks of November. Quite apart from Ireland, the Liberals were bitterly divided over the whole question of radicalism, Whigs such as Lord Hartington being quite unable to accept the radical proposals of candidates such as Joseph Chamberlain, who wanted to disestablish the Church of England, have free education for all, and reform the law relating to land ownership and rentals. But in spite of these divisions, the Liberals won by a substantial majority: 334 Liberal seats, with 86 Home Rulers, as opposed to a mere 250 Conservatives. 'The elections not good, though there are some striking Conservative victories,' the Queen told her journal.[34]

But then came the phenomenon known as the Hawarden Kite. With the Liberals in office, and the Grand Old Man as Prime Minister for the third time, Gladstone let it be known that, rather than simply being friendly towards the cause of Parnell, he was now a convert to the cause of Home Rule, and intended it to be the chief aim of his administration to bring it to pass.

He flew this 'kite' in the most extraordinary way – not by making a speech, or by telling the House of Commons, but by allowing his son Herbert to write a letter to *The Times*. It was written from Hawarden Castle, Mrs Gladstone's seat: 'Nothing would induce me to countenance separation, but if five-sixths of the Irish people wish to have a Parliament in Dublin, for the management of their own local affairs, I say, in the name of justice, and wisdom, let them have it.'[35]

This 'kite', flown into the air so casually, changed the skyline of British politics for a generation. When offering men places in his new Cabinet, Gladstone gave them a short memorandum, telling them of his decision to set up 'a legislative body to sit in Dublin and to deal with Irish as distinguished from imperial affairs'.[36]

John Morley, one day to become Gladstone's biographer, became Irish Secretary. His views had been no secret for a long time: he had advocated Ireland being given the same status as Canada or Australia, self-governing within the imperial umbrella. The complexion of the Liberal Party was changed completely by the alchemy of Home

Rule. Whereas over questions such as education and land reform the radicals and the old-fashioned Whigs were poles apart, over the Irish Question, Whigs like Harty Tarty and moderate Liberals such as Goschen found themselves to be the allies of radicals like Chamberlain and G. O. Trevelyan, who were rigidly Unionist. The new Government proposed two Irish Bills, one for dissolving the Act of Union, and another for creating an Irish assembly. Trevelyan and Chamberlain immediately resigned from the Cabinet.

The Queen watched the Government's discomfiture with a certain quiet satisfaction. She wrote to Vicky from Windsor Castle, 'Mr Gladstone only thinks of Irish affairs and nothing else. We have just heard Liszt who is such a fine old man. He came down here and played four pieces beautifully. What an exquisite touch.'[37]

On 8 April, the day after the Abbé Liszt had so delighted his Windsor audience, Gladstone presented his Home Rule Bill to the House of Commons. It was one of the most dramatic days in the history of Parliament, as decisive a moment in party politics as had been Peel's brave decision, in 1846, to abolish the tariffs on corn and thereby splinter the Conservative Party. Instantaneously, Gladstone lost Liberal mainstays such as Goschen and Hartington, as well as the radicals Chamberlain and Trevelyan. On 14 April, on the stage of the old Opera House in the Haymarket, there was a Unionist rally, where Lord Hartington and Goschen appeared on the same platform as Salisbury and W. H. Smith, a Conservative MP and grandson of the founder of the stationer's. Chamberlain, not yet ready to be seen in such company, organized a smaller group of radical Unionists – though he seemed to be in very great confusion about what sort of government he wanted for Ireland, switching from one day to the next from some sort of British 'federation' to thinking that Ireland might enjoy a status comparable to that of Canada.[38] From a narrowly political viewpoint, in terms of the interest of the Liberal Party, Gladstone seemed to have led his party over a cliff. One writer compared Gladstone to a desperate pirate burning his ship.[39] No wonder, at Hatfield, that the Cecils had the joke that the initials G.O.M. (Grand Old Man) stood for 'God's Only Mistake'. 'We hope to succeed in smashing the old lunatic,' wrote Lady Salisbury on 19 April.[40] As his seventy-seventh birthday approached, Gladstone became seriously worried that there would be no guests. It had been his custom to entertain the Prince of Wales on his birthday, but this year, he was afraid of asking Bertie and his son for fear that they would be compromised by seeming thereby to support Home Rule. The Duke of Argyll had already refused his invitation, and Gladstone feared that if he did ask the prince, Bertie would come into a room and find it empty, having expected to meet the peerage. In the event, Gladstone need not have worried. Bertie stayed away, but there were plenty of guests and Prince Albert Victor (Eddy) came and was, according to Gladstone, 'most kind'.[41]

For Gladstone, it was a matter of simple principle, and, as it was on the other side of the political divide for Lord Carnarvon, principle was not purely theoretical. If Home Rule would please the great majority of the Irish people, and bring peace to that troubled island, it was surely the practical as well as the idealistic solution? Invoking the prayer of Virgil's Aeneas, Gladstone repeated a tag which had been on the lips of Pitt when the Act of Union (of Irish and English Parliaments) was established:

> *Paribus se legibus ambae*
> *Invictae gentes aeterna in foedera mittant.*
> ('Under equal terms, let both nations, unconquered,
>   enter upon an everlasting compact' – *Aeneid*
>   XII.190–1.)

The Queen had nothing but contempt for party politics, and would have been perfectly happy to have a succession of coalitions, provided they promoted the agenda of popular Toryism: a strong monarchy, a strong Empire, a United Kingdom. During the tense days of April and May, she found it incomprehensible, both that the Liberal Unionists should hang back from open support of Lord Salisbury, and that he, for his part, should have gone silent after the Haymarket evening for fear of 'repelling a single Radical or Liberal auxiliary'. He did not want to split the anti-Gladstone vote.[42] To Goschen, a staunch Unionist and First Lord of the Admiralty in Gladstone's first administration, she wrote, 'It is sad, and I cannot help saying not creditable or pleasant fact [sic] that the Liberals do not wish to unite with the Conservatives at such a supreme moment of danger to the best interests of my great Empire.'[43]

One of the reasons that Queen Elizabeth II's visit to Ireland on 17–20 May 2011 made such an enormous impact was that, ever since Gladstone's attempt to pass Home Rule, there had been a perception that the British monarch had sided with the Unionists. Elizabeth's acknowledgement of faults and mistakes on both sides, and her bowing her head in silence beside a war memorial for the thousands of Irish servicemen who had given their lives in the First World War, was perhaps also a silent admission that Home Rule might not have been such a 'supreme danger' to the Empire, at that moment when Queen Victoria was emerging, in the 1880s, to be just such a public figurehead as Gladstone had wished her to be in the 1860s: a public monarch, who was prepared to parade herself before the people as a reassuring figurehead.

In March, she went to lay the first stone of the Medical Hall in London University. On 4 May, she opened the Colonial and Indian Exhibition at South Kensington with a formal entourage including 'the Duchess of Bedford, the Great Officers of State etc.'. She processed through huge marquees as the band played 'God Save the Queen'. She inspected serried rows of Lascars and Parsees and Indians in exotic costumes and uniforms. She teetered down an Indian carpet into the Albert Hall where an Indian choir sang the second verse of the National Anthem in Sanskrit. Lord Tennyson had composed a 'beautiful' ode, set to music by Sullivan, the solo being sung by Albani. After Albani had sung 'Home Sweet Home', there were rousing choruses of 'Rule Britannia'.[44] The Queen was an impenitent imperialist. She saw herself as the Mother of Nations, and had simply ceased to be the shrinking violet who would not appear in public. The wish of the Irish to regulate their own affairs and have their own Parliament was the first step towards the dissolution of the Empire. 'Lord Salisbury earnestly trusts,' he wrote, 'that your Majesty has not been fatigued by your great recent exertions. The ceremony in the Albert Hall was singularly successful, and gave an enormous deal of gratification to your Majesty's loyal subjects.'[45]

Far from being tired, Victoria headed off to Liverpool on 11 May to open the International Exhibition of Navigation, Commerce and Industry, the brainchild of the Mayor of Liverpool, David Radcliffe. 'The crowds were marvellous,' she wrote, '...the enthusiasm and perfectly deafening cheering inside the Exhibition as well as outside was more than I have ever seen... And they behaved so well – never pushed or crowded. And they looked so delighted only to see their little old Queen.' She knighted the Mayor on the steps of a high throne, and 80,000 schoolchildren were amassed to sing 'God Save the Queen', and the next day, Arthur and Liko were sent to St George's Hall to preside over a banquet.[46] This was monarchy such as had not been made visible for a generation, and the Queen was loving it.

When she saw the politicians who were staggering from all-night sessions in Parliament and watching the Irish Home Rule Bill being torn to shreds, she saw figures who were exhausted. Gladstone, when he came for his weekly audience, looked 'ill and haggard'.[47] Nor was she entirely confident yet in Salisbury's competence to carry the anti-Home Rule cause. Whereas she considered Gladstone's manifesto – 'Trust the Irish!' – 'a very foolish one', she was appalled by Salisbury's speech, which had 'done harm' itemizing nations that could not govern themselves: 'the Hottentots couldn't, the Indians couldn't and the Irish couldn't... Most unfortunate.'[48]

The vote on the Second Reading of the Home Rule Bill occurred during the night of 7–8 June. Parnell made a measured speech, and in his account of the proceedings, Gladstone wrote to the Queen, 'He was particularly impressive in the expression of the necessity for keeping within that body [an Irish Parliament] every Irishman, and he held that the Protestants would be a most valuable and essential element of the new system. Mr Gladstone humbly thinks that this speech, quietly delivered, which defies analysis, well deserves your Majesty's attention.' Gladstone himself made a speech of immense length ending, 'Think, I beseech you; think well, think wisely, think, not for the moment, but for the years that are to come, before you reject this Bill.' The rejection was quite narrow – only 30 votes in it (341 against 311).[49]

The night after she received this account at Balmoral, the Queen was sleepless – 'so worried and anxious'.[50] Gladstone asked the Queen to dissolve Parliament. Rosebery went to see the Queen in person on 10 June to explain that in view of Gladstone's age, he felt he could not resign over the issue, but should force a General Election instead. The Queen liked Lord Rosebery and found him 'excessively agreeable'.[51]

Gladstone then came North, making a slow progress, with speeches in South Lancashire and in Glasgow before reaching his constituency of Midlothian. The Queen wrote to upbraid him, saying that she was 'surprised' – always an opprobrious term in her vocabulary – 'that he should visit other places totally unconnected' with his constituents. He hit the shuttlecock back over the net, saying – not entirely convincingly – that he shared the Queen's dislike of the practice of speaking outside his constituency, and wondering whether she had noticed of recent years how figures such as Lord Salisbury and Lord Iddesleigh (formerly Sir Stafford Northcote) 'have established a rule of what may be called popular agitation by addressing public meetings from time to time'.[52] Touché. Only a week later in Leeds, Salisbury was rallying the anti-Irish faithful, a crowd of 5,000 in the Coliseum Theatre, during which he ridiculed Gladstone's 'spasmodic ejaculations'.[53]

Both men were on the hustings in all but name. British politics had changed, and the Queen's own willingness to play to the gallery and appear before massed audiences was part of this. Salisbury went to the Auvergne while the election was held, in June, his body scalding all over with eczema. The election was during harvest. Not surprisingly, the agricultural workers did not vote, and the overall turnout was low: 2,974,000 as opposed to the 4,638,000 who had voted in the November election. The results were: 316 Conservatives, 77 Liberal Unionists, 192 Gladstonian Liberals and 85 Home Rulers. Salisbury asked Hartington – a Liberal Unionist – to take the office of Prime Minister, offering to serve as his Foreign Secretary. But Harty Tarty 'combatted my arguments in his usual sleepy manner'.[54] So it was, that on 25 July, Lord Salisbury kissed hands and became the Prime Minister for the second time. He told his son, 'It is an office of infinite worry, but very little power.'[55]

Queen Victoria could not but be glad that her old enemy Mr Gladstone was to be relieved of that particular source of worry in this, of all years. For, as she had written in her journal on 20 June, at Balmoral, 'Have entered the fiftieth year of my reign and my Jubilee Year.'[56]

TWENTY TWO

'YOU ENGLISH'

Public display, that aspect of her role which Victoria had found so unbearable in the first decade of her widowhood, was something which she learned to exploit in order to strengthen the monarch's hand. Her instinct was still to shy away. When that radical stronghold, Birmingham, requested a royal visit in the Jubilee Year, she 'emphatically refused'. A week later, however, Salisbury, who knew how to manage her, persuaded her otherwise. She 'smiled on the proposal', and, as Ponsonby said, 'this change was entirely owing to Lord Salisbury's persuasion'.[1] It was a propitious beginning to the Jubilee, which was not merely a retrospective celebration, but also a demonstration of political intent. There was plenty of opposition in Britain to the very idea of monarchy, and in the world at large to the British Empire. The Golden Jubilee would be Lord Salisbury's answer to them, though he personally kept out of the limelight. When the new Dean of Westminster, George Bradley, put up a huge screen which made the Queen invisible in the Abbey, Lady Salisbury said she would like to hang him,[2] since the whole point of the celebration was to have the sovereign, and all that she stood for, on display.

The Jubilee Year started early in India, with a magnificent firework display in Calcutta in February. The viceroy was able to tell Queen Victoria, 'The natives of India are passionately fond of pyrotechnic displays, and on the 16th they were shown fireworks far superior to any that they had ever seen before. The principal feature was the outline of your Majesty's head, traced in lines of fire, which unexpectedly burst on the vision of the astonished crowd. The likeness was admirable, and caused an enormous shout of pleasure and applause.'[3] If the crowds in India showed such enthusiasm for their Empress, it was only to be expected that the good-hearted folk of London Town would do the same. In May 1887, however, when the Queen opened the People's Palace on the Mile End Road in the East End, she heard what she described to the Prime Minister as 'a horrid noise (quite new to the Queen's ears), "booing", she believes it is called'. Salisbury hastened to remind her that 'London contains a much larger number of the worst kind of rough than any other great town in the island'[4], and she could assure herself that the booers were 'probably Socialists and the worst Irish'.[5]

All the same, those organizing the Golden Jubilee celebrations must have felt a little nervous, lest the population might be less ecstatic in their delight than the more enthusiastic royalists might hope. Nor was it only the 'worst kind of rough' who were republican in sentiment. Only the previous year, at a parliamentary dinner held by the Liberal Party, over 100 of the guests had failed to stand for the royal toast, and hissing had been heard when it was proposed.[6]

There was scarcely an atmosphere of political stability. Lord Randolph Churchill had exhibitionistically resigned as Chancellor of the Exchequer because Salisbury would not let him spend enough on the navy. He was eventually succeeded by the Liberal Unionist Goschen – though only after Goschen had been shooed into Parliament via the safe Tory seat of St George's Hanover Square, vacated by its unselfish occupant Lord Algernon Percy. Stafford Northcote, the Foreign Secretary, had a heart attack and dropped dead in Salisbury's presence. At a time when, as Salisbury himself told the Queen, 'The prospect is very gloomy abroad, but England cannot brighten it… We have absolutely no power to restrain either France or Germany, while all the power and influence we have will be needed to defend our influence in the south-east of Europe.'[7]

Moreover, the Irish Question was not going to go away, simply because the Liberal Party – the one English party which had any chance of solving the problem – had just smashed itself into smithereens.

Nor could the Empress of India rest in the certain knowledge that all her Indian subjects were content with her dominion over them. Even as London was preparing for the Jubilee Parades, and the Jubilee Service in Westminster Abbey, the Emperor of Russia was reading the following letter addressed to himself: 'I am a patriot and seek only to deliver some 250,000,000 of my countrymen from this cruel yoke of the British rule.' The same pen had earlier issued 'proclamations' from a printing press in Paris, calling for the liberation of the 250 million, and asserting that he would return to the Punjab to reclaim his rightful inheritance. When flown with drink in the Irish and American Bar in the rue Royale, he had even been known to refer to the English monarch as 'Mrs Fagin', for, said he, 'she's really a receiver of stolen property'.[8] Who could this be, but the Maharajah Duleep Singh?

If anyone was entitled to complain that the British had stolen from India, it was he – for his precious and sacred diamond, the Koh-i-Noor, had been delivered as a gift from the East India Company to 'Mrs Fagin' in 1849 and was now locked up in the Tower of London. Lord Dalhousie had so rightly and memorably said, 'I regarded the Koh-i-Noor as something by itself, and with my having caused the Maharajah of Lahore, in token of submission, to surrender it to the Queen of England. The Koh-i-Noor has become in the lapse of ages a sort of historical emblem of conquest in India.'[9] The owner of the diamond had been depicted as a beautiful boy by Winterhalter, and his portrait hung on the walls of the Queen's palaces. He had been so entirely assimilated as to have undergone baptism, to have been established as a landowner with a great shooting estate at Elvedon in Suffolk, and to send his sons to Eton. But the svelte youth whose fleeting beauty was captured by Winterhalter had lost his hair and developed a paunch, and as well as becoming an old roué who haunted theatres and bars in London. He was also confronted by death. And he wanted to revert to the religion of his youth. He converted back to Sikhism, and dreamed of reclaiming his old territories in the Punjab. It was a threat which the British authorities took extremely seriously – so much so that when he set off for India by ship, he and his family were waylaid at Aden and sent home again. His long-suffering wife and children went to spend their few remaining thousands of pounds living at Claridge's. The maharajah went AWOL in France, and then, with a false passport, and a chambermaid from a London hotel who was carrying his baby, he set off for Russia to throw himself on the mercy of the Russian Emperor.

In the event, Duleep Singh's rebellion was a damp squib, but it provided an embarrassing sideshow to the Jubilee. The Amritsar police superintendent wired back to the India Office in London that, since the issuing of the maharajah's 'proclamations', 'the behaviour of the Sikhs has quite changed in the villages. They are defiant and insolent now to Mission ladies and order them out of their houses saying, "We do not want you"'.[10]

Queen Victoria, who had always nursed a soft spot in her bosom for the maharajah, urged her ministers and their underlings in the army and the Secret Service to proceed with gentleness. 'Some kind person should meet him at Paris and set him straight,' she said, 'pacify him and prevent his ruining his children.' She sagely cautioned that it would have 'a very bad effect in India if he is ill used'. Why not give him a peerage, she suggested, 'and then they could live as any other nobleman's family?'[11] The idea fell on Lord Salisbury's deafest of ears. Nevertheless, whenever she could get a letter through to him, the Queen persisted in calling herself 'your friend and perhaps the truest you have'.[12]

She had always felt awkward about taking the Koh-i-Noor; her fondness for Duleep Singh was personal and strong; and she had, in general, an affection for Indians. The English habits of circumlocution and understatement and suppressing feeling had never been hers. The Victoria who liked Brown's directness of talk and physicality, who wallowed in Disraeli's exotic vein of fantasy and poetic flattery, was revivified by contemplating her Indian subjects, much more so than when listening to the dry-stick pronouncements of Oxford-educated bishops and politicians. Moreover, did not the sacred city of Agra contain the most famous shrine of marital bereavement, the Taj Mahal, a monument which even the mausoleum at Frogmore could not quite rival? It was to Agra that application was made for two Indian servants to join Her Majesty's household.

One of the men selected was Mohammed Buksch, a sort of butler to General Thomas Dennehy, the political agent in Rajputna. The other was Abdul Karim, a clerk to the supervisor of Agra jail. Hearing that he had been chosen to serve as an orderly to Her Majesty, Karim supposed that he would be riding as her escort; this was what 'orderlies' did in the Indian Army. Kitted out in the most splendid uniforms which the best tailor in Agra could run up in a short time – deep red and blue tunics, with matching pugrees or waistbands, white trousers or salwars, and bejewelled turbans – Buksch and Karim were actually being hired to wait at table. They were to be little more than junior footmen, designed to add a little colour to the Queen's entourage as she received the homage of the many Indian dignitaries visiting London and Windsor for the Jubilee. These included the prodigiously rich (and largely westernized) Maharajah and Maharini of Coch Behar, Niprendra and Sunity Devi Narayan, a beautiful, dashing pair in their twenties, who brought their three children with them; as well as the very different, and deeply traditional Maharajah and Maharini of Baroda in modern-day Gujarat, the Maharajah of Indore, the Maharajah of Bharatpore, and many others.

When the Jubilee Parade was held in London, culminating in a Service of Thanksgiving in Westminster Abbey, Victoria found herself at the head of a divided, troubled nation. This fact was largely disguised by the pageantry which triumphantly displayed her as the grandest monarch in Europe and the Empress of the farthest-flung dominions in the world.

The Indian crowds had cheered the fireworks, but it took little to divert the householders of the Punjab into hostility towards the Christian missions, when they had read Duleep Singh's 'proclamations'. The crowds of London were loyalist, but there were many in the East End more inclined to boo. And likewise, the potentates of Europe who came to salute the Queen's fifty years on the throne were deeply divided among themselves, and profoundly ambivalent in their attitudes to British domination of the world.

What a glorious sight, however, these potentates made as they processed, uniformed and helmeted, through the streets of London. The sun shone gloriously. Triumphal arches festooned with crowns, shields and evergreens marked the parade route, and greenery and flags were intertwined round balconies. The procession was led by the Prince of Wales Hussars, the Horse Guards and the Life Guards, with drawn swords, brilliant in the sunlight. The Court, her children, the politicians had all implored the Queen to wear a crown as she processed in 'a handsomely gilt landau',[13] but she insisted upon wearing a bonnet. She was preceded by her aides de camps and equerries on horseback, and six carriages, a phalanx of military leaders, then six more carriages containing members of the extended Royal Family, the Master of the Horse, and then seventeen princes on horseback – three sons, five sons-in-law and nine grandsons. The old German Emperor Wilhelm I, aged over ninety, was too ill to attend, but all eyes in the crowd fell upon his son Fritz – Queen Victoria's son-in-law. For weeks beforehand, Willy had been bombarding the Queen his grandmother with telegrams, questioning his father's fitness to travel. When they reached London,[14] Willy and his wife Dona took great offence at one of the receptions at Buckingham Palace, since Dona was 'placed behind the black Queen of Hawaii!!'[15] But, although Willy's greed to succeed to the imperial title was tactless in its candour, he was right to warn Victoria: Fritz was a sick man, suffering, though he did not know it, from throat cancer.

Lord Lorne, Louise's husband, who had an eye for a beautiful soldier, believed that Fritz, who wore the pure white uniform and silver breastplate of the Pomeranian Cuirassiers, a steel, eagle-winged helmet on his head, the Order of the Garter slashed across his chest and a gold-inlaid field-marshal's baton in his hand, resembled 'one of the legendary heroes embodied in the creations of Wagner'.[16] Alas, even as he rode to the Abbey this latter-day Amfortas could feel death closing around him.

The Abbey service was beautifully conducted, with the ceremonial robes, worn forty-nine years earlier by the nineteen-year-old Victoria, draped symbolically over a chair as the choir sang Prince Albert's setting of the Te Deum. Of course, she would not have been Queen Victoria if, in the midst of so much jubilation, she had not felt 'great pain' as she thought of 'above all, the dear husband and father, two dear children, my dear Mother, my sister and so many others – and, also, [John Brown], the loyalest, best friend who so loyally and lovingly looked after me!'[17] As these thoughts passed through her head, the surviving children and grandchildren processed to kiss the old lady as she sat on the Coronation Chair of Edward III. Then it was back to the Palace to eat. The procession took so long that they did not sit down to luncheon until 4 pm, with the Queen seated between the King of Saxony and the King of Denmark. After a short rest to read her telegrams, she was led in to dinner, wearing a dress with 'the rose, thistle & shamrock embroidered in silver on it, & my large diamonds'.[18] On this occasion, she sat between the King of the Belgians and the King of Denmark. Similar junkettings took place the next day, when she distributed Jubilee medals to the assembled kings, princes, maharajahs and potentates. By evening, she had taken off for Windsor, where she took comfort in the presence of her two new Indian servants. 'The one, Mohamed Buxsh [sic], very dark with a very smiling expression... & the other, much younger, called Abdul Karim... much lighter, tall, & with a fine, serious countenance. His father is a native doctor at Agra. They both kissed my feet.'[19]

It is so typical of the Queen that the beginnings of this new passion, her last attachment, for Abdul Karim, began after the wearing days of public Jubilee ceremonial. Ever since childhood, she had been used to seclusion and quiet, and she needed people who were special to her alone. What did it matter if this child of someone who was little more than a prison pharmacist should have become 'the son of a doctor'? Already, as all her favourites had been, he was being scattered with Victorian fairy dust.

While Queen Victoria was having her feet kissed by Abdul Karim, the Crown Princess Victoria of Germany had retired to an hotel with her exhausted husband. The Wagnerian hero was suffering from a growth on his vocal cord, and one week after the Jubilee, this was removed surgically by Dr Morell Mackenzie. The growth was sent for examination in Berlin by Dr Rudolf Virchow, who found no evidence of malignancy, and the Queen conferred a knighthood on Dr Mackenzie, at his patient's request, for his agreement with this optimistic diagnosis. Vicky and Fritz took off on a restorative trip, extending into the autumn, in the Italian Tyrol. Since his father, Wilhelm, was visibly dying, there was great pressure placed upon them to return to Berlin, but Vicky thought 'It would be madness to spoil Fritz's cure'. He was all but speechless, and another lump had appeared on his throat. They moved south to the Italian Riviera at San Remo, and Sir Morell Mackenzie came out to examine the putrid throat again. This time, he was less sanguine. By now Professor von Schrötter from Vienna and Dr Krause from Berlin had descended on San Remo. Schrötter pronounced that the Crown Prince had incurable cancer. Krause, who knew Fritz's medical history, had insisted upon large doses of potassium iodide being administered before surgery. This was because, in 1869, at the opening of the Suez Canal by the Empress Eugénie, Fritz had been to bed with a Spanish beauty named Dolores Cada and contracted syphilis. Krause still held out a hope, albeit a small hope, that the throat condition was syphilitic, rather than cancer; but this hope was soon abandoned.[20] Mackenzie and the other doctors agreed that the growth was in fact malignant. When he was left alone with Vicky, Fritz broke down and wept. 'To think that I should have such a horrid, disgusting illness! That I shall be an object of disgust to everyone and a burden to you all! I had so hoped to be of use to my country… What will become of you? I have nothing to leave you! What will become of the country?'[21]

They returned to Germany very low in spirits.

Queen Victoria watched these developments with a very heavy heart. She was sympathetic to any woman on the verge of losing her husband; how much the more was she sympathetic to her firstborn daughter. Moreover, she had always sided with Fritz and Vicky's liberal political outlook, maintained with great courage and difficulty against the barrage of vilification and outright libels put out against them by the Bismarck camp. Nevertheless, the Queen still retained some affection for Willy, and she was not 100 per cent against him, as Vicky was. She still believed, furthermore, that she had a role to play in the pacification of Europe and the moderation of the German militaristic right wing.

Meanwhile, only four years after the demise of John Brown, the courtiers had new cause to squirm while, shamelessly eccentric as ever in her choice of favourites, the Queen wallowed in the company of Abdul Karim. Down the corridors of Osborne wafted the delicious aromas of spices which Abdul had brought with him from Agra: cloves, cinnamon, cumin, nutmeg and cardamom drowned out the pong of overboiled cabbage and mutton. To the amazement of the cooks, Abdul Karim had entered the kitchen and prepared the Queen a fine chicken curry, daal and fragrant pilau. She considered it 'excellent' and decreed that curries should be prepared regularly. Coming out of the dining room one day, she had said to Karim, 'Speak to me in Hindustani, speak slowly that I may understand it, as I wish to learn.' She had soon acquired a special scarlet morocco notebook from the royal stationers in which she noted down Hindustani phrases, and she and Abdul began to sit down, while he taught her the language. She arranged for him to have an hour's English lesson each day, so that he could converse with her. He explained to her the differences between Hindus and Muslims – he and Buksch were Muslim. He told her about the conflicts between Hindus and Muslims at Agra. By the time the autumn leaves were falling, the Empress of India found that, in the space of a few weeks, she had learned more of India, its languages, religions and customs, than she had known in seventy years of life.[22]

The Jubilee had demonstrated the huge popularity of the monarchy – in some quarters. It had not done anything to eliminate the differences in society, nor the inequality between rich and poor, nor the intractable problems of Ireland. Ample proof of this was given on 13 November 1887, known forever afterwards as Bloody Sunday. There had been a long depression in trade, the economy was languid, there was unemployment among the dockers, and disgruntlement in the East End which had booed the Queen earlier in the year. A massive demonstration formed in Trafalgar Square to protest against the Government's Irish policy. William Morris, the designer, poet and artist, was there with his fellow socialists and, as his future biographer, and Burne-Jones's son-in-law, J. W. Mackail wrote, 'no one who saw it will ever forget the strange and indeed terrible sight of that grey winter day, the vast, sombre-coloured crowd, the brief but fierce struggle at the corner of the Strand, and the river of steel and scarlet that moved slowly through the dusky swaying masses when two squadrons of the Life Guards were summoned up from Whitehall'.[23]

The soldiers who a few months before were conducting a little old lady in a bonnet through a pageant of imperialist patriotism, were now turned against the people of London. Alfred Linnell was one of those injured in the fight with police and soldiers, and when he died in hospital a huge public funeral was organized. It became a mass protest 'against what they described as the autocracy of the police... hired murderers in uniform and a ruling class trembling in its shoes'.[24]

1888 was, for the Germans, the year of the three emperors, or, as they called them, *der greise Kaiser, der weise Kaiser und der reise Kaiser*: the very old Emperor, the wise Emperor and the gadabout Emperor. This was because, in the very first few months of his reign, Wilhelm II made a visit with his navy to St Petersburg, went to Sweden and

Denmark, and then in October passed through Austria, called on the Emperor Franz Josef, en route for visits to the King of Italy and the Pope in Rome.

The spectacle of a young man passing out of his mother's or grand-mother's control is often to be seen in families. But the gadabout Emperor Willy's decisive rejection of his parents and their liberal values had immense consequences beyond the family circle of Hohenzollerns and Saxe-Coburgs, vast as that circle now was. Europe was now in a countdown to world war. In February 1888, there was yet another moment when it looked possible that Austria-Hungary and Russia would go to war over Bulgaria. Count Herbert Bismarck – son of old Otto – who had been voted immense sums by the Reichstag to increase the size of the German Army, made a bold diplomatic gesture. He published the secret contents of the Treaty which had been drawn up between Germany and Austria-Hungary after the Congress of Berlin in 1879. He was sabre-rattling, to persuade the Russians, on this occasion, to stand down. But, as Queen Victoria immediately saw, the terms of this treaty were calamitous. They committed Germany, in the event of war, to fight on the Austrian side against Russia. This, combined with the equally calamitous entente cordiale urged on by Bertie a little later in the century (which locked Britain and France into similarly precipitous treaty obliga-tions) was the recipe for universal conflict which caught flame in 1914. On 25 February 1888, the Queen wrote from Buckingham Palace to the Prime Minister that she thought 'you should remonstrate with Count Bismarck on this rash act which after all will probably end in trouble'.[25] How horribly right she was.

The willingness of the Germans and the British to hate one another was manifested by an unseemly wrangle, after Emperor Frederick's death, between Sir Morell Mackenzie and his German doctors; the case quickly turned into an international incident. Fritz's death of throat cancer, following a tracheotomy performed by Dr Bramann, was painful in the extreme. The tubes which they inserted into his throat did not fit, and however often they were changed, the discharge was stinking. Astonishingly, the German doctors who performed the operation were not, unlike Mackenzie, laryngologists.

After he died, on 15 June 1888, the doctors, in defiance of every medical code and all royal protocol, went public in their analysis of the case. Mackenzie gave an interview to a Dutch newspaper, in which he blamed the clumsy German surgeons. They responded with a sixty-two-page, black-bordered pamphlet entitled *Die Krankheit Kaiser Friedrich des Dritten*, in which the toadyism of the English doctor and his raising of false hopes were all spelt out. Mackenzie, not to be outdone, then published *The Fatal Illness of Frederick the Noble*, which sold 100,000 copies in a fortnight, and simultaneously there appeared an American and a French edition. He also threatened libel proceedings against any publisher who threatened to translate *Die Krankheit*. Behind the ultimately pointless question of which was the worst doctor on the case, and who was to blame for Emperor Frederick's horrible death, aged fifty-six, was the cruel suggestion that the Englishwoman – *die Engländerin* – Vicky had hastened his demise, or even wished it. It was all part of the general pattern of German politics from now onwards. 'Darling, darling unhappy Child,' wrote the Queen in Balmoral to the widowed Empress Frederick, 'I clasp you in my arms and to a heart that bleeds, for this is a double, dreadful grief, a misfortune untold and to the world at large.' 'It is too dreadful,' she wrote in another letter, 'to think of Willy & Bismarck & Dona being the supreme head of all now! Two so unfit and one so wicked.'[26]

The character of the new Emperor was partly to blame. In some moods, he was more English than the English, proud to be an admiral of the fleet, and affectionate about his grandmother on the Isle of Wight. On other occasions, the vehemence of his anti-English feelings appeared unbalanced, as when he had a nosebleed, and hoped he was losing every drop of his English blood. If you were English, it was never easy to know which Wilhelm you were going to meet. He could be genial, even humorous in a heavy kind of way. When he visited the British Fleet in the Mediterranean, he came on board a vessel and when he had been shown round, he said to the captain, one John Pipon, 'You are the only Captain in the British Fleet who has not offered me champagne.' The following New Year's Day, Captain Pipon received a postcard signed, 'With the best wishes of your thirsty friend William R and I'.[27] On the other hand, especially when he was dealing with his family, Wilhelm II could be vicious and mischievous. There was never any love lost between him and his uncle Bertie. When Bertie went over to Berlin for Fritz's funeral, 'nothing could have been nicer than his manner towards me... and we parted the very best of friends.'[28] Buoyed by the unusual cordiality of the relations between them, Bertie told his nephew that he was going to be in Vienna at the same time as Wilhelm in September. This letter received no reply, but the British Ambassador in Vienna – now our old friend from Rome, Sir Augustus Paget – was informed by the German Ambassador, Prince Reuss, that Wilhelm would not meet his uncle there, and indeed, 'preferred his room to his company'.[29]

It was hard to disentangle the reasons for this calculated insult. Some said that Bertie had been speaking too freely of his belief that Alsace and Lorraine, appropriated by Prussia in the war of 1870, should be returned to France. Others said that Willy had taken offence because his uncle had not written direct to express his wish to meet in Vienna, but had sent the message via a military attaché. Bertie replied that his words had been misrepresented, and that he had never said that Alsace and Lorraine should be given to France. 'It takes two to make a quarrel! And as I never had one with William in my life, I think I have reason to complain of the treatment which I received, which created a scandal at Vienna, when I was guest of the Emperor of Austria, and everybody imagined I was on bad terms with William, which as far as I was concerned was not the case.'[30]

Meanwhile, in Queen Victoria's life, the quiet routines of the Household continued. In the Jubilee Year, she took on, as well as the two Indian servants, a new Maid of Honour called Marie Adeane, aged twenty-four, the granddaughter of Lord Hardinge, a former lord-in-waiting, and the great-niece and niece of two equerries

– Augustus Liddell and Alick Yorke. She was very nervous to begin with, but as she was led up to the Queen by Lady Ely, she met an old lady who 'kissed me most affectionately on my cheek – and pinned a Maid of Honour badge – a miniature of herself in early days, surrounded by diamonds and mounted on a ribbon bow, the same texture and colour of the Order of the Bath – on my left shoulder'. Marie had the qualifications which were specified – fluency in French and German, ability to play piano duets with Princess Beatrice in the evenings, and with 'no shadow of any prospective engagement or incipient love affair'.

She quickly discovered the Queen's energy and appetite. In April 1888, when she and Lady Churchill, 'half dead with fatigue', had just arrived at Windsor, they were looking forward to a quiet dinner when, unannounced and unexpected, 'the Queen arrived at 8.30, looking as fresh as a daisy and not a bit the worse for her long journey; a few minutes later we were summoned to dine with her'. She was immediately struck by how much the Queen enjoyed her food and drink, and promised to get her mother to send cider for Her Majesty to sample. 'I have never tasted Perry and only cider once or twice in my life. Do you think your Mama would send me some?'

Marie was one of those who witnessed at first hand the grief of the German Empress when she arrived at Windsor in November – 'it was too sad for words, she came with the Queen and the Prince of Wales and walked into the hall quite slowly, all draped in crape, and her face quite invisible but I could see her trembling with grief and agitation, she shook hands with all of us, and kissed Ethel and Lady Ely, but never spoke a word. Then she pulled herself together and shook hands with each of the gentlemen before going upstairs.'[31]

Marie was among the courtiers who could watch at first hand the Queen's growing devotion to Abdul Karim, or, as he was now to be called, Munshi Hafiz Abdul Karim, the Queen's official Indian clerk and Muslim teacher. ('Munshi' is Hindustani for language teacher and/or secretary.) Other Indian menials were now engaged to wait at table. The Munshi's salary was increased to £144 per annum, and would rise to £250. Her Hindustani was improving. She could now say, 'You may go home if you like', and 'You will miss the Munshi very much' and 'Hold me tight' ('Ham ko mazbut Thamo').[32] Visitors and correspondents were treated to encomiums: 'I take a little lesson every evening in Hindustani and sometimes I miss writing by post in consequence,' she admitted to Vicky. 'It is a great interest and amusement to me. Young Abdul (who is in fact no servant) teaches me and is a vy. strict Master and a perfect Gentleman. He has learnt English wonderfully – and can now copy beautifully and with hardly any faults. He will I hope remain and be vy. useful in writing and looking after my books and things.'[33] The Munshi was 'very intelligent & useful', 'He is so good & gentle & understanding all I want & is a real comfort to me', 'such a good influence with the others… he and all the others set such a good example and so respectable'. She either did not notice, or for the time being chose to ignore the snobbish and racist feelings of the English servants and the courtiers, none of whom liked Karim, and some of whom already felt was John Brown in a turban.

Cordial as her personal relations always were with Lord Salisbury, Queen Victoria did not hold back from admonishment or disagreement. Traditionalist and monarchist as Salisbury was, he was also a shrewd housekeeper and he had his eye on the sheer extravagance of the Queen residing in Windsor, Balmoral and Osborne, and the Prince of Wales occupying the palatial Marlborough House and Sandringham; while the historic palaces of Kew, Kensington and Hampton Court remained unused. His attempts to make Her Majesty address this issue were not met with much success. He used Ponsonby as the conduit through which he fed to the Queen his cautious suggestion that she might consider getting rid of Kensington Palace. Her response was that 'it would never do to sell any Palace'. Ponsonby ventured to remind her that he had, 'by her order suggested to Mr Gladstone's and I think Lord Beaconsfield's Governments that they should buy Kew Palace and that both were ready to listen to some proposal. But it did not go further. The Queen said that the proposal was not to sell it outright but to sell it to the Crown Lands so that it should be taken in to Kew Gardens. This is true. Still, the Palace would have gone from the Sovereign.'[34] As the weeks trundled past, the matter surfaced from time to time. The Queen reiterated her refusal to contemplate selling either Kensington Palace or Hampton Court, but she was prepared to consider selling her interest in London's public parks, 'but would wish for a stipulation that Constitution Hill should not be converted into a public thoroughfare for omnibuses, carts and cabs'.[35]

Less salubrious London thoroughfares also came to the attention of the Queen, as of everyone else, that year, when the grisly murders of prostitutes in Whitechapel seized the public imagination. Salisbury, who felt that the Home Secretary, Henry Matthews, had demonstrated his inadequacy at Bloody Sunday, was now under pressure from the Queen. When Jack the Ripper – as the unknown murderer was nicknamed – carved up his third victim, the Queen wrote to complain that the Home Secretary's 'general want of sympathy with the feelings of the <u>people</u> are doing the <u>Government</u> harm'.[36] Matthews was eventually sacked and given a viscountcy to keep him out of harm's way, but not before a fifth woman fell victim to the Ripper's knife. The Queen upbraided Salisbury for not ensuring that there was better street lighting in the East End. 'All these courts must be lit and our detectives improved,' she said to him, while to the useless Matthews himself, she itemized the procedures which he should have instituted:

——Have the cattle boats and passenger boats been examined?

——Has any investigation been made as to the number of single men occupying rooms to themselves?

——The murderer's clothes must be saturated with blood and must be kept somewhere.

——Is there sufficient surveillance at night?

These are some of the questions that occur to the Queen on
reading the accounts of this horrible crime.[37]

In the modern vogue for historical detective fiction, almost every
ingenious variation on fact has been tried: it is fascinating to think
of the Queen herself as a detective. Meanwhile, it was to a prison far,
far away that her attention was diverted. The Munshi returned from
Agra after a visit home to ask her to obtain promotion for his old
boss, the prison superintendent Dr John Tyler. And while she was
about it, perhaps she could put in a word for his father Wuzeeruddin.
Never one to beat about the bush when it came to helping her
friends, she wrote, not to any mere district commissioner, but to the
Viceroy of India himself, Lord Lansdowne, instructing him to give
a pension to the Munshi's father. When he was slow in his replies,
and then expressed some misgivings, Lansdowne received a series of
telegrams. If promotion for Dr Tyler had to wait, well and good, but
would the viceroy not see that it was a matter of urgency to help the
Munshi's father? 'As regards Dr Wuzeeruddin,' she wrote, 'he wants
nothing, the Queen believes, but a pension to live comfortably after
30 years' service both as Military and Civil Doctor or rather Hospital
Assistant.'[38]

Throughout the early months of 1889, Salisbury's Government and the
Queen were agonizing over the German Emperor's expressed wish
to make a State Visit to Britain. Wilhelm II had still not apologized
for the insult to Bertie in Vienna, and Salisbury felt that, until some
apology was forthcoming, the British would lose face by accepting the
Emperor in an official capacity. Wilhelm wanted to come to the Isle of
Wight in Cowes week, and intended to arrive accompanied by a good
number of German naval vessels. Salisbury wondered whether the visit
could not be classified as 'private', a mere wish by a grandson to visit a
grandmother while on a boating trip. Wilhelm replied, not unwittily,
that 'he did not understand how the Emperor of Germany coming in

his fleet and being received by the Queen of the greatest naval power, with hers, could be called private'.[39] Ponsonby was sure that, by the time summer came, the quarrel with the Prince of Wales would have been 'made up', but as April drew to its end, the Queen remained adamant. 'The Emperor William refuses to take any step towards a reconciliation and the Prince of Wales cannot receive him. Her Majesty asks how, in that case, can she receive him. An affront to the Heir apparent is an affront to her and the Queen will not be trampled upon by her grandson who is instigated [sic] by two bad men.'[40]

In the event, it was Bertie who backed down. He withdrew his objection to the emperor's visit, provided that the Emperor withdrew his imputation. Wilhelm persisted in pretending that he had made no such imputation, and that therefore there was nothing to withdraw. While his grandmother wrote to him in official language, and, when quarrelling with him, used the third person, he always replied, 'Dearest Grandmama' – and signed himself 'Willy' thereby deflating her. 'The whole affair is absolutely invented,' he wrote to her at the end of May, 'there being not an atom of cause to be found. The whole thing is purely a fixed idea, which originated either in Uncle Bertie's own imagination or in somebody else's.' He added that, whoever put this idea in his uncle's head, 'I am very glad to hear that this affair has at last come to an end.'[41] Insult was added to injury when it was discovered that the Emperor was bringing in his suite his infamous adjutant, Colonel von Kessel. When the cipher went missing which was used to decode foreign messages, von Kessel had accused the Empress Frederick herself of having stolen it, in her capacity as an English spy. He had then mysteriously 'found' the key to the code in a drawer in his own table. 'Gustav von Kessel, with a wickedness & audacity I could hardly have credited <u>even</u> in <u>him</u>, now swears… that the cipher… <u>was not there when he last</u> looked through the table drawers & insinuates that it has been put there by someone in this house!!'[42] spluttered Vicky to her mother.

If the Vienna insult to Bertie and the accusation of espionage against his own mother were not enough to sour feelings against the young

Emperor, there was in progress a painfully unseemly quarrel between his father's doctors. This was no academic disagreement about the possible treatments for throat cancer. It was an unbecoming public row, fuelled in part by the worsening diplomatic relations between Britain and Germany, and also by the characters of those involved. Sir Edward Malet, the British Ambassador in Berlin, confided in Ponsonby, over a game of billiards at Osborne, that Dr Mackenzie was 'a most unprincipled and designing man', who had done no end of mischief, political and otherwise. Malet blamed Victoria's weakness; for, 'in spite of all her cleverness, anyone can get round her who fawns upon her'.[43] The symptoms of the poor late Emperor were now the stuff of international wrangling and unseemly half-truths being aired in the newspapers. Yet, in spite of all this, and in spite of the quarrel between Willy and Bertie, the German Emperor's planned visit to Britain went ahead.

Before his arrival, the Queen sent word to Berlin that she intended to make him an admiral of the British Fleet. Willy, when told of this honour by Malet, declared that he felt as Macbeth must have done when hailed by the witches as Thane of Glamis, Thane of Cawdor and 'Macbeth, that shalt be king hereafter!' He meant, simply, that he felt honour upon honour was being heaped on his head, but the words had unintended omen. The fine portrait of the kaiser in his admiral's uniform now hangs, rather hidden away, in a corridor of what was once the wing of Osborne House used – after the Queen's death – as a convalescent home for officers. How salutary it would have been if it had been on public display – in, say, the National Portrait Gallery in London – to remind the British and German public of their closeness. The Queen had made her grandson a British admiral because she wanted, almost above all things, to preserve the peace between the two peoples. Wilhelm appeared to take his rank quite literally, since he immediately drafted to his grandmother proposals for the navy of which he was now an officer. She should deploy more ships in Mediterranean waters; the Naval Vote should be £21 million, spread over four years, to counter the American navy-building. Such a programme was already in place. Whereas previous wisdom, since the Battle of Trafalgar, had decreed that the navy should be one-third bigger than the world's next largest (usually France), there was now a new yardstick, known as the Two-Power Standard. The Royal Navy was to be kept 'to a standard of strength equivalent to that of the combined forces of the next two biggest navies in the world'.[44] The arms race was on.

By the time he arrived at Osborne for Cowes week, the new admiral was in benign mood. To show that Germany could build ships too, the Emperor was accompanied by no fewer than twelve warships. He inspected the British Fleet – to some eyes it looked more as if he was snooping upon it – and throughout his visit, when presented to fellow naval officers, he lectured them about guns and armaments. To repay the courtesy paid to him by the British Crown, he made his grandmother colonel-in-chief of the Prussian First Dragoon Guards. He presented her with a bust of himself by Reinhold Begas, and on his cousin George, the future King George V, he bestowed the Order of the Black Eagle. Bertie, through gritted teeth, made the German Emperor a member of the Royal Yacht Squadron, the highest of accolades in sailing circles – equivalent to membership of the MCC in cricket.

It was a successful visit to Grandmamma in her 'quiet comfy old house', and even included a few nights with the Prime Minister in the rather grander setting of Hatfield. When he got home, he was still hugging himself with delight to be an admiral in the Royal Navy, 'and with keenest sympathy shall I watch every phase of its further development, knowing that the British ironclads, coupled with mine and my army, are the strongest guarantees of peace which Heaven may [sic] help us to preserve!'[45]

∞

His was not the only arrival that summer in Britain of a foreign potentate. A month after the German Emperor had come to Cowes, the Shah of Persia visited Windsor. When the visit was in prospect, the Queen had immediately foreseen the hideous possibility that she might be expected to foot the bill. 'This is odious,' she wrote to Salisbury. 'She positively refuses to be put to any expense on account of this political visit.'⁴⁶ Thereafter, whenever Salisbury tried to discuss arrangements about the shah's visit, she invariably responded with an account of royal poverty, pleading for Government money to be given not merely to her children, but to her grandchildren. 'Her Majesty believes that in the first year of her reign,' Ponsonby was asked to write to the Prime Minister, 'the Parliamentary Grants to members of the Royal Family amounted to nearly £300,000 a year whereas it is scarcely half that sum.'⁴⁷ (Those who have followed this narrative thus far will remember that in addition to her private money and income from the Duchy of Lancaster, the Queen received £385,000 from the Civil List, and that she had persuaded successive Prime Ministers to give at least £6,000 a year to each of her children.) This was simply her instinctive reaction when asked to part with any money.

As often happened with an event long dreaded, she quite enjoyed the shah's visit. He was stouter than when last seen, but spoke better French.⁴⁸ But they were all fatter. When the shah had gone, and she was spending a quiet day at Frogmore, she had to be carried up the steps of the mausoleum to commune with the spirit of the Prince Consort. Though the shah's visit had presumably cost some money, she had somehow managed to survive it without bankruptcy.

It was decided that there should be a new image of the Queen Empress upon the coinage. This must have stirred memories for Gladstone, who would almost certainly remember, when he was Chancellor of the Exchequer in 1860, an indignant Queen sending back designs for a new coinage again and again to the long-suffering modeller at the Royal Mint until a satisfactory image of herself was produced. 'The portrait is so frightful,' she had written in 1860, 'that the Queen cannot sanction it. She has given many sittings, corrected again and again, and still it is so bad… The Queen wishes more to be done, as

<u>all</u> her corrections have proved utterly useless, and she really cannot allow so bad a likeness of herself to be put into circulation.'⁴⁹ Her correspondence with Lord Salisbury upon the subject was conducted with less heat but no less fascination: she was, after all, superintending her last self-image. The three-quarters-view veiled matriarch was to be reproduced on coinage throughout the Empire. A coin is an enduring image; at the same time, it is a marker in an impermanent world. To be fixed on a coin is to be part of a succession of monarchs all of whom have passed onwards. As she grudgingly approved the new images of herself, she was yet again contemplating mortality.

There was a painful, and strange, incident in the second half of 1890, relating to the Queen's Indian servants. One afternoon in June, while staying at Balmoral, she climbed into the carriage which would take her to her Summer Cottage, wearing a certain brooch which had been given to her by the Grand Duke of Hesse. On the way back, the brooch was missing. It had been pinned to her shawl by Mrs Tuck, her dresser, who was upbraided by the Queen for forgetting the brooch. A search was then made of the cottage, and of the gravel outside, but no brooch turned up. Rankin, the footman on duty, said that he had seen Abdul Karim's brother-in-law, Hourmet Ali, who worked as one of the Indian servants, lurking around the cottage while the Queen had tea.

A month later, the servants were travelling back from the Earl of Fife's wedding at Buckingham Palace, and one of the other Indians, Mahomet, told Mrs Tuck that Hourmet Ali had stolen the brooch, and sold it to Wagland the jeweller in Windsor for six shillings. The next day, Mrs Tuck went to Wagland and asked if he had bought the brooch from an Indian, and the jeweller returned it, with a note stating what had happened. He said that the Indian had visited the shop several times and that he had eventually succumbed to his nagging and bought the item to 'save himself further annoyance'. Mrs Tuck thereupon took the note, and the brooch, to the Queen, and explained what had happened. The Queen was furious at the imputation that the dear Munshi's brother-in-law was a thief. Hourmet was a model of honesty. In India – so it was claimed later – it was considered perfectly honest to pick up items which had fallen on the ground and claim them as one's own. Mrs Tuck was abashed that the Queen was so 'dreadfully angry'. She was also taken aback by the words which the Queen had used. 'That is what you English call justice.'[50] You English. The Queen Empress had just celebrated her Golden Jubilee. She was nearly seventy years old and she had lived in Britain all her life. But with a part of herself she had never felt at home. Her empathy with the outcasts, and the non-English, with Highland Scots and with Indians, was natural, when one remembers her mother's loneliness and sense of strangeness in her years of widowhood in Kensington Palace. You English.

PART SEVEN

TWENTY THREE

'HER EXCELLENT YOUNG MUNSHI'

A NYONE IN THE Reading Room of the British Museum one April day in 1889 would have noticed the distinguished figure of the Archbishop of Canterbury, with his long grey hair swept back behind his ears, and his manly legs clad in black gaiters, taking the *Annual Register* for 1820 from the shelves. Had Mr Sherlock Holmes been there, he might have guessed what Archbishop Benson was doing, but luckily for the prelate, his morning's research went undetected. He was looking up the funeral of King George III. Having read the description, he then reached for the volume of 1837 and read the entry for the funeral of William IV. 'Ceremonial order and procession given, the Archbishop of Canterbury, the Lord Chancellor, the Heralds and the other dignitaries in the procession. The Dean of Windsor moved from the Communion Table to read the service after the sentence on committing the body to the grave...' He copied down the details, but this would never do. William IV had been king for little over seven years, and they could easily get away with giving him a quiet funeral at St George's Chapel, Windsor. What had happened to the man who gave away the Queen in marriage, the old Duke of Sussex? When did he die? '42? Ah, yes, 1843. The archbishop noted that Sussex had thought William IV's funeral was such a shambles that he had insisted upon being buried in the public cemetery at Kensal Green. His funeral, on 4 May 1843, followed 'the full service of the Established Church, read by the Bishop of Norwich, Clerk of the Closet to the Queen'. Once again, while this was of historical interest, it was scarcely of any use to Benson. He was being prudent, and planning Queen Victoria's funeral. There was no precedent in living memory. Not since George III had there been a monarch of comparable longevity; not since Queen Elizabeth had there been a sovereign so intimately bound up with the life, the politics and the collective emotions of the people of Britain. Of course, a responsible archbishop must make a plan.[1]

As destiny was to ordain, however, Edward White Benson was one of the many people of his time who died before the Queen. Though he was ten years her junior, he would expire aged sixty-seven during Morning Prayer at Hawarden Parish Church, in the company of the Gladstones, while the congregation was reciting the Lord's Prayer, on 11 October 1896.[2] Although, ever since the Golden Jubilee, the Queen's subjects had been haunted by the sense of an Ending – of their century, of their Queen, of their age – she lived a vigorous existence during the 1890s, albeit one in which she was frail, her eyesight became poor, and her stout frame became so obese that by the end of the decade she could hardly walk. And she continued to speak an unreformed Regency English. In Osborne, on Christmas Day 1891, she asked Sir Henry Ponsonby, 'Why the blazes don't Mr Macdonnell telegraph here the results of the election? He used to do so and now he don't.'[3] If William IV had lived in the age of the telegraph, it is just the sort of question, with 'don't' for 'doesn't', and the blunt 'why the blazes' which he would have asked. One sees here how much she had in common with her cousin the Duke of Cambridge, who likewise appeared in many ways to be a pre-Victorian. During a drought, he went to church and the parson prayed for rain. The duke involuntarily exclaimed, 'Oh God! My dear man, how can you expect rain with wind in the east?' When the chaplain, later in the service, said, 'Let us pray,' the duke replied, 'By all means.'[4]

While Benson planned her funeral, the unwitting Queen, still very much alive, was extending her house on the Isle of Wight. Osborne

House, designed by Prince Albert, was an airy, Italianate conception, having corridors adorned with classical statues, with cool spaces, with room on the walls for his exquisite collection of Trecento masters. Since the death of her aesthete husband, Victoria had managed to clutter all the interiors, crowding the tables with photographs in frames and plaster casts of her children and grandchildren's limbs. (Lord Rosebery once said that he thought the drawing room at Osborne the ugliest in the world until he saw the drawing room at Balmoral.[5]) But now her new interest in India must find architectural expression, so the Durbar Room was added to the house, a whole new wing in which Moghul-style plasterwork and arches festooned the great chamber. The design was that of Bhai Ram Singh, with the assistance of the director of the Lahore Museum, Lockwood Kipling, father of Rudyard. The carpet, like the Munshi, came from Agra. The Queen's Indian tastes were decidedly Moghul, and Punjabi in locality.

A Durbar is a court (the word comes from the Persian *darbar*), and at Osborne, Queen Victoria was embodying in plasterwork what Lord Beaconsfield had engineered in politics, a claim to British dominion of India and, by implication, the world. It was an extraordinary imaginative and political journey for the only child of Kensington Palace, with her dolls and her lonely German mother, to have made. A strange journey, too, for Britain. When Victoria was born, the King was the man who had lost the American colonies. When the time came for her bishops to enact the obsequies written out by Archbishop Benson, Victoria would be handing to her successor a global imperial sway.

The 1890 Durbar at Delhi, with its great procession of elephants through the Mori Gate, though it has perhaps been overshadowed in memory by such pageants as the 1911 Coronation Durbar, which we can see in film, must, nevertheless, have been a stupendous affair, and it gave this unambiguous message to the Indians: the British, the new Moghuls, are here to stay.

It was a message which both was and was not absorbed – as is starkly revealed in just one journal entry made by the Queen during one of her visits to the South of France, in March 1891. 'Received bad news from India, of a revolt at Manipur. The Commissioner from Assam, on his way there, was attacked & forced to retreat.' But then, on the very same day, she received a visit from the man who had called upon all 250 million of his fellow Indians to rise up against their Empress.

> Louise came to luncheon, after which I saw, in the small drawing-room below, the poor misguided Maharajah Duleep Singh, who had asked to see me, having some months ago humbly begged forgiveness for his faults & rebellion. He is nearly paralysed down his left side. He was in European clothes, with nothing on his head, & when I gave him my hand, he kissed it, & said, 'Pray excuse my kneeling'. His second son Frederick, who has a very amiable countenance, came over from Nice with him. I made the poor broken down Maharajah take a seat & almost immediately afterwards he broke into a most violent fit of weeping. I took & stroked his hand & he became calm & said, 'Pray excuse me & forgive my grievous faults,' to which I replied, 'That is all forgiven & past.' He complained of his health, & said he was a poor broken down man. After a few minutes' talk about his sons & daughters, I wished him goodbye & went upstairs again, very thankful that this painful interview was well over.[6]

No pain could be felt, by the Queen at least, in the presence of the Munshi, and nor could he be described as broken: indeed, with each promotion and increase in salary, he became plumper and more self-satisfied. In the spring, he developed a carbuncle on his neck, and the Queen kept up a steady flow of letters to Dr Reid: 'The Queen is much troubled about her excellent Abdul, who is so invaluable to her, and who has hitherto been so strong and well. She trusts Dr Reid is not anxious about him? He has always been so strong and well that she feels troubled at the swelling.'[7] Not content to leave the Munshi in the doctor's capable hands, the Queen visited him in his bedroom, which raised a few eyebrows. 'Queen visiting Abdul twice daily,' noted her doctor testily, 'in his room taking Hindustani lessons, signing her boxes, examining his neck, smoothing his pillows, etc.' No one suspected the Munshi, as they had evidently suspected John Brown, of impropriety with the Queen, but they were made anxious by so glaring a departure from the conventional. Queen Victoria was oblivious to conventions when it suited her, and she was besotted with her favourite. To Vicky, she gushed about the portrait of the Munshi which she had commissioned by the Austrian artist Heinrich von Angeli: the artist 'was so struck with his handsome face and colouring that he is going to paint him on a gold ground'.[8]

Fully aware that her children and courtiers would not treat Abdul kindly when she herself left the scene, Victoria determined to provide for him, and wrote to the Viceroy of India commanding him to give 'a grant of land to her really exemplary and excellent young Munshi, Hafiz Abdul Karim, who is quite a confidential servant – (and she does not mean in the literal sense, for he is not a servant) – and most useful to her with papers, letters, books, etc.'[9] Lord Lansdowne was uneasy about the request, since there was no precedent for such a grant being given to an Indian attendant. Land grants were normally only given in recognition of long military service. Then, some old soldier might be given land yielding a rent of, say, 300 rupees a year. Since he was often on tour, covering vast distances, the viceroy did not put the grant of land to the Munshi high on his list of tasks, but his sovereign did not allow him to forget it, and throughout that summer she sent a regular stream of letters and telegrams, insisting that the Munshi be given land yielding at least 600 rupees. Land was eventually found in the suburbs of Agra, and she also made it plain to Lord Cross, the Indian Secretary in the Cabinet, that the Munshi must be recognized officially as the Queen's Indian Secretary. It was a remarkable rise for a man still in his twenties, and who had only been hired so short a while previously as a waiter.

❧

The Munshi was not the only young man on the Queen's mind. She wanted to make Prince Albert Victor (Eddy), now aged twenty-six, a peer, but the difficulty was in the choice of a title. In considering the possibilities, she found the spirits of her 'wicked uncles' rising up to haunt her, like the ghosts in some Shakespearean play. York she 'positively refuses'. 'She would rather not Kent.' 'She would like Rothsey, but the Prince of Wales says no. And Gloucester raises shadows of Silly Billy.' In the end, the family agreed on Clarence and Avondale. 'Avondale is Scotch – George I was I believe Baron Avondale.'[10]

It was to be assumed that Eddy, the eldest son of the Prince of Wales, would one day become the King of England. His upbringing had not been without struggle – on behalf of his tutors and minders. Effort was not something he had ever demonstrated himself. Privately educated, he found difficulty with most academic subjects. Able to speak a little Danish (his mother's language), he was barely competent in French or German. He joined the 10th Hussars, but his army career was completely unsuccessful. They promoted him as far as major, and then his coevals began to be promoted above him, which caused embarrassment but no surprise. Indeed, the Prince of Wales thought Eddy's remaining in the army was 'simply a waste of time – & he has not that knowledge even of Military subjects which he ought to possess. His education & future has been a matter of some considerable anxiety for us & the difficulty in rousing him is very great.'[11]

Eddy was every bit as scandal-prone as his father. The old Queen complained to Vicky about Eddy's 'dissipations', causing Knollys, the Prince of Wales's private secretary, to exclaim to Ponsonby, 'I ask who is it tells the Queen these things?'[12] A good question, but the Queen was always a very accomplished collector of family gossip, and there was not much which passed her by.

In July 1889, the Metropolitan Police had raided a homosexual brothel in Cleveland Street, and the rent boys had given them the names of various illustrious clients, including an equerry of the

Prince of Wales called Lord Arthur Somerset. Arthur Newton, the somewhat sleazy solicitor employed by Somerset, hinted to investigators that if too much heat were put upon his client, he would reveal the name of an even more illustrious customer at the Cleveland Street establishment: P.A.V. (namely, Prince Albert Victor). There was never any firm evidence that Eddy was bisexual, let alone homosexual, but he was the sort of man to whom scandalous stories stuck like burrs. (In 1962, upon no evidence whatsoever, it was even claimed that he was Jack the Ripper.)

Eddy's emotional life on the surface took a more conventional pattern, with a succession of unsuccessful pursuits of women. He fell in love with Alicky, the sixth child of Princess Alice, but hers was to be a stranger destiny: to be Tsarina Alexandra Feodorovna of All the Russias, who would die in the cellar at Ekaterinburg. The Queen told Arthur Balfour that, apart from Alicky and Princess May of Teck, there were only three Protestant princesses in Europe who were suitable, and they were 'all three ugly, unhealthy and idiotic'.[13]

Eddy, with his instinct for the unsuitable, promptly fell in love, not with a Protestant, but with Princess Hélène of Orléans, daughter of the Count of Paris. Salisbury was horrified, and told the Queen that marriage to a Frenchwoman, even if she were to renounce her religion, would be highly unpopular with the British public. Because this seemed to be a genuine love match, however, it caught the fancy of the Queen, and when they went in person to plead with the old lady at Balmoral, she was almost tempted to accede to the match.

Almost, but not quite. She told Alix 'how troubled and agitated' she felt about the pair. Probably, if it had not been for Lord Salisbury, the Queen might have been tempted to let them marry. She promised that she would not give up hope 'and will do what I can'. As she told Alix, with whom she felt ever closer bonds,

> I fear you greatly understate the difficulties and obstacles which are manifold. By changing her religion only to be able to marry him, she will be furiously attacked and may be

tormented by the Roman Catholics and may be mistrusted by the Protestants, for the English and the Scotch think Roman Catholics (foolishly I admit) quite wicked and I fear they will be very angry. Then politically it might become very serious and involve the country in quarrels with France. If that foolish brother of hers were to make some attempt again [to become King of France] and fail, and came here and she were possibly Princess of Wales or even Queen and he went to her, it might involve England in war...[14]

It was a sad situation, since the Queen was, as she said, 'deeply' fond of Eddy, and liked Hélène 'so much' when she met her. Hélène, for her part, was genuinely in love. '*Je l'aimais tant,*' she told the Queen later, when Fate had dealt its hand with full cruelty, '*et j'ai peut-être été imprudente mais je n'ai pas pu faire autrement, je l'aimais tant*'.[15]('I loved him so much, and perhaps I was unwise but I could not have done otherwise, I loved him so much.')

As well as being warned off marriage by the politicians, the lovebirds were forbidden to marry by Pope Leo XIII, and a new bride had to be found for Eddy.

1891–2 was an *annus horribilis* for the Queen. Even the usually enjoyable jaunt to the Riviera was blighted. From the Grand Hotel in Grasse, Ponsonby wrote to the Prime Minister,

In this 'health' resort, we stand thus:

Pss. Beatrice	Cough and cold
Pce Henry	Measles
Lady Churchil	Cough
Miss Adeane	Swelled face
Sir H Ponsonby	Cough
Major Bigge	Cold

Worse was to follow. Four days later, the Queen's housemaid developed blood poisoning, having pricked herself accidentally with a needle. Dr Reid called in Dr Frank of Cannes and Dr Vidal of Grasse, and to everyone's horror they pronounced the poisoning to be incurable. The woman died. Then the Queen caught the cold which everyone else was suffering, 'but denies it. However she has lost her voice and it is very hoarse.'[16]

When they came home, it was to the seemingly unending cycle of scandal in which the Prince of Wales found himself. In September 1890, Bertie had been staying at Tranby Croft, the Yorkshire house of a shipowner called Sir Arthur Wilson. After dinner, the men played baccarat and a well-known clubman called Sir William Gordon-Cumming of the Scots Guards raised his stake having surreptitiously peeped at his cards. Five of the players saw him do this, and they decided, when the game was complete, to make him sign a statement promising that he would never play cards again. They in turn were sworn to secrecy to preserve his good name. Bertie was not one of the signatories, but he was a member of the party. Rumours hovered that it had in fact been Bertie who cheated at cards, and that Gordon-Cumming was covering for him. It was a puzzling affair, and as Bertie's biographer Jane Ridley suggests, it is superficially surprising that Bertie sided with his nouveaux-riches hosts and friends against an old Scottish family, the Gordon-Cummings. One possible motivation is that Bertie was angry with Gordon-Cumming, who had won £225 off him on an earlier evening, and had the temerity to be found in the arms of the prince's favourite mistress, Daisy Brooke.[17]

Daisy was not present at the Tranby Croft party. With her husband, she was attending the funeral of her stepfather, Lord Rosslyn, but when Bertie met up with her again, he spilled the beans about the card cheat. Not for nothing was Daisy known as the 'Babbling Brooke'. Within weeks, *le tout Londres* was gossiping about it. To preserve his good name, Gordon-Cumming brought an action for slander against the Wilson family. Bertie was to be summoned as a witness.

The Court was thrown into panic, and attempted damage-limitation. Would it not be possible to pre-empt a court case by having a secret military tribunal to establish the truth of what had happened at Tranby Croft? Would Gordon-Cumming's colonel-in-chief – none other than Bertie's brother Arthur, Duke of Connaught – not be able to put pressure on the man? The answer to both these questions was 'No'. Prince Arthur refused to intervene. 'Being the prince's brother it was more than ever incumbent on me not to allow myself to be used in a way that might cause the world to think that Cumming was to be sacrificed to the prince.'[18] Gordon-Cumming himself resigned from the army, so that scotched the idea of a military tribunal. The case was heard in public, on 1–2 June 1891. The solicitor general, Sir Edward Clarke, represented Gordon-Cumming, and he made mincemeat of the witnesses against him. One of them, Sir Edward Lycett Green, broke down altogether and admitted he could not remember the details of the baccarat game. As he won the case for his client, Clarke did not let the Prince of Wales off lightly. 'There is a strong and subtle influence of royalty, a personal influence which has adorned our history with chivalrous deeds; and has perplexed the historian with unknightly and dishonouring deeds done by men of character.'[19]

It could not have been worse publicity, not merely for the prince, but for the entire Royal Family: a Tory solicitor general, exposing the sleazy world in which Bertie moved, with its new-money house parties and its casual sexual mores.

Far worse than the Tranby Croft incident was the public exposure of Bertie's adulteries with Daisy Brooke. Some years earlier, Daisy had been in love with one of the Prince of Wales's equerries, Lord Charles Beresford. (One of his brothers, Lord Marcus, was Bertie's stud manager.) Though she had married Francis Greville, Lord Brooke (heir to the earldom of Warwick), when she was twenty, she had quickly tired of him and had many admirers, including Lord Randolph Churchill, Lord Blandford and Sir William Gordon-Cumming. Her passion for Charlie Beresford was something more serious. The pair were separated by his naval career. (He was the captain of HMS *Undaunted*, and it was his naval brigade which was sent, too late, to rescue General Gordon in 1882.) By 1886, Charlie's passion had died down and he had returned to his wife.

Some years later, in 1889, Daisy wrote Beresford an impassioned letter, begging him to return to her. In this letter, she represented his wife's pregnancy as a betrayal of herself, she told the story of their love, and she claimed that her children were in fact fathered by him. It was the sort of letter which almost begged to be read by the man's wife. Mina Beresford did indeed read it, and was appalled. She was also frightened that Daisy would be successful in persuading Lord Charles to resume his relations with her.

Clearly, the two women were heading for the most sensational public spat. It was time to call for that know-all, and manager of Victorian society secrets, George Lewis. This legendary solicitor (he would act for Bertie in the Tranby Croft case) had a finger in every pie, and knew everybody's secrets – a little like Mr Tulkinghorn in Dickens's *Bleak House*.

Bertie now entered the story. He had joined the queue of roués who were in love with Daisy, and her plight wrung his heart. In an unmarked cab, he visited George Lewis at 2 am, rousing him from his bed and begging him to destroy the letter which Daisy had so ill-advisedly written to Lord Charles. He then, a few days later, and more brazenly, called at the Beresford house, 100 Eaton Square, and asked them to show him the letter. Lord Charles upbraided the prince for 'a most dishonourable and blackguard action' in referring to the letter. He castigated Lewis for his 'sycophantic servility' in breaking a client's confidence by discussing the letter with Bertie.[20]

Charles Beresford rejoined HMS *Undaunted*, and was expected to be at sea for several months. Anyone who hoped that matters would die down in his absence was disappointed. His wife, and her sister Mrs Gerald Paget, wrote a spoof novelette of pamphlet length entitled *Lady River* about the Babbling Brooke. Not only did it reveal her amorous propensities, it actually quoted from the letter which Bertie had been so anxious to suppress, and it revealed her new position as the prince's *maîtresse en titre*. The pamphlet was soon being copied and handed round London drawing rooms, where guests, amid splutters of laughter, would be treated to readings after dinner.

As the *annus horribilis* of 1891 drew to a close, the Queen and the Prime Minister were directly involved with the affair. Lady Charles Beresford actually wrote to the Queen repeating a stipulation which she had already laid down to Bertie: that Daisy should be sent to live abroad for a year, as a *quid pro quo* for the return of her incriminating letter. 'My sister will not stop till she is exposed,' she warned. 'We can get rid of her with a scandal: those in authority can do without one.'[21]

After negotiations which involved Lord Salisbury, the Queen, Sir Schomberg McDonnell, Salisbury's secretary, and the two royal Private Secretaries, Francis Knollys and Henry Ponsonby, the letter was returned to Lady Brooke, and the society gossips found other things to chatter and giggle about. The stench of scandal was, nevertheless, overpowering, and, as Salisbury told the Queen that Christmas, 'The Prince and Princess of Wales are in terror that the whole row will crop up again, and I am afraid that Lady Charles Beresford won't remain quiet.' That was Salisbury. And, in a sentence which was so very highly revealing, Ponsonby replied, 'my path is clear at this moment. To prevent the Royal Family from rushing into any course without Lord Salisbury's advice.'[22]

But the horrors were not yet complete, and misery was to be brought not by scandal but by two other tragedies. In the same letter in which he was still agonizing about the Beresford affair, Ponsonby wrote from Osborne to the Prime Minister, 'There was a shoot in the covers yesterday. Four of the princes went out. Prince Christian was not shooting – only looking on, but close to his son who was shooting. A pheasant flying low came near him. The Duke of Connaught killed the pheasant but two of his pellets struck Prince Christian. One in the eye through the middle of it. We telegraphed to Lawson. But he said Eye must be taken out – and he took it out this morning. I believe we don't say it was the Duke of Connaught but everyone knows – and he's wretched about it.'[23]

This unpleasant episode was quite enough to cast a blight over the royal Christmas holiday, but worse was to follow. On the last day of the year, Queen Victoria's nephew Victor – son of her sister Feodore – died at St James's Palace – dear good honest Victor, who was only fifty-eight.

The one good piece of royal news that month had been the announcement, at the beginning of December, of Eddy's engagement to Princess May of Teck, the niece of the Queen's peppery old cousin the Duke of Cambridge.

George Cambridge's sister Mary Adelaide, May's mother, was a woman of extraordinary proportions. In 1857, when she was twenty-four, the American Minister to the Court of St James's had noted that Princess Mary Adelaide was a 'very fat, very thick set and very proud young lady'.[24] Later in life, Lord Cranborne (son of the Prime Minister) noted, when going on an expedition to see an Alpine glacier in the company of the princess, 'Of course, qua Royalty, she goes first, and where she can go, we may safely follow; neither is there any danger because no crevasse is large enough to swallow her up.'[25] Fond as she was of clothes and jewellery, and easy as it was in those days to swathe a female form in expensive stuffs from neck to toe, the obesity did pose problems when it came to finding her a husband. Even when she was seventeen, old King Leopold of the Belgians had been shocked by how she had 'grown out of all *Compass*'. Although she had hoped to marry a British peer, the Queen preferred the idea of 'some German Kammerherr or young officer! It wd. really be the best thing.'[26] They had eventually lighted upon Prince Franz of Teck, son of the morganatic marriage of Duke Alexander of Würrtemberg, with the Hungarian Countess Rhédey de Kis-Rhéde. Queen Victoria dismissed all worries about the pair not being *ebenbürtig* – of equal status. Such things did not matter in Britain. The pair had four children, of whom Princess May was the only daughter. (Her brothers were Dolly – Adolphus – Francis and Alexander.) Their father had an 'almost feminine' delight in interior decoration, which would be inherited by May.

The family grew up in Kensington Palace, where they survived on Princess Mary Adelaide's modest parliamentary annual emolument of £5,000. 'Fat Mary', as she was ungallantly known at Court, was an accomplished player on the Queen's good will, and Victoria found it hard to refuse, when confronted with open requests. She had to retrench in writing. 'The Duchess of Teck may have a carriage tomorrow,' the Queen had written as late as 1888 to Ponsonby, 'but Sir Henry must make it very clear it must not be asked for again.'[27] The Tecks were familiar figures at public functions, Drawing Rooms or Courts, he pencil thin and dark and trim, she ever-billowing, and, when she sat, often crunching, for she kept about her person a packet of Abernethy biscuits lest hunger overcame her between meals.

While she ate and swelled, and Duke Franz elegantly arranged cushions and rehung paintings in his exquisite interiors, Princess May had grown up to be a rather stiff but pretty girl, devoted to good works. The chief drama of her adolescence consisted in keeping the peace between Princess Mary Adelaide and her lady-in-waiting, Lady Geraldine Somerset, who hated Fat Mary, and was still painfully and unrequitedly in love with the brother, the Duke of Cambridge, who was morganatically married to an actress named Mrs Fairbrother and who had a succession of mistresses.

The Cambridges were very much poor relations, but Queen Victoria had always got on well with George. Although all her biographers stress Victoria's need, in marrying the virtuous Prince Albert, to escape the dissipations and clumsiness of her 'wicked uncles', there was always a distinctly Hanoverian side to her. George Cambridge was a throwback to the world of William IV and George IV, to a lack of stiffness and a lack of side which was always part of Victoria's character also. Though anxious for Princess May's brothers to join the Würrtemberg army,[28] a marriage between Eddy and May would keep things in the family at home. It also had the added advantage of annoying the Germans. Willy, now an open hate-object to his mother Vicky, had rather taken to Princess May of Teck, noting her beauty and charm. He had been pleased when his wife's brother, Ernst

Gunther, Duke of Schleswig-Holstein, had previously proposed to May. Vicky was triumphant when he met with a refusal: 'I am much amused that Dona turned up her nose at the <u>idea</u> of her <u>charming</u> brother thinking of May, whereas I know it as a fact that he <u>made</u> <u>démarches</u> to obtain her hand wh. <u>May refused</u> at <u>once</u>!'[29]

This hugely increased May's value in the marriage market. After initial fears that May was a superficial person – *oberflächlich*, some people had called her – Queen Victoria came to think she would make an ideal future Queen of England – for that, in choosing a wife for Eddy, was what they were selecting. 'I think she is a superior girl – quiet & reserved till you know her very well, – but she is the reverse of *oberflächlich*. She has no frivolous tastes, has been very carefully brought up & is well informed and always occupied.'[30]

The obvious hope was that this elegant young woman, much given to visiting soup kitchens and hospitals, would find some occupation for the feckless, chain-smoking Eddy, and somehow raise the sordid tone which hovered over the Prince of Wales's family and household. She seemed to be fond of him, as was Queen Victoria, but they were in a minority at Court, Randall Davidson, for example, being wearied by Eddy's 'readiness to talk at a moment's notice on any and every subject, and the inanity of his voluble platitudes gave one a painful notion of the encouragement he must usually meet with if he is led to chatter so sententiously'.[31]

In January 1892, that family assembled at Sandringham for a shooting party to celebrate Eddy's twenty-eighth birthday. It was bleak weather. The Princess of Wales and Princess May both had heavy colds, and many in the household actually had influenza. On 7 January, the day before his birthday, Prince Eddy felt ill while out shooting, and when his temperature soared, he went to bed in his little bedroom off a sombre, cold corridor – a room so small that when he lay in the bed by the window, he could stretch out and touch the mantelpiece. Princess May sat beside him. The next day, his birthday, he got up and tottered downstairs to look at his birthday presents, but he felt too ill for the entertainments which his parents had kindly, and rather childishly, arranged – a ventriloquist and a banjo-player. The next day, he developed inflammation of the lungs and the doctors recognized incipient pneumonia. By 13 January, he was delirious, yelling out 'Hélène, Hélène!' and talking wildly of Lord Randolph Churchill and Lord Salisbury and how much he loved his grandmother, the Queen. At 9.35 on the morning of 14 January, he died.

Even today, a visitor to the Albert Memorial Chapel at Windsor will feel a sense of shock when surveying Sir Alfred Gilbert's beautiful carved effigy of the Duke of Clarence and Avondale on his tomb, a figure in Hussars' uniform, unambiguously young and dead. Eddy's death was universally shocking, perhaps the more so because it came after so many scandals. In East Anglia, a ballad was circulated, and sung to the tune of 'God Bless the Prince of Wales'. For many years after Eddy's death, it was sung in pubs and at village gatherings:

> Alas, his soul it has departed,
> How solemn came the news,
> His parents broken hearted,
> Their darling son to lose.
> With sympathy and feeling,
> We one and all should say,
> God rest his soul in silence,
> And bless the Princess May![32]

As must often be the case in a dysfunctional family, the tragedy exacerbated feelings of alienation and anger between Queen Victoria and the stricken Bertie. 'The poor Parents, it's <u>too dreadful</u> for them to think of! & the poor young Bride!' she wrote to Ponsonby. Princess May responded fulsomely to the Queen's letter of condolence: 'How too dear & touching of you in the midst of your sorrow to write to poor little me.'[33]

Bertie begged his mother not to attend the funeral at Windsor because of the cold weather, and illness. Victoria took offence. 'I have read your letter which has distressed me very much. You have stopped my going... I feel quite ill at not going. Everybody expects me to go.'[34] Bertie responded with, 'Your telegram has deeply pained us as you have misunderstood the motive which urges us to beg you not to undertake a journey for so painful a ceremony on account of incurring considerable risk while this illness is flying about.'

Princess Beatrice and Princess Helena attended the funeral on behalf of their mother. The Prince and Princess of Wales received telegrams at a rate of 1,000 per day.[35]

Lord Salisbury's second administration, from 1886 to 1892, was one which had seen no major foreign war and comparatively easy diplomatic relations with the 'usual suspects' – Russia, Turkey, Germany. His hostility to Irish nationalism won him few friends in Ireland or America, but, as an exercise in holding the pass, it was successful. No socialist could have applauded Bloody Sunday, and many people must have considered that the manner in which a peaceful demonstration in Trafalgar Square was put down by armed mounted soldiers was, to say the least, draconian. There was a major London dock strike in 1889, led by the Irish-born Ben Tillett, which threatened the entire economy of the greatest commercial port in the world; both sides were so adamant that the dockers themselves came close to starvation, and the dispute was only solved through the patient mediating skills of Cardinal Manning. It was not surprising that within a year of Salisbury leaving office, the Independent Labour Party had been formed.

But neither Salisbury nor the Queen were under any illusions about the need for any Government, even one as benignly intentioned as theirs, to put down its opponents, at home or abroad, with violence where necessary.

Purging the mind of any sentimental illusions about the Salisbury Government of 1886–92, it is yet possible to see it as the most perfect example of the Victorian constitutional monarchy in action. Salisbury revered Queen Victoria, but he knew how to manage her. Though their relationship lacked any of the girlish excitement which animated her relationship with Disraeli, it was both a friendship and a near-perfect working relationship. When you read the correspondence between this pair, who were at the apex of the world's richest and most powerful Empire, it is like watching a mighty, well-oiled machine in motion. Of course, there were tensions – whose journey with the Queen was there which lacked potholes and interruptions? She was everlastingly on the cadge for more funds – for children and grandchildren; and even for Lord Salisbury, she felt she could get away with a minimalist public programme of engagements. But it was a machine which worked.

From the moment he took office as Secretary of State for India in the late 1870s, Salisbury had mastered the technique of asking her advice on trivial matters while he pursued his larger policies. He recognized how passionately the Queen, in common with most royal personages, was obsessed by honours, titles, medals and uniforms. The question of whether British officers should wear medals bestowed upon them by foreign potentates, and upon what occasions such lacked tact or dignity, could keep the old lady going for weeks. And there was also the simple question of who should receive knighthoods, baronetcies, deaneries, bishoprics and the many other baubles in her gift. A particularly comic instance of this – which actually occurred during Salisbury's brief first period of office – was the awarding of a knighthood to Chubb the locksmith. Ponsonby complained, 'Sir Chubb is the locksmith. I presume he was knighted for his Politics or Philanthropy and not for his locks – Hart the Queen's locksmith is furious, and sneers at Chubb's philanthropy.'[36]

So they happily worked together, the aristocratic Prime Minister and the Queen Empress. By the time of the General Election, in the summer of 1892, Salisbury had become as invaluable to the Queen in her old age as a sage and trustworthy personal adviser, as had Melbourne been to her in her youth.

The most dramatic episode, in this phase of the unfolding Irish tragedy, was undoubtedly the divorce of Mrs O'Shea from Captain O'Shea. Quite unknown to the political classes, let alone the public,

Charles Parnell, the leader of the Irish Home Rulers, had been living with Mrs O'Shea since 1880. She was long estranged from her husband, a spendthrift officer in the Hussars. In 1889, Mrs O'Shea inherited a fortune from an aunt, and O'Shea wanted a share of it. He sued for divorce, citing Parnell as the co-respondent. The Catholic Church in Ireland and the Northern Nonconformists who formed so sturdy a part of Gladstone's Liberal power base were alike scandalized. Home Rule was made an even remoter possibility. 'You cannot remain Parnellite and remain Catholic,' one Meath priest told his congregation.[37] Parnell defied public opinion and married Katherine O'Shea, but it was a short-lived marriage. Having addressed a political meeting in the rain at Kilkenny in September 1891, he became ill, returned to England and died in Brighton on 6 October. Another death which had its effect on the fortunes of the Liberals was that of the 7th Duke of Devonshire. His heir, Harty Tarty, left the Commons and took his seat in the Lords. He was succeeded as Liberal Leader in the Commons by Joseph Chamberlain, a figure even more violently Unionist than he. Hartington himself, before he became 8th duke, had already appeared on a platform in Liverpool with Salisbury, defending the Union, thereby scuppering any chances of a reconciliation between Liberal Home Rulers and Liberal Unionists. With all this in the background, it was in some ways surprising that the Conservatives lost the election in August 1892. The Queen was dismayed by the results: 268 Conservatives, with 272 Liberals and 45 Liberal Unionists, 81 Irish Nationalists and, for the first time in history, 2 Independent Labour MPs, Keir Hardie and J. W. Burns.

Far from moving with the times, Queen Victoria had reverted to pre-1832 ways of thinking about the electoral system. Rather than recognizing that Salisbury had lost in the polls, she thought that he 'appeared to acquiesce too much in the result of the elections'[38]. To Vicky, she wrote, 'It seems to me a defect in our much famed Constitution, to have to part with an admirable Government like Lord Salisbury's for no question of any importance, or any particular reason, merely on account of the number of votes.'[39]

With such distressing evidence of the democratic process in action, it was all the more important to ensure the succession to the throne. Victoria was in no doubt at all that, after a decent interval, poor Princess May of Teck should be married off to Prince Eddy's younger brother George – 'so nice, sensible, and truly right-minded'[40] – before a more eligible royal bachelor in Europe scooped her up. George, who would one day be King George V, was made Duke of York – in spite of his grandmother's earlier objection to reviving the title, with all its memories of her moronic uncle of that name. George had it in mind to marry his cousin Missy, the daughter of Affie, Duke of Edinburgh, but this was hastily overruled. A straightforward naval officer, George was sent off to Heidelberg for a couple of months to perfect his German, and then he was ready to be married.

The wedding was fixed for 6 July 1893.

The only problem, in the weeks running up to the nuptials, was the rumour which circulated about the Duke of York being already married, and his wife alive. No evidence for this wild idea was ever produced, but it occupied much of the archbishop's time as he prepared for the ceremony. It had been a sordid, difficult, time for the monarchy. Benson, as he drafted his words to the young couple, must have had in mind the plethora of stories of Cleveland Street homosexual brothels, of the fast country-house set, cheating at cards and at marriage, as he prepared to marry the future King George and Queen Mary.

'This is an age,' he wrote, 'and this a people, which in spite of many outward changes, still, in its heart of hearts, looks to the highest to do the common duties of all better than them all… The first element of Society is the Family. The one prayer of all is that no blessing, no peace, no strength of the Family may be lacking to the Future which is in the hand of God for you.'[41]

6 July turned out to be a sweltering hot day. Bertie, as father of the groom, nevertheless had time, during the frenzy of wedding service,

wedding breakfast and Royal Family dinner, to sneak off for an hour with his mistress, the Babbling Brooke.[42]

Outside the Royal Chapel, enormous crowds waited to see the arrival of the royal guests, and of the bride who only a year earlier had been the subject of tragic ballads as she buried her fiancé Eddy. Encouraged by Lord Salisbury and Archbishop Benson, the Royal Family put on such a display as the politicians of the 1870s had yearned for, but which in those days the Widow of Windsor had always refused. As if in reply to the socialists, to the scandal-sheets, to the satirical pamphlets and to the sneering lawyers with their distressing grasp of the rules of baccarat and the names of Bertie's nouveaux-riches friends, the great Royal Establishment put on a wedding procession which thrilled the masses. There they all were in the bright sunshine of the Mall, Silver Stick-in-Waiting, Gold Stick, maids of honour, grand dukes, the Captain of the Yeomen of the Guard and the Master of Buckhounds. Four carriages trotted the short distance from the Palace to the Chapel Royal at St James's Palace, the last of which contained the Duchess of Teck and the Queen. And when it was all over, the Queen and her family appeared on the balcony of Buckingham Palace to wave the young couple goodbye.[43]

It was the Queen's appearance, however, as she came into the small chapel, which made the greatest impression upon her archbishop. Benson wrote in his diary:

The Bishops of London and Rochester and I (with others) were standing in front of the Altar. I could scarcely believe my eyes when the Queen entered the Chapel by the lower end. There she was alone and began to walk up alone. The Duchess of Teck and her grandson of Hesse were behind her. On she came, looking most pleasant, slightly amused, bowing most gracefully to either side as she came, her black silk almost covered with wonderful lace, and lace and a little crown with chains of diamonds on her head, walking lame and with a tallish stick. She looked Empire, gracious Empire…[44]

TWENTY FOUR

'WHAT A FUNNY LITTLE WOMAN'

L EST ANYONE SHOULD have been under the impression that Great Britain had a monarch who was 'above politics', the Court Circular in *The Times* informed readers that she had accepted Lord Salisbury's resignation 'with much regret'.[1]

In the past, the Queen's instinct, upon hearing that Mr Gladstone had won an election, had always been to seek some alternative Liberal as Prime Minister. In 1868, 1880 and 1886, she had asked Lord Hartington to form an administration over Gladstone's head. In 1892, Lord Hartington had become the Duke of Devonshire, and split with Gladstone over the Irish Question, so she could no longer look to him to save her. She would have liked to ask Lord Rosebery, one of her favourite politicians among the younger generation, despite his political views which she regarded as 'almost Communistic'. Ponsonby, however, dissuaded her, and she bowed to the inevitable, which was 'to have that dangerous old fanatic thrust down her throat'.[2]

During the election campaign, Gladstone had been making a speech at Chester when a 'middle-aged bony woman' threw a piece of gingerbread which caught him in his left eye – the one eye which he still found 'serviceable'. Like many humourless people, Gladstone was everlastingly prone to mishaps which were difficult to take quite seriously. Had he been half blinded by a stone or a gun, it would have been simply sad; but for so serious a person to be injured by a sweetmeat bordered on farce. For the rest of his life, he saw the world through a fog. At the end of August, shortly after becoming Prime Minister, he was walking in his park at Hawarden when a 'dangerous cow'[3] knocked him to the ground. She 'might have done serious damage. I walked home with little difficulty & have to thank the Almighty.'[4]

The Grand Old Man, who had been sitting in Parliament since 1833, was eighty-three years old. He told Morley, his Chief Secretary for Ireland (and future biographer), that 'his general health was good and sound, but his sight and his hearing were so rapidly declining, that he thought he might almost any day have to retire from office'.[5] The Queen noted that he was 'very deaf and aged'.[6] She told Davidson that she found interviews with the old man 'rather a farce, as she is as anxious as she can be to avoid reference to politics... We therefore confine ourselves to correspondence'.[7]

Something which could have united them was the death of their friend-in-common Lord Tennyson. Gladstone had been at Eton with Arthur Hallam, the friend whose premature death occasioned the lyrics of *In Memoriam*; and the old Prime Minister lent his letters from Hallam to the Queen – a fact she found touching. There seemed no obvious candidate to succeed Tennyson in his role as Poet Laureate. His personal friendship with Prince Albert and the Queen in their early days on the Isle of Wight, his reign-of-William-IV clothes and diction, his firm adherence to vague religious hopes and his necro-philiac obsession with the dear departed dead made him so perfect a poet of the Queen's reign that he was quite literally irreplaceable. Tennyson himself had remarked that of the younger poets, only Rudyard Kipling had 'fire in his belly'. Algernon Charles Swinburne was an avowed atheist and would never have been acceptable to the Queen; nor would William Morris, who added communism to the sin of religious unbelief. So, the laurel crown gathered dust. Victoria could find no brow worthy of it, and Gladstone, ever-conscious that he had but a short time in office before his sight and hearing altogether faded, pressed on with the formation of his Government

and the advancement of the cause dearest to his heart: Home Rule
for Ireland. In fact, this was an ambition doomed before it began, and
his last, short administration was dominated by decisions concerning
East Africa, Egypt, and the increase in the Royal Navy.

Gladstone's Cabinet contained three future Prime Ministers: H.
H. Asquith became Home Secretary, Henry Campbell-Bannerman
the Secretary of State for War, and, after pleading and persuading
from the Prince of Wales and the Queen, Lord Rosebery accepted
the post of Foreign Secretary.

Gladstone had wanted to offer a Cabinet seat to Henry
Labouchere, but the Queen insisted that she would not accept him,
unless he severed connections with his lucrative newspaper *Truth*,
a radical sheet which only a couple of years before had suggested
that Buckingham Palace be converted into a home for fallen women.
Since 'Labby' would never give up his paper, the Queen knew that
her conditions should never be met. Radicals were not the only ones
on this occasion who questioned whether she had been within her
constitutional rights to determine the composition of the Cabinet.
Ponsonby agreed with the Queen that she 'had a perfect right
according to the Constitution to dismiss Gladstone which means
dismissing his ministers. But he thinks that when once appointed
she cannot dismiss any one minister serving under a Prime Minister.
Of course the conversation was "academic" as to dismiss a ministry
would be impossible as long as they have a Majority in Parliament.'[8]

Gladstone clung to office long after he was physically incapable of it.
Morley likened his unwillingness to resign to 'the resistance of a child
or an animal to an incomprehensible (and incredible) torment'.[9]

Rosebery and the Queen together were under no illusions about
the crises facing Britain. Britain was undergoing a severe recession.
Labour relations were poor. The success of the dockers in their long

strike of 1889 had inspired other workers to join trades unions – the numbers were approaching 2 million. In 1893, 30,440,000 days' work were lost in industrial stoppages. Agriculture was in apparently terminal decline. Prices had fallen by 40 per cent since 1890 and wages had been cut by as much as 25 per cent.

When he visited Windsor Castle in December, Rosebery had 'poured out to her on the subject' of Home Rule. 'She says he told her that in his opinion the Home Rule Attempt is impossible... Lord Rosebery begs her on no account to mention Uganda to Mr Gladstone as he is quite rabid on the subject and desires to abandon it without scruple – a policy to which Rosebery is steadfastly opposed.'[10]

The area of Uganda was being administered by the British East Africa Company. Captain Frederick Lugard arrived in the Kingdom of Buganda, one of the main Ugandan states, in 1890 and found a chaotic situation: feuds between French Catholic and English Protestant missionaries, inter-tribal conflict, appalling atrocities being committed by King Mwanga. The British East Africa Company could not afford to go on losing £40,000 per annum, and it wanted to pull out of Uganda. If it did so, Lugard argued, there would be massacres. Only the British Government was in a position to intervene.

Gladstone and the other anti-imperialists in the Cabinet were against Government intervention. Rosebery did not agree. He realized that the 'Scramble for Africa' was on among the European powers and that if Britain did not dominate East Africa, it would fall into the hands of the French. It was largely this, and a certain deviousness, which enabled him to get his way, despite the arguments of Liberals, such as Sir William Harcourt, who argued that, unlike India, Africa could never be profitable to Britain. English settlers, argued Harcourt, 'could never get these savages to work for them. These savages are not like the mild Hindoo with whom you can do as you please.'[11]

Largely through sleight of hand, Rosebery got the Cabinet to agree to 'postpone' withdrawal from Uganda, while in effect establishing it as a British dominion. He likewise strengthened the position of the British in Egypt, having no wish to preside over a repetition of the fiascos of ten years earlier, of a restless Egypt and the British humiliated by Gordon being murdered in the Sudan. Thus, for all his 'Communistic' radicalism, Rosebery was really an impenitent imperialist. And once he had decided, after the bitter bereavement of losing his beloved wife Hannah, to accept the post of Foreign Secretary and re-enter politics, there was no one else in the Liberal Party who could withstand his advance.

Gladstone's attempt to achieve Home Rule for Ireland before he retired was, as Rosebery had told the Queen in December, doomed to failure. Rosebery, however, continued to support it, since, as he told her in June 1893, there was no realistic alternative, for 'were the hope of Home Rule to be removed, the latent forces of anarchy and revolution would break out with renewed horror'.[12]

He was right in both his prophecies: Gladstone's Bill would fail, and Ireland would descend into violent anarchy. But the unforeseen coup de grâce which brought an end to Gladstone's parliamentary career was not Ireland, nor imperialism, but a combination of ill health and the increase in the Navy Estimates.

When the Queen asked the old man about the condition of Britain's defence, Gladstone was overcome with a near gastric calamity, only just able to leave the royal presence and reach a bathroom before diarrhoea and vomiting overtook him.

The French and the Russian navies had greatly increased in recent years, and those two nations were now allies. Germany was also building up its navy, and there was overwhelming pressure on Earl Spencer, First Lord of the Admiralty, to increase the British naval capacity. Crucial technological advances had been made between the late 1880s and the early '90s, not least the change from cordite to gunpowder as a propellant. Many naval vessels were still using obsolete muzzle-loading guns, only five vessels carrying the more modern breach-loaders. In the summer of 1893 two of the best British battleships, the *Victoria* and the *Camperdown*, collided in the Mediterranean. Ominously, it was the *Victoria* which sank, and with it Gladstone's career. He had, rather nobly and with great obstinacy, opposed the majority in his Cabinet who wanted an expensive refurbishment of the Royal Navy.

As the row gathered pace, Gladstone's eyesight faded to the point where he could scarcely see. He knew that his resignation was inevitable, but he decided to let Rosebery and friends sweat a little. 'I am now like the sea in swell after a storm, bodily affected, but mentally pretty well anchored. It is bad: but oh how infinitely better than to be implicated in that [navy] plan,' he told his diary. And then he went to recuperate in Biarritz, a favoured resort. There he made notes on the plan to introduce a new tax – (always an abomination to him) – death duties – to pay for the arms race, to which he refused to subscribe. He wrote, 'Above all, I cannot and will not add to the perils and the coming calamities of Europe by an act of militarism which will be found to involve a policy, and which excuses thus the militarism of Germany, France or Russia. England's providential part is to help peace, and liberty of which peace is the nurse. This policy is the foe of birth. I am willing to see England dare [?illegible] the world in arms: but not to see England help to set the world in arms.'[13]

Did the Grand Old Man ever write a grander sentiment? Morley – known by his mocking colleagues as the Grand Old Maid – was surely not hyperbolic when he began his chapter on Gladstone's fourth administration with a quotation from the first book of the *Iliad*: 'Two generations of mortal men had he already seen pass away, who with him of old had been born and bred in sacred Pylos, and among the third generation, he held rule.'[14]

The Queen, who was also capable of greatness in her own way and at certain times, perhaps never behaved with less dignity than she did at the time of Gladstone's resignation. She who accepted the weeping and rebellious Maharajah Duleep Singh back into her love; she who asked Lord Carnarvon to dinner, in spite of her early fury over his Cabinet resignation; she who forgave the young Davidson his impertinent advice to suppress her memoir of Brown; and who was all smiles – after six months of 'no speaks' with Princess Beatrice – could not, for a quarter of an hour, rise to the occasion and pretend to be civil to this mighty statesman, this eighty-four-year-old embodiment of the nineteenth-century political story.

On 3 March 1894, she was to hold a Council at Windsor Castle. Both the Gladstones stayed overnight with the Ponsonbys, and Mrs Gladstone as well as her husband had an audience with the Queen after breakfast. 'She was very much upset, poor thing, & asked to be allowed to speak, as her Husband "could not speak". This was to say, which she did with many tears, that whatever his errors might have been, "his devotion to Your Majesty and the Crown were very great". She repeated this twice, & begged me to allow her to tell him that I believed it, which I did, for I am convinced it is the case, though at times his actions might have made it difficult to believe. She spoke of former days & how long she had known me & dearest Albert. I kissed her when she left.'[15]

Part of the trouble, in the relationship between Victoria and Gladstone, was one of simple shyness. Gladstone could not 'speak', and Victoria was reduced to stiltedness in his company. But there was also a deep personal dislike, which she was not gracious enough to conceal. In her reply to his letter of resignation, the Queen did not express a word of thanks to him. 'She trusts he will be able to enjoy peace and quiet with his excellent and devoted wife in health and happiness, and that his eyesight may improve. The Queen would gladly have conferred a peerage on Mr Gladstone but she knows he would not accept it.' This was no way to sign off a great national hero. Gladstone let it be known that he was 'a good deal hurt and does not wish to receive any further communications'.[16]

He was still having bad dreams about the Queen two years later, and he left instructions to his family that, after his death, they should 'to keep in the background the personal relations of the Queen and myself in these later years, down to 1894 when they died a kind of natural death'.[17]

When he did die, in May 1898, Victoria's children remonstrated with their mother for her failure to see his greatness. 'Poor Mr

Gladstone was often your Minister and though it was impossible always to agree with him, yet he was a great Englishman and it is fitting to do honour to his memory as such' – so wrote the Empress Frederick. The Queen belted the shuttlecock back over the net at once: 'I cannot say that I think he was a great Englishman. He was a clever man, full of talent, but he never tried to keep up the honour and prestige of Great Britain. He gave away the Transvaal, he abandoned Gordon, he destroyed the Irish Church and tried to separate England from Ireland and to set class against class.'[18]

By way of reparation, at the State Funeral in Westminster Abbey, two of the pall-bearers were Bertie, the Prince of Wales, and his son George, Duke of York. Bertie made a point of speaking to Mrs Gladstone after the service.[19] Gladstone himself, to the end, had persisted in finding the ungraciousness and the vitriol of the Queen's animosity difficult to understand. There was, he wrote, 'something of mystery, which I have not been able to fathom, and probably never shall'.[20]

Perhaps the simplest explanation was one she gave to Marie Mallet, her Maid of Honour. 'She said she has always disliked politics & does not consider them a woman's province, but that the Prince Consort forced her to take an interest in them, often to her disgust & that since he died she has tried to keep up the interest for his sake... Mr Gladstone had caused her more pain & anxiety than any of [her Prime Ministers], so often insisting upon measures which she felt & knew were mistakes & dangerous & which have turned out to be so!'[21]

When Gladstone finally resigned, the Queen defied convention and did not ask the incumbent Prime Minister's advice about his choice of a successor. It was in effect Ponsonby who had to consult with the senior Liberals, and act as an intermediary with the Queen.[22] There was tremendous in-fighting in the Liberal Party, between radicals and imperialists, pro- and anti-Home Rulers. Before the old man went, Sir William Harcourt – who frequently dined with Ponsonby

– told Gladstone that he must 'bring up his heaviest guns to cover our retreat and proclaim war against the H of Lords'.[23] Those on the left of the party wanted Harcourt as Prime Minister, even though Rosebery, as well as being the Queen's choice, was undoubtedly the more popular politician in the country at large.[24]

The Queen was watching the march of radicalism with horrified fascination. The Independent Labour Party had been founded in Bradford in 1893 – 'the most important political event of the nineteenth century', according to one of its founder members, Philip Snowden. Keir Hardie, a working-class Lanarkshire miner and son of a Clydeside shipworker, took his seat in the Commons in August 1892. He refused to wear parliamentary 'uniform' of a silk top hat, frock coat and starched collar. Instead, he wore tweeds and a deerstalker hat. He was actually the sort of straight-talking Scotsman that Queen Victoria in other contexts would have liked, but she could not like what he said in Parliament.

On 23 June 1894, the Duchess of York gave birth to a son, and the House of Commons drafted a congratulatory address. Keir Hardie asked that they should add to this address a message of condolence to the families of 251 miners who had just been killed in a pit disaster at Pontypridd, South Wales. The request was refused, and Hardie made the speech which undoubtedly cost him his seat (West Ham) at the next election.

> From his childhood onward this boy will be surrounded by sycophants and flatterers by the score. [Cries of 'Oh! Oh!'] and will be taught to believe himself as of a superior creation. [Cries of 'Oh! Oh!'] A line will be drawn between him and the people whom he is to be called upon some day to reign over. In due course, following the precedent which has already been set, he will be sent on a tour round the world, and probably rumours of a morganatic alliance will follow [Loud cries of 'Oh! Oh!' and 'Order!'] – and the end of it all will be that the country will be called upon to pay the bill. [Cries of 'Divide!'][25]

The Queen talked about this speech 'with great horror'.[26] She would have been even more horrified if she had known with what uncanny accuracy Keir Hardie was predicting the life and fortunes of the future King Edward VIII, whose antics landed the monarchy in what his mother called 'a pretty kettle of fish'.

'Nothing can prevent Asquith from leading the Liberal Party when I am out of the way,' said Harcourt to his son Loulou, and this would eventually prove to be the case. H. H. Asquith, a clever, Balliol-educated Yorkshire lawyer, and a young Welsh solicitor called David Lloyd George, who had entered the House in a by-election in 1900, would dominate the politics of the left in Britain until the Independent Labour Party of Keir Hardie had assembled enough seats to become the Opposition, and eventually the Government, after the First World War. No monarchist at this date would ever have been able to predict that these developments would not lead to a British republic. Victoria's 'horror' at Keir Hardie was understandable, as was her belief that Gladstone's gerontic radicalism had opened the doors towards it. She would entirely have endorsed Lord Salisbury's view that 'Gladstone's revolutionary appeals to the jealousy of the poor will do much harm'.[27]

For the Queen's part, although she did not approve of Rosebery's politics, she was very fond of him 'personally... and prefer him [in] certain [respects] to Lord Salisbury. He is so much attached to me personally'.[28]

She had an almost maternal feeling towards him, and felt able, as she would never have done to Disraeli, to tell him to curb his cynical sense of humour, which animated many of his public utterances. It is not true that Victoria was humourless, but when it came to irony or country-house larkiness, she drew a blank. Everything she heard, for example, about the Souls – the 'set' who included Arthur Balfour, Margot Asquith, the Duchess of Rutland et al – made her say, 'they really should be told not to be so silly!'[29] She detected some of this 'silliness' in Rosebery. She presumed to speak in the name of his late wife, 'one who can no longer be a comfort and support to him and who she [knows] felt very anxious on this subject [radicalism]'.[30] As for his speeches out of Parliament, 'he should take a more serious tone and be, if she may say so, less jocular, which is hardly befitting a Prime Minister'.[31] Far from resenting these pieces of advice, Rosebery evidently liked his monarch's motherly attentions, and her repeated worry that he was not getting enough sleep – which was a persistent problem throughout his year or so of premiership.

Naturally, she protested when his 'Communistic' opinions went against her better instincts. As he told her in the autumn of 1894, 'the cry in the Liberal Party is for the abolition of the House of Lords or of its veto'. For his part, he had long believed that 'the House of Lords, as at present constituted, cannot continue to exist'. The Queen was 'much put out and perturbed'[32] by the suggestion of modifying the power of the Lords over the Commons. While Rosebery pointed out how intolerable it was that a largely Tory House of Peers could always veto the resolutions of an elected House of Commons, the Queen felt any gesture towards Lords reform was 'mischievous in the highest degree. Is <u>Party</u> to go before the interests of the Country?'[33] As it happened, she need not have worried. The difficult question of dealing with the Tory bias of the House of Lords, as opposed to the elected Commons, was to be addressed by George V in the early years of his reign; and advocates of root and branch reform of the Lords waited over 100 years before their dreams were realized.

A matter over which the Queen was surprisingly much more sympathetic was the resignation as commander-in-chief of her dear old cousin the Duke of Cambridge. The Duke was seventy-six and he had held this post for the past thirty-nine years. Many was the letter which the Queen had fired off on his behalf to the first Gladstone Government, protesting at the abolition of purchase as a system of selecting officers; protesting against the abolition of flogging; howling against the winds of change whenever they blew.

A Royal Commission, set up in 1888, had delivered a report on army reform in 1890, recommending the abolition of the post of commander-in-chief, to be replaced by a group of five senior officers responsible to the War Ministry. This was a recommendation only partially implemented by the Rosebery Government, and the post remained. Although the Queen agreed in principle that Cousin George should be replaced, she probably understood better than the younger politicians that it would be difficult to get him to go quietly. Having said he would leave, the duke then asked for a pension of £2,000 p.a. on top of the £12,000 voted to him annually by Parliament merely for being the Duke of Cambridge. 'I am not a rich man, but a very poor one', spluttered the duke. 'I will lose my occupation and position. And for what? Because the Government thinks a change is necessary. The Queen sent me a Patent in 1887 giving me the office for life and I have done nothing discreditable since then. As to the question of my age it is an unmerited insult'.[34]

The Queen, naturally, assumed that Cousin George would be succeeded in the role by her son the Duke of Connaught. When the truth dawned on her that they intended to appoint a non-royal commander-in-chief, she confessed that it was 'painful' to her, and asked for Rosebery's assurance that 'the Duke of Connaught will not later on be debarred from that office'.[35] They gave the post to one of the Queen's bêtes-noires, Garnet Wolseley, and he was succeeded in 1901 by Lord Roberts. On both occasions, poor Arthur, Duke of Connaught, always Queen Victoria's favourite son, felt 'vexed'.[36] One of his sons-in-law became the King of Sweden.

It was exactly twenty years before Archduke Franz Ferdinand was assassinated in Sarajevo, and we can watch the characters in the drama involved in the outbreak of world war growing into their roles. In the Liberal Party, Asquith, Grey, Lloyd George – members of the fateful Cabinet which could see no way out of their doom-laden treaty obligations with France and Russia and against Austria-Hungary – were all coming to the fore. In the wider Royal Family, we see the players waiting in the wings.

In April 1894, Queen Victoria visited Coburg. 'When the dear old Festung came in sight, I could but think of my beloved Albert's joy when we approached Coburg the first time'.[37] The German Emperor was in town, and had brought with him a squadron of the Prussian regiment of Dragoons – of which his grandmother was colonel-in-chief – for her to inspect when she dismounted from her train.

Her son Affie, Duke of Edinburgh, was now the Duke of Saxe-Coburg-Gotha. He had been more successful in his naval career, than Prince Arthur, Duke of Connaught, was in his army career. In June 1893, he was Commander-in-Chief of the British Fleet, stationed at Devonport, and an admiral of the fleet. But then Prince Albert's dissipated old brother Ernst died in Coburg, and Affie's naval duties came to an end. Since Bertie, for obvious reasons, had resigned the title of heir to the Duchy of Saxe-Coburg-Gotha and since Ernst II and Alexandrine were childless, the title passed to the Duke of Edinburgh.

He immediately lost his £15,000 per annum as an English royal duke, and as a German one he did not find it always easy – there was much resentment in Germany against the arrival of a foreigner, as he was perceived. When his mother arrived to see him in April 1894, he was already installed as the duke with his nice Russian wife Marie. A huge contingent of the family was staying at the Schloss Ehrenberg for the wedding of Ducky – Affie's daughter Victoria Melita – to Ernst Ludwig of Hesse-Darmstadt, the son of the ever-lamented Princess Alice. He was the last person, as it happened, ever to hold that office. It was not to be a happy marriage: Ducky found the constraints of an unreformed petty German Court at Darmstadt intolerable. She forgot to answer letters, forgot to return visits to boring old relations and was regarded as too skittish; Louis was irascible with her, and there were many rows. She was horse-mad, and would ride out into the woods, forgetting appointments. Louis particularly hated a frisky stallion called Bogdan, her favourite horse whom no one but she could ride. Eventually, the squabbling pair divorced in 1901.

Even on her wedding day, poor Ducky was less interesting to the rest of the family than her sister Alicky. The day after Ducky and Ernst were married, Queen Victoria had just had her breakfast in the Schloss Ehrenberg when Ella burst into the room: 'Alicky and Nicky are engaged!'[38]

So, while Ducky went off for seven years of stultifying boredom in Darmstadt, her two sisters were now both bound for Russia. Ella was already the Grand Duchess Elisabeth. Alicky was to become Alexandra Feodorovna. Queen Victoria took an active role in training her for her new role, for her husband, Nikolai Alexandrovich, as Tsarevich, was the heir to the Empire of All the Russias. Quite how soon he would become the Emperor, and Alicky the Empress, none of them could have guessed. It is almost unbearably poignant to see the photographs taken in the summer of 1894 of the betrothed Nicky and Alicky. He, more or less the double of his cousin George, Duke of York, stares heedless at the camera, while she, blank-faced, clutches the handle of an umbrella.

Shortly after the wedding in Coburg, Alicky came to England to spend an extended period with her elder sister Victoria (mother of the future Earl Mountbatten of Burma and grandmother of the future Prince Philip, Duke of Edinburgh) and with her grand-mother the Queen. She was accompanied by Mlle Schneider, who was teaching her Russian, and after initial religious instruction by the Bishop of Ripon, Dr Carpenter, an expert on the Eastern Churches, she was handed over to the emperor's confessor, Father Yanishev, who received her into his Church. Queen Victoria oversaw all this, and also arranged for the sisters to enjoy themselves; the great Eleonora Duse performed in Ibsen's *The Master Builder* in a special perfor-mance at Windsor Castle, and they went into London to see Sarah Bernhardt act in a play called *Adrienne Lecouvreur*. Both sisters agreed that La Duse was infinitely the more impressive of the two theatrical legends.[39]

The carefree life did not last long. The forty-nine-year-old Emperor, Nicky's father Alexander III, was an autocrat who made

Queen Victoria's occasional outbursts against radicalism seem mild. He regarded parliamentary government as 'the great lie of our time'. As for juries, he thought they should be abolished 'in order to restore the significance of the court in Russia'. He was scarcely preparing his son, or his people, for the progressive future, and with his mentor, the Ecclesiastical Censor Pobedonostsev – the mastermind behind the excommunication of the novelist Tolstoy – he would happily have undone all the comparatively liberal reforms of his father. 'The voice of God orders us to stand boldly by the task of governing,' he wrote in one of his royal proclamations.[40] Even Lord Salisbury would have appeared radical beside Alexander III.

Rosebery stayed at Balmoral with the Queen for two nights in October 1894. It was as unlike Mr Gladstone's farcical visits as possible. Whereas the Grand Old Man was sometimes not spoken to at all during his visits to the Deeside Schloss, Rosebery spent the afternoons and evenings freely chatting with the Queen, about the Chinese–Japanese war then in progress, and about the sudden deterioration in health of the Russian Emperor, which, apart from the personal grief which it would cause Victoria's granddaughter Alicky, was clearly a potential calamity in terms of international politics. He had nephritis, and, as the medical bulletins became more and more pessimistic, the Prince of Wales set out to pay his last respects. The Emperor died at Livadia on 31 October. Nicky was now the Tsar. Less than a month after his father's death, he married Alicky in an elaborate ceremony at St Petersburg. Victoria was now the grandmother of two of the most powerful imperial houses in Europe – Germany and Russia. Two of the central players in the tragedy of 1914, Wilhelm of Germany and Nikolai Alexandrovich of Russia, were now on the stage. In the Tobolsk province of Siberia, a weird sexual maniac-cum-mystic named Rasputin was beginning his married life and fathering three children. In Alicky's genes, though she did not know it, lurked the fatal capacity to pass on haemophilia to a male child.

In each of the years he was Prime Minister, Rosebery's horse won the Derby: Ladas in 1894, and Sir Visto in 1895. The Queen's lady-in-waiting, Eliza Waterpark, was an aunt by marriage of Rosebery, married to his uncle Bouverie Primrose. It was very much through Uncle Bouverie that Rosebery had developed his interest in racing and horses. 'What do you say to Lord Rosebery winning the Derby and to his being Prime Minister,' Eliza wrote proudly to her sister in June 1894.[41] But within a year, though his luck as a racehorse owner never seemed to desert him, he was a political spent force. There was a characteristic witty acknowledgement of this in Rosebery's choice of title when he was elevated to the English peerage in 1895 – Baron Epsom of Epsom. 'I never did have power,' he bitterly remarked of his time in office.[42]

Rosebery was premier for little over a year. He was too thin-skinned for the office, and when his popularity waned, he had not got the necessary insensitivity to withstand the unceasing criticism of him coming from Labouchere and the other radicals. Moreover, the year of his premiership, 1894–5, coincided with one of the most unpleasant scandals of the Victorian era, the persecution of Oscar Wilde by the 'Scarlet Marquess' of Queensberry.

The son of the Scarlet Marquess was Viscount Drumlanrig – Drummy, a blond, blue-eyed, rather dim Guards officer who had been educated at Harrow. When Rosebery was still at the Foreign Office, it was suggested that he take on Drummy as a private secretary, and that Drummy be made an English peer. He was given the title Lord Kelhead, and made a lord-in-waiting, a courtier's role, but one which entitled him to vote, and swell the all-too-thin Liberal ranks, in the House of Lords.

It was a definite risk, to reward Drumlanrig in this way. His father had been excluded from the House of Lords on the grounds of his atheism. Scottish peers did not all sit in the House as of right. They elected a fixed number from among their group, and Queensberry, who had made himself offensive in many ways, scuppered his chances of election when he insisted upon distributing atheist literature on the red leather benches before prayers.

Violent in his temper, and with a bee in his bonnet about homosexuality, he felt immediate resentment at his son being given a peerage; and his crude mind assumed that the title of Kelhead was given as a reward for sexual favours. Rosebery had definitely passed through a homosexual phase at Eton, where his tutor, William Johnson Cory, a fine poet and translator who expounded the virtues of Greek love, had been asked to leave because of his over-effusiveness to the boys. (He does not seem to have indulged in any impropriety more intimate than sending them love letters and rubbing his whiskers against their cheeks while they recited Anacreontics.)

Rosebery was a devoted husband to Hannah de Rothschild, and had, in adult life, shown a keen appreciation of women's beauty; but a whiff of his adolescent self hung about him, and although he was hetereosexual in practice, there were rumours. He had that habit of witty speech, brilliant off-the-cuff jokes and a very faint air of camp which can be wrongly mistaken for homosexuality. Queensberry bombarded Rosebery with highly abusive letters, addressing one such missive to 'The Jew Pimp'. When Rosebery escaped to Bad Homburg in Austria, Queensberry pursued him, chasing him through the town, and informing 'everyone, even ladies, of the direful things he was going to do to that boy pimp and boy lover Rosebery'.[43] For so shy and inward a man as Rosebery to quote this fact does suggest that he was completely innocent of the charges made by Queensberry. At the same time, the marquess was persecuting Oscar Wilde, who was in love with Drumlanrig's brother Lord Alfred Douglas, and accusing Wilde of being 'a damned cur and coward of the Rosebery type' – a phrase which was read out in court in Wilde's defence when the poet-playwright's sordid pursuit of under-age working-class male prostitutes was read out in court. Though Wilde's defence counsel intended to demonstrate the marquess's lack of reason, it was a phrase which did not do Rosebery any good.

Drummy got engaged to Alix Ellis, daughter of one of the Prince of Wales's equerries. Loulou Harcourt maliciously said this 'makes the institution of marriage ridiculous!'[44] In October 1894, during a shooting party in the Quantocks, he was found dead. He was killed with a single bullet which passed through the mouth and shattered the skull. To do this, Drummy would have had to be holding the loaded gun pointing upwards, a strange thing to do unless he intended suicide.[45]

There was never any evidence of a homosexual relationship between Drummy and Rosebery, and if there had been, Loulou and the other malice-merchants in the Liberal Party, all of whom had come to hate Rosebery, would not have held back from supplying it. But in the climate of that particular year or two, in which Wilde's fate was sealed, it did not help the Prime Minister's standing, and probably contributed to the sleepless nights which, in the end, exhausted him to the point of collapse.

Victoria was appalled by the implication, made by the coroner in his inquest, that Drumlanrig's death might not have been accidental.[46] In her surviving journals, transcribed by Princess Beatrice, the Queen merely says how 'dreadfully shocked' she was to hear 'that that charming Lord Drumlanrig whom we all liked so much was accidentally killed'[47]. Admittedly, the month of October 1894 was dominated, for the Queen, by anxiety about the last weeks of the Emperor of Russia, but she was an obsessive gossip and took a keen interest in the private lives of her small Court. Silence on the subject of the inquest into Lord Drumlanrig's sad death, and the lack of speculation about the death of her lord-in-waiting suggests that, when she came to 'transcribe' Queen Victoria's journals, Princess Beatrice might have, as so often, omitted potentially interesting material.

In the event, the Rosebery Government fell on a parliamentary technicality. The War Minister, Henry Campbell-Bannerman, had not ordered enough cordite, the new smokeless propellant used in all the new guns being manufactured for the armed forces, and the

Commons gave a vote of censure for his inefficiency. But the real reason for the routing of Rosebery was Ireland.

In the House of Lords in March, Salisbury, with a Cecil deviousness of which his old ancestor Lord Burghley would have been proud, remarked, almost casually, that since the question of Home Rule now appeared to be in suspense, there should be a General Election on the issue, since it could not be passed into law until the wishes of the English, as well as of the Irish, people be tested. Salisbury was not usually noted for his enthusiasm for democracy, but he knew very well, not only that the majority of the British public were against Home Rule for Ireland, but so was Rosebery, and so were all the Liberal Unionists.

One wonders if Rosebery was committing political suicide or simply being extraordinarily careless when he replied that, 'The noble marquess made one remark on Irish Home Rule with which I confess myself in entire accord. He said that before Irish Home Rule is concluded by the Imperial Parliament, England as the predominant member of the partnership of the three kingdoms will have to be convinced of its justice and equity.'[48]

More than seventy of Rosebery's Liberal MPs, especially those on the Celtic fringes, were ardent supporters of the Home Rule measure. His airy agreement with the Leader of the Tories in this manner merely broadened what was to become an unbridgeable abyss between the Liberal Unionists and the rest. Salisbury spent the next few months sounding out Liberal Unionists and five of them agreed to serve in his Cabinet, if Rosebery's Government collapsed: the Duke of Devonshire (Harty Tarty), Hicks Beach, Joseph Chamberlain, Goschen and Henry James (not the American novelist but Lord James of Hereford, serving as Salisbury's Chancellor of the Duchy of Lancaster). In the election which followed Campbell-Bannerman's Commons censure, there was a Tory landslide, with such figures as Harcourt, Asquith and Morley losing their seats. One ominous result of all this was that Joseph Chamberlain, dynamic Birmingham radical, but fervent imperialist, chose the Cabinet post of Colonial

Secretary. Salisbury was surprised; he had offered Chamberlain any job he liked, and had assumed that the businessman would have wanted to be Chancellor of the Exchequer. With wild miscalculation, Salisbury believed Chamberlain's interest in the colonies to be 'entirely theoretic'.[49]

All the pieces and players were now in place for the final act of the Victorian drama, and for a calamitous imperialist war.

Meanwhile at Court, focus was, as so often, not pointing, as Chamberlain was, towards Africa, but towards India. At Christmas 1894, the new viceroy, Lord Elgin (grandson of the purchaser of the Parthenon Marbles), was what the Queen would call 'surprised' to receive a card inscribed with an appalling poem: 'With hearts of gold/ And a breath of May,/And a wish from my heart/To yours Today'. The poem was by Ellis Walton (not, surely, a candidate for the still vacant Poet Laureateship), and the card was signed: 'To Wish You a Happy Christmas from M. H. Abdul Karim, Windsor Castle'.[50]

Lord Elgin did not acknowledge this extraordinary communication, and the Queen was soon asking him why not. He resolutely refused to do so. His aide de camp had been Fritz Ponsonby, the twenty-seven-year-old son of Sir Henry, who came back to England in January. Sir Henry had attended his royal mistress at Osborne for the last time. The story went round that he looked at her intently, and remarked, 'What a funny little woman you are.' The Queen was supposed to have answered, 'Sir Henry, you cannot be well,' and rang the bell.[51]

Back in Osborne Cottage with his wife Mary, Sir Henry suffered a paralytic stroke. For a while, he was completely unconscious. When he came to himself, his right arm and leg were paralysed, his speech was incoherent, and it was clear that he would never be well again. He led an invalid existence for most of that eventful year.

Fritz, however, who now took up the post of a junior equerry, had news for the other courtiers. While he had been in India, the Queen had asked him to visit the Munshi's father, the 'surgeon general' in Agra whom she had insisted upon giving an honour – Khan Bahadur – in the recent New Year Honours. Fritz had been interested to discover that the surgeon general was not in fact a doctor at all, but the apothecary in the jail.

When told of the fact, the Queen hotly denied it, and informed Fritz that he must have seen the wrong man. Fritz was banished from her dinner table for a year. He was, meanwhile, told to write to Lord Elgin and discover the reason for his failure to acknowledge the dear Munshi's Christmas card. He received a reply via the viceroy's secretary pointing out how 'impossible it would be for an Indian Viceroy to enter into correspondence of this kind'.

The Household, meanwhile, noted that Rafiuddin Ahmed, a radical Muslim Indian lawyer and journalist with links to Afghanistan, had befriended the Munshi. They feared that the Queen was showing secret Indian papers to the Munshi and that these were in turn being 'leaked' to radical groups in Afghanistan.

The Queen at this date still refused to wear spectacles and had taken to complaining that modern ink was very faint, so it would have been possible for an unscrupulous person to read her private documents without her being especially aware of the fact. She certainly needed someone to read her papers for her.

During the annual visit to the Riviera, one of the local newspapers had described the Munshi as a servant. A correction had to be printed, dictated by the man himself, which stated that 'The Munshi, as a learned man and the Queen's Indian Secretary, and preceptor in Hindustani, is one of the most important personages "*auprès de la Reine*", having several men under him, and being often privileged to dine with his Royal Mistress and pupil.' The Household were incensed, and Fritz Ponsonby sent the cutting to Lord Elgin. When the party moved on to Darmstadt, the Queen gave instructions to the Empress Frederick that she should show the Munshi round the Schloss – 'kindly remember that he is my Indian Secretary and considered as a gentleman in my suite... He can take no meat and only a little milk and fruit cld. be offered him... I hope I am not being troublesome.'[52]

It was sad that Sir Henry Ponsonby could not enjoy these stages of the Munshi comedy, for he had always, very typically, showered the Munshi with half-ironical courtesy and he loved it when the Queen behaved unreasonably. Sir Arthur Bigge, though a good private secretary to her majesty, did not quite possess Ponsonby's lightness of touch.

Henry Ponsonby had become Victoria's private secretary during the first premiership of Gladstone, and he had seen her through a period of momentous political change. No one could gag Queen Victoria, exactly, but Ponsonby's wit and common sense had saved her from many a mishap; and, particularly when the Liberals were in office, he was able to calm down politicians whose feelings were wounded by royal rebuke. He was also a superb go-between within the Royal Family itself, and, together with Knollys, a defuser of rows, a muffler of scandal, above all a patently good-hearted man whose laughter could often persuade wounded parties not to nurse self-important grievances. He understood the Queen, and although he must indeed have thought her a funny little woman, his amusement at her antics was nearly always contained within the carapace of loyalty, and she could have had no wiser or firmer ally. With a weaker, or stupider, private secretary, the Queen could have got herself, and the monarchy, into grave trouble, particularly since the second Disraeli Government when she made no secret of her capricious Toryism.

He was just short of seventy when he had his stroke. Probably the strain of Gladstone's resignation, and the resulting political excitations, had added work and stress to Ponsonby's weakened constitution. One of his simplest and most vital political assets was that he wrote with a clear hand – unlike Queen Victoria, many of whose scribbled instructions and comments to her ministers were not just difficult to read, but totally illegible. Without Ponsonby's accompanying letters, it would have been impossible to understand, much of the time, what the monarch was saying. The Queen had noticed a change, for the last six months, in his normally clear handwriting; and she had been disturbed by lapses in his memory.[53]

For the whole of 1895, he was an invalid, and at eight in the morning on 21 November, in his bed at Osborne Cottage, he died. Rather bluntly, the Queen remarked, 'He was dead to me ten months ago.'[54]

TWENTY FIVE

DIAMOND JUBILEE

O NE OF THE many delusional quirks of the German Emperor was his belief that he still enjoyed a cordial relationship with his grandmother Queen Victoria. In fact, by the mid-1890s, her patience with Willy had worn very thin, her hostility towards his militaristic postures matching the ominous swell of anti-Germanism in British public opinion. The growing hostility between the two cousin-nations was thrown into painful relief by events in Africa.

British troops had occupied the Cape in 1795, and by 1814, through conquest and purchase (£6 million), the British had ousted the former European settlers there, who were overseen by the Dutch East India Company. Between 1836 and 1840 7,000 Dutch settlers (the Boers) had made the Great Trek, emigrating from Cape Colony into the great plains beyond the Orange River, and across them into Natal, and up into the Zoutpansberg and the northern part of the Transvaal. They wanted freedom from the British; they wanted to practise their austere form of Protestantism; and they wanted to be allowed to enforce a very different attitude to the indigenous African population. The British white settlers were scarcely, by twenty-first-century standards, egalitarian in their attitudes to the Africans, but for the Boers, the superiority of the whites to the blacks was a matter of doctrine, and they wished to be able to maintain a system of slavery.

The initial reaction of Britain had been that the Boers were breaking a firm agreement, for which money had exchanged hands, and that they were liable to the jurisdiction of British courts. Little by little, however, the Boers established a republic at Pietermaritzburg. Natal was eventually annexed to Britain, and by the middle of the nineteenth century, the independence of the Transvaal had been recognized. In 1854, at the Treaty of Bloemfontein, Britain recognized the existence of the Orange Free State. South Africa was now made up of five states – the Cape, Natal and British Kaffira being British; the Transvaal and Orange Free State being Boer.

The next major development was the occupation by Europeans of Bechuanaland – what was later to be Botswana. Cecil Rhodes now rose to pre-eminence: a completely new figure in history, though one perhaps intuited, in his quest for power-through-gold, and domination-through-mines, in the more lurid music-dramas of Richard Wagner: a businessman-of-war, inspired by a crazed belief in Social Darwinism, and a belief that the Anglo-Saxon race would civilize the world while making themselves prodigiously rich. During Gladstone's Government, he had got permission from Westminster to annex Bechuanaland and establish British sovereignty there against the claims of the Boer incursions and the Germans. When Wilhelm II complained to Rhodes that Germany had entered the Scramble for Africa too late, and that, if Britain took Bechuanaland as well as South Africa, there would be nothing left, Rhodes replied, 'Yes, there is, Your Majesty – Asia Minor and Mesopotamia.' He ignored the fact that these territories were in the Ottoman Empire.[1]

Of course, what had quickened the excitement of the Scramble was the lust for gold, added to which was the discovery, from 1870 onwards, of the Kimberley Diamond Fields. Johannesburg, built on the southern slopes of the Witwatersrand, was founded in 1886, with a population of 3,000. Within a decade, the population had swollen to over 50,000 whites, with a virtual slave population of Africans to work the mines, and 7,000 British Indians working in various menial capacities. Gold mines created an unsightly greedy sprawl for fifty miles around the centre of the city. Here was a parable, an emblem upon African soil, of nineteenth-century European greed and Mammon worship.

The non-Boers living in this republic founded on the principle of raping the earth, accumulating riches and exploiting their fellow men were only there to make money. These *Uitlanders* or foreigners felt that they had a raw deal from the Boers, whose nationalist leader was Paul Kruger. They had no votes, but they were taxed, and the Uitlander mine owners had to pay enormous duties to the Kruger Government. It was still worth their while, however, as fortunes were being made overnight. What had begun, at the time of the Great Trek, as a stout-hearted republic formed for agriculturalists had become the richest spot on earth.

Cecil Rhodes, who thought that everything by right should belong to the British Empire, managed to create in his mind the notion that the mine owners of Johannesburg were being 'exploited' by the Boers. He now had a champion in the heart of the British Government: Joseph Chamberlain, the sixty-year-old Birmingham businessman and radical. Salisbury soon changed his view that Chamberlain's interest in the colonies was purely 'theoretic'; Rhodes had always recognized the truth about Chamberlain. A petition was got up, signed by 35,000 Uitlanders, outlining their grievances. They wanted Westminster to intervene on their behalf with Paul Kruger. There was a genuine fear of an Uitlander uprising in Johannesburg. Both sides in South Africa had been piling up arms for some years; and the Boers were armed to the teeth with Mauser rifles and Krupp artillery purchased from Germany.

A crazy scheme now formed in the mind of Rhodes, and of the Chartered Company which was administering Bechuanaland, and of which Rhodes was the leading light. The company's administrator was Dr Leander Starr Jameson, an Edinburgh-trained medical man. It was proposed that Jameson would lead a small private army, assembled by Rhodes, from Pitsani, 180 miles from Johannesburg; 470 mounted men, 120 Bechuanaland police, 8 machine guns and 3 pieces of artillery was all they had. Naturally, if they had been successful, and had they captured Johannesburg for the British, it is highly probable that Jameson and Rhodes would have been welcomed to London as heroes by Chamberlain and Salisbury. But it was a botched plan from the start. Jameson's army was halted on the fourth day of their ride at Krugersdorp by a deadly artillery barrage from the Boers. On 2 January, they were manoeuvred into a trap at Doornkop and they laid down their arms.

The Jameson Raid left many South Africans, on both sides, with the impression that the matter would not end there; that a war between the British and the Boers was now inevitable. What gave the issue an even more dangerous international colouring was the reaction of the German Emperor. Chamberlain went through the motions of denouncing the raid; but he must surely have been in on the plot beforehand. He must have said, in effect, to Rhodes – if it succeeds, the Jameson Raid is a British triumph; if it fails, it is Rhodes's and Jameson's disaster. Wilhelm II raised the temperature of the whole affair by sending Kruger a very public telegram: 'I sincerely congratulate you that, without appealing for the help of friendly Powers, you with your people, by your own energy against the armed hordes which, as disturbers of the peace broke into your country, have succeeded in re-establishing peace and maintaining the independence of your country against attacks from without.'[2]

Wilhelm sent this telegram having held a Council of State with his Chancellor, Foreign Minister and three others, as that Foreign Minister, Marschall von Biberstein, admitted, a quarter of a century afterwards.[3]

Queen Victoria had by now become a complete jingoist. Cecil Rhodes was received at Court as a great hero. When the Empress Eugénie met him at dinner with Queen Victoria in 1894, she was agog to converse with him, but could scarcely get near, so eager were the English royalties to monopolize him.[4] The Queen, in this fever of imperialism, was therefore happy to receive that republican radical Joseph Chamberlain, her Colonial Secretary, at Osborne House and considered him 'very interesting in all he told me about the Transvaal, and is very firm and sensible'.[5] Fritz Ponsonby was amused to see Joe, with his slicked-back, pomaded hair, his monocle and his winged collar, 'talking earnestly and deferentially to the Queen, when I remembered the firebrand he had been'.[6]

Rhodes was clearly guilty. He resigned his premiership of the Cape. Rhodes's brother and four others involved in the raid were put on trial in the Transvaal and condemned to death. The world now saw Britain as a buccaneer race who had colluded in the raid. 'Dr Jim', as Jameson was nicknamed, was brought back to London for trial and served fifteen months in Holloway Prison. He returned to South Africa, and later in life became a privy councillor and a baronet; as Premier of the Cape he was one of the key figures in the unification of South Africa. It was often said that Kipling wrote his poem 'If' as a celebration of Dr Jim's character, and even if that were not true, it is surely revealing that anyone said it at all: it shows Jameson's standing in the eyes of the British public.

Beatrice Webb was one of the founders of the Labour Party, of the London School of Economics and of the *New Statesman*. Admittedly, she was biased by a passionate and unrequited love for Joseph Chamberlain, but she was not far from the truth when she wrote in her diary, 'Joe Chamberlain is today the National Hero… In these troubled times, with every nation secretly disliking us, it is a comfortable thought that we have a government of strong resolute men, not given either to bluster or vacillation, but prompt in taking every measure to keep us out of a war and to make us successful should we be forced into it.'[7]

If Queen Victoria's eyes were upon the Transvaal at this time, they were also on West Africa. It was here, on what was known as the Gold Coast, in Ashanti, that a very different type of British imperialism was on display from the swashbuckling antics of Cecil Rhodes and Dr Jameson. In the strange way in which quite disparate events coalesce, the crippling dullness of the Queen's daily life and the violent doings of some West African tyrant kings conjoined to produce a Victorian family tragedy.

By now, the tiny household at Balmoral and at Osborne was locked in routines of a quite numbing tedium. Marie Mallet, maid of honour, wrote to her mother from Balmoral in November 1896, 'our life is as monotonous as possible and were it not for the little jokes amongst ourselves, we should expire from dullness'.[8] General Sir Michael Biddulph, when groom-in-waiting, frequently got upbraided by his monarch for not being able to think of sufficient synonyms for 'went for a drive in a carriage', when composing the Court Circular. Sometimes she was accompanied by Princess Beatrice and her children, the golden-haired Ena, one day to become Queen of Spain, and the eldest, Alexander, who resembled Little Lord Fauntleroy.[9] The truth was, she did the same thing every day. She breakfasted at ten, then she went for a drive in a carriage. She lunched at two, then she went for a drive in a carriage or her little pony chair. 'It was a great crime,' Fritz Ponsonby remembered, 'to meet her in the grounds when she was out in her pony chair, and of course we all took very good care that this should never happen. If by any unlucky chance we did come across her, we hid in the bushes.' As the younger Ponsonby made clear, this was not just applicable to the equerries and junior courtiers. Home Secretary, Sir William Harcourt, while walking with old Sir Henry Ponsonby, considered taking cover on such an occasion, but since he was over six feet four inches in height, the two distinguished gentlemen turned back on their walk, rather than committing the solecism of meeting the Queen.[10] The dinners were usually attended by very few people. 'A great deal... depended on what mood the Queen was in; when she was rather preoccupied and silent, dinner was a dismal affair, but when she was inclined to talk and interpose with witty remarks, it went with a swing. Once an earnest clergyman described what he had seen in the East End of London, and by way of showing how overcrowded the houses were, said that in one house he visited, he found that seven people slept in one bed. The Queen dryly remarked, "Had I been one of them I would have slept on the floor".[11] Usually a tiny number would assemble at dinner and if an abrasive character such as the Empress Frederick was not present to check the Queen's assertions, they would sit politely while she displayed what the cleverer present considered her 'deplorable' literary taste. 'On the subject of Marie Corelli, the Queen said she would rank as one of the greatest writers of the time, while the Empress thought her writings were trash.'[12] Sometimes, the equerries were allowed off and the Queen simply dined with Princess Beatrice and her husband.

The strain on Liko's patience was immense. This extremely energetic, handsome and perfectly intelligent man, aged thirty-seven, had nothing to do. It was at this point that troubles in West Africa came to a head.

King Prempeh of Ashanti had seized power after a bloody civil war. His 'election' as monarch was endorsed by the British-controlled Gold Coast Government. But no one pretended that Prempeh was a model of Prince Albert-style constitutional monarchy. Human sacrifices were commonplace, and raids were made on neighbouring tribespeople to replenish Prempeh's supply of slaves, in which he did swift and ruthless trade. The Ashanti people came to the Gold Coast administrators and begged the British to intervene. At first they refused, but the situation was so extreme that the case for intervention became overwhelming. An ultimatum was issued to Prempeh, which he ignored. And it was then that an expeditionary force, under the command of Colonel Francis Scott, was formed. It consisted of the 2nd Yorkshire regiment, a special service corps made up of several British regiments from the United Kingdom, the 2nd West India regiment and some African soldiers from the Gold Coast and Hausa.

On 11 November, Lord Wolseley asked the Queen's permission for Prince Christian Victor, son of Princess Helena and Prince Christian Victor of Schleswig-Holstein, to join the expedition, and the Queen granted the request. Christian had been given a modern education, by the royal standards of the time; he had attended Wellington (where he captained the XI), Sandhurst and Magdalen College,

Oxford, and he became an officer in the 60th King's Royal Rifles, doing active service in India. ('We are going to punish some frontier tribes who have been firing on and robbing British subjects,' he wrote excitedly, aged twenty-three, to his grandmother the Queen, from Rawalpindi in 1891, 'it will be rather a novel experience for me to see shots exchanged in reality, but I must say I am looking forward to it immensely.'[13])

When he reached the West African coast, Christian Victor wrote to Queen Victoria, 'I can't imagine how people live here; there is nothing to do.'[14] His uncle Liko, who had often suffered from the same failure of imagination on the Isle of Wight, was now in danger of some kind of marital trouble in London. Whether it was an affair, or whether, as his son the Marquess of Carisbrooke later said, he was being 'pursued by a woman',[15] Liko felt it would be a good thing to get out of England, and he asked Victoria's permission to join the Ashanti expedition. She answered firmly that it would 'never do'. But, in spite of trying to get Sir James Reid to pronounce that the West African climate would not suit him – and how right she was – the Queen eventually yielded to Princess Beatrice's plea that Liko 'smarted under his enforced inactivity, and this was about the only occasion which presented no difficulties, as he would go as a volunteer without usurping anyone's place'.[16]

On 6 December, he knelt before the Queen and kissed her hand, and the next day he boarded a troop train at Aldershot. The Royal Family at home entered that ominous week of the year which would culminate on the dreaded 14 December, anniversary of the deaths of the Prince Consort and of Princess Alice. On that date in 1895, however, Princess May went into labour at York Cottage, Sandringham, and gave birth to a boy, who was named Albert, and later became George VI.

On Christmas Day, two troop ships, the *Coromandel* and the *Manilla*, arrived at Cape Coast Castle – the latter boat containing Prince Henry – Liko. The previous day, Major Pigott, of Prince Christian Victor's regiment, had been shooting in the bush and secured a good bag which 'swelled the menu very opportunely' when they ate their delayed Christmas dinner. Next day, accompanied by 1,000 bearers, the expedition made its way inland towards Jakuma and Akroful. Commanding the native levies was a Major R. S. S. Baden-Powell – later to be famous in the South African war, and as founder of the Scout movement. As they proceeded, two of the African kings sent their submission to the British without fighting. The heat and humidity were oppressive – as Christian Victor wrote to his colonel from the swamps, 'the climate here is beastly'. Baden-Powell, with his native forces, marched through thick jungle to Bekwai, which cut off King Prempeh, who, with his Queen-mother, immediately sought palaver with the British. This was not granted until they reached Kumasi.

If the Jameson Raid and the attitudes of Rhodes represent the British Empire at its most questionable, the march of Sir Francis Scott and such men as Baden-Powell surely showed the British at their patient best, as a peacekeeping force. Not a shot was fired, and the appalling violence and tyranny of King Prempeh was replaced by a much more humane and better organized colonial regime.

The cost, in the first stage of the enterprise, was the health of those Europeans who had exposed themselves to the swamps. At Prahsu, Liko's camp commandant Major Ferguson died of swamp fever, and a few days later, Prince Henry was himself overcome by malaria. Prince Christian Victor reached Kumasi, which Liko did not, and he there also succumbed to fever. He was ill for three days and recovered. His uncle, Prince Henry, however, was less lucky. He was put aboard HMS *Blonde*, and it was hoped he would reach England alive. He died on 20 January. The cable between Bathurst and Accra had broken down, and it was only on 22 January that the news reached Osborne, and the Queen poured out sorrow into her journal: 'Our dearly loved Liko has been taken from us! Can I write it? He was so much better, and we were anxiously awaiting the news of his arrival at Madeira. What will become of my poor child [Beatrice]? All she said, in a trembling voice, was, "The life is gone out of me." She went back to her room with Louischen [Duchess of Connaught] who as well as dear Arthur, has been most tender to her.'[17]

Since he had died on board ship, and no adequate funerary arrangements were in place, a makeshift tank was constructed out of biscuit tins, and when the body was placed into it, the metal casket was filled up with rum. Some fool told his children, who had nightmares for months afterwards. It was a miserable time. Princess Louise arrived and terribly upset her sister by calmly announcing that Liko had always been her confidant and that Beatrice was 'nothing to him'. Louise's husband, Lord Lorne, after his stint in Canada where his Governor-Generalship had been less than successful, was now a Unionist MP for South Manchester. The couple saw less and less of one another, and she was a 'loose cannon'. Her deliberately bitchy remark to her sister was no doubt prompted by the fact that, only five weeks before, Beatrice had persuaded the Queen to summon Randall Davidson to 'talk to' Louise about her embarrassing closeness, not to Liko, but to Sir Arthur Bigge – now the Queen's private secretary.[18] Meanwhile, at Sandringham, there was the awkward question of whether to go ahead with the christening of the new baby.

The burial took place on 5 February, an icy day, at Whippingham Parish Church, where they had been married. In the darkening afternoon, the relentless drive still had to take place, and Lady Leila Erroll was lady-in-waiting at the Queen's side. The Queen was slumped in morose silence. Lady Erroll tried to say that we should all meet our loved ones in Heaven. The Queen answered monosyllabically, 'Yes.' Warming to her theme, Lady Erroll added, 'We will all meet in Abraham's bosom.' The Queen snapped back, 'I will not meet Abraham.' In her journal that evening, the Queen wrote, 'Dear Leila, not at all consolatory in moments of trouble.'[19]

Probably the most important item on the domestic political agenda that year was the Education Bill – which was eventually dropped because the Liberals threatened to filibuster it. The Bill was intended to improve the general condition of education, and to remove some of the abuses in the system left by the original 1870 Act. Instead of the elementary schools being under the control of local boards (some of which were of Dickensian ineptitude), it proposed a centralized system in which school inspectors could guarantee the quality of local schools throughout the kingdoms. Most crucially, the new Bill intended to give strength and encouragement to the Nonconformist schools – the so-called Voluntary schools. It was in some ways strange, given this fact, that the Liberals, who were supported by so many Nonconformists, should have opposed the Bill. The reason was that Asquith, who led the opposition in debate, was primarily a secularist, and he hoped to drive a wedge between the Churchmen and the Nonconformists in the House. In fact, as the Bishop of London said, 'in 1870, the State cut itself off altogether from religious instruction in its schools; it would not recognise the subject, it would not inspect the children in their knowledge of it'. This was all very much in accordance with that great schools inspector (and poet) Matthew Arnold's 'liberalism', that is agnosticism. 'In 1896,' went on the bishop, 'the State comes forward to declare by Act of Parliament that it abandons this neutral attitude, that it recognises the right of the parent to decide the religious teaching which his child shall receive.'[20] The Queen was very much of this view also, and when the Government decided to drop the matter she wrote in the first person – very unusual in official communications with Prime Ministers and always a sign of extreme strength of feeling – 'I cannot refrain from expressing my deep regret at the Cabinet's decision to drop the Education Bill.'[21]

In the same session of Parliament, the Conservatives repealed the Red Flag regulations relating to the newfangled automobiles. In 1896, Parliament decreed it was now possible for drivers of the new contraptions to do so without a pedestrian parading in front of them with a warning scarlet banner. Thus it was that Victoria, who had been born in the Pickwickian age of stagecoaches and seen the birth and growth of the railways, should have lived to see motor travel recognized in English law. In the same year, 1896, Karl Benz built his first car.

Many of these parliamentary events were chronicled to the Queen not by the Prime Minister, but by his languid tall, nephew, First Lord of the Treasury Arthur Balfour. (The ease with which he found political promotion – and he succeeded his uncle Robert Salisbury as Prime Minister – gave rise to the expression 'Bob's Your Uncle'.) A fascinating figure, Balfour, who wrote one of the best works of religious philosophy in English – *The Foundations of Belief* (1895) – was much liked by the Queen. He was probably one of the first, if not the first, politicians to cycle in London. One aspect of his character dismayed her, however – his fondness for golf. One Sunday afternoon at Osborne, he was planning a round of golf: a foursome with the Duke of York (later George V), Sir Arthur Bigge and Ponsonby junior. The Queen sent for Balfour to discuss some political matter after luncheon and then asked him what he was about to do. Balfour replied that he was going for a walk. Unfortunately, she then sent for the Duke of York and asked him the same question – in the case of the honest sailor-prince, eliciting a completely truthful answer. 'The Queen was much amused at catching him out, as she expressed it, "telling a fib".'[22]

The death of Archbishop Benson[23] precipitated the inevitable fall of episcopal dominoes: for if Bishop X was translated to Canterbury, his see had in turn to be filled with Bishop Y, and nearly all the senior appointments in the Church were filled by translation, rather than by the consecration of a candidate not yet a bishop. The Queen would have liked Davidson either to fill Benson's role at Canterbury, or to fill the role of Bishop of London – for it was London's Dr Temple who was eventually sent to Lambeth Palace. Lord Salisbury had been minded to promote the Bishop of Peterborough, Mandell Creighton, to Canterbury. He was undoubtedly the cleverest and wittiest bishop on the bench. (His *Life of Queen Elizabeth* remains a classic.) But there were too many things against him from the Queen's point of view. He was distinctly High, and he was rumoured to be something of a lady's man. 'His manner is not good,' admitted Salisbury.[24] The Queen was against promoting Dr Temple: 'His age is far too advanced to undertake such an arduous post; and his eyesight is most defective, he can hardly see anything below him.'[25] She urged Salisbury to promote her favourite Davidson, the forty-eight-year-old Bishop of Winchester. (She had chosen Davidson as Bishop of Rochester in 1891, and he was translated to Winchester in '95.)

It was typical of Salisbury's ability to get his own way, and to manipulate the Queen, that within a week she had abandoned her objections to Temple 'though she retains her personal opinion as to his fitness'.[26] The point she made about Temple's age – eight years older than his predecessor who had just dropped dead during Matins – was surely a strong one. In a certain way, though, in so far as the later part of this reign was working towards a climacteric, a mighty change in which, before she died, she was to set her seal upon her age, there was some fittingness in choosing Temple. Bushy-eyebrowed headmaster of that school which knew its glory age in Queen Victoria's reign and supplied so many of its bishops, soldiers, imperial administrators and poets – Rugby – Temple represented Prince Albert's religion: Liberal Protestantism. So liberal had he been, indeed, as a contributor to the famous Broad Church collection *Essays and Reviews*, that there were protests at his consecration to the episcopate. His was not the austere High Churchmanship of Salisbury, but it represented perhaps the Christianity most representative of the governing class, who had not quite abandoned the Faith, but did not like anything which smacked too strongly of dogma, still less of Catholicism. Creighton, with his sense of humour and his taste for the grotesque, was a much better Bishop of London, much better at providing leadership to a diocese by now so full of 'bells and smells'. His successor at Peterborough, equally apt as a representative of another aspect of the age, was Edward Glyn, married to Lady Mary Campbell, a sister-in-law of Princess Louise. Post-First World War, there would be little room in the Church of England for Trollope's Archdeacon Grantly.

With the right bishops in place, with a politician whose views so conveniently dovetailed with the Queen's in her final years, what a pity they did not make Rudyard Kipling the Poet Laureate. He would probably have refused it, as he did when offered it by George V, but Tennyson was surely right to say he had fire in his belly, and he was the perfect unofficial laureate of late Victorian imperialism. Instead, cynical Salisbury, a brilliant man who could afford from a great intellectual height to be amused by philistinism, placed the laureate crown on the brow of the absurdly moustachioed Alfred Austin, a Catholic journalist of High Tory persuasion with scarcely even pretension to poetic gifts. Alfred Austin's poem 'Jameson's Ride', the first published after he had succeeded to Tennyson's laureateship, surely scraped into a new low point, even by the undistinguished history of laureate verse.

> I suppose we were wrong, were madmen,
> Still I think at the Judgment Day,
> When God sifts the good from the bad men,
> There'll be something more to say.
> We were wrong, but we aren't half sorry;
> And as one of the baffled band,
> I would rather have had that foray
> Than the crushing of all the Rand.

Even Salisbury was a bit embarrassed, pretending, when he wrote to the Queen (who had been 'surprised' by the poem), not to have seen it, but 'he has heard it strongly condemned by many persons both from a political and a literary point of view'.[27] The wag Sir Owen Seaman explained the appointment neatly when he wrote:

> At length a callous Tory chief arose,
> Master of caustic jest and cynic gibe,
> Looked round the Carlton Club and lightly chose
> Its leading scribe.[28]

On Wednesday, 23 September 1896, the Queen noted in her journal, 'Today is the day on which I have reigned longer by a day than any English sovereign, and the people wished to make all sorts of demonstrations, which I asked them not to do until I had completed the sixty years next June.'[29] She was in Balmoral for the momentous day. On every hill, there were bonfires. Every church rang its bells. The men of the Crathie and Ballater Volunteers lined the darkened roads with blazing torches, to greet an illustrious pair who had come to visit the Queen: the new Emperor and Empress of Russia. The welcoming party consisted of the old Duke of Cambridge, the Duke and Duchess of York, and a Guard of Honour of the Black Watch.

The figures who stepped from their carriage into the Scottish night air were not the same as the carefree lovers Alicky and Nicky who had enjoyed their courtship at Osborne and Windsor two years before. With sadly little preparation, they had been thrust into the role of absolute autocrats, aged only twenty-seven in his case, twenty-three in hers. Their Coronation, in May 1896, had been a disaster. Half a million people had assembled on the Khodinsky Plain, a large park outside Moscow. As Coronation mugs, cakes and sweetmeats were distributed, people surged forward and began to be trampled underfoot. As some were pushed forward, and others tried to escape, the crowd got out of control, and mounted troops were brought in. They were meant to restore order, but they made things worse, with hundreds now being trampled underfoot. In the end, more than 3,000 people had been killed. This terrible accident cast a pall of gloom over the opening of the reign, as the newly crowned Nicholas II and Alexandra Feodorovna appeared on this scene of chaos and were shown into the Imperial Pavilion in the park, even as corpses and wounded were being carried away by the hundred. Their distress was deep, they visited hospitals and the afflicted, but no one had felt happy on their day of crowning.

The Alicky who had grown up in Darmstadt as Princess Alice's little English girl, fed on rice pudding and baked apples, was not recognizable in the stiff, sad Russian Empress who stayed at Balmoral.

Her grandmother the Queen had, with crashing tactlessness, noted that the day of their visit coincided with the anniversary of the Fall of Sevastopol, and put on a small exhibition of trophies won from the Imperial Russian Armies in 1855. The young people viewed them with humourless solemnity. Nicholas II hated Balmoral; he hated being surrounded by all his wife's extended German family; and he disliked being taken out for sport in the freezing wet weather. They had no luck in finding a stag and only managed to shoot a brace of grouse. As the rain pelted against the windows, Alexandra Feodorovna was morosely silent indoors. Her sister, Lady Milford Haven ('Victoria B.'), wrote:

> I watched Nicky once at a luncheon saying to Ernie [their brother Ernest Ludwig, last reigning Grand Duke of Hesse and the Rhine], how he envied his being a constitutional monarch on whom the blame for all the mistakes made by his ministers was not heaped. Under other circumstances, Nicky would have made a remarkably good constitutional Sovereign, for he was in no way narrow minded, nor obsessed by his high position. If you could have boiled down Nicky and William [Wilhelm II, Emperor of Germany] in one pot you would have produced an ideal Emperor of Russia. His father's dominating personality had stunted any gifts for initiative in Nicky.[30]

Davidson had, with perhaps pardonable gush, given the Queen's fondness for him, and her longevity, remarked that 'your Majesty should wield a personal and domestic influence over the thrones of Europe absolutely without precedent in the history of Christendom… It can be no small matter to the world's life that the occupants of the imperial thrones of Germany and of Russia should at such a juncture bear the relation they do to your Majesty.'[31] But, as the Balmoral visit made clear to everyone, the influence of 'Gangan' – as the toddler David, future Edward VIII, was calling her during this bleak holiday – was on the wane.

Nicky and Alicky were being transformed, by the rigidity of the system into which they had been forced, and by the weakness of their characters, into unsuccessful autocrats, doomed to become martyrs. Today, they are actually saints of the Russian Orthodox Church, and the faithful queue in Russian churches to light candles before their icons. Such a transformation of their grandmother is never quite imaginable, partly because, however much in small and domestic matters she liked to be an autocrat, the system in which Victoria was operating was not one which could ever freeze her into an icon or hack her down as a martyr. Not that confusion was always to be avoided. Arthur Wagner, the eccentric and wealthy Brighton clergyman who built so many High churches in that seaside town, grew short-sighted and a little vague in his old age. Being driven past the statue of Queen Victoria erected to commemorate her Diamond Jubilee, he murmured, 'To think that I should have lived to see the day when the Brighton Corporation erected a statue of Our Dear Lady.'[32]

In Queen Elizabeth I's reign, Protestant devotees such as Edmund Spenser had made her into a *Faerie Queene*, almost an ersatz Madonna. Queen Victoria, who was horrified by churches such as 'Father' Wagner's in Brighton, had, nevertheless, developed into a figurehead: not a gilded icon such as would one day depict the Russian Emperor and his wife, but a potent symbol all the same. '*L'histoire d'un homme, c'est l'histoire d'une époque*',[33] as one of his most fervent admirers began his biography of General de Gaulle. For many who lit the bonfires in Britain in September 1896, Victoria had come to embody their own experience of their times. This is different from personal admiration, just as it is certainly different from the veneration owing to a saint. But for hundreds of thousands of people throughout the world, Queen Victoria had become something more than simply an old lady in a bonnet. She had transcended autocracy and become the role model for all future successful constitutional monarchs, a beloved figurehead reflecting back to the people themselves their own experiences of passing time and, perhaps also, their own values, their own sense of the sacred. These things are very hard to define.

∽

Nor is it to belittle such feelings, still less the old lady who was the focus of them, to enjoy, as her courtiers did, the rich comedy of the Queen's character, which remained in all its vivid outline until the end of her days.

What a pity she never met Proust![34] Her life on the Riviera was abounding in the sort of characters about whom he wove his imaginative web. As when, in 1887, the Countess of Paris passed through Biarritz and told Princess Beatrice that her mother-in-law, the Queen Regent (*soi-disante*), was 'burning with desire to visit our Queen, but would not put her foot in a country which had insulted her husband'.[35] At Cimiez, in April 1897, the Queen found herself staying in the same hotel as the great Sarah Bernhardt: as venerated for her acting as she was celebrated for her rackety life of love. (Bertie, as the Queen was no doubt completely aware, had become obsessed by her when she did a London season in 1879, attending her performances night after night; though she was only a flirtation, she was invited to his Coronation years later, and placed with Mrs Keppel, Jennie Churchill and the other mistresses in the chancel gallery nicknamed the 'King's Loose Box'.[36])

Inevitably, therefore, Queen Victoria was a little torn when she found herself staying in the same hotel: the side of her nature which relished the theatre, and which liked to have set eyes upon contemporary celebrities, was at war with the prudish mother of the prodigal son. In the end, she relented, and a small stage was erected in her reception room in the hotel. Bernhardt performed a half-hour piece entitled *Jean Marie*, and the Queen found it 'quite marvellous... She appeared much affected herself, tears rolling down her cheeks. She has a most beautiful voice and is very graceful in all her movements.' The two legends met for a few moments after the performance, and Victoria said she hoped Bernhardt was not tired. '*Cela m'a reposé*,'[37] was the reply. The Queen removed one of her pearl bracelets and put it on the wrist of La Bernhardt, and the actress took off one of hers and presented it to the Queen, together with a photograph.

The hotel they had chosen for the 1897 Riviera jaunt, the Excelsior Regina Hotel at Cimiez, near Nice, was a new one. Lord Salisbury was himself a devotee of the Riviera, where he had a house, and where he enjoyed tea parties with the Queen. Salisbury had 'questioned the salubrity'[38] of a place as yet untried. The punctilious Dr Reid, however, had visited the building site during construction to make sure that they were installing proper drains, and could assure the Prime Minister that 'I have for nearly a year been giving constant attention to the progress of the new hotel'. It had electric lighting, and superb views of the Mediterranean. He had also found a doctor in Cimiez whom he deemed to be 'a physician of the highest standing'.[39]

As it happened, this holiday, for all the pleasure which the Queen invariably derived from the scenery, and the company, on the Riviera, was clouded by a row brought to a head by James Reid himself. For, the Household had reached boiling point over the question of the Munshi. Before they all set out, Reid had told the inner circle – Marie Mallet, Jane Churchill, Fritz Ponsonby, Arthur Bigge, Harriet Phipps – that the Munshi was yet again suffering from gonorrhoea; that the Queen was insisting upon the Munshi, yet again, accompanying the royal party to Cimiez; and that it was expected that they should dine with him. A majority of the Household, led by Fritz Ponsonby, said that if this happened, they would go on strike; and it was agreed that the Queen should be told. They fixed on Harriet Phipps as their spokesperson.

With very great courage, Miss Phipps crossed the courtyard at Windsor and approached the Queen's sitting room. The Queen was seated at her writing table behind a large pile of state papers, which she was closely perusing through the spectacles which – though she had been given them some years before – she had only recently consented to wear. As Harriet Phipps falteringly explained the position, the Queen's anger mounted. Her hand came out across the table and she swept everything onto the floor – papers, mementoes, pens, glass ink-pots, framed photographs all went flying. The child was mother to the woman; just such storms by the infant in Kensington Palace had alarmed her widowed mother, the Duchess of Kent, and convinced Lehzen that she had never known so 'passionate and naughty' a child. The Queen had her way, and the Munshi came with the Household to the South of France.

Although he had not been invited, the Munshi's radical friend Rafiuddin Ahmed joined the party after two days. At the Prime Minister's request, the Household expelled him after forty-eight hours; the Queen demanded that Salisbury apologize, or at least explain to Ahmed that he was being expelled because he was a journalist, and not because he was suspected of being a spy.

By now there was a formidable anti-Munshi alliance: Fritz Ponsonby and Dr Reid were the most vociferous among the courtiers, but none of the courtiers liked the Munshi, and the Prince of Wales, who, together with all Victoria's children, hated the man, proposed that they should collect details about the Munshi's family to discredit him in the eyes of the Queen. The viceroy was appealed to, and once more, details of the Munshi's original deceptions were wired back to England: the father being a pharmacist at the jail in Agra and not a doctor... But nothing new was unearthed.

Reid then tried a truly extreme measure. So stubborn was the Queen being, he said, in a formal letter to her, that 'there are people in high places, who know Your Majesty well, who say to me that the only charitable explanation that can be given is that Your Majesty is not sane'.[40] If Reid thought this would cow the granddaughter of the mad George III, he was very much mistaken. She flew into a 'most violent passion' and said she thought they were all behaving 'disgracefully'. Reid then wrote to the Munshi himself accusing him of being a liar. In words which can still make the reader cringe, over a century after they were written, Reid wrote, 'You are from a very low class and never can be a gentleman. Your education is nil. To be called "Secretary" is perfectly ridiculous.' He went on to say that the police were investigating him, and to accuse the Munshi of trying to cheat the Queen. 'If the Queen were to die and any letters of hers were found in your possession no mercy will be shown you. The Queen does not know all I have told you because it would shock her greatly to know how completely you have deceived her and what a scoundrel you are, and she hopes it may be possible for you to stay with her still. But this can only be if your "position" is altogether taken away.'[41] The Munshi did not know that the police, and the Prime Minister, suspected Rafiuddin of spying, so much of Reid's letter would have been incomprehensible to him. He retreated into silence.

The Diamond Jubilee of Queen Victoria must represent, in the eyes of many, the very summit of British power in the world. The British dominated Asia – not only did they govern India, but they had annexed Upper Burma in 1886. In West and East Africa the British had colonized far greater areas than had any other European power. In spite of the setback of the Jameson Raid, few could have seen that the Boers, even when armed with German weapons, provided much of a rivalry to British power in South Africa. The enormous fertile tracts of Bechuanaland remained under British sway. Further afield across the globe, the dominions of Australia, New Zealand and Canada looked to the Queen as to their Head of State. Although the balance of power in Europe was precarious, Britain remained, not least because of the strength of her navy, a superpower, and Victoria was the grandmother of two of the most powerful European emperors.

Yet the poetic antennae of that most imperialist of all great British writers sensed that an apex was what it was: that after the Diamond Jubilee, Britain had nowhere to go but down. In one of his finest political hymns, Rudyard Kipling, thirty-two years old, wrote:

> Far-called, our navies melt away;
> On dune and headland sinks the fire:
> Lo, all our pomp of yesterday
> Is one with Nineveh and Tyre![42]

The situation in Europe was by now so tense that an assembly of crowned heads, such as had marked the Golden Jubilee of 1887, posed diplomatic problems. How would the German Emperor be received, only a year after the calculated insult of his telegram to Paul Kruger? Europe, moreover, was in the middle of a major crisis, in some respects the most dangerous it had seen since the Crimean War. In February 1897, Colonel Vassos landed in Crete and hoisted the Greek flag in defiance of Turkish occupation of the island. By April, Greece and Turkey were at war, a war which Turkey would win. But it had a far wider effect than in the actual areas of conflict – namely, on the alliance of the European powers. Although liberals in Germany, such as the Dowager Empress (Vicky), supported Greece, her country was heavily committed to Turkey. 'What my feelings are when I read of the encouragement given to Turkey by Germany and by the German officers in the Turkish Army, you can imagine,' Vicky told her mother. 'The Turks are a fearful foe, not for Russians or European troops, but for the Greeks. They are like wild beasts in their cruelty.'[43] The matters unresolved by Gladstone's pamphlet on the Bulgarian atrocities once more flared up to divide Europe. Did the Europeans – as cynics such as Salisbury and power-brokers such as the German Emperor desired – simply back Turkey? Or were there issues of human rights, and of a common religion, which meant that in the end Christian must side with Christian against Muslim? These matters would shake up, and split up, the Concert of Europe, with Russia, endlessly hungry for influence in Turkey and emotionally in favour of strengthening Orthodoxy, fatally, but naturally, inclined to side against Germany.

As was now so often the case, because of the wide net of royal intermarriage throughout Europe, it was not merely political: it was a family affair. During the last Jubilee, Sophie, the seventh child of Vicky and Fritz, had met the Crown Prince Constantine of Greece. 'Is there a chance of Sophie's marrying Tino of Greece?'[44] the Queen had loosely asked a year later, while busily encouraging the match. It had duly taken place, and Sophie, the sister of the man who was now the Emperor – Willy – had married in Athens, with half the crowned heads of Europe present. 'Tino of Greece' on his father's side was the nephew of the King of the Hellenes and, on his mother's side, of the Tsar of Russia. When Sophie converted to the Orthodox faith, Willy and Dona banished her from Germany forever. 'Sophie made an awful scene in which she behaved in a simply incredible manner,' Willy wrote to Queen Victoria, in an attempt to justify himself. But for his grandmother, his behaviour was that of 'a tyrant and bully'. 'It is all grievous and sad and if I do not say more about it all it is because I do not wish to add fuel to the flames,' Victoria wrote.[45]

With this familial and political rift ever-widening, there would be too much diplomatic complexity for the uniformed princes of the European dynasties to trit-trot behind the old lady's landau and be mistaken for Lohengrin. The world was a very different place from that of 1887.

'I feel deeply for the Queen's anxiety,' Salisbury told Sir Arthur Bigge.[46] It was Joseph Chamberlain, the Colonial Secretary, who came up with the idea that the Diamond Jubilee should be made into a gigantic celebration of British imperial power: that, rather than inviting any European Heads of State, they should parade through the streets of London the different races of the Empire – soldiers from Borneo, Cyprus, Hong Kong, Canada, New Zealand, South Africa. Rather than the European powers sitting down and trying to work out a way to avert total calamity, how much easier it was, in Salisbury's great dictum, to 'leave ill alone', and to put on a parade.

Rather than heeding the sombre mood of the young Kipling's words, they hired a dud bishop – Bishop Walsham How of Wakefield – to write a Jubilee Hymn, and Sir Arthur Sullivan set it to music. Today, the hymn is forgotten, and How (who died on a fishing holiday in County Mayo a couple of months after the Jubilee) is now remembered only for two things: one, he wrote the popular hymn 'For All the Saints, who from their Labours Rest'; and two, he was the fool, in 1895, who solemnly ordered a fire to be lit in his grate by a parlourmaid, so that he could burn Thomas Hardy's novel *Jude the Obscure*. Hardy, a parsimonious man, was scandalized that a fire should have been lit in the summer months. If the bishop was going to burn his book, it would surely have been better to wait until the first cold day of autumn.

Very few people in London, on the day of the Jubilee itself, would have had any of Kipling's misgivings about the durability of Empire. The Queen came up from Windsor on 21 June 1897, and stayed the night at Buckingham Palace. £250,000 had been spent on London street decorations,[47] mingling thousands of tiny gas jets – a novelty when the Queen was young – with the totally newfangled electric light bulbs. In Whitehall, London County Council had erected an immense stand, costing £25,000, which illustrated the material progress of the reign. It was equipped with ladies' rooms and flush lavatories and telephones. One witness, sitting on the right wing of the stand set up under the National Gallery – to the north end of Trafalgar Square – looked down upon a 'sea of horses and men, forests of plumes and lances'. As far as you could see, on either side of the enormous stand in Whitehall, 'it was one mass of galleries and people to the very roofs'.[48] The Queen was terrified that there would be a repetition of the disaster which had attended Alicky and Nicky's Coronation in Moscow, and she sent repeated letters and telegrams to the Home Office. She need not have worried. Although the crowds were immense, there were no calamities.

> At quarter past eleven, the others being seated in their carriages long before, and having preceded me a short distance, I started from the State entrance in an open State landau drawn by eight creams, dear Alix, looking very pretty in lilac, and Lenchen sitting opposite me. I felt a good deal agitated, and had been so all these days, for fear anything might be forgotten or go wrong. Bertie and George C. rode one on each side of the carriage, Arthur (who had charge of the whole military arrangements) a little in the rear. My escort was formed from the 2nd Life Guards and officers of the native Indian regiments, these latter riding immediately in front of

my carriage. Guard of Honour of Blue-jackets, the Guards, and the 2nd West Surrey Regiment (Queen's) were mounted in the Quadrangle and outside the Palace.

Before leaving I touched an electric button, by which I started a message which was telegraphed throughout the whole Empire. It was the following: 'From my heart I thank my beloved people, May God bless them!'[49]

Such moments in London's history happen rarely, which is perhaps why they are so powerful. Modern royalty appears publicly much more often than Queen Victoria did, and even then, the effect is extraordinary on the Big Days, such as Queen Elizabeth II's Diamond Jubilee, or the funeral of her mother Queen Elizabeth. On such occasions, there is a palpable demonstration of union between Monarch and People, in which the politicians and the state functionaries play only an incidental role – even though it is by construction, or evolution, of a relatively benign political system which allows to flourish the almost organic relationship between Crowned Head and populace.

In the case of Queen Victoria, the intensity of crowd reaction was especially strong, because she made public parade of herself so seldom. The emotional atmosphere was overpowering on that hot, sunny day. The Queen, dressed in grey and black, but smiling and bowing, held a parasol above her and bowed her smiling head to left and right as the landau passed through the streets of London – Constitution Hill, to Hyde Park Corner; then along Piccadilly, down St James's Street to Pall Mall, past all the clubs, into Trafalgar Square, up the Strand and into Ludgate Hill to St Paul's. ('One misses Temple Bar,'[50] she noted.) Often, as the landau made its way, the procession stopped, and the crowd sang 'God Save the Queen' over and over again. She was now too stout and too arthritic to contemplate moving into the cathedral, let alone negotiate the aisle. She therefore decreed that the Service of Thanksgiving should be held on the cathedral steps while she sat in her landau, while the old favourites – the Te Deum, the Old Hundredth and, yet again, the National Anthem – were sung.

There followed a gruelling series of events, all of which, however tiring, she seemed to enjoy. On the day after the Jubilee Parade, she went to the swelteringly hot Ball Room in Buckingham Palace to receive loyal addresses from the two Houses of Parliament. The journey to Paddington Station in the afternoon was, once again, through dense crowds – 10,000 elementary schoolchildren had been brought to sit in the stands occupied the previous day by grown-ups, and loyal addresses from London School Boards were presented. Upon arrival at Slough, there were more loyal addresses, with the Lord Lieutenant of Buckinghamshire standing on a special dais, and children from the British Orphan Asylum presenting a bouquet. At the end of the week, there was a garden party at Buckingham Palace; for, although there were no crowned heads attending, London had swarmed with royalties and Russian, Italian and German princes and princesses mingled with the likes of Sir Henry Irving and great musicians such as Albani and Tosti. At Windsor, there were more inspections of colonial troops and police – from Hong Kong, a delegation of the police force; from West Africa, a troop of Houssas [sic] – 'fine looking men, but very black'.[51] Best of all, she liked the Sikhs, 'very fine, handsome men', and she was able, with the Indian troops, to exchange words of Hindustani.[52] Then, at Windsor, there was a garden party for Members of the House of Commons. In the first week of July, there was a Council at Windsor to swear in the colonial premiers as privy councillors. On 8 July, Mandell Creighton, now the Bishop of London, wrote a memorandum to the Queen about the Jubilee Ceremonies that 'no ceremonial recorded in history was ever more impressive, more truly national, or expressed more faithfully sentiments which were deeply and universally felt... The proceedings throughout were charged with strong personal feeling. It was not the grandeur, the dignity, or the display which were impressive: it was the intimacy and the sincerity of the respect and affection towards the Queen which was in the air.'[53]

What Creighton wrote was surely true, and it was a tribute to the very distinctive nature of the Queen's character: this ability, which she had tapped since the publication of her Highland journals, while living the life of a virtual recluse, to communicate with her people. For a busy monarch of the twenty-first century, the round of garden parties following the 1897 Jubilee would read like Business as Usual. For Queen Victoria they were a rarity. One of her biographers, Giles St Aubyn, says that 'the ensuing fortnight was one of the busiest of Queen Victoria's life'.[54] It is quite a funny sentence, partly because it is probably true. In terms of public engagements, and fulfilling functions which a modern royal personage would take in their stride every single month, this probably was one of the Queen's busiest fortnights. It is a sentence which also gives the modern reader pause. If you have been reading this book from its beginning, you will have been noticing that this is one of the most remarkable of all the remarkable features of the Queen's character: the idleness, which in the 1860s and early 1870s drove ministers to despair, and at times appeared to threaten the very existence of the British monarchy.

It was not, as we have seen, a total idleness, since she kept a gimlet eye on foreign affairs and on domestic politics throughout, even at her lowest moments of despair. But the diurnal tedium of her life, which drove courtiers to distraction, is in itself a very remarkable fact. Apart from being the Queen, she had done so very little. It is one of the things which make her such a completely fascinating figure for a biographer, since she compels us to concentrate upon *her*, rather than upon her deeds. The tempting thing, when trying to make sense of any human life, whether famous or obscure, is to concentrate upon outward activities. Queen Victoria does not allow us to do that, since, apart from being expert in watercolours and a fairly avid reader of popular fiction, she did not really 'do' anything: certainly not in the second half of her life. What a poet of her times once called 'those years and years of world without event' made up her drama. So, as well as her life being that of her own times, as must be the case of a monarch in her position, her life was also that of the inner woman, of whom – from the letters and the journals – we have so vivid a sense.

Meanwhile, all through the summer came yet more signals of mortality. The old Duchess of Atholl – one of the first friends Victoria and Albert had made in Scotland, and later a Mistress of the Robes – had died in May. And in October, Mary Adelaide, Duchess of Teck – Fat Mary – was called to her reward, from White Lodge in Richmond Park, surrounded by a loving family, including her son-in-law the Duke of York, the Princess of Wales and her children. Her husband, the poor Duke of Teck, was present in body, but the mind which had planned the exquisite garden and chosen so many beautiful wallpapers and cushion covers, was now wandering, no one knew where.

Though her Cambridge parents were buried in the family vault at Kew, Princess Mary Adelaide had often expressed her dread of its damp, and her hope that she would be allowed to repose in the Royal Vaults at St George's Chapel, Windsor.[55] It was for permission that this might happen that the Duchess of York now wrote to the Queen, who was at Balmoral. Of course, the permission was granted, but the intestate demise of her Cambridge cousin sharpened Queen Victoria's mind, and she realized that she should leave very detailed instructions for her own burial.

On 9 December, at Windsor, as the solemn season approached in which Prince Albert's death was always commemorated, the Queen wrote out instructions, and gave them to Reid, with the command that they were to be carried always, by 'the one who may be travelling with me'.

When Michaela Reid – the doctor's granddaughter-in-law – wrote her excellent account of Queen Victoria's relationship with her last medical practitioner, and revealed this wish list to the world, the strongest possible pressure was placed upon her by the Queen's descendants to keep them secret, with, for example, Princess Margaret writing to Lady Reid trying to prevent publication. To those who are obsessed with John Brown, the motive for this unsuccessful blocking-attempt would be a simple one. Among the many and detailed instructions which the Queen gave was that she should be buried with 'a plain gold wedding-ring which had belonged to the mother of my dear valued servant and friend Brown and was given him by her in '75 – which he wore for a short time and I have worn constantly since his death – to be on my fingers'.[56]

This is indeed a striking request, suggesting that, whatever the nature of her deep devotion to Brown, it was something much more profound than that felt by many old ladies for their servants. Like all the other evidence relating to Brown, however, it is far from definitive, and it certainly does not prove, or disprove, the truth of the strange deathbed confession of Norman Macleod that he had married the pair when Minister at Crathie. For beside the coffined figure, with the ring of old Mrs Brown on her finger, there were to be wedged a whole crateful of mementoes, including 'the hair of our valued friend Baron Stockmar who died in 1863', another locket 'containing the hair of the late Countess Blücker [sic]', and another 'containing the hair of my dear friend Lady Augusta Stanley'. Together with 'a pocket handkerchief of my faithful Brown' and 'a coloured profile photograph in a leather case of my faithful friend J. Brown' was to be 'some souvenir of my faithful wardrobe maid Annie McDonald to be near me, & anything else which Beatrice should wish to add'.

Parents who put a certain type of imaginative child to bed find they are unable to do so without adding not merely one favourite teddy bear, but the favourite book, the favourite dog on wheels, the much-needed and half-chewed blanket: so many things crammed into the bedding that it is hard to know where the child will find to sleep. Beatrice and the doctor would have found it very hard to fit the casket out with all the treasures with which the Queen wished to be tucked up – 'a piece of Balmoral heather, a painted profile photograph of my dearest Husband, always on my dressing table, & a coloured photograph of my dearest Beatrice, & one of her dear husband, and photographs of all my dear children, & their husbands & wives & of my grandchildren in frames'. There was also to be one of Prince Albert's cloaks, a shawl 'worked by my dearest daughter Alice'.

The glorious lack of minimalism about these instructions, the fervent need to carry clutter into the vaults of the Frogmore Mausoleum and, emblematically at least, to take them with her into eternity, shows the extent to which Queen Victoria was a be-er more than a do-er, a contemplative not an active personality. She never ceased to be the solitary child with a hundred dolls, imprisoned not only in her mother's apartments at Kensington Palace, but also inside her own overpowering psyche. The clutter of trinkets was but the outward and visible sign of the cloud of witnesses she carried in her head – her mother, her husband, her children and her friends.

Strangely enough, the intensely personal quality of the Jubilee ceremonial, noted by Mandell Creighton, and her secret wishes for her burial tell the same story. She was not an artist or a poet, but she had the poet's ability to recreate the world on her own terms, to carry it around with her, up to and beyond the grave. Far from alienating her people, in the end, by some weird paradoxical royal magic, it drew them. There remains something not merely fascinating, but loveable about this intensely strong character.

TWENTY SIX

'THIS ENGLAND'

WHEN SIR HERBERT Kitchener came to Balmoral in 1896, he did not make a good impression. After dining with the Queen, her Maid of Honour, Marie Mallet, felt that he was

> either a woman hater or a boor, for he would hardly utter to us ladies, in spite of many and tremendous efforts… To the Queen after dinner he talked much and showed off some Sudanese trophies he has brought as presents to Her Majesty – chain armour, probably medieval, hammers, spears & a crusader's sword with the motto "Do not draw me without reason. Do not sheathe me without honour" in old Romanesque [sic] on the blade… My own impression of K. is that of a resolute but cruel man, a fine soldier, no doubt, but not one of the type that tempers justice with mercy – he has a low, narrow forehead – very blue eyes & a fine figure.[1]

The first stage of the reconquest of the Sudan had been accomplished by Kitchener just before this visit to Balmoral. He went back the following year, with a much bigger army, and with the full backing of the Queen and Parliament – and with the backing of Salisbury, who had hitherto been sceptical about the wisdom of burdening Britain with the government of the Sudan. Having been converted, Salisbury was determined to make its conquest quite unambiguous, and at the end of 1897, he instructed Major J. R. L. Macdonald to advance northward along the White Nile from Uganda with a force of Sudanese askaris, while Kitchener came down from the north-west. By 1898, the army of the Khalifah, against whom Kitchener had now been fighting for over two years, on and off, had still not been overcome. With 7,500 British and 12,500 Egyptian troops and a flotilla of gunboats transported by the Nile, Kitchener now advanced upon the Khalifah, and confronted him on the plains of Omdurman. He had the Maxim gun: the first machine gun, pioneered in Britain in the mid-1880s and used with great effect in colonial wars since that time – for example, by Lugard in subduing Buganda.

> Whatever happens, we have got
> The Maxim Gun, which they have not

as Hilaire Belloc bitterly wrote in 'The Modern Traveller'. One of the British cavalrymen, riding with the 21st Lancers, was Lord Randolph Churchill's son Winston Spencer Churchill, who was reminded, when he saw the enemy, of a twelfth-century crusader army. The death toll among the askaris was 11,000, with 16,000 wounded. The British casualties were 47 killed, 382 wounded. Churchill himself, who took part in a cavalry charge, was disgusted, as was most civilized opinion. It had been a massacre, more than a battle. Churchill was especially revolted by the fact that the wounded askaris were simply left on the battlefield to die. Kitchener's troops moved the short distance into the middle of Khartoum, where the looting was led by Kitchener himself. Many of the Khalifah's followers were shot without trial or even inquiry. Sir John Maxwell, the major who was largely responsible for these shootings, commented that he regarded 'a dead fanatic as the only one to extend any sympathy to'.[2]

Kitchener came home to Britain covered in glory, and was rewarded by a peerage. This time, he was a great social success at Balmoral, dining with the Queen and Arthur Balfour. Kitchener told them about the battle, and amused the company by saying that

at the end of the battle he had 'two thousand women on his hands'
– presumably because their husbands had been shot. Asked what the
women were like, he replied, 'Very much like all women, they talked
a great deal.'[3] Queen Victoria, as if to prove the point, monopolized
the conversation, and replayed the humiliations of '82 and the Death
of Gordon at Khartoum. She recalled how furious Gladstone had
been that she sent him the telegram of rebuke *en clair*; but she had
sent it deliberately, so that everyone should know what she thought
of him.

The next day, Kitchener said he would not go out after luncheon
because he had to write a speech for the Guildhall, and he was no
public speaker. Balfour said there would be no difficulty about this,
and that he would be more than happy to write Kitchener's speech
for him. Fritz Ponsonby took the general the finished speech, which
was received with great mirth. 'Why, the whole place would scream
with laughter at such beautiful language coming from me.' But he
was grateful, nevertheless, and translated Balfour's delicate phrases
into his own round unvarnished idiom.[4] Kitchener's visit had brought
out a somewhat Boadicean side of the Queen's character, which she
perhaps needed; for, the last years of her life were to be dominated
by a war.

Successful Britain may have been in managing to subdue the
religious enthusiasts who followed the Sudanese successor to the
Mahdi. The Dutch Calvinists of the Transvaal would prove a tougher
nut to crack. The obsession with General Gordon, displayed by
the Queen when she conversed with Kitchener, was shared by the
population of Britain at large. Dr Watson, when he shared rooms
with Sherlock Holmes, put up a newly framed picture of Gordon
in 1893 (in the story entitled 'The Cardboard Box'). George William
Joy's 1885 painting *Gordon's Last Stand* (currently in Leeds City Art
Gallery) was an icon reproduced in countless schoolrooms and homes
throughout the British Empire. Victoria's determination was that
such a martyrdom should never happen again. Although Salisbury
was a man who was reluctant to intervene in any international affairs,

and a natural pessimist hesitant to go to war, he nevertheless deplored Gladstone's policy of making peaceful negotiation instead of war – he called it 'the Quakerization of Mankind'.[5]

Alfred Milner, who had become the Governor of the Cape Colony in 1897, was in many ways a walking parable of what had happened to Britain during the last decades of Victoria's reign. A Liberal, Balliol graduate and pupil of Benjamin Jowett, Milner had worked on the *Pall Mall Gazette* as a journalist under John Morley and W. T. Stead. As a politician, he had been a safe pair of hands as Chairman of the Board of the Inland Revenue. Then his old radical partner in politics, Chamberlain, sent him to South Africa to be Governor of the Cape Colony. The fervour of his imperialism outstripped that of Chamberlain. From the start, Milner was in favour of teaching the Boers a lesson, subduing them, making them accept British suzerainty over the Transvaal.

The whole situation was complicated by the huge wealth of the gold and diamond mines around Johannesburg, and by the fact that the Uitlanders, 'the foreigners' who had been drawn to all this wealth, had not come from one place but from Britain and from various countries of Central Europe. Half the Jews who gravitated to Johannesburg were from Germany or German-speaking Central Europe. Since many of them did not have the vote in their own country, they were not especially bothered by the lack of franchise for Uitlanders in the Transvaal, and they were refreshed by the Boers' lack of anti-Semitism, compared with the attitudes with which they had grown up in Europe.[6] The Jews tended to distance themselves from the complaints and grievances of the British Uitlanders. In many respects they were better off under Boer rule.

Behind the quarrels of Uitlanders and the Boers was the bigger question of whether Britain ruled the whole of South Africa. And behind the quarrel between Britain and the Boers lay the bigger question of Britain and the rest of the world. The German Emperor's telegram to Kruger, congratulating him on scotching the Jameson Raid, made that clear enough, even though Wilhelm was a divided self, part hating his English mother and her nation, part aspiring to be closer to Queen Victoria than any of her grandchildren. Another grandchild, Prince Leopold's daughter Alice, recalled having breakfast at Windsor after hostilities had broken out in South Africa, when the Queen 'received a letter from William telling her how she should ruin the Boer War! She had been enraged at the Kruger Telegram, but this piece of presumption aroused her most violent indignation.'[7]

The war was not inevitable. In the end, it boiled down to the question of whether the British Government could live with the fact that there were two Boer republics in South Africa, with very different laws and ways of life from those obtaining in the British colonies. In the end, the British desire to dominate the whole of Southern Africa was what drove Salisbury on to prosecute the war. In the Victorian heyday, the electorate had boxed and coxed between two tempting alternatives: the Liberal programme of extending the franchise and making Government accountable to the electorate – this was what made people vote for Gladstone; and the Tory jingoism of Disraeli, which cheered the Queen into believing she was the Empress of India, and the voters into thinking that they ruled the waves. In the latter days of the Queen's reign, Joseph Chamberlain combined both these British ideals. He was a jingoistic democrat. The public enthusiasm for the war was not universal, but it was immense.

On 18 December 1898, a burly, drunken Englishman called Tom Edgar got into a fight with another Englishman in Johannesburg. The police arrived and Edgar ran for home. He was pursued and the Boer police got into a scuffle. Edgar was shot dead. As Major General Butler – Commander-in-Chief of the British forces in South Africa – said, 'Had this drunken brawl occurred in any city in the world out of the Transvaal it would have occasioned no excitement outside of the people immediately concerned in it.'[8] When he came to London to explain the situation, Butler reminded the British politicians that Johannesburg was 'the most corrupt, immoral and untruthful assemblage of beings at present in the world'.[9]

As far as Chamberlain was concerned, however, that was not the point. The Boer policeman who shot the British man received no reprimand or discipline. A petition demanding justice was signed by 21,684 Uitlanders. They delivered it, not to Paul Kruger, but to Queen Victoria.

It came at a time of yet another family crisis for her. 23 January 1899 was scheduled as a day of celebration in Coburg: the silver wedding of the duke, Alfred, and his wife Marie of Russia. Their son Alfred ('Young Affie'), born at Buckingham Palace in 1874, had been an officer in the Guards. After his father succeeded to the dukedom of Coburg, he had followed his parents to Germany. When he was less than twenty, the Court Circular had announced, on 28 January 1895, that he was betrothed to the Duchess Elsa Matilda Marie, elder twin daughter of Duke William Eugene of Württemberg. This marriage never took place. Young Affie's life remains something of a mystery. Some have asserted that he contracted a secret marriage with Mabel Fitzgerald, the granddaughter of the Duke of Leinster. It seems certain that he was suffering from syphilis, contracted while a Guards officer, and that by the time of his parent's silver wedding party, Young Affie was suffering from general paresis of the insane. As the family gathered at Coburg, Affie shot himself with a revolver, but failed to kill himself. He was moved to the Martinsbrunn Sanatorium in Gratsch, near Meran (Merano) in the South Tyrol, where he died on 6 February, aged twenty-four. His father, who went to see the corpse – what Victoria called 'the dear remains' – was shocked by the sight, but the next day, he wrote to his mother, 'I have returned from praying near my dear boy who looks so peaceful. I am broken-hearted, but we start tonight with the remains for Gotha.'[10]

The Queen in middle age would have been prostrated by such an event occurring in her family. In old age, Victoria was buoyant. Despite missing the Munshi (who was on a year's leave of absence in India), she consoled herself by continuing with the annual visit to Cimiez and a few weeks in the luxury of the Excelsior Regina Hotel. By the time she returned, South Africa was closer than ever to war.

By May 1899, Milner – in a communiqué which became known as the Helot Dispatch – compared the plight of the Uitlanders with that of slaves in Ancient Greece. Kruger and Milner met for talks in June, but the Bloemfontein Conference broke up in failure. By June, the Prime Minister was being shown a copy of the *Daily Telegraph* demanding war. Salisbury knew that this demand, apparently written by a journalist, had in fact been drafted by Chamberlain himself.[11]

It was a bad time for Salisbury. His wife suffered a stroke on 6 July. (She would die on 20 November 1899.) Though most of the Cabinet wanted to move cautiously with regard to the Transvaal, the war momentum was strong. Salisbury wanted negotiations with Kruger to last long enough to allow troop ships to reach the South African ports. Dining at Osborne in late August, Salisbury told the table that he thought Kruger 'will go on for his own people pretending not to give in but will not go to war as it would put an end to himself'.[12]

So confident were the British of victory in the event of war, that there were only 12,000 British troops in South Africa when the Boers eventually attacked, and started their War of Independence on 11 October. There were 38,000 Transvaalers and Free Staters in the field, ready to fight. The first engagement happened when a small force led by Koos de la Rey moved across the Transvaal border and captured an armoured train bringing arms to Mafeking.

Meanwhile, troops were being mustered from all over the Empire – from India, from Australia, New Zealand and Canada. Eventually 365,693 imperial troops were assembled to fight 82,242 South Africans.

Among the British troops were Prince Christian Victor, the thirty-two-year-old son of Lenchen and Christian of Schleswig-Holstein. He had been an officer in the 60th King's Royal Rifles since 1888. As a staff officer under Kitchener, he had been at the Battle of Omdurman – 'the grandest sight I have ever witnessed'.[13] Now he was off to South Africa. On the night before he sailed, his parents and sisters took him to Her Majesty's Theatre to see Shakespeare's *King John*. He told his mother how much he had been impressed by the lines

> This England never did, nor never shall
> Lie at the proud foot of a conqueror...[14]

A little over a year later, he died of malaria and was buried at Pretoria – the first British royal personage to be buried in Africa.

The Duchess of York's brother Alexander (Alge, later Earl of Athlone) also served in the Boer War with the Inniskilling Dragoons (though his own regiment was the 7th Hussars). He was mentioned in dispatches (as he had been in the Matabele War of '96), and was eventually awarded the Distinguished Service Order.[15] So, like most army families, the Queen was deeply and personally involved with the war, following it on a daily, and sometimes an hourly, basis.

Sir Redvers Buller arrived at Cape Town with a huge army in December 1899. He had told the Queen before he left England that he did not think there would be much hard fighting. He divided the forces into three: General Sir William Gatacre was to defend the Cape Colony; Field Marshal Paul Methuen was to relieve Kimberley; and Buller himself was to march on Ladysmith.

Only three weeks after the death of Lady Salisbury, there began what came to be known as Black Week. First, General Gatacre's men were ambushed at Stormberg and surrendered to the Boers. Then Lord Methuen's 1st Division was defeated by Piet Kronje at Magersfontein, and failed to relieve Kimberley. On 15 December, Buller's army was roundly defeated by Louis Botha at the Battle of Colenso. Balfour went to Windsor at the end of that week to explain the defeats to the Queen. It was traditionally her own 'Black Week', containing as it did the fateful 14 December on which she had lost a husband and a daughter. Balfour, however, found Victoria indomitable. 'Please understand that there is no one depressed in this house; we are not interested in the possibilities of defeat. They do not exist.'[16]

Salisbury promptly sacked Buller, leaving him in charge of the army in Natal, and placed the campaign under the charge of Field Marshal Roberts – 'Bobs' – which as the Queen rightly pointed out, had been her wish all along. Bobs's son had just been killed at Colenso. ('Our loss is grievous,' he told the Queen, 'but our boy died the death he would have chosen.'[17])

Although there would continue to be opposition to the war, and pro-Boer factions among a liberal-minded, or perverse, minority, Black Week united the great majority of British people. Tens of thousands of men besieged the recruiting depots. The Lord Mayor of London formed the City of London Imperial Volunteers. It soon comprised a battery of artillery, a battalion of infantry and two companies of mounted infantry – 1,500 men in all. It contained nine barristers, seven architects, two bankers, thirty civil servants. This was the first time in British history that social classes other than the very highest and the very lowest formed part of the fighting force.[18]

Another consequence of Black Week was that it was decided to arm native Africans to fight the Boers. The socialist leader Keir Hardie made a speech in which he said, 'We are breaking faith with every nation in Europe in arming the blacks to fight against white men.'[19] The Queen would not have agreed. She never felt more imperialist than in her last years; never more certain that her dominion embraced all the peoples where the British flag had been planted.

TWENTY SEVEN

'VALE DESIDERATISSIME!'

URING 1900, THE fortunes of war turned, largely through the
skill of General Roberts. In January, the Boers, with inadequate
forces, tried to storm Ladysmith. They were driven back and a month
later their unsuccessful siege was relieved by Roberts. Thereafter, the
Boers were on the run. Roberts marched into Bloemfontein and took
charge of the vitally important railway. By the end of May he had
entered Johannesburg. Mafeking was relieved on 17 May, to huge
rejoicing: it 'filled the whole country with wild delight', said the
Queen.[1] By September, Kruger had fled South Africa for Portuguese
territory. The war would not end before the Queen's death. Roberts
had achieved the victory, however, and the 'mopping up' was left to
Kitchener. Three hundred thousand more troops were sent out to
South Africa to help him defeat the last remnant of guerrilla forces.
It was during this phase of the war that the British earned international hatred, not least for their invention of the concentration camp,
as a means of containing the half- – sometimes completely – starved
women and children of the Boer farmers.

Roberts, his return delayed by a broken arm, began the journey home.

The war took its toll on the Queen, as did the relentless succession of
family illnesses and bereavements. Vicky had been plagued by what

she believed to be lumbago, ever since falling from a horse in 1898. In 1899, she was too ill to attend Queen Victoria's eightieth birthday celebrations. It was cancer of the spine. Soon, she needed to be carried everywhere, and as she admitted, 'every movement is painful'.[2]

At the end of July, news came from Coburg that her brother Alfred had died of cancer of the larynx. 'What a mercy darling Alfred did not know the nature of his illness and the utter hopelessness of it,' Vicky wrote to her mother. 'Dear Alfred was spared mental pain and anxiety and like Fritz he was convinced he <u>would</u> improve! This is a mercy, though in my own case, I prefer to know <u>exactly</u> how the matter stands.'[3]

It was a hard thing for an old mother to bear – Alice dead, Leopold dead, Affie dead, and Vicky dying. Affie's only son Alfred had died aged twenty-four in 1899. The dukedom of Saxe-Coburg-Gotha, which had been renounced by Arthur, Duke of Connaught, therefore passed to the heir of the next brother, Leopold: to Charles Edward, then a schoolboy. Coburg, that nest of European kings and queens, was now searching on the playing fields of Eton for a duke.

The enfeebled Queen managed to inspect some of the returning troops from South Africa. She sat in a carriage on 29 Novermber, in an archway of Windsor Castle, and for the last time, her beautifully clear, bell-like voice was heard in public. 'Alas!' she told them, 'the joy at your safe return is clouded over by the memory of sad losses of many a valuable life which I, in common with you all, have to deplore.' Next day, also seated in a carriage, she watched a march-past of 240 Canadian troops. The Canadian officers dined with her afterwards.[4] She waited in Windsor until the sacred 14 December. When she crossed the Solent for her usual Osborne Christmas, her lady-in-waiting Lady Churchill remarked to her maid that the Queen appeared to be 'a dying woman'.[5]

In fact, it was Lady Churchill who would die first. The Queen was weak throughout Christmas, and, most uncharacteristically, had almost no appetite, often taking only a little whisky in her milk (or milk in her whisky). On Christmas Day, Dr Reid came to tell her that

Lady Churchill, who had been a lady of the bedchamber since 1854, had died of heart failure during her sleep. The Queen took the news quite calmly. Four days later, to broth, Benger's Food and warm milk, she was able to add 'a little cold beef, which is the first I have had for weeks and I really enjoyed it!'[6]

The death of Lady Churchill, and appalling weather, did little for the Queen's spirits. She was well enough on New Year's Day, 1901, to go with her son Arthur, Duke of Connaught, and her granddaughter Thora[7] to visit convalescent soldiers in a nursing home nearby. Tiny Lord Roberts, his arm still in a sling, eventually arrived. It was forty-two years since he had been one of the first recipients, at her hands, of the Victoria Cross. She now invested him as a Knight of the Garter, and told him that she intended him to have an earldom. But when he returned for another audience on 15 January, the Queen had taken a turn for the worse. She was confused in her mind. The next day, she took to her bed. Reid noted that the right side of her face appeared to be partially paralysed. He also noted that it was the first time in twenty years as her personal physician that he had seen her in her bed. She had clearly suffered a stroke, and for the next week, as she stayed in bed and became weaker, the family began to make its way to the Isle of Wight to take their leave. Among them was Willy, who, although virtually estranged from his mother, was devoted to his grandmother, and determined to speak with her before she died.

The Queen, now blind and semi-conscious, was only just able to swallow. The three daughters – Lenchen, Louise and Beatrice – knelt at her side, telling her who was coming and going: Randall Davidson reading the prayers for the dying; the doctors – Reid, Powell, Barlow; various ladies-in-waiting. Reid administered oxygen.

Reid also whispered to the Prince of Wales, 'Would it not be well to tell her that her grandson the Emperor is here too?'[8] Bertie decided not. 'It would excite her too much.' His sisters had been right to keep the fact from dear Mama that the hated Willy was in the room.

Wilhelm was, however, her grandson, and the son of her beloved firstborn. He had been standing next to her bedside all day, without telling the Queen that he was there, and without remonstrating with his uncles and aunts for their possessive behaviour. Inevitably, during a protracted death, there are breaks in the proceedings, when the onlookers obey calls of nature, and when maids and nurses attend to the bedding. Later in the morning, Reid went up to the Emperor and told him he was going to take him to the bedside when no one else was there. Wilhelm asked Dr Reid, 'Did you notice this morning that everybody's name in the room was mentioned to her except mine?'

There was a phase later in the day when, for about three hours, the Queen was alone with maids and nurses. During this time, she awoke and asked for the Vicar of Whippingham, Mr Smith, to be brought to her. While this was being arranged, Dr Reid went to ask the Prince of Wales's permission to take the German Emperor to see his grandmother. At last, Bertie relented. When Reid told the Queen that Wilhelm was there, she smiled, through her hazy dream, and said, 'The Emperor is very kind.'

By 4 pm, Reid gave his verdict to the family – 'The Queen is sinking.' Emperor Wilhelm had remained throughout this period. The Queen opened her eyes and said, 'Sir James, I am very ill.' The doctor assured her she would soon be better. She turned her eyes towards the picture of the Entombment of Christ which hung over the chimneypiece. Her pulse remained steady, regular. As the end approached, Reid moved her into a sitting position. The German Emperor knelt on the opposite side of the bed. Scotland and Germany, the two lands in which this most English of monarchs felt most at home, clasped her in her final breath. She died at 6.30 pm, supported by the arms of James Reid and her grandson Willy. Vicky, the Dowager Empress, had been too ill to be present. She lay in Schloss Friedrichshof in Kronberg, dying of cancer, learning Greek verbs: modern Greek, since she was vainly hoping to visit her daughter Sophie, Crown Princess of Greece, in Athens. She died in August that year. She too, like her mother and namesake, gave strict instructions about her laying out. The corpse of this German Empress was to be stripped naked and wrapped in the Union Jack, and buried according to the rites of the Church of England.

Queen Victoria's body had never been seen by her doctors. They were forbidden, in her lifetime, even to touch her with a stethoscope, an instrument from which she felt a peculiar aversion. Dr Reid was astounded to see, as he prepared the Queen for her last journey to Windsor, that she had had a ventral hernia and a prolapse of the uterus. It is not uncommon, especially for a woman who bore nine children, but it must have been in the highest degree uncomfortable, and there is no way of knowing at this distance of history how long she endured the condition.[9]

The elaborate instructions regarding her coffin arrangements were followed to the letter, the doctor and dresser filling the casket with the required collection of votive offerings and souvenirs before the lid was sealed. Of course, the family knew nothing of what the coffin contained. This was in itself emblematic: there was so much of the Queen's inner life which would always remain a mystery to her children. Reid placed a bunch of flowers in the Queen's hand to conceal the photograph of John Brown which it was clutching, and then he allowed her children to come to pay their respects. The Prince of Wales generously let the Munshi come in to say goodbye. Then the lid was put on, and screwed down. The box which contained Victoria, her childhood memories, her loves and passions, the inner consciousness of which she had an artist's awareness, and an almost novelistic skill at recording in her journals, was now hidden away. What was being borne from the Isle of Wight to the mainland was the Queen Empress, the Emblem of Empire, the Crowned Head of a beleaguered nation still at war.

The coffin was taken to Trinity Pier and borne across the Solent in the Royal Yacht *Alberta*, followed by King Edward VII, aboard *Victoria and Albert*. The Emperor Wilhelm followed in his imperial yacht, wearing the uniform of an English admiral. As they approached the ships of the Royal Navy in Portsmouth Harbour, they were also dwarfed by the gigantic German battleships which had accompanied the Emperor. Throughout the voyage, guns thundered their salute. The sea was choppy. Mist had cleared from the morning, and as the *Alberta* came within the shadow of Nelson's *Victory*, the sun was beginning to set in a glorious blaze.

Next morning, the coffin continued its journey to London by train. People knelt beside the railway track[10] as they saw the train pass. When she reached the capital of her Empire, the Queen was, rather typically, just passing through. Not for her an elaborate State Funeral at Westminster Abbey. Londoners could merely see the procession of a woman changing trains – a coffin being borne from Victoria[11] to Paddington Station. As befitted the head of the army, and the daughter of a soldier, she had ordered that it should be a military funeral, and that it should be white, not black. The coffin was placed on a gun carriage at the station and accompanied by eight cream horses. The coffin was covered with a white pall, with the Imperial State Crown, Orbs, Sceptre and Collar of the Garter upon it. She was followed by the King of England, and by his brother, all in uniform, by the German Emperor, by King George I of the Hellenes, by King Carlos of Portugal, King Leopold II of Belgium, by the crown princes of Germany, Romania, Greece, Denmark, Norway, Sweden and Siam, by the Archduke Franz Ferdinand of Austria-Hungary (whose assassination thirteen years later would precipitate the outbreak of world war), by the Grand Duke Michael Alexandrovich, and by the Duke of Aosta.

At the Queen Empress's request, hangings from the London windows were not black, but purple, tied with white satin bows. The music was not Handel's funeral march, but Chopin, Beethoven and Highland laments. The music was far from continuous, and what struck many observers was the silence of the capital as the coffin passed by. An Empire was almost numb with surprise. Only the very old could remember a time when there had been no Queen Victoria.

Another gun carriage was waiting at the station in Windsor. Here the horses were frisky, kicking and plunging so violently that they managed to break their harness. The front of the procession had already set off and reached Windsor High Street. Admiral Sir

Michael Culne-Seymour, meanwhile, back in the station forecourt, was shouting, 'My boys will soon put things right.' Fritz Ponsonby obtained the King's permission to unharness the gun carriage, and have it dragged up the hill by the Blue Jackets. Sir Arthur Bigge exploded with rage and said he was 'ruining the ceremony'.[12] The gun carriage was, however, manhandled up the slope to the steps of St George's Chapel. The Duke of Cambridge, whose views of this muddle can be very readily imagined, shuffled along behind on the arm of his son Adolphus. More or less a full complement of the Royal Family were present, except for the Duke of York – the future King – who was suffering from measles.

The late Queen would have been delighted by the sub-arctic temperature of St George's Chapel. After a short service, her coffin was taken to the Albert Memorial Chapel, where it remained, surrounded by the recumbent effigies of the Prince Consort, of Prince Leopold and of Prince Eddy. Officers of the Grenadiers and the Life Guards shared the honour of standing guard, four at a time, one at each corner of the coffin, for two days and two nights. As they changed the guard, the senior member of the old guard would say, 'I commit to you the charge of the body of her late Majesty Queen Victoria, Queen of Great Britain and Ireland, Empress of India, together with the Regalia of the British Empire.'

On Monday afternoon, the coffin – which everyone could now see was very small, like that of a child – set off on its last journey to Frogmore, where the final part of the burial service from the Book of Common Prayer was read. Above the door of the shrine, the Queen had had inscribed, in 1862, the words, 'Farewell most beloved! Here at last, will I rest with thee; with thee in Christ I will rise again'.[13] Of the mourners, the two most visibly affected were the Princess of Wales – our future Queen Mary – and the sixteen-year-old Duke of Albany, Charlie – Prince Leopold's son. His was to be perhaps the strangest destiny of all the grandchildren of the Queen. An Old Etonian who had grown up at Claremont, he became the Herzog Karl Eduard when still a teenager. He did sterling work for the

Red Cross, and magnificently restored the Veste, the old castle at Coburg where Luther had taken refuge during the religious wars. A German patriot, he fought against his grandmother's family in the First World War, and in the 1920s was a supporter of the right against the tide of republicanism and communism. Fatefully, he became an Obergruppenführer in the SA, perhaps the only Old Etonian so to do.[14]

All these strange things lay in the future as Charlie dabbed his sixteen-year-old eyes at Frogmore, and as the other mourners came outside the afternoon air was flecked with light snow.

Before he went home, the German Emperor was given a dinner at Marlborough House in London by his uncle the King. In his speech of thanks, Willy, that divided personality, had left his Prussian militarist self in his luggage with his swords and helmet. He spoke with the conciliatory vision of his grandfather Prince Albert. 'We ought to form an Anglo-German alliance,' he said. 'You to keep the seas while we would be responsible for the land; with such an alliance, not a mouse could stir in Europe without our permission, and nations would, in time, come to see the necessity of reducing their armaments.'[15]

The fates heard his words and mocked. With the kindliest and most peaceable of intentions, his uncle Edward VII urged his politicians not merely to promote an entente cordiale with France, but to forge alliances from which, in the end, there appeared to be no escape; so it was that when, within less than fourteen years of Queen Victoria's funeral, the Russians and the Austrians went to war, nearly all the nations represented at her funeral were drawn, on different sides, into the self-destructive inferno.

A different, a new, a post-Victorian world was coming into being, as the snow fell upon the locked mausoleum. The Boer War was brought to an end. Edward VII defied all his parents' worst fears and, for his short reign, became a popular King.

For him, and for his surviving siblings, the sheer strength of Queen Victoria's personality was almost overwhelming. He closed Osborne House. Half of it became the Royal Naval College for young cadets, and the other half, a convalescent home for retired officers. In the years after his mother's death, he did his best to gather up as much written evidence as he could in order to destroy it. The correspondence with Disraeli was brought over from Hughenden, and heavily pruned. Her letters to Dr Profeit concerning John Brown were eventually tracked down and destroyed. 'Baby', aka Princess Beatrice, busily set to work 'copying' dear Mama's journals and censoring as she went. Within days of his mother's death, Bertie, with his pot hat on his head and his wiry long-haired white fox terrier, Caesar, at his heels, strode around the rooms at Windsor Castle, and at Buckingham Palace, destroying as he went. 'Alas,' Queen Alexandra wrote to the dying Empress Frederick, 'during my absence, Bertie has had all Beloved Mama's rooms dismantled and all her precious things removed.'[16] Busts and statues of John Brown were smashed. (His statue at Balmoral was removed to a remote corner of the estate.) The papers of the Munshi were burned. All the relics of the Prince Consort were sent to Windsor Castle. In rooms where smoking had always been strictly forbidden, the bronchitic King coughed and blew cigar smoke. 'I don't know about A-rr-t but I think I know something about Arr-angement,'[17] he said in his guttural German voice, as he rehung pictures, and heaped framed photographs into bins.

He could not, however, remove her from the one place where she caused him the most torment – the inside of his head. Edward VII's iconoclasm could destroy a few shreds of evidence, and he had it in his power to 're-aRRange' some rooms. Victoria herself, however, would not go away. She remains a figure of extraordinary vividness. Those who had lived in the later part of her reign tried to articulate the paradox, from Kipling's bitter 'Widow of Windsor' poem, to many a more sentimental tribute. The frisson, the paradox, was to be found in the contrast, between the 'funny little woman' in a bonnet, who appeared to do next to nothing, and the mighty Empire whose hub and, in a sense, controller she was.

There were many during her lifetime, just as there have been many since, who took it upon themselves to expound the secrets of a successful constitutional monarchy. Victoria confounded, and confounds, most of these wiseacres, by actually doing extraordinarily little, and by entertaining views of the monarchy which were sometimes 'sensible' and Whiggish, and sometimes as capricious as W. S. Gilbert's Mikado. Whether the system helped to save her or she the system is probably an unanswerable question. Her fascination increases, rather than diminishes, with the passing of the years. This is partly, when we view her funeral procession, because constitutional monarchy is so obviously a system to be preferred to the ones adopted in many of the countries over which her unfortunate descendants tried, vainly, to exercise jurisdiction. As Europe discarded its monarchies and moved through the 1920s and '30s, the refugees tended to be moving from communist Russia and Nazi Germany towards monarchist London, and not the other way around.

So Victoria as the great defender and womb of European monarchies remains of perennial interest. It would not be so extraordinarily fascinating, however, were it not for the fascination of the Queen Empress herself. Those who visited her in the latter decades of her life might have made pleasantries about her, smiled at the vehemence of her opinions, observed her vacillations between well-grounded common sense and sheer caprice. In her presence, however, they felt something like awe. Anyone who has tried to write about her develops this sense too. It is something quite other than sentimental deference to royalty for its own sake. Almost none of the crowned heads who followed her coffin through the streets of Windsor could inspire it. The awe is for Queen Victoria the woman. Step over the carpet to that plump little figure who sits at her table, state papers or a Hindustani grammar open in front of her, the Munshi or Princess Beatrice at her side. You are approaching someone of great kindliness, someone of a far sharper intelligence than you would quite have guessed, and someone who – contrary to the most tedious of all the clichés about her – was easily amused. But you are also, if you have your wits about you, more than a little afraid. You are in the presence of greatness.

NOTES

1 AUTHORS

1 J. A. Froude, *Thomas Carlyle: A History of His Life in London 1834–1881*, London, Longmans, Green, 1884, Vol. I, p. 90.
2 Ibid.
3 Roger Fulford, *Royal Dukes: Queen Victoria's Father and 'Wicked Uncles'*, pp. 226 ff.
4 Froude, Vol. I, p. 135.
5 'Did he really say, "We authors, Ma'am?"'The story has never been authenticated, but it deserves to be true'. Robert Blake, *Disraeli*, n. p. 493.
6 Yvonne M. Ward, *Censoring Queen Victoria*, p. 9.
7 Giles St Aubyn, *Queen Victoria: A Portrait*, p. 601.
8 *The Times*, 19 December 1890.
9 Papers of the 3rd Marquess of Salisbury, Hatfield, Sir Henry Ponsonby to Lord Salisbury, 22 December 1890.
10 Battersea Papers, BL Additional MS 47,909, 24 April 1922.
11 Ibid., 29 February 1931.
12 A recent lively biography of Princess Louise by Lucinda Hawksley – the great-great-great-granddaughter of Charles Dickens – rehearses many of the rumours: that Louise had affairs with, among others, the sculptor Joseph Edgar Boehm, with her brother-in-law Prince Henry of Battenberg and with the courtier Sir Arthur Bigge. When the author applied to the Royal Archives at Windsor Castle, she was told, 'We regret that Princess Louise's files are closed.' (Hawksley, *The Mystery of Princess Louise*, p. 2.) So, the rumours remain rumours.

2 ZOOLOGY

1 *Letters of Countess Granville*, pp. 196–7, quoted Cecil Woodham-Smith, *Queen Victoria. Her Life and Times, Volume 1, 1819–1861*, p. 51.
2 See Daniel Schönpflug 'One European Family?' in Karina Urbach (ed.), *Royal Kinship, Anglo-German Family Networks, 1815–1918*, quoting Andreas Kraus, 'Das Haus Wittelsbach und Europa', and Lucien Bély, *La société des princes XVIe–XVIIIe siècle* (Paris, Fayard, 1999).
3 John Martin Robinson, *The Dukes of Norfolk* (Chichester, Phillimore, 1995),

p. 1, says that the family line 'cannot be traced further than the reign of Edward I' and quotes Gibbon: 'The proudest families are content to lose in the darkness of the middle ages the tree of their pedigree.'

4 Though the source of the huge increase in royal wealth was the Duchy of Lancaster; see p. 341.

5 John Davis, 'The Coburg Connection', in Urbach (ed.), *Royal Kinship*, p. 102.

6 Karl Marx, *Kritik des Hegelschen Staatsrechts*, 1843: *Werke*, Karl Marx and Friedrich Engels (eds.), Vol. I, p. 310.

7 Dulcie Ashdown, *Queen Victoria's Family*, p. 36.

8 Sidney Lee, *Queen Victoria, A Biography*, p. 17.

9 David Duff, *Edward of Kent*, p. 85.

10 Ibid., p. 109.

11 See the excellent *The Prince and His Lady* by Mollie Gillen.

12 Both quoted in Duff, *Edward of Kent*, p. 238.

13 Quoted ibid., p. 230.

14 Quoted Elizabeth Longford, *Victoria R.I.*, p. 20.

15 Dulcie Ashdown, *Queen Victoria's Mother*, p. 48.

16 D. M. Potts and W. T. W. Potts, *Queen Victoria's Gene: Haemophilia and the Royal Family*, p. 64.

17 Ibid., p. 72.

18 I espoused it in my book *The Victorians*, acknowledging my debt to Potts and Potts.

19 Kate Williams, *Becoming Queen*, p. 139.

20 Ibid., p. 140 (slightly emended).

21 All the above, Duff, *Edward of Kent*, p. 224.

22 Lee, p. 18.

23 Duff, *Edward of Kent*, p. 279.

3 'IT IS ONE STEP'

1 A. C. Benson and Viscount Esher (eds.), *The Letters of Queen Victoria 1837–1861*, Vol. I, p. 10.

2 RA/VIC/MAIN/Z/128/185.

3 Lee, p. 30.

4 Roger Fulford (ed.), *Dearest Child: Letters between Queen Victoria and the Princess Victoria 1858–1861*, pp. 111–2.

5 RA/VIC/MAIN/Z/128/1.

6 RA/VIC/MAIN/Z/128/2.

7 RA/VIC/MAIN/Z/128/3.

8 Fulford, *Royal Dukes*, p. 58.

9 Benson and Esher, *Letters*, Vol. I, p. 10.

10 Ibid., p. 11.

11 Ibid.

12 *Oxford Dictionary of National Biography*, Vol. 13, p. 76, K. D. Reynolds, 'Elizabeth, Marchioness Conyngham'.

13 J. G. Lockhart, *Life of Sir Walter Scott*, p. 690.
14 Lee, pp. 29–30.
15 Quoted Woodham-Smith, p. 54, quoting RA Y 203/81.
16 Quoted ibid., p. 73.
17 RA/VIC/MAIN/Z/128/7–9.
18 Conroy Papers, Balliol College, Oxford.
19 www.measuringworth.com
20 Benson and Esher, *Letters*, Vol. I, p. 18.
21 Woodham-Smith, p. 72, quoting a translation of RA M4/16, Duchess of Clarence to Duchess of Kent, 12 January 1830.

4 'WHITE LITTLE SLAVEY'

1   Marquess of Anglesey, *One Leg: The Life and Letters of Henry William Paget, First Marquess of Anglesey, KG*, pp. 227–30; see also Prochaska, *Royal Bounty: The Making of a Welfare Monarchy*, p. 54.
2   Anglesey, p. 230.
3   Viscount Esher (ed.), *The Training of a Sovereign*, p. vii.
4   Charles Greville, *The Greville Memoirs, 1814–1861*, ed. Lytton Strachey and Roger Fulford, Vol. II, p. 119.
5   Ibid., p. 307.
6   Ibid., p. 36.
7   Prochaska, p. 58.
8   Greville, Vol. III, p. 147.
9   Ibid., p. 192.
10 Lee, p. 31.
11 Viscount Esher (ed.), *The Girlhood of Queen Victoria: A Selection of Her Majesty's Diaries between the years 1832 and 1840*, Vol. I, p. 29.
12 Jane Ridley, *Bertie*, p. 9.
13 David Cecil, *Melbourne*, p. 388.
14 Conroy Papers, Balliol College, Oxford.
15 All the strongly phrased insults come from various documents in the Conroy Papers, Balliol College, Oxford.
16 RA/M7/67, Prince Charles Leiningen's memorandum, quoted Longford, p. 56.
17 RA/VIC/MAIN/ADD/A11/18, Lord Liverpool's memorandum, quoted Longford, p. 57.
18 Boyd Hilton, *A Mad, Bad, and Dangerous People?*, pp. 430–1 and Antonia Fraser, *passim*.
19 Dugald Stewart, *Lectures on Political Economy*, ed. Sir William Hamilton (Edinburgh, 1855, 2 vols.), Vol. II, p. 374.
20 Jonathan Parry, *The Rise and Fall of Liberal Government in Victorian Britain*, pp. 43–4.
21 Esher, *Girlhood*, Vol. I, p. 44.
22 Ibid., pp. 134–5.
23 Ibid., p. 133.

24 Katherine Hudson, *A Royal Conflict: Sir John Conroy and the Young Victoria*, p. 62.
25 RA Y79/35, King Leopold of the Belgians to Queen Victoria, 9 March 1854, quoted Hudson, p. 104.
26 Journal, 26 February 1838.
27 RA M7/42, Baron Stockmar to the Duchess of Kent, transcribed Hudson, p. 102.
28 Benson and Esher, *Letters*, Vol. I, p.48, 13 May 1836.
29 RA Y88/11, 17 May 1836.
30 Esher, *Girlhood*, Vol. I, p. 159.
31 Ibid., p. 161.
32 Benson and Esher, *Letters*, Vol. I, p. 19.
33 Greville, Vol. III, pp. 309–10.
34 Esher, *Girlhood*, Vol. I, p. 190.
35 Ibid., p. 191.
36 RA/VIC/ADD/A11/12.
37 Woodham-Smith, p. 135.
38 Esher, *Girlhood*, Vol. I, p. 193.
39 RA Melbourne papers, 20 June 1837, quoted Philip Ziegler, *King William IV*, p. 289.
40 *Oxford Dictionary of National Biography*, Vol. 13, p. 78, K. D. Reynolds, 'Elizabeth, Marchioness Conyngham'.
41 Greville, Vol. III, p. 375.
42 Esher, *Girlhood*, Vol. I, p. 196.
43 Ibid.

5 'THE IGNORANT LITTLE CHILD'

1 Conroy Papers, Balliol College, Oxford.
2 Ibid.
3 Ibid.
4 Journal, 7 February 1838.
5 Lord Byron, 'Remember Thee, Remember Thee'.
6 David Cecil, p. 227.
7 Superficially, because beneath the surface Melbourne and all the Whigs would have fought to the death to defend themselves against radicals, plebeians, trades unions – anything which diminished their power in any way. Their only reason for siding with the liberals was self-preservation.
8 Quoted L. G. Mitchell, *Lord Melbourne, 1779–1848*, p. 211. Hertfordshire Record Office, Panshanger MSS, D/ELb, f. 35.
9 Journal, 15 October 1838.
10 Journal, 22 April 1838.
11 Journal, 21 January 1838.
12 Journal, 10 October 1838.
13 Journal, 3 December 1838. This Mrs Lamb was the natural child of Lady Elizabeth Foster, later Duchess of Devonshire.

14 Journal, 5 July 1839.
15 Journal, 6 February 1839.
16 Journal, 1 January 1839.
17 Hilton, *A Mad, Bad, and Dangerous People?*, p. 558.
18 All the quotations, unless otherwise stated, relating to this day come from Queen Victoria's journal, 28 June 1838.
19 Journal, 24 June 1838.
20 Journal, 19 April 1838.
21 Benson and Esher, *Letters*, Vol. I, p. 121.
22 Ibid.
23 Journal, 16 July 1839.
24 Journal, 8 July 1839.
25 Journal, 5 November 1839.
26 Journal, 3 July 1839.
27 Journal, 1 November 1838.
28 Journal, 6 February 1839.
29 Journal, 1 August 1838.
30 Journal, 3 February 1839.
31 Journal, 10 July 1839.
32 Journal, 25 April 1838.
33 Journal, 7 July 1839.
34 Journal, 10 July 1839.
35 Quoted Mitchell, p. 241.
36 Journal, 10 August 1839.
37 Journal, 12 May 1839.
38 Benson and Esher, *Letters*, Vol. I, p. 175.
39 Ibid., 11 May 1839, p. 172.
40 Journal, 20 June 1837.
41 Benson and Esher, *Letters*, Vol. I, p. 177.
42 Ibid., 12 October 1839, p. 188.
43 Journal, 1 November 1839.
44 Journal, 5 November 1839.
45 Benson and Esher, *Letters*, Vol. I, 15 October 1839, p. 188.
46 Ibid., 24 October 1839, p. 190.
47 Journal, 26 July 1843.

6 'TOO HASTY AND PASSIONATE FOR ME'

1 See the *Daily Telegraph*, 24 September 2013, where the monarch was photographed in conversation with the Prime Minister of New Zealand. A photograph in frame of the Duke and Duchess of Cornwall is on the table. Toy corgis are to be seen in the foreground. And on either side of the chimneypiece hang the Brocky drawings. The images themselves are to be found in Jonathan Marsden, *Victoria & Albert: Art and Love*, p. 62.
2 T. R. Hooper (ed.), *Memoirs of Ebenezer and Emma Hooper*, p. 185.

3   Hooper, p. 186.
4   Journal, 1 January 1840.
5   Robert Rhodes James, *Albert, Prince Consort*, p. 90.
6   Journal, 10 February 1840.
7   Journal, 11 February 1840.
8   Sir Theodore Martin, *The Life of His Royal Highness The Prince Consort*, Vol. I, p. 55.
9   Quoted Robert Rhodes James, p. 104.
10 Ibid., p. 107.
11 RA/VIC/MAIN/Y/54/3, quoted Frank Eyck, *The Prince Consort: A Political Bigraphy*, p. 24.
12 Journal, 1 December 1840.
13 Robert Rhodes James, pp. 126–7 quoting RA/VIC/MAIN/Y/154/100, RA/VIC/ADDU/2/4, ff.2 and 5.
14 Ibid., p. 127 quoting RA U2/4.
15 Paul Thomas Murphy, *Shooting Victoria: Madness, Mayhem, and the Rebirth of the British Monarchy*, pp. 54–64.
16 Ibid., pp. 181–2.
17 Ibid., p. 207.
18 Hermione Hobhouse, *Thomas Cubitt, Master Builder*, p. 375.
19 Ibid., p. 135.
20 Peel Papers, BL Additional 40,437, f. 251, 2 November 1843.
21 Ibid., f. 376, 2 November 1843.
22 Ibid., f. 193, 7 September 1843.
23 Ibid., f. 201, 8 November 1843.
24 Journal, 2 December 1843.
25 Kate Colquhoun, *A Thing in Disguise: The Visionary Life of Joseph Paxton*, p. 123.
26 Ibid., pp. 124–6.
27 Hobhouse, *Cubitt*, p. 316 and passim.
28 Quoted ibid., p. 377.
29 J. N. D. Kelly and M. J. Walsh, *Oxford Dictionary of Popes*, p. 313.
30 Albert to Peel, Peel Papers, BL 212, f. 280, 19 October 1841, quoted Emma Winter, 'Albert and Fresco Painting' in Franz Bosbach and John R. Davis (eds.), *Prinz Albert. Ein Wettiner in Grossbritannien*, p. 152.
31 Leah Kharibian, *Passionate Patrons: Victoria and Albert and the Arts*, p. 43.
32 Ibid., p. 41.
33 Winter, in Bosbach and Davis, p. 158.
34 Journal, 6 May 1842.
35 Journal, 2 September 1842.
36 Ibid.
37 Journal, 5 September 1842.
38 Journal, 7 September 1842.
39 Journal, 1 October 1844.
40 Journal, 1 May 1843 – the German for 'wheelchair' is Rollstuhl.

41 Journal, 4 May 1843.
42 Journal, 1 June 1844.
43 Journal, 3 June 1844.
44 Journal, 22 June 1846.
45 Journal, 23 January 1846.
46 Hansard, Third Series, Vol. LXXXIII, p. 94.
47 Ibid., p. 310.
48 Hansard, Third Series, Vol. LXXXIV, p. 347.

7 *I PURITANI*

1 Peel Papers, BL Additional 40,441, f. 324.
2 Ibid.
3 Journal, 8 September 1846.
4 Ibid.
5 Journal, 25 June 1846.
6 Journal, 10 June 1846.
7 Journal, 6 July 1846.
8 *Oxford Dictionary of National Biography*, Vol. 48, p. 300, John Prest, 'Lord John Russell'.
9 E. L. Woodward, *The Age of Reform, 1815–1870*, p. 352.
10 Journal, 5 July 1846.
11 See Karina Urbach, 'Albert and Palmerston' in Bosbach and Davis, pp. 83–93.
12 Ibid., p. 86, quoting Staatsarchiv Coburg LA A7206.
13 David Brown, *Palmerston and the Politics of Foreign Policy, 1846-1855*, quoting PRO 30/22/7 ff. 343–5, Russell Papers.
14 Urbach, in Bosbach and Davis, p. 88.
15 Quoted Brown, *Palmerston and the Politics of Foreign Policy*, p. 93.
16 Hansard, Third Series, Vol. XCVII, 1 March 1848, pp. 121–3.
17 David Brown, *Palmerston: A Biography*, p. 310.
18 Ibid.
19 Journal, 24 December 1846.
20 Richard Ormond and Carol Blackett-Ord, *Franz Xaver Winterhalter and the Courts of Europe, 1830–70*, p. 38.
21 For my account of the children's education, I follow Woodham-Smith, pp. 265–9.
22 Ibid., p. 265.
23 Marsden, p. 78, quoting the *Athenæum*, 1847, p. 496.
24 Ormond and Blackett-Ord, p. 40.
25 Journal, 31 January 1848.
26 Journal, 25 February 1848.
27 Journal, 29 February 1848.
28 Ibid.
29 Journal, 25 February, 1848.
30 Woodham-Smith, p. 285, letter dated 16 March 1848.

31   Journal, 1 March 1848.

32   Journal, 25 February 1848.

33   Journal, 29 February 1848.

34   Journal, 27 February 1848.

35   Dorothy Thompson, *The Chartists*, p. 307.

36   Journal, 6 March 1848.

37   Journal, 7 March 1848.

38   Journal, 6 April 1848.

39   Robert Rhodes James, p. 188.

40   Journal, 21 April 1848.

41   Journal, 4 April 1848.

42   Journal, 11 February 1848.

43   Journal, 27 May 1848.

44   Journal, 7 September 1848.

45   Journal, 8 September, 1848.

46   Ibid.

47   Journal, 19 September 1848.

48   Ibid.

49   Journal, 22 June 1846.

50   Journal, 24 November 1848.

51   Journal, 25 November 1848.

8 HALLELUJAH CHORUS

1   HM Queen Victoria, *Leaves from the Journal of Our Life in the Highlands, from 1848 to 1861*, p. 161.

2   Ibid., p. 159.

3   Ibid., p. 169.

4   Roger Swift and Christine Kinealy (eds.), *Politics and Power in Victorian Ireland*, p. 14.

5   Christine Kinealy, 'Queen Victoria and Ireland' in Swift and Kinealy, p. 27.

6   Quoted Robert Rhodes James, p. 192.

7   'The Torchlit Ball at Corriemulzie' is one of the Queen's many lyrical descriptions of Highland dancing in the *Leaves*.

8   Alfred Tennyson, 'Locksley Hall', *The Poems of Tennyson*, ed. Christopher Ricks, Vol. 2, p. 128.

9   Benson and Esher, *Letters*, Vol. II, p. 223.

10   Ibid., p. 285.

11   Journal, 19 January 1851.

12   Journal, 16 January 1851.

13   Journal, 12 January 1851.

14   Benson and Esher, *Letters*, Vol. II, p. 281.

15   Journal, 27 January 1851.

16   BL Gladstone Papers, 14 March 1870.

17   Owen Chadwick, *The Victorian Church*, Vol. I, p. 298.

18   Journal, 29 January 1851.

19 Journal, 27 June 1850.

20 Journal, 2 March 1850.

21 Hansard, Third Series, Vol. CXII, p. 443.

22 Benson and Esher, *Letters*, Vol. II, p. 256.

23 Journal, 21 March 1850.

24 Quoted Michael Leapman, *The World for a Shilling: How the Great Exhibition of 1851 Shaped a Nation*, p. 165.

25 Ibid., p. 205 and passim.

9 'GODLIKE MEN'

1   Colquhoun, p. 187.

2   Stanley Weintraub, *Albert, Uncrowned King*, p. 263.

3   J. Matthews, M. G. Wiebe, et al (eds.), *Benjamin Disraeli Letters*, Vol. VI, p. 77.

4   Quoted Theodor Zeldin, *France, 1848–1945*, Vol. I, pp. 502–3.

5   Benson and Esher, *Letters*, Vol. II, p. 366.

6   Zeldin, Vol. I, p. 506.

7   Quoted Jasper Ridley, *Napoleon III and Eugénie*, p. 314.

8   Antoine D'Arjuzon, *Victoria et Napoléon III. Histoire d'une amitié*, p. 83.

9   Karl Marx and Friedrich Engels, *Werke*, Vol. VIII, p. 115.

10 Bertrand Russell, *The Autobiography*, p. 22.

11 Journal, 18 September 1852.

12 Benson and Esher, *Letters*, Vol. II. p. 386.

13 Ibid., p. 383.

14 Angus Hawkins, *The Forgotten Prime Minister: The 14th Earl of Derby*, Vol. II, p. 39.

15 Journal, 16 September 1852.

16 Charles Tennyson, *Alfred Tennyson, by His Grandson*, p. 271.

17 Tennyson, 'Ode on the Death of the Duke of Wellington', *Poems*, Vol. II, p. 290.

18 Karl Marx on the 18th Brumaire.

19 Ralph R. Frerichs, 'Anaesthesia and Queen Victoria', UCLA Department of Epidemiology, School of Public Health (3), 2001.

20 Journal, 22 April 1853.

21 Benson and Esher, *Letters*, Vol. II, p. 397.

22 Ibid., p. 367.

23 Ibid., p. 407.

24 Woodham-Smith, p. 347, quoting RA/ADD/A19/37, 6 January 1853.

25 Longford, p. 243.

26 Victoria transcribed Lady Augusta's letter with this description in her journal, 1 February 1853.

27 Benson and Esher, *Letters*, Vol. II, 23 March 1853, p. 442.

28 Greville, Vol. I, p. 106, 15 November 1853.

29 Lambert, pp. 83–100.

30 Journal, 23 September 1853.

31 See James Pope-Hennessy, *Queen Mary*, p. 101, for Victoria's obsession with

Württemberg, and the possibility of one of her family becoming its grand duke.

32 Journal, 23 September 1853.

33 Benson and Esher, *Letters*, Vol. II, 16 October 1853, p. 457.

10 AT WAR

1   Alan Mallinson, *The Making of the British Army*, p. 274 and passim.

2   Ibid., p. 265.

3   Journal, 11 March 1854.

4   Journal, 11 November 1854.

5   Journal, 12 November 1854.

6   Ibid.

7   BL Herries Papers, Additional MS 57414 f. 13.

8   Ibid., f. 15.

9   Ibid., f. 17.

10 Ibid., f. 17.

11 Ibid., f. 14.

12 Ibid., f. 67.

13 Ibid., f. 82.

14 Michael Alexander and Sushila Anand, *Queen Victoria's Maharajah*, p. 168.

15 Hawkins, Vol. II, p. 109.

16 Journal, 4 February 1855.

17 Journal, 5 February 1855.

18 Martin, Vol. III, p. 382.

19 Benson and Esher, *Letters*, Vol. III, p. 122.

20 Journal, 13 April 1855.

21 Journal, 15 April 1855.

22 Benson and Esher, *Letters*, Vol. III, p. 118.

23 Journal, 16 April 1855.

24 Ibid.

25 Longford, p. 251.

26 Quoted d'Arjuzon, p. 123.

27 Quoted Edith Saunders, *A Distant Summer*, p. 49.

28 *The Times*, 24 August 1855.

29 Saunders, p. 138.

30 Ibid., p. 140.

31 Ibid., p. 42.

32 Hannah Pakula, *An Uncommon Woman: The Empress Frederick, Daughter of Queen Victoria, Wife of the Crown Prince of Prussia, Mother of Kaiser Wilhelm*, p. 52.

33 Ibid., p. 50.

11 'SCOLDER AND SCOLDED'

1   Count Egon Casar Corti, *The English Empress: A Study in the Relations Between Queen Victoria and Her Eldest Daughter, Empress Frederick of Germany*, Vol. I, p. 30.

2   RA/VIC/MAIN/Z/261.
3   RA/VIC/MAIN/Z/140, ff. 30–1 (translation from German). Original letter destroyed by Princess Beatrice, but photocopy survives.
4   RA/VIC/MAIN/Y/206, Sir James Clark's diary, 15 February 1856.
5   RA/VIC/MAIN/Z/491, ff. 4–5.
6   RA/VIC/MAIN/Z/142.
7   RA/VIC/MAIN/Y/206, Sir James Clark's diary, 5 February 1856.
8   Journal, 19–31 July 1856 passim.
9   RA/VIC/MAIN/Z/140, ff. 33–5, Windsor Castle, 5 November 1856.
10 RA/VIC/MAIN/Z/261, f. 51v.
11 Ibid., f. 1r.
12 Ibid., f. 28v.
13 Ibid., f. 1r.
14 Ibid., f. 18r.
15 Vincent A. Smith, *Oxford History of India*, pp. 588–9.
16 Muriel E. Chamberlain, *Lord Aberdeen: A Political Biography*, p. 524.
17 RA/VIC/MAIN/Z/261, f. 9v.
18 Journal, 3 August 1857.
19 Journal, 6 August 1857.
20 Journal, 9 August 1857.
21 Journal, 25 August 1857.
22 Journal, 14 October 1857.
23 Journal, 25 January 1858.
24 Pakula, p. 79.
25 Ibid., p. 82.
26 Ibid., p. 83.
27 *O mon Dieu, mon Dieu*, M. de Courcel, quoted *Geoffrey Madan's Notebooks*, ed. J. A. Gere and John Sparrow, p. 48.
28 *Dearest Child*, p. 31.
29 Roger Fulford, *The Prince Consort*, quoting 'Royal Archives' (unspecified), p. 76.
30 Quoted Weintraub, *Albert*, p. 340.
31 Bodleian MS. Eng. Lett. D. 267, f. 30.
32 Quoted Fulford, *Prince Consort*, p. 210.
33 Quoted Weintraub, *Albert*, p. 340.
34 Madan, p. 111.

12 NERVE DAMAGE

1   Martin, Vol. II, p. 58.
2   Staatsarchiv Coburg, A.Y. 28. N.9 (translation).
3   Fulford, *Royal Dukes*, p. 257.
4   Golo Mann, *Deutsche Geschichte des 19. und 20. Jahrhunderts*, p. 110.
5   Ibid., p. 144.
6   Hawkins, Vol. II, p. 154. In general, most of the information about the fall of the Government and Derby's re-election comes from Hawkins.

7   Journal, 20 February 1858.
8   Chamberlain, p. 523.
9   Aberdeen in the Gurney Papers (Norfolk County Record Office, quoted Chamberlain).
10   A. N. Wilson, *The Victorians*, p. 214.
11   Quoted Michael Maclagan, *'Clemency' Canning: Charles John, 1st Earl Canning, Governor-General and Viceroy of India, 1856–1862*, p. 140.
12   RA/VIC/MAIN/Z/261, f. 50v.
13   Ibid., f. 51r and v.
14   RA/VIC/MAIN/Y/206, Sir James Clark's diary.
15   RA/VIC/MAIN/Z/261, f. 87r.
16   Quoted Woodham-Smith, p. 405.
17   Ibid.
18   RA/VIC/MAIN/Z/261, f. 90.
19   *Dearest Child*, p. 73.
20   Ibid., p. 79.
21   Ibid., p. 94.
22   Ibid., p. 108.
23   Ibid., p. 115.
24   Quoted Woodham-Smith, p. 395.
25   *Dearest Child*, p. 139.
26   Ibid.
27   Ibid., p. 141.
28   Ibid., p. 154.
29   Ibid., p. 136.
30   Ibid., p. 138.
31   For most of the above, Pakula, pp. 123–7.

13 *'ARME FRAU'*

1   Robert Rhodes James, pp. 242–3, no reference, but quoting Woodham-Smith, RA/VIC/MAIN/140/60–2.
2   RA/VIC/MAIN/Z/130/113.
3   RA/VIC/MAIN/Z/128/48.
4   Benson and Esher, *Letters*, Vol. III, p. 335.
5   *Dearest Child*, p. 354.
6   Benson and Esher, *Letters*, Vol. III, p. 335.
7   Quoted Rhodes James, p. 243 without a reference.
8   *Dearest Child*, p. 308.
9   Ibid., p. 254
10   Ibid., p. 171.
11   Ibid., p. 212.
12   Ibid., p. 236.
13   Ibid., p. 258.
14   Ibid., p. 149.
15   Ibid., p. 245.

16 Ibid., p. 318.
17 RA/VIC/MAIN/Z/140, f. 46–51 (translated from German).
18 RA/VIC/MAIN/Z/491, f. 8.
19 *Dearest Child*, p. 289.
20 Benson and Esher, *Letters*, Vol. III, p. 348.
21 Ibid., p. 349.
22 Ibid., p. 356.
23 Sir Philip Magnus, *King Edward the Seventh*, p. 39.
24 Ibid., pp. 40–41.
25 RA/VIC/MAIN/Z/491, f. 35.
26 RA/VIC/MAIN/140, f. 63, translated from German, no date, but it must
    come from about this period.
27 RA/VIC/MAIN/Z/491/25v and 26r.
28 RA/VIC/MAIN/Z/491/23r.
29 Ibid.
30 RA/VIV/MAIN/Z/290/56 and 57.
31 RA/VIC/MAIN/Z/290/58.
32 Volume Two is missing.
33 RA/VIC/MAIN/Z/132, f. 111.
34 Ibid., f. 107.
35 RA/VIC/MAIN/Z/128, f. 7.
36 He uses the English word 'nervousness' in an otherwise German letter (of
    6 June 1860) promising to do 'everything I can to help you get over your
    nervousness'. *Nervosität* in German, the word he is clearly thinking of,
    is semantically closer to *Angst* and actual nervous collapse than the mild
    English noun. RA/VIC/MAIN/140, f. 64.
37 RA/VIC/MAIN/Z/491, f. 43.
38 Ibid., f. 9r.
39 RA/VIC/MAIN/491, f. 7. All references to the last volume of
    Reminiscences are 491.
40 Weintraub, *Albert*, p. 401.
41 This perception is largely owing to the ingenious researches of Helen
    Rappaport. See her *Magnificent Obsession*.
42 *Dearest Child*, p. 308.
43 Ibid., p. 310.
44 Journal, 26 August 1861.
45 *Dearest Child*, p. 365.
46 Longford, p. 289.
47 *Dearest Child*, p. 365–6.
48 Weintraub, *Albert*, p. 406.
49 Quoted ibid., p. 406.
50 All the quotations above are from Queen Victoria's journal on the relevant
    dates.
51 RA/VIC/MAIN/Z/140.
52 RA//VIC/MAIN/Z/142/14 December.

53 RA/VIC/MAIN/Z/143/14 December.
54 *Dearest Child*, p. 375.

14 'THE QUEEN'S GRIEF STILL SOBS'

1   RA/VIC/MAIN/Z/491, f. 32.
2   Ibid., f. 18v.
3   Quoted by John Martin Robinson in his excellent *Windsor Castle, A Short History*, p. 133 – but he does not say whose words they are!
4   Roger Fulford (ed.), *Dearest Mama: Letters between Queen Victoria and the Crown Princess of Prussia, 1861–1864*, pp. 101–2.
5   Journal, 21 September 1863.
6   Staatsarchiv Coburg, 13 April 1863, No. 944.
7   Journal, 19 November 1863.
8   Quoted Gerard Noel, *Princess Alice, Queen Victoria's Forgotten Daughter*, p. 91.
9   The joke was that he only knew three people who had ever understood the Schleswig-Holstein Question: the Prince Consort, who was dead, a German professor, who had gone mad, and himself, who had forgotten it.
10 Martin, Vol. II, p. 56.
11 '*dieser Dummkopf von Kronprinz*' – Mann, p. 374.
12 *Dearest Mama*, p. 35.
13 Gladstone Papers, 28 April 1862.
14 St Aubyn, *Queen Victoria*, p. 333.
15 Ibid.
16 *Dearest Mama*, p. 115.
17 Ibid., p. 65.
18 Ibid., p. 85.
19 Book of Common Prayer: Solemnization of Matrimony.
20 Noel, p. 79.
21 *Dearest Mama*, 18 June 1862, p. 78.
22 Ibid., p. 84.
23 Ibid., p. 85.
24 Charlotte Zeepvat, *Queen Victoria's Youngest Son*, p. 48, quoting RA Add U 143/Reel 1.
25 *Dearest Mama*, pp. 234–5.
26 Ibid., p. 128.
27 Ibid.
28 Magnus, p. 66.
29 Staatsarchiv Coburg, 29 March 1863 (translation), 28. B.18. A.W. 27, Nr 942.
30 Journal, 7 March 1863.
31 Magnus, p. 67.
32 Ibid., p. 68.
33 G. E. Buckle, *The Letters of Queen Victoria, 1862–85*, Second Series, Vol. I, p. 55.

34 Ibid., p.186.
35 Ibid., p. 97.
36 Ibid., p. 100.
37 Coburger Hausarchiv, A I 28 b 18 A W 27 Nr. 950 Sm (translation).
38 Journal, 9 November 1863.
39 Buckle, Second Series, Vol. I, p. 104.
40 Journal, 3 September 1863.
41 Ibid.
42 Ibid.
43 Personal observation and conversation with the guide in the Schloss Ehrenberg – to whom apologies, as I did not write down his name.
44 Journal, 4 September 1863.
45 Zeepvat, p. 53.
46 Staatsarchiv Coburg (translation).
47 Journal, 26 September 1863.
48 Buckle, Second Series, Vol. I, p. 116.
49 Journal, 20 November 1863.
50 Journal, 4 December 1863.
51 Journal, 6 January 1864.
52 Journal, 15 January 1864.
53 Ibid.
54 Buckle, Second Series, Vol. I, p 143.
55 Jane Ridley, p. 84.
56 Buckle, Second Series, Vol. I, p. 151.
57 Ibid., p. 152.
58 Ibid., p. 153.
59 Ibid., p. 159.
60 *Dearest Mama*, p. 296.
61 Ibid., p. 301.
62 Ibid., p. 320.
63 Keith A. P. Sandiford, *Great Britain and the Schleswig-Holstein Question, 1848–64*, p. 3.
64 Quoted Woodward, p. 320.
65 John Vincent (ed.), *Disraeli, Derby and the Conservative Party: Journals and Memoirs of Edward Henry, Lord Stanley, 1849–1869*, p. 317.
66 BL Waterpark Papers, 1864.
67 Ibid., 21 September 1864.
68 Purves Papers, quoted Raymond Lamont-Brown, *John Brown, Queen Victoria's Highland Servant*, p. 105.
69 Lamont-Brown, p. 105.
70 Buckle, Second Series, Vol. I, p. 255.
71 Roger Fulford (ed.), *Your Dear Letter: Private Correspondence of Queen Victoria and the Crown Princess of Prussia, 1865–1871*, p. 22.
72 Lamont-Brown, p. 107.
73 Ibid., p. 119.

74 Journal, 12 September 1863.
75 Brown, *Palmerston: A Biography*, p. 475.
76 Quoted Woodward, p. 175.

15 'I COULD DIE FOR YE'

1   Hawkins, Vol. II, p. 419.
2   Ibid., p. 421.
3   Pope-Hennessy, p. 585.
4   Quoted Deirdre Murphy et al, *Victoria Revealed*, p. 19.
5   Journal, August 22, 1867.
6   *Daily Telegraph*, 24 August 1867.
7   The epithet is considered. There *are* no better diaries!
8   Duff, *Victoria in the Highlands*, p. 15.
9   Lamont-Brown, p. 26.
10 Who could well be the author of this book.
11 Lamont-Brown, p. 95.
12 *Your Dear Letter*, p. 48.
13 Buckle, Second Series, Vol. I, pp. 328–9.
14 Ibid., p. 327.
15 *Your Dear Letter*, p. 63.
16 Vincent, p. 264, dated 9 August 1866.
17 *Your Dear Letter*, p. 74.
18 Vincent, p. 338, dated 9 August 1866.
19 *Your Dear Letter*, p. 59.
20 BL Clarendon Papers, A.5.1.9. f. 261.
21 Pakula, and *Your Dear Letter*, p. 79.
22 *Your Dear Letter*, p. 68.
23 Ibid., p. 69.
24 Buckle, Second Series, Vol. I, p. 356.
25 Pakula, p. 243.
26 RA Add U/2, 1 February 1867, quoted Noel, p. 135.
27 DA LAL, 19 July 1866, quoted Noel, p. 135.
28 Vincent, p. 305.
29 Ibid., p. 326, dated 31 December 1867.
30 *Your Dear Letter*, p. 161.
31 John Morley, *The Life of William Ewart Gladstone*, Vol. I, p. 204.
32 Ibid., passim.
33 *Your Dear Letter*, p. 174.
34 Ibid., p. 175.
35 BL Gladstone Papers, 12 February 1869.
36 Blake, p. 504.
37 *Your Dear Letter*, p. 185.
38 Morley, Vol. II, p. 192.

16 'MEIN GUTER TREUER BROWN'

1 BL Gladstone Papers, 6 January 1869.
2 Mallinson, p. 290.
3 *Dictionary of National Biography*, Supplement 1901–1911, pp. 94–7, Ernest Marsh Lloyd, 'George William Frederick Charles'.
4 Though some of these, such as the Duke of Cambridge wine bar in Oxford, have been replaced with portraits of the twenty-first-century William, Duke of Cambridge, a very different character.
5 Anthony Powell, *Faces in My Time*, p. 149.
6 *Dictionary of National Biography*, Supplement 1901–1911, p. 94, Ernest Marsh Lloyd, 'George William Frederick Charles'.
7 RA/VIC/MAIN/E/57/9, 8 February 1867.
8 Ibid.
9 RA/VIC/MAIN/E/58/37, 2 March 1869.
10 BL Gladstone Papers, 31 January 1869.
11 Ibid.
12 BL Gladstone Papers, 12 June 1869.
13 BL Gladstone Papers, 9 June 1869.
14 Ibid.
15 BL Gladstone Papers, 11 June 1869.
16 Ibid., 6 July 1869.
17 BL Gladstone Papers, two separate letters, 16 September 1869, both written from Balmoral.
18 Ibid., 1 November 1860.
19 Coburger Hausarchiv, A. 1. 28b18. AW 27 Nv.1039.
20 Zeepvat, p. 66, quoting RA Add A30/336.
21 Hawkins, Vol. II, p. 350.
22 Vincent, p. 314. 'Browns' was slang for coppers, pennies and halfpennies.
23 BL Gladstone Papers, 9 June 1869.
24 Louisa, Countess of Antrim, *Recollections*, quoted Lamont-Brown, p. 107.
25 Coburger Hausarchiv, A1 28b18 AW 27 Nv1023.
26 Blunt Papers, Fitzwilliam Museum, Cambridge, MS 9 4–6, 1909, quoted Lamont-Brown, pp. xiii–xiv.
27 Lamont-Brown, p. 121.
28 *Saturday Review*, April 1867.
29 Patrick Jackson (ed.), *Loulou: Selected Extracts from the Journals of Lewis Harcourt*, p. 82.

17 A PEOPLE DETACHED FROM THEIR SOVEREIGN

1 Quoted Michael Howard, *The Franco-Prussian War*, p. 48.
2 Kimberley, 'Journal of Events during the Gladstone Ministry', quoted K. Theodore Hoppen, *The Mid-Victorian Generation, 1846–1886*, pp. 602–3.
3 *Your Dear Letter*, p. 272.
4 Buckle, Second Series, Vol. II, p. 13.
5 Ibid.

6   BL Gladstone Papers, 10 February 1870.
7   Ibid., 8 May 1870.
8   William M. Kuhn, *Henry and Mary Ponsonby: Life at the Court of Queen Victoria*, p. 71.
9   BL Gladstone Papers, 12 September 1870.
10   Reid Papers. The account, given by the Empress to Sir James Reid orally in 1895, is printed in Michaela Reid, *Ask Sir James: The Life of Sir James Reid, Personal Physician to Queen Victoria*, pp. 267–70.
11   Dr Thomas Evans, *Avec l'empereur et l'imperatrice. Memoires* (Paris, Plon, 1910), quoted Pierre Milza, *Napoléon III*, p. 593.
12   Buckle, Second Series, Vol. II, p. 126.
13   Buckle, Second Series, Vol. II, p. 133.
14   See Corelli Barnett, *Britain and Her Army, 1509–1970*, p. 301.
15   Kuhn, p. 145.
16   BL Gladstone Papers, 30 August 1871.
17   Ibid., 9 June 1880.
18   Ibid., 10 February 1870.
19   Ibid., 27 April 1882.
20   Ponsonby Papers, RA/VIC/ADD/A/36.
21   William Kuhn: 'Queen Victoria's Civil List: What Did She Do With It?', *The Historical Journal* (1993), pp. 645–5, Cambridge University Press; The Duchy of Lancaster Website; Harold Hyde Walker, *History of Harrogate under the Improvement Commissioners, 1841–1884* (Harrogate, Manor Press, 1886), esp. p. 182.
22   BL Gladstone Papers, 27 August 1870.
23   Ibid., 7 October 1870.
24   Ibid., 17 August 1871.
25   Ibid., 15 August 1871.
26   Hansard, Third Series, Vol. CCVIII, pp. 654, 703 and 786.
27   *Your Dear Letter*, p. 287.
28   Ibid., p. 295.
29   Ibid., p. 296.
30   Ibid., p. 300.
31   Quoted Jane Ridley, p. 142.
32   Ibid.
33   Jane Ridley, pp. 146–7.
34   Noel, p. 172.
35   BL Gladstone Papers, 8 December 1871.
36   Ibid., 11 December 1871.
37   Ibid., 24 December 1871 (Ponsonby to Gladstone).
38   Ibid., 24 December 1871 (Gladstone to Ponsonby).
39   Fulford, Roger (ed.), *Darling Child: Private Correspondence between Queen Victoria and the Crown Princess of Prussia, 1871–1878*, p. 31.
40   Ibid.
41   BL Gladstone Papers, 2 May 1872.

42 Ibid., 5 August 1872.
43 Buckle, Second Series, Vol. II, pp. 190–1.
44 Journal, 29 February 1872.
45 Quoted Lamont-Brown, p. 168.
46 *Darling Child*, p. 38.
47 Buckle, Second Series, Vol. II, p. 215.
48 Ibid., p. 217–8.
49 *Darling Child*, p. 48.
50 BL Gladstone Papers, 3 October 1872.

18 'YOU HAVE IT, MADAM'

1   Corti, *The English Empress*, p. 189.
2   Jane Ridley, p. 167.
3   Vincent, p. 317.
4   *Darling Child*, p. 112–3 and passim. See also St Aubyn, *Queen Victoria*, p. 480.
5   Zeepvat, p. 122, quoting RA Z264/2; QV to Leopold, 19 October 1873.
6   Ibid., p. 116. The pun had been used before, more aptly, in Queen Victoria's girlhood, of Bishop Fisher of Salisbury. If the Queen heard of Lewis Carroll's joke, it will have awoken uncongenial memories: the Kingfisher's niece was Lady Conroy.
7   Zeepvat, p. 126.
8   *Darling Child*, p. 86.
9   Jane Ridley, p. 136.
10 BL Additional MS 47,909, Princess Louise to Lady Battersea, 1900.
11 *Darling Child*, p. 124.
12 The reticular family connections, to the second and third generations, become ever closer from now onwards: the Tsarina was the aunt of Alice's husband Louis of Hesse-Darmstadt; she was also the aunt of Prince Henry of Battenberg, who would become in time another of Queen Victoria's sons-in-law.
13 *Darling Child*, p. 101.
14 Ibid., p. 103.
15 BL Gladstone Papers, 30 July 1873.
16 *Darling Child*, p. 120.
17 Ibid., p. 124.
18 *Oxford Dictionary of National Biography*, Vol. 53, pp. 651–7, Peter T. Marsh, 'Archibald Campbell Tait', quoting RA/VIC/Z173/12, 19 February 1884.
19 Tait Papers, Lambeth Palace, 11 January 1874.
20 Ibid.
21 Ibid.
22 Buckle, Second Series, Vol. II, p. 290.
23 Stanley Weintraub, *Victoria, Biography of a Queen*, p. 379.
24 Blake, p. 507, quoting RA, D.6.12, 30 January 1875.
25 Alexander Heriot Mackonochie, *A Memoir by E.A.T.* (London, Kegan Paul, 1890), p. 58.

26 BL Gladstone Papers, 23 December 1873.
27 Ibid.
28 Ibid.
29 Ibid., 11 August 1869.
30 Chadwick, Vol. II, p. 322.
31 Ibid., p. 319.
32 R. C. K. Ensor, *England, 1870–1914*, p. 31.
33 John Vincent (ed.), *Derby Diaries, 1869–78* (Cambridge, Cambridge University Press, 1995), p. 221 (5 June 1875), quoted Jane Ridley, p. 172.
34 BL India Office, MSS Eur C 144/12/64, Salisbury to Northbrook, 22 July 1875, quoted Jane Ridley, p. 177.
35 *The Times*, 7 December 1875.
36 Buckle, Second Series, Vol. II, p. 432.
37 *Darling Child*, p. 204.
38 *The Times*, 17 July 1830.
39 Blake, p. 562.
40 *Darling Child*, p. 207.
41 Blake, p. 563.
42 Corti, *The English Empress*, p. 220.
43 Journal, 14 March 1876.
44 Carnarvon Papers, BL Additional MS 60926, anecdote told at Highclere, August 1886, by George Russell who heard it from the witness.
45 Blake, p. 584.
46 Buckle, Second Series, Vol. II, p. 417.
47 Tom Hughes, 'Victorian Calendar', posted on http://victoriancalendar. blogspot.co.uk/, 3 August 2011.
48 Ibid.
49 Corti, *The English Empress*, p. 223.
50 Tsarina Maria to her brother Prince Alexander of Hesse-Darmstadt, ibid., p. 221.
51 Ibid., p. 222.
52 Buckle, Second Series, Vol. II, p. 466.
53 Bismarck, *Gedanken und Erinnerungen*, quoted Corti, *The English Empress*, p. 226.
54 Blake, p. 593.
55 Ibid., p. 605.
56 *Darling Child*, p. 251.
57 Carnarvon Papers, BL Additional MS 60757, f. 57, 30 June 1878.
58 Buckle, Second Series, Vol. II, p. 542.
59 Corti, *The English Empress*, p. 237.
60 Ibid., p. 232.
61 Ibid., p. 234.
62 Paget Papers, BL Additional MS51205, ff. 91–2, 11 February 1878.
63 Corti, *The English Empress*, p. 242.
64 Ibid., p. 244.

65　This was the occasion when Bismarck remarked '*Der alte Jude, das ist der Mann!*'

66　Papers of the 3rd Marquess of Salisbury, Hatfield, 3 September 1879.

67　Corti, *The English Empress*, p. 246.

68　Blake, p. 649.

19 'PROSTRATE THOUGH DEVOTED'

1　Paget Papers, BL Additional MS 51205, 16 July 1878.

2　Ibid., 24 June 1878.

3　Ibid.

4　Reid, p. 208.

5　Noel, p. 237 ff.

6　Ibid.

7　Hansard, Third Series, Vol. CCCLVIII, p. 275, 17 December 1878.

8　Journal, 14 December 1878.

9　Journal, 24 May 1879.

10　Ibid.

11　Buckle, Second Series, Vol. III, p. 312.

12　Byron Farwell, *Queen Victoria's Little Wars*, opening sentence.

13　Blake, pp. 670–1.

14　Coburger Hausarchiv, Nr 1223. Author's translation.

15　Roger Fulford (ed.), *Beloved Mama: Private Correspondence of Queen Victoria and the German Crown Princess, 1878–1885*, p. 73.

16　Journal, 5 February 1880.

17　*Beloved Mama*, p. 72.

18　Ibid., p. 73.

19　Ibid., p. 75.

20　Hugh Seton-Watson, *The Russian Empire, 1801–1917*, p. 427.

21　Corti, *The English Empress*, p. 246.

22　Paget Papers, BL Additional MS 51205, f. 122.

23　Ibid., 3 December 1878.

24　Dilke Papers, BL Additional MS 43874, 17 February 1884.

25　Ibid., ff. 13–14, 8 June 1885.

26　*Beloved Mama*, p. 97.

27　Ibid., p. 98.

28　Ibid., p. 97.

29　The period of Disraeli's second administration – 1874–80 – was perhaps unique in British popular literary history. Both the Prime Minister and the Viceroy of India (Bulwer Lytton, author of *The Last Days of Pompeii* etc.) were bestselling novelists, while, from August 1877, the First Lord of the Admiralty was the stationer and railway-kiosk bookseller W. H. Smith. Smith was satirized as 'The ruler of the Queen's Nav-ee' in Gilbert and Sullivan's *HMS Pinafore*.

30　Ripon Papers, BL Additional MS 43,510, 30 November 1880.

31　Blake, p. 745.

32 Ibid., p. 747.
33 Ibid., p. 748.
34 Ibid., p. 750.
35 BL Waterpark Papers, 19 April 1881.

20 'GRACIOUS CONFIDENCES SO FRANKLY GIVEN'

1   George Bell, *Randall Davidson, Archbishop of Canterbury*, Vol. I, p. 56.
2   A. C. Benson, *Edward White Benson, Archbishop of Canterbury*, Vol. I, p. 553.
3   Ponsonby Papers, RA/ADD/A/36.
4   BL Gladstone Papers, 22 May 1880.
5   Ibid., 16 April 1880.
6   Dilke Papers, BL Additional MS 43874.
7   BL Gladstone Papers, 3 January 1883.
8   Journal, 2–4 March 1882.
9   *Beloved Mama*, p. 116.
10 BL Gladstone Papers, 3 May 1882.
11 Dilke Papers, BL Additional MS 43874, June 1881.
12 BL Gladstone Papers, 18 June 1880.
13 Hansard, Third Series, Vol. CCLIV, 9 July–2 August 1880.
14 RA Add A30/581, 5 January 1881, quoted Zeepvat, p. 200.
15 BL Gladstone Papers, 26 March 1882.
16 Duff, *Hessian Tapestry*, pp. 87–8.
17 Ibid., p. 88.
18 BL Gladstone Papers, 19 March 1883.
19 All the above, and most of the information about Sir James Reid, from Reid, *Ask Sir James*, passim.
20 Reid's diary, 21 March 1883.
21 James Lees-Milne, *Ceaseless Turmoil, Diaries 1988–1992*, p. 199.
22 Lamont-Brown, passim.
23 He was Chichester Fortescue, elevated to the peerage in 1874, the Irish Secretary in Gladstone's First Cabinet. He was a valuable ally to Gladstone over the Irish Question, and a witty diarist.
24 Carlingford Papers, Somerset Country Record Office, Lord Carlingford's journal, 30 May 1883.
25 Victor Mallet (ed.), *Life with Queen Victoria, Marie Mallet's Letters from Court, 1887–1901*, 9 October 1895.
26 BL Gladstone Papers, 2 May 1883, Ponsonby to Gladstone.
27 Ibid., passim.
28 Bell, Vol. I, p. 57.
29 Ibid., p. 18.
30 Davidson Papers, Lambeth Palace, 27 January 1884.
31 Ibid., Queen Victoria's letter to Davidson, Osborne, 28 June 1884.
32 Ibid.
33 This and subsequent quotations from Davidson's correspondence are from Bell, Vol. I, p. 94.

34 Longford, p. 455.
35 Carnarvon Papers, BL Additional MS 60923. Journal, 10 December 1884.
36 Paget Papers, BL Additional MS 51205, f. 6.
37 Zeepvat, p. 226.
38 Ibid., pp. 227–8.
39 Dilke Papers, BL Additional MS 43,874, f. 137.
40 Zeepvat, p. 233.
41 Ibid., p. 237.
42 Knightley Papers, British Library 29 March 1884.
43 Dilke Papers, BL Additional MS 43874, 29 March 1884.
44 Ensor, p. 87.
45 Papers of the 3rd Marquess of Salisbury, Hatfield, 20 October 1884.
46 Ibid., 29 October 1884.
47 Journal, 24 November 1884.
48 Buckle, Second Series, Vol. III, p. 581, 27 November 1884.

21 'AN INFLAMMATORY ATMOSPHERE'

1   Journal, 28 March 1884.
2   Duff, *Hessian Tapestry*, p. 197.
3   Arthur Ponsonby, *Henry Ponsonby, Queen Victoria's Private Secretary, His Life from His Letters*, p. 303.
4   Duff, *Hessian Tapestry*, information in the Family Tree at the end of the book.
5   Ibid., p. 197.
6   An example of which is kept in Sir James Reid's scrapbook.
7   Dilke Papers, BL Additional MS 43874, f. 13, 30 December 1884.
8   Duff, *Hessian Tapestry*, p. 201.
9   Dilke Papers, BL Additional MS 43874, f. 13, 30 December 1884.
10 Longford, p. 479.
11 *Beloved Mama*, p. 180.
12 Tennyson, *Poems*, Vol. III., p.133.
13 Quoted ibid., p. 134.
14 Duff, *Hessian Tapestry*, p. 223.
15 Roger Owen, *Lord Cromer: Victorian Imperialist, Edwardian Proconsul*, p. 177.
16 Ibid., p. 194.
17 *Beloved Mama*, p. 159.
18 Quoted Owen, p. 200.
19 Ibid., p. 209.
20 Buckle Second Series, Vol. III, p. 597.
21 Ibid., p. 598.
22 Ibid., p. 617.
23 Journal, 11 March 1885.
24 BL Gladstone Papers, 10 April 1885.
25 Ibid., 31 May 1885.

26 Journal, 14 March 1885.
27 Buckle, Second Series, Vol. III, p. 633.
28 BL Gladstone Papers, 18 June 1885.
29 Roberts, p. 351.
30 Ibid., p. 339.
31 Ibid., p. 353.
32 Buckle, Second Series, Vol. III, p. 705.
33 Roberts, p. 350.
34 Journal, 2 December 1885.
35 *The Times*, 12 December 1885.
36 Morley, Vol. III, p. 220.
37 Agatha Ramm (ed.), *Beloved and Darling Child: Last Letters between Queen Victoria and Her Eldest Daughter*, p. 32, 7 April 1886.
38 Morley, Vol. III, p. 239.
39 Ibid., p. 243.
40 Roberts, p. 382.
41 Morley, Vol. III, p. 244.
42 Roberts, p. 383.
43 G. E. Buckle, *The Letters of Queen Victoria, 1886–1901*, Third Series, Vol. I, pp. 111–2.
44 Journal, 4 May 1886.
45 Buckle, Third Series, Vol. I, p. 117.
46 *Beloved and Darling Child*, p. 32.
47 Buckle, Third Series, Vol. I, p. 117.
48 Ibid., p. 132.
49 Ibid., p. 142.
50 Journal, 8 June 1886.
51 Journal, 10 June 1886.
52 Buckle, Third Series, Vol. I, p. 149.
53 Roberts, p. 389.
54 Ibid., p. 392.
55 Ibid., p. 393.
56 Journal, 20 June 1886.

22 'YOU ENGLISH'

1 Papers of the 3rd Marquess of Salisbury, Hatfield, Ponsonby to Salisbury, 21 January 1887.
2 Roberts, p. 462.
3 Buckle, Third Series, Vol. I, p. 277.
4 Roberts, p. 462.
5 Buckle, Third Series, Vol. I, p. 308.
6 Longford, p. 504.
7 Roberts, p. 430.
8 Alexander and Anand, p. 257.
9 Quoted Christy Campbell, *The Maharajah's Box*, p. 41.

10 Alexander and Anand, p. 211.
11 Campbell, p. 128.
12 Ibid., p. 60.
13 Buckle, Third Series, Vol. I, p. 322.
14 Pakula, p. 444.
15 Ibid.
16 Pakula, p. 445.
17 Coburger Hausarchiv, Nr. 1293 (translation).
18 Journal, 21 June 1887.
19 Journal, 23 June 1887.
20 Reid, p. 261.
21 Pakula, p. 448.
22 Sharbani Basu, *Victoria and Abdul: The True Story of the Queen's Closest Confidant*, p. 78 and passim.
23 J. W. Mackail, *The Life of William Morris*, p. 201.
24 Ibid., p. 203.
25 Papers of the 3rd Marquess of Salisbury, Hatfield, 25 February 1888.
26 *Beloved and Darling Child*, p. 76.
27 Bodleian Library MS Dep. D.837, Robert Collier, 2nd Baron Monkswell, Royal Anecdotes.
28 Buckle, Third Series, Vol. I, p. 489.
29 Ibid.
30 Ibid.
31 Mallet Papers, Balliol College, Oxford.
32 Basu, p. 84.
33 Ibid., p. 81.
34 Papers of the 3rd Marquess of Salisbury, Hatfield, 25 February 1888.
35 Ibid., 1 March 1888.
36 Roberts, p. 507.
37 Quoted Basu, p. 90.
38 Ibid., p. 91.
39 Papers of the 3rd Marquess of Salisbury, Hatfield, 18 April 1889.
40 Ibid., 24 April 1889.
41 Ibid., 28 May 1889.
42 RA/Z/43/31, Crown Princess of Prussia to Queen Victoria, 30 October 1888, quoted Pakula, p. 509.
43 Reid, p. 263–4.
44 Roberts, p. 540.
45 E. F. Benson, *The Kaiser and English Relations*, p. 79.
46 Papers of the 3rd Marquess of Salisbury, Hatfield, 31 December 1888.
47 Ibid., 1 March 1889.
48 Buckle, Third Series, Vol. I, p. 507.
49 BL Gladstone Papers, 4 July 1860.
50 Basu, p. 96.

23 'HER EXCELLENT YOUNG MUNSHI'

1   Benson Papers, Lambeth Palace, Vol. 72.
2   Benson, *Edward White Benson*, Vol. II, p. 776.
3   Papers of the 3rd Marquess of Salisbury, Hatfield, 25 December 1891.
4   Princess Marie Louise, *My Memories of Six Reigns*, p. 19.
5   Sir Frederick Ponsonby, *Recollections of Three Reigns*, p. 15.
6   Journal, 31 March 1891.
7   Basu, p. 102.
8   Ibid., p. 104, quoting RA/VIC/ADDU/32, 17 May 1890.
9   Ibid., quoting IOR MSS/Eur/D558/1 Telegram No. 28, Queen Victoria to Lansdowne, Windsor, 11 July 1890.
10 Papers of the 3rd Marquess of Salisbury, Hatfield, 21 May 1890.
11 Pope-Hennessy, p. 193.
12 Ibid.
13 Roberts, p. 549.
14 Papers of the 3rd Marquess of Salisbury, Hatfield, Queen Victoria to Princess Alexandra, copy of letter, 30 August 1890.
15 Kronberg Archives, 19 November 1892, quoted Pope-Hennessy, p. 199.
16 Papers of the 3rd Marquess of Salisbury, Hatfield, 18 April 1891.
17 Jane Ridley, p. 286.
18 Ibid., p. 286–7.
19 Ibid., p. 289.
20 Quoted Sushila Anand, *Daisy, The Life and Loves of the Countess of Warwick*, p. 43.
21 Papers of the 3rd Marquess of Salisbury, Hatfield, 22 December 1891.
22 Ibid., 27 December 1891.
23 Ibid.
24 Pope-Hennessy, p. 32.
25 Kenneth Rose, *The Later Cecils*, p. 52.
26 Pope-Hennessy, p. 36.
27 Ibid., p. 60.
28 Ibid., p. 103.
29 Ibid., p. 185.
30 Ibid., p. 208.
31 Lambeth Palace, Davidson's diary, New Year 1888.
32 Pope-Hennessy, p. 224.
33 Ibid., p. 226.
34 Jane Ridley, p. 296 quoting RA VIC/Z475/198, draft telegram, 18 January 1892.
35 Ibid., p. 296.
36 Papers of the 3rd Marquess of Salisbury, Hatfield, 11 August 1885.
37 R. F. Foster, *Modern Ireland, 1600–1972*, p. 424.
38 Roberts, p. 580.
39 Ibid., p. 578.
40 *Beloved and Darling Child*, p. 142.

41 Benson Papers, Lambeth Palace.
42 Jane Ridley, p. 305.
43 Benson Papers, Lambeth Palace, programme of the wedding.
44 Benson, *Edward White Benson*, Vol. II, p. 531.

24 'WHAT A FUNNY LITTLE WOMAN'

1 *The Times*, 15 August 1892.
2 Arthur Ponsonby, pp. 216–7.
3 The cow's head is preserved in the Glynne Arms, Hawarden.
4 Quoted H. C. G. Matthew, *Gladstone 1875–1898*, p. 331.
5 Morley, Vol. III, p. 373.
6 Buckle, Third Series, Vol. II, p. 187.
7 Lambeth Palace, Davidson Papers, 11 December 1892.
8 4 September 1892, quoted Longford, p. 520.
9 Leo McKinstry, *Rosebery: Statesman in Turmoil*, p. 270.
10 Lambeth Palace, Davidson Papers, 10 December 1892.
11 McKinstry, p. 241.
12 Ibid., p. 265.
13 Matthew, p. 351.
14 Morley, Vol. III, p. 369.
15 Journal, 3 March 1894.
16 Jackson, 4 March 1894, p. 222.
17 Morley, Vol. III, p. 410.
18 *Beloved and Darling Child*, pp. 214–5.
19 Matthew, p. 385.
20 Ibid., p. 358.
21 Mallet Papers, Balliol College, Oxford, June 1896.
22 Buckle, Third Series, Vol. II, p 373 where Rosebery writes 'Lord Rosebery… thought it his duty to inform Your Majesty through Sir Henry Ponsonby of some at least of the objections he sees to his attempting the task of reconstituting the Government' etc etc.
23 Jackson, p. 219.
24 'By far the most popular politician in the country' – McKinstry, p. 267.
25 Hansard, Third Series, Vol. CCCLVIII, p. 275.
26 Jackson, p. 235.
27 Roberts, p. 580.
28 *Beloved and Darling Child*, p. 178.
29 Mallet Papers, Balliol College, Oxford, 8 November 1895.
30 Buckle, Third Series, Vol. II, p. 381.
31 Ibid., p. 404.
32 Ibid., p. 430.
33 Ibid., p. 431.
34 Quoted McKinstry, p. 372.
35 Buckle, Third Series, Vol. II, p. 504.
36 *Dictionary of National Biography*, 1941–50, p. 19.

37 Buckle, Third Series, Vol. II, p. 393.
38 Journal, 20 April 1894.
39 Duff, *Hessian Tapestry*, p. 236.
40 Seton-Watson, pp. 461–3.
41 BL Waterpark Papers, 10 June 1884.
42 *Dictionary of National Biography*, 1922–1930 p. 696.
43 McKinstry, p. 360.
44 Jackson, p. 238.
45 McKinstry, p. 364.
46 Ibid., pp. 364–5.
47 Journal, 20 October 1894.
48 Hansard, Third Series, Vol. CCCLXI, p. 85.
49 Roberts, p. 604.
50 Basu, p. 156.
51 Quoted Kuhn, p. 237.
52 RA/VIC/ADDU/32, 27 April 1895, quoted Basu, p. 169.
53 Kuhn, p. 237.
54 Mallet Papers, Balliol College, Oxford, 21 November 1895.

25 DIAMOND JUBILEE

1   Lawrence James, *The Rise and Fall of the British Empire*, p. 259.
2   Quoted Ensor, p. 232.
3   1922, see Ensor, ibid.
4   Bodleian Library, MS Dep. D. 837, Robert Collier, 2nd Baron Monkswell, Royal Anecdotes.
5   Buckle, Third Series, Vol. III, p. 19.
6   Frederick Ponsonby, *Recollections*, p. 42.
7   Beatrice Webb, *The Diary of Beatrice Webb*, Vol. II, 5 January 1886, p. 88.
8   Mallet Papers, Balliol College, Oxford, 6 November 1896.
9   Duff, *Hessian Tapestry*, p. 246.
10 Frederick Ponsonby, *Recollections*, p. 12.
11 Ibid., p. 23.
12 Ibid., p. 51.
13 T. Herbert Warren, *Christian Victor, The Story of a Young Soldier*, p. 142.
14 Warren, p. 220.
15 Duff, *Hessian Tapestry*, p. 390.
16 Journal, 18 November 1895.
17 Buckle, Third Series, Vol. III, p. 25.
18 Reid Papers, 19 November 1885. 'After dinner had talk in my rooms with Bishop of Winchester who had been sent for by the Queen and Pss Beatrice to speak to Bigge about his relations with Pss Louise and had done so'. Bigge, as Lord Stamfordham, was the much-trusted private secretary to Kings Edward VII and George V.
19 Princess Marie Louise, p. 145.
20 *Morning Post*, 19 June 1896.
21 Buckle, Third Series, Vol. III, p. 55.

22 Frederick Ponsonby, *Recollections*, p. 45.
23 Described in Chapter 23.
24 Buckle, Third Series, Vol. III, p. 95.
25 Ibid.
26 Ibid., p. 99.
27 Buckle, Third Series, Vol. III, p. 24.
28 *In Cap and Bells* (London, New, York, J. Lane, 1900).
29 Buckle, Third Series, Vol. III, p. 79.
30 Quoted Duff, *Hessian Tapestry*, p. 249.
31 Buckle, Third Series, Vol. III, p. 77.
32 Colin Stephenson, *Merrily on High* (London, Darton, Longman and Todd, 1972), p. 27.
33 François Mauriac, *De Gaulle* (Paris, Grasset, 1964), p. 11.
34 He made many a sly reference to Bertie, as when the Duchesse de Guermantes says, 'I find King Edward charming, so simple and much cleverer than people think. And the Queen is, even now, the most beautiful thing I've ever seen in the world.' 'But, Madame la Duchesse,' said the prince, who was losing his temper and did not see that he was giving offence, 'you must admit that if the Prince of Wales had been an ordinary person, there isn't a club that wouldn't have blackballed him, and nobody would have been willing to shake hands with him...' etc.
35 Papers of the 3rd Marquess of Salisbury, Hatfield, 12 March 1887.
36 Jane Ridley, p. 368.
37 Buckle, Third Series, Vol. III, p. 152.
38 Papers of the 3rd Marquess of Salisbury, Hatfield, February 1897.
39 Ibid.
40 Reid Papers, quoted Basu, p. 189.
41 Basu, p. 218.
42 *Rudyard Kipling's Verse* (London, Hodder & Stoughton, 1940), p. 326.
43 *Beloved and Darling Child*, p. 202.
44 *Beloved and Darling Child*, p. 74.
45 Ibid., p. 91, St Aubyn, *Queen Victoria*, p. 559.
46 Buckle, Third Series, Vol. III, p. 151.
47 Longford, p. 20.
48 E. C. F. Collier (ed.), *A Victorian Diarist: Later Extracts from the Journals of Mary, Lady Monkswell*, p. 30.
49 Buckle, Third Series, Vol. III, p. 175.
50 Ibid., p. 175.
51 Ibid., p. 186.
52 Ibid., p. 187.
53 Ibid., p. 191.
54 St Aubyn, *Queen Victoria*, p. 548.
55 Pope-Hennessy, p. 338.
56 All references to the burial instructions are from Reid Papers.

26 'THIS ENGLAND'

1   Mallet Papers, Balliol College, Oxford, 17 November 1896.
2   Lawrence James, p. 283.
3   Frederick Ponsonby, *Recollections*, p. 43.
4   Ibid., p. 44.
5   Roberts, p. 716.
6   Byron Farwell, *The Great Boer War*, p. 32.
7   HRH Princess Alice, Countess of Athlone, *For My Grandchildren*, p. 100.
8   Farwell, *The Great Boer War*, p. 31.
9   Ibid., p. 32.
10 *Beloved and Darling Child*, p. 225.
11 Roberts, p. 722.
12 Ibid., p. 730.
13 Warren, p. 274.
14 Ibid., p. 299.
15 HRH Princess Alice, Countess of Athlone, p. 114.
16 Farwell, *The Great Boer War*, p. 142.
17 Ibid., p. 141.
18 Ibid., p. 143.
19 Roberts, p. 750.

27 *'VALE DESIDERATISSIME!'*

1   *Beloved and Darling Child*, p. 251.
2   Pakula, p. 587.
3   Ibid., p. 588.
4   Weintraub, *Victoria*, p. 630.
5   Ibid.
6   Quoted Reid, p. 199.
7   Daughter of Lenchen, named Helena Victoria but always known as Thora. She never married and gave herself up to good works, such as the YWCA. One of her last public appearances was at the wedding of Princess Elizabeth to Prince Philip of Greece in 1947.
8   This and subsequent quotations from Victoria's deathbed, Reid, p. 210–11.
9   Ibid., p. 212.
10 St Aubyn, *Queen Victoria*, p. 598.
11 Ibid. I find this rather puzzling, since the train from Portsmouth normally comes in to Waterloo!
12 St Aubyn, *Queen Victoria*, p. 599.
13 *Vale desideratissime! Hic demum Conquiescam tecum, tecum in Christo consurgeam.*
14 Harald Sandner, *Hitlers Herzog: Carl Eduard von Sachsen-Coburg und Gotha – die Biographie* (Aachen, Shaker Media, c. 2010).
15 John Röhl and Sheila de Bellaigue, *Wilhelm II, The Kaiser's Personal Monarchy*, p. 193.
16 Jane Ridley, p. 351.
17 Ibid.

BIBLIOGRAPHY

Manuscript Collections

Aberdeen Manuscripts: Correspondence of the 4th Earl of Aberdeen, British Library

Acland Manuscripts: Letters from members of the Royal Family, MSS Acland d. 1–3, Bodleian Library, Oxford

Battersea Papers: Royal correspondence of Lady Battersea, particularly with Princess Louise, Additional MS 47,909, British Library

Benson Papers: Correspondence and notes of Archbishop Benson, Lambeth Palace Library

Bentley Papers: Anecdotes concerning the Royal Family, Dep. D. 837, Bodleian Library, Oxford

Carlingford Papers: Diary and correspondence of S. Chichester-Fortescue, 1st Lord Carlingford, Somerset County Record Office, Taunton

Carnarvon Papers: Journals of Lord Carnarvon, British Library, Additional MSS 60923–60934

Clarendon Papers: Papers and correspondence of Lord Clarendon, Foreign Secretary, MS Clar. Dep. C. 87, Clar dep c. 500–555, etc, Bodleian Library, Oxford

Coburger Hausarchiv: Copious correspondence from Queen Victoria, especially to her sister-in-law Alexandrine

Conroy Papers: Diaries and correspondence of Sir John Conroy and family, Balliol College, Oxford

Davidson Papers: Diaries, correspondence and other memorabilia of Archbishop Davidson, Lambeth Palace Library

Dilke Papers: Additional MS 43874, British Library

Gladstone Papers: Royal correspondence, Loan MS 73. 1–27, 1845–1894, British Library. In addition, the Gladstone Papers are the most extensive archive in the British Library and I have read widely in them

Hatfield Papers: Correspondence and papers of the 3rd Marquess of Salisbury, including many letters from Queen Victoria, Hatfield House

Herries Papers: President of the Board of Control, East India Company, Additional MS 57414, British Library

Howley Papers: Sermons and letters of Archbishop William Howley including sermon preached to Victoria on her confirmation, MS 45471-2, Bodleian Library, Oxford

Hughenden Manuscripts: Papers and correspondence of Benjamin Disraeli, Bodleian Library, Oxford

Iddesleigh Papers: Papers of Sir Stafford Northcote, later Lord Iddesleigh, especially Additional MS 50,013, British Library

Longley Papers: Photographs, notes and correspondence of Archbishop Longley, Lambeth Palace Library

Mallet Papers: Diaries of Marie Mallet, Maid of Honour to Queen Victoria, Balliol College, Oxford

Martin Papers: Letters to Sir Theodore Martin relating to his life of the Prince Consort, MS 41706, also correspondence MS Eng Lett. D.267, Bodleian Library, Oxford

Milner Papers: Letters from Queen Victoria to Viscount Milner, Bodleian Library, Oxford

Max Müller Papers: Letters between Professor Müller and the Queen or her Secretaries, MS Eng d. 2350, Bodleian Library, Oxford

Paget Papers: Royal correspondence, Additional MSS 51205-51249, British Library; Papers of James Howard Harris, 3rd Earl of Malmsbury, Additional MSS 51206-51207; and Correspondence of Sir Augustus Paget, Additional MSS 51205-51236, British Library

Peel Papers: Extensive correspondence between Peel and Prince Albert and with Queen Victoria, Additional MSS 40,430 ff., British Library

Ponsonby Papers: Correspondence of 1st Baron, Arthur Ponsonby and Frederic Edward Grey Ponsonby, Bodleian Library, Oxford. The extensive correspondence of Henry and Mary Ponsonby, with daily records of life at Court, are housed in the Royal Archive

Reid Papers: Extensive diaries, scrapbooks, letters and other documents in the possession of Sir Alexander Reid, Bt.

Ripon Papers: Diaries and correspondence of Lord Ripon, Viceroy of India. Additional MSS 43,510 ff., British Library

Royal Archives, Windsor Castle: Papers of the Duchess of Kent, of Queen Victoria and her family, and many of the other members of the Royal Family. Queen Victoria's journal, transcribed (and heavily 'edited' by Princess Beatrice) is available online at http://www.queenvictoriasjournals.org/home

Stanley Correspondence: Letters to Arthur Penryn Stanley and Lady Augusta Stanley, MS 41644, Bodleian Library, Oxford

Tait Papers: Diaries, sermons and correspondence of Archbishop Tait, Lambeth Palace Library

Waterpark Papers: Albums, diary and correspondence of Lady Waterpark, Additional MS 60750 etc., British Library

Printed Sources

Airlie, Mabell, Countess of, *Thatched with Gold*, ed. Jennifer Ellis, London, Hutchinson, 1962

Albert, Harold A., *Queen Victoria's Sister: The Life and Letters of Princess Feodora*, London, Robert Hale, 1967

Alexander, Grand Duke of Russia, *Once a Grand Duke*, London, Cassell, 1932

Alexander, Michael, and Anand, Sushila, *Queen Victoria's Maharajah*, London, Phoenix Press, 2001 [first published 1980]

Ames, Winslow, *Prince Albert and Victorian Taste*, London, Chapman and Hall, 1967

Anand, Sushila, *Daisy, The Life and Loves of the Countess of Warwick*, London, Portrait, 2008

Anand, Sushila, *Indian Sahib: Queen Victoria's Dear Abdul*, London, Duckworth, 1996

Anglesey, Marquess of, *One Leg: The Life and Letters of Henry William Paget, First Marquess of Angelsey, 1758–1854*, London, Leo Cooper, 1961

Anon., *Coorg and its Rajahs, By an Officer formerly in the service of His Highness Veer Rajunder Wadeer, Rajah of Coorg*, London, John Bumpus, 1857

Anon., *Uncensored Recollections*, Philadelphia, J. B. Lippincott, 1924

Antrim, Louisa, Countess of, *Recollections*, London, 'King's Stone' Press, 1937

Argyll, George Douglas, 8th Duke of, *Autobiography and Memoirs*, 2 vols., London, John Murray, 1906

d'Arjuzon, Antoine, *Victoria et Napoléon III. Histoire d'une amitié*, Biarritz, Atlantica, 2007

Arnold, Jacques, *The Royal Houses of Europe: The Family Tree of HH Franz, Duke of Saxe-Coburg-Saalfeld*, West Malling, Patricia Arnold, 2006

Aronson, Theo, *The Fall of the Third Napoleon*, Indianapolis, Bobs Merrill Co. Ltd, 1970

Aronson, Theo, *A Family of Kings*, London, Cassell, 1976

Aronson, Theo, *Grandmama of Europe*, London, Cassell, 1972

Aronson, Theo, *The Kaisers*, Indianapolis, Bobs Merrill Co. Ltd, 1971

Aronson, Theo, *Queen Victoria and the Bonapartes*, London, Cassell, 1972

Aronson, Theo, *Victoria and Disraeli*, London, Cassell, 1977

Arthur, George, *Not Worth Reading*, London, Longmans, Green, 1938

Ashdown, Dulcie M., *Queen Victoria's Family*, London, Robert Hale, 1975

Ashdown, Dulcie, M., *Queen Victoria's Mother*, London, Robert Hale, 1974

Aston, Major General Sir George, *HRH The Duke of Connaught and Strathearn*, London, Harrap, 1929

Athlone, HRH Princess Alice, Countess of, *For My Grandchildren*, Cleveland, World Publishing Co., 1966

Auchinloss, Louis, *Persons of Consequence: Queen Victoria and Her Circle*, New York, Random House, 1979

Balsan, Consuelo Vanderbilt, *The Glitter and the Gold*, London, Heinemann, 1953

Barker, R. Auriol, *Illustrated Guide to Osborne*, containing Blunt, Anthony F., *A Catalogue of the Pictures, Porcelain and Furniture in the State Apartments*, London, Her Majesty's Stationery Office, 1952

Barnett, Corelli, *Britain and Her Army, 1509–1970. A Military, Political and Social Survey*, London, Allen Lane and Penguin Press, 1970

Barraclough, Geoffrey, *The Origins of Modern Germany*, Oxford, Basil Blackwell Publishing, 1952

Basu, Sharbani, *Victoria and Abdul: The True Story of the Queen's Closest Confidant*, Stroud, The History Press, 2010

Battiscombe, Georgina, *Queen Alexandra*, London, Constable, 1969

Beaver, Patrick, *The Crystal Palace 1851–1936: A Portrait of Victorian Enterprise*, London, Hugh Evelyn, 1970

Beckett, John, *The Rise and Fall of the Grenvilles. Dukes of Buckingham and Chandos, 1710 to 1921*, Manchester, Manchester University Press, 1994

Bell, George, *Randall Davidson, Archbishop of Canterbury*, 2 vols., London, Oxford University Press, 1935

Belliappa, C. P., *Victoria Gowramma, the Lost Princess of Coorg*, New Delhi, Rupa & Co., 2012

Benson, A. C., *Edward White Benson, Archbishop of Canterbury*, 2 vols., London, Macmillan and Co., 1899

Benson, Arthur Christopher, and Esher, Viscount (eds.), *The Letters of Queen Victoria 1837–1861*, 3 vols., London, John Murray, 1908

Benson, E. F., *The Kaiser and English Relations*, London, Longmans, 1936

Bernstorff, Count, *The Memoirs of Count Bernstorff*, tr. E. Sutton, London, Heinemann, 1936

Bird, Anthony, *Paxton's Palace*, London, Cassell, 1976

Birke, Adolf M., and Kluxen, Kurt, *Viktorianisches England in deutscher Perspektive*, Munich/New York/ London/Paris, K. G.Saur, 1983

Blake, Robert, *Disraeli*, London, Eyre and Spottiswoode, 1966

Bosbach, Franz and Davis, John R. (eds.), *Prinz Albert. Ein Wettiner in Grossbritannien*, Munich, K. G.Saur, 2004

Bourne, Kenneth, *Palmerston, The Early Years, 1784–1841*, London, Allen Lane, 1982

Brown, David, *Palmerston: A Biography*, New Haven/London, Yale University Press, 2010

Brown, David, *Palmerston and the Politics of Foreign Policy, 1846–1855*, Manchester/New York, Manchester University Press, 2002

Brown, Ivor, *Balmoral. The History of a Home*, London, Collins, 1955

Buckle, G. E. (ed.), *The Letters of Queen Victoria, 1862–85*, Second Series, 3 vols., London, John Murray, 1926–8

Buckle, G. E. (ed.), *The Letters of Queen Victoria, 1886–1901*, Third Series, 3 vols., London, John Murray, 1930–2

Bülow, Bernhard Fürst von, *Denkwürdigkeiten*, 4 vols., Berlin, Verlag Ullstein, 1930

Campbell, Christie, *The Maharajah's Box: An Imperial Story of Conspiracy, Love and a Guru's Prophecy*, HarperCollins, 2001

Campbell, Susan, 'The Genesis of Queen Victoria's New Kitchen Garden', *Garden History Journal*, 1984, pp. 100–19

Cecil, Algernon, *Queen Victoria and Her Prime Ministers*, London, Eyre and Spottiswoode, 1953

Cecil, David, *Melbourne*, London, Constable, 1961

Chadwick, Owen, *The Victorian Church*, 2 vols., London, Adam & Charles Black, 1970–2

Chamberlain, Muriel E., *Lord Aberdeen. A Political Biography*, London and New York, Longman, 1983

Chambers, James, *Charlotte and Leopold*, London, Old Street Publishing, 2007

Christopher, Prince of Greece, *Memoirs of HRH Prince Christopher of Greece*, London, The Right Book Club, 1938

Collier, E. C. F. (ed.), *A Victorian Diarist: Later Extracts from the Journals of Mary, Lady Monkswell*, London, John Murray, 1946

Colquhoun, Kate, *A Thing in Disguise: The Visionary Life of Joseph Paxton*, London, Fourth Estate, 2003

Corti, Egon Caesar, Count, *The Downfall of Three Dynasties*, tr L. Marie Sieveking and Ian F. D. Morrow, London, Methuen & Co., 1934

Corti, Egon Caesar, Count, *The English Empress. A Study in the Relations between Queen Victoria and Her Eldest Daughter, Empress Frederick of Germany*, tr. E. M. Hodgson, London, Cassell & Son, 1957

Corti, Egon Caesar, Count, *Leopold I of Belgium. Secret Pages of European History*, tr. Jospeh McCabe, London, T. Fisher Unwin, 1923

Davis, H. W. C., *The Political Thought of Heinrich von Treitschke*, London, Constable and Co. Ltd, 1914

de Decker, Michel, *Napoléon III ou l'Empire des sens*, Paris, Belfond, 2008

Dennison, Matthew, *The Last Princess: The Devoted Life of Queen Victoria's Youngest Daughter*, London, Weidenfeld & Nicolson, 2007

Dennison, Matthew, *Queen Victoria: A Life of Contradictions*, London, HarperCollins, 2013

Detrez, Raymond, *Historical Dictionary of Bulgaria*, 2nd edn, Lanham, Maryland/Toronto/Oxford, The Scarecrow Press, Inc., 2006

Dowe, Dieter (ed.), *Europe in 1848. Revolution and Reform*, New York/Oxford, Berghahn Books, 2001

Duff, David, *Edward of Kent. The Life Story of Queen Victoria's Father*, London, Stanley, Paul & Co. Ltd, 1938

Duff, David, *Hessian Tapestry*, London, Frederick Muller, 1967

Duff, David, *The Life Story of HRH Princess Louise, Duchess of Argyll*, London, Stanley Paul & Co., 1940

Duff, David, *Victoria in the Highlands*, London, Muller, 1968

Duff, David, *Victoria Travels*, London, Muller, 1970

Ebart, Paul von, *Luise, Herzogin von Sachsen-Coburg-Saalfeld*, Minden, Westfalia, J. C. C. Bruns Verlag, 1903

Emden, Paul H., *Behind the Throne*, London, Hodder & Stoughton, 1934

Ensor, R. C. K., *England, 1870–1914*, Oxford, Clarendon Press, 1936

Epton, Nina, *Victoria and Her Daughters*, London, Weidenfeld & Nicolson, 1972

Ernle, Lord, *Whippingham to Westminster*, London, John Murray, 1938

Esher, Viscount (ed.), *The Girlhood of Queen Victoria. A Selection of Her Majesty's Diaries between the years 1832 and 1840*, 2 vols., London, John Murray, 1912

Esher, Viscount (ed.), *The Training of a Sovereign*, London, John Murray, 1914

Eyck, Frank, *The Prince Consort: A Political Biography*, Bath, Cedric Chivers, 1959

Farwell, Byron, *The Great Boer War*, London, Allen Lane, 1973

Farwell, Byron, *Queen Victoria's Little Wars*, London, Allen Lane, 1973

Ferguson, Frank, and McConnel, James (eds.), *Ireland and Scotland in the Nineteenth Century*, Dublin, Four Courts Press, 2009

Feuchtwanger, Edgar, *Albert and Victoria. The Rise and Fall of the House of Saxe-Coburg-Gotha*, London, Hambledon Continuum, 2006

Fleming, G. H., *Lady Colin Campbell: Victorian 'Sex Goddess'*, Adlestrop, Windrush Press, 1989

Foster, R. F., *Modern Ireland, 1600–1972*, London, Allen Lane, 1988

Fraser, Antonia, *Perilous Question, The Drama of the Great Reform Bill, 1832*, London, Weidenfeld & Nicholson, 2013

Fraser, Flora, *Princesses: The Six Daughters of George III*, London, John Murray, 2004

Froude, J. A., *Thomas Carlyle: A History of His Life in London 1834–1881*, 2 vols., London, Longmans, Green, 1884

Fulford, Roger (ed.), *Beloved Mama: Private Correspondence of Queen Victoria and the German Crown Princess, 1878–1885*, London, Evans Bros., 1981

Fulford, Roger (ed.), *Darling Child: Private Correspondence of Queen Victoria and the Crown Princess of Prussia, 1871–1878*, London, Evans Bros., 1976

Fulford, Roger (ed.), *Dearest Child: Letters between Queen Victoria and the Princess Victoria 1858–1861*, London, Evans Bros., 1964

Fulford, Roger (ed.), *Dearest Mama: Letters between Queen Victoria and the Crown Princess of Prussia 1861–1864*, London, Evans Bros, 1968

Fulford, Roger, *The Prince Consort*, London, Macmillan, 1949

Fulford, Roger, *Royal Dukes: Queen Victoria's Father and 'Wicked Uncles'*, London, Duckworth, 1933

Fulford, Roger (ed.), *Your Dear Letter: Private Correspondence of Queen Victoria and the Crown Princess of Prussia, 1865–1871*, London, Evans Bros., 1971

Gash, Norman, *Aristocracy and People*, London, Edward Arnold, 1979

Gash, Norman, *Mr Secretary Peel*, London, Longman, 1961

Gash, Norman, *Politics in the Age of Peel*, London, Longman, 1953

Gash, Norman, *Sir Robert Peel*, Harlow, Longman, 1985

Gaunt, Richard A., *Sir Robert Peel: The Life and Legacy*, London, I. B.Tauris, 2010

Gieger, Etta K., *Die Londoner Weltausstellung von 1851: im Kontext der Industrialisierung in Grossbritannien*, Essen, Blaue Eule, 2007

Gillen, Mollie, *The Prince and His Lady. The Love Story of the Duke of Kent and Madame de St Laurent*, London, Sidgwick & Jackson, 1970

Girouard, Mark, *The Return to Camelot*, New Haven, Yale University Press, 1981

Greville, Charles, *The Greville Memoirs, 1814–1861*, ed. Lytton Strachey and Roger Fulford, 8 vols., London, Macmillan, 1936

Grey, Lieutenant-General the Hon. C., *The Early Years of His Royal Highness The Prince Consort, compiled under the direction of Her Majesty the Queen*, London, Smith, Elder and Co., 1867

Guedalla, Philip, *The Queen and Mr Gladstone*, London, Hodder & Stoughton, 1933

Hardie, Frank, *The Political Influence of Queen Victoria*, Oxford, Oxford University Press, 1970

Hawkins, Angus, *The Forgotten Prime Minister: The 14th Earl of Derby*, 2 vols., Oxford, Oxford University Press, 2008

Hawksley, Lucinda, *The Mystery of Princess Louise*, London, Chatto & Windus, 2013

Heinz, Marianne, et al, *3 x Tischbein und die europäische Malerei um 1800*, Munich, Hirmer Verlag, 2005

Hilton, Boyd, *The Age of Atonement*, Oxford, Oxford University Press, 1988

Hilton, Boyd, *A Mad, Bad, and Dangerous People? England 1783–1846*, Oxford, Clarendon Press, 2006

Hobhouse, Christopher, *1851 and the Crystal Palace: an Account of the Great Exhibition and Its Contents*, London, John Murray, 1937

Hobhouse, Hermione, *The Crystal Palace and the Great Exhibition: a History of the Royal Commission for the Exhibition of 1851*, London, Athlone Press, 2002

Hobhouse, Hermione, *Prince Albert: His Life and Work*, London, Hamish Hamilton, 1983

Hobhouse, Hermione, *Thomas Cubitt, Master Builder*, London, Macmillan, 1971

Holland, Sydney, Viscount Knutsford, *In Black and White*, London, Edward Arnold, 1926

Hooper, T. R. (ed.), *Memoirs of Ebenezer and Emma Hooper*, Guildford, Billing and Sons, 1905

Hoppen, K. Thedore, *The Mid-Victorian Generation, 1846–1886*, Oxford, Clarendon Press, 1998

Housman, Laurence, *Victoria Regina, A Dramatic Biography*, London, Jonathan Cape, 1934

Howard, Michael, *The Franco-Prussian War. The German Invasion of France, 1870–71*, London and New York, Methuen, 1961

Hubbard, Kate, *Serving Victoria, Life in the Royal Household*, London, Chatto & Windus, 2012

Hudson, Katherine, *A Royal Conflict: Sir John Conroy and the Young Victoria*, London/Sydney/Auckland, A John Curtis Book/Hodder & Stoughton, 1994

Huntly, Marquis of, *Auld Acquaintance*, London, Hutchinson, n.d.

Jackson, Patrick (ed.), *Loulou: Selected Extracts from the Journals of Lewis Harcourt (1880–1895)*, Madison, New Jersey, Fairleigh Dickinson University Press, 2006

James, Lawrence, *The Rise and Fall of the British Empire*, London, Little, Brown, 1994

James, Robert Rhodes, *Albert, Prince Consort*, London, Hamish Hamilton, 1983

Kelly, J. N. D, and Walsh, M. J., *Oxford Dictionary of Popes*, revised edn, Oxford, Oxford University Press, 2010

Kharibian, Leah, *Passionate Patrons: Victoria and Albert and the Arts*, London, Royal Collection Publications, 2010

Kitson Clark, George, *The Making of Victorian England*, London, Methuen, 1962

Kitson Clark, George, *Peel and the Conservative Party*, 2nd edn, London, Frank Cass & Co., 1964

Kuhn, William M., *Henry and Mary Ponsonby: Life at the Court of Queen Victoria*, London, Duckworth, 2002

Lambert, Andrew, *The Crimean War: British Grand Strategy Against Russia 1853-6*, Farnham, Ashgate, 2011

Lambton, Antony, *The Mountbattens*, London, Constable, 1989

Lamont-Brown, Raymond, *John Brown, Queen Victoria's Highland Servant*, Stroud, Sutton Publishing, 2000

Leapman, Michael, *The World for a Shilling: How the Great Exhibition of 1851 Shaped a Nation*, London, Headline, 2001

Lee, Sidney, *Queen Victoria, A Biography*, London, Smith, Elder & Co., 1904

Lees, William Nassau, *Indian Musalmans: being Three Letters reprinted from 'The Times' with an Article on the late Prince Consort*, London, Williams & Norgate, 1871

Lees-Milne, James, *Ceaseless Turmoil, Diaries 1988–1992*, London, John Murray, 2004

Lockhart, J. G., *Life of Sir Walter Scott, Bart.*, 2nd edn, Edinburgh, Adam and Charles Black, 1853

Longford, Elizabeth, *Victoria R.I.*, London, Weidenfeld & Nicolson, revised edn, 1987 [first published 1964]

Lyden, Anne M., *A Royal Passion. Queen Victoria and Photography*, Los Angeles, J. Paul Getty Museum, 2014

McClintock, Mary Howard, *The Queen Thanks Sir Howard*, London, John Murray, 1946

MacDonagh, Oliver, *Early Victorian Government, 1830–1870*, London, Weidenfeld & Nicolson, 1977

Mackail, J. W., *The Life of William Morris*, London, Longmans, 1901

McKinstry, Leo, *Rosebery: Statesman in Turmoil*, London, John Murray, 2005

Maclagan, Michael, *'Clemency' Canning: Charles John, 1st Earl Canning, Governor-General and Viceroy of India, 1856–1862*, London, Macmillan, 1962

Madan, Geoffrey, *Geoffrey Madan's Notebooks*, ed. J. A Gere and John Sparrow, Oxford, Oxford University Press, 1984

Magnus, Sir Philip, *King Edward the Seventh*, London, John Murray, 1964

Mallet, Victor (ed.), *Life with Queen Victoria, Marie Mallet's Letters from Court, 1887–1901*, London, John Murray, 1968

Mallinson, Allan, *The Making of the British Army*, London, Bantam Press, 2009

Mandler, Peter, *Aristocratic Government in the Age of Reform*, Oxford, Clarendon Press, 1990

Mann, Golo, *Deutsche Geschichte des 19. und 20. Jahrhunderts*, Frankfurt am Main, Fischer Taschenbuch Verlag, 2003 [first published 1958]

Marie of Battenberg, Princess, [Princess Marie zu Erbach-Schonberg], *Reminiscences*, London, Allen and Unwin, 1925

Marie Louise, Princess, *My Memories of Six Reigns*, London, Evans, 1956

Marsden, Jonathan (ed.), *Victoria and Albert, Art and Love*, London, Royal Collections Publications, 2010

Martin, Sir Theodore, KCB, *The Life of His Royal Highness The Prince Consort*, 5 vols., London, Smith, Elder and Co., 1875–80

Marx, Karl, and Engels, Friedrich, *Werke*, Berlin, Dietz Verlag, 1960

Matson, John, *Dear Osborne*, London, Hamish Hamilton, 1978

Matthew, H. C. G., *Gladstone, 1875–1898*, Oxford, Clarendon Press, 1995

Matthews, J., Wiebe, M. G., et al (eds.), *Benjamin Disraeli Letters*, 6 vols., Toronto/Buffalo, University of Toronto Press, 1982–2009

Maurois, André, *King Edward and His Times*, London, Cassell, 1933

Maxwell, The Right Hon. Sir Herbert, *The Life and Letters of George William Frederick Fourth Earl of Clarendon, K.G., G.C.B.*, 2 vols., London, Edward Arnold, 1913

Maxwell, The Right Hon. Sir Herbert (ed.), *The Creevey Papers*, London, John Murray, 1912

Mechtold, Rudi, *Die Queen, die Windsors und die Rosenau, Katalog für der Ausstellung, 2004*, Coburg, Landesbibliothek, 2004

Milza, Pierre, *Napoléon III*, Paris, Perrin, 2004

Mitchell, L. G., *Lord Melbourne, 1779–1848*, Oxford, Oxford University Press, 1997

Moore, D. C., *The Politics of Deference*, Aldershot, Hampshire, Gregg Revivals, 1984

Morley, John, *The Life of William Ewart Gladstone*, 2 vols., London, Edward Lloyd, 1908

Mount, Ferdinand, *Umbrella, A Pacific Tale*, London, Heinemann, 1994

Murphy, Deirdre, and Lee, Prossner, et al, *Queen Victoria Revealed: 500 Facts about the Queen and Her World*, ed. Sarah Kilby, Surrey, Historic Royal Palaces, 2012

Murphy, Paul Thomas, *Shooting Victoria: Madness, Mayhem, and the Rebirth of the British Monarchy*, London, Head of Zeus, 2012

Neale, The Rev. Erskine, *Life of His Royal Highness Edward, Duke of Kent*, London, Richard Bentley, 1850

Nelson, Michael, *Queen Victoria and the Discovery of the Riviera*, London/New York, I. B. Tauris, 2001

Netzer, Hans-Joachim, *Albert von Sachsen-Coburg und Gotha. Ein deutscher Prinz in England*, Munich, Verlag C. H. Beck, 1988

Nevill, Ralph, *The Reminiscences of Lady Dorothy Nevill*, London, Edward Arnold, 1906

Nicholas of Greece, Prince, *My Fifty Years*, London, Hutchinson, 1926

Noel, Gerard, *Princess Alice, Queen Victoria's Forgotten Daughter*, London, Constable, 1974

Oman, Sir Charles, *Things I have Seen*, London, Methuen, 1933

Ormond, Richard, and Blackett-Ord, Carol, *Franz Xaver Winterhalter and the Courts of Europe, 1830–70*, London, National Portrait Gallery, 1987

Owen, Roger, *Lord Cromer: Victorian Imperialist, Edwardian Proconsul*, Oxford, Oxford University Press, 2004

Pakenham, Thomas, *The Boer War*, London, Weidenfeld & Nicolson, 1979

Pakula, Hannah, *An Uncommon Woman: The Empress Frederick, Daughter of Queen Victoria, Wife of the Crown Prince of Prussia, Mother of Kaiser Wilhelm*, New York, Simon and Schuster, 1997

Parry, Jonathan, *The Rise and Fall of Liberal Government in Victorian Britain*, New Haven and London, Yale University Press, 1993

Phillips, John A. S. (ed), *Prince Albert and the Victorian Age*, Cambridge, Cambridge University Press, 1981

Plowden, Alison, *The Young Victoria*, London, Weidenfeld & Nicolson, 1981

Ponsonby, Arthur, *Henry Ponsonby, Queen Victoria's Private Secretary, His Life from His Letters*, London, Macmillan and Co., 1943

Ponsonby, D. A., *The Lost Duchess. The Story of the Prince Consort's Mother*, London, Chapman and Hall, 1958

Ponsonby, Sir Frederick [Lord Sysonby], *Recollections of Three Reigns*, London, Eyre and Spottiswoode, 1951

Ponsonby, Sir Frederick [Lord Sysonby], *Sidelights on Queen Victoria*, London, Macmillan, 1930

Ponsonby, Sir Frederick [Lord Sysonby] (ed.), *Letters of the Empress Frederick*, London, Macmillan, 1928

Pope-Hennessy, James, *Queen Mary*, London, George Allen and Unwin, 1959

Postgate, Raymond, *The Story of a Year: 1848*, London, Cassell, 1955

Potts, D. M., and Potts, W. T. W., *Queen Victoria's Gene: Haemophilia and the Royal Family*, Stroud, Sutton Publishing, 1995

Powell, Anthony, *Faces in My Time*, London, Heinemann, 1980

Prest, John, *Lord John Russell*, London, Macmillan, 1972

Price, Munro, *The Perilous Crown: France between Revolutions, 1814–1848*, London, Macmillan, 2007

Priesner, Rudolf, *Herzog Carl Eduard zwischen Deutschland und England: eine tragische Auseinandersetzung*, Gerabronn, Hohenloher Druck- und Verlagshaus, 1977

Prochaska, *Royal Bounty: The Making of a Welfare Monarchy*, New Haven, Yale University Press, 1995

Ramm, Agatha, *Germany 1789–1919, A Political History*, London, Methuen & Co Ltd, 1967

Ramm, Agatha (ed.), *Beloved and Darling Child*, Stroud, Sutton, 1991

Rappaport, Helen, *Magnificent Obsession: Victoria, Albert and the Death that Changed the Monarchy*, London, Hutchinson, 2011

Reid, Michaela, *Ask Sir James: The Life of Sir James Reid, Personal Physician to Queen Victoria*, London, Hodder & Stoughton, 1987

Reinhardt, Volker, and Lau, Thomas, *Deutsche Familien, Historische Portraits von Bismarck bis Weizsaecker*, Munich, Verlag C. H. Beck, 2005

Rennell Rodd, Sir James, *Social and Diplomatic Memories*, London, Edward Arnold, 1923

Ridley, Jane, *Bertie*, London, Chatto & Windus, 2012

Ridley, Jasper, *Lord Palmerston*, London, Constable, 1970

Ridley, Jasper, *Napoleon III and Eugénie*, London, Constable, 1979

Roberts, Andrew, *Salisbury, Victorian Titan*, London, Weidenfeld & Nicolson, 1999

Robinson, John Martin, *Windsor Castle, A Short History*, London, Michael Joseph, 1996

Röhl, John C. G., *Wilhelm II. Der Aufbau der persönlichen Monarchie, 1888–1900*, Munich, Verlag C. H.Beck, 2001

Röhl, John C. G., tr. Jeremy Gaines and Rebecca Wallach, *Young Wilhelm: The Kaiser's Early Life, 1859–1888*, Cambridge, Cambridge University Press, 1998

Röhl, John C. G., and de Bellaigue, Sheila, *Wilhelm II, The Kaiser's Personal Monarchy, 1888–1900*, Cambridge, Cambridge University Press, 2004

Rose, Kenneth, *The Later Cecils*, London, Weidenfeld & Nicolson, 1975

Roumania, Queen of, *The Story of My Life*, 3 vols., London, Cassell, 1933

Russell, Bertrand, *The Autobiography. 1872–1914*, London, George Allen and Unwin, 1967

Russell, George W. E., *Collections and Recollections*, London, Nelson, 1903

St Aubyn, Giles, *Edward VII: Prince and King*, London, Collins, 1979

St Aubyn, Giles, *Queen Victoria: A Portrait*, Sinclair Stevenson, 1991

St Aubyn, Giles, *The Royal George*, London, Constable, 1963

Sandiford, Keith A. P., *Great Britain and the Schleswig-Holstein Question, 1848–64: A Study in Diplomacy, Politics, and Public Opinion*, Toronto and Buffalo, University of Toronto Press, 1975

Sandner, Harald, *Das Haus Sachsen-Coburg und Gotha*, Coburg, Neue Presse, 2002

Saunders, Edith, *A Distant Summer*, London, Sampson, Low, Marston & Co. Ltd, 1946

Scheeben, Elisabeth, *Ernst II, Herzog von Sachsen-Coburg und Gotha. Studien zu Biographie und Weltbild eines liberalen deutschen Bundesfürsten in der Reichsgründungszeit*, Frankfurt am Main/Bern/New York/Paris, P. Lang, 1987

Schindling, Anton, and Ziegler, Walter, *Die Kaiser der Neuzeit, 1519–1918*, Munich, Verlag C. H.Beck, 1990

Seton-Watson, Hugh, *The Russian Empire, 1801–1917*, Oxford, Clarendon Press, 1967

Simms, Brendan, *The Impact of Napoleon*, Cambridge, Cambridge University Press, 1991

Smith, Vincent, *Oxford History of India*, 4th edn., ed. Percival Smith, Oxford, Oxford University Press, 1981

Somerset, Anne, *The Life and Times of William IV*, London, Weidenfeld & Nicolson, 1980

Sotnick, Richard, *The Coburg Conspiracy*, London, Ephesus Publishing, 2008

Southgate, Donald, *The Passing of the Whigs, 1832–1886*, London, Macmillan, 1962

Stansky, Peter (ed.), *The Victorian Revolution*, New York, Watts, 1973

Strachey, Lytton, *Queen Victoria*, London, Chatto & Windus, 1921

Strickland, Agnes, *Queen Victoria: From Birth to Bridal*, London, Henry Colburn, 1840

Stuart, Dorothy Margaret, *Daughter of England*, London, Macmillan, 1951

Stuart, Dorothy Margaret, *The Mother of Victoria*, London, Macmillan, 1941

Swift, Roger, and Kinealy, Christine (eds.), *Politics and Power in Victorian Ireland*, Dublin, Four Courts Press, 2006

Taylor, A. J. P., *The Course of German History*, London, Hamish Hamilton, 1945 [revised edn London, Methuen, 1961]

Tennyson, Alfred (ed. Ricks, Christopher), *The Poems of Tennyson*, 3 vols., London, Longman, 1969

Tennyson, Charles, *Alfred Tennyson, by His Grandson*, London, Macmillan, 1968

Teyssier, Arnaud, *Louis-Philippe, Le dernier roi des Français*, Paris, Perrin, 2012

Thompson, Dorothy, *The Chartists*, Hounslow, Temple Smith, 1984

Thompson, Dorothy, *Queen Victoria: Gender and Power*, London, Virago, 1982

Ullrich, Volker, *Die nervöse Grossmacht: Aufstieg und Untergang des deutschen Kaiserreichs, 1871–1918*, Frankfurt am Main, S. Fischer Verlag, 1997

Urbach, Karina, *Queen Victoria, Eine Biografie*, Munich, Verlag C. H. Beck, 2011

Urbach, Karina (ed.), *Royal Kinship, Anglo-German Family Networks, 1815–1918*, Munich, K. G. Saur, 2008

Vallone, Lynne, *Becoming Victoria*, New Haven/London, Yale University Press, 2001

Van der Kiste, John, *Dearest Vicky, Darling Fritz: Queen Victoria's Eldest Daughter and the German Emperor*, Stroud, Sutton Publishing, 2001

Van der Kiste, John, *Sons, Servants and Statesmen: The Men in Queen Victoria's Life*, Stroud, Sutton Publishing, 2006

Victoria, HM Queen, *Leaves from the Journal of Our Life in the Highlands, from 1848 to 186*, London, Smith, Elder & Co., 1868

Victoria of Prussia, Princess, *My Memoirs*, London, Eveliegh Nash and Grayson Ltd, 1929

Vincent, John (ed.), *Disraeli, Derby and the Conservative Party: Journals and Memoirs of Edward Henry, Lord Stanley, 1849–1869*, Hassocks, Sussex, The Harvester Press, 1978

Wangenheim, Rita von, *Baron Stockmar. Eine coburgisch-englische Geschichte*, Coburg, Hirsch-Verlag, 1996

Ward, Yvonne, *Censoring Queen Victoria: How Two Gentlemen Edited a Queen and Created an Icon*, London, Oneworld Publications, 2014

Warner, Marina, *Queen Victoria's Sketchbooks*, New York, Crown Publishers, 1979

Warren, T. Herbert, *Christian Victor, The Story of a Young Soldier*, London, John Murray, 1903

Warwick, Frances, Countess of, *Afterthoughts*, London, Cassell, 1931

Webb, Beatrice, *The Diary of Beatrice Webb, Volume Two: All the Good Things of Life*, ed. Norman and Jean Mackenzie, London, Virago, 1983

Webster, Sir Charles, *The Foreign Policy of Palmerston, 1830–1841*, London, G. Bell and Sons, 1951

Weintraub, Stanley, *Albert, Uncrowned King*, London, John Murray, 1997

Weintraub, Stanley, *Victoria, Biography of a Queen*, London, Unwin Hyman, 1987

Williams, Kate, *Becoming Queen*, London, Hutchinson, 2008

Wilson, A. N., *The Victorians*, London, Hutchinson, 2002

Windsor, HRH The Duke of, *A King's Story: The Memoirs of HRH the Duke of Windsor, KG*, London, Cassell, 1951

Witheridge, John, *Excellent Dr Stanley*, Norwich, Michael Russell, 2013

Woodham-Smith, Cecil, *Queen Victoria. Her Life and Times. Volume I, 1819–1861*, London, Hamish Hamilton, 1972

Woodward, E. L. *The Age of Reform, 1815–1870*, Oxford, Clarendon Press, 1938

Zeepvat, Charlotte, *Queen Victoria's Youngest Son: The Untold Story of Prince Leopold*, Stroud, Sutton Publishing, 1998

Zeldin, Theodore, *France, 1848–1945*, Oxford, Clarendon Press, 2 vols., 1973–7

Ziegler, Philip, *King William IV*, London, Cassell, 1971

Ziegler, Philip, *Mountbatten, The Official Biography*, London, Collins, 1985

INDEX